PSHIRE

MERRIMACK R.

ESSEX

Salisbury
Newburyport
Cherry Hill
Res.
**Parker
River N.W.R.**
Plum Is.          Cape Ann
Boxford     Ipswich     Rockport

IDDLESEX

CONCORD R.
SUDBURY R.

Lynnfield     Kettle Is.
House Is.
Marblehead

**Great
Meadows
N.W.R.**
Concord
Cambridge          Nahant

**Boston**

Blue Hills
Sharon

NORFOLK

Scituate

STELLWAGEN
BANK

Uxbridge

PLYMOUTH

Bridgewater

Duxbury
Beach
Plymouth Beach
Plymouth     Manomet

Race Point     Provincetown

Cape Cod Bay

Wellfleet

First Encounter Beach          Eastham
Coast
Guard
Beach

BRISTOL

TAUNTON R.

Middleborough

Lakeville
Ponds

Myles
Standish
S.F.

Cape Cod
Canal

Sandy Neck

Orleans

ODE

LAND

Westport

Bird Is.

C A P E     C O D

Barnstable          Chatham

Morris Is.

**Monomoy
N.W.R.**

Buzzards
Bay          Falmouth

Penikese Is.     Elizabeth Islands

Chappaquiddik

Muskeget
Tuckernuck

Nantucket
Sound

MARTHA'S
VINEYARD

Nomans Land

NANTUCKET

Block Is.

Nantucket
Shoals

# Birds of Massachusetts

With gratitude to
Margaret and F. Gregg Bemis,
ardent birders and conservationists

We also wish to acknowledge the generous support of
The Webster Foundation
and
The William P. Wharton Trust

# BIRDS of MASSACHUSETTS

Richard R. Veit
and
Wayne R. Petersen

*Illustrated by*
Barry W. Van Dusen

***NATURAL HISTORY of NEW ENGLAND SERIES***
Christopher W. Leahy, General Editor

Massachusetts Audubon Society

**Library of Congress Cataloging-in-Publication Data**

Veit, Richard R., 1957–
    Birds of Massachusetts / Richard R. Veit and Wayne R. Petersen;
illustrated by Barry W. Van Dusen.
      p.   cm.—(Natural history of New England series)
    Includes bibliographical references (p.    ) and index.
    ISBN 0-932691-11-0 (hard cover)
    1. Birds—Massachusetts.   I. Petersen, Wayne R., 1944–
II. Title  III. Series.
QL684.M4V45  1993
598.29744—dc20                        93-2931
                                              CIP

For Ruth P. Emery, the "Voice of Audubon,"
without whose unsurpassed enthusiasm and
meticulous avian record keeping
this book could never have been written

# Contents

# List of Illustrations

# Foreword

*by Roger Tory Peterson*

Massachusetts has always treasured history and tradition, yet the state often leads the way in exploring new directions. This has been particularly true of its involvement with the natural world—which many of us regard as the "real world."

The Massachusetts Audubon Society's first president, William Brewster (1851–1919), held impeccable credentials as an old Bostonian, and he also helped revolutionize the study and protection of bird life. Born in the year Audubon died, he developed what today would be described as a systematic ornithological data base. He was one of the first American field men to understand the value of keeping detailed consistent records, so that future bird population trends could be compared with an empirical (rather than a merely anecdotal) past.

Brewster was also a player in the American conservation movement. Encouraged by a group of dedicated women activists (who were also blessed with the best Brahmin credentials), he agreed to be the first president of the Massachusetts Audubon Society, which was founded in 1896 to halt the wanton slaughter of egrets, terns, and other birds, whose plumes were commanding great sums as hat decorations.

Brewster himself wrote an authoritative book on Massachusetts bird life—*Birds of the Cambridge Region* (1906)—but it was not until 1925, with the publication of *Birds of Massachusetts and Other New England States* by Edward Howe Forbush (1858–1929), that the first comprehensive summary of the state's avifauna was published. As state ornithologist from 1908 to 1920, Forbush built on Brewster's powerful synthesis of science and conservation. Arriving at a time when Americans were beginning to appreciate birds without insisting on shooting them first, and charged with protecting the "useful" birds of Massachusetts, Forbush may respectfully be thought of as an ornithological PR man. He developed a prodigious correspondence with virtually everyone in New England who had something to say on the subject of birds. He showed conclusively that, contrary to popular prejudice, *most* birds were more useful than harmful, thus helping to end the brutal and baseless destruction of birds of prey and other supposed avian vermin.

But Forbush's greatest achievement was to set his immense store of knowledge down in three large volumes. *Birds of Massachusetts and Other New England States* is the seminal work to which all subsequent Massachusetts bird books inevitably refer. Brilliantly illustrated by the young Louis Agassiz Fuertes, these hefty green volumes became essential in the library of anyone interested in natural history and showed indisputably, to the citizens of the Commonwealth, the splendor, fascination, and value of their native bird life.

As a teenager, nearly 70 years ago, I was to meet this legendary author when I attended my first convention of the American Ornithologists' Union (AOU) in New York City. In Dr. Frank Chapman's office on the fifth floor of the American Museum, Forbush showed us the original watercolors for his soon-to-be-published classic. Perched on a small stepladder so all could see, he showed us the Fuertes paintings plate by plate. Also in the room that day was a 35-year-old assistant curator, who was to be the next titan in the American ornithological pantheon. His name was Ludlow Griscom.

Returning to New York a year later to take up my art education, I often saw Griscom in action at the bimonthly meetings of the Linnaean Society, which he dominated. He was always a good show and just a bit austere in keeping a tight rein on a half dozen young upstarts who called themselves the Bronx County Bird Club (Joseph Hickey and Allan Cruickshank were charter members). Although he felt kindly toward these younger men, his cross-examinations were ruthless when they reported Three-toed Woodpeckers and other unlikely finds. I became the first non-Bronx member of this exclusive little group.

Griscom was our god, and his *Birds of the New York City Region* was our bible. Every one of us could quote chapter and verse. We used his terminology and even his inflection when we pronounced something as "unprecedented" or "a common summer resident." It was quite logical that we should choose Griscom for our role model, for he represented the new field of ornithology. He bridged the gap between the shotgun ornithologist of the old school and the modern birder with binoculars and telescope.

In 1927 Griscom left the American Museum for a position on the scientific and administrative staff of Harvard's Museum of Comparative Zoology (MCZ) in Cambridge, Massachusetts, and it was not until 1931 when I went to Boston to teach school that our paths crossed again. He wasted no time introducing his high-pressure methods to the leisurely birdwatchers of the Nuttall Ornithological Club of Cambridge—then, as now, the oldest bird club in the country—and especially to the young members of the Harvard Bird Club, whose field trips I joined as often as possible. Griscom spent the rest of his life in Massachusetts continuing to uphold the state's best ornithological traditions: as a scientist and curator at the MCZ and a founder of the Boston Museum of Science; as a conservationist who was an active board member and honorary vice president of Massachusetts Audubon for many years; and as the consummate teacher and mentor of a whole generation of passionate field ornithologists. Immersed as he was in the traditions of Brewster, Forbush, and other great American ornithologists of the past, Griscom was also the greatest revolutionary of them all.

It is impossible to overestimate Ludlow Griscom's influence on the astonishing popularity that birds and birdwatching have attained in the modern era. He had the vision to combine the intrinsic fascination of birds, the lure of the list, and advances in the technology of optical equipment into an irresistible new sport. And then, having invented the game, he fielded a succession of brilliant birders to demonstrate how it should be played.

Had it not been for Ludlow Griscom and his disciples, I could never have produced the Peterson field guides. These super birders taught me the fine points of field recognition while I, trained academically as an artist, attempted to pull things together and give them visual form. It was during those Boston years that I wrote and illustrated my first field guide. After it was turned down by four New York publishers, it was accepted by Houghton Mifflin in Boston because the editor, Francis Allen, a member of the Nuttall Club and a skilled Griscom-trained birder, saw the validity of my schematic approach. Within a few decades, birding was transformed from an arcane preoccupation of a few academics and wealthy eccentrics to the favorite pastime of millions.

The fruits of Griscom's hundreds of dawn-to-well-after-dark field trips in Massachusetts were regional works on the birds of Concord, Nantucket, and Martha's Vineyard and the immediate antecedent of the present work, *Birds of Massachusetts*, coauthored with Dorothy E. Snyder. A slender volume of just under two hundred pages, modestly subtitled *An Annotated and Revised Checklist*, it displays all the Griscom "field marks": a thorough search and analysis of every scrap of the literature on the subject; a strict code of authenticity in accepting records; an admirable economy of language; and a crisp, articulate style that seems to convey the very essence of each species in relationship to Massachusetts. Like *Birds of the New York City Region*, *Birds of Massachusetts* quickly became gospel.

Sadly, Griscom died before witnessing the full flowering of modern-day birding that he, to a great extent, had stimulated. It is a little daunting to compare the small fraternity of Griscom disciples and Audubon Society members that made up the birding community through the 1960s with today's throng of avid binocular addicts armed with not one but several field guides, communicating with each other on CB radios, subscribing to at least one birding magazine, and dialing state and national birding hotlines on their car phones. This burgeoning interest in birds has contributed greatly to our knowledge of the distribution and abundance of many species. With many more birders using ever more sophisticated guides and equipment, we were bound to discover "new" hawk migration routes, recognize Eurasian stints more often, and learn which areas of ocean White-faced Storm-Petrels frequent during which months. But our new-age bird mania and the data it has generated have also created a distinct new challenge for writers of comprehensive, annotated state and regional check-lists. And this brings us to the achievement of Richard R. Veit and Wayne R. Petersen, authors of this splendid new *Birds of Massachusetts*.

In the 37 years since Griscom and Snyder's book was published, approximately seventy-five species have been added to the Massachusetts list, about thirty new breeding species have been confirmed, and the size of the avian record has increased by orders of magnitude because of the enormous increase in active note-taking birders, many of whom even the demanding Griscom would have had to qualify as "competent observers." Gleaning this immense archive, analyzing the pattern of records for trends in occurrence, and then rearticulating the whole Massachusetts avian record in a readable format: these were the tasks that faced Dick Veit and Wayne Petersen beginning in 1979. I believe that Brewster, Forbush, and Griscom would be amazed at the extent of the present record and gratified by the professional manner in which these two scholarly field ornithologists have displayed it.

A book of this kind does not need to be explained to those who will own it; its contents are self-evident. But I am particularly impressed with the meticulous quality of the species accounts, the well-wrought introductory essays on Massachusetts "birding regions" and aspects of the Massachusetts avifauna, and the fine illustrations and cover art by up-and-coming young natural history artist Barry Van Dusen.

As befits the traditions of the Bay State, this handsome and exacting new *Birds of Massachusetts* both builds on the venerable ornithology of the Commonwealth and breaks new ground. It is an impressive addition to the ornithological literature and will certainly be a model for other states to follow.

*July 10, 1992*
*Old Lyme, Connecticut*

# Acknowledgments

The data upon which the species accounts are based was collected by hundreds of talented people; we cannot overemphasize the importance of their contribution. However, neither can we mention them all by name. Most of the significant records within the text are credited to either individuals or the original references where the records were cited. To everyone who has submitted field notes at one time or other, but whose name we have not mentioned within the text, we extend both thanks and apology.

The one person who indirectly contributed more time to the preparation of this book than any other was Ruth P. Emery. During her 29 years of employment at the Massachusetts Audubon Society and for 12 years thereafter, Ruth compiled a lion's share of the records that appear in the text. To this day, her carefully prepared reporting slips fill many shelves in the attic of Massachusetts Audubon headquarters. Because Ruth wrote down virtually everything that was reported, we have had access to both the edited compilations of records that appeared in such publications as *Records of New England Birds* and *Bird Observer* and the "raw data."

# Acknowledgments

During the final stages of editing, Margaret Argue and Boots Garrett generously gave their time in checking bird records against original sources. Our warm thanks for their efforts.

The following people took the time to thoroughly read various versions of the manuscript, or portions of it, and kindly contributed insightful comments and unpublished records of their own: Kathleen S. Anderson, Wallace Bailey, James Baird, Bradford Blodget, P.A. Buckley, Richard A. Forster, Jeremy J. Hatch, Richard S. Heil, Seth Kellogg, Trevor L. Lloyd-Evans, Blair Nikula, Ian C.T. Nisbet, Paul Roberts, and William C. Russell. To thoughtfully read a manuscript of this length is an enormously time-consuming exercise, and one that the authors sincerely appreciate.

Davis W. Finch and Cloe Mifsud provided Veit access to those records compiled by Finch while he served as editor for the Northeastern Maritime Region for *American Birds* magazine. For access to unpublished shorebird manuscripts, special thanks go to Brian A. Harrington.

Richard K. Walton and Simon A. Perkins provided much encouragement, contributed insightful conversation, and attended to numerous bothersome details during the production of this work. In addition, Simon's artful editing of the section "Regional Descriptions of Massachusetts" provided a useful backdrop for the entire text.

The following curators were most helpful in providing access to the collections in their charge: John Nove (Peabody Museum, Salem); Dr. Raymond A. Paynter, Jr. (Museum of Comparative Zoology, Cambridge); and Donald Salvator (Boston Museum of Science). Also, Joseph R. Jehl, Jr., Allan R. Phillips, and Bruce A. Sorrie contributed their expertise in verifying the identification of several critical specimens.

Veit wishes to acknowledge support provided by John P. Ebersole, Jeremy J. Hatch, and Michael A. Rex in their capacity as graduate advisors at the University of Massachusetts, Boston, where an early version of this book constituted a master's thesis.

For useful and entertaining discussions in office, tavern, and field, we thank Dennis J. Abbott, Peter Alden, Edith and Clinton Andrews, Ralph Andrews, Dorothy Arvidson, F.G. Buckley, Robert Fox, Carl Goodrich, J.A. Hagar, F.R. Hamlen, W.W. Harrington, Karsten Hartel, Sibley Higginbotham, Norman P. Hill, Vernon Laux, Joseph Kenneally, Christopher W. Leahy, Kevin Powers, Tudor Richards, Robert Smart, P. W. Smith, Robert Stymeist, Peter Vickery, and Soheil Zendeh. From the very start of the project, Richard A. Forster was always available to share his vast knowledge of Massachusetts birds and to offer particularly thoughtful criticism whenever it was needed.

Roger Tory Peterson's willingness to provide a lively and reflective foreword to the book was most appreciated. Without Roger's seminal influence, it is unlikely that either author would have developed his enduring passion for birds.

In the early stages of this manuscript, Charlotte Smith had the stamina as a typist to put up with Veit's unreasonable demands and endless input of yellow pads. During the final months of production, Laura Giard and Cynthia Fraser similarly accommodated Petersen's never-ending manuscript changes with patience, understanding, and good humor. Thank you to these unsung heroes.

For technical assistance with the species maps, we thank David Stemple and Judy Smith for their invaluable advice and many hours spent at a computer terminal.

To Barry Van Dusen, illustrator and book designer, go special kudos for the high quality and aesthetic beauty of the book's appearance. Petersen particularly appreciates Barry's willingness to make numerous artistic changes in order to capture the essence of the species in the illustrations.

David Ford deftly guided the book through the tangles of printing and final publication, and to him go our admiration and thanks.

Editing a gigantic compendium of dates, numbers, localities, and names can be an overwhelming task. Fortunately for the authors, Ann Hecker cheerfully and willingly took on the job and with unfailing and meticulous precision ensured the accuracy of every line in the text. With assistance from Betty Graham, Nancy Ludlow, and Elizabeth Daly, grammatical uniformity was ensured, and John Mitchell helped with substantive editing for a particularly challenging section. Our sincerest thanks to all.

Veit particularly thanks Marcia Litchfield for enduring support and interest, and Juliet, Geddes, Simon, and Blair Perkins for guinea hens, broken shear pins, Joker, and Red Cap Ale.

A special expression of gratitude goes to Christopher W. Leahy whose expertise, contributions, advice, sense of humor, optimism, and confidence in the value of the project made Petersen's existence both endurable and pleasant during the final months of production. Without Chris's support and guidance, *Birds of Massachusetts* might never have become a reality.

For his sustained enthusiasm and his understanding of the importance of the project, we thank Dr. Gerard A. Bertrand, president of the Massachusetts Audubon Society.

Barbara Braun survived six years of editing and proofreading and has the sincerest appreciation of the senior author for putting up with it all. In the same spirit, the junior author wishes to warmly acknowledge Betty Petersen for more than 25 years of support and encouragement in helping to make a dream come to fruition.

*Razorbill*

# Regional Descriptions of Massachusetts

*edited by Simon Perkins*

*In this chapter, the faunal diversity of Massachusetts is described in terms of eight regions: Berkshire County, the Connecticut River valley, Worcester County, Essex County, the Sudbury River valley, the greater Boston area within Route 128, southeastern Massachusetts, and Cape Cod and the Islands. Some of the regions, such as Greater Boston, are defined by arbitrary boundaries while others, such as Cape Cod and the Islands, have greater biotic integrity. Several authors contributed to this section as follows: Douglas McNair (Berkshires); Simon Perkins (Introduction, Connecticut River valley, Worcester County, Essex County, and Greater Boston); Richard Walton (Sudbury River valley); Wayne Petersen (Southeastern Massachusetts); and Richard Veit and Richard Forster (Cape Cod and the Islands).*

## Introduction

Massachusetts contains a remarkably rich flora and fauna within a relatively small geographical area. This wealth is largely attributable to a combination of the state's varied topography and geology, its latitude, and its coastal location.

The topography and geology of Massachusetts reflect abundant evidence of the last period of glaciation. On a local scale, many ponds and lakes persist today where the ice gouged and pitted the underlying rock, and numerous eskers, moraines, drumlins, and monadnocks rise from the landscape. The islands of Nantucket and Martha's Vineyard lie at the point where the last glaciers reached their southernmost limit of advance, and both islands exhibit classic examples of terminal moraines and sandy outwash plains.

On the broadest scale, the topography of Massachusetts follows a gradual east to west incline, and from the low coastal plain of the southeast to the 3,491-foot summit of Mt. Greylock in the Berkshires, the Connecticut River valley represents the most significant interruption in this gentle ascent.

Altitude and latitude play an especially critical role in producing the state's high faunal diversity. Massachusetts lies at a latitude where a cooler, northern "Canadian" life zone approaches a milder, southern "Carolinian" life zone. This geographical position combined with a broad elevational range creates highly divergent habitats within a relatively small area.

At one end of the ecological spectrum, Hooded Warblers and King Rails, species more typical of southern swamplands, occasionally breed in southeastern Massachusetts, while other southern representatives such as Red-bellied Woodpeckers and Acadian Flycatchers occupy southern segments of the Connecticut and Housatonic river valleys.

At the other end of the spectrum, in the highest hills on the Hoosac Plateau and within the northern Berkshire Hills, altitude recapitulates latitude, and some of the faunal elements there closely resemble those more typical of northern New England. In these areas, Blackpoll Warblers nest in dense spruce forests, and Olive-sided Flycatchers and Rusty Blackbirds breed within the cool confines of boreal bogs.

Between these two ecological extremes, an extensive transitional zone forms the state's biological core, and the ecotypes that approach from the north and south gradually blend into that core within deep and complex interdigitations. The forests within this transitional zone typically contain trees such as oaks, ashes, hickories, hemlock, and White Pine, and bird species commonly associated with these forests include Red-eyed Vireos, Great-crested Flycatchers, Scarlet Tanagers, and Ovenbirds.

Massachusetts owes a great deal of its avian diversity to the proximity of the sea. Oceanic species in the offshore waters, along with numerous coastal species, contribute to this diversity, as do the many migrant species that use the coast as their primary route of passage. Massachusetts' coastal waters are not uniform in temperature. The cold, coastal waters of the Gulf of Maine are bounded to the south by Cape Cod, while the tropical, northbound Gulf Stream glances off the continental slope a mere 150 miles south of Nantucket. Consequently, just as the terrestrial avifauna reflects the transitional nature of the region, so too does the array of pelagic species. For example, cold-water species such as the Northern Fulmar and Manx Shear-water occur in close proximity to warm-water species such as the Cory's and Audubon's shearwaters.

## Berkshire County

Berkshire County, the westernmost county in Massachusetts, is notably hilly and rugged and has an average elevation of just under 1,500 feet. The county is comprised of three major physiographic regions: the Berkshire Hills, the Taconic Range, and the Berkshire Valley.

The Berkshire Hills, a southerly extension of Vermont's Green Mountains, form a ridge down the eastern half of the area. Three peaks in this range that exceed 2,500 feet are Mt. Borden, Mt. Busby, and Mt. Monroe. The Taconic Range, which extends for 150 miles from west central Vermont to southeastern New York, forms the western boundary of the county. This range is steep and narrow, with maximum elevations of 2,602 feet at Mt. Everett and 2,793 feet at Mt. Berlin. Mt. Greylock, located on a spur of the Taconic Range, has the most interesting ornithological history of the Berkshire County mountains. It is the highest point in southern New England (3,491 feet) and hosts several plant species that are unusual or that occur nowhere else in Massachusetts (for example, Braun's Holly Fern). Blackpoll Warblers breed within the extensive stands of Red Spruce and Balsam Fir near the summit, and "Bicknell's" Gray-cheeked Thrushes nested there as recently as 1973.

The Berkshire Valley, which lies between the Taconic Range and the Berkshire Hills, is composed largely of limestone. The valley, which is characterized by many cultivated pastures and rocky outcrops, contains the headwaters of the Housatonic River. The Hoosic River, a tributary of the Hudson River, flows northwest toward Vermont and New York through the narrow northern portion of the Berkshire Valley. A scenic river, the Hoosic winds through some of the most rugged parts of Berkshire County near Mt. Greylock and the northwest escarpment of the Berkshire Hills.

Berkshire County lies within the transitional zone of the eastern continental forest. Its forested hills contain mostly secondary-growth hardwoods, although a few tracts are believed to represent "old growth" where some trees are more than a century old. The dominant tree species are beech, hemlock, Sugar Maple, and Yellow Birch, while Red Spruce is prevalent at higher elevations in the northern townships. Southern Berkshire County is characterized by oaks, hickories, ash, and Red Maple. White Pine is the dominant conifer of the southern part of the county but is gradually replaced by spruce in more northern areas. The largest stands of spruce and Balsam Fir are found at the summit of Mt. Greylock and at one or two adjacent sites, where the plant communities assume a character typical of more northern life zones.

There are numerous marshes, swamps, and bogs in Berkshire County, and dense growths of alders and willows are commonplace in the poorly drained wetlands of the Berkshire Hills. Since their reintroduction in the 1930s, Beavers have helped to create many new wooded swamps and several birds, especially Great Blue Herons and Eastern Bluebirds, have benefited from the consequent increase in dead trees made available for nesting by the activity of the Beavers.

Curiously, the original forests of Berkshire County were never well described. During the middle of the 18th century, approximately 80 percent of the forests were cleared for lumber and firewood, and the resulting landscape was then converted to agriculture. By the 1820s, settlers began leaving Berkshire County to head west after having depleted the soils to a point that agriculture was no longer profitable. This exodus accelerated after the Civil War, and the abandonment of farms has continued to the present. Fields and pastures quickly reverted to secondary growth but were eventually cleared again during the late 19th and early 20th centuries. During that same period, the state began purchasing land on which to construct reservoirs and establish state forests. Unfortunately, much of the original spruce forest of the northern townships was not preserved; however, many areas have since been reforested with plantations of spruce.

Bird species typical of northern habitats that breed more commonly in Berkshire County than elsewhere in Massachusetts include the Great Blue Heron, Common Merganser, Common Snipe, Yellow-bellied Sapsucker, Alder Flycatcher, Olive-sided Flycatcher, Common Raven, Swainson's Thrush, Golden-crowned Kinglet, Blackpoll Warbler, Mourning Warbler, and Rusty Blackbird.

During migration, the central Berkshire Valley contains the best habitat in the county for herons, waterfowl, and shorebirds. Lake Onota, Richmond Pond, Pontoosuc Lake, Stockbridge Bowl, Lake Cheshire, and Laurel Lake are especially attractive to these birds. Of these, Lake Onota has historically been the best. The Pittsfield Sewer Beds were among the best inland sites in Massachusetts for attracting birds during the period from 1945 to 1960, but, since being replaced by more modern facilities, they no longer provide suitable habitat.

During fall, migrating hawks may be observed from such prominent hills as Mt. Busby in North Adams, Fobes Hill in Windsor, Lenox Mountain in Lenox, Monument Mountain in Stockbridge, and Baldwin Hill in South Egremont. The Berkshire Hills Country Club in Pittsfield and Berry Pond in the Pittsfield State Forest have also been especially productive for hawk watching in recent years.

Certain uncommon or rare winter visitors from farther north occur more frequently, or in greater numbers, in Berkshire County than elsewhere in the state. Such species include the Bohemian Waxwing and winter finches such as the Pine Grosbeak, Common Redpoll, and Red and White-winged crossbills.

## Connecticut River Valley

The Connecticut River valley forms a deep natural divide between the hills of Berkshire County and the remaining eastern two-thirds of Massachusetts. The valley is formed from a fertile floodplain flanked by a series of high hills and ridges. Four large tributaries feed into the Connecticut River, forming the largest drainage of any river in New England.

The primary soils are composed of rich sediments. These have been deposited during seasonal flooding of the river, as well as over a much larger time scale during the period immediately following the Pleistocene glaciation, when all but the highest peaks were submerged within a series of vast melt-water lakes. These fertile soils support some of the most extensive and active farms in Massachusetts. The most important yields are corn, tobacco, and dairy products.

The source of the Connecticut River is located at the Connecticut Lakes in northern New Hampshire. The river reaches Long Island Sound roughly 350 miles south at Old Saybrook and Old Lyme, Connecticut. By the time the river has reached the border of Massachusetts, it has fallen from nearly 2,000 feet in elevation to about 200 feet above sea level and has become slow and wide. During the river's 60-mile run through the Commonwealth, the valley widens further, measuring roughly eight miles across in Greenfield and about twenty miles across at the Connecticut border.

Though most of the valley lies within a transitional zone, traces of southern or northern elements may be found where the river approaches the borders of Connecticut and New Hampshire. The valley forms a corridor along which extend marginal tongues of southern plant communities that reach as far north as Longmeadow. There, Sugar Maple, Eastern Hemlock, and ashes may be found along with more southern species such as Tulip Poplar and Chestnut Oak. Similarly, birds typical of eastern transitional forests such as Red-eyed Vireos and Scarlet Tanagers may be found with southern species such as Red-bellied Woodpeckers and Acadian Flycatchers. Near the New Hampshire border, traces of boreal forest may be found at the higher elevations farthest from the river. Tree species there include Red Spruce and Balsam Fir, and attendant breeding bird species typically include Golden-crowned Kinglets, Yellow-rumped Warblers, and White-throated Sparrows.

The most conspicuous topographical features within the Connecticut River valley include Mt. Tom, Mt. Toby, and Sugarloaf Mountain, as well as the entire Holyoke Range. In 1955, Mt. Tom supported the last native-nesting pair of Peregrine Falcons in the state, and, since 1989, a hacked pair of Peregrines has bred successfully on the Monarch Place building in downtown Springfield.

Along the river's margins, oxbow lakes remain where the river once followed a different course, and swales, marshes, and meadows are now found where ancient lakes once flanked the main channel. The marshes provide breeding habitat for several uncommon and local breeders, such as the American Bittern and Common Moorhen, as well as other marsh obligates, such as the Virginia Rail, Sora, and Marsh Wren.

Bald Eagles have recently become an important addition to the list of breeding birds in the valley. In 1989, an eagle that was hacked at the Quabbin Reservoir built a nest with a "wild" bird at Barton Cove in Turners Falls and has been nesting there each year since.

During years when rodents are abundant, the open agricultural fields may support the largest numbers of inland wintering Short-eared Owls to be found anywhere in the state. These same fields also attract large concentrations of open-country winterers such as Horned Larks and Snow Buntings.

The valley's greatest ornithological virtues are most apparent during migration seasons. Edward H. Forbush called the valley, "the principal inland highway of bird migration within the New England states." Indeed, the Common Nighthawk illustrates this point well because the great majority of all nighthawks that pass south through the state each autumn follow the Connecticut River valley.

Many geese and certain sea ducks, such as scoters, that move along the Atlantic Coast in spring, turn inland up the Connecticut River to their breeding quarters on northern lakes. Likewise, wood-warblers bound for forests in Canada and northern New England follow this same spring route, stopping to feed in the Red and Silver maples and willows along the river's shoreline.

In late summer, when water levels drop, migrant shorebirds often pause to feed and rest on the river's exposed margins and sandbars. Under similar conditions in winter, large numbers of gulls, primarily from local landfills, collect in these same areas. These gatherings occasionally attract species rarely seen inland such as Glaucous, Iceland, and Lesser Black-backed gulls. In the fall, migrant Canada Geese, and, occasionally, Snow Geese, alight to feed in the valley's many cornfields.

Migrating hawks ride winds that are deflected upward against steep ridges such as those along the Holyoke Range. Mt. Tom was one of the first hawk watching localities discovered in Massachusetts, and today the site remains popular among birders seeking views of migrant raptors. Species that are especially prevalent there during migration include Ospreys, Broad-winged, Red-tailed, and Sharp-shinned hawks, and, in more recent years, Turkey Vultures.

## Worcester County

Worcester County marks the first significant transition point between the low, relatively flat coastal plain and the higher, hillier interior. Located slightly east of a point midway between Boston and the state's western border, the county's margins extend from New Hampshire to Connecticut and Rhode Island and are bounded to the east by the towns of Ashburnham, Harvard, Southboro, and Blackstone. The county's western border roughly bisects Quabbin Reservoir from north to south.

A central plateau extending from the White Mountains in New Hampshire southward through the county forms the broadest topographical feature within the area. Above this plateau project several conspicuously higher monadnocks, the most prominent of which are Mt. Wachusett in Princeton, at 2,006 feet, and Mt. Watatic in Ashburnham, at 1,832 feet.

Quabbin Reservoir, the largest body of fresh water in the state, has become ornithologically significant since its creation in the 1930s. Wachusett Reservoir in Clinton, Sterling, and West Boylston is the second largest body of fresh water in the county and serves as a holding reservoir for

*Northern Shrike*

7

Quabbin water bound for points east. The largest rivers in Worcester County include the Blackstone, which flows from the city of Worcester roughly southeast through Uxbridge and thence into Rhode Island, and the Nashua, which flows northward into the Merrimack River.

The flora and fauna are generally transitional in nature, yet certain northern species are readily found within the county near the New Hampshire border. On the summit of Mt. Watatic in Ashburnham, for example, Red Spruce grows in profusion, and birds commonly associated with this forest type are found nesting there. These include the Winter Wren, Golden-crowned Kinglet, and Magnolia Warbler. But even in the absence of spruce growth, Worcester County provides conditions suitable for certain northern species of birds. Where the relatively low, flat land of eastern Massachusetts meets the higher terrain within Worcester County, several species of birds reach the southern and eastern limit of their breeding range within the state. These include the Yellow-bellied Sapsucker, Common Raven, and Black-throated Blue Warbler.

Common Loons reach the southeasternmost limit of their breeding range in North America in Worcester County, where nearly all known pairs nest on the Quabbin and Wachusett reservoirs. Wachusett Reservoir is also the only inland nesting site in Massachusetts for the Herring Gull.

Aside from loons, Quabbin supports several other notable avian elements. Probably the most celebrated is the Bald Eagle. Since a hacking program was initiated in 1982, six pairs of eagles have established territories within Quabbin, and at least three of those pairs have raised young. Additionally, up to 50 individuals, most presumably from more northern populations, spend a portion of the winter at Quabbin.

In summer months, during years of unusually low water at Quabbin, grassy flats emerge in portions of the reservoir and provide excellent feeding habitat for shorebirds. Among the more than twenty species of shorebirds recorded there, the most noteworthy species have included the Hudsonian Godwit, Baird's Sandpiper, and Buff-breasted Sandpiper. In 1989, Quabbin also became the first and only known nesting area in the state for the Cerulean Warbler. Since then, nesting pairs have bred in two different areas within the mature deciduous forest around the reservoir.

In the late 1970s, Mt. Wachusett and Mt. Watatic were discovered to be two of the premier fall hawk watching stations in the state. The majority of the raptors recorded at those sites each autumn are Broad-winged Hawks, though Sharp-shinned Hawks and Ospreys are also often well represented. Peak Broad-winged numbers occur within a typically narrow window of dates in mid-September, when a maximum single-day count may exceed 10,000 individuals.

## Sudbury River Valley

The Sudbury River valley has a tradition rich in both cultural and natural history. Over the course of time, significant changes in both floral and faunal populations have occurred. Many of these changes can be attributed to centuries of nearly continuous human habitation, first by native Americans and later by European colonists. In the past century and a half, there has been a succession of naturalists working in the valley. For example, the bird life has received the particular attention of such men as Henry David Thoreau, William Brewster, and Ludlow Griscom. Perhaps nowhere in North America is there a lengthier ornithological record.

The Sudbury River is a part of a watershed defined by the drainage area of the Sudbury, Assabet, and Concord rivers. Two of these rivers, the Sudbury and the Assabet, arise near Cedar Swamp in the town of Westboro. The Assabet follows a northerly course, while the Sudbury begins its course in an easterly direction. In Concord, the Sudbury and the Assabet join to become the Concord River, which then flows into the Merrimack River in Lowell for the river's final descent to the Atlantic Ocean.

The portion of this river system that has received the most attention from local and visiting naturalists, and the part that will be the focus of this discussion, includes those sections of the Sudbury and Concord rivers that flow through Framingham, Wayland, Sudbury, Concord, and Carlisle. The topography of this area, formed mainly during the Pleistocene glaciation, includes the flat, broad floodplain and adjacent river meadows through which the meandering river makes its course, as well as the nearby uplands with their gently sloping hills, eskers, drumlins, kettleholes, and kames. The valley's wetlands contain a great variety of aquatic plants, including pondweeds, water lilies, duckweeds, Pickerelweed, Arrow Arum, scattered stands of cattails, and thickets of Buttonbush, willow, and alder. Over the last quarter century, Purple Loosestrife has colonized the river meadows and now dominates certain stretches of the river edge. Red Maples are abundant along the edge of the floodplain, and Silver Maples and Swamp White Oak grow in a number of localities. The maturing, second-growth transitional woodlands of the valley include most of the typical hardwoods of central New England—oaks, maples, hickories, and birches, as well as softwoods such as White Pine and Eastern Hemlock. Unfortunately for bird diversity, the field and pasture habitat that was so prevalent just three decades ago is now very limited in extent, and the few fields that remain are rapidly growing up to shrub communities that are often dominated by invasive European Buckthorn.

The most productive birding habitats in the valley are the rivers, cattail marshes, Red Maple swamps, fields, agricultural plots, and a few of the maturing, second-growth forests. Areas that contain a combination of these habitats include the Heard's Pond area in Wayland, Nine Acre Corner on Route 117 in West Concord, and the impoundments of the Great Meadows National Wildlife Refuge in Concord.

The Sudbury River valley is a particularly fine area in which to observe a large variety of migrating birds. Waterfowl are often conspicuous in both spring and fall and are usually most numerous along the rivers, as well as at

Heard's Pond and Wash Brook in Wayland, at Nine Acre Corner, and in the Great Meadows impoundments. Among spring arrivals, diving ducks such as Ring-necked Ducks, Common Goldeneyes, and Common and Hooded mergansers are often particularly conspicuous, as are dabblers such as Wood Ducks, both teal species, and American Black Ducks.

The Great Meadows impoundments also serve as an important staging area for waterfowl in the fall, and among the more interesting migrants are American Wigeon, Northern Pintails, Gadwalls, and Northern Shovelers. Late in the season, American Coots may also be found there feeding with the ducks. During years of low water, the Great Meadows refuge is also attractive to fall migrant shorebirds. Species regularly recorded include Lesser Golden-Plovers, Lesser Yellowlegs, Least and Pectoral sandpipers, and Common Snipe. Shorebirds may also be found during fall migration in the agricultural fields at Nine Acre Corner. This locality is equally productive in the fall for finding large flocks of Red-winged Blackbirds and sparrows. Within the latter group, Savannah, Swamp, and Song sparrows are usually most numerous, but Lincoln's and White-crowned sparrows also appear regularly in small numbers.

During late April and May, the best spot for observing migratory birds is in the vicinity of Heard's Pond. There, Griscom Woods (the area between Heard's Pond and Wash Brook) and Heard Farm are consistently productive. Noteworthy during this season are many species of wood-warblers and Rusty Blackbirds. In rainy weather, large mixed flocks of swallows often feed over the pond.

The valley's extensive marshlands have become increasingly valuable as a refuge for certain wetland species, particularly because this habitat is gradually disappearing in many Massachusetts areas. Both Soras and Virginia Rails are summer residents within the cattail marshes of Wash Brook and the Great Meadows impoundments, and more sporadic breeders include Pied-billed Grebes, American and Least bitterns, King Rails, and Common Moorhens.

In these same wetland locales, Marsh Wrens and Swamp Sparrows are very numerous, and, along the rivers, the Wood Duck population is thriving because the ducks have readily taken advantage of the many nest boxes provided by the U.S. Fish and Wildlife Service.

## Essex County

Essex County is arguably the most ornithologically rich area in Massachusetts. This wealth was first thoroughly chronicled in the 1905 Nuttall Ornithological Club publication, *The Birds of Essex County*, by Dr. Charles W. Townsend. This book, and its 1920 supplement, remains the definitive work on the subject.

Occupying the northeasternmost corner of Massachusetts, Essex County is bounded to the north by New Hampshire and to the east by the Atlantic Ocean. The county's variety of topographical and geological features includes low, rolling hills, numerous ponds and lakes, large marshes, several large rivers, and a complex coastline. The character of the coastline varies from long, sand beaches, such as those at Salisbury, Plum Island, and Ipswich, to rugged, rocky headlands such as those at Cape Ann, Marblehead Neck, and Nahant. Most of the larger rivers, including the Parker and Ipswich, terminate at estuaries that are dominated by extensive *Spartina* marshes. The county's two largest freshwater marshes are located in Lynnfield and along the Ipswich River, primarily in Wenham.

Much of today's Essex County landscape appears virtually unchanged since its most recent reformation during the Pleistocene glaciation. For example, a great terminal moraine in the area known as "Dogtown" forms the bulk of the interior portions of Gloucester and Rockport, and numerous drumlins remain scattered throughout the county. Conspicuous examples of the latter include Great Neck in Ipswich and Hog Island in Essex.

Like that of most of Massachusetts, the vegetation in Essex County reflects the transitional nature of the region. The relatively mild coastal winters allow the growth of certain southern plants such as Laurel Magnolia, which gives its name to a village in Gloucester, while cold pockets in some interior areas of the county support various northern hardwoods and Black Spruce-Tamarack bogs.

One of the epicenters for migrant birds in the state is the area that encompasses the Parker River National Wildlife Refuge on Plum Island and the Merrimack River estuary in Newburyport Harbor. There, each spring and fall, great assemblages of migrants convene to feed and rest, shorebirds being particularly abundant. The salt marshes and the many shallow pannes therein provide resting areas for thousands of sandpipers and plovers, and, when the tide is low, Newburyport Harbor offers expansive mud flats on which these waders feed. During autumn migration, Plum Island is the most important stopover point in New England for Long-billed Dowitchers.

Under favorable wind conditions in spring, hawk flights are easily observed on Plum Island, particularly when Sharp-shinned Hawks and American Kestrels follow the coast northward. Likewise, migrant passerines often concentrate at the coast, where they stop to feed and rest among the Choke Cherry, Beach Plum, and bayberry thickets within Plum Island's dune hollows.

The Merrimack River estuary attracts many wintering waterfowl and may also support a dozen or more Bald Eagles each winter.

In the last century, during the height of farming in Massachusetts, much of Essex County was pasture land. Today, most of that farmland has succeeded to secondary forest, but remnants of the Common Pastures in Newbury and West Newbury still maintain a modest variety of grassland birds. One or two pairs of Upland Sandpipers return to the area each summer, as do a few pairs of Eastern Meadowlarks and many Bobolinks. In the winter, Rough-legged Hawks and Short-eared Owls occasionally forage for rodents over the more extensive fields.

The large tract of mature forest around Crooked Pond in Boxford attracts a wide variety of woodland species. Among these residents, species with strong southern affinities, such as the Louisiana Waterthrush, breed in close proximity to northern species such as the Winter Wren. Many raptors nest there as well. These include Northern Goshawks, Cooper's Hawks, Red-shouldered Hawks, Great Horned Owls, and Barred Owls.

Crane Beach in Ipswich, in addition to being the site where Charles J. Maynard collected the first specimen of "Ipswich" Sparrow in 1868, is also an important nesting stronghold for Piping Plovers.

Across Ipswich Bay lies Cape Ann, which, by virtue of its projection into the Atlantic Ocean, provides one of the best vantage points in Massachusetts from which to view the passage of storm-driven seabirds. The rugged outer shores of Gloucester and Rockport are also reliable locations for finding uncommon winter visitors such as King Eiders, Harlequin Ducks, Purple Sandpipers, and Iceland and Glaucous gulls.

Cape Ann's peninsular configuration is shared by Marblehead Neck and Nahant to the south. That configuration and the presence of dense pockets of vegetation in all three areas serve to concentrate migrant land birds in both spring and fall. Historically, these three peninsulas have proven to be among the most productive "migrant traps" in the state.

Lynnfield Marsh, the county's most extensive cattail marsh, is an important nesting site for a host of threatened marsh birds. Within this one wetland, species that breed either sporadically or regularly include the American Bittern, Least Bittern, Common Moorhen, and King Rail.

## Greater Boston

The area encompassed within the loop of Route 128, an area loosely referred to as the Greater Boston area, is an ornithologically significant region in its own right. In fact, the birds of Greater Boston have received considerable attention, beginning with William Brewster's *Birds of the Cambridge Region*, in 1906, and later followed by Horace Wright's *Birds of the Boston Public Gardens*, in 1909. Not only has this area proven to be historically rich in bird life, but even today it continues to support a rich avifauna, despite its highly residential character.

For the purposes of this discussion, Greater Boston includes the townships inside Route 128, except those within Essex County, which are treated elsewhere in this section. The terrain making up Greater Boston forms a shallow basin that drains toward Boston Harbor via three main rivers: the Charles, the Neponset, and the Mystic. At the periphery of this basin, the land rises to high points at the Middlesex Fells to the north, Arlington Heights to the west, and Great Blue Hill in Milton to the south. At 635 feet, Great Blue Hill is the highest point in eastern Massachusetts. Other conspicuous topographical features include an unusually high number of drumlins. Indeed, much to the curiosity of geologists, the majority of all identified drumlins in Massachusetts are located inside Route 128.

Despite the disturbances caused by extensive human activity throughout the region, the basic components of a wide variety of habitats remain intact. The Middlesex Fells and the Blue Hills Reservation represent two of the least disturbed and most extensively wooded tracts within the area, and both support a healthy assortment of woodland species. Among these, the more noteworthy examples include the Pileated Woodpecker, Winter Wren, Worm-eating Warbler, and Louisiana Waterthrush. Additionally, the Blue Hills support the easternmost nesting pairs of Turkey Vultures.

Areas such as Mt. Auburn Cemetery in Cambridge and Logan International Airport are examples of habitats that have been greatly altered by humans but that are nevertheless valuable oases for birds within an otherwise inhospitable urban desert. Mt. Auburn Cemetery is recognized nationally as one of the premier locales in eastern North America for witnessing the spring passage of migrant wood-warblers, while the airport supports a surprising array of bird species. Logan Airport is presently the northernmost breeding site in the United States for the American Oystercatcher; the extensive grassland there annually holds several pairs of breeding Upland Sandpipers; and, throughout the winter months, particularly in flight years, Logan may attract the largest concentrations of Snowy Owls anywhere in the lower 48 states.

Various long-legged waders, such as the Snowy Egret, Black-crowned Night-Heron, and Glossy Ibis, nest on several islands in Boston Harbor, and the harbor itself supports large numbers of wintering waterfowl, including thousands of Brant and Common Eiders.

Fowl Meadow in Milton and Canton is the only extensive freshwater wetland in Greater Boston. Unfortunately, its drainage pattern has been significantly altered over the years, yet several wetland species including the American Bittern, Virginia Rail, and Marsh Wren continue to breed within its margins.


## Southeastern Massachusetts

Southeastern Massachusetts, as defined in this section, is comprised of Plymouth and Bristol counties. Descriptions of this region's avifauna have been illuminated in the works of notable ornithologists such as Arthur C. Bent at the turn of the century and by the systematic studies conducted at the Manomet Bird Observatory in Plymouth since its inception in 1969.

Most of the topography of Plymouth County was formed during the last glacial period. The landscape is gently undulating and contains only a few hills, the highest point in the area being the Pine Hills of Plymouth, where the remains of a terminal moraine reach 395 feet. The coastline of Plymouth County consists of gradually sloping sand or cobble beaches interspersed between gravel bluffs or granitic headlands. Examples of the latter are found in Cohasset and Scituate.

The most prevalent forest types in southeastern Massachusetts are pine-oak associations, comprised of either Scrub Oak and Pitch Pine or mixed oak and White Pine. In poorly drained areas, particularly within river floodplains, Red Maple or Red Maple-White Pine forest dominates.

Several habitat types found in southeastern Massachusetts warrant particular mention. The coastal plain, which lies eastward of a line that runs roughly from Duxbury southwestward to Fall River, is a major physiographic feature. The predominant ecological community found on the plain is a pine-oak association, and the best example of this habitat is found in the barrens of Myles Standish State Forest in Plymouth. These pine-oak barrens are periodically swept by forest fires, thus providing nesting conditions that are found in few other areas in the state. Among the more characteristic and abundant bird species of the pinelands are Common Nighthawks, Whip-poor-wills, Fish Crows, Hermit Thrushes, Brown Thrashers, Nashville, Pine, and Prairie warblers, Rufous-sided Towhees, and Vesper Sparrows.

Two plant communities that support local populations of birds with northern affinities are Red Maple and coastal White Cedar swamps. Outstanding examples of these communities are found in Hockomock Swamp in the West Bridgewater-Raynham area, Little Cedar Swamp in East Middleboro, Acushnet Cedar Swamp in New Bedford, and Pine Swamp in Raynham. Breeding bird studies in some of these areas have revealed the regular presence of Brown Creepers, Winter Wrens (rare), Northern Waterthrushes, Canada Warblers, and White-throated Sparrows.

Another area of ecological importance came into existence during the 1970s at the expense of the Great Cedar Swamp in Halifax and Middleboro. The conversion of swamp forest to vast open cornfields and hayfields by the Cumberland Farms food store chain produced grassland habitat that was previously scarce in southeastern Massachusetts. With the creation of this habitat came a new and varied assortment of grassland birds. Upland Sandpipers now breed nearly annually, and from May through October migrant shorebirds typically include large numbers of Killdeers and Pectoral Sandpipers. In winter, hawks and Short-eared Owls routinely hunt over the extensive fields. A less extensive area that attracts many of these same species is the Daniel Webster Wildlife Sanctuary in Marshfield.

The North, Taunton, and Westport rivers all provide adequate habitat for aquatic species, and the Lakeville ponds represent particularly important feeding areas for a variety of migrant waterfowl, most notably Ring-necked

Ducks and scaup. The lower Taunton River in the Assonet-Somerset area of Bristol County can be an especially important wintering area for Canvasbacks, which occasionally number in the hundreds. Bald Eagles have also become increasingly frequent visitors to the Lakeville ponds.

Major concentrations of migratory shorebirds at Third Cliff in Scituate and on the beaches of Plymouth and Duxbury are highlighted by the midsummer buildup of Red Knots, Black-bellied and Semipalmated plovers, Ruddy Turnstones, Sanderlings, Semipalmated and Least sandpipers, and Dunlins. Winter aggregations of Purple Sandpipers on the rocky ledges off North Scituate and Cohasset are among the largest in Massachusetts. A few beaches support modest breeding populations of Piping Plovers and Least Terns, and a historically important tern colony at Plymouth Beach continues to support a large colony of Common Terns, along with a few pairs of Arctic and Roseate terns. The largest tern colony in the state, and one of the two largest Roseate Tern colonies in North America, exists on Bird Island off the entrance to Marion Harbor in Buzzards Bay.

Clark's Island in Duxbury Bay is the site of a large heron rookery that has been active since at least the early 1970s. The first Glossy Ibises to nest in Massachusetts were found at Clark's Island in 1974, and a few pairs continued to breed there irregularly through the 1980s. This colony has supported a few pairs of Great Egrets and Little Blue Herons, in addition to greater numbers of Snowy Egrets and Black-crowned Night-Herons.

The coastal waters of Plymouth County are visited annually by a great variety of seafowl. From high headlands such as Gurnet Point in Duxbury and Manomet Point in Plymouth, tremendous migratory flights of sea ducks may be witnessed in the fall as the birds enter Cape Cod Bay from the north. Most numerous are scoters, eiders, Oldsquaws, and Red-breasted Mergansers. Many thousands of Common Eiders usually spend the winter in Duxbury Bay and Plymouth Harbor, due largely to an increased growth of mussel beds in those waters over the last 20 years. In spring, Duxbury Bay is also a major staging area for northbound Brant.

Extensive freshwater marshes are scarce in southeastern Massachusetts. Nonetheless, marshes large enough to support wetland birds are found in the Cherry Hill Conservation Area in Marshfield, along the Eel River in Plymouth, and along the larger, regional rivers such as the North and Nemasket rivers. Within these marshes, American Bitterns and Virginia Rails routinely occur, and the cattail marshes along the North River contain one of the largest Marsh Wren colonies in the state.

In addition to supporting those species previously described, southeastern Massachusetts represents the northern distributional limit, or local center of abundance, for several species of Massachusetts birds. In this category belong the Northern Bobwhite, Fish Crow (summer only), Carolina Wren, White-eyed Vireo, and Pine, Prairie, and Hooded warblers (irregular in Bristol County).

## Cape Cod and the Islands

Cape Cod and its offshore islands, including the Elizabeth chain, Nantucket, and Martha's Vineyard, were formed by the glaciers of the Pleistocene period. Terminal moraines are found on the northern portions of central Cape Cod, as well as on Nantucket, Martha's Vineyard, and the Elizabeth Islands. The Cape and Islands are characterized by moderately hilly ground liberally pocked with kettle ponds, which were formed by the melting of stranded ice blocks left by the receding glaciers. Some of these kettle ponds have succeeded to Red Maple swamps or sphagnum bogs, and some of the swamps are attractive to migrant land birds in spring and fall.

Outwash plains, which make up the southern sections of central Cape Cod and the southern portions of Nantucket and Martha's Vineyard, are formed from gravel that was carried south by the meltwaters of the receding glaciers, and the "great ponds" of Martha's Vineyard and Nantucket are the remnants of rivers that drained the glaciers. The high bluffs of Gay Head on Martha's Vineyard, North Truro on Cape Cod, and Sankaty Head on Nantucket are formed from the debris that was pushed ahead of, and deposited by, the advancing glaciers.

The sandy soils of Cape Cod and the Islands support forests composed primarily of oaks and Pitch Pine, though as recently as the turn of the century these areas were virtually treeless due to systematic clearing for farming. On Nantucket, through this period, extensive moorlands were maintained by and for sheep, as well as for the purpose of attracting huntable migratory shorebirds such as Lesser Golden-Plovers and Eskimo Curlews.

This unique coastal heathland habitat persists in Massachusetts today only in certain portions of outer Cape Cod, Nantucket, and Martha's Vineyard and on several of the Elizabeth Islands such as Pasque and Nashawena. Distinctive plants associated with this habitat type include Broom Crowberry, Golden Heather, Poverty Grass (*Hudsonia*), and Bearberry.

Regrettably, many of these moors are being overgrown with shrubby thickets, Pitch Pine, and Scrub Oak, and are increasingly threatened by human development. What moors remain, however, support some of the few breeding Northern Harriers and Short-eared Owls still remaining in southern New England, along with most of Massachusetts' nesting Grasshopper Sparrows.

Dense thickets of Bayberry, Beach Plum, Poison Ivy, Blackberry, Catbrier, and roses serve as habitat for some of the most conspicuous breeding passerines of Cape Cod and the Islands. These include Rufous-sided Towhees, Gray Catbirds, Common Yellowthroats, and Song Sparrows.

The more exposed shorelines of Cape Cod and the Islands are changing continually due to the combined effects of rising sea level, current action, and storms. Points and small islands appear and disappear at irregular intervals. One of the best documented and most dramatic examples of this gradual evolution is shown by Monomoy Island off Chatham. Historically, the area has varied among an extension of North Beach, an extension of Morris Island, a separate island, and a series of islands.

Monomoy is one of the most spectacular migratory stopover areas in Massachusetts. Both North and South Monomoy consist entirely of sand, and together they extend approximately eight miles south into Nantucket Sound from Chatham. Among the ornithological features that have attracted attention to Monomoy over the years are the large numbers of migratory shorebirds that feed on the flats at the north end, the migrating passerines that periodically accumulate around the ponds and thickets at the south end, and the history of nesting gulls and terns on both islands.

Because of Monomoy's dual status as a National Wilderness Area and a National Wildlife Refuge, the island's safety from development is ensured. Despite this, the quality of the tidal flats at the north end seems to have declined in recent years. The numbers of shorebirds reported feeding on these flats were apparently almost ten times higher in the 1940s than they are today. A possible explanation is that increased exposure to the ocean since the breaching of the north end in 1960 and Inward Point in 1978 has altered the sediment contents of the flats. Observers who recall birding at Monomoy when it was still connected to Morris Island in Chatham remark that the flats were much muddier then. Today, those same flats are mostly bare sand, except at the very edge of the adjacent salt marsh.

Provincetown, at the tip of Cape Cod, also attracts a diverse array of migrating birds. Along the outer beach, especially near Race Point, the number of seabirds that are attracted to schools of fish near offshore tidal rips can be impressive in any season. In spring, the Beech Forest attracts many species of passerines, while, in fall, the thickets and marshes between the airport and Race Point occasionally trap multitudes of land birds, especially during foggy or rainy weather.

Several agricultural fields, most notably those at Hillside Farm in Truro and those behind the Barnstable County Courthouse in Orleans, have dense growths of seed-bearing weeds that regularly attract large numbers of sparrows and other weed-loving species in fall.

Cape Cod has some of the largest salt marshes in Massachusetts, including the Great Marsh at Sandy Neck in Barnstable, the marshes at Wellfleet Bay Wildlife Sanctuary, and Nauset Marsh in Eastham. All three contain nesting populations of Sharp-tailed Sparrows and Seaside Sparrows and, irregularly, a few Clapper Rails.

Penikese Island supports a small but persistent colony of Leach's Storm-Petrels that represents this species' southernmost population in the western Atlantic Ocean. A single brooding Manx Shearwater was also found on Penikese in 1973, and, nearby on the Weepecket Islands, a pair of Great Cormorants was found nesting in 1984. These latter two records, like that for the petrel, represent the southernmost breeding records for each species on the Atlantic Seaboard.

Muskeget Island, situated about five miles west-northwest of Nantucket, is of particular interest because of its history of nesting seabirds. During the 1800s, Muskeget harbored enormous colonies of Common and Roseate terns. After the terns were decimated by plume traders, Muskeget became the largest Laughing Gull colony in the Northeast during the 1940s, only to be eventually replaced by colonies of Herring and Great Black-backed gulls two decades later.

*Manx Shearwater*

# Aspects of Massachusetts Bird Life

## PELAGIC BIRDS AND COLONIAL WATERBIRDS

### History of Pelagic Bird Study

The scientific study of pelagic birds in Massachusetts began in 1884 when Captain Joseph W. Collins published, "Notes on the methods of capture of various species of seabirds that occur on the fishing banks off the eastern coast of North America which are used as bait for catching codfish by New England fishermen," in a report to the United States Fish Commission. His paper graphically describes the practice of using shearwaters for fish bait, as well as providing information about the seasonal occurrence and abundance of seabirds on Georges Bank. Collins' notes were the first to chronicle the winter abundance of Northern Fulmars on Georges Bank—a fact otherwise undocumented prior to the 1960s. In addition, his descriptions of the arrival and departure dates of jaegers, skuas, and a number of more common seabird species can hardly be improved upon today.

In the years following Collins' initial publication, other ornithologists gradually contributed to the growing understanding of the status of pelagic birds in Massachusetts. For example, Spencer F. Baird (1887) reported a massive influx of Cory's Shearwaters and jaegers in Buzzards Bay during the fall of 1886, and, during the period between 1910 and 1920, Herbert K. Job and Walter H. Rich conducted pelagic bird studies off Cape Cod. Much of their work was later cited in Arthur C. Bent's *Life Histories of North American Birds* (1922) and William B. Alexander's *Birds of the Ocean* (1955).

Offshore trips in search of birds were continued by Ludlow Griscom, who went to sea from Chatham and Rockport 60 times between 1932 and 1954. Griscom's detailed journals clearly reflect the variation in seabird abundance from season to season and from year to year, in addition to providing an invaluable basis for comparison with more recent trips. Beginning in the 1960s, the Brookline Bird Club and the Massachusetts Audubon Society initiated the tradition of running regular boat trips to Stellwagen Bank, Jeffries Ledge, and Pollock Rip, and, by the 1970s, public whale watching excursions offered ready access to these same waters. Beginning in the 1980s, occasional overnight charter trips were being made to the continental shelf edge in the vicinity of Hydrographer Canyon. As a result of these various investigations, Massachusetts has enjoyed nearly continuous coverage of its offshore waters for almost a century.

## Pelagic Studies

Prior to the 1970s, most of the at-sea studies of pelagic birds off Massachusetts were conducted opportunistically, usually aboard chartered fishing boats that visited the inshore fishing banks, such as Stellwagen Bank and Pollock Rip. More recently, Kevin D. Powers (1983) published the results of a quantitative survey of the marine birds of Georges Bank and the Gulf of Maine that has proven to be invaluable during the preparation of the present work. Powers' study, which was conducted under the auspices of the Manomet Bird Observatory, relied on data gathered by a corps of experienced observers aboard research vessels and Coast Guard ships. This study provided seabird distribution maps by season, as well as yielding information about what areas of the pelagic waters off Massachusetts are especially attractive to foraging seabirds. For example, Powers' data clearly shows that in spring, Red Phalaropes aggregate in great numbers to feed on fish eggs that are concentrated at the shelf-break front of Georges Bank and that staggering numbers of seabirds regularly cluster around commercial fisheries operations, especially on the perimeter of Georges Bank. The MBO study also provided information on habitat selection by marine birds, such as the offshore separation by surface water temperature of Greater and Cory's shearwaters.

## Land-based Studies

The convoluted coastline of Massachusetts provides ample opportunity for studying the migrations of seabirds, especially when storms deflect their movements within sight of land. Halibut and Andrew's points on Cape Ann, Sandy Neck in Barnstable, First Encounter Beach in Eastham, Race Point in Provincetown, and the east and south shores of Nantucket have been the most consistently productive places from which to watch during northeasterly gales. Observers have also found that strong northeasterly winds regularly trap seabirds in Cape Cod Bay and that the birds will typically circle the bay in a counterclockwise direction in an attempt to gain exit to the sea at Provincetown as long as the high winds persist. If the winds shift to the northwest, the trapped pelagic birds are then deflected toward the easterly shores of Cape Cod Bay, thus making their exit passage most visible at First Encounter Beach in Eastham. In fact, some of the most notable shore counts of certain pelagic birds ever made on the Atlantic Coast of the United States (e.g., jaegers, skuas, Sabine's Gull) have been made at this location.

Furthermore, some of the best information on the irregular incursions of alcids, such as the Thick-billed Murre and Dovekie, have been most often detected by land-based observations. For example, it was Dorothy Snyder's careful and repeated observations of Dovekies at Cape Ann during the 1950s that revealed that their famous southward incursions are not necessarily caused by storms, because large numbers were noted during days with little or no wind, or with light breezes from the southwest (Snyder 1953). Despite the examples cited above, the only systematic effort to study Massachusetts seabirds from shore has been an autumn sea watch, intermittently conducted by the Manomet Bird Observatory (Petersen 1971), which was primarily designed to monitor scoter migration.

## The Sand Lance Connection

Beginning in the 1970s, an important shift occurred in the local distribution and abundance of a number of Massachusetts seabirds, largely in response to an explosion in the population of the bait fish called the Sand Lance (*Ammodytes* sp.). Sherman et al (1981) documented this population explosion of Sand Lances, which began during 1975 and 1976. The attendant response in seabird numbers was observable within two years, when Stellwagen Bank swarmed with shearwaters and jaegers during the fall of 1977. At the zenith of their abundance, Sand Lances were most conspicuous in shallow waters, both very close to shore and over the shallower parts of the offshore fishing banks. Off Cape Cod and Nantucket, the greatest numbers appeared during the spawning season between November and March. At times during the period of maximum abundance, thousands of Herring Gulls and Black-legged Kittiwakes gathered along Cape Cod and Nantucket beaches to feast on the ubiquitous fish, right in the breaking surf. In summer and early fall, shearwaters, terns, and jaegers concentrated in unprecedented numbers at Stellwagen Bank and at Pollock Rip off Chatham. Although seabird numbers seemed greatest during the late 1970s, seasonal counts remained inflated into the early 1980s. During this same time period, Razorbills began occurring in unprecedented numbers in winter, and, for a series of years, the Cape Cod Christmas Bird Count held the national high count record for this species.

Apparently, a somewhat comparable event occurred during the fall of 1886 (Baird 1887), when large numbers of Cory's Shearwaters and jaegers entered Buzzards Bay in pursuit of superabundant numbers of Herring (*Clupea harengus*). This event lasted only one season, unlike the Sand Lance explosion, which persisted for nearly a decade and attracted a diversity of seabird species.

## Seabird and Wading Bird Colonies in Massachusetts

Some of the most exhaustive population and ecological studies of colonial waterbirds ever undertaken have focused on seabirds nesting in Massachusetts. In particular, the relationship between nesting gulls and terns has received considerable attention as a conservation and management issue.

Up until the latter portion of the 19th century, enormous numbers of Common and Roseate terns nested on Muskeget and Penikese islands. The numbers of birds in these great colonies were severely depleted by plume hunters between 1880 and 1905, after which time protective measures were taken and the species began to increase. By the 1920s, however, Herring Gulls had extended their breeding range south from Maine into Massachusetts, soon to be followed by Great Black-backed Gulls in the 1940s. These range expansions by gulls eventually usurped many of the most desirable nesting sites previously occupied by the terns. As a result, terns have been forced to use suboptimal breeding sites, many of which are highly susceptible to predation by Black-crowned Night-Herons, Great Horned Owls, and several mammalian predators. Human intervention to discourage predators has become a necessity in order to ensure the survival of the terns.

In addition to the numerous tern and gull colonies found on the Massachusetts coast, the southernmost breeding colony of the Leach's Storm-

Petrel occurs on Penikese Island, although the number of nesting pairs has been reduced to fewer than 20 following the island's colonization by gulls in the 1930s. Besides the storm-petrels, the first pair of Manx Shearwaters ever found nesting in North America was discovered breeding under a wooden plank at Penikese Island in 1973 (Bierregaard et al 1975), but the species has not returned since.

The Double-crested Cormorant is another seabird that has greatly expanded its breeding range and increased its numbers in recent years, although the causes remain obscure. The species was the subject of an intensive study in Maine from 1910 to 1950 (Gross 1944), during which time the population was controlled because it was believed that the birds competed with commercial fishermen.

After being afforded protection in Maine beginning in the mid-1950s, cormorant numbers in Massachusetts steadily increased until the early 1970s, at which point the number of local breeding pairs doubled about every three years, at least until 1982 (Hatch 1984). Since then, the rate of increase has apparently diminished, although the overall spread of the species continues, not only in New England, but also elsewhere in North America. Whether this dramatic population explosion will have deleterious effects on other colonial waterbird species remains to be seen.

Long-legged wading birds have also enjoyed a general increase in numbers in Massachusetts since Griscom and Snyder described their status in 1955. A trend began in the 1970s when three species—Tricolored Heron, Cattle Egret, and Glossy Ibis—expanded their breeding ranges northward to Massachusetts, while several other species increased in numbers and established a number of new nesting rookeries along the coast. Slightly later than the range expansion and population explosion shown by the coastal nesting herons, egrets, and ibises, Great Blue Herons began to increase at inland breeding sites, and, by 1991, 37 active rookeries were known throughout the state (Blodget, pers. comm.).

A characteristic of all colonial waterbirds, especially terns and long-legged wading birds, is the frequency with which the breeding colonies change location. Changing ecological conditions, the arrival of competitive or predatory species, and direct human disturbance are all factors that contribute to these shifts. The figure on page 25 depicts the largest and most significant coastal colony sites in the Commonwealth, while the table on page 24 indicates the species composition and numbers of pairs in each colony during the period 1984 to 1985 (Andrews 1990).

## Principal Waterbird Colonies on the Massachusetts Coast

| Colony Name | Double-crested Cormorant | Great Egret | Snowy Egret | Little Blue Heron | Cattle Egret | Black-crowned Night-Heron | Glossy Ibis | Laughing Gull | Herring Gull | Great Black-backed Gull | Roseate Tern | Common Tern | Arctic Tern | Least Tern |
|---|---|---|---|---|---|---|---|---|---|---|---|---|---|---|
| Milk Island | 717 | – | – | – | – | – | – | – | 1330 | 700 | – | – | – | – |
| Kettle Island | – | – | 33 | 4 | – | 18 | 11 | – | 437 | 46 | – | – | – | – |
| House Island | – | – | – | – | – | – | – | – | 280 | 75 | – | – | – | – |
| Eagle Island | – | – | 2 | – | 2 | 42 | – | – | 375 | 50 | – | – | – | – |
| Egg Rock | 304 | – | – | – | – | – | – | – | 135 | 62 | – | – | – | – |
| Spectacle Island | – | 1 | 40 | – | – | 60 | 10 | – | 920 | 36 | – | – | – | – |
| Middle Brewster Island | 92 | – | 124 | – | – | 270 | – | – | 1400 | 110 | – | – | – | – |
| Calf Island | – | – | 25 | – | – | 50 | 1 | – | 810 | 149 | – | – | – | – |
| Shag Rocks | 886 | – | – | – | – | – | – | – | 17 | 3 | – | – | – | – |
| Clark's Island | – | 2 | 127 | 1 | – | 235 | – | – | 1813 | 156 | – | – | – | – |
| Plymouth Beach | – | – | – | – | – | – | – | – | – | – | 6 | 1114 | 6 | 17 |
| Gray's Beach | – | – | – | – | – | – | – | – | – | – | 64 | 856 | – | – |
| Dead Neck/ Sampson's Island | – | – | 1 | – | – | 20 | – | – | 300 | 90 | 53 | 168 | – | 15 |
| New Island | – | – | – | – | – | – | – | 254 | – | – | 40 | 1540 | 6 | – |
| North Monomoy Island | – | – | – | – | – | – | – | 800 | 570 | 63 | 2 | 1200 | 3 | 2 |
| South Monomoy Island | – | – | 85 | – | – | 82 | – | – | 13,951 | 4933 | – | – | – | 35 |
| Bird Island | – | – | – | – | – | – | – | – | – | – | 1650 | 810 | – | – |
| Ram Island | – | – | – | – | – | – | – | – | 500 | 90 | – | – | – | – |
| Weepecket Islands | 1135 | – | – | – | – | – | – | – | 658 | 130 | – | – | – | – |
| Nashawena Island | – | – | 30 | – | – | 20 | – | – | 930 | 200 | 2 | 145 | – | 68 |
| Penikese Island | – | – | – | – | – | – | – | – | 383 | 8 | – | – | – | – |
| Sarson Island | – | – | 2 | – | – | – | – | – | 175 | 5 | – | 250 | – | – |
| Nomans Land | – | – | 13 | – | – | 60 | – | – | 1200 | 200 | 3 | 150 | – | 1 |
| Muskeget Island | – | – | – | – | – | – | – | – | 250 | 750 | – | – | – | – |
| Tuckernuck Island | – | – | – | – | – | – | – | – | 800 | 400 | – | – | – | 200 |
| Coatue | – | 1 | 11 | – | – | 42 | – | – | 970 | 679 | – | – | – | – |
| Quaise | – | 1 | 45 | – | – | 9 | – | – | – | – | – | – | – | – |

Numbers of pairs from *Coastal Waterbird Colonies, Part 1: Maine to Virginia 1984–1985*, compiled by Ralph Andrews, U.S. Fish and Wildlife Service, Newton Corner, MA, 1990.

## Principal Waterbird Colonies on the Massachusetts Coast

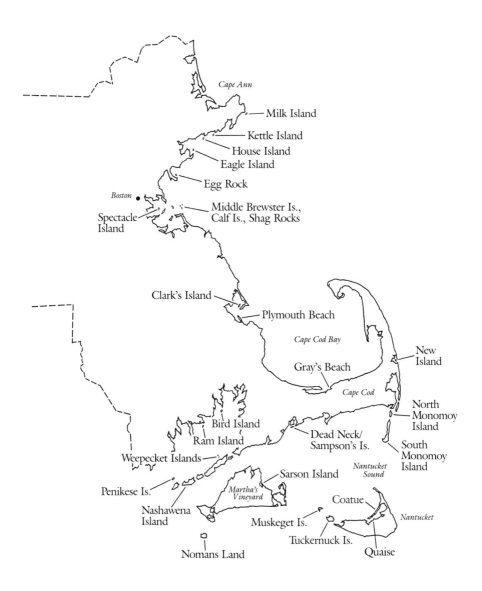

*Cape Ann*

Milk Island

Kettle Island
House Island
Eagle Island

Egg Rock

*Boston*

Spectacle
Island

Middle Brewster Is.,
Calf Is., Shag Rocks

Clark's Island

Plymouth Beach

*Cape Cod Bay*

New
Island

Gray's Beach

*Cape Cod*

North
Monomoy
Island

Bird Island

Dead Neck/
Sampson's Is.

Ram Island

South
Monomoy
Island

Weepecket Islands

*Nantucket
Sound*

Sarson Island

Penikese Is.

*Martha's
Vineyard*

Coatue

Nashawena
Island

Muskeget Is.

*Nantucket*

Tuckernuck Is.

Nomans Land

Quaise

# RECENT CHANGES IN
# MASSACHUSETTS BIRD LIFE

A number of Massachusetts bird populations have significantly changed since the publication of Griscom and Snyder's *Birds of Massachusetts* in 1955. In some cases, the causes of these changes are obvious, but, in other cases, the reasons are obscure. The list that follows is comprised of 41 Massachusetts breeding species whose numbers in the state have significantly increased during the last 30 years.

| | |
|---|---|
| Common Loon | Great Black-backed Gull |
| Double-crested Cormorant | Mourning Dove |
| Great Blue Heron | Barn Owl |
| Great Egret | Red-bellied Woodpecker |
| Snowy Egret | Acadian Flycatcher |
| Little Blue Heron | Willow Flycatcher |
| Cattle Egret | Fish Crow |
| Glossy Ibis | Common Raven |
| Mute Swan | Tufted Titmouse |
| Canada Goose | Carolina Wren |
| Gadwall | Blue-gray Gnatcatcher |
| Turkey Vulture | Northern Mockingbird |
| Osprey | Blue-winged Warbler |
| Bald Eagle | Cerulean Warbler |
| Northern Goshawk | Worm-eating Warbler |
| Peregrine Falcon | Northern Cardinal |
| Wild Turkey | Brown-headed Cowbird |
| American Oystercatcher | Orchard Oriole |
| Willet | House Finch |
| Wilson's Phalarope | Evening Grosbeak |
| Herring Gull | |

Some of the increases are the direct result of human intervention. For example, hacking programs aimed at restoring extirpated populations of Bald Eagles and Peregrine Falcons in the northeastern United States have successfully reinstated these species to the list of Massachusetts breeding birds. Likewise, the erection of nesting platforms and breeding boxes, especially on Martha's Vineyard, has dramatically increased local populations of Ospreys and Barn Owls. In a different fashion, introduced species such as the Mute Swan and House Finch have steadily colonized the region from populations originating on Long Island, New York, in the early 1900s and 1940s respectively. Similarly, the Wild Turkey has now been reestablished in a number of forested areas throughout the state as a result of stocking efforts by the Massachusetts Division of Fisheries and Wildlife.

During the 1970s, a number of southern coastal nesting species began to spread northward into New England. Most notable of these were the Great Egret, Snowy Egret, Little Blue Heron, Cattle Egret, Glossy Ibis, American Oystercatcher, and Willet. Oystercatchers and Willets were apparently reclaiming ancestral breeding areas following recovery from hunting pressure, but the colonization by the herons is more difficult to explain. It has been proposed that severe drought conditions in the southern states may have triggered a major northward dispersal that ultimately resulted in new colony formation to the north. However, the periodic summer incursions of herons and egrets to Massachusetts were known long before the 1970s (Cottrell 1949), so it is possible that a general population increase south of New England was responsible for this range expansion.

In the case of Herring and Great Black-backed gulls, local populations steadily swelled following the initial colonization of Massachusetts during the 1920s and 1940s, respectively. An abundance of open landfills and a burgeoning fishing industry coupled with the practice of disposing of fishing wastes near coastal fishing ports provided a readily exploited food source, while the region's many offshore islands served as suitable nesting areas for the expanding populations. Currently, gull numbers appear to be more stable and are probably close to the carrying capacity of the region.

The majority of recent increases in Massachusetts bird populations involve southern species. It is possible that global warming and associated long-term climatic changes may be responsible for some of these population shifts. The Carolina Wren, for example, has long been at the northern periphery of its range in southern New England. Forbush (1929) described how this species has always had a history of increasing and decreasing in response to winter severity. A series of mild winters would allow Massachusetts populations to increase, only to get knocked back by a good old-

*Carolina Wren*

fashioned New England winter. By the 1990s, however, the Carolina Wren reached an all-time population high in the Commonwealth. Along with a milder climate, the tremendous increase in winter bird feeding has probably facilitated the spread of such species as the Tufted Titmouse and Northern Cardinal and possibly, to a lesser extent, the Red-bellied Woodpecker and Carolina Wren.

Forest fragmentation is another factor that has contributed to the present abundance of at least one species—the Brown-headed Cowbird. As extensive tracts of woodland are fragmented by power lines, roadways, subdevelopments, and industrial complexes, increased amounts of forest edge are created that benefit the peculiar breeding strategy of the cowbird. As nest parasites, cowbirds rely on smaller passerine species for hosts. With the steady opening of eastern forests, cowbirds have now gained increased access to many forest breeding birds that were in the past geographically isolated or ecologically insulated from their parasitism. Recent studies have shown a rising incidence of nest parasitism in forest-nesting passerine birds, and genuine concern has arisen over the long-range future of certain host species (Terborgh 1989).

At the same time that some bird species have been increasing in abundance or expanding their range into New England, other species have been declining or have been undergoing range contractions. The following list includes 24 species whose local declines have been most dramatic since 1955.

| | |
|---|---|
| Pied-billed Grebe | Arctic Tern |
| American Bittern | Short-eared Owl |
| American Black Duck | Whip-poor-will |
| Northern Harrier | Olive-sided Flycatcher |
| Cooper's Hawk | Eastern Bluebird |
| Red-shouldered Hawk | Gray-cheeked Thrush |
| King Rail | Golden-winged Warbler |
| Common Moorhen | Northern Parula |
| Piping Plover | Vesper Sparrow |
| Upland Sandpiper | Grasshopper Sparrow |
| Roseate Tern | Bobolink |
| Common Tern | Eastern Meadowlark |

One of the dangers in drawing up a list of increasing or decreasing bird species is that there are often short-term or periodic fluctuations in bird populations that are contrary to the long-term trend. For example, certain species (e.g., Cooper's Hawk, Eastern Bluebird) that are clearly enjoying a population increase at the time of writing have actually been in a state of decline throughout most of the period since 1955. The increase or stabilization of numbers for these species remains for future field students to monitor.

Some population declines seem to be readily explainable. As marshland

and grassland habitats are developed, become polluted, or succeed ecologically, certain species that depend upon them have steadily declined. In
fact, nearly half of the species listed as declining are associated with these
two habitats. Roseate Terns, on the other hand, have suffered from competition with expanding gull populations for nesting space and from increased
pressure from predators. Similarly, the Piping Plover, once a frequent nester
on nearly every sandy beach in Massachusetts, is now listed as federally
threatened on the Atlantic Coast, largely as a result of competition with
humans and their off-road vehicles, as well as predation pressure similar to
that facing the terns.

One of the greatest threats facing certain Neotropical migrant species is
the alarming rate of tropical forest destruction and its impact on species that
utilize that habitat during the winter. It has been suggested that a number
of North American passerine species may be declining as a result of this
habitat alteration. Of equal concern regarding these same species is the
steady fragmentation of temperate zone forest in eastern North America. As
a result of these two processes, and associated predation and parasitism
factors, many songbird species are undoubtedly diminishing in abundance;
but our ability to properly measure the phenomenon is limited by the
absence of long-term baseline data with which to compare present populations. For a current and cogent discussion of these problems, the reader is
referred to Terborgh (1989) and Hagan and Johnston (1992). Neotropical
migrant species breeding in Massachusetts that are being affected by these
processes include the Whip-poor-will, Olive-sided Flycatcher, Gray-cheeked
Thrush, Golden-winged Warbler, and Northern Parula.

The Golden-winged Warbler may represent the most complex case of any
declining bird species in Massachusetts. It is facing the destruction of its
tropical wintering habitat, ecological change in its breeding range, increased
nest parasitism by Brown-headed Cowbirds, and competition from an
expanding Blue-winged Warbler population. Which of these factors will
ultimately prove to be the most significant in influencing the demise of this
lovely parulid remains to be seen.

# MIGRATION AND VAGRANCY

## *Migration*

The seasonal and periodic movements of bird populations are such dynamic aspects of the avifauna of Massachusetts that no treatment of the Commonwealth's birds would be complete without a discussion of migration. So much has been learned about the mechanics of migration during the past half century that it is now possible to characterize the process more precisely than ever before. The comments that follow apply in many ways to the migration of birds anywhere in eastern North America, although the geographical position and topographic configuration of Massachusetts inevitably produces effects that are regionally specific. For information pertaining to the migration of specific species, the reader is referred to the individual species accounts.

Aside from the protracted summer and fall migration of shorebirds, most of the major migrational activity through Massachusetts occurs between mid-March and early June and late August through mid-November. There are, however, irregular winter irruptions of northern hawks, owls, and finches that fall outside these periods, in addition to the annual arrivals and departures of a variety of migratory summer and winter residents.

Although it had long been assumed that "wind drift" was responsible for the preponderance of migrant songbirds along the coast in fall, a pattern did not emerge until coordinated coastal bird-banding studies (e.g., Baird et al 1959) demonstrated that the majority of these coastal migrants were immatures. Soon afterward, John Richardson (1972), who was studying bird migration in eastern Canada, observed that the majority of the fall migrant passerines initiating nocturnal departures from eastern Canada do so in a southwesterly direction on nights when favoring tailwinds (i.e., northeasterly) are blowing in the intended flight direction of the migrants. Most heavy coastal migrant fallouts, however, occur following the passage of Canadian-born cold fronts with attendant north*westerly* winds—winds that would seem unsuitable for migrants desiring to follow a southwesterly course. Richardson's radar work did reveal, however, that on most evenings following the passage of a cold front, there were consistently large numbers of departing migrants, even when winds were not from the optimal directions. The pattern suggested by these observations is that large numbers of inexperienced immature birds are likely to initiate nocturnal migration under suboptimal conditions. Under such suboptimal wind conditions, the migrants are wind drifted southeastward to the coast where they either precipitate into coastal migrant traps or continue out to sea, where many undoubtedly perish.

A related discovery elucidated by radar is the fact that large fallouts of migrants, regardless of the season, are not necessarily reflective of a heavy

*White-crowned Sparrow*

nocturnal passage the preceding evening. It is only when migrants are confronted with adverse conditions (e.g., rain, fog, or a wind shift) that they are forced to alight, occasionally in spectacular numbers. Just such an event occurred in May 1948 when heavy rain squalls unexpectedly overtook nocturnal migrants passing over eastern Massachusetts during the height of spring migration. At the time, observers on the ground had the erroneous impression that a record-breaking migration had taken place the previous evening. In actuality, the unfavorable weather simply interrupted what might otherwise have been an average night's passage.

A peculiar variation of fall migration involves the regular appearance of species in Massachusetts long after the majority of their populations have migrated south. Typical examples include the Yellow-billed Cuckoo, Common Nighthawk, Chimney Swift, Barn Swallow, and several warbler species. These tardy individuals, along with various "lingering" passerines that often show up at bird feeders in early winter, are probably more than simply late fall migrants. More likely, they are "reverse migrants" that arrive in Massachusetts during late October and November following weather conditions accompanied by strong southerly winds (Heil 1981). Their origin is undoubtedly south of New England, but the precise causes of their unseasonal northward migration remain unclear.

The geographical location and topographical features of Massachusetts also have an affect on the behavior and distribution of migrants. Ludlow

Griscom (1949) suggested that the Connecticut and Housatonic river valleys represent the primary passerine flyways through the Commonwealth in spring, as well as describing a concentration of spring migrants in "a narrow east-west belt from Canton and Milton through Brookline to Cambridge and Belmont. East of Milton [the migration] amounts to nothing and peters out westward to Lincoln and Concord, amounting again to nothing in the central uplands. North of Boston [the flight] hits the coast and is well developed only in the eastern half of Essex County." More recent radar studies have demonstrated that migration ordinarily occurs on a much broader front than described by Griscom, although the radar work of Nisbet and Drury (1967) does convincingly demonstrate that passerines migrating over Massachusetts in spring do so on a northeasterly bearing, the eastern edge of the flight typically falling on a line between Providence, Rhode Island, and Cohasset, i.e., roughly paralleling the eastern seaboard of the United States. Therefore, in areas such as river valleys where grounded migrants concentrate, it is probably the configuration of the landscape and the availability of food and cover that concentrates them more than the fact that they are following predetermined migration corridors or flyways.

The annual passage of diurnal raptors is another migratory event of considerable interest to birders. In the fall, especially during September, occasionally spectacular hawk flights develop at favored concentration points such as Mount Tom in the Connecticut River valley and Wachusett Mountain in Worcester County. Extensive observations during hawk migration seasons have shown that hawks alter their flight lines considerably from day to day in response to varying wind conditions and the height and density of cloud cover. While it is true that hawks often follow "leading lines" (e.g., coastlines, ridge tops, and river valleys) under certain conditions, most birds typically migrate on the same sort of broad fronts as those described for passerines. These variations in flight patterns readily explain the great fluctuations in counts of migratory hawks from year to year.

There is also much evidence to indicate that many waterfowl, shorebirds, and several other waterbird groups make inland passages over New England in great numbers. Very often, rainy weather forces flocks of Snow Geese and various shorebirds to alight in flooded pastures and cornfields during March and April, while in the fall, muddy-edged ponds and reservoirs or exposed sandbars in the Connecticut River attract a variety of shorebirds. In years of high water, when exposed flats are unavailable for resting and feeding, these species pass through unnoticed. Similarly, during October and November, modest numbers of loons, grebes, scoters, and other sea ducks alight in the larger interior water bodies such as the Quabbin and Wachusett reservoirs in central Massachusetts and Berkshire County lakes such as Onota and Pontoosuc.

Coastal shorebird migration has always been one of the great ornithological attractions of Massachusetts. The favored areas in Essex, Plymouth, and

Barnstable counties afford extensive habitat that seasonally supports tens of thousands of migrants. During the protracted autumn migration between early July and mid-November, great waves of shorebirds annually arrive on calendar schedules that vary from species to species. These migrations are divided into two peaks, the first consisting of adult birds that leave their arctic and subarctic breeding grounds soon after their precocial young have hatched and the second comprised of juveniles. The occurrence of optimum passage of weather fronts can influence the timing of these flights, and relative breeding success in the North also influences the ratio of age classes present at a given time.

Perhaps most noteworthy in describing Massachusetts shorebird migration is the fact that certain notably uncommon species occur almost exclusively in fall (e.g., Hudsonian Godwit, Western Sandpiper, Baird's Sandpiper, Buff-breasted Sandpiper, and Long-billed Dowitcher), while several very common or abundant fall migrants are much less common in spring (e.g., Lesser Yellowlegs, Whimbrel, and Semipalmated Sandpiper). These differences are due to variations in the routes used by these species at different times of the year and also to a larger total number of birds migrating in fall.

## Vagrancy

Avian vagrancy is an especially fascinating phenomenon. Vagrant birds are ones that have wandered, been blown, or been otherwise transported to localities beyond their normal range. Ornithologists generally believe that the occurrence of vagrant birds probably results from various factors, including variations in the reproductive success within a species' population, navigational dysfunction, displacement by wind, and responses to perturbations in the environment of the vagrant species involved. Regardless of the precise causes, the search for, and discovery of, vagrant birds has for many years been a source of pleasure for birders worldwide.

In discussing the hypotheses that attempt to explain avian vagrancy, it is inadvisable to attribute isolated vagrant occurrences to a singular mechanism or factor. Instead, it is advisable to view vagrancy as a phenomenon with very likely several factors interacting in ways that cause individual birds to be displaced in time and space.

Nearly 60 years of uninterrupted compilation of Massachusetts bird records has provided the authors with a data base that may be unequalled in North America. The advantage of this continuous record is that it provides the opportunity to establish a possible link between the incidence of vagrancy and avian reproductive success. This correlation is especially noticeable in the case of certain rare migrant and vagrant species from western North American that appear in Massachusetts during autumn.

By using Breeding Bird Survey data, it is possible to approximate the relative annual reproductive success of certain species throughout their breeding range (Robbins et al 1986). When Breeding Bird Survey data for the years 1965 to 1979 was compared with the relative annual fall occurrence in Massachusetts of six western species (i.e., Western Kingbird, Western Tanager, Black-headed Grosbeak, Clay-colored Sparrow, Lark Sparrow, Yellow-headed Blackbird), a positive correlation emerged. For three species (i.e., Western Kingbird, Clay-colored Sparrow, Yellow-headed Blackbird) for which high reproductive success was specifically noted during the 1965 to 1979 period (op cit), there was a relative increase in the number that appeared in Massachusetts during the autumns of the same time period. The notion that an increase in the production of young may have been responsible for an increase in Massachusetts records seems plausible. Other vagrant occurrences may result from similar, but less recognizable, increases in reproductive success within a vagrant's breeding range.

Another attempt to explain vagrancy involves a set of hypotheses proposed by David DeSante (1973, 1983) and summarized by Roberson (1980). These hypotheses suggest that defective orientation and navigation mechanisms may account for avian geographical displacement. DeSante suggests that if a bird inherits faulty genetic orientation and navigation information, the defect can manifest itself behaviorally as either disorientation or misorientation. Disoriented birds have failed to inherit a basic navigational compass direction or else have failed to learn a consistent compass reference point. Such disoriented individuals are likely to migrate in random directions, or else they consistently fly downwind regardless of the compass direction.

Misorientation, in contrast with disorientation, may manifest itself in one of three ways: as 180-degree, simple, or mirror-image misorientation. Birds exhibiting 180-degree misorientation follow a northward heading in fall that would actually be more appropriate for their spring migration. Vagrants from the south that appear in Massachusetts in fall (e.g., Fork-tailed Flycatcher, Painted Bunting), as well as more frequent "reverse migrants" (e.g., Yellow-throated Warbler, Prothonotary Warbler), may reflect this type of misorientation.

Birds exhibiting simple misorientation may inherit an inappropriate migration compass direction, or else they learn an incorrect compass reference point. Because such individuals are able to maintain a compass direction, even if it is inappropriate, birds manifesting this condition are likely to show up during the principal seasons of migration. Conversely, disoriented individuals, because of their inability to maintain a fixed compass bearing, frequently take significantly longer to cover comparable distances and may occur well outside established migration seasons.

Birds with mirror-image misorientation are thought to inherit the correct angular compass deviation but relate it to the compass reference point with the wrong east-west (right-left) sense (DeSante 1983). For example, a bird exhibiting mirror-image misorientation that might be expected to migrate on a southeast heading might follow a southwest heading instead. DeSante's (1973) studies have attempted to predict the frequency and timing of vagrant eastern warblers in California, but his hypotheses have never been applied in an effort to explain the pattern of occurrence of certain western vagrants in Massachusetts.

Weather, especially wind, is still another way of attempting to explain the appearance of vagrant birds that appear miles outside their normal range. For example, birders have little difficulty in reconciling the appearance in Massachusetts of southern seabirds (e.g., White-tailed Tropicbird, Sooty Tern, Bridled Tern) following the passage of hurricanes originating in the tropics; or the occurrence in spring of southern species (e.g., Swallow-tailed Kite, Mississippi Kite, Wilson's Plover) that "overshoot" their breeding range while migrating north on southwesterly airflows. It is similarly plausible to suppose that vagrant birds migrating with faulty navigation and orientation mechanisms may be wind drifted, just as are many immature individuals of more regularly occurring species. The displacement of vagrants by wind transport has been articulated by various workers (e.g., McLaren 1981, Wilson 1988).

In addition to wind, a number of other environmental factors seem to correlate well with the incidence of vagrancy, as well as with other more predictable bird movements. For example, changing food availability has been demonstrated to determine when irruptions of crossbills (Benkman 1987) will take place; and drought conditions in prairie grasslands may cause eastward displacements in summer of disrupted breeders such as Scissor-tailed Flycatchers, Dickcissels, and Lark Buntings (Petersen 1988). Similarly, environmental irregularities in the marine environment such as El Niño events in the Pacific Ocean and the movement of Gulf Stream eddies in the Atlantic Ocean may account for vagrant records of certain pelagic species (e.g., Swallow-tailed Gull in California, Band-rumped Storm-Petrel in Massachusetts).

At least some of these attempts to explain avian vagrancy are predicated upon the notion that bird populations may respond to environmental changes by somehow redistributing themselves. For example, in 1955 Ludlow Griscom and Dorothy Snyder described the Massachusetts status of the Tufted Titmouse as that of a "rare vagrant from the south," yet today, this species is one of the most numerous birds in suburban Massachusetts. It is probable that events occurred either within the historic range of the titmouse, or in the continental environment, that suddenly permitted the expansion of its range parameters. Various environmental or climatic factors, or species population fluctuations, undoubtedly lie behind other more recent range expansions of birds previously described as Massachusetts vagrants (e.g., Tricolored Heron, American Oystercatcher, Red-bellied Woodpecker). Global warming, increased winter bird feeding, reduced persecution, increased survival of young, a shortage of food, and increased population pressure at the heart of a species' range are all factors that may cause birds to disperse. Initially, dispersive individuals may be thought of as vagrants; however, for some species, these vagrant individuals actually represent pioneer colonists. For this reason, future bird record keepers and ecologists would be well advised to monitor carefully the occurrence of vagrant birds because in some cases they represent far more than genetic accidents or misguided migrants.

A final point to emphasize when discussing vagrancy is the role played by coastlines and coastal islands. Regardless of the mechanisms or factors responsible for displacing vagrant birds, vagrants often appear to travel until they encounter an environmental barrier (e.g., the ocean, a lakeshore, a desert). In Massachusetts, as well as elsewhere in New England, the coast and offshore islands have consistently proven to be the places where the greatest number of vagrants are found. These areas serve as "land's end" to misguided birds, and some of the better known spots (e.g., Plum Island, Monomoy Island, Nantucket) have for many years been favorite places to seek unusual birds.

# Sources of Data

## Historical Resources

No fewer than 16 books have been published on the birds of Massachusetts. During the 19th century, seminal works covering all species occurring in the state included those by Edward A. Samuels (1864) and Joel A. Allen (1878), followed early in the 20th century by a complete annotated checklist by Reginald H. Howe and Glover M. Allen (1901). However, by far the most complete work ever published on Massachusetts birds was *Birds of Massachusetts and other New England States* by Edward H. Forbush. Printed in three volumes between 1925 and 1929, this classic continues to be one of the most comprehensive state bird books ever published.

Forbush's work provided detailed information on life history, status, and plumage descriptions for every bird species occurring in Massachusetts. While serving as the Massachusetts state ornithologist from 1908 to 1920, Forbush witnessed firsthand the gross excesses of the market gunning and plume hunting eras. This persecution of birds provided the impetus needed for writing the books, which specifically attempted to document the economic importance and usefulness of birds rather than chronicling their demise. As a strong advocate of bird conservation, Forbush hoped to elicit public support for bird protection through the information presented in his magnificent volumes.

Because Forbush was such a strong spokesman for bird protection, he could not readily advocate the collecting of birds for specimens. As a result, his volumes include a number of records based on sight reports only, a circumstance for which he was later criticized by Griscom and Snyder (1955) in their efforts to update his monumental work.

In spite of this fact, the Forbush volumes contain a wealth of information on the historical fluctuations of Massachusetts bird populations, along with some of the most comprehensive data ever compiled on the habitat use and breeding biology of birds in the Commonwealth. In fact, some of the information on the natural history of Massachusetts birds in the present work is drawn from Forbush (e.g., egg dates).

Following Forbush's epic work in the 1920s, two comprehensive books on Massachusetts birds appeared in 1955. The first of these, *Birds of Massachusetts* by Ludlow Griscom and Dorothy E. Snyder, was an annotated checklist that described the status of all species and subspecies of birds that had occurred in the state up until 1955. In this checklist, the authors accepted as authentic only those bird species represented by extant specimens that they had personally examined, identifiable photographs, or sight records of "easily identified species, supported by the multiple observations of competent observers and appropriate as to date and place."

This highly conservative approach to assembling an unimpeachably accurate record of Massachusetts bird life has been criticized, especially by those whose records fell into oblivion because of its austerity. In a few instances (e.g., the probable incursion of Western Grebes on the Northeast coast in the 1940s), valid and noteworthy records may, indeed, have been obscured by Griscom's rigid "code of authenticity." On the whole, however, the clarity and validity brought to the record of the Massachusetts avifauna by Griscom and Snyder was a heroic undertaking of inestimable value and far outweighs any perceived errors of omission.

Ludlow Griscom was a pivotal figure in the development of field ornithology as a means of contributing to the scientific record and as a popular hobby, not just in Massachusetts and New York where he was most active, but throughout North America. His exceptional talent for identifying birds in the field had a profound influence on Roger Tory Peterson's efforts while he was creating his landmark book, *A Field Guide to the Birds*, in 1934. In addition to his legendary energy, enthusiasm, and charismatic personality, Griscom brought to birding a new obsession with accuracy, careful record keeping, and doing one's homework. Among his key insights was that the best field observers were those who were aware of all possibilities, and he advised his companions always to expect the unexpected. For example, a flock of Bonaparte's Gulls might just contain a Common Black-headed Gull, a vagrant from Eurasia, which Griscom himself first found at Newburyport Harbor in 1930. These personal qualities and standards of birding behavior electrified a host of bright young protégés from the 1920s to the 1950s, and they continue to be strongly influential within today's vastly enlarged birding community.

In addition to possessing extraordinary field skills, Griscom maintained copious notes and records. One of his journals contained a complete account of his activities for every day afield; a second contained lists of all birds seen for each day in the field; and a third was an annotated list of all Massachusetts birds, which was updated every time something new or different was encountered. He was very objective in describing the birds that he saw, and even years later one can read his field descriptions and confidently reach conclusions concerning the identity of the species he observed.

The second book coincidentally published in 1955 was Wallace Bailey's *Birds in Massachusetts*. Also an annotated checklist, Bailey's work presented a more liberal description of the status of the state's avifauna. Bailey relied heavily upon records published in *Records of New England Birds* and tended to assume that the majority of the published records were correct. His work proved especially useful in specifically defining the occurrence periods of birds in Massachusetts for the present work.

Other previous Massachusetts bird books focused on the status of birds in single counties or within specific geographic regions—e.g., Berkshire County, Walter Faxon and Ralph Hoffman (1900) and Douglas McNair (1978); Essex County, Charles W. Townsend (1905, 1920); Cambridge and vicinity, William Brewster (1906); the Connecticut River valley, Aaron C. Bagg and Samuel A. Eliot (1937); Nantucket, Ludlow Griscom and Edith Folger (1948); Concord region, Ludlow Griscom (1949) and Richard K. Walton (1984); Martha's Vineyard, Ludlow Griscom and Guy Emerson (1959); Cape Cod, Norman P. Hill (1965) and Wallace Bailey (1968).

## Periodicals

The species accounts, which comprise the bulk of the text, are largely based on records extracted from several primary journals, as well as information derived from the previously listed existing works on Massachusetts birds. The following is a list of the most important of these journals.

| | |
|---|---|
| *The Bulletin of the Massachusetts Audubon Society* | 1935–1958 |
| *Bulletin of New England Bird Life* (published by the New England Museum of Natural History) | 1936–1944 |
| *Records of New England Birds* (published by the Massachusetts Audubon Society) | 1945–1961, 1964–1968 |
| *Bird Observer* (formerly *Bird Observer of Eastern Massachusetts* until 1987) | 1973-present |
| *Bird News of Western Massachusetts* | 1966-present |
| *American Birds* (formerly *Audubon Field Notes* until 1970) | 1971-present |
| *The Chickadee* (annual journal of the Forbush Bird Club) | 1930-present |

## Censuses

Several data sources consistently referred to in the text represent information collected during organized census efforts rather than by individual observers, so a brief description of each census follows.

> Christmas Bird Count (CBC)—a winter census taken within a circular area 15 miles in diameter. Christmas Bird Counts are conducted during the period extending approximately one week before to one week after Christmas so that three entire weekends are included. Each CBC is held on a single calendar day. Groups of observers attempt to provide uniform coverage of the count circle and then combine their totals at the end of the day. There are approximately 29 CBCs conducted in Massachusetts each year, the results of which are published annually by the National Audubon Society in *American Birds*.

> Breeding Bird Census—a census conducted in June using the same rules as a Christmas Bird Count.

> Massachusetts Audubon Society May Bird Walks—informal counts of birds, made in May by single groups of observers within the boundaries of a specified town.

> Take a Second Look (TASL)—a volunteer census program originally established by the journal *Bird Observer* for the purpose of censusing water birds in the Boston Harbor area. Each TASL census represents a single calendar day's effort.

## Bird Records

A final and invaluable source of data for the current project were the files and records of the late Ruth P. Emery. Ruth Emery established and maintained an exhaustive bird record keeping system for about 40 years. She began compiling Massachusetts bird records in 1944 while she was employed by the Massachusetts Audubon Society. Her filing system made use of individual species report slips that were assembled in taxonomic order by both month and year. These meticulously filed records represent a principal source of data for much of the present work, especially for the years during which no records for eastern Massachusetts were published (1961–1963 and 1969–1972). Emery continued this herculean effort until 1983, when, for reasons of declining health, she passed the processing of reports on to the field editors of *Bird Observer* magazine. Without Ruth Emery's perseverance and attention to detail, the authors would have had great difficulty in discerning many of the changes in bird populations that are chronicled in the text.

## *Acceptance of Sight Records*

Prior to the establishment of the Massachusetts Avian Records Committee in 1991, Massachusetts had no formal procedure for evaluating the validity of sight reports. The present authors were therefore confronted with the often-difficult task of sorting and evaluating certain weakly documented reports, some of which undoubtedly represented authentic additions to the state bird record, from the erroneous sight reports that inevitably find their way into the published annals of field ornithology. Griscom and Snyder solved this problem by holding all observers, including themselves, to the rigorous standards previously mentioned on page 38. Unless a given record met the letter of this standard, it was discarded or relegated to the purgatory of the Hypothetical List, *even when the authors believed the identification in question to have been correct.* While this effectively prevented the inclusion of bad records, it also arbitrarily excluded a number of good records.

To be satisfactorily corroborated, certain species (e.g., skuas, *Calidris* sandpipers) will always require the best possible documentation such as photographs, detailed field notes, and confirmation by more than one competent observer. Moreover, in certain cases (e.g., some *Empidonax* flycatchers), even the best evidence short of a specimen will not suffice to authenticate a record. On the other hand, there are instances of highly distinctive birds (e.g., an adult Terek Sandpiper), seen under good conditions by experienced observers of known competence, that the authors believe merit inclusion among the authentic species of Massachusetts, even when such a record may represent a first for Massachusetts. We have approached the selection of these few cases conservatively and, while we acknowledge that the process is necessarily subjective, we believe that the overall accuracy of the list benefits from it.

## *Massachusetts Breeding Bird Atlas Project*

In 1974, the Massachusetts Audubon Society and the Massachusetts Division of Fisheries and Wildlife jointly initiated a six-year Breeding Bird Atlas Project (MBBAP) to map the distribution of all bird species nesting in Massachusetts between 1974 and 1979. Thanks to the efforts of hundreds of volunteer participants, Massachusetts Audubon was able to compile thousands of observations of breeding bird activity throughout the state.

In order to organize and plot the data gathered during the atlas period, the survey used 7.5-minute-series U.S. Geological Survey topographic quadrangle maps. Each of the 186 Massachusetts maps was further divided into six, 9.2-square-mile sections, or blocks. Observers visited a block as many times as possible during the six-year period in an effort to determine which bird species were "possible," "probable," or "confirmed" breeders within the area. Specific bird behavior criteria based upon similar efforts in Great Britain (Sharrock 1976) were prepared so that each species found in a block could be assigned to one of these three breeding categories. The ultimate goal of the project was to raise as many breeding species to the "confirmed" level as possible.

Data presented on 133 maps in the text represents only the presence or absence of breeding species, not the size of the population in each block. Symbols on the maps indicate the highest level of breeding confirmation that was attained for each block at the end of the 1974–1979 atlas period. The breeding status for each species is represented on the maps as follows: "confirmed" (▲); "probable" (■); "possible" (▪).

The maps that appear in the text are based upon data gathered during the MBBAP and were carefully chosen as those that still accurately reflect each species' current pattern of distribution and status. Maps for species for which significant range expansions or contractions have occurred since 1979 have been omitted, and the reader should rely upon the text for a summary of the current breeding status.

*Red-bellied
Woodpecker*

# Definition of Terms
and Abbreviations

For Massachusetts breeding species, every account includes the subheadings **Range, Status, Breeding,** and **Nonbreeding.** For species that do not breed in Massachusetts, the subheading **Occurrence** is used in place of **Breeding** and **Nonbreeding.** The specific content of these subheadings is described below.

**Range:** Each species' range description is preceded by the name of the primary zoogeographic realm in which the species occurs (e.g., Nearctic, Palearctic), followed by a brief summary of the species' overall geographic distribution. For polytypic species, emphasis is given to the particular subspecies that regularly occurs in Massachusetts. For those species for which more than one clearly definable subspecies has been recorded in the Commonwealth, appropriate notes are included at the end of the species account.

**Status:** This section describes the overall status, frequency of occurrence, and relative abundance of the species in Massachusetts at different times of the year.

43

It is difficult to develop a terminology that is uniformly applicable to all bird species occurring within a particular region. This difficulty is largely related to differences in the distribution and abundance patterns of various birds. For example, some species range widely over large areas while others aggregate into large flocks at specific sites. Bull (1964) discusses this problem at length and appropriately gives as an example a comparison between the abundance of Northern Gannets and Red-eyed Vireos in New York.

Which species is the more numerous species in Massachusetts? Although birders may see thousands of gannets in a day off Cape Cod in fall, they could probably never in a lifetime see that many vireos in Massachusetts, even though thousands of Red-eyed Vireos undoubtedly breed in the state every year. Because of these distributional and abundance differences, the criteria that have been adopted in the present work include a combination of descriptive terms that will collectively provide the reader with a precise impression of the status for each species.

For each account, a set of terms is used to describe the species' *overall status* in Massachusetts, its *frequency of occurrence*, and its *relative abundance* during times when it is present in the state. Although these terms attempt to quantify the general status of each bird species in Massachusetts, they are by no means absolutely precise.

*Overall Status:*

*Resident*—a species that remains within the same geographical area for the entire year, or an entire season (e.g., a winter resident remains in the same area for the entire winter).

*Migrant*—a species that appears in Massachusetts for less than an entire season during a round-trip journey between established breeding and wintering ranges (e.g., Cape May Warbler). A partial migrant is a species with some members of the population that are migratory and some that are sedentary (e.g., Blue Jay).

*Visitor*—a species that occurs regularly in Massachusetts, usually at the same time of year, but not on a round-trip journey between breeding and wintering ranges (e.g., southern herons that visit Massachusetts in late summer but do not breed in the state).

*Vagrant*—a species that occurs in Massachusetts at irregular intervals and whose normal range does not encompass Massachusetts.

*Frequency of Occurrence:*

*Regular*—a species that occurs in Massachusetts every year in the same season(s).

*Irregular*—a species that does not occur in Massachusetts every year, or only occurs at unpredictable intervals.

*Relative Abundance:*

The following terminology has been adopted to quantitatively describe the relative abundance of each species. All abundance ratings are based on what is believed to be the true status of a species, which may sometimes be quite different from the impression gained by a single observer while working in the field. In addition, the abundance terms are often used with modification (e.g., "fairly common" or "very uncommon") to provide a relative sense to the abundance codes.

*Abundance Terms*

| | | |
|---|---|---|
| Abundant | 500–1,000 | per day per locality |
| Very Common | 100–499 | per day per locality |
| Common | 10–99 | per day per locality |
| Uncommon | 1–9 | per day per locality |
| Rare | 1–10 | per season per locality |

**Breeding** and **Nonbreeding:** Within each of these subsections, an indication of relative abundance is provided for each season during which the species occurs in Massachusetts. Sample counts showing the maximum number of individuals that have been recorded per day per locality in Massachusetts are included, along with outstandingly early and late occurrence dates. For species that do not breed in Massachusetts, the detailed status description appears under the heading **Occurrence**.

## *Abbreviations*

The abbreviations that follow are used consistently throughout the book.

| | |
|---|---|
| AB | *American Birds* |
| ABC | Allen Bird Club |
| AFN | *Audubon Field Notes* |
| AK | *The Auk* |
| AMNH | American Museum of Natural History |
| AOU | American Ornithologists' Union |
| ASNH | Audubon Society of New Hampshire |
| BB | *British Birds* |
| BBC | Brookline Bird Club |
| BBS | Breeding Bird Survey |
| BMS | Boston Museum of Science |
| BNWM | *Bird News of Western Massachusetts* |
| BOEM | *Bird Observer* (formerly *Bird Observer of Eastern Massachusetts*) |
| CBC | Christmas Bird Count |
| CCBC | Cape Cod Bird Club |

| | |
|---|---|
| cf | compare |
| DWWS | Daniel Webster Wildlife Sanctuary |
| EMHW | Eastern Massachusetts Hawk Watch |
| et al | and others |
| FBC | Forbush Bird Club |
| fide | by the faith of |
| GBBBC | Greater Boston Breeding Bird Census |
| GMNWR | Great Meadows National Wildlife Refuge |
| HBC | Hoffman Bird Club |
| in litt. | in literature |
| IRWS | Ipswich River Wildlife Sanctuary |
| MAS | Massachusetts Audubon Society |
| MBBAP | Massachusetts Breeding Bird Atlas Project |
| MBO | Manomet Bird Observatory |
| MCCBBC | Mid-Cape Cod Breeding Bird Census |
| MCZ | Museum of Comparative Zoology (Harvard University) |
| MDFW | Massachusetts Division of Fisheries and Wildlife |
| MNWS | Marblehead Neck Wildlife Sanctuary |
| ms | unpublished manuscript |
| MSSF | Myles Standish State Forest |
| MVBBC | Martha's Vineyard Breeding Bird Census |
| NBBC | Nantucket Breeding Bird Census |
| op cit | in the work cited previously |
| pers. comm. | personal communication |
| PBC | Paskamansett Bird Club |
| PRNWR | Parker River National Wildlife Refuge |
| PMS | Peabody Museum of Salem |
| RNEB | *Records of New England Birds* |
| SSBC | South Shore Bird Club |
| SUASCO | Sudbury, Assabet, Concord river watersheds |
| TASL | Take a Second Look |
| USFWS | United States Fish and Wildlife Service |
| USNM | United States National Museum |
| VO | various observers |
| WBWS | Wellfleet Bay Wildlife Sanctuary |

Black-capped
Chickadee

# Species Accounts

*The species accounts make up the principal content of the book. More than simply an annotated checklist, the accounts provide a complete summary of the status and pattern of occurrence of all bird species known to have been definitely recorded in Massachusetts through the year 1991. Confirmed escapes from captivity (e.g., Bar-headed Goose) have been omitted.*

*A statistical summary follows.*

| | |
|---|---|
| *Total species:* | *460* |
| *Regular breeding species:* | *196* |
| *Rare breeding species (fewer than five records):* | *10* |
| *Introduced species:* | *5* |

# Red-throated Loon   *Gavia stellata*

**Range:** Holarctic; in North America, breeds from Northern Ellesmere Island south to northeastern Alberta, northern Manitoba, eastern Quebec, and northern Newfoundland. In the East, winters on the Atlantic Coast from Maine to Florida and also along the Gulf Coast.

**Status:** Common to abundant migrant. Uncommon to rare winter resident; very rare in midsummer.

**Occurrence:** Red-throated Loons usually outnumber Common Loons during migration at coastal vantage points in both spring and fall and are also more restricted to coastal waters than that species (Powers & Cherry 1983). The peak of the spring migration occurs from late March to late April. *Spring maxima:* 1,120, Monomoy, 28 April 1941 (fide Griscom); 750, Gay Head, Martha's Vineyard, 5 April 1979 (Laux); 300 +, Low Beach, Nantucket, 7 April 1963 (Andrews). The fall migration is more protracted and typically extends from mid-October to mid-December. *Fall maxima:* 1,600, Sandy Neck, Barnstable, 7 November 1977 (Pease); 1,000, Nauset, Eastham, 30 November 1957 (Armstrong et al); 940 in one hour, Rockport, 15 December 1956 (Isleib); 762 +, Rockport, 19 October 1975 (Brown).

The number of wintering Red-throated Loons varies from year to year, but the highest counts—e.g., 375, Nantucket CBC, 31 December 1978—occur in the early winter along the southeast coast. Counts later in the winter are much lower, so it is unusual to see more than ten per day per locality.

Inland, Red-throated Loons are scarce in spring—e.g., eight records for Berkshire County between 11 April–18 May (McNair 1978). In fall, most counts are of single individuals, although very occasionally many more are seen together—e.g., 150, Turners Falls, Gill, 12 November 1985 (Fairbrother); 9, Pittsfield, 8 November 1959 (Eliot); 4, Brookfield, 18 November 1962 (McMenemy).

# Pacific Loon   *Gavia pacifica*

**Range:** Holarctic; breeds from eastern Siberia, northern Alaska, and southern Baffin Island south to central Yukon and the south shore of Hudson Bay. Winters mainly on the Pacific Coast from southeastern Alaska to Baja California; much more rarely east to the Atlantic Coast.

**Status:** Rare winter visitor.

**Occurrence:** Reports of this species have raised more eyebrows and generated more arguments than perhaps any other bird species in Massachusetts, not only because of possible confusion with Common Loons, but also because of the overall uncertainty concerning the status of Pacific and Arctic loons on the Atlantic Coast of North America. The species has been reported in Massachusetts practically every year since the 1940s, yet it has never been adequately photographed or collected here. Among the more convincing reports since 1960 are: 1 alternate plumage, Manomet, 24 April 1969 (Fox, Smart); 1 in prealternate molt, Marblehead, 4 May 1961 (Snyder); 1, Rockport, 31 January 1963 (Snyder, Ingalls); 1 alternate plumage, Plum Island, 20 May 1976 (Jenkins); 1, Provincetown, 2–3 October 1976 (Bailey, Goodrich, Nikula); 1, Woods Hole, 1 January 1977 (Smart, Abbott); 1, Race Point, Provincetown, 18 February 1978 (Veit, Litchfield); 1, Plum Island, 23 December 1979–27 January 1980 (Petersen, Soucy, et al); 1, Gay Head, Martha's Vineyard, 23 March 1980 (Kleiner et al); 1, Salisbury, 20 February 1982 (Brown); 1, Plum Island, 23 March 1982 (Heil); 1, Salisbury, 28 November 1982 (Clayton); 1, Quincy, 11–18 January 1983 (Brown, Emery, et al); 1, Rockport, 21 January 1983 (Forster, Bertrand); 1, Gloucester, 25 January 1983 (Drummond et al); 1, Plymouth, 29 October 1984 (Evered 1985); 1 prealternate molt, Duxbury Beach, 10 March 1991 (Petersen, Fox, Kenneally, Leggett).

**Remarks:** Specimens from elsewhere on the Atlantic Coast have proven to be *G. pacifica*. Because *G. arctica* of Eurasia and northern Alaska could also occur, the specific identification of birds in any plumage is extremely critical. The acquisition of a Massachusetts specimen would be most desirable in order to positively document the occurrence of this species in the state.

# Common Loon   *Gavia immer*

**Range:** Holarctic; in North America, breeds from central Alaska, southern Baffin Island, and Greenland south to northwestern Montana, southern Ontario, and southern New England. In the East, winters mainly along the coast from Maine to Florida and Texas.

**Status:** Rare and local breeder. Common to very common migrant at the coast; uncommon inland; uncommon winter resident.

**Breeding:** It is difficult to ascertain the breeding status of the Common Loon in Massachusetts before 1890, for despite Forbush's comments (1925) that it "nested about many ponds in Massachusetts," there is apparently little evidence to support this statement. Indeed, there appear to be only three confirmed 19th-century records. However, loons were quick to discover the Quabbin Reservoir, and 1 pair with 2 young was seen at New Salem, 30 June 1943 (Allison), three years before the reservoir was completely full. Between 1943 and 1974, mature adults were reported annually with only one proven nesting: 1 pair and 2 young, 28 July 1959 (Albertine).

Since 1975, loons have bred, or attempted to breed, annually in Massachusetts. In 1984, the Common Loon was designated a species of special concern by the Massachusetts Natural Heritage and Endangered Species

Program, and because of disturbance by humans, powerboats, and Raccoon predation, a special warden was appointed to monitor the breeding activities of the Quabbin Reservoir loons. Also in 1984, a pair of loons bred successfully at Wachusett Reservoir (Blodget). By 1991, there were nine pairs breeding at several Massachusetts locations (fide Blodget). *Egg dates:* 2 June–10 August (Maine, New Hampshire).

**Nonbreeding:** There is a sizeable nonbreeding population of Common Loons in Massachusetts during the summer. These birds are largely sub-adult, oiled, or injured individuals, most of which are found off Cape Cod and the Islands, with a few also appearing on inland lakes. Summering loons occasionally are found in sizeable loose aggregations—e.g., 60, Sandy Neck, Barnstable, throughout July 1979 (Pease); 49, Nantucket Sound, August 1941 (Maclay); 30, Monomoy, 8 July 1975 (BOEM).

The migration period of the Common Loon is protracted, extending in spring from mid-March to early June and in fall from late August to December. Most birds migrate close to shore and are readily counted from such coastal vantage points as Cape Ann, Manomet Point, Provincetown, and Nantucket. *Spring maxima:* 150, Sandy Neck, Barnstable, 24 May 1982 (Pease); 125, Cape Cod Bay, 18 April 1982 (Nikula); 88, Muskeget Island, 21 May 1981 (Heil); 65, Nantucket, 18–20 April 1947 (fide Griscom); 50 migrating north-northeast, off Provincetown, 26 May 1979 (Petersen). *Fall maxima:* 340, Rockport, 5 November 1983 (Heil); 240, Rockport, 8 November 1977 (Heil); 217, Andrews Point, Rockport, 6 October 1962 (Snyder); 344 recorded passing Manomet Point, throughout October 1968 (MBO).

Inland, migrants are regularly seen passing overhead in May and September—e.g., 23, Mt. Wachusett, 17 September 1982 (Roberts). They often put down on lakes and ponds, usually because of inclement weather—e.g., 54, Lake Onota, Pittsfield, 19 May 1945 (Snyder, Hendricks); 63, Lake Onota, Pittsfield, and Stockbridge Bowl, 12 November 1979 (Goodrich, Minneci). In winter, Common Loons are thinly distributed along the coast and are most numerous off Nantucket and Martha's Vineyard—e.g., 355, Nantucket CBC, 31 December 1978; 300, Martha's Vineyard, 28 December 1981 (Petersen). These numbers dwindle markedly by midwinter, and it is unusual to see more than thirty to fifty during February at either Nantucket or Martha's Vineyard. Common Loons are rare inland in winter, and their presence or absence is directly related to the availability of open water.

# Pied-billed Grebe   *Podilymbus podiceps*

**Range:** Nearctic and Neotropical; breeds from British Columbia, northern Manitoba, southern Quebec, and Nova Scotia south to Baja California and southern Florida. East of the Rockies, winters from southern New England (rarely) south to the West Indies and Central America.

**Status:** Rare, local, and declining breeder; fairly common migrant and irregular in winter.

**Breeding:** Since 1955, Pied-billed Grebes have declined substantially as breeders in Massachusetts, due in part to the destruction of freshwater marshes. Probably fewer than twenty pairs currently breed in Massachusetts. For a number of years, Parker River National Wildlife Refuge was one of the most consistent breeding localities—e.g., 4 families, July 1973 (Soucy, Petersen). *Egg dates:* 23 April–28 June.

**Nonbreeding:** Pied-billed Grebes are among the first Massachusetts breeding birds to return in the spring, with the vanguard often appearing by the middle of March. Concentrations of spring migrants are seldom recorded away from known breeding localities—e.g., 11, Wayland, 16 April 1990 (Perkins). In fall, peak counts are reported from large freshwater ponds during late September and October—e.g., 30, Plum Island, 29 September 1968 (BBC); 24, Martha's Vineyard, 18–20 October 1963 (Keith et al); 22, Monomoy, 12 October 1956 (Gendall); 18, Lakeville, 28 October 1979 (SSBC). Migrants are occasionally reported at sea—e.g., 1, Stellwagen Bank, 13 September 1980 (Raymond).

During mild seasons, when ponds and bays remain unfrozen, Pied-billed Grebes are capable of surviving the entire winter in Massachusetts. Most birds are found on Cape Cod and the Islands, but there are midwinter records from inland localities—e.g., 1 Springfield, 9–21 February 1966 (Longley); 1, Stockbridge Bowl, 26 January–2 February 1980 (Goodrich); 1, Cheshire Lake, throughout February 1980 (Minneci). *Winter maximum:* 90, Cape Cod CBC, 29 December 1974.

# Horned Grebe  *Podiceps auritus*

**Range:** Holarctic; in North America breeds chiefly from central Alaska, southern Keewatin, and northern Manitoba south and east to central Wisconsin and southeastern Ontario; also on Anticosti Island and the Magdalen Islands, Quebec. On the Atlantic Coast, winters from Nova Scotia to Florida, primarily on salt water.

**Status:** Uncommon to very common migrant and winter resident. Abundance varies considerably from year to year.

**Occurrence:** Horned Grebes are most numerous in Massachusetts coastal waters and in sheltered bays and harbors. In recent years, they have become relatively scarce in winter, and in some years maximum counts have not exceeded ten birds at any one locality. *Spring maxima:* 550, Plum Island, 3 April 1960 (Gardler); 400, Plum Island, 4–30 April 1955 (deWindt, Burnett); 200, Chatham, 31 March 1974 (Nikula). *Fall maxima:* 1,000 +, upper Buzzards Bay, 15 November 1975 (Petersen, Sorrie). Winter numbers of Horned

Grebes are highly variable from year to year, and in recent years there seems to have been a steady decline. *Winter maxima:* 2,000, Plum Island, 1 February 1964 (BBC); 1,170, Newburyport CBC, 22 December 1957; 300 + , Sandy Neck, Barnstable, 12 January 1975 (Petersen).

Inland, Horned Grebes are of regular occurrence on reservoirs and lakes in small numbers during spring and fall migration—e.g., 50, Lake Onota, Pittsfield, 24–25 April 1971 (Goodrich); 74, Central Valley Lakes, Berkshire County, 6 November 1955 (fide McNair); 32, Quabbin Reservoir, 2 November 1968 (Yenlin); 24, Ludlow Reservoir, 24 October 1964 (Chagnon et al).

# Red-necked Grebe  *Podiceps grisegena*

**Range:** Holarctic; in North America breeds from northwestern Alaska, northwestern Saskatchewan, and western Ontario south to South Dakota and southern Quebec. In eastern North America, winters along the Atlantic Coast from Newfoundland to Florida, with most in the northern portion of the range.

**Status:** Erratic; occasionally very common to abundant migrant; uncommon winter resident in coastal waters. Rare to uncommon inland.

**Occurrence:** The numbers of migrant Red-necked Grebes in Massachusetts seem to vary considerably from year to year, especially in spring. In this season, the birds apparently move north to coastal Massachusetts during March and April from wintering grounds farther south on the Atlantic Coast. Local coastal flocks gradually increase in size prior to making an overland migration to interior North America. *Spring maxima* (1977): 306, Hull to Brant Rock, 5 March (Higginbotham); 192, Manomet, 2 March (MBO Staff); 87, Dennis, 13 March (Nikula); (1979): 2,000, Cape Cod Bay, 4 April (McNair); 250, Manomet, 4 April (MBO staff).

Summer records are rare—e.g., 1, Gloucester, 15–22 July 1962 (Rice); 1 dead, South Wellfleet, 30 August 1979 (Heil); 1, Rockport, 21 June 1981 (Stangel); 1, Monomoy, 12 August 1981 (Trull). In the fall, there is a scattering of September records, but most migrants occur in late October and November. *Fall maxima:* 37, Rockport, 16 November 1976 (Veit); 24, Plymouth, 25 October 1974 (Groves, Houghton). In winter, up to a dozen individuals are routinely encountered at favored coastal localities. *Winter maxima:* 136, Quincy CBC, 18 December 1988; 120, Nantucket CBC, 1 January 1989.

Inland, from one to five Red-necked Grebes are often found on large lakes and reservoirs in both spring and fall—e.g., 69, Lake Congamond, Southwick, 15 April 1984 (Kellogg); 25, Lake Onota, Pittsfield, 24–25 April 1971 (Goodrich).

# Eared Grebe  *Podiceps nigricollis*

**Range:** Holarctic and Ethiopian; in North America breeds from central British Columbia, southern Saskatchewan, and western Minnesota south to Baja California and southern Texas. Winters within the breeding range and south to Colombia. Rare but regular on the Atlantic Coast, mainly in late fall and winter.

**Status:** Rare visitor.

**Occurrence:** Prior to 1955, there were only eight records of this western species in Massachusetts, including two specimens: 1, Rockport, 4–25 February 1950 (Griscom, Morgan, PMS #7391); 1, Monomoy, 27 September 1953 (Morgan, Griscom, BMS #20367). Since then, the species has occurred almost annually, most often along the coast, between November and March. An especially long-lived individual was seen each winter between 1964 and 1968 at Bass Rocks, Gloucester.

Excluding those Gloucester reports, there have been over twenty-five local records of Eared Grebes since 1955, spanning the dates 2 September to 24 May, in addition to three summer records: 1, Monomoy, 9 August–29 October 1967 (Rhome et al); 1 (likely the same individual), Monomoy, 26 July–2 October 1968 (Garrey, Blodget); 1, Gloucester, 20 June–7 August 1990 (Leahy, VO). There are two inland records: 1, Horn Pond, Woburn, 20 October–13 November 1968 (Everett et al); 1, Wachusett Reservoir, Clinton, 19–24 May 1980 (Blodget).

# Western Grebe  *Aechmophorus occidentalis*

**Range:** Nearctic; breeds from northern Alberta and southwestern Manitoba south, sporadically, to central California, southwestern Colorado, and southwestern Minnesota. Winters mainly on the Pacific Coast from Alaska to Baja California. Rare but regular visitor to the Atlantic Coast.

**Status:** Rare visitor; mostly in winter.

**Occurrence:** Lacking specimen evidence, Griscom and Snyder (1955) regarded all sight records of Western Grebes in Massachusetts as hypothetical, and they suggested the possibility of confusion with the Great Crested Grebe (*Podiceps cristatus*) of Eurasia. Between 1934 and 1946, at least seventeen Western Grebes were reported in Massachusetts, including incidences of single birds inland: Agawam, 15 December 1934 (Allen 1937); Springfield, 29 February 1936 (Allen 1937). Following 1946, the publication of all reports was suspended until a specimen could be obtained. However, pronounced flights seem to have occurred from 1934 to 1936 and in 1946. During the winter of 1946–1947, a flock of 10 to 12 birds was seen in Gloucester (fide Harrington).

Selected Massachusetts records since 1955 are: 1–2, Magnolia-Marblehead, 21 January–18 March 1973 (Goodrich, Forster); 1, North Scituate, 5–6 February 1973 (Moore et al); 1, Plymouth-Duxbury, 11–14 March 1973 (Maxim, Corwin); 1, Orleans, 10 April 1976 (fide Bailey); 1, Plum Island, 22 November 1979–27 January 1980 (Harper, Wiggin, Nove, et al); 1, Nantucket, 28–29 December 1979 (Buckley, Able); 1, Nantucket, 2–3 January 1982 (Komar et al); 1, Scituate, 22 March–4 April 1982 (Campbell et al); 1, Duxbury, 28 November to 31 December 1982 (Petersen, Clapp, et al); 1, Scituate, 28 November 1982–8 May 1983 (Petersen et al); 1, Nahant, 15 May 1983 (Heywood, Stymeist).

This enumeration reveals a clustering of records in certain years (1972–1973, 1979–1980, 1982–1983), similar to the flights that seem to have occurred in earlier years. Reports of Western Grebes in Massachusetts have all fallen in the period between November and April. Several Massachusetts records since 1955 probably represent the same individual seen repeatedly on subsequent occasions.

**Remarks:** To date, all Massachusetts reports of Western Grebes pertain to birds in the dark morph, now considered a species distinct from birds in the light morph, which are currently called Clark's Grebes (*Aechmophorus clarkii*).


# Black-browed Albatross  *Diomedea melanophris*

**Range:** Southern oceans between 30 and 65° S latitude; breeds at South Georgia, the Falkland Islands, Ildefonso and Diego Ramirez islands near Cape Horn, and also on islands in the Indian and Pacific oceans. Atlantic Vagrants have reached Great Britain, Greenland, and the Atlantic Coast of North America.

**Status:** Vagrant: three sight records.

**Occurrence:** Before 1970, all albatross reports from the Atlantic Coast of North America pertained to the Yellow-nosed Albatross whereas those from Great Britain referred, without exception, to the Black-browed Albatross. Since that time, there have been a number of sight records, but no photographs or specimens, of Black-browed Albatrosses from eastern North America. There are three such records from Massachusetts—i.e., 2 (probably subadults) seen from shore at Bird Island, Marion, 28 June 1972 (Hatch, Conca); 1 subadult, Nantucket-Hyannis ferry, 16 September 1973 (Veit); 1 adult, Jeffrey's Ledge, 20 miles east of Newburyport, 11 July 1976 (Heil, Kasprzyk, Garrett). What was presumably the same bird was carefully observed on 24 July 1976 (Heil) as it flew northeastward across the Plum Island causeway and then out to sea.

# Yellow-nosed Albatross   *Diomedea chlororhynchos*

**Range:** Southern Atlantic and Indian oceans between 20 and 45° S latitude; breeds at Tristan da Cunha and Gough Island in the Atlantic and St. Paul Island in the Indian Ocean. Vagrant to the western North Atlantic.

**Status:** Vagrant: two sight records.

**Occurrence:** The two Massachusetts sight records of Yellow-nosed Albatrosses occurred in May and June, the months in which most other North American individuals have been reported (McDaniel 1973). The records are: 1 subadult, seen from shore at Bird Island, off Marion, 7 May 1971 (Nisbet); 1 adult, Cultivator Shoal, northwestern Georges Bank, 14 June 1976 (Loughlin). An unidentified albatross seen from a boat off Gay Head, Martha's Vineyard, 2 July 1972 (Nisbet) may well have been the same individual seen in 1971 in upper Buzzards Bay.

# Northern Fulmar   *Fulmarus glacialis*

**Range:** Holarctic; breeds in Novaya Zemlya, Franz Josef Land, Spitsbergen, and Jan Mayen Island south and west to the British Isles, Iceland, East Greenland, and southeastern Newfoundland. In the Canadian Arctic, breeds east to northern Greenland and south to central Baffin Island. The nominate race winters south regularly to Georges Bank and rarely south to Maryland and North Carolina.

**Status:** Common to abundant winter resident offshore. Irregular, but at times common, within sight of land, mainly during storms.

**Occurrence:** Griscom and Snyder (1955) and Bailey (1955) concurred that the Northern Fulmar was a rare vagrant to Massachusetts; "the spectacular increase in Great Britain" referred to by Griscom and Snyder (op cit) was not realized on this side of the Atlantic Ocean until the 1960s. By 1973, breeding fulmars were recorded in Newfoundland, and, since then, there have been increasing numbers in New England offshore waters. During the course of pelagic research initiated in 1976 by MBO, the numbers of wintering fulmars on Georges Bank and in the Gulf of Maine reflected this increase.

Since 1975, observations of Northern Fulmars from shore have similarly increased. Powers (1983) has shown that, on average, the largest numbers are found off New England between December and March. ***Maxima*** (offshore): 3,000, northeast peak of Georges Bank, 26 January 1977 (Powers); 2,500, southern Gulf of Maine, 16 January 1978 (Veit). In some years, sizeable concentrations persist on Georges Bank until mid-June—e.g., 8,000 +, around a commercial fishing fleet, northern edge of Georges Bank, 11 June 1978 (Veit). Fulmars are regularly found over inshore waters in May and June and again in October. *Inshore maxima:* 500 +, Jeffrey's Ledge, 8 October 1978 (Phinney, ASNH); 300 +, First Encounter Beach, Eastham, 8 January 1977 (Nikula, Goodrich); 250 +, Provincetown, 25 September 1977 (Veit, Perkins, Vickery, Litchfield); 100, 20–30 miles east of Chatham, 1 February 1962 (fide Bailey); 88, Massachusetts Bay, 1–4 November 1976 (Lloyd-Evans); 65, Rockport, 22 September 1977 (Perkins); 60, Stellwagen Bank, 30 October 1976 (Petersen, H. D'Entremont, et al); 60, Stellwagen Bank, 26 May 1979 (Petersen). The only inland records of fulmars in Massachusetts are: 1 shot through the thighs and picked up alive, Worcester, 29 December 1938 (Brown, see Parker 1939); 1 after hurricane, Wachusett Reservoir, Clinton, 27 September 1985 (McMenemy).

**Remarks:** All specimens from Massachusetts, including those collected offshore, are of the nominate race, *F. g. glacialis*, which is the form that has increased so dramatically during the past 150 years and recently colonized Newfoundland.

# Black-capped Petrel   *Pterodroma hasitata*

**Range:** Tropical Atlantic Ocean; breeds on Hispaniola and Cuba; ranges at sea north to Cape Hatteras, North Carolina, and south to Brazil; accidental to the Gulf of Maine.

**Status:** Vagrant: three sight records.

**Occurrence:** The first Black-capped Petrel to be recorded in Massachusetts waters was identified on the southeastern portion of Georges Bank (40° 58′N, 66° 35′W), 23 March 1977 (Lambert 1977). In 1991, two additional occurrences were carefully documented: 1 photographed, southwest corner of Stellwagen Bank, 22 April (Highley, photos on file at MAS); 1 during Hurricane Bob, off South Sunken Meadow Beach, Eastham, 19 August 1991 (Heil, Smith). Because this species occurs regularly in continental slope waters off Cape Hatteras (Lee 1984), future records should be anticipated, especially during late summer and fall when warm core eddies periodically drift north from the Gulf Stream.

# Cory's Shearwater   *Calonectris diomedea*

**Range:** Primarily Palearctic; the race *C. d. borealis* breeds on the Azores, Canary, Salvage, and Madeira islands; occurs at sea west to the North American coast and south to Brazil and South Africa.

**Status:** Common to abundant summer and fall visitor to waters south of Cape Cod, occasionally entering Cape Cod Bay. Abundance fluctuates considerably from year to year (Veit 1976).

**Occurrence:** Cory's Shearwaters are most abundant off our coast from July to October. The largest numbers usually concentrate along the 50-fathom contour, approximately 30 to 40 miles south of Nantucket and Martha's Vineyard (Powers 1983). Occasionally, very large numbers are seen from the south shores of those islands.

Because of their preference for warm water (18° C +), Cory's Shearwaters are generally rare north of Cape Cod, although in some years they penetrate deep into the Gulf of Maine, presumably at times when surface temperatures there are higher than normal. Baird (1887) reported that between late September and early November 1886, enormous schools of Sea Herring (*Clupea vulgaris*) entered Buzzards Bay and were accompanied by thousands of Cory's Shearwaters. During the 1970s, concentrations of Cory's Shearwaters south of Nantucket appear to have been attracted by schools of Sand Lances (*Ammodytes* sp.), which were driven to the surface by Bluefish.

Peak numbers of Cory's Shearwaters usually occur from early summer to midfall. *Maxima:* 7,000, Nantucket, 15 July 1979 (Perkins); 5,500, Nantucket, 10 July 1980 (Perkins); 4,000 +, Nantucket, 1–6 October 1968 (Soucy, Jodrey); 4,000, off Martha's Vineyard, 15 July 1981 (Laux); 2,500 +, Eastham, 4 November 1979 (Nikula); 2,200, Tuckernuck Island, 18 October 1981 (Veit); 2,000, 50 miles south of Martha's Vineyard, 28 June 1981 (Laux). *Extreme dates:* 1, Nantucket, 4 April 1976 (E. and C. Andrews); to 1, Barnstable, 16 December 1976 (Pease); 1, North Beach, Orleans, 16 December 1979 (Goodrich, Harris).

Inland, an "immature male" was found dying in Peru, Berkshire County, 28 September 1938 (Hendricks 1939).

**Remarks:** The race *C. d. diomedea,* which breeds on islands in the Mediterranean (Bourne 1955), has been collected three times off Long Island, New York (Bull 1964) and could occur regularly in the western Atlantic.

# Greater Shearwater   *Puffinus gravis*

**Range:** Atlantic Ocean; breeds on Tristan da Cunha and, in small numbers, in the Falkland Islands (Woods 1970). Spends May to November in the North Atlantic Ocean.

**Status:** Common to abundant summer and fall resident offshore.

**Occurrence:** Maximum counts of arriving Greater Shearwaters from the South Atlantic are indicated by the following figures: 50,000, northern edge of Georges Bank, 11 June 1978 (Veit); 30,000, Hydrographer Canyon, 18–22 June 1977 (Laux); 20,000, Southeastern Georges Bank, 1–14 June 1977 (Veit).

Occasionally, tremendous fall flocks of staging adults, or nonbreeders possibly lingering because of a superabundance of food, are recorded. *Fall maxima:* 200,000 near 40° 58′N, 67° 00′W, 11 November 1977 (Powers &

Van Os 1979); 40,000, Provincetown, 25 September 1977 (Veit, Perkins, Litchfield, Vickery); 18,000, Stellwagen Bank, 11–25 October 1981 (VO); 15,000 (during a period of maximum abundance of Sand Lances [*Ammodytes* sp.]), eastern shore of Cape Cod, 7–11 November 1981 (Heil, Nikula, Petersen).

Greater Shearwaters have been recorded in every month except January and April; however, they are very rare outside the traditional summer and early fall period. Most unusual are the following winter records: 1, Great South Channel, 8 February 1977 (MBO); 1, Georges Bank, 4 March 1976 (Lloyd-Evans).

All inland records have come in the wake of hurricanes, as shown by the following records: 1, Wellesley, 10 August 1887 (Howe & Allen 1901); 1 picked up dead, Montgomery, 21 September 1938 (Griscom & Snyder 1955). Unlike Cory's Shearwaters, Greater Shearwaters are not readily attracted to schooling bait fish near shore; therefore, maximum counts from land are usually associated with onshore gales. *Extreme dates* (for shore-based sightings): 1, Plum Island, 8 May 1976 (Johnson); 1, Plum Island, 27 December 1972 (Alexander).

## Sooty Shearwater  *Puffinus griseus*

**Range:** Mainly Pacific and Atlantic oceans; breeds on islands off Tasmania, New Zealand, and southern South America. Migrates to North Pacific and North Atlantic oceans between May and September.

**Status:** Fairly common to abundant offshore visitor, occasionally common within sight of land. Usually greatly outnumbered by Greater Shearwaters, except in May and early June.

**Occurrence:** Sooty Shearwaters regularly arrive on the fishing banks off New England by mid-May and usually reach peak densities during June. Most birds depart by late summer, as the population gradually shifts northeastward toward Europe. As with Greater Shearwaters, an influx of presumed nonbreeders is often apparent in late fall. During May and June, Sooty Shearwaters are regularly seen within sight of land, particularly off Cape Cod and the Islands during storms and in foggy weather, when they sometimes enter bays and estuaries.

The largest numbers of Sooty Shearwaters occur offshore with the arrival of the summering population. *Maxima:* 14,400, northern edge of Georges Bank, 7 June 1978 (Veit); 4,000, southeastern Georges Bank, 1–14 June 1977 (Veit). Counts closer to shore and from the beaches average 100 to 200 but are occasionally much higher—e.g., 2,500, off Chatham, 12 June 1984 (Nikula, Leahy, et al); 1,450, off Chatham, 4 June 1978 (Petersen et al); 800, Provincetown, 25 September 1977 (Veit, Litchfield, Perkins, Vickery); 200,

Monomoy, 4 June 1973 (Nisbet). Late fall maxima are consistently lower—e.g., 40 +, North Truro to Provincetown, 14 November 1975 (Veit, Russell, McCaskie); 15, Eastham to Provincetown, 6 November 1976 (Petersen, Forster). Sooty Shearwaters are rare in Massachusetts waters before mid-May and after November, so the following records are exceptional: 1, Gulf of Maine, 27 January, 1977 (Powers); 1, Gay Head, Martha's Vineyard, 14 March 1979 (Laux); 1, Eastham, 28 April 1978 (Laux); 1, Eastham, 17 December 1978 (Petersen, Donahue, Anderson); 1, Barnstable, 21 December 1975 (Pease).

# Manx Shearwater   *Puffinus puffinus*

**Range:** Mainly Palearctic; breeds in Iceland, the British Isles, islands off Brittany, and in the Azores, Madeira and the Salvages. Breeding has also been confirmed in North America—in Massachusetts in 1973 and in Newfoundland in 1976 (AB 31: 1110). Of common occurrence off northeastern North America between May and October. Winters off southeastern South America.

**Status:** One breeding record; uncommon to fairly common offshore visitor.

**Breeding:** The first breeding record of the Manx Shearwater in North America was confirmed when a nest containing a single young was found at Penikese Island, 6 June 1973 (Ben David, Bierregaard, see AB 28: 135). No additional proof of nesting has been obtained in Massachusetts.

**Nonbreeding:** As recently as 1957, Manx Shearwaters were considered to be of only casual occurrence anywhere in North America, with only five specimens recorded (AOU 1957, Griscom & Snyder 1955), three of these from Massachusetts: 1 picked up dead, Edgartown, Martha's Vineyard, 2 September 1950 (Griscom & Snyder 1955); 1 collected, off Chatham, 13 August 1953 (Griscom, Morgan, MCZ #280747); 1 collected, off Chatham, 20 August 1955 (Bowen, Morgan). The species has steadily increased since then, so that by 1980 sightings of 50 birds per day were not unusual. Manx Shearwaters are more coastal in their distribution than the larger shearwaters, and maximum counts in Massachusetts are either of birds seen from shore or from boats on the inshore fishing banks, especially Stellwagen Bank.

Farther offshore, Manx Shearwaters are usually encountered singly, with daily totals rarely exceeding five on Georges Bank. Although the species has been reported in every month except February—including, 1, Barnstable, 28 January 1973 (Pease)—the largest numbers occur between July and September. *Maxima:* 200, Stellwagen Bank, 18 July 1988 (Nielsen); 120, Barnstable, 12 August 1979 (Trull); 50 +, Stellwagen Bank, 23 August 1981 (BBC,

Drummond); 50 +, Provincetown, 25 November 1979 (Trull, Kasprzyk).
*Spring maxima:* 6, Barnstable, 25 May 1976 (Pease).


## Audubon's Shearwater   *Puffinus lherminieri*

**Range:** Pantropical; in the western Atlantic breeds in the Bahamas; also in the Greater and Lesser Antilles. Nonbreeders occur north in Gulf Stream waters to southern New England.

**Status:** Uncommon but regular visitor to warmer waters near the continental slope in summer. Moribund individuals have occasionally been found on Cape Cod and the Islands during late July and August.

**Occurrence:** Before extensive seabird studies were initiated by the Manomet Bird Observatory in 1976, Audubon's Shearwaters were known from Massachusetts only as beached stragglers—e.g., 1 picked up dead, Chilmark, Martha's Vineyard, 13 August 1937 (Olney, Minot, MCZ #291305); 1 picked up alive, Squibnocket, Martha's Vineyard, 27 July 1967 (Stevenson). Increased pelagic coverage indicates that a recent clustering of records in late summer seems to correspond to the highest surface temperatures of the year in the waters south of Nantucket and Martha's Vineyard (Gordon 1956). Additional records other than those collected by MBO are: 2, 55 miles south of Nantucket, 27 July 1980 (Heil); 2, Hydrographer Canyon, 2 September 1982 (Veit, Russell, et al); 3, Hydrographer Canyon, 22 August 1983 (Stymeist, Petersen, Veit, et al); 15, Hydrographer Canyon, 20 August 1984 (Veit, Petersen, et al); 15, Hydrographer Canyon, 19 August 1985 (Petersen et al).


## Wilson's Storm-Petrel   *Oceanites oceanicus*

**Range:** Breeds on the Antarctic Continent and on islands of the Scotia Arc north to South Georgia. In the Atlantic Ocean, spends May to September north to Labrador, Iceland, and the British Isles.

**Status:** Abundant offshore resident from June to mid-September.

**Occurrence:** This species and the Greater Shearwater are the two most numerous and widespread pelagic birds in the offshore waters of Massachusetts during the summer months. Although stragglers have been recorded as early as April and as late as November, the bulk of the population is present between late May and August, when 1.5 million birds have been estimated to occur in the shelf waters off the northeastern United States (Powers 1983). Manomet Bird Observatory surveys beginning in 1976 found that the "greatest densities were consistently found in the western Gulf of Maine south to the Great South Channel and east along the northern edge of Georges Bank" (Powers 1983).

This distribution is occasionally modified by the presence of major fishing operations near the continental slope, which serve to attract the storm-petrels—e.g., 50,000 carefully estimated in the vicinity of the Soviet Silver Hake fishery, southeastern Georges Bank, 1–14 June 1977 (Veit). Counts of 1,000 to 5,000 birds are typical for single-day boat trips to the coastal fishing banks off Cape Cod and Cape Ann, although abundance varies considerably from year to year. This species is much rarer inland than the Leach's Storm-Petrel, with only two known records: 1 specimen, Berkley, 16 August 1907 (MCZ #251082); 1 after Hurricane David, Dalton, Berkshire County, 7 September 1979 (specimen examined by Forster).

## White-faced Storm-Petrel   *Pelagodroma marina*

**Range:** Widespread in subtropical waters of the Atlantic and Pacific oceans. *P. m. hypoleuca* breeds in the Salvages (near the Canary Islands), and *P. m. eadesi* breeds in the Cape Verde Islands. Both subspecies have been collected off Massachusetts (Buckley & Wurster 1970, Gordon 1955a, Ridgway 1885).

**Status:** Rare but regular visitor to the vicinity of the continental slope south of Massachusetts; vagrant farther inshore.

**Occurrence:** The pelagic distribution of White-faced Storm-Petrels in the Atlantic is poorly known. However, the accumulated records off the East Coast of the United States suggest that they occur regularly over the continental slope during the period from late August to early October. In fact, all of the Massachusetts records, with one exception, are from a restricted oceanographic zone lying between the 100- and 1,000-fathom depth contours. The records are: 1 *P. m. hypoleuca* collected, 40° 34′N, 66° 09′W (near southeastern Georges Bank), 2 September 1885 (Ridgway 1885); 1, 30 miles north of Cape Cod, 1 October 1946 (Abbot 1946); 1 *P. m. eadesi* collected, 39° 48′N, 71° 02′W (about 75 miles south southwest of Gay Head, Martha's Vineyard), 18 August 1953 (Gordon 1955a); 1–3, 38° 54′N, 69° 30′W (about 90 miles south of Nantucket), 29 August 1967 (Wurster). A more recent series of records from Hydrographer Canyon includes: 1, 2 September 1982 (Russell, Veit, et al—photo at MAS); 1 *P. m. hypoleuca* collected, 10 September 1982 (Backus, USNM #572200); 2, 22 August 1983 (Abbott, Stymeist, Petersen, Veit, et al); 1, 19 August 1985 (Petersen et al); 1, 7 September 1985 (Petersen et al).

## Leach's Storm-Petrel   *Oceanodroma leucorhoa*

**Range:** Widespread in the North Atlantic and North Pacific oceans; breeds in the northwest Pacific and in the North Atlantic from southern Labrador and southern Iceland south to Massachusetts and the British Isles. Atlantic birds winter south to the coasts of Brazil and Liberia.

**Status:** One small nesting colony on Penikese Island in Buzzards Bay. Uncommon to occasionally common migrant; most numerous more than 50 miles from shore. Rare inland, usually following severe and sustained gales.

**Breeding:** Leach's Storm-Petrels have nested at Penikese Island since at least 1933 (Townsend & Allen 1933). Between the 1930s and 1950s, J.A. Hagar (pers. comm.) estimated that 120 pairs bred at Penikese, both in natural burrows in the soil and in crevices of an old foundation. They have steadily declined since then and seem now to breed only in the foundation. Recent estimates suggest that at least 5 to 10, and possibly as many as 30 pairs, now breed on the island. The decline since the 1950s may be the result of predation by nesting gulls or disturbance by recent human activities.

The presence of the Penikese Island colony may account for a number of inshore sightings during the summer—e.g., 1, Gay Head, Martha's Vineyard, 14 July 1967 (Sears, Keith); 1, from the Nantucket Ferry, 29 June 1968 (Chalif); 1, Chappaquiddick, Martha's Vineyard, 14 July 1967 (Sears, Keith); 3–4, off Chatham, 13 August 1973 (Petersen, Goodrich, Harrington); 3, Nantucket, 19 June 1974 (Crompton, Veit); 2, Nantucket, 23 June 1974 (Crompton, Veit); 1, Nantucket Sound, 20 June 1975 (Veit). Otherwise, most Leach's Storm-Petrels are found far offshore during the summer, with a concentration south of the continental slope (Powers 1983). During the summers of 1982 and 1983, the remains of at least 20 Leach's Storm-Petrels were found in pellets regurgitated by Short-eared Owls at Monomoy (Holt), suggesting that the petrels might be prospecting for nesting sites in that area.

**Nonbreeding:** Leach's Storm-Petrels migrate offshore during early May and from late September to November. Small numbers appear close to shore, but the majority remain at sea, except during severe storms. High counts in spring are unusual because severe storms rarely coincide with major northward movements of the species. *Spring maxima:* 10,000+ seen during an unseasonal snowstorm, Cape Cod Bay, 10 May 1977 (Petersen, Forster, Anderson); 200 during a storm, Sandy Neck, Barnstable, 11 June 1977 (Pease). During the summer, the largest counts are near the continental slope: 200, southeastern Georges Bank, 1–14 June 1977 (Veit); 150+, southeastern Georges Bank, 19–20 August 1985 (Petersen et al); 100, Hydrographer Canyon, 20 August 1984 (Veit, Petersen, et al). A rare exception is a count of 350+, off First Encounter Beach, Eastham, 13 August 1979 (Ni-

*Although few people have ever seen it on its Massachusetts nesting grounds, the highly pelagic **Leach's Storm-Petrel** maintains its southernmost breeding terminus in eastern North America on tiny Penikese Island in Buzzards Bay.*

kula). High counts in fall are invariably associated with storms and normally occur between late September and late November. *Fall maxima:* 100, Provincetown Harbor, 17 September 1933 (R.T. Peterson); 100, Sandy Neck, Barnstable, 15–16 October 1955 (Ferguson et al). There is a scattering of records from December and January; most noteworthy is a group of 15 storm-petrels (probably Leach's) seen during a gale, Pleasant Bay, Chatham, 27 January 1937 (Bishop).

Leach's Storm-Petrels are regularly blown inland by severe storms and hurricanes. The maximum number recorded under such conditions was after the hurricane of 21 September 1938, when several were seen at Northampton (Eliot) and Southwick (fide Bagg) and 3 to 4 others elsewhere in the Connecticut River valley. Singles were found in Cambridge and Lincoln after Hurricane Carol, 31 August 1954 (RNEB), and in Quincy and Hingham after Hurricane Donna, 13 September 1960 (RNEB). The farthest inland record for Massachusetts is: 1 shot, Ashmore Reservoir, Hinsdale, 19 October 1894 (Bagg & Eliot 1937).

# Band-rumped Storm-Petrel   *Oceanodroma castro*

**Range:** Tropical and subtropical portions of the Atlantic and Pacific oceans; in the North Atlantic, breeds in the Azores and the Salvage, Madeira, Cape Verde, Ascension, and St. Helena islands. Regular summer visitor to the continental slope off southeastern North America (Lee 1984).

**Status:** Vagrant or rare visitor; two sight records.

**Occurrence:** On a chartered pelagic bird trip, a Band-rumped Storm-Petrel was carefully identified near Hydrographer Canyon, 40° 12′ N, 69° 02′ W, 20 August 1984 (Veit, Petersen, Smith, Vaughan, et al). The location of this sighting, in 80° F water and near the shelf-break, is similar oceanographically to a region off Cape Hatteras where numerous Band-rumped Storm-Petrels have been recorded (Lee 1984). A second sighting involved two birds in the same vicinity, 19 August 1985 (Petersen, Haney, et al).

# White-tailed Tropicbird   *Phaethon lepturus*

**Range:** Pantropical; breeds in Bermuda, the Bahamas, and the Greater and Lesser Antilles. Ranges at sea northwest to the coast of the United States, but rarely north of North Carolina.

**Status:** Vagrant: at least seven records.

**Occurrence:** Most records of this species from the Northeast have been during or after hurricanes. The following spring records are exceptional: 1 picked up alive, Harwichport, 25 April 1944 (Baker, BMS #X03–178); 1 seen flying up the Merrimack River, Haverhill, 26 May 1940 (Harris, Pulsifer, Cole). The Haverhill report should perhaps be conservatively considered as tropicbird sp., given the precedence of Red-billed Tropicbirds (*P. aethereus*) in the Northeast during the period May to June (Lee et al 1981). There are three records of dead birds from Nantucket after Hurricane Donna (13 September 1960): 1 immature, 13 September 1960 (Heywood); 1, 14 September 1960 (Andrews, Boyd); 1, 24 September 1960 (Andrews, Boyd). The three specimens are in the collection of the Maria Mitchell Association on Nantucket. Other records are: 1 unidentified tropicbird, 75 miles southeast of Nantucket, 20 August 1984 (Veit, Petersen, Osborne); 1, Cockle Cove, South Chatham, 27 September 1985 (Nikula, Trull); 1 captured alive and later released in Bermuda, Byfield, 28 September 1985 (Abusamara); 1 photographed, Hydrographer Canyon area, 4 September 1986 (Haney, Bowen, et al).

## Red-billed Tropicbird   *Phaethon aethereus*

**Range:** Pantropical; breeds in the Caribbean region from Puerto Rico and the Virgin Islands through the Lesser Antilles south to Tobago, Grenada, and Panama. Ranges at sea casually north to the Atlantic Coast of North America to Florida and North Carolina.

**Status:** Vagrant: three records (perhaps the same individual).

**Occurrence:** An adult Red-billed Tropicbird was first noted flying below the cliffs at Gay Head, Martha's Vineyard, 15 September 1986 (Rosenwald [see Rosenwald 1986], Arvidson 1986) where it remained to be observed by hundreds of people until 26 October. What was presumed to be the same bird returned to the same location from 6 to 30 August 1987 (VO) and 14 June to 4 July 1988 (Davis, Laux). The occurrence of this elegant vagrant triggered a series of intriguing articles on the broader topic of vagrant origins (see Veit 1988, Wilson 1988, Veit 1989).

## Brown Booby   *Sula leucogaster*

**Range:** Pantropical; breeds throughout the West Indies and on other islands in the tropical Atlantic. Ranges north regularly to the Dry Tortugas, Florida. Otherwise, rare vagrant north of the tropics, north to Nova Scotia.

**Status:** Vagrant: two records.

**Occurrence:** An adult Brown Booby apparently obtained on Cape Cod was found in the Boston Market, 17 September 1878 (BMS #12204), following "one of the most southerly hurricanes on record"—a storm that was centered over Trinidad on 1 September and crossed Long Island, New York, on 12 September (Bull 1964). Another adult was seen after a southerly storm off North Beach, Chatham, 30 May 1946 (Griscom, Mason, et al). Two additional sight records off Monomoy in September and October are less convincing and do not satisfactorily eliminate possible confusion with Northern Gannets.

# Northern Gannet   *Sula bassanus*

**Range:** Palearctic; in North America, breeds on Bonaventure Island and the Anticosti Islands, Quebec; the Magdalen Islands, Quebec; on Cape St. Mary, Baccalieu Island, and Funk Island, Newfoundland; also on islands off Iceland and in the British Isles. North American birds winter at sea between New England and the Gulf of Mexico.

**Status:** Abundant migrant and winter resident offshore.

**Occurrence:** Powers (1983) estimated that 168,000 Northern Gannets winter in shelf waters off the northeastern United States, and Nettleship (1976) estimated a North American breeding population of 65,000 birds. It would appear that Powers' estimate accounts for a substantial proportion of the North American population. In midwinter, most Gannets seen off the Massachusetts coast are adults; the immature birds move farther south and account for most sightings in the Gulf of Mexico (Duncan & Havard 1980). During midwinter, Northern Gannets occasionally aggregate near the continental slope, but this may be a result of their attraction to the fishing trawlers that frequent the area.

Peak numbers of gannets are seen from shore during migration in early spring and late fall. Many high counts involve storm-driven birds passing coastal vantage points, while others are of birds that remain inshore to feed on schooling bait fish for extended periods of time. *Spring maxima:* 2,000, Truro, 30 March 1961 (Bailey); 1,500 + , Muskeget Island, 10 May 1981 (Heil); 1,000, Truro, 7 May 1983 (Nikula); 750, Nantucket, 5 May 1958 (Eaton); 500 per hour, Nauset Light, 27 March 1977 (Nikula, Goodrich); 500, Sandy Neck, Barnstable, 27 April 1973 (Pease).

A few immature Northern Gannets summer in Massachusetts waters, and counts of 1 to 5 birds per day are not unusual in July and August. *Summer maximum:* 20, Stellwagen Bank, 11–12 June 1982 (Hallowell). *Fall maxima:* 15,000 + , Monomoy (including many in Nantucket Sound), 20 November 1973 (Veit, Brown); 12,000 + , First Encounter Beach, Eastham, 25 October 1983 (Nikula); 11,845, Cape Cod CBC, 17 December 1978; 10,000 + in two hours, First Encounter Beach, Eastham, 19 November 1986 (Petersen); 8,000 + , North Truro-Provincetown, 14 November 1975 (Veit, Russell, McCaskie); 5,000, Outer Cape Cod, 7–11 November 1981 (Heil, Petersen); 3,300, Sandy Neck, Barnstable, 10 October 1982 (Clapp).

During January and February, gannets are usually uncommon within sight of land; however, storms occasionally push hundreds close to outlying points, such as Nantucket. Inland records: 1 captured alive, Enfield, 11 October 1917 (Griscom & Snyder 1955); 1, Westwood, 16 March 1958 (Foster); 1 hit by a car, Cheshire, 5 December 1960 (Hendricks); 1, GMNWR, 6 October 1964 (Garrey et al); 1 captured and photographed, Adams, 14–16 October 1964 (Kulish); 1 immature, GMNWR and Lincoln (possibly the same individual), 16 October 1980 (Holland, Lowe, et al); 1, Raynham, 23 June 1984 (Sorrie); 1, photographed flying up the Connecticut River, Hadley, 24 January 1990 (Yeskie).

# American White Pelican   *Pelecanus erythrorhynchos*

**Range:** Primarily western Nearctic; breeds in southern British Columbia and from northeastern Alberta and southwestern Ontario south to southeastern California and South Dakota; also in southeastern Texas. Winters from California, the Gulf Coast states and Florida south to Guatemala.

**Status:** Rare visitor.

**Occurrence:** Prior to 1960 there were only six American White Pelican records in Massachusetts. Since that time, the species has become increasingly frequent in the state, with the majority of records coming from the coast, especially Cape Cod and the Islands. Records through 1983 include: 1 specimen, Gloucester, 1886 (PMS #6017); 1 specimen, Cohasset, 5 October 1876 (MCZ #291130; listed by Griscom & Snyder 1955 as "lost" and taken in North Scituate); 1 picked up dead, Sandwich, 13 May 1905 (fide Brewster); 1, Plymouth, 15 September 1945 (Foster); 1, Nantucket, 2 July 1950 (Coffin et al); 2, North Truro, 23–24 April 1953 (Watts, Howes, et al); 2, Cockle Cove, Chatham, 1–25 October 1961 (Drew, Bailey, et al); 1, Orleans, 8 December 1963 (Cochran et al); 1, Martha's Vineyard, 12–26 October 1974 (Ben David et al); 1, Nantucket, 18–23 October 1974 (Dennis, Andrews); 1, West Harwich, 21 December 1974–14 February 1975 (Smith, VO); 1, Truro-Chatham, 31 October–7 December 1978 (Boardman et al); 1, Plum Island, 4–15 June 1981 (VO); 1, Belle Isle Marsh, East Boston, 15 May 1983 (Zendeh, Jackson); 1 captured alive, Springfield, 9 December 1983 (fide Kellogg). Since 1983, American White Pelicans have been of nearly annual occurrence in Massachusetts.

# Brown Pelican   *Pelecanus occidentalis*

**Range:** Southern Nearctic and Neotropical; breeds from North Carolina to Florida, along the Gulf Coast to Texas, in the northern Bahamas, in Cuba, and south to Panama. Vagrant north along the East Coast to Massachusetts.

**Status:** Vagrant: twelve records.

**Occurrence:** Most Brown Pelicans have occurred in Massachusetts in fall. Curiously, they have not been recorded after the major hurricanes that brought numbers of other southeastern coastal species to Massachusetts, except in 1960. The records are: 1 shot out of a flock of 13, Nantucket, 1867 (Griscom & Snyder 1955); 1, Ipswich, 1867 (LeBaron); 1, Ipswich, 1922 (Maynard); 1, Cataumet, 28 August 1933 (Brooks 1934); 1, off Gay Head, Martha's Vineyard, 4 July 1946 (Maher et al); 1, Martha's Vineyard, 25 September 1958, and remaining for three or four days (fide Emerson); 1, off Plymouth Beach, 13 September 1960 (Fox); 1, Monomoy, 23 September 1962 (Hager, fide Bailey); 1 photographed, Norton's Point, Martha's Vineyard, 28 September 1985 (Laux et al); 1, Nantucket Harbor, 28 September 1985 (Pokras); 1 landed on fishing boat, Georges Bank, 29 September 1985 (fide Wilson); 1 captured alive, Nahant, 11 November 1988 (Wasserman, MCZ #332838).

# Great Cormorant  *Phalacrocorax carbo*

**Range:** Cosmopolitan; in the North Atlantic, breeds in western Europe, Iceland, and Greenland, and, in North America, at numerous sites around the Gulf of St. Lawrence, along the coast of Nova Scotia, and in central coastal Maine (1983 on). Winters within the breeding range and south to Delaware, irregularly to South Carolina.

**Status:** Rare breeder. Common to very common migrant and winter resident. Occasional and increasing inland in small numbers.

**Breeding:** Single pairs of Great Cormorants successfully bred at the Weepecket Islands off Naushon Island in 1984 (Hatch) and in Boston Harbor in 1985 (Hatch). Both this species and the Double-crested Cormorant have steadily increased in Massachusetts waters during the past 75 years, and Hatch (1982a) has shown a continuous, although somewhat erratic, increase in wintering Great Cormorant numbers throughout the Northeast.

**Nonbreeding:** Great Cormorants are primarily winter residents, which are most abundant from December to March at locations such as Outer Brewster Island in Boston Harbor, on islands off Cohasset and Cape Ann, and in the Woods Hole area. Their distribution seems to be defined by their preference for rocky shores, so they are relatively uncommon over much of Cape Cod and the Islands. Early fall migrant Great Cormorants have appeared at Sandy Neck, Barnstable, 27 August 1981 (O. and N. Komar, D'Entremont) and Monomoy (2), 28 August 1975 (Goodrich, Nikula); however, the main fall arrival begins with the appearance of immature birds in mid-September, somewhat ahead of the adult population, which stabilizes by late November. ***Winter maxima:*** 726, Boston Harbor, 8 March 1981

(TASL); 700, Vineyard Sound, 25 January 1953 (Butler); 600, Nahant-Winthrop, 5 December 1982 (Stymeist). Large winter concentrations also occur in Vineyard Sound (Hatch, pers. comm.). Wintering birds normally depart by mid-April, although stragglers routinely linger into the summer—e.g., 3 immatures, Boston Harbor, 8–9 June 1979 (Grugan, Petersen); 2 subadults, Plymouth, 8 July 1979 (Petersen, Sorrie); 2 immatures, Outer Brewster Island, summer 1982 (Hatch, Veit); 2 adults, Gloucester, July 1982 (Leahy); 4 immatures, North Scituate, 15 July 1983 (Petersen). The breeding population will likely continue to increase, especially because the number of summering nonbreeders appears to be increasing. As Great Cormorants have become more numerous throughout the year in Massachusetts, there has been a corresponding increase in inland records, at least as far westward as the Connecticut River valley.

# Double-crested Cormorant  *Phalacrocorax auritus*

**Range:** Nearctic; breeds from central Alberta, central Manitoba, the shores of the St. Lawrence River, and southern Newfoundland south, locally, to the Salton Sea, California, New Mexico, Kentucky, and Long Island, New York. Winters in eastern North America from southern New England south to Florida and the Greater Antilles.

**Status:** Abundant breeder and migrant; rapidly increasing. Rare but increasingly regular in winter.

**Breeding:** Hatch (1982a) showed that Double-crested Cormorants were breeding on the Boston Harbor Islands circa 1500 A.D., as evidenced by bones of both adult and young birds found in Indian middens. According to Hatch, cormorants subsequently declined and were entirely extirpated as breeders by the early 19th century. A pronounced population increase began near the beginning of the 20th century. Nesting was recorded in Maine in 1893 and 1925; in Boston in 1940 (53 nests, Hagar 1941a); in Salem Harbor in 1942 (2 nests, Burnett); and on the Weepecket Islands (in Buzzards Bay) in 1946 (Griscom & Snyder 1955).

Drury (1973a) demonstrated that the rate of population growth of Double-crested Cormorants in Maine was most pronounced from 1925 to 1940, when the number of nesting pairs increased from about 100 to over 13,000. Between 1944 and 1953, a control program was undertaken in Maine in response to complaints from fishermen that the birds were eating too many fish, but the eradication program appeared to coincide with a natural decline in the population. From the early 1950s until 1972, the total New England population again increased slowly from 9,700 to 15,000 pairs, but Massachusetts Bay colonies declined from 715 to 325 pairs. Hatch (op cit) has shown that the Boston Harbor population more than doubled between

1977 and 1981, from 1,000 to 2,510 pairs, and that it has approximated an exponential increase since 1972. By 1982, the entire nesting population of Massachusetts numbered 5,173 pairs (Hatch), 1,000 of these on the Weepeckets and the rest on islands between Boston Harbor and Cape Ann. *Egg dates:* 5 April–late June.

**Nonbreeding:** The first northbound migrants appear in late March, but the highest counts are recorded during late April. The vast majority of migrants are seen at the immediate coast, but flocks moving north are of regular occurrence inland as well. *Spring maxima:* 1,300, North Scituate, 27 April 1980 (Brown); 400 migrating north, Sudbury River valley, throughout April 1984 (Forster); 389, Plum Island, 27 April 1983 (Roberts); 300 +, Scituate, 9 April 1977 (Veit); 300, Foxboro, 29 March 1982 (Brown); 172, Littleton, 13 April 1978 (Baird); 100, Framingham, 15 April 1982 (Ryan). Rare in Berkshire County; the maximum there is: 41, Sheffield, 12 April 1980 (HBC).

In fall, migrants are much more numerous than in spring, both on the coast and inland. The fall flight of Double-crested Cormorants crosses the base of Cape Ann and the eastern part of the state on a line between Boston and Narragansett Bay, which makes them uncommon as migrants on outer Cape Cod and the Islands (Nisbet & Baird 1959). *Fall maxima:* 5,000 +, Plum Island, 8 October 1977 (Stymeist); 4,400, Plum Island, 11 October 1978 (Roberts); 4,000 +, Plum Island, 13 October 1979 (Kasprzyk); 3,200 +, Salisbury, 24 September 1980 (Heil); 2,350, Plum Island, 5 October 1978 (Roberts); 850, Middleboro, 23 October 1980 (Anderson); 225, Mt. Wachusett, 18 September 1977 (Roberts).

There were no proven midwinter records of Double-crested Cormorants prior to 1976. Concurrent with their increase as breeders, they are now appearing with more frequency than ever before, including: six reports, January 1979 (BOEM); 1, Martha's Vineyard, 28 February 1979 (Laux); 1, Nantucket, 16 February 1981 (Veit). By 1987, 25 were counted on the Greater Boston CBC.

# Anhinga  *Anhinga anhinga*

**Range:** Nearctic and Neotropical; breeds in North America from central and eastern Texas, western Tennessee, north-central Mississippi, southern Alabama, and coastal North Carolina south to Florida; also in Cuba and in Middle and South America. Winters in the southeastern United States from central South Carolina to Florida and the Gulf Coast southward to Cuba, Middle America, and South America.

**Status:** Vagrant: at least two satisfactory sight records.

**Occurrence:** There are at least two convincing reports of Anhingas occurring in Massachusetts: 1 female soaring, Nahant, 25 May 1987 (Forster,

Seeckts); 1 male soaring, Lincoln, 18 April 1991 (Nisbet). In both cases, the observers had previous experience with Anhingas, as well as with similar confusing species, and their written documentation of each sighting warrants the inclusion of the species in this text (see Forster 1987a).

# Magnificent Frigatebird  *Fregata magnificens*

**Range:** Pantropical; breeds on islets off the west coasts of Baja California and Central America, on widely scattered islets in the West Indies (north to the Bahamas), and on islets off the coast of Brazil. Ranges regularly to southern Florida; vagrant elsewhere on the East Coast of North America.

**Status:** Vagrant: eleven records.

**Occurrence:** Unlike other vagrant seabirds of tropical origin, Magnificent Frigatebirds in Massachusetts are usually not associated with tropical storms or hurricanes. The records are: 1 collected after a southerly gale, New Bedford, 17 October 1893 (MCZ #291309); 1 seen during a storm, Nahant, 15 May 1938 (Emilio, Foye, Alexander, Lawson); 1 adult male, Nantucket, 8 September 1951 (Davis et al); 1 immature photographed, Chatham, 17–18 June 1960 (Drew, Bailey); 1 female, Nantucket, 7 July 1966 (Gleick); 1 immature, Woods Hole, 9 July 1966 (Garrey); 1, Eastham, 13 July 1966 (fide Forster); 1 immature, Naushon Island, 20 August 1967 (Garrey et al); 1, Nantucket, 11–12 May 1969 (Faunce, E. and C. Andrews); 1 immature after Hurricane Belle, North Chatham, 11 August 1976 (fide Bailey); 1, Penikese Island, 31 May 1979 (Masch). Future frigatebirds should be carefully scrutinized because the Lesser Frigatebird (*F. ariel*) has been photographed in Maine (Snyder 1961).

# American Bittern  *Botaurus lentiginosus*

**Range:** Nearctic; breeds in eastern North America from northern Manitoba and Newfoundland south to central Oklahoma and North Carolina. Winters along the coast from Massachusetts south to the Gulf Coast.

**Status:** Uncommon breeder and declining; uncommon migrant and rare and erratic in winter.

**Breeding:** American Bitterns have declined substantially in Massachusetts since the 1960s, probably in large part due to the gradual disappearance of extensive cattail marshes. To illustrate this decline, 24 pairs of bitterns were estimated breeding in Newbury during the summer of 1953 (deWindt); whereas, between 1976 and 1980, the Massachusetts Breeding Bird Atlas project confirmed only 17 instances of breeding in the entire state. The area of highest nesting density is apparently still in northeastern Essex County, and the species is rare on the southeastern coastal plain. Secondary strong-holds are in the Sudbury River valley, at scattered localities in interior Plymouth County, and in Berkshire County. The breeding population usually arrives by the middle of April, but residents become hard to locate after they stop calling. *Egg dates:* 1 May–13 June.

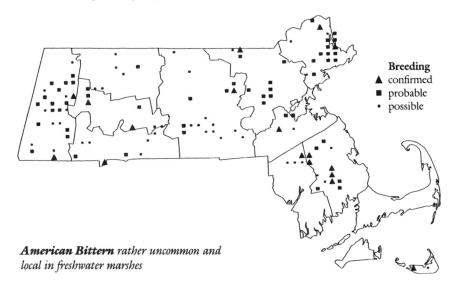

Breeding
▲ confirmed
■ probable
• possible

*American Bittern* rather uncommon and local in freshwater marshes

**Nonbreeding:** After the breeding season, American Bitterns frequent coastal salt marshes, where high counts for the year are often made. *Maxima:* 20, Plum Island, 15 October 1966 (BBC); 16, Plum Island, 12 November 1977 (Martin). A few hardy birds attempt to survive the winter, most often on Cape Cod and the Islands. *Winter maxima:* 5, eastern Massachusetts, February 1974 (BOEM); 4, Eastham, 20 January 1968 (Forster); 3, Chatham, 25 January 1968 (Copeland).

# Least Bittern   *Ixobrychus exilis*

**Range:** Nearctic and Neotropical; breeds in eastern North America from eastern North Dakota, eastern Maine, and southern New Brunswick south to Texas and Florida. Winters from southern Texas and Florida south to northern South America.

**Status:** Rare and local breeder and uncommon migrant.

**Breeding:** As breeding birds, Least Bitterns are restricted to extensive cattail marshes. They have declined in recent years because many of these marshes have been destroyed. Though never numerous in Massachusetts, the Least Bittern has a secretive nature that has made confirmation of its breeding especially difficult. Historic breeding locations include: Pilgrim Lake, North Truro, 1892 (Hill 1965); Cambridge and Lexington, circa 1900 (Brewster 1906); the Sudbury River valley, 1877–1881, and in the 1940s–1950s (Griscom 1949); and Pittsfield, 1955 (E. and A. Fitz).

Currently, Least Bitterns breed most consistently at Plum Island, at Great Meadows National Wildlife Refuge in Concord, and along the Sudbury River in Wayland, probably with a conservative total of no more than 5 to 6 pairs at those three localities. Other localities where birds have been recorded during June and July are Chestnut Hill, Brookline (O. and N. Komar), Peabody (Heil), West Harwich (Hines), Marshfield (Petersen), and Whitman (Petersen), suggesting that breeding may have occurred at those localities as well. There are no recent nesting records from Worcester County west to the Berkshires, although individuals have been seen in suitable habitat in May in Pittsfield. *Egg dates:* 1–29 June.

**Nonbreeding:** Nesting Least Bitterns appear to arrive during mid-May and depart by mid-August, but there are a remarkable number of sightings from strikingly atypical habitats and outside this time period between March and December—e.g., 1 caught alive, Scituate, 18 March 1980 (Keating, fide Petersen); 1, Quabbin, 24 March 1968 (Clark); 1, Rockport, 3 April 1973 (Bannon); 1 banded, Marion, 5 April 1975 (Mock); 1 caught alive, Barnstable, 6 April 1975 (Bailey); 1, Monomoy, 17 May 1977 (Roberts); 1, Monomoy, 5 September 1964 (Bailey); 1, Wellfleet, 22 October 1967 (Bailey); 1, Plum Island, 3 November 1973 (Petersen, Forster). The only winter record is: 1 moribund individual, Fall River, 18 February 1939 (Hadfield).

# Great Blue Heron  *Ardea herodias*

**Range:** Nearctic; breeds from southeastern British Columbia, northern Alberta, east to the Gaspé Peninsula, and northern Nova Scotia south, at least locally, throughout the United States to the Gulf Coast and Florida; also in Middle America and the Greater Antilles. Winters, on the Atlantic Coast, from Massachusetts south to the West Indies.

**Status:** Uncommon and local breeder, common migrant on the coast; uncommon and erratic winter resident.

**Breeding:** Unlike other herons, Great Blue Herons do not nest on offshore islands in Massachusetts, but are restricted to isolated stands of dead trees in ponds, usually created by beaver dams, where they are apparently relatively free of predation. Because of the remoteness of many of these colonies, it is possible that Griscom and Snyder (1955) may have overlooked some of them. However, they did mention that Great Blues nested in tall pines in the Harvard State Forest in Petersham from 1925 to 1938, but that the colony was abandoned when the 1938 hurricane toppled the trees.

Recent census data, however, makes unambiguous an increase in the Massachusetts breeding population during the last two decades. For example, in 1989, Blodget (pers. comm.) determined that 266 nesting pairs of Massachusetts Great Blue Herons produced a total of 683 young in 22 colonies from Middlesex County westward. *Egg dates:* early April–late May.

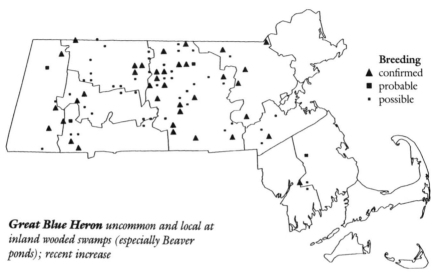

**Breeding**
▲ confirmed
■ probable
· possible

*Great Blue Heron uncommon and local at inland wooded swamps (especially Beaver ponds); recent increase*

**Nonbreeding:** In both spring and fall, loose flocks of Great Blue Herons are often seen migrating overhead throughout the state. Obvious spring migrants appear chiefly from mid-March to mid-April. *Spring maxima:* 59, West Bridgewater, 11 April 1980 (Higginbotham); 9, Sudbury River valley, 12 April 1980 (Forster). Fall migrants concentrate on coastal salt marshes in October and November, especially at Plum Island and Nauset, when peak counts for the year are often made. *Fall maxima:* 100, Nauset, Eastham, 8 October 1973 (VO); 100, Plum Island, 7 October 1979 (SSBC); 80+, Plum Island, 29 September 1976 (Heil); 56 migrating south, Ipswich, 19 October 1983 (Heil); 26 arriving from the north, Nantucket, 17 October 1979 (Veit, Litchfield); 16 migrating, Sudbury, 28 September 1964 (Baird).

Great Blue Herons regularly attempt to winter in Massachusetts—e.g., 60+, Outer Cape, 22 February 1975 (Petersen); 58, Orleans, 19 January 1975 (Laux)—with the number surviving depending upon the relative severity of the season. In Berkshire County, there is only one instance in which an individual survived through February (McNair 1978).

# Great Egret   *Casmerodius albus*

**Range:** Cosmopolitan; breeds in eastern North America along the Atlantic Coast from Massachusetts to Florida, along the Gulf Coast, and north along the Mississippi River drainage to southern Minnesota. Winters along the Atlantic Coast from Virginia to Florida and Texas, and also in the West Indies and northern South America.

**Status:** Uncommon and local breeder; fairly common migrant and visitor.

**Breeding:** Before 1960, Great Egrets were the most regular of the southern herons to occur in Massachusetts. Since that time they have been greatly outnumbered by Snowy Egrets, due to an explosive range expansion by the latter species. Like the Little Blue Heron, the Great Egret was considered an accidental visitor from the south at the beginning of the 20th century, with only seven specimens collected between 1865 and 1920 (Griscom & Snyder 1955). Between 1921 and 1955, Great Egrets appeared more regularly in Massachusetts, with major flights in 1921, 1937 (about 200 birds recorded), 1940, 1946, and 1948. The 1948 incursion was by far the largest, with more than 1,500 birds seen at 130 localities in Massachusetts. Most occurred between early July and October and were distributed as follows: 400 in Norfolk, Bristol, and Plymouth counties; 375 in Berkshire County (Cottrell 1949); 225 in Essex County; 200 in Middlesex County and Boston; 157 on Cape Cod and the Islands; 85 in Worcester County; and 65 in the Connecticut River valley. No flights of this magnitude have been recorded since, nor have Great Egrets been recorded inland in such abundance.

The species first nested in Massachusetts in 1954 and 1955 at the South Hanson Swamp, Plymouth County. Three or four nests were found there in 1954 (Whiting, Higginbotham), and one pair with two young was observed in 1955 (Goodell et al). The birds apparently did not return in subsequent years. In 1956, two pairs were found at House Island, Manchester (Drury et al), and a nest with two eggs was seen there 14 July 1957 (Helms). They were next recorded breeding in 1974, when 1 to 2 pairs were found at Clark's Island, Duxbury, 13 July (Petersen). Three nests were found at Clark's Island, July 1975 (Harrington), and ten nests were found in 1978 (Forster). By 1977, the total state nesting population was six pairs: 3, Clark's Island; 2, Dead Neck–Sampson's Island, Cotuit; 1, House Island, Manchester (Erwin & Korschgen 1979, Forster), and in 1984, 5 pairs were counted statewide (Andrews 1990). Great Egrets appear to be gradually increasing in Massachusetts—e.g., two pairs were found nesting on Spectacle Island in Boston Harbor, 1981–1982 (Hatch, Petersen); 25 pairs, Kettle Island, Magnolia, 1990 (Perkins). *Egg dates:* 3 May–mid-June.

**Nonbreeding:** Great Egrets now appear every year in small numbers, but the explosive dispersal flights of the 1930s and 1940s have not been repeated. Early migrants, e.g., 1, Eastham, 17 March 1957 (Wood) and 1, Middleboro, 17 March 1979 (Petersen), are often associated with southerly storms. Spring migrants usually arrive in early April, with the highest counts always occurring near the coast. *Spring maxima:* 22, eastern Massachusetts, April 1977 (BOEM); 10, Westport, 21 April 1975 (Brown). The species is scarce inland in spring, e.g., five records from Berkshire County since 1953, and only somewhat more frequent in the Connecticut River valley.

Fall peaks usually occur at coastal salt marshes and at evening roosts between late August and early October. *Fall maxima:* 170, Plum Island, 27 August 1989 (Abrams); 38, Westport, 11 October 1982 (Stymeist); 32, Westport, 29 September 1985 (Petersen); 30 +, Westport, 29 August 1976 (O'Hara). Inland records in the fall are slightly more numerous than in spring, e.g., 15, GMNWR, 1–16 August 1957 (Vaughan, M. and A. Argue).

Coincidental with their establishment as breeders in Massachusetts, there has been an increasing tendency for Great Egrets to linger into early winter, the latest being: 1, East Orleans, 28 February 1973 (Bailey).

## Little Egret   *Egretta garzetta*

**Range:** Mainly Palearctic; breeds in southern Europe, Africa, and Madagascar, and from Southeast Asia south to New Guinea. Winters principally in Southeast China and the African and Australian regions.

**Status:** Vagrant: two records.

**Occurrence:** The first United States record for the Little Egret was established when an adult in nonbreeding plumage appeared among a flock of Snowy Egrets at Plum Island, 12 August 1989 (Forster, VO [see Forster 1989]). Subsequently, the bird appeared briefly in Ipswich, 18 August (Forster), only to reappear at Plum Island several days later. During the latter weeks of its stay on Plum Island, it consorted and roosted with Snowy Egrets and was seen by hundreds of people prior to its departure on 10 September. Photos documenting the occurrence of this species in Massachusetts are on file at Massachusetts Audubon. The second record is: 1 in breeding plumage, Nantucket, 14 May–31 July 1992 (Perkins, VO, see photo AB 46:498).

## Snowy Egret   *Egretta thula*

**Range:** Nearctic and Neotropical; breeds along the Atlantic Coast of North America from southern Maine to Florida, along the Gulf Coast, north along the Mississippi River to southern Illinois, and, erratically, in Kansas, Minnesota, and Oklahoma. Winters mainly in the southern portion of the breeding range, north to Virginia and south to northern South America.

**Status:** Locally common breeder; common to abundant migrant and summer visitor.

**Breeding:** Considered a rare vagrant from the south until 1948, the Snowy Egret is now the state's second most common nesting heron. Between 1926 and 1947, only six individuals were reported in Massachusetts. Then, during the major heron incursion of 1948, which also included Little Blue Herons and Great Egrets, thirty Snowy Egrets were found, mostly in eastern Massachusetts but including two in southern Berkshire County, 24 July–15 August. Since 1948, Snowy Egrets have occurred regularly in Massachusetts each summer and in steadily increasing numbers. More than any other species of heron, the Snowy Egret is restricted to the immediate coast.

Snowy Egrets first bred in Massachusetts in 1955, when a pair hatched two young at Quivet Neck, East Dennis, 17 July (Shaub et al), although the species has not been reported nesting there since. Between 1961 and 1967, from 1 to 3 nests were found annually around Menemsha Pond, Martha's Vineyard. By 1968, 45 pairs were estimated breeding at Martha's Vineyard, including 25 pairs at Cape Pogue (Woodruff). A major and continuing population increase began in the late 1960s. Erwin and Korschgen (1979) found 459 pairs of Snowy Egrets breeding in Massachusetts in 1977—220 of these at House Island, Manchester; 68 at Clark's Island, Duxbury; 59 on islands in Boston Harbor; and the remainder in eight small colonies on Cape Cod and the Islands.

Subsequent estimates suggest that the population continues to be expanding rapidly: in 1978, 250 pairs were estimated at House Island (Forster), and 241 nests were counted at Clark's Island (Davis). During the summer of 1983, 82 nests were found at the north end of South Monomoy Island (Holt et al). In 1984, estimates suggested that the total Massachusetts nesting population was 538 pairs (Andrews 1990). Virtually all breeding Snowy Egrets in Massachusetts build their nests amid colonies of the more numerous Black-crowned Night-Heron. The nests are either on small offshore islands or among dense thickets on barrier beaches. *Egg dates:* early May–18 July.

**Nonbreeding:** The first spring migrant Snowy Egrets normally appear along the coast in the last days of March—earliest, Chatham, 12 March 1955 (Mosher)—with peak counts coming from either rookeries or nearby roosts—e.g., 350, Plum Island roost, 25 May 1981 (Stymeist). During the summer, Snowy Egrets are common and widespread in coastal salt marshes; their numbers gradually build at coastal roosts until a peak is reached in late August and early September, most often at Plum Island. *Fall maxima:* 1,076, Plum Island, 16 August 1988 (Stymeist); 985, Plum Island, 26 August 1978 (Heil); 880+, Plum Island, 23 August 1978 (Kasprzyk). While numbers at the Plum Island roost fluctuate from year to year, counts have consistently exceeded 500 birds from 1977 on. Snowy Egrets have been scarce inland since the 1948 influx, with no Berkshire County records since then and only sporadic records of from 1 to 5 birds in the Connecticut River valley during the month of August. Most Snowy Egrets have left the state by November; however, there are winter records as follows: 1 survived the winter, Eastham, 1974–1975 (Petersen, Bailey); 1, Eastham, 8 January 1976 (Bailey); 4, Buzzards Bay CBC, 18 December 1976; 1, Nantucket CBC, 3 January 1982.

# Little Blue Heron  *Egretta caerulea*

**Range:** Nearctic and Neotropical; breeds along the Atlantic Coast from southern Maine to Florida and from central Oklahoma, southern Illinois, and central Alabama south to the West Indies and northern South America. Eastern birds winter from South Carolina and the Gulf Coast south to South America.

**Status:** Rare and local breeder; irregular, sometimes fairly common, late summer visitor and migrant.

**Breeding:** Little Blue Herons were first found breeding in Massachusetts in 1940 and 1941 (Hagar 1941b) in a Black-crowned Night-Heron colony at Tilden's Island in Marshfield. One pair fledged two young in 1940, and, of 3 pairs present in 1941, 2 seemed to be nesting, and 1 nest that fledged 3 young was found. Nesting was not again confirmed until 1974, when 5 pairs and 10 immatures were seen at Clark's Island in Duxbury Bay (Harrington, Petersen, Anderson), and 2 to 4 pairs were found breeding at House Island, Manchester (Leahy). Erwin and Korschgen (1979) found 19 nesting pairs of Little Blue Herons in Massachusetts during the summer of 1977, including 6 pairs at Big Ram Island, Westport; 5 pairs at House Island; and 3 pairs at Clark's Island. While this total of 19 pairs for Massachusetts remained fairly stable between 1977 and 1983, some shifting between individual colonies did occur. The House Island birds deserted by 1980 (Heil), but 2 pairs were found at nearby Kettle Island in 1982 (Hatch, Veit). By 1984, only 5 pairs could be located breeding in Massachusetts (Andrews 1990). Maximum estimates for any one colony include: 10 nests, Clark's Island, July 1975 (Harrington); 15 pairs estimated, House Island, 24 July 1976 (Forster). *Egg dates:* Uncertain; probably most in May.

**Nonbreeding:** Little Blue Herons were considered accidental from the south in Massachusetts until the early part of the 20th century (Howe & Allen 1901). Between 1881 and 1955, irregular flights of Little Blue Herons occurred during the late summers of 1881 (6 reported), 1899, 1921, 1929 (42 in Essex County), 1937, 1939 (33 + in eastern Massachusetts), 1940, 1944, 1946, and 1948.

During July and August 1948, in a flight of unprecedented proportions, thousands of herons occurred in the northeastern United States. The most common species of that flight were Great Egrets and Little Blue Herons, although other species appeared in lesser numbers. Curiously, the concentration of sightings was in the inland portions of New England, from southern Connecticut through central Massachusetts and north into northern Vermont, New Hampshire, and southwestern Maine. The highest count of Little Blue Herons for Massachusetts was 250 in the Sudbury River valley, including a roost of 189 birds, 7 August (Morgan). Only two of the 189 were adults; all the rest were in juvenal plumage. From elsewhere in the state, 70 Little Blue Herons were found in Essex County during August; 130 in Norfolk, Bristol, and Plymouth counties; 24 on Cape Cod and the Islands; 17 in Worcester County; 50 in the Connecticut River valley; and 150 in Berkshire County. A total of 700 birds was reported from 50 localities in Massachusetts, while the grand total for New England from 85 localities was 1,100. "Practically all individuals were in the white plumage, there being only a handful of adults, and none in pied plumage" (Cottrell 1949). No counts approaching this magnitude have been recorded since, despite the much more regular occurrence of the species in Massachusetts.

Migrant Little Blue Herons in spring occur from late March through mid-May; the earliest birds—e.g., 1, Orleans, 17 March 1983 (Cook et al)— usually arrive following warm fronts from the south. *Spring maxima:* 6, Manchester, 9 April 1977 (Parsons); 5, Marshfield, 6 May 1968 (Judge et al). Numbers gradually increase throughout the summer until reaching an annual peak in August, when the largest numbers are seen entering evening roosts, such as the one at Plum Island. *Fall maxima:* 30, Plum Island, 3 September 1977 (Perkins, Vickery); 17, Squantum, 6 August 1976 (Janes). Always rare inland, Little Blues curiously seem to outnumber Snowy Egrets in the Connecticut River valley. There is only one spring record for Berkshire County since 1948: 1, Pontoosuc Lake, Pittsfield, 14 May 1944 (Eliot, Snyder). The species is rare after midfall, but there are at least six December records since 1974, including: 2, Plum Island, 3–16 December 1983 (Heil). The only midwinter record is: 1 lingering individual, Eastham, 18 February 1975 (Petersen, Forster, Bailey).

## Tricolored Heron   *Egretta tricolor*

**Range:** Nearctic and Neotropical; resident along the North American coast from southern New Jersey to Florida and Sonora, Mexico; also breeds north to southern Maine. Breeding birds between Maine and New Jersey migrate to the southeastern United States during winter.

**Status:** Rare breeder; uncommon migrant and visitor.

**Breeding:** Three pairs of Tricolored Herons raised young at House Island, Manchester, summer of 1976 (Forster, Petersen, Leahy), and a single pair was reported there during 1977 (Erwin & Korschgen 1979). They have not been reported nesting since then.

**Nonbreeding:** Griscom and Snyder (1955) considered Tricolored Herons to be of hypothetical occurrence in Massachusetts, listing six sight records between 1940 and 1955, the first being: 1, Ipswich, 7–15 September 1940 (Allen 1941). Since 1955, Tricolored Herons have been of nearly annual occurrence during both spring and fall in Massachusetts. Reports of single birds range from: 1, South Harwich, 3 April 1973 (Nikula) to 1, Plum Island, 4 December 1966 (Emery). Most birds first appear during late April and May, with peaks occurring in late August and September. *Maxima:* 7, Plum Island, 3 September 1977 (Perkins, Vickery); 6 after a hurricane, Chilmark, Martha's Vineyard, 15 September 1960 (Keith). The majority of Tricolored Heron records are coastal, but there are at least three records from the Connecticut River valley and one from Berkshire County—i.e., 1, Northampton, 17 April 1971 (Gagnon); 1, Connecticut River valley, summer of 1981 (fide Kellogg); 1–2, Longmeadow, 13–20 July 1983 (fide Kellogg); 1, Williamstown, 19–20 May 1966 (Whitehead).

## Reddish Egret   *Egretta rufescens*

**Range:** Chiefly Nearctic; breeds in coastal Texas, in the Florida Keys, and in the Bahamas, Cuba, and Hispaniola. Disperses northward to southern Illinois, Colorado, and Massachusetts.

**Status:** Vagrant: three records.

**Occurrence:** The first occurrence of a Reddish Egret in Massachusetts was an adult in the dark morph discovered at Monomoy, 30 May 1953 (Smart, Snyder, Stephenson), where it remained until 3 June and was carefully studied by Griscom, Morgan, and Drury. More recent records are: 1 dark morph photographed, WBWS, South Wellfleet, 12 May 1991 (Haley, VO, see AB 45: 415); 1 immature, Chappaquiddick, Martha's Vineyard, 5–29 July (Laux, VO); 1 (same individual), 30 July–20 September 1992 (Reid, VO).

## Western Reef-Heron   *Egretta gularis*

**Range:** Ethiopian; breeds along the west coast of Africa between 20° N and the Equator. Vagrant to the Azores, the Cape Verde Islands, Spain, and North America.

**Status:** Vagrant: one record.

**Occurrence:** The only documented record of this African species for North America is of an individual in the dark morph discovered at the Quaise Marsh, Nantucket, 26 April 1983 (Andrews), and positively identified from photographs by Alec Forbes-Watson and Robert Ridgely. The bird remained until 13 September 1983 and was studied and photographed by many hundreds of observers. Plumage characteristics indicated that it was undergoing its first pre-alternate molt during June and July. Some Western Reef-

Herons are known to stray well outside of their normal range during spring (Cramp et al 1977), and, because they are not known to be kept in captivity in North America, there is no reason to consider this individual anything other than a bona fide vagrant. Smith's observation of two Western Reef-Herons in Barbados (AB 38: 254–256) supports the supposition that these herons are crossing the Atlantic on their own.

# Cattle Egret   *Bubulcus ibis*

**Range:** Originally Ethiopian, now cosmopolitan; breeds in eastern North America, at widely scattered sites from North Dakota and Nova Scotia south to Texas and Florida. Increasing and expanding its range very rapidly. Winters from Texas and Florida south to the West Indies and northern South America.

**Status:** Rare and local breeder; fairly common migrant and visitor in some years.

**Breeding:** In 1974, Leahy established the first breeding record for the state when he found 2 to 4 pairs nesting at House Island, Manchester. That colony subsequently increased to 10 pairs by 1976 and 1977 (Forster, Erwin & Korschgen 1979), but by 1980 the colony had been deserted (Heil). In June 1982, 5 nests were found on nearby Eagle Island (Hatch, Veit). In a statewide coastal census in 1984, only 2 pairs could be located, both on Eagle Island (Andrews 1990). Apparently, the Massachusetts nesting population of Cattle Egrets has yet to exceed 10 pairs. *Egg dates:* late May–early June.

**Nonbreeding:** The first Cattle Egret collected in North America was taken in Sudbury, 23 April 1952 (Morgan, Drury, Stackpole, MCZ #279088). One was later seen in Cambridge, 27–28 November 1952 (Nuner), and a second was shot by a hunter in North Truro, 28 November 1952. That specimen was mounted as a trophy at the Hyannis Sportsmen's Club (Griscom & Snyder 1955). Another was seen at Newbury, 25–29 April 1954 (Snyder et al). These Massachusetts records, and one from Cape May, New Jersey, 25 May 1952, resulted in closer examination of egrets in Florida, which revealed the presence of a number of Cattle Egrets there (Peterson 1954). The first records for the New World, from Guyana and Suriname in the late 1870s, were dismissed as escaped captive birds. The evidence appears to suggest, however, that Cattle Egrets arrived in South America during the late 1800s and reached Florida by at least 1930 (Davis 1960).

Massachusetts records gradually increased in frequency during the late 1950s—e.g., 10, South Dartmouth, 9 May 1959 (Fernandez). The first major flights occurred in 1961, 1962, and 1964. In 1961, about 14 were reported in Massachusetts between 23 April and 27 May, including: 5, Salisbury, 21 May

(Gardler, Forster). In 1962, at least fifty-eight were found in the state, including: 14, Wayland; 9, Bridgewater; 3, Ashley Falls; several, Housatonic River valley—all between late April and late May (RNEB). In 1964, a major incursion occurred during the period 6 to 12 May, when about 40 were found in eastern Massachusetts, plus 3 in Charlton, 12 May (Jacobs), and 12 in Lancaster, 17 May (Harris). They have steadily increased since that time; however, their numbers fluctuate considerably from year to year.

Cattle Egrets ordinarily arrive during April, although late March records occur with increasing frequency, usually following periods of unseasonably mild weather—e.g., 1, Boston, 20 March 1984 (Nisbet); 2, Nantucket, 20 March 1983 (Vermilye, Andrews). The number of spring migrants reported each year in Massachusetts far exceeds the small nesting population. *Maxima:* 155, throughout Massachusetts, 5–17 May 1964 (RNEB); 100 (a most unusual total for Berkshire County), West Stockbridge, 4 May 1972 (Ryan); 78, eastern Massachusetts, September 1977, including 38 at Marshfield and 15 at Ipswich (BOEM); 44, Ipswich, 1 August 1976 (Berry); 44, South Dartmouth, 8 August 1976 (Hamlen); 18, Ipswich, 1–20 May 1973 (Berry et al). Late records include: 1, 160 miles southeast of Boston, 18 October 1964 (Doyle, fide Baird); 1, Boston Public Garden, 16–17 October 1966 (Connelly); 1, Worcester, 8–14 November 1966 (Kofciusko, Kleber); 1, Wellfleet Center, 1 December 1966 (Bailey); 1 captured, Chappaquiddick, Martha's Vineyard, 10 December 1967 (*Vineyard Gazette*). In recent years, Cattle Egrets have become increasingly frequent during late November and December, especially on Nantucket and Martha's Vineyard. The single winter record is: 5, Westport, 28 January 1978 (Laux).

## Green-backed Heron   *Butorides striatus*

**Range:** Nearctic; breeds, in eastern North America, from North Dakota, southern Ontario, southern Quebec, and southern New Brunswick south to western Mexico and Florida. Winters mainly from the Gulf Coast states south to northern South America.

**Status:** Uncommon breeder and fairly common migrant.

**Breeding:** Unlike the many species of Massachusetts herons that breed colonially, Green-backed Herons nest singly, usually in wooded swamps near open water. A historic exception is a loose colony of 10 nesting pairs in a maple swamp near Fresh Pond, Cambridge, May 1896 (Brewster 1906). More recently, 1 or 2 pairs have occasionally been found associated with

*First collected in North America in Wayland in 1952, the **Cattle Egret** is a highly successful colonist from the Old World. By 1974, this species was breeding in Massachusetts, and its range currently extends to parts of southern Canada.*

coastal heron colonies (e.g., Quaise, Nantucket). McNair (1978) estimated the breeding population of Berkshire County to be about 30 pairs. *Egg dates:* 5 May–17 June.

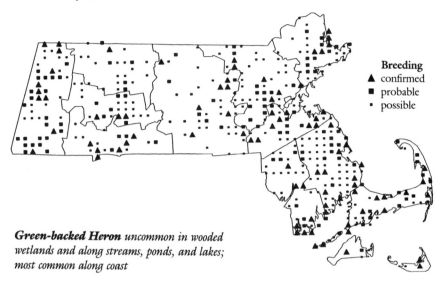

**Breeding**
▲ confirmed
■ probable
· possible

*Green-backed Heron uncommon in wooded wetlands and along streams, ponds, and lakes; most common along coast*

**Nonbreeding:** Green-backed Herons ordinarily arrive in late April and early May—earliest date, 1 found dead, Middleboro, 13 April 1973 (S. and S. Peak)—and depart by early October. Maximum counts for the year occur during post-breeding dispersal in August. Most notable of these counts are the numbers reported from a wooded swamp created by the SUASCO flood-control dam on the Assabet River in Westboro. In 1974, 57 were counted there on 25 August and 64 on 31 August (Jenkins). Such counts are exceptional anywhere in the Northeast. *Other maxima:* 17, Plum Island–Newburyport, 20 May 1962 (deWindt); 15, South Dartmouth, 26 August 1978 (Hamlen); 14, Sharon, 6 September 1980 (Clapp); 13, Eastham, 27–30 August 1978 (Forster). The species is rare in winter, but there are at least seven December records and two for January—e.g., 1, Cambridge, 16 December 1979 (Crofoot, Leverich); 1, Sudbury, 30 December 1979–1 January 1980 (Forster); 1, Cohasset, 1 January 1960 (Harrington); 1, Gloucester, 1 January 1968 (D'Entremont).

# Black-crowned Night-Heron  *Nycticorax nycticorax*

**Range:** Cosmopolitan; breeds throughout much of temperate North America, but lacking from mountainous regions and the Great Plains. On tic Coast, breeds from New Brunswick to Florida and winters from .setts south.

**Status:** Locally common to abundant breeder and migrant; uncommon in winter.

**Breeding:** Black-crowned Night-Herons have declined substantially as breeders in the Northeast since the turn of the century. In June 1920, Gross counted 2,536 nests in a colony at Sandy Neck, Barnstable (Gross 1923), and 1,500 pairs were estimated at Hyannis in 1895 (Brewster). Both of these colonies were abandoned around 1940 (Hill 1965). Night-herons were also common breeders in the Connecticut River valley at one time; the largest colony was at Pine Point, Springfield, where several hundred pairs were said to nest during the 1920s and 1930s. H. E. Woods banded a maximum of 296 fledglings there on 21 June 1931 (Bagg & Eliot 1937). These authors also cite records of additional colonies in the Connecticut River valley during the latter part of the 19th century, none of which were as large as the one at Pine Point. The decline of the Black-crowned Night-Heron is probably attributable to the direct disturbance of rookeries, shooting, and the use of DDT and other pesticides during the 1950s and 1960s.

Since 1940, night-heron colonies have become much smaller and more widely dispersed, and none have existed farther inland than about 20 miles from the coast. Erwin and Korschgen (1979) found 1,958 breeding pairs in the state, with the largest colonies at House Island, Manchester (600 pairs); Nantucket (400 pairs); Clark's Island, Duxbury (250–300 pairs); Dead Neck–Sampson's Island, Cotuit (231 pairs); and Peddocks Island in Boston Harbor (150 pairs). The remaining pairs were found on Cape Cod and the Islands, except for 33 pairs on Spectacle and Middle Brewster islands in Boston Harbor. Since 1977, the population seems to have increased slightly, and breeding has been recorded in at least two additional sites. Erwin and Korschgen (op cit) underestimated the heronry at Clark's Island, where between 200 and 350 pairs of night-herons have nested since 1975 (Davis & Parsons 1982). During a 1984 coastal census, 973 pairs were located in Massachusetts (Andrews 1990). More recently, at least two sizable colonies were located at Nantucket in 1990 (fide Perkins), along with 250 pairs at Monomoy, 21 June 1990. *Egg dates:* 10 April–30 June.

**Nonbreeding:** Black-crowned Night-Herons assemble in roosts following the breeding season. These roosts are sometimes widely separated from any nesting colony. A traditional roost is on the west edge of Nauset Marsh in Eastham, where 75 to 100 birds are usually present during late summer and fall. One of the larger post-breeding assemblages noted in recent years occurs annually at the dam on the Charles River in Watertown, where 201 birds were counted on 1 July 1976 (Luck). The birds gather at that locality to feed on Alewives, which concentrate at the base of the dam. Inland, Black-crowned Night-Herons are now uncommon, and counts of more than five in Worcester County or farther west in fall are unusual.

Black-crowned Night-Herons frequently survive mild winters on Cape

Cod and the Islands, but they are rarely seen in that season north to Boston Harbor and Essex County. There are no recent records of overwintering inland. Statewide Christmas Bird Count totals for Massachusetts have steadily declined—e.g., 188 in 1974 to 16 in 1983 (Heil 1983a). *Winter maxima:* 32, Quincy, 28 January 1974 (Brown); 20, Eastham, throughout February 1973 (Petersen, Pease); 15, Eastham, throughout February 1974 (Nikula); 6, Eastham, throughout February 1974 (Nikula).

# Yellow-crowned Night-Heron  *Nycticorax violaceus*

**Range:** Nearctic and Neotropical; breeds along the Atlantic Coast from Massachusetts to Florida, and north, in the Midwest, to Oklahoma, southeastern Kansas, western Wisconsin, and southern Indiana. Winters on the Gulf Coast and on the Atlantic Coast north to North Carolina.

**Status:** Rare but probably regular breeder; uncommon spring migrant and late summer visitor.

**Breeding:** The first confirmed breeding of the Yellow-crowned Night-Heron in Massachusetts was at Ipswich in 1928, when 1 of 4 young fledged was collected by Townsend (1929). The species was also suspected of breeding at Provincetown in 1891 on the basis of adults present from 19 April–8 July and an adult and immature collected on 18 July (Griscom & Snyder 1955). One pair nested more or less regularly near Damon's Point, Marshfield, from the 1930s until at least the 1950s (Griscom & Snyder 1955), and a pair bred at Chatham in 1940 and 1941 (op cit). More recently, the repeated summer occurrences of adult birds accompanied by immatures in late summer at Plum Island, Westport, Martha's Vineyard, Nantucket, and Centerville suggest that breeding may now occur regularly in those areas. Yellow-crowned Night-Herons are solitary nesters, not usually associating with the colonial Black-crowned Night-Heron, which makes them especially difficult to confirm as breeders. *Egg dates:* Uncertain, probably June.

**Nonbreeding:** Before 1940, the Yellow-crowned Night-Heron occurred less regularly than it does today, but overall its status has changed little over the last 40 years. The most frequent observations of the species in Massachusetts are of immature birds in late summer and fall, along with a few reports of adults in spring. Most records are from large coastal salt marshes, but individuals have been recorded inland even as far west as Berkshire County.

Presently, the Yellow-crowned Night-Heron regularly occurs in small numbers as a migrant and a late summer visitor. The earliest records are: 1, Rockport, 14 March 1962 (Bloombergh, Johnson); 1 adult found dead, Marshfield, 2 April 1983 (Clapp). *Maxima:* 6, Plum Island, 16 May 1981 (Drummond et al); 6, Squantum, 28 August 1973; 5, Marshfield, 21 May 1956 (Vaughan); 8 coastal reports, September 1954 (Griscom & Snyder 1955).

Yellow-crowned Night-Herons are rare but regular between July and October. The farthest inland record is from New Marlboro in Berkshire County, 1–10 July 1978 (Langeveld et al). There are three December coastal records of immatures, plus an exceptional record of: 1 adult, Bourne, 17 February 1965 (Briggs).

# White Ibis  *Eudocimus albus*

**Range:** Nearctic and Neotropical; breeds, in North America, along the Gulf and Atlantic coasts, north to southern North Carolina. Vagrant north to Ontario and Newfoundland.

**Status:** Vagrant: seventeen records, all since 1954.

**Occurrence:** Because White Ibises were unrecorded in Massachusetts before 1954, it seems likely that the recent increase in records may be associated with the general northward range expansion exhibited by several other species of southern herons. Records include: 3 adults (perhaps hurricane-drifted), Plum Island, 26 September 1954 (Paine, Ames); 1, Wrentham, 4 August 1956 (Howard, Sands, Bussewitz); 1 adult found dead in a snowbank, Nantucket, 18 February 1965 (Andrews); 3 immatures flying northeast, Westhampton, 12 May 1974 (Lynes); 1, Orleans, 19 August 1975 (Goodrich, Nikula); 1 immature, Dartmouth, 23 August–14 September 1975 (Petersen); 1, Weymouth, 11 July 1977 (Richman, Morano); 1 immature, Cohasset–North Scituate, 20 July–28 August 1977 (Forster, Sabin, Osborne); 1, Plum Island–Newburyport, 29 June–28 July 1979 (VO); 1 adult, Nantucket, 19 August 1983 (Bazakas, fide Andrews); 1 adult, No Man's Land and Squibnocket, Martha's Vineyard, 1 June 1984 (Sorrie, Andrews); 1 adult, Truro, 27 March 1986 (Everett); 1 adult (possibly the same bird), Marshfield, 31 March 1986 (Clapp); 2 adults, Middleboro, 21–29 March 1989 (Paine, Aversa, Drew, VO); 1 immature, Weymouth, 17 April 1989 (Breen, fide Clapp); 1 immature, Longmeadow, 5 August 1989 (Withgott); 1 adult, Hadley, 15 April 1990 (Yeskie).

# Glossy Ibis  *Plegadis falcinellus*

**Range:** Cosmopolitan; breeds, in North America, along the East Coast from southern Maine to Florida. Winters mainly in Florida and South Carolina.

**Status:** Very common local breeder; locally common migrant.

**Breeding:** Glossy Ibises were first found breeding in Massachusetts in 1974, when 4 to 6 pairs with 15 young were seen at Clark's Island, Duxbury Bay, 13 July (Petersen, Anderson, Harrington), and 2 to 4 pairs were found at

House Island, Manchester, 18 July (Leahy). Peak densities were reached in 1976–1977, when approximately 170 pairs bred in Massachusetts, distributed as follows: 107 pairs, House Island, 1977 (Erwin & Korschgen 1979); 60 pairs, Clark's Island, 1976 (Davis & Parsons 1982); 4 pairs, Boston Harbor Islands, 1976 (Hatch 1982b). Since then, they have declined substantially; the House Island colony was entirely abandoned by 1979, while the Clark's Island colony diminished to 15 pairs by 1981 (Hatch, op cit). There was no apparent reason for this decline. A statewide nesting total of 22 pairs was established in 1984 (Andrews 1990). *Egg dates:* probably June.

**Nonbreeding:** Glossy Ibises have been recorded annually in Massachusetts since 1947. Before then, they occurred only at very irregular intervals with the following flights recorded: 5 specimens taken, Cambridge, Concord, and Middleboro, early May 1850 (Griscom & Snyder 1955); at least 30 recorded, including a flock of 20 in Cambridge, 14 July 1878 (Brewster). The first state records after 1878 were: 1, Edgartown, 5–7 May 1932 (Worden); 1, Ipswich, 21 May 1932 (R. T. Peterson). Peak numbers of Glossy Ibises appear from mid-April to mid-August—earliest, 1 found dead, Beverly, 5 March 1973 (Lazell)—the largest counts coming from the Plum Island marshes and nearby farmlands in Ipswich. They are usually uncommon elsewhere on the coast and rare at any time far inland. *Spring maxima:* 254, Ipswich, 25 April 1977 (Parsons); 180, Plum Island, 24 April 1976 (Forster). *Fall maxima:* 94, Plum Island, 8 August 1979 (Kasprzyk); 94, Plum Island, 6 August 1980 (Stymeist). This species usually departs by early September—latest, 1, Logan Airport, East Boston, 1 January 1991 (Smith); 1, Plum Island, 5 December 1990 (Perkins)—considerably earlier than most other southern herons. There are about a dozen records, mostly of single birds between April and August, and ranging westward to Berkshire County. A most exceptional total was: 42, Pittsfield, 2 May 1972 (Dennis).

# White-faced Ibis   *Plegadis chihi*

**Range:** Western Nearctic; breeds from central California, eastern Oregon, and southern North Dakota south and east to southern Louisiana. Winters from southern California and Texas south to South America.

**Status:** Vagrant: three or four records.

**Occurrence:** All Massachusetts records of White-faced Ibises are of adults in breeding plumage: 1, Essex, 24–27 April 1984 (Forster); 1, Plum Island, 10 June 1990 (Saporito et al); 1 (possibly the same individual) photographed (see AB 44: 1113), Topsfield, 24 June 1990 (Perkins); 1, Holden, 25–27 July 1990 (Blodget).

# Wood Stork   *Mycteria americana*

**Range:** Nearctic and Neotropical; breeds in coastal Georgia, peninsular Florida, Texas, and Central and South America. Rare vagrant north to New England and the Great Lakes.

**Status:** Vagrant: four to five records.

**Occurrence:** Early records of Wood Storks from Massachusetts include: 1 collected, Georgetown, 19 June 1880 (Hale); 1 collected, Seekonk, 17 July 1896 (BMS #12936); 1 collected, Chilmark, 26 November 1918 (BMS #12392); 3, Rockport, 28 June–3 August 1955 (Robinson et al; photo in RNEB 11: 137). More recently, on 18 November 1963, a flock of 11 Wood Storks was reported at Plymouth Beach (Foster). A rash of sightings on Long Island during the period 1958–1962 (Bull 1974) perhaps lends added credence to the last report.

# Greater Flamingo   *Phoenicopterus ruber*

**Range:** Chiefly Neotropical and Ethiopean; breeds in the Bahamas and Greater Antilles, on the northeastern coast of South America, and in the Galapagos Islands. Vagrant to the eastern United States.

**Status:** Vagrant: eleven or more records, some of which may represent escaped aviary birds.

**Occurrence:** A number of Greater Flamingos were seen in New England during 1964 and 1965. Although they were summarily dismissed as being escapees at the time, the concentration of records in late August and in May could also suggest dispersal by wild birds. Vagrant flamingos were recorded in Bermuda during September to December in the latter part of the 19th century (Wingate 1973) and, more recently, have been seen in Newfoundland (7 November 1977), Nova Scotia (October 1969), and New Brunswick (November 1973).

The Massachusetts records are as follows: 1, Nantucket, 20–31 August 1964 (Harris, Andrews); 1, Lenox, 23–24 August 1964 (Hutchinson, Sanborn); 1, Natick, August 1964 (photo at MAS); 1, Plum Island and Ipswich, 16 September–25 October 1964 (Kingman, Fowler, VO); 1, Westport, 22 May 1965 (Eddy); 1, Auburndale, 23 May 1965 (Eddy); 1, Norwell, 23 May 1965 (Guild); 1 flying south, Nauset Beach, Eastham, 1 June 1965 (Shaw); 1, Quabbin, 12 August 1965 (fide Emery); 1, Duxbury, August 1965 (fide Emery); 1, Nauset-Monomoy, August 1965 (fide Emery); 1, Salisbury, 18 December 1965 (Preston); 1, Barnstable, 21 October 1967 (Gesner); 1, Sandwich, 23 November 1967 (Alves). Interestingly, there have been no reports of flamingos in Massachusetts since 1967, despite a continued increase in aviary populations in the Northeast.

# Fulvous Whistling-Duck  *Dendrocygna bicolor*

**Range:** Cosmopolitan; in North America, breeds in southern California and along the Gulf and Atlantic coasts, north to North Carolina. Disperses northward, irregularly, to New England and the Canadian Maritime Provinces.

**Status:** Vagrant: appears irregularly throughout the year.

**Occurrence:** The first flock of Fulvous Whistling-Ducks to appear in Massachusetts was: 6 (1 shot), Chilmark, 22 December 1962 (fide Keith). This record closely followed a rash of occurrences in the northeastern United States during the period between 1955 and 1961 (Baird 1963). An individual was found dead in Dennis, 3 March 1965 (Bailey), but the species remained unrecorded again until 1974, after which there were the following records: 10, Edgartown, 3 July 1974 (Ben David); 3, Rowley, 21 July–5 August 1974 (Petersen, Forster, et al); 5, Monomoy, 30 May 1975 (Nikula, Goodrich, Laux); 1, South Natick, 7–10 June 1975 (Timberlake, Lund); 6, Plum Island, 13 June 1975 (Gardler); 1 shot (of 7), Marshfield, October 1975 (specimen to MBO); 4, Eastham, 18 November 1975 (Clem); 10, Plum Island, 6 November 1977 (Oliver et al); 10, Plum Island, 7 November 1978 (Abbott); 4 shot, Nantucket, 28 November 1979 (Derr, Andrews); 2, Uxbridge, 8–10 December 1979 (FBC); 1 badly decomposed specimen, Nantucket, 20 March 1980 (Reilly, Tooker); 2 photographed, Monomoy, 7 August 1983 (Everett); 1, Nantucket, 9 October–7 November 1986 (Werner, Beattie, et al); 2, Plum Island, 19 August 1989 (McHale).

# Tundra Swan  *Cygnus columbianus*

**Range:** Nearctic; breeds from northern Alaska east to southwestern Baffin Island and south along the shores of Hudson Bay to northeastern Manitoba. Winters on the Pacific Coast and on the Atlantic Coast between Chesapeake Bay and South Carolina.

**Status:** Rare migrant; more frequent in fall. Occasional in winter.

**Occurrence:** Tundra Swans appear in Massachusetts chiefly from late October to early December and more rarely from March to early April. They are most frequently seen on Cape Cod and the Islands, where they prefer shallow glacial ponds, but are also of regular occurrence at inland sites. McNair (1978), for example, listed 4 spring and 6 fall records from Berkshire County. *Spring maxima:* 4 flying north, Pittsfield, 22 March 1920 (S. W. Bailey); 3, Acoaxet, 5 March 1966 (D'Entremont et al). *Fall maxima:* 28, Eastham, 28 October 1917 (Blaney); 17, Plum Island, 20 November 1958 (Stanwood, Knight); 7, Monomoy, 17 November 1985 (Nikula). Twenty-four were reported in Massachusetts during November 1959. Recent flocks have not generally exceeded 6 to 7 birds. Since 1973, from 1 to 7 swans have regularly wintered along the coast, most often on the Islands.

## Mute Swan   *Cygnus olor*

**Range:** Palearctic; introduced to North America. Mainly resident along the East Coast between Massachusetts and Virginia and also, sporadically, around the Great Lakes.

**Status:** Very common resident in southeastern Massachusetts; uncommon, but increasing, north to Essex County.

**Breeding:** In 1955, Mute Swans were considered rare vagrants to Massachusetts, deriving from feral stocks, which at that time bred from Long Island east to southeastern Rhode Island (Griscom & Snyder 1955). By 1965, they bred irregularly at Falmouth (Hill 1965, p. 64) and were apparently firmly established on Martha's Vineyard as well (113 adults and 44 young, Chilmark, 18 August 1965 [Hancock]). They have steadily increased since that time and were first found nesting at Ipswich and Magnolia between 1974 and 1984. *Egg dates:* 15 April–early June.

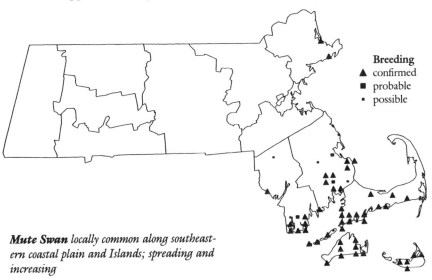

**Breeding**
▲ confirmed
■ probable
• possible

*Mute Swan locally common along southeastern coastal plain and Islands; spreading and increasing*

**Nonbreeding:** Although most Mute Swans are found along the immediate coast, there are at least five records from Berkshire County—maximum: 5, Pontoosuc Lake, Pittsfield, 10 November–7 December 1978 (Collins). Mute Swans are controversial in that they have been accused of destroying local waterfowl habitat because of their excessive appetites as well as their aggressive behavior. **Maxima:** 314, Martha's Vineyard CBC, 30 December 1984; 150, Westport, 2 May 1982 (Gove).

## Greater White-fronted Goose  *Anser albifrons*

**Range:** Holarctic; *A. a. flavirostris* breeds in western Greenland and winters in Iceland; *A. a. gambeli* breeds from northern and central Alaska east to northeastern Hudson Bay and winters chiefly in California, Mexico, Louisiana, and Texas. Both of these subspecies occur as vagrants to the Atlantic Coast of the United States.

**Status:** Vagrant: apparently all but two of the records since 1954 are of the Greenland race.

**Occurrence:** Griscom and Snyder (1955) listed five extant specimens of *A. a. flavirostris* from Massachusetts, four of which were immature, taken at Nantucket, Abington, North Truro, Martha's Vineyard, and Plymouth. They also listed the following sight records: 2 immatures, Monomoy, 17 January–15 February 1937; 1 immature, Fresh Pond, Cambridge, 12 November–1 December 1945 (Elkins et al). These individuals all had yellowish bills. Pink-billed white-fronted geese, probably *A. a. gambeli*, have been seen at Plum Island, 27 March–1 May 1954 (Griscom et al) and 5, Newburyport, 8–28 February 1982 (Altman, Heil, et al). The records (sixteen plus) since 1954 principally fall into the period between mid–September and November and March through April. The majority of these records involve orange-billed birds, presumably of the race *A. a. flavirostris*.

As with a number of waterfowl species, the possibility of captive escapees cannot be ruled out. Nonetheless, the frequency and pattern of records suggest that the majority of Greater White-fronted Goose records probably represent wild birds.

## Snow Goose  *Chen caerulescens*

**Range:** Nearctic; breeds in northern Canada from northern Ellesmere Island south to northern Mackenzie and northern Ontario. Winters in central California, on the Gulf Coast, and in the Chesapeake Bay area.

**Status:** Common to abundant migrant; rare in winter.

**Occurrence:** Snow Geese are generally most numerous in Massachusetts during April, when as many as several thousand birds occasionally gather in the Plum Island marshes prior to completing their northward migration. There are no major stopover areas in Massachusetts other than Plum Island, but flocks of 200 to 400 birds are frequently seen migrating overhead anywhere in the state, especially in the Connecticut River valley during

April and early May. In fall, flocks of Snow Geese are smaller than those in spring, and they do not generally linger in large numbers at Plum Island during that season. *Spring maxima:* 3,000–4,000 (including 3–4 blue morphs), Plum Island, 18–30 April 1976 (Forster); 2,500 (including 3 blue morphs), Plum Island, 12–15 April 1979 (BOEM); 1,700, over Pittsfield, 6 April 1979 (Ferren); 1,000, over Pittsfield, 5 April 1972 (Wannamaker); 660, Sudbury, 29 March 1981 (Forster); 600+, Brewster, 9 March 1954 (Hill); 500+, Florence, 31 March 1968 (Gagnon). *Fall maxima:* 3,500 migrating, Lanesboro, 12 November 1979 (MacDonald); 700+, Northampton, 17 November 1968 (Hubley et al); 700, Plum Island, 18 October 1979 (Blanchard); 500 in a cornfield, Sheffield, 11–12 October 1975 (fide McNair). In winter, a few Snow Geese have survived the entire season on Cape Cod and the Islands, and more rarely elsewhere. *Winter maxima:* 10 (all blue morphs), Eastham, 10 January 1964 (Beale); 3, Newburyport, winter 1959–1960 (RNEB).

**Subspecies:** The majority of Snow Geese that occur in southern New England are of the northeastern breeding subspecies, *C. c. atlantica*, in which the proportion of dark morph birds is low. The smaller, more southerly race, *C. c. hyperboreus*, is highly dimorphic, having a blue and a white morph. Thus, most records of blue morph Snow Geese, and an undetermined proportion of Snow Geese that occur here, are presumably of the smaller race. *Maxima* (blue morph): 12, Newburyport, early December 1957 (deWindt); 10, Eastham, 10 January 1964 (Beale); 8, Ipswich, 11 February 1970 (Payson); 5, Nantucket, 9 October 1979 (Litchfield).

# Brant  *Branta bernicla*

**Range:** Holarctic; breeds, in North America, in arctic Canada from northern Ellesmere Island south to northern Alaska, northern Mackenzie, Devon Island, and southwestern Baffin Island. Birds breeding east of about 110° W are *B. b. bernicla*, which winter on the Atlantic Coast; those breeding west of 10° are *B. b. nigricans*, which winter mainly on the Pacific Coast.

**Status:** Locally abundant migrant and winter resident.

**Occurrence:** Before a severe Eelgrass (*Zostera marina*) blight in 1931 (Griscom & Snyder 1955) drastically depleted the principal food supply for Brant, they were very abundant in coastal Massachusetts—e.g., 25,000–40,000 reported in the spring of 1930 (Phillips 1932). Because they subsisted almost entirely upon Eelgrass during the winter up until the time of the blight, the disappearance of that plant from coastal waters resulted in their mass starvation. It has been suggested (Palmer 1976), however, that other factors coincidental with the Eelgrass blight, particularly reproductive failure, may have contributed to the decline following the blight. During the early

1930s, maximum counts of only 50 to 100 birds were reported for Cape Cod (Hill 1965). Brant have steadily increased since then, due possibly to the regeneration of the Eelgrass beds, but they are no longer as abundant as they were during the early part of the 20th century.

During migration, which takes place in April and May and again from October to November, Brant are frequently seen in large flocks both on the coast and more rarely inland. Most inland counts are of birds flying overhead; the birds alight only occasionally during periods of inclement weather. *Spring maxima:* 4,500, Monomoy, 11 May 1974 (Veit et al); 2,400, Plymouth, 2 April 1975 (Clough); 25, Onota Lake, Pittsfield, 18 May 1952 (fide McNair). *Fall maxima:* 5,000 +, Eastham-Orleans, 11 November 1978 (Veit et al); 2,000 +, Eastham-Brewster, 31 October 1981 (SSBC, Petersen); 400, Wachusett Reservoir, 18 October 1978 (fide Blodget); 200, over Brookfield, 23 October 1978 (Blodget); 200, over Florida, 27 October 1940 (Benchley, Hagar); 150, over Mt. Greylock, 27 October 1940 (Benchley, Hagar).

The major wintering areas for Brant in Massachusetts are in Boston Harbor, southeastern Cape Cod Bay between Eastham and Brewster, and Duxbury Bay; winter numbers seem to fluctuate considerably from year to year. *Winter maxima:* 7,487, Cape Cod CBC, 19 December 1976; 5,066, Boston Harbor, 7 January 1984 (TASL). Usually, a few Brant, frequently crippled or immature birds, spend the entire summer in Massachusetts, most often on Cape Cod—maximum, 8, WBWS, throughout August 1974 (Bailey).

**Subspecies:** The "Black Brant," *B. b. nigricans*, has been recorded on at least nine occasions in Massachusetts: 1 collected, Monomoy, spring 1883 (Griscom & Snyder 1955); 1, Monomoy, 15 April 1902 (op cit); 1, Brewster, 23–24 November 1947 (Griscom et al); 1, Brewster, 28 October 1951 (Griscom et al); 1 banded, Monomoy, 9 November 1952 (Smith); 1, Brewster, 28 February 1953 (Griscom et al); 1, Duxbury, 4 May 1973 (Petersen, Goodrich, Forster); 1, Chatham, 16–29 February 1975 (Petersen, Proctor, Kenneally, Fox); 1 shot, Chatham, 23 December 1981 (Kinsella).


# Barnacle Goose  *Branta leucopsis*

**Range:** Palearctic; breeds in eastern Greenland, Spitsbergen, and Novaya Zemlya. Regular vagrant to eastern North America, south to North Carolina, and inland as well.

**Status:** Vagrant: one old and several recent records; several proved to be escaped captive birds.

**Occurrence:** A Barnacle Goose was shot out of a flock of 3 at North Eastham, 1 November 1885 (BMS #17635). Sight records have generally been dismissed as being escaped caged birds; however, 1 recorded at Wachusett

Reservoir, 4 November 1979 (Blodget), certainly occurred at an appropriate date for a wild bird. The most plausible recent record of a bird assumed to be wild is: 1, New Bedford, 18 December 1988–25 January 1989 (Mock, VO), which arrived and consorted with 2 Greater White-fronted Geese of the Greenland race, *Anser albifrons flavirostris*. More disconcerting was a group of 6 birds at Osterville, 18 January–22 March 1991 (Barber, VO), which were ultimately determined to be of captive origin (Arvidson 1991a, b).

## Canada Goose  *Branta canadensis*

**Range:** Nearctic; *B. c. canadensis* breeds chiefly in Labrador and Newfoundland and winters in southern Newfoundland and Nova Scotia and along the East Coast from coastal New Hampshire south to North Carolina. Feral birds breed intermittently along the Atlantic Coast of the United States.

**Status:** Fairly common breeder; abundant migrant and common winter resident on the coast.

**Breeding:** Feral Canada Geese, mainly of the race *B. c. moffitti* (Heusmann, pers. comm.), are now firmly established and widespread as breeders in the state. They nest commonly around inland farm ponds and in salt marshes on the coastal plain. Sample nesting densities include: 12 nests, Muskeget Island, May 1981 (Heil); 5 nests on 2-acre Bird Island, 23 April 1984 (Forster); 481 birds, GBBBC, 17 June 1979. *Egg dates:* April–June.

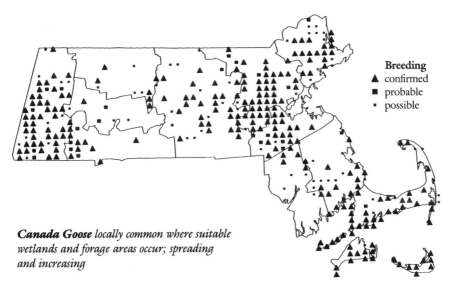

Breeding
▲ confirmed
■ probable
· possible

*Canada Goose locally common where suitable wetlands and forage areas occur; spreading and increasing*

**Nonbreeding:** During early spring and late fall, large numbers of migrant Canada Geese pass over Massachusetts or stop to feed on coastal salt marshes and tidal flats. Peak counts of migrants generally occur in March and April and again in November, when regular counts of 1,500 to 2,000 occur at Plum Island. *Fall maxima:* 4,575, Plum Island area, 13 November 1964 (USFWS); 600 migrating south, Mt. Wachusett, 27 September 1980 (Petersen).

The late fall and winter population reached a peak about 1950, when over 7,000 were counted in the Eastham-Brewster area in early January (Griscom & Snyder 1955), but counts of that magnitude have since declined. Since the mid-1950s, maximum counts from the principal concentration areas at Plum Island and Cape Cod have remained rather constant at 3,000 to 5,000 birds for each locality during November and December. The Massachusetts Division of Fisheries and Wildlife censused the Canada Geese wintering in the state during the Christmas Bird Count period in 1983–1984. They found 21,705 Canada Geese and estimated that 10,000 to 12,000 of those were feral residents. At inland sites (areas more than five miles distant from salt water), a total of 8,576 geese was found, of which 7,500 were thought to be feral. The highest concentration of inland geese was in the Sudbury-Concord-Assabet River drainage (Heusmann, pers. comm.).

The number of Canada Geese that survive the winter in Massachusetts depends directly upon the extent of ice cover on ponds, bays, and marshes. *Winter maxima:* 3,552, Cape Cod CBC, 19 December 1976; 3,044, Concord CBC, 2 January 1983; 2,042, Plum Island, 7 January 1982 (Spencer); 634, Framingham, 3 February 1980 (Forster). Inland wintering flocks are much smaller than those on the coast, e.g., 200, Berkshire County, 1979–1980, a season that was exceptional for its lack of snow cover (McNair 1978).

**Subspecies:** An extralimital subspecies, the "Richardson's" Canada Goose (*B. c. hutchinsii*), has been reported on several occasions in Massachusetts—e.g., 1 collected, Bridgewater, 8 October 1910 (MCZ #275911); 1 collected, Squibnocket Pond, Martha's Vineyard, 13 December 1958 (Austin, fide Kleber); 1, Orleans, 26 January–late February 1977 (Petersen et al); 1, Plum Island, 17 April 1977 (Veit, Litchfield); 1, Concord, 22 October 1989 (Perkins).

# Common Shelduck  *Tadorna tadorna*

**Range:** Chiefly western Palearctic; breeds west to Great Britain; vagrant to Iceland and the Faeroes and, possibly, North America.

**Status:** Vagrant: two records, perhaps not of wild birds.

**Occurrence:** An immature female Common Shelduck was collected near the mouth of the Essex River, Ipswich, 5 October 1921 (Tobey, PMS #6103). Another was shot at Squibnocket Pond, Martha's Vineyard, late November 1964 (Frye).

## Wood Duck  *Aix sponsa*

**Range:** Eastern Nearctic; breeds from central Manitoba and Nova Scotia south to Florida and Texas. Winters mainly south of Virginia and Nebraska, but also along the immediate coast north to Cape Cod.

**Status:** Common and widespread resident and migrant.

**Breeding:** Wood Ducks are fairly common breeders throughout the state; their abundance is determined by the availability of artificial nesting boxes. Consequently, some of the largest counts of Wood Ducks have been recorded at the Great Meadows National Wildlife Refuge in Concord, where an active Wood Duck program has been maintained for years, and in southeastern Massachusetts, where cranberry bog reservoirs provide ideal nesting habitat. In the western portion of the state, Wood Ducks breed in mature wooded swamps, where they prefer natural cavities for nesting (Grice & Rogers 1965). *Summer maxima:* 150, GMNWR, 19 July 1977 (Forster); 46 young and 163 eggs found in 14 boxes, Carlisle, 23 May 1959 (Greenough); 17 occupied boxes, Carlisle, May 1960 (Greenough). Post-breeding aggregations, occasionally numbering in the hundreds, occur between late July and September. *Egg dates:* late March–14 June.

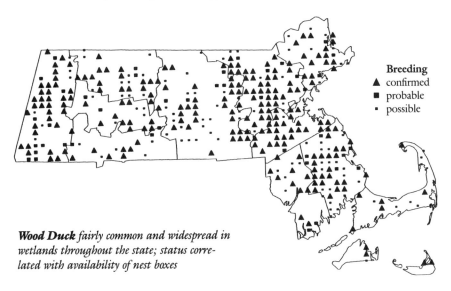

Breeding
▲ confirmed
■ probable
• possible

*Wood Duck fairly common and widespread in wetlands throughout the state; status correlated with availability of nest boxes*

**Nonbreeding:** Spring migrants normally first appear in early March; however, it is difficult to distinguish fall migrants from local residents, but increases in late October and November probably reflect the arrival of fall migrants. Wood Ducks have occasionally been observed from ships at sea, and not infrequently flying to land from the ocean—mainly during October and November, but also occasionally in April—e.g., 1 flying southwest,

roughly 90 miles southeast of Nantucket, 11 December 1979 (MBO staff).
*Fall maxima:* 800, Norfolk, 4 October 1989 (Cassie); 220, Central Valley
Lakes of Berkshire County, 3 October 1959 (HBC); 200, Lake Onota,
Pittsfield, 18 October 1947 (HBC); 200, Concord, 18 August 1959 (Freeland);
125, South Hanson, 10 October 1981 (Petersen). Winter survival occurs
regularly on Nantucket and Martha's Vineyard but is unusual elsewhere.
*Winter maximum:* 28, Nantucket CBC, 3 January 1981.

## Green-winged Teal   *Anas crecca*

**Range:** Holarctic; breeds from north-central Alaska and central Labrador
south to California and Nova Scotia, with a disjunct breeding population
between eastern Massachusetts and northern New Jersey. Winters in the
southeastern United States, north to Cape Cod.

**Status:** Uncommon and local breeder; common to abundant migrant;
irregular winter resident.

**Breeding:** Green-winged Teal were first confirmed breeding in Massachusetts at Plum Island in June 1954 (Nightingale), and females with young
have been found in the Plum Island-Ipswich area annually since 1974. In
1971, nesting birds were recorded west to Berkshire County, where at least 8
additional pairs have subsequently bred (McNair 1978). Breeding has also
been recorded at widely scattered localities throughout the state, including
Monomoy, Nantucket, and Martha's Vineyard. *Egg dates:* mid-May–30
June.

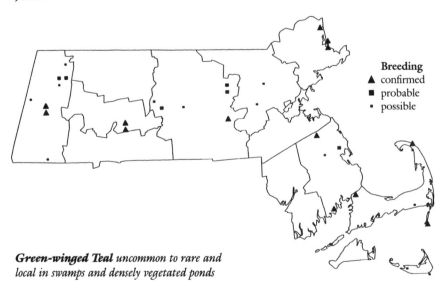

**Breeding**
▲ confirmed
■ probable
· possible

*Green-winged Teal uncommon to rare and
local in swamps and densely vegetated ponds*

**Nonbreeding:** In spring, Green-winged Teal are most abundant in Massachusetts during late March and April. *Spring maxima:* 300, Marshfield, 2 April 1978 (Petersen et al); (Berkshire County): 24, Lake Onota, Pittsfield, 18 April 1964 (fide McNair). Peak fall counts often occur earlier than for other species of puddle ducks—usually by early October, although in some years the peak counts are not recorded until December. *Fall maxima:* 5,000, PRNWR, 2 November 1965 (USFWS); 4,869, Plum Island, 9 October 1981 (Spencer); 48, Richmond Pond, Berkshire County, 15 November 1970 (fide McNair). Green-winged Teal are particularly common in coastal salt marshes, especially those at Plum Island and Monomoy.

Green-winged Teal are generally uncommon in winter, with a few regularly surviving along the coast. *Winter maximum:* 250 + , Nantucket, 28 December 1975 (Andrews et al).

**Subspecies:** The "Eurasian" Green-winged Teal (*A. c. crecca*) has occurred regularly in Massachusetts since at least the late 1940s (Griscom & Snyder 1955). They have been reported annually since the mid-1960s, mostly during the main flight of *A. c. carolinensis* in late March to early May and again in late October to November. Most records are of single birds except: 2, Plum Island, 24 March 1955 (Crompton et al); 2, Newburyport–Plum Island, April 1955 (Griscom et al); 2, Marshfield, 2 April 1978 (Petersen, Flaherty). A *carolinensis* x *crecca* hybrid was seen at Newburyport Harbor, 27 April 1965 (Forster), and another at Plum Island, 26–27 April 1975 (Forster).

# American Black Duck  *Anas rubripes*

**Range:** Eastern Nearctic; breeds from northeastern Saskatchewan and northern Labrador south to northeastern Illinois and northeastern North Carolina. Winters in the eastern United States, north to Nova Scotia.

**Status:** Common and widespread breeder. Very abundant migrant and very common, but declining winter resident.

**Breeding:** American Black Ducks breed throughout the state wherever there is suitable habitat, which may vary from open salt marshes to densely wooded swamps. At many inland localities, breeding American Black Ducks seem to have been displaced by Mallards. *Summer maxima:* 1,450, Newburyport, late August 1956 (Pelletier, Nightingale); 496, Clinton, 8 August 1974 (Blodget). *Egg dates:* 2 April–24 May.

**Nonbreeding:** The American Black Duck is one of the most ubiquitous species of waterfowl in Massachusetts, reaching maximum numbers on the coastal salt marshes of Essex County and Cape Cod. The population using the Newburyport–Plum Island marshes, which has been carefully monitored by the U.S. Fish and Wildlife Service since at least the 1950s, reaches a peak density during late March and late November. During the spring migration

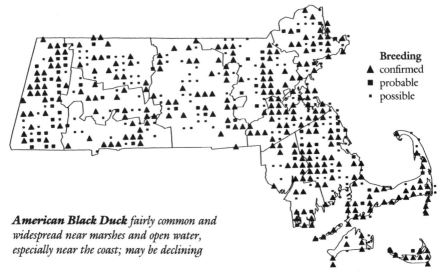

*American Black Duck fairly common and
widespread near marshes and open water,
especially near the coast; may be declining*

in March and April, there has been an apparent decline since 1955. In 1958,
deWindt estimated 10,000 American Black Ducks along the Merrimack
River, 25–26 March; since then, counts during that season have seldom
exceeded 2,000 birds. This may reflect either depletion by hunting or
increased winter mortality due to severe weather. J.A. Hagar (pers. comm.)
suggested that the reduction in the number of aquatic organisms in northeastern ponds and lakes due to acid rain may be largely responsible for
this decline. At inland localities where they do not winter, American Black
Ducks usually arrive as soon as the ponds and rivers open up, and in fall
they depart by late December.

Regular censuses of the Plum Island marshes indicate that black ducks
have substantially declined as migrants and winterers in eastern Massachusetts. The highest totals of American Black Ducks ever recorded in Massachusetts were during the mid- and late 1950s—e.g., 21,000 counted during
an aerial survey between the Essex River and the New Hampshire border, 18
November 1955 (Nightingale). The highest comparable counts made in
recent years are: 16,650, Plum Island, 24 November 1972 (Petersen, Goodrich); 13,500, 13 December 1981 (Heil). Most recent counts in that area have
been much lower than that. The Newburyport CBC generally records 4,000
to 7,000 black ducks, except for high totals of 28,034, 22 December 1968;
13,402, December 1971; 13,392, December 1962. Although the evidence is
somewhat equivocal, these data are consistent with recent analyses of bag
totals by the U.S. Fish and Wildlife Service, which suggest a continuing
decline in the Northeast beginning in the early 1960s (Heusmann, pers.
comm.).

On Cape Cod, the situation is similar. The maximum count there was:
2,000, Brewster, 27 November 1948 (Griscom), and recent totals for the

Cape Cod CBC have generally not exceeded that total. Maximum counts for Berkshire County are: 400, Richmond Pond, 14–21 November 1970 (fide Addison); 200, Richmond Pond, 22 November 1964 (fide McNair).

## Mallard  *Anas platyrhynchos*  .

**Range:** Holarctic; breeds from Alaska, southern Quebec, and southern Maine south to southern California, northern Mexico, and Virginia. Many eastern birds are feral. Some feral birds are resident; others migrate to the southeastern United States.

**Status:** Very common to abundant resident and migrant.

**Breeding:** Mallards have greatly increased in Massachusetts since about 1910. This increase includes both wild and feral populations. Waterfowl surveys at the Parker River National Wildlife Refuge have not indicated a major change in status at that locality between the late 1950s and the early 1980s: e.g., 1,121, 25 October 1958 (USFWS); 1,053, 10 December 1981 (USFWS). Mallards are presently ubiquitous in Massachusetts; the introduction of feral birds into the area has resulted in much hybridization with American Black Ducks and with various barnyard waterfowl, particularly Muscovy and Peking ducks. Many areas that formerly hosted nesting American Black Ducks have now become overrun by Mallards.

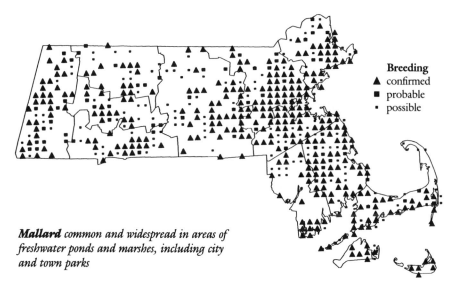

Breeding
▲ confirmed
■ probable
• possible

*Mallard common and widespread in areas of freshwater ponds and marshes, including city and town parks*

**Nonbreeding:** Peak counts of Mallards are generally obtained in November and December, when an influx of migrants from the Northwest augments the local population during that season—e.g., 1,682, Greater Boston CBC,

16 December 1979; 740, Springfield CBC, 28 December 1963; 77, Sudbury River valley, 3 November 1982 (Walton). Representative summer maxima include: 325, PRNWR, 15 August 1989 (Petersen); 263, PRNWR, 3 June 1982 (Spencer); 220, Clinton, 2 August 1974 (Blodget).

## Northern Pintail *Anas acuta*

**Range:** Holarctic; breeds, in eastern North America, around the southern perimeter of Hudson Bay and from the Great Lakes northeast along the St. Lawrence River to northeastern Quebec and western Nova Scotia. Winters in the southeastern United States, north along the coast to Cape Cod.

**Status:** Very uncommon to rare local breeder. Common migrant; local and irregular in winter.

**Breeding:** One or two pairs of Northern Pintails have nested at Clark's Pond, Ipswich, almost annually since 1961, following their introduction at the Ipswich River Wildlife Sanctuary in Topsfield during the late 1950s. The most recent successful nesting report in that area is of a pair seen with 10 young at Plum Island throughout June 1975 (Emery et al). In 1984 there were at least 3 to 4 pairs nesting at Monomoy, and 30 individuals were counted there, 31 July 1983 (Nikula). *Egg dates:* late May–17 July.

**Nonbreeding:** Pintails are most common in coastal localities, such as Plum Island and Monomoy. In spring they arrive during late February or March, with peak counts in late March and then again in November. Some remain to winter during particularly mild seasons. *Spring maxima:* 300, Salisbury–Plum Island, March 1958 (deWindt); 130, Plum Island, 26 March 1977 (Heil). *Fall maxima:* 795, Plum Island, 23 November 1981 (Spencer); 200, Plum Island, 12 November 1983 (Prybis); 140, Plum Island, 8 October 1984 (Stymeist); 125, Monomoy, 11 November 1985 (Nikula). There are no records of more than 10 birds at any locality in Berkshire County and not more than 30 in the Sudbury River valley (fide Walton).

## Garganey *Anas querquedula*

**Range:** Chiefly Palearctic; breeds throughout temperate Eurasia west to Great Britain. Winters in Asia, Africa, and Australia. Vagrant to North America.

**Status:** Vagrant: three records.

**Occurrence:** A male Garganey was discovered at Plum Island, 4 May 1968, where it remained until 25 May (Wade, VO). At the time, the bird was suspected of being an escapee—a conclusion that in retrospect seems less likely. Another male discovered at Marshfield, 1 April 1978 (Flaherty, Petersen, VO) remained until 18 April. The third record was a subadult male present at Plum Island, 11 May to 1 July 1985 (Stymeist et al). The North American pattern of occurrence of this species, with most records from April to May, strongly suggests that these records represent birds of wild origin (see Spear et al 1988).

# Blue-winged Teal  *Anas discors*

**Range:** Nearctic and Neotropical; breeds from central Alaska, central Manitoba, central Ontario, southern Quebec, and Nova Scotia south to northeastern California, southern New Mexico, central Louisiana, and eastern North Carolina. Winters along the Atlantic and Gulf coasts from North Carolina and Texas south to central Peru and Argentina.

**Status:** Uncommon breeder and common migrant; rare in winter.

**Breeding:** Blue-winged Teal are widespread, although not very numerous, breeders in Massachusetts. The highest densities of nesting pairs are: 8 pairs, Newburyport, 30 May 1961 (deWindt); 5–6 pairs, Monomoy (fide Hill 1965). Three to four nesting pairs have also been recorded for the Connecticut River valley and Berkshire County (fide McNair). Blue-winged Teal prefer to nest either in cattail marshes or in *Phragmites* stands at the uppermost reaches of salt marshes.

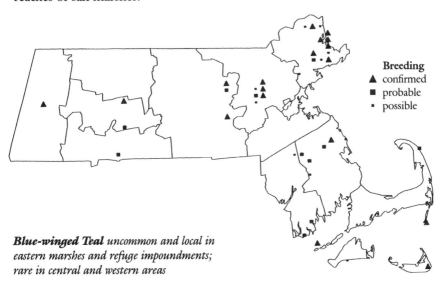

**Breeding**
▲ confirmed
■ probable
· possible

*Blue-winged Teal uncommon and local in eastern marshes and refuge impoundments; rare in central and western areas*

**Nonbreeding:** Migrants often concentrate at Plum Island, Great Meadows National Wildlife Refuge in Concord, and Monomoy. Most spring migrants appear in late March and April; fall peaks occur in late September and early

October. *Spring maxima:* 150, PRNWR, 18 April 1965 (USFWS Survey).
*Fall maxima:* 300, Plum Island, 6 September 1981 (Heil); 150, PRNWR, 25
September 1965 (USFWS Survey); 75, Lake Onota, Pittsfield, 14 September
1941 (Hendricks).

Blue-winged Teal occur much less frequently in winter in Massachusetts
than Green-winged Teal. In many seasons, none are recorded; however, up
to three birds successfully wintered in Sandwich in most years between 1973
and 1979 (Pease). Other winter records are: 2, Lakeville, 8 February 1975
(Higginbotham); 8, Marshfield CBC, 27 December 1975; 5, Bridgewater, 16
December 1976 (Flaherty); 2, Yarmouth, throughout the winter of 1990–1991
(Hamilton).

# Cinnamon Teal  *Anas cyanoptera*

**Range:** Nearctic and Neotropical; breeds in western North America, east to
eastern Montana, Wyoming, and Nebraska. Winters from central California
east to central Texas and south to northern South America. Vagrant to the
Atlantic Coast.

**Status:** Vagrant: two sight records.

**Occurrence:** Single drake Cinnamon Teal were seen at the south end of
Monomoy, 11 May 1978 (Mott), and on Martha's Vineyard, 12 May 1983
(Laux). The coincidence of dates suggests that these birds were wild.

# Northern Shoveler  *Anas clypeata*

**Range:** Holarctic; breeds, in North America, mainly in the Northwest,
south and east regularly to northeastern Manitoba, western Wisconsin, and
western Kansas. There also are scattered breeding records in northeastern
North America, around the Great Lakes, and east to New Brunswick, Prince
Edward Island, Massachusetts, Long Island, New York, and northern New
Jersey. Winters from southern British Columbia to northern New Mexico
and the Gulf Coast, and on the Atlantic Coast to South Carolina, south to
northern South America and the West Indies.

**Status:** Rare and local breeder. Fairly common migrant at Plum Island and
Monomoy; uncommon or rare elsewhere.

**Breeding:** Northern Shovelers nested at Monomoy in 1974 (French) and at
Plum Island in 1975 and 1977 (Forward, Berry); additional nestings have
probably occurred at Monomoy.

**Nonbreeding:** Northern Shovelers have steadily increased in the state since
the 1920s, when they were considered very rare by Griscom and Snyder

(1955). The highest counts of shovelers are invariably from Plum Island and Monomoy, but they are now increasingly regular inland to the Sudbury River valley, the Connecticut River valley, and Berkshire County. *Spring maxima:* 12, Onota Lake, Pittsfield, 19 April 1965 (fide McNair); 8, Monomoy, 5 May 1974 (Bailey). *Fall maxima:* 84, PRNWR, 9 October 1981 (Spencer); 74, Monomoy, 2 December 1990 (Perkins); 52, Monomoy, 20 November 1973 (Brown, Veit); 26, GMNWR, 4 November 1978 (Gove); 10, Monomoy, 2 January 1973 (Forster). A sample of winter records includes: 8, Yarmouth and Barnstable, throughout January 1976 (Pease, Laux); 3, Nantucket CBC, 1 January 1984; 1, Springfield, 19 January–12 February 1968 (LeShure); 1, Plymouth, 27 December 1984–28 February 1985 (Petersen).

# Gadwall  *Anas strepera*

**Range:** Holarctic; breeds in North America from southern Alaska, central Manitoba, and southern Quebec south to central California, northern Texas, and northwestern Iowa; sporadically east to the Atlantic Coast, north to Prince Edward Island, and south to North Carolina. Winters mainly in the southeastern United States, north occasionally to Massachusetts.

**Status:** Locally uncommon breeder and common migrant; rare in winter.

**Breeding:** Until about 1930, Gadwalls were considered rare vagrants from the West, at which time, largely through protection, they began to appear regularly in Massachusetts during spring and fall. Between 1930 and 1965, they gradually increased but nonetheless remained uncommon in the state. In August of 1957, Richard Borden introduced 27 young Gadwalls to his ponds near the Great Meadows National Wildlife Refuge in Concord. In April of 1965, 50 more birds were released. Following the 1965 release, 7 pairs nested in Concord. However, the species has not been found nesting in Concord since that time (Borden & Hochbaum 1966). By the early 1970s, Gadwalls were nesting at Plum Island and Penikese Island (1972), and, by 1975, the species was established in Ipswich and on Martha's Vineyard and Monomoy. *Egg dates:* late May–July.

**Nonbreeding:** In spring, migrant Gadwalls appear in Massachusetts in late March and begin migrating south after the first freeze. *Spring/summer maxima:* 250 +, Stage Island Pool, Plum Island, 10 July 1981 (Heil); 115 adults and 8 young, Plum Island, July 1977 (Heil); 104, PRNWR, 3 June 1982 (Spencer). *Fall maxima:* 300 +, Plum Island, 11 August 1979 (Heil); 200, Clark's Pond, Ipswich, 29 November 1973 (Alexander); 55, GMNWR, 22 November, 1978 (Walton). *Winter maxima:* 47, Newburyport CBC, 23 December 1979; 45, Plum Island, 6 January 1974 (McClellan); 35, Salem, 5–31 January 1979 (Heil); 30, Plymouth, 4–31 January 1981 (Petersen et al). The maximum count for Berkshire County is: 7, Lakes Onota and Pontoosuc, 2 November 1975 (fide McNair).

# Eurasian Wigeon   *Anas penelope*

**Range:** Chiefly Palearctic; breeds west to Iceland and east to Kamchatka and the Komandorskyie Islands. Rare but regular migrant and winter visitor on both coasts of North America.

**Status:** Rare but regular migrant.

**Occurrence:** Eurasian Wigeon have occurred regularly in Massachusetts since at least 1920. They are usually found among flocks of American Wigeon in areas where that species is most numerous. Favored localities for Eurasian Wigeon include the larger ponds on Nantucket, Martha's Vineyard, Cape Cod, Plum Island, and several ponds in Plymouth County.

Most birds are found between October and December, but records in April and early May are increasingly frequent. Two recent late spring records from Essex County and Cape Cod are most unusual: 1, Newburyport Harbor, 31 May–5 June 1980 (Arrigo et al); 1, Plum Island, 23–31 May 1981 (VO). *Maxima:* Griscom and Snyder (1955) state that up to "9 drakes in one day" were found on the ponds of Martha's Vineyard during the years 1920 to 1950, and Griscom and Emerson (1959) cite a record of "43 on Poucha Pond, Martha's Vineyard, 11 November 1940; this included a solid flock, separate from the abundant American Wigeon and Redhead, and contained many presumed females" (W. and B. Cottrell, Parker). This last count far exceeds any other for eastern North America. Recent maxima have been much lower: 5, Nantucket CBC, 18 December 1977; 4, Nantucket, throughout December 1975 (Andrews).

There are at least three recent midsummer records: 1 male, Monomoy, 27 June 1984 (Holt, Lortie, et al); 1 male in pre-eclipse molt, Plum Island, 2 July 1982 (Heil); 1 male, Plum Island, 21 August 1986 (Harper et al).

# American Wigeon   *Anas americana*

**Range:** Nearctic; breeds mainly in northwestern North America, south and east to James Bay, northern Minnesota, and western Nebraska; scattered breeding records in the Northeast, east to Prince Edward Island, Nova Scotia, Maine, Massachusetts, and Delaware. Winters in the southeastern United States, north to Massachusetts.

**Status:** Rare and local breeder. Uncommon spring and locally common fall migrant; fairly common winter resident.

**Breeding:** One pair of American Wigeon nested at Penikese Island, June–August 1972 (Nisbet), and there are at least two confirmed nestings on Monomoy, 1981 (French) and 1983 (Holt, Lortie). *Egg dates:* June.

**Nonbreeding:** American Wigeon were uncommon transients in the state until 1890, when a pronounced increase was detected, which persisted until the early 1940s. The maximum counts for that period were: 3,000, Squib-nocket Pond, Martha's Vineyard, November 1919 (Phillips; in Griscom & Emerson 1959); 2,900, Martha's Vineyard, 29 November 1941 (Griscom & Snyder 1955). The American Wigeon wintering population crashed badly in the mid-1940s. Apparently, a September storm in 1944 opened to the sea many of the fresh ponds on Nantucket and Martha's Vineyard, killing the vegetation upon which the wigeon fed (Griscom & Emerson 1959). Since then, wigeon have gradually increased, but they have never regained their former abundance in Massachusetts.

Since the late 1950s, American Wigeon have become more numerous at the Great Meadows and the Parker River refuges during migration than they are on Cape Cod and the Islands. This may reflect improved habitat at the refuges as well as a deterioration of Vineyard and Nantucket ponds, which have been repeatedly breached by the sea.

During spring migration in Massachusetts, numbers of nonwintering birds in April rarely exceed 50. In the fall, wigeon arrive during September, reach peak densities in late November, and remain in Massachusetts until their preferred ponds freeze over. Some almost always winter on the Islands, with up to 200 birds surviving if the ponds remain open. *Fall maxima:* 1,408, PRNWR, 20 November 1958 (Nightingale); 1,250, GMNWR, 12 October 1958 (Forster); 455, Nantucket, 25 October 1979 (Veit, Litchfield). Inland: 50, Williams Reservoir, North Adams, 22 October 1967 (Whitehead et al) is the maximum for Berkshire County, where they are even less numerous in spring, e.g., 35, Richmond Pond, 2–3 April 1954 (Schumacher).

# Canvasback  *Aythya valisineria*

**Range:** Nearctic; breeds from central Alaska, northern Mackenzie, and southeastern Manitoba south to northern California, northern Colorado, and northern Minnesota. Winter range has varied considerably since 1900; usually found in bays and large lakes east to Lake Ontario, Quebec (formerly), and southeastern Massachusetts south to Florida and the Gulf Coast.

**Status:** Local and occasionally abundant winter resident and uncommon migrant.

**Occurrence:** The abundance of Canvasbacks in Massachusetts during fall and winter has varied dramatically during the historical period. They were scarce before 1900, but a "sudden increase started in 1905, after which flocks of 100 to 150 birds appeared on the ponds of Cape Cod, Nantucket, and Martha's Vineyard" (Fay 1910). Between 1910 and 1950, Canvasbacks were of regular occurrence and were apparently fairly common on ponds in southeastern Massachusetts. Griscom and Snyder (1955) refer to a decline beginning in 1950; it was apparently only a temporary fluctuation, however, because Canvasbacks were once again common by the mid-1960s, and abundant by the mid-1970s, when counts of 2,000 to 2,500 were regular during the winter in the Taunton-Assonet area.

Although Griscom spoke of spring and fall migrants, it seems more likely that most Massachusetts Canvasbacks represent arriving and departing winter residents. The birds move around considerably during the winter season according to local ice conditions and changing food supply. *Maxima:* 4,000, Assonet, 22 February 1981 (Emerson); 2,500, Somerset, 26 January 1975 (Athearn); 2,500, Assonet, 13 December 1975 (Hill); 1,500, Assonet, 7 February 1978 (Petersen, Anderson). The wintering population consistently numbered between 2,000 and 4,000 birds during the period 1975–1981. Representative counts from elsewhere in the state include: 700, Cambridge, 5 November 1988 (Perkins et al); 633, Cape Cod CBC, 19 December 1976; 300, Nantucket, 20 November 1980 (Veit); 230, Winthrop, 9 December 1979 (BBC); 107, Cambridge, 30 October 1982 (Barton). In Berkshire County, Canvasbacks occur as migrants from mid-March to mid-May, and again in November. Maximum counts there are: 84, Lake Onota, Pittsfield, 29 November 1969 (Sanborn); 99, Richmond Pond, 23 November 1976 (Burg, Sanborn).

# Redhead   *Aythya americana*

**Range:** Nearctic; breeds mainly in northwestern North America, south and east to northwestern Iowa and east central Manitoba. There are also disjunct breeding populations in Wisconsin and Michigan and scattered breeding records east to New Brunswick and Long Island, New York (many of these the result of stocking). In the eastern North America, winters north to southern Massachusetts, Lake Ontario, and northern Illinois.

**Status:** Local and erratic, but at times common migrant and winter resident.

**Occurrence:** Redheads have been markedly erratic in Massachusetts during the historical period. Periods of lavish abundance from 1900 to 1910 and 1922 to 1928 on Martha's Vineyard and Nantucket were followed by periods during which no Redheads could be found. These variations in winter abundance can be attributed to the saltwater breaching of the fresh ponds on Nantucket and Martha's Vineyard, which killed much of the pond vegetation on which the ducks fed. Redheads are especially fond of Wild Celery (*Vallisneria spiralis*), which was introduced to the ponds on Martha's Vineyard during the 1880s (Forbush 1916) and was killed by intrusions of salt water into the ponds.

Griscom and Snyder's (1955) statement that up to 12,000 Redheads were present on Martha's Vineyard during the early 20th century seems to be based on the ambiguous account by Forbush (1916) that, "Mr. Brown says that two thousand Redheads remained in Antires Pond during the coldest weather of January and February, 1910, and that he has seen more than ten thousand Ducks in Edgartown Great Pond at one time, and perhaps two thousand in the other ponds in the same time period." It is unclear whether the ducks referred to were Redheads or other species, but it is clear that very large numbers of Redheads, far exceeding any recent totals, were found on Martha's Vineyard during the early 20th century.

Currently, Redheads are still found more commonly on Nantucket and Martha's Vineyard than elsewhere in Massachusetts. They were uncommon until the late 1960s, when a pronounced increase began. The population reached a peak in 1975–1976, but the causes of the increase are uncertain. Away from Nantucket, Redheads have occurred in some numbers north to Eastham, Falmouth, and Plymouth, but they are uncommon elsewhere in the state. The maximum for Berkshire County is: 12, Lake Onota, Pittsfield, late October-November 1948 (fide McNair). Redheads generally arrive in October and November and then remain for the entire winter if ponds remain open. There is little evidence of spring migration. *Maxima:* 800, Nantucket, 19 November 1976 (Andrews); 638, Nantucket CBC, 28 December 1975; 220, Falmouth, 2 February 1980 (Soucy); 115, Falmouth, 27 February 1976 (Nikula). Redheads have occasionally been seen north to Essex County in winter, e.g., 2, Plum Island, 23 January 1977 (Veit).

# Ring-necked Duck *Aythya collaris*

**Range:** Nearctic; breeds from southern Alaska, northeastern Manitoba, and central Labrador south to eastern California, central Minnesota, central New York, and western Massachusetts. Winters from southern Massachusetts south to the Gulf Coast.

**Status:** Rare and local breeder. Locally common to very common spring and abundant fall migrant. Regularly winters in small and variable numbers in southeastern Massachusetts and on the Cape and Islands.

**Breeding:** Ring-necked Ducks have been confirmed nesting on at least three occasions in Massachusetts: e.g., 1 nest with 11 eggs, GMNWR, Concord, 22 May 1947 (Chandler 1953, Hagar); 1 female with a brood of chicks, Ashfield, early July 1978 (Forster, fide Bates); 1 female with a brood of chicks, Ashfield, early July 1979 (Forster, fide Bates). *Egg date:* 22 May.

**Nonbreeding:** Spring migrants are found from early March to late April, usually in wooded swamps, stump ponds, and on reservoirs. *Spring maxima:* 507, Boylston, 25 March 1990 (Blodget); 400, South Hanson, 3 March 1991 (Petersen); 336, Sudbury River valley, 9 April 1978 (Forster); 200, South

Hanson, 13 March 1981 (Petersen); 200, Carver, 28 March 1982 (Briggs); 125, Lake Pontoosuc, Pittsfield, 30 March 1954 (Dunbar et al). Summer records of nonbreeders include: 1, Monomoy, 30 July–1 August 1964 (Harrington et al); 1, Brookline, 14 June 1975 (Agush); 1, Lakeville, 26 June 1977 (Petersen, Anderson).

In fall, when Ring-necked Ducks are most numerous in Massachusetts, they arrive in late August on large ponds in the Lakeville area—earliest: 4, 9 August 1980 (Petersen)—and reach maximum densities in early November. They are less numerous on Cape Cod and the Islands than on the mainland; however, a reservoir excavated in 1982 at West Newbury has proven attractive to Ring-necked Ducks in recent years. From 1975 to the present time, increasingly large numbers have been recorded in fall at Lakeville. *Fall maxima:* 1,650, Lakeville, 3 November 1985 (Petersen); 1,500, Lakeville, 1 November 1981 (Petersen); 1,250, Lakeville, 19 October 1979 (Petersen); 500 +, West Newbury, 6 November 1982 (CBC); 103, Central Valley Lakes, Berkshire County, 10 October 1977 (fide McNair). In winter, numbers seldom exceed 200—e.g., 210, Mid-Cape Cod CBC, 27 December 1988—with the highest counts usually occurring on Cape Cod.

**Remarks:** A probable Ring-necked Duck x Redhead hybrid was identified in Middleboro, 27 March 1977 (Petersen, Forster).

## Tufted Duck  *Aythya fuligula*

**Range:** Chiefly Palearctic; breeds west to Iceland and east to the Komandorskiye Islands. Regular visitor in small numbers on both coasts of North America.

**Status:** Vagrant: rare, but almost regular.

**Occurrence:** Tufted Ducks have occurred in many consecutive seasons at both Newburyport and Falmouth beginning in 1954. They generally associate with both Greater and Lesser scaup. At Newburyport, a male remained from 24 January to 15 February 1954 (Eliot, Crompton, deWindt). Up to 3 birds were seen there from January to March, 1959 through 1962 and 1975 to 1976. *Maximum:* 3 (2 males and 1 female), Newburyport, 20–28 February 1960 (deWindt, Drury). At Falmouth, a male was first seen 21 February–6 March 1960 (Kelley et al) and was seen subsequently each winter until 1968, and once again in 1976. Two (1 male and 1 female) were also present there during the winters of 1965–1966 and 1966–1967.

Other records of Tufted Ducks in Massachusetts include: 1 especially tame bird, Marshfield, February–April and November 1954 (Ames); 1 male, Westport Harbor, 14 May 1966 (Athearn); 1 male, Little Quitticas, Lakeville, 19 January 1975 (Petersen, Anderson); 1 male, Sesachacha Pond, Nantucket,

16–18 February 1975 (Conner, Andrews); 1 male, Salisbury, 17–28 February 1975 (Holland, Treacy); 1 male, Lake Assawompsett, Lakeville, 8 November 1975 (Petersen, Sorrie); 1, Cockeast Pond, Westport, 27 January–13 March 1983 (Pyburn, Garrett, et al); 1 male, Chatham, 27 March–3 April 1983 (Tait, VO); 1, Monomoy, 27 July–23 October 1983 (Vose et al); 1 male, Sandwich, 17 December to 28 February 1989 (Nielsen, VO).

## Greater Scaup  *Aythya marila*

**Range:** Holarctic; breeds from central Alaska and northern Mackenzie east to the southern shores of Hudson Bay, Ungava Bay, Labrador, Anticosti Island, and southeastern Newfoundland. In eastern North America, winters from the Great Lakes and Newfoundland south to Florida and the Gulf Coast.

**Status:** Common to abundant migrant and winter resident, greatly outnumbering Lesser Scaup throughout most of the state in all seasons.

**Occurrence:** The relative abundance of the two scaup species has changed considerably over the last 100 years. Between 1890 and 1920, Lesser Scaup were more abundant than they are today, always greatly outnumbering Greater Scaup on fresh water, both inland and on the Cape and Islands. For example, Phillips (Forbush 1916) found that 80 percent of the scaup shot on Wenham Lake during the years 1905 to 1908 were Lessers. Today, Greater Scaup greatly outnumber Lesser Scaup in all locations, with the possible exception of certain ponds favored by Lesser Scaup at Lakeville and on Cape Cod and the Islands during late fall and winter.

Greater Scaup are most abundant on large saltwater bays and harbors and, to a lesser extent, on large freshwater lakes. In Massachusetts the species has declined since the 1950s, particularly in Newburyport Harbor and Quincy Bay. *Spring maxima:* 15,000, Newburyport, 19 April 1954 (deWindt); 11,795, Boston Harbor, 25 March 1979 (Brown). Inland: 600, Pittsfield, 1 April 1953 (Dunbar). *Fall maxima:* 3,000, Wollaston Bay, 13 October 1961 (Higginbotham). Inland: 386, Central Valley Lakes, Berkshire County, 26 November 1977 (McNair et al). *Winter maxima:* 20,000, Wollaston Bay, 26 December 1959 (Quincy CBC); 15,000, Somerset, 27–28 February 1957 (Proctor et al); 12,000, Revere, throughout January 1974 (Veit et al). Inland: 1, Pittsfield, 30 January 1963 (Vincent, Smith). Single, non-breeding Greater Scaup are routinely reported along the coast during mid-summer—maximum: 7, Salisbury, 22 July 1960 (deWindt).

## Lesser Scaup  *Aythya affinis*

**Range:** Nearctic; breeds from central Alaska and northern Mackenzie south to northern Idaho, northeastern Colorado, and northwestern Minnesota, and sporadically east to southern Ontario. Winters mainly in the southeastern United States, north occasionally to southeastern Massachusetts.

**Status:** Fairly common to locally abundant migrant and winter resident.

**Occurrence:** Prior to 1920, Lesser Scaup were much more numerous in Massachusetts than they are today. It is thought that Lesser Scaup suffered more from hunting pressure than Greater Scaup because of the Lesser's preference for small freshwater ponds and cattail marshes, places more readily accessible to hunters than the open bays favored by Greater Scaup. The only places in Massachusetts where Lesser Scaup are still numerous are certain ponds in Falmouth, Lakeville, and Nantucket.

In certain areas (e.g., Falmouth and Lakeville) this species occasionally occurs in mixed flocks with Greater Scaup, thereby complicating the identification of birds in these flocks. *Spring maxima:* 435, Falmouth, 16 April 1989 (Perkins); 85 +, Lakeville, 21 March 1976 (Petersen et al). In Berkshire County, McNair (1978) states that proven maxima have not exceeded 20 in spring or 30 in fall since 1929 but that Lesser Scaup may have been commoner before that time. *Fall maxima:* 660, Falmouth, 29 October 1977 (Clarke); 300, Lakeville, 15 November 1975 (Petersen); 250, Martha's Vineyard, 28 December 1981 (Petersen). *Winter maxima:* 340, Falmouth, 1 February 1975 (Blodget); 220, Mattapoisett, 6 January 1976 (Brown). There has only been one convincing record of Lesser Scaup in Massachusetts between June and August since 1955: 1, Monomoy, 1 August 1987 (Petersen). The earliest fall arrival is: 2, Monomoy, 2 September 1984 (Petersen).

# Common Eider  *Somateria mollissima*

**Range:** Holarctic; breeds, in eastern North America, on islands along the coast of Labrador, Newfoundland, eastern Quebec, Nova Scotia, and Maine. Winters from Newfoundland south regularly to Chesapeake Bay, with the majority off southern New England.

**Status:** Several recent breeding records in Buzzards Bay and Boston Harbor. Very abundant migrant and winter resident off Cape Cod and the Islands; locally common to abundant elsewhere along the coast.

**Breeding:** Between 1973 and 1975, 175 Common Eider chicks were introduced to Penikese Island, from nests in Casco Bay, Maine (Stanton 1979). Some of these birds have established themselves as breeders, and they are gradually colonizing the neighboring Elizabeth Islands—e.g., 10 pairs, Penikese Island, and 3 pairs, Nashawena Island, 1983 (Hatch). Additional breeding attempts include four pairs of rehabilitated oil casualties at Penikese Island in 1979: 4 nests, 30 May–July (Masch, fide Petersen). The only breeding evidence in locations other than the Elizabeth Islands is the sighting of 1 female eider with 3 downy chicks near the Shag Rocks in outer

Boston Harbor in 1982 (Hatch, Litchfield), and the discovery of a nest with eggs in 1984 at Bird Island, Marion (Nisbet). The continuing increase in numbers of summering birds suggests the possibility of a further increase in breeding records, particularly on the Boston Harbor Islands.

**Nonbreeding:** A major segment of the population of *S. m. dresseri* has traditionally wintered on the shoals off Cape Cod, and estimates of these aggregations have remained relatively constant since 1890. Hill (1965) documented the dramatic increase in the great flocks off Monomoy from 15,000 in 1940 to 500,000 in 1951. In March 1952, massive numbers of eiders were killed by oil leaking from two tankers, the Pendleton and the Fort Mercer, both of which ran aground off Chatham during World War II (Burnett & Snyder 1954). The losses were temporary, however, because by 1960 the eider population off Monomoy had again swelled to 500,000. Although the population has seemed to remain more or less stable since that time, in some years the birds disperse over such large areas that accurately estimating their numbers is extremely difficult.

Flocks of Common Eiders, mostly subadult males, have regularly summered in such places as outer Boston Harbor, Duxbury Bay, and Monomoy, and on the various islands off Cape Cod and Essex County since at least 1955—e.g., 1,200 +, Great Brewster Island, 25 July 1981 (Petersen); 250, Duxbury Beach, 6 July 1978 (Heil); 75, Monomoy, throughout July 1966 (Forster).

The migration route followed by Common Eiders is strictly coastal. Major northward departures in spring have never been recorded, but large flights of southbound birds are a common sight during October and November. There are only eight known inland records for Massachusetts: 1 adult male found dead, Weston, 6 April 1963 (C. Harrington); 1, Holyoke, 22 September 1966 (Yenlin); 2, Agawam, 1–9 January 1971 (Kellogg); 1 immature male, Charlton, 3–4 May 1980 (Meservey, Blodget); 1, Turners Falls, 21–29 April 1986 (Markham); 1 male, Gilbertville, 7 May 1986 (Lynch); 1, South Quabbin, 8 October 1988 (Gagnon); 1, Wachusett Reservoir, 2 November 1991 (Nielsen, Stymeist).

Since 1955, Common Eiders have not only regained their former numbers off Cape Cod, but they have also appeared along the coast of mainland Massachusetts, particularly in Boston and Plymouth harbors, in far greater abundance than ever previously reported. The Monomoy flock is probably a much less cohesive unit than Hill (1965), Griscom and Snyder (1955), and Bailey (1955) implied. Judging from a number of shore-based estimates of flock size, it seems that the birds wintering in that area regularly travel to the shoals off Nantucket and Martha's Vineyard, and perhaps even into Cape Cod Bay. Therefore, the lack of estimates on the order of magnitude of half a million perhaps more accurately reflects dispersal than decline.
*Winter maxima* (since 1955): 300,000–500,000 estimated from land, off the

east shore of Nantucket, 1–2 January 1983 (Buckley, Boyle, Gove, Stymeist); 250,000, Elizabeth Islands, 30 December 1960 (Morgan); 20,000, Duxbury Bay, 21 December 1974 (Petersen); 18,507, Marshfield CBC, 26 December 1982; 18,000, Nahant-Winthrop, 6 December 1978 (Heil); 18,000, Winthrop, 15 November 1979 (Heil, Stymeist).

**Subspecies:** There are at least three Massachusetts specimens of *S. m. borealis*, which normally only winter south to Nova Scotia: e.g., 1 shot, Muskeget, 15 March 1890 (BMS #16252); 1 shot, Newburyport, 16 November 1933 (Nelson, fide Griscom & Snyder 1955); 1 picked up dead, Martha's Vineyard, 16 June 1946 (Zimmer, Chalif 1947). Several specimens, reportedly intermediate between *S. m. dresseri* and *S. m. borealis*, have been picked up dead on Cape Cod (Griscom & Snyder 1955).

# King Eider  *Somateria spectabilis*

**Range:** Holarctic; breeds in the Arctic, south in North America to the southwestern shore of Hudson Bay and southern Baffin Island. Winters mainly along the coast, from southern Labrador south to Chesapeake Bay and North Carolina.

**Status:** Uncommon to rare but regular winter resident on the coast.

**Occurrence:** King Eiders are most frequently observed off the rocky shores north of Boston, particularly at Cape Ann and Nahant, but they are also of regular occurrence in small numbers on the South Shore, Cape Cod, and the Islands. Occasionally, small flocks have been reported, but more frequently 1 to 5 individuals are seen per day per locality. Single birds are regularly seen migrating north with flocks of scoters during late April and early May. *Maxima:* Griscom and Snyder (1955) mention a flock of 42 seen from a boat off Cape Ann but give no date. Additional maxima: 27, Rockport, 27 December 1959 (Snyder); 17, near the Dry Salvages off Rockport, 27 December 1936 (Griscom). Recent counts have been much lower, usually not exceeding 10, except: 19 (all females and young males), Rockport (Sanborn, Rhome), and 13–19 (including 1 adult male), Nahant, winter of 1970–1971 (Forster, Gardler). Recent high counts from the southeastern coast include: 6 (3 males, 3 females), East Orleans, throughout March 1974 (Petersen); 4 +, Nantucket, 1–2 January 1983 (Andrews, Stymeist, et al).

Although the species is rare before late October and after early May, there are a few records of King Eiders in Massachusetts during the period June to August: e.g., 1 immature male, Monomoy, 22 August 1954 (Griscom); 1 immature male, Monomoy, 30 August 1964 (Forster); 1, Nahant, 19–23 June 1966 (Murphy); 1 female, Nauset, Eastham, 25 July–September 1974 (VO); 1, Monomoy, 11 August 1974 (VO); 1 immature male, Martha's Vineyard, 20 June 1981 (Laux); 1 immature male, Chatham, 21–30 August 1983 (Hines et al). The only inland records are: 1 collected, Lake Nippenicket, Bridgewater, 21 October 1899 (MCZ #275912); 10, Lake Pontoosuc, Pittsfield, 27 April 1991 (Shampang, photo in AB 45:416).

## Steller's Eider   *Polysticta stelleri*

**Range:** Northeastern Palearctic and northwestern Nearctic; breeds east to the arctic coast of Mackenzie, the Shumagin Islands, and the Alaska Peninsula. Winters, in North America, south to the Kenai Peninsula. Vagrant elsewhere in North America.

**Status:** Vagrant: one record.

**Occurrence:** An adult male Steller's Eider was found in Scituate, 29 March 1977 (Vernon). It remained until 7 April and was carefully studied by hundreds of observers. At the time, this represented the fourth record for eastern North America, with previous ones from Baffin Island, the Gulf of St. Lawrence, and Maine (AB 31: 973).

## Harlequin Duck   *Histrionicus histrionicus*

**Range:** Holarctic; in eastern North America, breeds in southeastern Baffin Island, Labrador, and along the north shore of the Gulf of St. Lawrence, south to the Gaspé Peninsula. Winters from Newfoundland south to Chesapeake Bay.

**Status:** Uncommon winter resident on the coast; very rare inland.

**Occurrence:** Harlequin Ducks tend to return year after year to the same preferred wintering sites. Traditional Massachusetts localities include the rocks off the Hammond Castle in Magnolia, the Glades at North Scituate, the east shore of Cape Cod at East Orleans, and the Squibnocket Cliffs at Martha's Vineyard. Generally, they prefer rocky, granitic shores such as those at Cape Ann; however, on Cape Cod and the Islands, they frequent stretches of beach where only scattered rocks exist. *Maxima:* Griscom and Emerson (1959) wrote of flocks numbering up to 35 off Squibnocket at Martha's Vineyard—i.e., 35, 26 February 1941 (Benchley)—and they point out that birds at that locality were first seen in 1896. Additional maxima: 30, Squibnocket Point, 4 January 1949 (Leigh); 20, Magnolia, 2 March 1964 (Stowe); 14, Nantucket, 15 February 1976 (Andrews). Griscom and Snyder (1955) mention an inland specimen from Hudson that is no longer extant. The only other inland records are: 1, on the Sudbury River, Saxonville, 14–24 February 1957 (Gleason et al); 1, Round Pond, Lynn, 26 February 1964 (Cartwright). While Harlequin Ducks are rare before November and after early May, there are a few summer records: e.g., 1 immature male, Plymouth, 9 July–late August 1974 (Sorrie et al); 1 male, Manchester, 23 June 1980 (Weissberg).

## Oldsquaw   *Clangula hyemalis*

**Range:** Holarctic; breeds in arctic North America south to northeastern Manitoba, northern Quebec, southern Labrador, and southern Greenland. Winters in southern Greenland, and, in eastern North America, on the Great Lakes and along the coast from Newfoundland to Florida and Texas.

**Status:** Abundant migrant and locally abundant winter resident; rare migrant inland.

**Occurrence:** Oldsquaws regularly concentrate at Newburyport Harbor during spring migration in April and May. *Spring maxima:* 4,000+, Newburyport Harbor, to April 1976 (Veit); 4,000+, Newburyport Harbor, 9 April 1978 (Heil). Inland: 14, Hinsdale, 19 April 1954 (fide McNair). Oldsquaws are scarce in summer, mostly occurring on Cape Cod and the Islands. *Summer maximum:* 5, Stage Island, Chatham, throughout June 1977 (Nikula).

In fall, heavy flights may occur along the coast from October to mid-November. *Fall maxima:* 5,900 migrating south, Andrews Point, Rockport, 5 November 1983 (Heil). Inland: 44, Connecticut River valley, 6–20 November 1982, with a single locality maximum of 20 at Quabbin, 7 November (fide Kellogg). Otherwise, counts of over 5 Oldsquaws at inland locations are unusual.

The annual late fall and winter concentration of Oldsquaws off Nantucket Island is one of the most spectacular ornithological phenomena that occur in Massachusetts. Beginning in late November, tens of thousands of Oldsquaws can be seen from the island, although the numbers generally decline during the course of the winter. They spend the night in Nantucket Sound, then fly to feeding grounds on the Nantucket Shoals during the day, so the passage past Nantucket, Tuckernuck, and Muskeget islands takes place both at dawn (heading south) and at dusk (heading north). Nantucket totals vary considerably from night to night, so a comparison between years is difficult. There has been a minimum of 50,000 birds wintering there since the mid-1970s, except during the exceptionally severe seasons of 1977–1978 and 1980–1981, when Nantucket Sound completely froze over. *Winter maxima:* 178,958, Nantucket CBC, 2 January 1988; 81,525, Nantucket CBC, 1 January 1983; 73,500 flying south past West Head, Tuckernuck, 13 December 1975 (Veit).

## Black Scoter   *Melanitta nigra*

**Range:** Holarctic; breeds in northeastern Siberia, Alaska, and, disjunctly, in east central Quebec and southwestern Labrador. Winters, in eastern North America, from southern Newfoundland to Florida and the Gulf Coast.

**Status:** Abundant migrant and uncommon to fairly common winter resident on the coast; uncommon migrant inland.

**Occurrence:** The Black Scoter is usually not as numerous as the Surf Scoter during the fall coastal migration but is the only scoter to occur in large numbers inland in that season, where flocks are occasionally forced to alight during periods of inclement weather. The species is uncommon north of Cape Cod and Nantucket Sound, but in winter it can be locally numerous at those localities. *Spring maxima:* 8,500, Chilmark, 5 April 1961 (Keith); 8,000, Martha's Vineyard, 12 April 1981 (Laux); 800 +, Plum Island, 1 May 1976 (Berry); 800, Truro, 8 April 1979 (Petersen). Inland, Black Scoters are rare in spring, most records being of singles in late April and early May. *Fall maxima:* (see table in White-winged Scoter account) 40,000, Monomoy, 11 November 1952 (Bailey); 5,000, Monomoy, 29 October 1959 (Bailey); 1,840 flying south, Rockport, 8 November 1959 (Snyder). Inland, they were generally unrecorded in numbers before the late 1960s and early 1970s, when hundreds were seen in Berkshire County. Previous inland maximum: 118, Onota Lake, Pittsfield, 22 October 1944 (Snyder). Recent inland maxima: 1,000, Onota Lake, Pittsfield (Addison); 300, Mt. Williams Lake, 17 October 1970 (Whitehead); 775, Pittsfield, 19 October 1972 (Goodrich). *Winter maxima:* 9,608, Martha's Vineyard CBC, 28 December 1986; 610, Nantucket CBC, 2 January 1982.

A few Black Scoters regularly spend the summer along the coast—e.g., 12, Dennis, 7 August 1968 (Everett); 4, Chatham, 13 August 1955 (Hayes).

## Surf Scoter  *Melanitta perspicillata*

**Range:** Nearctic; breeds from western Alaska east to James Bay, central Quebec, and western Labrador. Winters, in eastern North America, on the Great Lakes (a few) and along the Atlantic Coast from southern Newfoundland to Florida and the Gulf Coast.

**Status:** Common spring and abundant fall migrant and uncommon winter resident on the coast; rare migrant inland.

**Occurrence:** The Surf Scoter is the most numerous scoter to occur during fall migration in Massachusetts, but frequently the least numerous in winter and also the least frequent species to occur inland. *Spring maxima:* 1,000, Chilmark, Martha's Vineyard, 5 April 1961 (Keith); 250, Eastham, 27 March 1982 (Nikula). Inland, the species is rare, with never more than 6 reported in Berkshire County (McNair 1978). *Fall maxima:* (see table in White-winged Scoter account) 20,000, Monomoy, 29 October 1959 (Bailey); 12,050, Rockport, 5 November 1983 (Heil); 10,000, Monomoy, 7 December 1960 (Bailey); 9,055, Rockport, 21 October 1961 (Snyder). Inland: 25, Onota Lake, Pittsfield, 17 October 1970 (fide McNair); 6, Acton, 20 October 1964 (Sprong); 6, Quabbin, 20 October 1968 (Yenlin).

In winter, the Surf Scoter is uncommon and local, with counts rarely exceeding 50; in this season it is most numerous in Buzzards Bay and off Martha's Vineyard—e.g., 2,076, Buzzards Bay CBC, 19 December 1981; 200, Marion, 13 January 1976 (Gove); 40, Martha's Vineyard 17–20 February 1978 (Sargent).

The Surf Scoter is the least common scoter to occur in summer—e.g., 6, Manchester, 11 July 1956 (Easton). Otherwise, there are occasional counts of 1 to 6 individuals, mostly from Monomoy or Cape Ann.

# White-winged Scoter   *Melanitta fusca*

**Range:** Holarctic; breeds from northwestern Alaska, the Mackenzie Delta, and northeastern Manitoba south to northeastern Washington and southeastern Manitoba, and also from Hudson Bay east to Labrador and Newfoundland. Winters, in eastern North America, on the Great Lakes (a few) and along the Atlantic Coast from Newfoundland to Florida.

**Status:** Abundant migrant and winter resident on the coast; rare migrant inland.

**Occurrence:** The White-winged Scoter is the most abundant wintering scoter in Massachusetts; yet, it is usually outnumbered during migration by the Surf Scoter and sometimes by the Black Scoter, especially among migrant scoter flocks entering Cape Cod Bay. Winter aggregations of White-winged Scoters are found most frequently in Nantucket Sound, whereas migrants can be watched from most any vantage point along the coast (Petersen 1970, 1983). Most of the birds migrate during October and again in April and early May. The White-winged Scoter follows the Black Scoter in its frequency of occurrence inland. *Spring maxima:* 5,000, Eastham, 27 March 1982 (Nikula); 3,000 flying northeast up Buzzards Bay past Gooseberry Neck, Westport, 8 May 1977 (Veit, Litchfield). Inland: 121 forced down by rain, Onota Lake, Pittsfield, 24 May 1948 (Hendricks). Otherwise, counts of over 10 at inland locations are unrecorded. *Fall maxima:* The following October totals of scoters counted passing Manomet Point provide the most recent accurate information at hand on coastal fall scoter migration (data compiled by Petersen).

OCTOBER SCOTER TOTALS AT MANOMET POINT

|                      | 10/67  | 10/68  | 10/75  | 10/76  |
|----------------------|--------|--------|--------|--------|
| White-winged Scoter  | 7,558  | 6,988  | 3,700  | 3,974  |
| Surf Scoter          | 9,200  | 13,555 | 10,600 | 18,904 |
| Black Scoter         | 10,915 | 2,112  | 8,900  | 2,524  |
| TOTAL                | 27,673 | 22,655 | 23,200 | 25,402 |

Inland: 41, Onota Lake, Pittsfield, 26 October 1962 (fide McNair); 25, Quabbin, 15 October 1967 (Yenlin); 11, Quabbin Dam, 20 October 1963 (Albertine).

High counts for the year usually occur in prewinter gatherings—e.g., 100,000, off Monomoy, 29 October 1959 and 2 December 1960 (Bailey). Recent counts have been considerably lower—e.g., 15,000, Nantucket Sound, 28 November 1974 (Veit); 9,000 +, Monomoy, 28 October 1973 (Harrington, Petersen). *Winter maxima:* 15,000, Woods Hole, 27 February 1966 (Garrey et al); 5,000, Nantucket, 17 February 1976 (Jackson); 3,600, Brewster, 29 December 1973 (Kenneally).

The White-winged Scoter is the most frequently observed scoter species in summer—e.g., 50, Lynn Beach, 10 June 1961 (Snyder); 10, Monomoy Point, 23 July 1955 (Earle et al).

# Common Goldeneye   *Bucephala clangula*

**Range:** Holarctic; breeds, in North America, from central Alaska, northern Labrador, and Newfoundland south to northern Washington, northern Michigan, and central Maine. Winters, in eastern North America, from Newfoundland and the Great Lakes south to Florida and Texas.

**Status:** Very common to abundant migrant and winter resident on the coast; common migrant inland.

**Occurrence:** Common Goldeneyes are locally abundant in large salt bays and harbors such as those at Newburyport, Plymouth, Nantucket, and Chatham. Because goldeneyes seem to be more tolerant of ice than many other ducks, peak counts often do not occur until mid- to late winter, when they are driven out of northern interior lakes. Inland, they may be found on rivers, large lakes, and reservoirs. The peak migration periods are during March and early April and late October and November. *Spring maximum:* 4,500, Newburyport, 9 April 1978 (Heil). *Fall maximum:* 700, PRNWR, 22 October 1964 (USFWS Census). *Winter maxima:* Between 1,000 and 5,000 have been counted at Newburyport between early January and March most winters since at least 1954. Other winter maxima: 3,117, Nantucket CBC, 31 December 1978; 2,539, Cape Cod CBC, 28 December 1958. Inland maxima: 150 +, Lakeville, 21 February 1984 (Briggs); 125, Pittsfield, 26 November 1977 (McNair); 75, Pittsfield, 9 April 1950 (fide McNair).

There are a number of records of single Common Goldeneyes summering in coastal localities.

# Barrow's Goldeneye   *Bucephala islandica*

**Range:** Chiefly Nearctic, although also breeds in Iceland; breeds, in eastern North America, in northern Labrador and winters along the coast from the

Gulf of St. Lawrence south regularly to Massachusetts, more rarely to Long Island and New Jersey.

**Status:** Uncommon winter resident on the coast and rare migrant inland.

**Occurrence:** Barrow's Goldeneyes almost invariably occur among flocks of the more abundant Common Goldeneye at coastal localities between November and April, but singles are also occasionally found inland during migration. The slight increase of records in recent years probably reflects increased observer familiarity with plumages other than that of the adult male.

Barrow's Goldeneyes are rare before late November—e.g., 1, Monomoy, 30 October 1971 (Petersen)—and after early April—e.g., 1, Springfield, 17 April 1955 (LeShure). *Maxima:* 12, Newburyport, 23 March 1980 (Heil); 9–10, Nantucket, 27 November 1980 (Perkins); 9, Plymouth Harbor, 22 January 1978 (Petersen et al). Inland, there are at least twelve records of single birds, including three from Berkshire County, which span the dates 2 November to 8 January and 26 March to 17 April (BNWM).

# Bufflehead *Bucephala albeola*

**Range:** Nearctic; breeds in the northwestern interior of North America, south and east to southern Ontario and central Quebec. One nesting record for Vermont. In eastern North America, winters in the southern United States and north along the Atlantic Coast to southern Nova Scotia and southern Newfoundland.

**Status:** Abundant migrant and winter resident on the coast; fairly common migrant inland.

**Occurrence:** Buffleheads are most numerous in sheltered bays and harbors along the coast, but they also occur regularly inland in rivers and on ponds, lakes, and reservoirs. The peak migration periods are during March and April and October and November. *Spring maxima:* 1,200–1,500, Nahant, 23 April 1975 (Gardler). Inland: 26, Lake Onota, Pittsfield, 24 April 1978 (fide McNair). *Fall maxima:* 1,350, Nahant, 17 November 1948 (Griscom); 850, Nahant, 11 November 1958 (Nisbet); 850, Nahant, 29 November 1975 (Forster, Buckley). On Cape Cod, Buffleheads have increased dramatically during the past 50 years, as evidenced by increased CBC totals. *Winter maxima:* 2,490, Buzzards Bay CBC, 16 December 1978; 1,150, Cape Cod CBC, 21 December 1975; 1,121, Cape Cod CBC, 19 December 1982. Inland: 100, Lakeville, 29 October 1980 (Petersen); 79, Central Valley Lakes of Berkshire County, 11 November 1977 (McNair).

The Bufflehead is rare in summer—e.g., 1 female, Plymouth, 30 July 1969 (Petersen); 1, Chatham, 5 July 1976 (Nikula, Goodrich); 2, Wachusett Reservoir, throughout summer of 1984 (Blodget).

# Hooded Merganser    *Lophodytes cucullatus*

**Range:** Nearctic; breeds sporadically in eastern North America from Central Manitoba, southern New Brunswick, and Nova Scotia south to Louisiana and central Georgia. Winters in the southeastern United States, north along the coast to southeastern Massachusetts.

**Status:** Uncommon and local breeder; fairly common migrant, most numerous in fall. Uncommon but regular in winter on Cape Cod and the Islands.

**Breeding:** Hooded Mergansers nest in wooded swamps and secluded Beaver ponds in Berkshire, Worcester, and Middlesex counties, and in cranberry bog reservoirs and stump ponds in southeastern Massachusetts. Because Hooded Mergansers frequently lay their eggs in Wood Duck boxes, the Wood Duck management program may well be benefitting the Hooded Merganser population in the state. *Egg dates:* 30 March–early June.

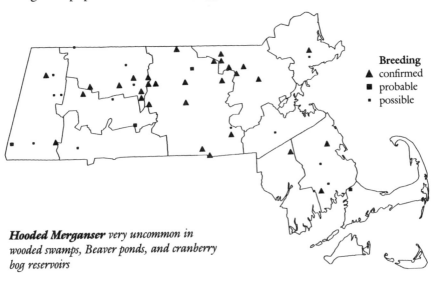

Breeding
▲ confirmed
■ probable
• possible

*Hooded Merganser very uncommon in wooded swamps, Beaver ponds, and cranberry bog reservoirs*

**Nonbreeding:** Hooded Mergansers are rather evenly distributed throughout the state during migration, although the largest counts are usually made in the southern Connecticut River valley and southeastern Massachusetts. Hooded Mergansers prefer secluded ponds surrounded by wooded swamps in migration, but they regularly use salt ponds in winter. *Spring maxima:* 30, Wood's Pond, Berkshire County, 31 March 1978 (fide McNair). *Fall maxima:* 225, Ludlow Reservoir, 23 November 1964 (LeShure); 200, Ludlow Reservoir, 19 November 1966 (Soja, Yenlin); 120, Bourne, 16 December 1978 (Petersen); 99, East Falmouth, 16 December 1978 (Nikula). *Winter maxima:* 344, Buzzards Bay CBC, 21 December 1985; 120, East Falmouth, 15 December 1979 (Heil).

# Common Merganser *Mergus merganser*

**Range:** Holarctic; breeds, in North America, from southern Alaska and central Labrador south to the Great Lakes, Massachusetts, and New York, and more rarely to Pennsylvania. Winters, in eastern North America, from the Great Lakes and Newfoundland south to central Texas and Georgia.

**Status:** Rare breeder. Common to abundant migrant and winter resident.

**Breeding:** Common Mergansers have been confirmed breeding in Massachusetts on over a dozen occasions since the 1940s—all in Berkshire County, the Connecticut River valley, and Worcester County. Breeders have most often been found on large rivers or remote ponds. *Egg dates:* June–early July.

**Nonbreeding:** Common Mergansers prefer large expanses of open water, such as the larger reservoirs of the inland portions of the state and the larger saltwater bays and rivers in the coastal sections. The species is one of our most hardy waterfowl, regularly lingering inland until the very last expanse of fresh water has frozen over, when they occasionally then move to salt water. They are most numerous in Massachusetts between October and early April. *Spring maxima:* 500, Milton, 11 April 1980 (Brown); 300+, Brewster, 7 March 1977 (Nikula). *Winter maxima:* 1,235, Plymouth CBC, 23 December 1982; 1,083, Cape Cod CBC, 29 December 1974; 200+, Nauset, Eastham, 20 January 1968 (Rich); 59, Agawam, 25 February 1968 (Yenlin).

# Red-breasted Merganser *Mergus serrator*

**Range:** Holarctic; breeds, in North America, from central Alaska and central Labrador, south and east to the Great Lakes, central Maine, and Nova Scotia, and rarely south along the coast to Long Island, New Jersey, and possibly to North Carolina. In eastern North America, winters in the Great Lakes and along the Atlantic Coast from Newfoundland to Texas.

**Status:** Rare breeder. Very abundant migrant and abundant winter resident on Cape Cod and the Islands; less numerous elsewhere along the coast and uncommon inland.

**Breeding:** Red-breasted Mergansers apparently nested regularly on Monomoy between 1877 and 1955 (Griscom & Snyder 1955). During the summer of 1966, Veit observed a family of ducklings on the beach at Tuckernuck Island that were probably this species, but it was not until 30 July 1978 that the Red-breasted Merganser was again confirmed at Monomoy when 4 adults and 1 chick were seen (BBC, Jackson). The only other recent evidence of breeding was obtained when 2 adults and 10 young were observed at Duxbury Beach, 30 June 1989 (Clapp). Because the species is regularly found in summer in Essex County and around the Elizabeth Islands, breeding could also occur in those areas from time to time. The only known Essex County breeding record occurred in Ipswich in 1916 (Griscom & Snyder 1955). Pairs recorded in Berkshire County during June and July of 1940, 1941, and 1948 may have been misidentified Common Mergansers, because Red-breasteds have never been known to breed south of extreme northern New England at inland locations (Bull 1974).

**Nonbreeding:** In some years, especially since 1978, Red-breasted Mergansers have exceptionally abundant in the shallow waters off Cape Cod, Nantucket, and Martha's Vineyard. Tens of thousands have congregated there during November and December, perhaps to feed upon Sand Lances (*Ammodytes* sp.), which were abundant in those waters during the 1970s and early 1980s (see comments under Herring Gull). The peak migration periods are from late March to May and again in October and November. These are the only seasons during which the species is regular at inland sites. *Spring maxima:* 15,000, Cape Cod Bay between Provincetown and Wellfleet, 31 March 1984 (Nikula); 2,500, Falmouth, 17 March 1979 (Nikula); 2,300 +, Wellfleet-Provincetown, 8 April 1979 (Petersen); 1,800, Nantucket, 21 March 1980 (Veit); 1,800, Nantucket, 18 April 1981 (Heil). Inland: 22, Woods Pond, Berkshire County, 1 May 1934 (Hendricks). *Fall maxima:* 12,000, Truro, 5 November 1978 (Petersen); 10,000, Nantucket, 28–29 November 1981 (Veit); 8,590 moving south, Rockport, 5 November 1983 (Heil); 8,000, Truro, 6 November 1977 (Petersen). Inland: 35, Lake Pontoosuc, Pittsfield, 18 November 1967 (HBC). *Winter maxima:* 16,855, Martha's Vineyard CBC, 30 December 1984; 14,272, Cape Cod CBC, 22 December 1985; 8,636, Nantucket CBC, 3 January 1987; 7,000, Nantucket, 30 December 1978 (Heil); 6,688, Nantucket CBC, 1 January 1983; 1,800 +, Martha's Vineyard, 23 February 1978 (Petersen).

# Ruddy Duck   *Oxyura jamaicensis*

**Range:** Nearctic and Neotropical; breeds mainly in western North America, east to central Manitoba and northwestern Iowa. Sporadic breeding records east to Maine, New Hampshire, and Massachusetts and south along the coast to North Carolina and Florida. Winters in the southeastern United States, north along the coast to southeastern Massachusetts.

**Status:** Breeds erratically at Plum Island and Monomoy. Locally common to occasionally abundant fall and very uncommon spring migrant; rare in winter.

**Breeding:** Ruddy Ducks formerly bred in Massachusetts at North Truro in 1890 and West Newbury in 1931 (Griscom & Snyder 1955). Since 1968, from 1 to 4 pairs have occasionally bred at Plum Island—e.g., 1978, 1984 (Forward, Emery, et al)—and at least one pair has bred at Monomoy off and on since about 1974 (Bailey, VO). *Egg dates:* June–July.

**Nonbreeding:** Ruddy Duck numbers in Massachusetts have fluctuated considerably since 1900. The most recent peaks were between 1930 and 1945, when more than one thousand were occasionally seen on Martha's Vineyard, and during the mid-1970s, when hundreds were found in the Lakeville ponds. In other years, very few were reported, so maximum counts did not exceed 20 to 30 birds. Ruddy Ducks have traditionally been most numerous on the large, shallow ponds of southeastern Massachusetts and Martha's Vineyard and are typically uncommon or rare elsewhere in the state. In spring, counts generally reflect the gradual departure of wintering birds rather than any pronounced influx of migrants. In Berkshire County, where they do not winter, they occur between early April and mid-May; the largest number ever seen together there was 4 (McNair 1978). *Fall maxima:* 1,200, Squibnocket Pond, Martha's Vineyard, 2 December 1937 (Hagar); 637, Lakeville, 11 November 1976 (Petersen, Higginbotham); 400, Lakeville, 8 November 1981 (Petersen). Inland: 38, Central Valley Lakes in Berkshire County, 6 November 1971 (Gagnon et al).

# Masked Duck   *Oxyura dominica*

**Range:** Chiefly Neotropical; breeds north to southern Florida and southern Texas. Vagrant to Massachusetts, Wisconsin, Vermont, New Jersey, Maryland, and Tennessee.

**Status:** Vagrant: one record.

**Occurrence:** A male Masked Duck in breeding plumage was collected at Malden, 27 August 1889 (Cory, AK 6: 336). The specimen is currently at the Field Museum of Natural History in Chicago. Although some have suggested that this bird may have escaped from captivity, Masked Ducks were not known to have been kept in captivity in the 1800s, are generally difficult to keep, and are prone to northward dispersal after breeding (Johnsgard & Hagemeyer 1969). It is therefore likely that the 1889 bird was a wild individual.

# Black Vulture   *Coragyps atratus*

**Range:** Southeastern Nearctic and Neotropical; resident in North America north to northern New Jersey, southeastern Pennsylvania, southern Ohio, Indiana, and Illinois; extending northward. Wanders north frequently, occasionally to Maine, New Brunswick, and Nova Scotia.

**Status:** Rare visitor; over thirty records since 1954 and nearly annual in occurrence.

**Occurrence:** Records of Black Vultures in Massachusetts are remarkably evenly distributed both in time and space. Griscom and Snyder (1955) mention at least thirteen specimens and several sight records before 1955. Since then, Black Vultures have occurred in every month of the year, with the greatest number of reports in July and October. Records exist for every county in the state. All of the records pertain to single birds, except: 2, Montague, 20 March 1965 (Morgan). Black Vultures have occasionally been seen together with Turkey Vultures—e.g., 1 with 7 Turkey Vultures, West Harwich, 24 April 1978 (Laux)—but more frequently they are seen alone. On several occasions they have remained to feed at garbage dumps over a period of several days.

# Turkey Vulture   *Cathartes aura*

**Range:** Nearctic and Neotropical; widespread in temperate North America. Breeds, in the northeastern United States, north to northern Vermont and New Hampshire. Northern breeders migrate to the southeastern United States.

**Status:** Rare breeder and fairly common migrant. Some birds occasionally overwinter. Increasing in recent years.

**Breeding:** Turkey Vultures were first recorded breeding in Massachusetts in 1954, when a nest with 2 chicks was found on 29 August on Long Mountain in Tyringham (Bliven, Regnier). They have increased steadily since then. Recent documented instances of breeding are: 1 with 2 eggs, Otis, 26 May 1969; 1 nest, Mt. Lizzie, Quabbin, 1975; 1 nest, Barre, 1976 (Swedberg); 2 nests, Blue Hills, Milton (where breeding has occurred regularly since), 1982 (Smith). All of these nests failed, apparently due to predation by Raccoons. However, Turkey Vultures are so frequently observed during the breeding season in Massachusetts—up to 50 per day in the Quabbin area—that it seems probable that many nests have been overlooked. Adults with flying young have been regularly observed at Mt. Wachusett during summer since 1980 (Roberts). *Egg date:* 26 May.

**Nonbreeding:** Migrating Turkey Vultures have become a routine sight in Massachusetts during early spring and late fall, east to Cape Cod and more rarely to the Islands. Maximum counts are all from the Quabbin Reservoir, where the birds occasionally aggregate at dusk in roosts during both spring and fall. Records of birds during midwinter have been frequent enough in recent years to suggest that some birds may be resident in western Massachusetts, as well as in the Blue Hills, Milton. Spring migrants typically arrive during late March, and fall migrants occur mainly in September. A few are seen until early November in eastern Massachusetts. *Spring maxima:* 75, eastern Massachusetts, April 1978 (BOEM); 55, Quabbin, 1 April 1979

(Brown); 41, Granville, 19 April 1987 (EMHW); 17, Provincetown, 12 May 1987 (Nikula); 8, outer Cape, 19 April 1981 (Nikula); 7, South Harwich, 24 April 1978 (Laux); 7, South Wellfleet, 24 April 1981 (Bailey). **Fall maxima:** 43, Mt. Wachusett, throughout September 1980 (Roberts); 23, Mt. Wachusett, 15 September 1983 (Roberts); 15, Mt. Wachusett, 5 September 1982 (Roberts); 4, Eastham, 24 October 1976 (Forster, Petersen). **Winter maxima:** 20 at roost, South Dartmouth, 13 February 1991 (Aversa); 8, Blue Hills, Randolph, winter 1990–1991 (Smith, VO); 2, Southwick, 9 January 1965 (Hubley); 1, Nantucket, 7–8 January 1980 (Andrews).

# Osprey  *Pandion haliaetus*

**Range:** Cosmopolitan; breeds, in North America, across much of Canada and along the Atlantic Coast from southern Labrador and Newfoundland to Florida. Winters from Florida and Texas south through the West Indies and Central America to Argentina.

**Status:** Locally common breeder; fairly common migrant.

**Breeding:** The coast of southern New England, from eastern Long Island and Connecticut to the islands south of Cape Cod, has always supported a substantial nesting population of Ospreys. As many as one thousand pairs bred in that area until about 1940. This total included 40 to 50 pairs in Massachusetts, mainly in the Westport River estuary and on Martha's Vineyard (Spitzer & Poole 1980). Curiously, few have ever nested on the coast between Cape Cod and southern Maine, perhaps due to a lack of suitable nesting sites or appropriate feeding areas.

Between the 1940s and the 1960s, the northeastern Osprey population declined substantially due to drastically lowered hatching success (Ames & Mersereau 1964, Henny & Wight 1969). The number of active nests in the Long Island–Cape Cod area declined from 814 in 1940 to 90 in 1970 (Spitzer & Poole 1980). In 1970, there were fewer than 10 successful nests in Massachusetts, all of them along the Westport River. This reduced breeding success has been conclusively attributed to the accumulation of DDT and DDE residues within the Ospreys' tissues, which resulted in the birds' inability to properly metabolize calcium for their eggshells (Spitzer et al 1978). The thin-shelled eggs either broke or failed to hatch due to overheating.

Since a federal ban on the use of DDT was enacted in 1972, the northeastern Osprey population has steadily increased so that in some areas of Massachusetts the number of breeding pairs now exceeds pre-DDT levels. This additional increase is partly due to the provision of human-made nesting platforms in areas where Ospreys could not otherwise find predator-free nesting sites.

In 1983, there were approximately 60 active Osprey nests in Massachusetts: 30 along the Westport River, 18 on Martha's Vineyard, 2 on Nantucket, about 5 along the southern shore of Cape Cod, and 1 to 2 in the Lakeville area. By 1990, the total number of nests in the state reached 190 (fide MDFW). The erection of additional nesting platforms on Cape Cod and the Islands has allowed a further population increase in that area, and it seems likely that Ospreys will continue to extend their breeding range north of there, given the present trend. *Egg dates:* 2 May–early July.

**Nonbreeding:** Ospreys are common during both spring and fall at coastal and inland hawk-watching vantage points. Spring migration occurs mainly during April, and fall migration during October. *Spring maxima:* 51, Mt. Tom, 19 April 1975 (Roberts 1990); 31, Mt. Tom, 30 April 1956 (op cit); 29, Mt. Watatic, 17 April 1988 (op cit); 28, Mt. Wachusett, 18 April 1983 (op cit). These counts are comparable to those made during the 1940s and 1950s. *Fall maxima:* 347, Mt. Wachusett, 1–29 September 1988 (EMHW); 271, Mt. Wachusett, 1–30 September 1987 (EMHW); 176, Mt. Wachusett, 23 August–6 October 1980 (Roberts); 66, Mt. Tom, 20 September 1963 (Forster); 46, Mt. Wachusett, 13 September 1978 (Roberts).

Ordinarily Ospreys are absent from Massachusetts in winter. However, there are some early winter records—e.g., 1, Wayland, 1 January 1964 (Tolman)—and eleven records for December, including: 1, Chicopee, 29 December 1965 (Maclachlan); 1, South Natick, 15 December 1990 (Kile); 1, South Hadley, 5 December 1968 (Warner); 2, Quabbin, 2 December 1962 (Hubley).

# American Swallow-tailed Kite  *Elanoides forficatus*

**Range:** Southeastern Nearctic and Neotropical; breeds, in North America, in peninsular Florida, southern Alabama, Mississippi, Louisiana, and north at least to North Carolina. Winters in South America. Vagrant north to New England and the Great Lakes.

**Status:** Vagrant: at least eighteen records; increasing in regularity.

**Occurrence:** The Swallow-tailed Kite has occurred in Massachusetts most often along the southeast coast in the wake of unusually warm weather and accompanying southwesterly winds during late April, May, and June. First recorded in spring in Massachusetts when 1 was observed in Cohasset, 17 May 1940 (May). Unusually early spring records include: 1, Great Island, West Yarmouth, 8 March 1991 (Forg); 1 picked up dead, Holbrook, 9 April 1974 (Fordham, MCZ #330420). There are only two fall records: 1, West Newbury, 25 September 1882 (Newcomb, PMS #6107); 1, Boston Fenway, 29 September 1959 (Garnwell).

# Black-shouldered Kite  *Elanus caeruleus*

**Range:** Cosmopolitan; in North America, mainly resident from Oregon south to Baja California and from Oklahoma and western Louisiana south to central Argentina and Chile. Expanding range northward and increasing in the United States.

**Status:** Vagrant: one record.

**Occurrence:** A Black-shouldered Kite was carefully studied as it fed and perched near Edgartown Great Pond, Martha's Vineyard, 30 May 1910 (Keniston, Fay, Brown; Fay 1910).

# Mississippi Kite  *Ictinia mississippiensis*

**Range:** Southeastern Nearctic; breeds from western Kansas and western Texas east to southern Illinois, northern South Carolina, and northern Florida. Rapidly expanding its range. Winters in Central and South America. Wanders, with increasing frequency, north to New England and the Great Lakes.

**Status:** Vagrant: twenty records.

**Occurrence:** Mississippi Kites have occurred in Massachusetts with increasing regularity since the 1960s. The first record—i.e., 1 immature, Lincoln, 5 July 1962 (Baird)—was followed by increasingly regular reports beginning in the late 1970s. Most sightings are from southeastern Massachusetts, especially Cape Cod, with the majority of records falling in the period between late April—i.e., 1, Granville, 27 April 1987 (Kellogg)—and June. The only fall occurrences are: 1 juvenile found in moribund condition, Easton, 1 September 1982 (Smith, MCZ #331366); 1 adult, Bolton, 14 September 1987 (Salmela); 1, Ipswich, 5 September 1988 (Parsons, Corley). The increase in Massachusetts observations correlates with the documented range expansion of the species in the Southeast (Parker & Ogden 1979).

# Bald Eagle  *Haliaeetus leucocephalus*

**Range:** Nearctic; breeds from Alaska east to Newfoundland and south along the Atlantic Coast to Nova Scotia and Maine; also in Florida and

*Seriously depressed as a breeding bird throughout much of North America by the 1960s, the **Bald Eagle** was among several raptor species hard hit by the overuse of pesticides. Following the ban on DDT and in response to a hacking program started in 1982, eagles began nesting at Quabbin Reservoir in 1989.*

▷

north along the coast to New Jersey. In winter, birds of both populations disperse widely.

**Status:** Rare migrant and breeder; uncommon winter resident.

**Breeding:** The original breeding of the Bald Eagle in Massachusetts is based only on vague historical records. R. T. Fisher found a nest at Cheshire Reservoir in Berkshire County sometime prior to 1900 (Faxon & Hoffman 1900), and eagles possibly bred on Mt. Tom and Mt. Toby in the Connecticut River valley during the early 1800s (Bagg & Eliot 1937). Hill (1965) mentions that a pair nested at Snake Pond, Sandwich, in the years 1900–1905 (Cobb), and he implies that Brewster knew of other nesting records.

   Although the Bald Eagle had long been extirpated as a nesting species in the state, recent efforts to reestablish this species as a breeder in Massachusetts have involved introducing young eagles to a hacking tower at Quabbin Reservoir (1982–1986) as well as elsewhere in the Northeast. Between the years 1982 and 1988, 41 Bald Eagle chicks were hacked from artificial nest platforms at Quabbin Reservoir by the Massachusetts Division of Fisheries and Wildlife and the U.S. Fish & Wildlife Service, in the hope that the birds would eventually return to breed at Quabbin. The hacking effort proved successful when 2 pairs first produced 3 young at Quabbin in 1989.

**Nonbreeding:** In winter since 1951, Bald Eagles have appeared at Quabbin Reservoir, where they feed upon the carcasses of deer stranded on the ice. They have historically wintered regularly along the Merrimack River and at Newburyport Harbor, and, more recently, they have frequented the Lakeville ponds. Numbers declined between 1955 and 1978, when Bald Eagle populations generally were substantially reduced by pesticide contamination. Recent high counts include: 61, throughout Massachusetts, 12 January 1990 (midwinter Bald Eagle Survey, MDFW); 36, Quabbin Reservoir, 8 January 1988 (midwinter Bald Eagle Survey, MDFW); 20–24 per day, Quabbin Reservoir, 15–30 August 1951 (Campbell); 22, Quabbin Reservoir, 11 January 1980 (Swedberg et al); 7, Merrimack River in Newburyport, December 1980–February 1981 (Heil et al).

   Bald Eagles have occurred as migrants and post-breeding wanderers throughout the state in every month of the year. Usually only single birds are encountered, but occasionally more are seen—e.g., 4 immatures, Chatham, 19 May–8 June 1964 (Holland, Dennis). They are of regular occurrence during September along inland mountain ridges, as well as from August to December on Outer Cape Cod and the Islands.

# White-tailed Eagle *Haliaeetus albicilla*

**Range:** Palearctic; breeds west to Iceland and east, rarely, to the westernmost Aleutian Islands. Vagrant elsewhere in North America.

**Status:** Vagrant: three records.

**Occurrence:** Although the White-tailed Eagle has not subsequently occurred in North America outside of Alaska, the following Massachusetts records occurred at a time when the species was more numerous and widespread. The first record was of an immature that flew aboard the Dutch steamer *Arundo* as it passed the Nantucket Lightship, 14 November 1914. The bird was taken alive to the New York Zoological Park, where it apparently lived for some time (Crandall 1915). Unfortunately, the specimen was apparently not preserved (Eisenmann, in litt.).

Two sight records of adult White-tailed Eagles in Massachusetts are well documented: 1, Newburyport Harbor, 10 February 1935 (Griscom et al); 1, Newburyport Harbor, 15–30 January 1944 (Griscom, Emery, M. and A. Argue, VO).

# Northern Harrier   *Circus cyaneus*

**Range:** Holarctic; breeds, in eastern North America, from northeastern Manitoba and northeastern Quebec south to northern Texas and eastern Virginia. Winters from South Dakota and Massachusetts south to Florida and Texas.

**Status:** Rare and local breeder, mainly on islands off Cape Cod, but occasionally inland as well. Fairly common migrant and winter resident.

**Breeding:** Northern Harriers have decreased considerably as breeders in Massachusetts since 1955. Their decline is probably due to habitat destruction and ecological succession in the open fields and pastures where they prefer to nest. In Berkshire County they bred regularly until at least 1950. A pair was present in Windsor during the summers of 1958 through 1960 (McNair 1978), and one was also seen there 25 June 1983 (Petersen). In the Connecticut River valley, the last nest found was at Mt. Hermon in 1932 (Bagg & Eliot 1937), while in Worcester County, a pair at New Braintree, throughout July 1990 (McMenemy), was the most recent probable inland nesting in the state. In Essex County, a nest with 5 eggs was found at Andover, 27 May 1956 (Root). Hill (1965) estimated that 8 to 10 pairs bred on Cape Cod.

Between 1974 and 1979, Massachusetts Breeding Bird Atlas workers found harriers nesting only on Nantucket, Martha's Vineyard, and the smaller islands of Tuckernuck, Muskeget, No Man's Land, Pasque, and Penikese. Those islands all have extensive open moorland and large microtine rodent populations. As of 1989, it was estimated that no more than 30 to 50 pairs of Northern Harriers bred in Massachusetts (Blodget, pers. comm.). *Egg dates:* mid-May–mid-June.

**Nonbreeding:** During migration in April and from September to November, Northern Harriers are regularly seen both on the coast and along inland ridges. *Spring maxima:* 30, Plum Island, 16 April 1988 (EMHW); 23, Plum Island, 26 April 1981 (EMHW) *Fall maxima:* 53, Mt. Wachusett, 6 September–2 November 1980 (Roberts); 52, Mt. Wachusett, 3–25 September 1989 (EMHW); 42, Mt. Wachusett, September 1987 (EMHW); 19, Nantucket, 6–8 October 1984 (SSBC). During the winter, harriers are concentrated along the outer coast, both in the Salisbury–Plum Island area and on Cape Cod and the Islands. In some years, they are also regular, at least into early winter, in the Connecticut River valley and over extensive farm fields in other inland areas. *Winter maxima:* 37, Nantucket CBC, 30 December 1984; 32, Nantucket CBC, 2 January 1988; 23, Cape Cod CBC, 17 December 1978; 9, Plum Island–Salisbury, 18 February 1980 (Heil); 4, Concord CBC, 21 December 1975.

## Sharp-shinned Hawk  *Accipiter striatus*

**Range:** Nearctic; breeds from northwestern Alaska and southern Labrador south to California and northeastern Georgia. In eastern North America, winters north to central Michigan and Nova Scotia.

**Status:** Very rare and local breeder. Common to very common migrant; uncommon winter resident.

**Breeding:** Sharp-shinned Hawks have markedly declined as breeders in Massachusetts since the turn of the century. Griscom and Snyder (1955) attributed this decline to the destruction of forests during the late 1800s. However, it seems that they have not increased as breeding birds along with the regeneration of forests in western Massachusetts. There have been only a few confirmed instances of breeding in Massachusetts since 1955: e.g., 1 nest with 3 eggs, Marshfield, 24 June 1982 (Veit, Heil); 1 pair with young, Wellfleet, summer of 1988 through 1990 (Green). Other probable instances of breeding include: 1 pair with 3 young, Framingham, September 1976 (Forster); 1 adult carrying food, Mt. Watatic, 30 June 1977 (Roberts); 1 adult carrying food, Otis, 3 August 1978 (McNair); 1 adult performing display flight, Northfield, 9 July 1979 (Forster); 1 adult carrying food, Middleboro, 23 May 1981 (Petersen, Anderson). *Egg dates:* May 3–24 June.

**Nonbreeding:** Sharp-shinned Hawks are most conspicuous in Massachusetts during migration, when hundreds are sometimes seen from various hawk migration lookouts in the state, both inland and on the coast. Usually, more are seen at inland sites, but the highest numbers ever recorded are from Cape Cod and Martha's Vineyard. During winter, Sharp-shinned Hawks are most common in the southeastern part of the state, where they are attracted to groups of passerines at feeding stations. *Spring maxima:*

289, Plum Island, 2 May 1987 (EMHW); 212, Plum Island, 1 May 1987 (EMHW); 165, Truro, 6 May 1984 (Nikula et al); 130+, Truro, 8 May 1983 (Nikula et al); 126, Plum Island, 26 April 1981 (Roberts); 96, Plum Island, 1 May 1978 (McClellan); 60+, Truro, 9 May 1979 (Nikula). *Fall maxima:* 1,100, Gay Head, Martha's Vineyard, 2 October 1982 (Laux); 1,009, Marconi Station, South Wellfleet, 20 September 1981 (Forster, Clapp); 400, Fobes Hill, Windsor, 28 September 1977 (McNair); 353, Mt. Wachusett, 17–23 September 1978 (Roberts); 162, Mt. Wachusett, 23 September 1979 (Roberts); 160, Mt. Wachusett, 17 September, 1978 (Roberts). *Winter maxima:* 18, Cape Cod CBC, 22 December 1985; 16, Cape Cod CBC, 17 December 1989; 13, Cape Cod CBC, 16 December 1979; 7, Nantucket CBC, 2 January 1982.

## Cooper's Hawk   *Accipiter cooperii*

**Range:** Nearctic; breeds, in eastern North America, from central Manitoba and western Nova Scotia south to Florida and Texas. Winters within the southern portion of the breeding range, north to Minnesota and southern New England.

**Status:** Rare and local breeder; uncommon migrant and winter resident.

**Breeding:** During the Breeding Bird Atlas Project (1974–1979), only two pairs of Cooper's Hawks were confirmed nesting in the state: 1 with 3 young, Lancaster, 6 June 1978 (Merriman); 1 nest, Stowe State Forest, June and July 1978 (Olmstead). Other recent confirmed instances of breeding include: 1 nest, Newbury, 17 July 1955 (deWindt); 1 nest, Belmont, 1960 (Drew); 1 nest, Charlton, 1983 (Meservey); 1 nest, Newburyport, 5–9 July 1984 (Petersen, Heil, Melvin); 1 nest, South Natick, summers of 1987–1988 (Landre et al); 1 nest, Middleboro, June 1989 (Petersen); 1 nest, Boxford, June 1990 (Aversa).

**Nonbreeding:** Cooper's Hawks have declined dramatically in the Northeast since 1955, when Griscom and Snyder (1955) had already detected a drop in local numbers. The decrease has in part been coincidental with an increase in Northern Goshawks in Massachusetts, and it is possible that subtle changes in local ecology have favored the goshawk. Migrating Cooper's Hawks move through Massachusetts during March and April, and again in September and October, but recent maximum counts are lower than they were 30 years ago. *Spring maxima* (prior to 1955): 22, Mt. Tom, 22 April 1950 (Smart); 13, Essex County, 29 April 1953 (Elkins, Wellman). More recent spring maxima: 10, Mt. Tom, 15 April 1976 (Roberts 1990); 10, North Truro, 1 May 1987 (EMHW); 5, Plum Island, 15 April 1960 (Roberts 1990). *Fall maxima:* 15, Mt. Tom, 21 September 1949 (Bagg); 5, Mt. Wachusett, 17 September 1982 (Roberts); 3, Ashburnham, 3 October 1982 (Roberts).

Usually present in small numbers in winter—e.g., 3, Concord CBC, 30 December 1978.

## Northern Goshawk   *Accipiter gentilis*

**Range:** Holarctic; breeds, in eastern North America, from northeastern Manitoba and northern Labrador south to southern Manitoba, northern New Jersey, and Pennsylvania. Winters from southeastern Manitoba and Nova Scotia south to Nebraska and Virginia.

**Status:** Uncommon resident and migrant on the mainland; rare migrant on the Islands.

**Breeding:** Goshawk numbers fluctuate in abundance in Massachusetts from year to year but have been steadily increasing since the mid-1950s, both as breeders and winterers. In 1955, they were largely restricted to western Massachusetts as breeders, but they now nest regularly throughout the state, east to Boxford, Framingham, Newbury, Marshfield, and Middleboro. Aside from a single nesting attempt in Centerville, 3 July 1990 (Collins), they have not yet been found breeding on Cape Cod or the Islands, where they are much less common than they are on the mainland, even during fall and winter. McNair (1978) lists fourteen nesting records for Berkshire County beginning in 1960. At least thirty-three nests were found through-out Massachusetts during the Breeding Bird Atlas Project between 1974 and 1979. *Egg dates:* 1 April–10 May.

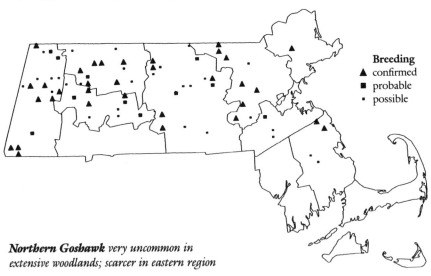

Breeding
▲ confirmed
■ probable
• possible

*Northern Goshawk very uncommon in extensive woodlands; scarcer in eastern region*

**Nonbreeding:** Goshawks migrate at irregular intervals and are therefore infrequently observed from regular hawk migration observation points.

***Spring maxima:*** 5, Mt. Tom, 30 April 1956 (Roberts 1990); 4, Mt. Tom, 1 April 1975 (op cit); 3, Ashburnham, 1 April 1984 (EMHW). Occasionally they irrupt southward in numbers, perhaps during years when food is scarce farther north, such as in 1973–1974. ***Fall maxima:*** 4, Ashburnham, 27 October 1979 (Petersen). ***Winter maxima*** (examples): 13, eastern Massachusetts, January 1978 (BOEM); 11, eastern Massachusetts, January 1974 (BOEM).

## Red-shouldered Hawk   *Buteo lineatus*

**Range:** Nearctic; in eastern North America, breeds from central Minnesota and southern New Brunswick south to Texas and Florida; also in Mexico. Winters north to southern Wisconsin and southeastern Massachusetts.

**Status:** Uncommon breeder; most numerous west of Worcester County. Uncommon migrant; rare to uncommon in winter.

**Breeding:** Although recent counts of migrant Red-shouldered Hawks are lower than they were formerly, it is not clear that they have declined as breeders since 1955. As an illustration of their abundance in Massachusetts, Holt found 23 and 21 active nests during May 1959 and 1960, respectively, in the town of Andover; in 1978, 7 nests were found in Otis (MacDonald). Also in 1978, at least 8 other pairs were located in Berkshire County (McNair). The species' preference for lowland deciduous forests and swampy woodlands often makes the birds inconspicuous when nesting. In western Massachusetts, Red-shoulders have a strong affinity for woodlands adjacent to Beaver ponds. They are absent as breeders from Cape Cod and the Islands, with one exception: probable nest and young observed, Nashawena Island, June 1975 (fide Sorrie). ***Egg dates:*** 3 April–5 June.

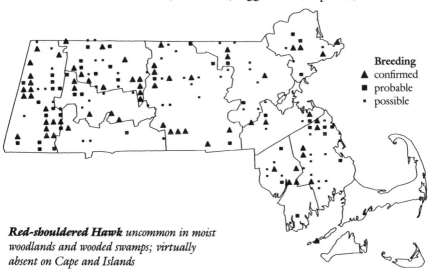

Breeding
▲ confirmed
■ probable
· possible

*Red-shouldered Hawk uncommon in moist woodlands and wooded swamps; virtually absent on Cape and Islands*

**Nonbreeding:** Red-shouldered Hawks migrate between mid-March and April and in October and early November, the timing coinciding with the migration of the Red-tailed Hawk. They are uncommon to rare on Cape Cod and the Islands. *Spring maxima:* 267, Mt. Tom, 28 March 1950 (Smart); 114, Mt. Tom, 22 March 1929 (Roberts 1990); 58, Sudbury River valley, 19 March 1954 (Wellman); 53, Mt. Tom, 20 March 1976 (Roberts 1990); 15, Mt. Tom, 25 March 1963 (Elkins); 8, Mt. Wachusett, 21 April 1979 (Roberts); 8 + adults, Truro-Provincetown, 27 March 1976 (Nikula, Goodrich). The Red-shouldered Hawk has evidently not decreased as a fall migrant. *Fall maxima:* 32, Mt. Tom, 21 October 1951 (Elkins); 32, Mt. Watatic, 27 October 1979 (Petersen); 22, Mt. Watatic, 24 October 1982 (Roberts).

Because of their retiring and sedentary nature and their preference for mature forests, Red-shouldered Hawks are easily overlooked during winter. They are rare on Cape Cod in winter. *Winter maxima:* 5, Bridgewater, 15 February 1981 (SSBC); 4, Concord, throughout February 1959 (Alden).

# Broad-winged Hawk *Buteo platypterus*

**Range:** Nearctic; breeds in central Alberta and Saskatchewan and from southern Manitoba and New Brunswick south to eastern Texas and northern Florida. Winters in southern Florida and in Central and South America.

**Status:** Fairly common breeder and abundant migrant on the mainland. Rare breeder and uncommon migrant on Cape Cod.

Breeding
▲ confirmed
■ probable
· possible

*Broad-winged Hawk fairly common in mature deciduous woodlands; absent on Islands*

**Breeding:** Broad-winged Hawks have increased since the early part of this century, probably due to the maturation of forests. Presently, they are fairly common breeders in the state, especially from Worcester County westward, in both deciduous and mixed woodlands. As evidence of their abundance as a breeding species, 15 active nests were found in Andover during May 1960 (Holt). McNair (1978) alleged that it is the most common nesting hawk in Berkshire County.

**Nonbreeding:** Migrating flights of Broad-winged Hawks are an immensely popular and spectacular attraction for hawk watchers throughout the Northeast. Their migration is precisely timed each year so that the bulk of birds pass north in spring through Massachusetts between 20 and 30 April and south in fall between 12 and 20 September. The number of birds seen each year depends on weather patterns, which determine the altitude at which the hawks migrate and the precise path that they follow. The largest autumn flights in Massachusetts have been recorded during northeasterly (not northwesterly) winds, which apparently provide optimum tail winds. When a low cloud ceiling prevents the hawks from ascending beyond visible range, the flights can be spectacular.

The vast majority of migrants are seen over inland mountain ranges, except in late spring, when flocks of yearling individuals regularly appear on Cape Cod under certain conditions. *Spring maxima:* 1,300, Mt. Tom, 27 April 1944 (Bagg); 1,104, Granville, 20 April 1986 (Kellogg); 712, Mt. Tom, 25 April 1964 (Forster); 549, Mt. Tom, 24 April 1945 (Bagg); 528, Mt. Tom, 29 April 1945 (Elkins); 383, Mt. Holyoke, 20 April 1986 (Roberts 1990); 288, North Truro, 1 May 1987 (op cit); 146, Petersham, 22 April 1979 (fide Roberts); 129, Mt. Wachusett, 22 April 1979 (Roberts). Strong and sustained southerly winds occasionally generate modest flights on Cape Cod—e.g., 70, Provincetown, 9 June 1976 (Heil); 50, Truro, 12 May 1977 (Bailey); 50, Provincetown, 2 June 1979 (Lipke). *Fall maxima:* 19,912, Mt. Wachusett, 13 September 1983 (AB 38: 176); 12,424, Southwick, 13 September 1983 (Kellogg); 10,086, Mt. Wachusett, 13 September 1978 (Roberts 1979); 5,996, Mt. Tom, 16 September 1960 (Elkins). Perhaps owing to the precise timing of the Broad-wing's migration, extremely early and late records are unusual—e.g., 1, Boxboro, 23 March 1975 (Brown); 1, Concord, 2 November 1903 (BMS #15614); 1, Wellfleet, 18 November 1959 (Bailey).

# Swainson's Hawk   *Buteo swainsoni*

**Range:** Nearctic; breeds in the Great Plains, east to southeastern Minnesota and eastern Iowa. Winters in northern South America and, regularly, in small numbers, in southern Florida. Vagrant to the Atlantic Coast.

**Status:** Vagrant: at least ten modern sight records.

**Occurrence:** During the period 1872–1892, when Swainson's Hawks were more numerous and widespread than they are today, four specimens were collected in Massachusetts: 1, Hamilton, 20 April 1872 (Butler); 1, Salem, 28 October 1889 (Newcomb); 1, Wayland, 12 September 1876 (Allen); 1, Essex, 29 May 1892 (Brewster). Oddly, the latter three of these are of the comparatively rare dark morph. Griscom and Snyder (1955) mention three additional sight records between 1893 and 1925, but reject some fifteen records from between 1930 and 1955, including four attributed to Griscom himself.

Since 1955, Swainson's Hawks have been reported at least twenty-five times, and, although some of these reports may have been valid, most lack documentation. Reports that seem unquestionable are: 1 light adult, Ipswich, 21–22 February 1960 (Snyder); 1, Wellfleet, 27 November 1964 (Smart, Fox, Armstrong); 1 light adult, Plum Island, 12 October 1965 (Petersen); 1 light adult, Newbury, 4 March 1975 (Laux, Goodrich, Nikula, Harris); 1 second-year subadult, Westover Air Force Base, Springfield, 12 October 1977 (Blakeney); 1 immature, Forest Park, Springfield, February–March 1978 (Gagnon); 1 immature, Framingham, 15 September 1979 (Forster); 1 immature, Buck Hill, Milton, 4 May 1980 (Veit, Perkins, Litchfield); 1 adult, Plum Island, 15 April 1988 (Soucy); 1 immature, Middleboro, 10–21 October 1988 (Harrington, Leggett, VO).

# Red-tailed Hawk  *Buteo jamaicensis*

**Range:** Nearctic; breeds virtually throughout temperate North America, north to northern Manitoba and northeastern Quebec; also south to Panama. Winters north to southern Maine and the Great Lakes.

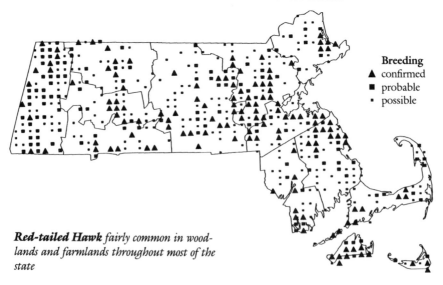

**Breeding**
▲ confirmed
■ probable
· possible

***Red-tailed Hawk*** *fairly common in woodlands and farmlands throughout most of the state*

**Status:** Uncommon, but conspicuous resident; fairly common winter resident, especially in eastern Massachusetts and the Connecticut River valley.

**Breeding:** Red-tailed Hawks are uncommon breeders throughout most of the state. They are found in a diversity of habitats, including mature mixed forests, open farmlands with adjacent woodlots, and Pitch Pine barrens on Cape Cod and the Islands. During the breeding season, they are remarkably inconspicuous, in contrast to winter, when they are frequently seen on exposed perches along highways and field edges. There is at least one record of a pair nesting on a utility pole—Whitman, 1981 (Petersen)—although they most typically select White Pines for nesting sites. *Egg dates:* 30 March–30 April.

**Nonbreeding:** Red-tailed Hawks migrate earlier in spring and later in fall than most other hawks. Peak migration time for them is late March and late October to November. Because of this schedule, they are frequently under-counted during migration due to lack of coverage at hawk lookouts at those times of the year. Nonetheless, a number of individuals seen during September hawk watches, and often dismissed as residents, are, in all probability, migrants (Roberts, pers. comm.). *Spring maxima:* 54, Mt. Tom, 29 March 1950 (Smart); 54, Granville, 17 March 1985 (Kellogg). *Fall maxima:* 198, Mt. Tom, 6 November 1937 (Hagar); 73, Pittsfield, 4 November 1989 (Perkins); 58, Mt. Wachusett, 23 October 1982 (Roberts).

In Massachusetts, Red-tailed Hawks are most numerous, or at least most conspicuous, during winter. The largest numbers are concentrated at the edges of open hunting areas, such as the periphery of large salt marshes, farm fields, and river meadows, and in the moorlands of Nantucket and Martha's Vineyard. *Winter maxima:* 91, Concord CBC, 28 December 1980; 84, Concord CBC, 27 December 1987; 64, Greater Boston CBC, 17 December 1989; 40, Bridgewater area, 15 February 1981 (SSBC, Petersen); 32, Newburyport CBC, 2 January 1983; 32, Nantucket CBC, 1 January 1983.

# Rough-legged Hawk  *Buteo lagopus*

**Range:** Holarctic; breeds, in North America, in arctic Canada, south to extreme northeastern Manitoba, northern Quebec, southern Labrador, and interior Newfoundland. Along the Atlantic Coast, winters south regularly to North Carolina, more rarely to the Gulf Coast and Florida.

**Status:** Irruptive; rare to occasionally fairly common winter resident and migrant.

**Occurrence:** Rough-legged Hawks migrate south in large numbers at irregular intervals. It seems likely that such incursions occur during years when their food supply in the north is depleted. Major flights to Massachusetts occurred during the periods: 1870–1887 (68 killed in one winter, Northampton and Hatfield [Damon, Bagg & Eliot 1937]); 1953–1954; 1960–1961; 1961–1962; 1964–1965; 1970–1971; 1971–1972; 1977–1978; 1980–1981; and 1989–1990. It is possible that excessive shooting during the late 1800s may have seriously depressed the population of these birds at the time; however, like Snowy Owls, Rough-legged Hawks are very prolific in some years, and it would seem that they have had an opportunity to recover. During the late 1800s, Rough-legged Hawks were most numerous in the Connecticut River valley, although in recent years they have been most common over the salt marshes of northeastern Essex County; at Daniel Webster Wildlife Sanctuary in Marshfield; on farm fields in Middleboro; and on the moors of Nantucket and Martha's Vineyard.

*Maxima:* (since 1955): 15, Sudbury River valley, 13 February 1965 (Forster); 12, Salisbury, 1 November 1964 (Vaughan); 12, Salisbury, 11 January 1981 (Arvidson); 8, Bridgewater, 15 February 1981 (SSBC); 7 migrating south in two hours, Salisbury, 8 November 1981 (Robinson et al). Fifty-four were reported in eastern Massachusetts during December 1977 (BOEM). *Extreme dates:* 1, Calf Island, Boston Harbor, 29 June 1966 (Weaver, Kadlec, Mott); 1, Monomoy, 9 June 1976 (Forster, Nisbet); 1, West Newbury, 22 May 1971 (Petersen et al).

# Golden Eagle   *Aquila chrysaetos*

**Range:** Holarctic; breeds, in eastern North America, from northeastern Manitoba and northern Quebec south to southern Manitoba and the Gaspé Peninsula; irregularly in Maine, New Hampshire, and northeastern New York. Winters at widely scattered localities in the southeastern United States, rarely north to Massachusetts.

**Status:** Rare but regular migrant and winter resident.

**Occurrence:** Golden Eagles have appeared during every month of the year in Massachusetts, but most are seen as migrants during April and May and from October to November. They are somewhat more frequent in the Connecticut River valley and the Berkshires than elsewhere but are of regular occurrence east to Essex County, Cape Cod, and, more rarely, Nantucket. *Spring maxima:* 3, Ashley Falls, 27 May 1960 (Bailey); 2, Mt. Tom, 19 April 1956 (Edison et al). *Fall maxima:* 3, Littleton, 14 September 1979 (Baird); 2, Petersham, 16 September 1990 (Baird).

In recent years, 1 to 3 Golden Eagles regularly winter in the wilder portions of the Quabbin Reservoir—e.g., 3, 28 February 1982 (Petersen et al); 3, 8 January 1983 (Forster). Golden Eagles are also occasionally found on the Islands; there are at least three records for Martha's Vineyard, all during

December (Griscom & Emerson 1959), including: 1 (which collided with high-tension wires and was electrocuted, specimen at the Maria Mitchell Association), Nantucket, 9–15 November 1962 (Andrews); 1 immature, Naushon Island, 9 January 1983 (Hatch). Additional records from mainland southeastern Massachusetts include: 1 subadult, Dartmouth, 19 February 1973 (Petersen, Goodrich); 1 adult, Lakeville, 5–13 March 1983 (Petersen).

## Eurasian Kestrel   *Falco tinnunculus*

**Range:** Palearctic; breeds west to the Shetland Islands; winters from Scotland to Africa (*F. t. tinnunculus*). Vagrant to North America.

**Status:** Vagrant: one record.

**Occurrence:** A female Eurasian Kestrel was collected at Nantasket Beach, Hull, 29 September 1887 by Foster H. Brackett (Cory 1888). This was the first North American record, but, subsequently, three have been reported in Alaska, two in New Jersey, and one in New Brunswick. The Massachusetts specimen is now located in the Cory collection at the Chicago Natural History Museum.

## American Kestrel   *Falco sparverius*

**Range:** Nearctic; breeds from central Alaska and southwestern Newfoundland south to Baja California, southern Texas, and northern Georgia. Winters, in eastern North America, north to central Michigan, southern Ontario, and northern New England.

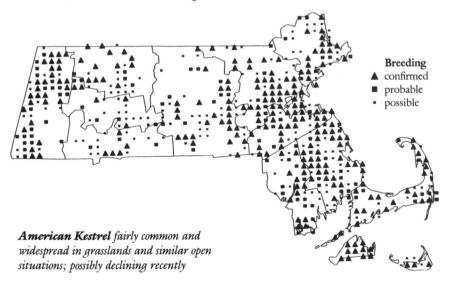

**Breeding**
▲ confirmed
■ probable
• possible

*American Kestrel fairly common and widespread in grasslands and similar open situations; possibly declining recently*

**Status:** Fairly common resident and common migrant.

**Breeding:** This is one of the few species of raptors whose population seems to have increased since the turn of the century. Griscom and Snyder (1955) noted an increase between 1900 and 1955, and current migratory totals are considerably higher than they were during the first half of the century. American Kestrels breed throughout the state in open country and are least numerous in the heavily wooded sections of Berkshire and Worcester counties. Sample maxima include: 13 active nests, Andover, 31 May 1960 (Holt); 15, GBBBC, 18 June 1977. *Egg dates:* 27 April–26 May.

**Nonbreeding:** Many American Kestrels migrate along the immediate coast in spring, but in fall most seem to travel southwest along the inland mountain ridges. Peak numbers occur in late April and September. *Spring maxima:* 904 counted, eastern Massachusetts (800 of these from Plum Island), April 1978 (EMHW); 339+, Plum Island, 12 April 1978 (Roberts); 250, Plum Island, 27 April 1989 (Clifford); 172, Plum Island, 18 April 1982 (Roberts); 100, Wellfleet, 20 April 1975 (Nikula); 95, Wellfleet, 18 April 1982 (Nikula); 33, Mt. Wachusett, 23 April 1983 (Roberts). *Fall maxima:* 74, Mt. Tom, 25 September 1965 (Yenlin); 53, Mt. Wachusett, 17 September 1981 (Roberts et al); 40+, Nantucket, 18 September 1973 (Stymeist, Fox, Baird). *Winter maxima:* 27, Millis CBC, 19 December 1987; 26, Bridgewater, 15 February 1981 (SSBC Raptor Survey); 25, Nantucket CBC, 29 December 1979; 23, Greater Boston CBC, 20 December 1981.

# Merlin  *Falco columbarius*

**Range:** Holarctic; breeds, in North America, from Alaska and northern Labrador south to eastern Oregon and New Brunswick. Winters in the eastern United States from southern Texas, the Gulf Coast, and South Carolina, casually north to the Canadian border; also south to northern South America and the West Indies.

**Status:** Uncommon to fairly common migrant; winters in small numbers on Nantucket, Martha's Vineyard, and outer Cape Cod, rarely north to Boston.

**Occurrence:** Merlins migrate through Massachusetts from late April to early May and again from mid-September to early October. The majority of Merlins are seen at the immediate coast, but a few also occur inland. *Spring maximum:* 20, Plum Island, 25 April 1970 (Roberts 1990). *Fall maxima:* 12, Essex County, 25 September 1949 (Griscom); 11, Nantucket, 24–25 September 1985 (Forster); 7, Nantucket, 8 October 1979 (Veit).

Griscom and Snyder (1955) dismissed many winter reports of Merlins in the Northeast. Although at inland locations many Merlins reported in winter prove to be some other species, they regularly winter in small numbers in southeastern Massachusetts, especially on Cape Cod and the Islands, and one or two have also wintered at Plum Island within the decade (Roberts pers. comm.). *Winter maxima:* 9, eastern Massachusetts (including singles north to Bridgewater and Amesbury), January–February 1980 (BOEM); 5, Nantucket, 2 January 1977 (Andrews, Veit). In Berkshire County, a female Merlin was killed and mounted in Adams, 23 January 1961, and sent to the Berkshire Museum (Hendricks), and another immature male flew into a window in Dalton, 1 March 1978 (fide McNair).

# Peregrine Falcon   *Falco peregrinus*

**Range:** Nearly cosmopolitan; breeds, in North America, in the Canadian Arctic, between latitudes of approximately 63° and 73° N, and in southern Greenland. Hand-reared birds have been released and are now breeding at scattered localities in the Northeast. Winters from the southern United States, sparingly north to New England, south to southern South America.

**Status:** Rare and local breeder. Rare to uncommon, but regular migrant; rare, but increasing, in winter. Most numerous on the coast.

**Breeding:** Peregrine Falcons nested in Berkshire County (at least 5 separate sites) up until 1957 (Hagar 1969). They also nested at Mt. Tom until 1955 and at four other localities in the Connecticut River valley during the period 1930 to 1940. They then disappeared as a result of pesticide contamination and did not breed again in Massachusetts until enticed to do so as a result of a hacking program initiated in the 1980s. In 1984, six Peregrine Falcon chicks were successfully hacked from a specially constructed platform in downtown Boston by the Massachusetts Division of Fisheries and Wildlife, in hopes that they would return in future years to breed. By 1989, single pairs of Peregrine Falcons were successfully nesting in Boston and Springfield.

**Nonbreeding:** In spring, most Peregrine Falcons are reported between late March and mid-May, mainly on the coast. During the fall migration, most birds are seen between late September and early November, particularly on Cape Cod and the Islands. There has been a pronounced increase in the number of migrants seen annually since the 1980s. *Spring maxima:* 9, Scituate, 25 April 1969 (Litchfield); 6, Plum Island, 15 April 1960 (Forster). *Fall maxima:* 12, Nantucket, 5–18 October 1979 (Veit, Litchfield); 10, Martha's Vineyard, 12 October 1982 (Brown). During the winter, up to 4 were reported during February in Massachusetts in three separate years: 1955, 1962, and 1965 (RNEB). Most of these were on the coast, but one, in 1962, was in Springfield. Since the late 1970s, from 1 to 3 individuals have overwintered on Cape Cod and Nantucket and in downtown Boston.

# Gyrfalcon   *Falco rusticolus*

**Range:** Holarctic; breeds, in North America, in arctic Canada from northern Ellesmere Island south to the Mackenzie River Delta, extreme northeastern Manitoba, northern Quebec, and northern Labrador. Winters south, occasionally, to New Jersey, Pennsylvania, and southern Michigan.

**Status:** Rare but regular migrant or winter visitor.

**Occurrence:** Since 1955, Gyrfalcons have been reported in Massachusetts, more or less regularly, with all but a few being on the coast between Essex County and Cape Cod. Of those for which the color phase was described, the majority have been gray or intermediate, with dark- and white-phase birds being the least frequently reported; however, an increase in the proportion of white birds since the early 1960s has been unambiguous (fifteen out of twenty-five reported before 1955 were dark, compared to six out of thirty reported since then). Interestingly, six of the seven white Gyrfalcons that have occurred in the state have appeared between mid-February and April, as follows: 1, East Milton, 11 February 1959 (Higginbotham); 1, South Dartmouth, 25 April 1966 (Raymond); 1, Plum Island, 23 March 1969 (Petersen, Goodrich); 1, Ipswich-Essex, 12–18 March 1976 (Hotz, Nove, Donahue); 1, Plum Island, 15 December 1976–31 January 1977 (Brophy et al); 1, Cambridge-Boston, 6–19 March 1977 (Hooper, Smith, et al). Many of the Gyrfalcons reported in fall are dark, and some have proven to be misidentified young Peregrine Falcons. The earliest fall record is: 1, Monomoy, 26 October 1974 (Bailey). One bird wintered at Monomoy from 1972–1973 until 1975–1976 (Clem, Bailey, Goodrich, et al). Recent inland records include: 1, Hadley, 20–31 December 1981 (Trull, Stemple); 1, Quabbin Reservoir, 15–25 February 1982 (Gagnon et al); 1, Northampton, March–April 1991 (fide Surner).

# Ring-necked Pheasant   *Phasianus colchicus*

**Range:** Originally eastern Palearctic; introduced to North America and elsewhere. Resident in the East from northern Minnesota and northwestern Missouri east to the Atlantic Coast, from northern Nova Scotia south to southern New Jersey and southeastern Pennsylvania.

**Status:** Common and widespread resident; populations regularly restocked.

**Breeding:** Resident Ring-necked Pheasants are found throughout the state, including Nantucket and Martha's Vineyard, wherever there is open country. Pheasants are often concentrated in cornfields during fall and winter. The species regularly breeds where it survives hunting pressure and winter kill. *Egg dates:* late April–late June.

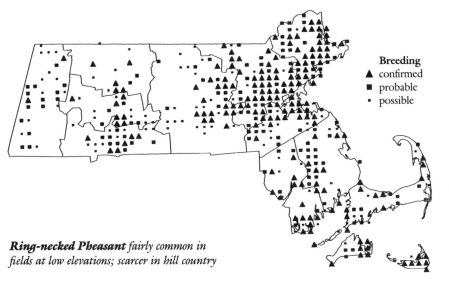

**Ring-necked Pheasant** *fairly common in fields at low elevations; scarcer in hill country*

**Nonbreeding:** As with the Ruffed Grouse, most of the highest pheasant counts of the year are made on the annual CBC. *Maxima:* 474, Concord CBC, 1 January 1970; 346, Concord CBC, 2 January 1967; 211, Greater Boston CBC, 16 December 1979; 30–40 in one flock, Wayland, 1 January 1961 (Davidson).

## Ruffed Grouse  *Bonasa umbellus*

**Range:** Nearctic; *B. u. umbellus* is resident from central New York and southeastern Massachusetts south to eastern Pennsylvania and New Jersey;

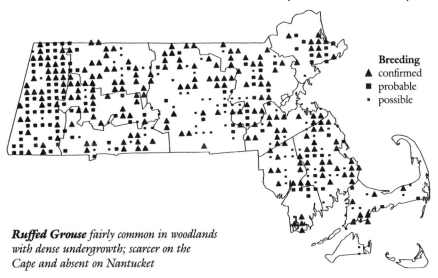

**Ruffed Grouse** *fairly common in woodlands with dense undergrowth; scarcer on the Cape and absent on Nantucket*

*B. u. togata* is resident from northeastern Minnesota and Nova Scotia south to northern Wisconsin, central New York, and western and northeastern Massachusetts.

**Status:** Fairly common resident in wooded areas.

**Breeding:** Resident Ruffed Grouse are found in a variety of woodland habitats in Massachusetts, from the mature deciduous and mixed forests of the western part of the state to the pine barrens and Scrub Oak forests of Plymouth County and Cape Cod. Populations fluctuate irregularly from year to year. In some years, grouse have been found in heavily urbanized areas. *Egg dates:* 1 April–late July (most in May).

**Nonbreeding:** Probably the best indicator of population fluctuation from year to year is the data gathered on the CBC. As an example of this variation, the average number of Ruffed Grouse recorded on the Concord CBC from 1960 to 1983 was 16; however, the range was 2 to 52. Closer evaluation of grouse data suggests that the species is cyclical in its abundance.

# Wild Turkey   *Meleagris gallopavo*

**Range:** Nearctic; range modified through overhunting, clearing of forests, and restocking; resident in the eastern United States from Vermont and Pennsylvania to Arkansas and Florida; absent from the higher mountains.

**Status:** Fairly common resident, especially in western Massachusetts, following repeated stocking efforts since at least the 1950s.

**Breeding:** Wild Turkeys were extirpated as breeding birds in Massachusetts by about 1850 (Griscom & Snyder 1955). They were introduced at Naushon Island in 1929, 1938, 1939, and 1940, and in the Myles Standish State Forest, Plymouth, in 1966; however, no turkeys have been reported in those areas for more than ten years—e.g., last seen on Naushon in 1976 (Hatch). Turkeys were introduced in the Quabbin area during the 1950s, and as many as 25 to 40 birds have been seen there in groups through the 1980s. Many seen during the last 20 years are derived from Pennsylvania stocks released in Berkshire County, where the species is now well established. The stocked population of Wild Turkeys in northwestern Massachusetts was composed of an estimated 1,500 birds by 1982 (MDFW). Wild Turkeys are now sufficiently established that an open hunting season was initiated in 1982. By 1990, a number of newly stocked populations had become established in eastern Massachusetts. *Egg dates:* April.

**Nonbreeding:** The highest turkey counts of the year generally occur when the birds are concentrated in winter flocks. *Maxima:* 142, Northern Berkshire CBC, 17 December 1988; 116, Northern Berkshire CBC, 15 December 1990; 72, Quabbin CBC, 28 December 1991; 67, Athol CBC, 15 December 1990.

# Northern Bobwhite   *Colinus virginianus*

**Range:** Nearctic; resident from southeastern South Dakota, northern Michigan, and southeastern Massachusetts south to eastern Texas and northern Florida.

**Status:** Locally common resident.

**Breeding:** The abundance and distribution of the Northern Bobwhite in Massachusetts is now largely contingent upon the stocking of birds by private hunting clubs. Outside of southeastern Massachusetts, bobwhite populations entirely composed of introduced birds. Even there, specimens taken recently differ from the large, heavy, and pale New England quail that were originally native in Massachusetts (Griscom & Snyder 1955). Present Northern Bobwhite populations have recently been augmented through stocking programs at Plum Island, in the Sudbury River valley, southern Connecticut River valley, and Berkshire County, and on Nantucket and Martha's Vineyard. *Egg dates:* 20 May–2 September.

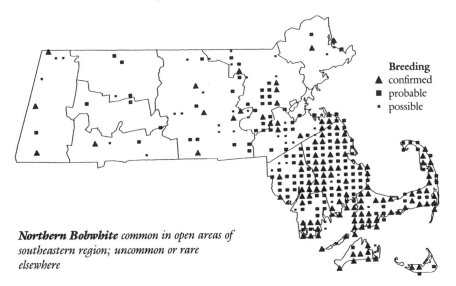

Breeding
▲ confirmed
■ probable
• possible

*Northern Bobwhite common in open areas of southeastern region; uncommon or rare elsewhere*

**Nonbreeding:** The highest annual counts of Northern Bobwhites come from southeastern Massachusetts. *Maxima:* 74, Mid-Cape Cod CBC, 28 December 1989; 73, Martha's Vineyard CBC, 29 December 1991; 48, Cape Cod CBC, 17 December 1989.

# Yellow Rail   *Coturnicops noveboracensis*

**Range:** Nearctic; breeds in eastern Alberta, Mackenzie, and Manitoba east, very sporadically, to New Brunswick and Maine. Winters along the Gulf

Coast from Texas to Florida and north along the East Coast to North Carolina.

**Status:** Rare migrant.

**Occurrence:** Yellow Rails are among the rarest of the North American rails and occur in Massachusetts only as migrants, principally during fall. They are very particular about habitat choice. Ideally, they prefer wet fields with fine, rank grasses 1 to 2 feet tall, but they also occur during migration in *Spartina* grass at the uppermost reaches of salt marshes, especially where fresh creeks spill into salt marshes, such as along the South River in Marshfield.

Apparently, Yellow Rails formerly occurred more frequently in Massachusetts than they do today. Forty-four specimens taken between 1867 and 1937 are extant at the MCZ, BMS, and PMS. Of forty-one of these specimens in the MCZ and BMS, thirty-seven were collected in the fall (15 August–19 November) and three in the spring (4 April–9 May). The distribution of specimens by month is: April, 2; May, 1; August, 1; September, 18; October, 15; and November, 3. The favored localities for these birds, which were usually hunted with the help of a trained dog, were: the Sudbury River meadows, 4 specimens; Wayland, 5 specimens; and Marshfield, 8 specimens. All were taken in eastern Massachusetts, but that is probably an artifact of lack of coverage in the western part of the state.

Since 1955, Yellow Rails have been recorded in fall as follows: 1, Nauset, Eastham, 14 October 1964 (Bailey); 1 immature, which flew aboard a fishing boat (and was taken to the Felix Neck Wildlife Sanctuary, 28 August, where it was banded and released), Little Georges Bank, 24 August 1973 (Sargent, Ben David, Keith); 1, Sandy Neck, Barnstable, 15 September 1979 (Pease); 1 road-killed, Provincetown, 14 September 1980 (fide Bailey); 1, Fort Hill, Eastham, 26 October 1980 (Petersen, Sorrie); 1, Fort Hill, Eastham, 13 October 1985 (SSBC); 1, Scituate, 26 September 1987 (Petersen); 1, Chatham, 21 November 1988 (Nikula); 1, Dorchester, 15 October 1989 (Donovan, Lomar). There have also been the following winter records: 1, Nauset, Eastham, 21 February 1954 (Fox, Morgan); 1, West Barnstable, 7 December 1954 (Heath); 1, Chatham, 28 December 1954 (Long); 1, North Beach, Chatham, 13 January 1982 (fide Forster); 1 found dead, Neponset River, Dorchester, 30 January 1992 (Donovan).

# Black Rail   *Laterallus jamaicensis*

**Range:** Nearctic; breeds in two disjunct areas: in freshwater marshes of the midwestern states between Kansas and northwestern Ohio and in extensive salt marshes along the northwest coast of Florida, along the Atlantic Coast from Florida to Long Island, and also in California. Winters mainly on the Gulf Coast of Texas and Louisiana.

**Status:** Vagrant: four records since 1955.

**Occurrence:** All records of the New England "Kicker" mentioned in Griscom and Snyder (1955) probably refer to Virginia Rails and should be disregarded (see Kellogg 1962). The report of Black Rails nesting in Chatham in 1884–1885 should not be rejected; however, no competent ornithologist ever saw the birds. Griscom and Snyder (1955) mention five specimens of Black Rails for Massachusetts, two of which were extant at the BMS in 1955; the dates of the specimens spanned 16 May 1904–26 August 1920. Griscom, Emery, and several others flushed a Black Rail at Newburyport, in the "Plum Bush" marshes, near the airport, 31 August 1945. The only records since then are: 1, Rockport, 22 April 1958 (Kieran); 1, Chatham, 13 September 1959 (Freeland, Bachrach); 1 picked up freshly dead in a backyard, Nantucket, 31 March 1978 (Bartlett, specimen to Maria Mitchell Association). A rail, very likely this species, was heard calling "kickee-doo" in the Rowley Marshes before dawn, 24 May 1976 (Heil et al).

# Clapper Rail  *Rallus longirostris*

**Range:** Nearctic and Neotropical; breeds, in eastern North America, along the Atlantic and Gulf coasts from Massachusetts south to southern Florida and west to southern Texas; also in the West Indies, Mexico, and South America. Winters regularly north to New Jersey.

**Status:** Rare breeder and uncommon but regular visitor.

**Breeding:** Clapper Rails have been known to breed in Massachusetts since at least 1955. Confirmed nesting records are as follows: 1 pair and 10 young, Yarmouthport, 3 July 1955 (Robbins et al); 1 nest with 10 eggs, Barnstable, 17 June 1956 (Hill); 1 nest with 10 eggs, Eastham, 26 June 1956 (Clem et al); 1 female with 2 young, Plum Island, 26 August 1957 (Eldredge); 1 pair with 4 young, Ipswich, 20 July 1960 (Wood et al); 1 adult with 3 young, Nantucket, July 1974 (Andrews, Veit). Six birds were heard calling in Barnstable during June 1976 (Pease). *Egg dates:* 17–26 June.

**Nonbreeding:** Clapper Rails have occurred regularly in Massachusetts since at least 1949. Most of the records probably involve nonbreeding wanderers because the largest numbers recorded are always in fall and early winter. The Clapper Rail is especially rare away from the immediate coast, but there is one inland record for Massachusetts: 1, Hardwick, 4 September 1933 (fide Griscom & Snyder 1955). *Maxima:* 7 +, South Wellfleet, 16 October 1976 (Jackson, Stymeist); 7, Eastham, 3 January 1954 (Cape Cod CBC). There are fewer than twenty records of Clapper Rails during January and February in Massachusetts, including birds north to Gloucester—e.g., 2, 8 January 1967 (SSBC); a maximum of 7, southeastern coastal plain, January 1974 (BOEM).

# King Rail  *Rallus elegans*

**Range:** Nearctic and Neotropical; breeds, in North America, in lowlands from southeastern North Dakota, central Michigan, and Massachusetts south to Texas and Florida. Winters north irregularly to Long Island, Massachusetts, and southern Illinois.

**Status:** Rare and secretive breeder; possibly extirpated. Rare migrant and winter visitor or resident.

**Breeding:** The confirmed breeding records of King Rails in Massachusetts, which are the northernmost on the Atlantic Seaboard, are as follows: 1 pair seen with a brood of young, Sandwich, 1880 (Jones); 2 adults and 1 immature, Pontoosuc Inlet, Pittsfield, 11 June–13 September 1948 (Vreeland et al); 2 adults and 2 immatures, Pontoosuc Inlet, Pittsfield, 19 May–11 August 1949 (Vreeland et al); 1 pair with 9 chicks, Newburyport, 11–15 July 1953 (deWindt et al); 1 pair and 1 young, Pontoosuc Inlet, Pittsfield, 25 July 1954 (Schumacher); 1 adult and 5 young, Newburyport, 1956 (deWindt); 1 adult with 4 chicks, Rowley, 21 July 1960 (deWindt); 2 pairs, Newburyport, 1961 (fide Emery); 1 adult with 3 chicks, Lynnfield, 15 May 1963 (Thurston); 1 adult and 1 chick, Wayland, 8 August 1965 (King); 1 adult and 7 young, Lakeville, 17 July 1976 (Turner); 1 adult with 1 juvenile, South Wellfleet, 25 July 1979 (Heil).

Breeding has not been confirmed since 1979, but calling birds were recorded during the summer at Plum Island in the late 1960s to mid-1970s; at Wellfleet Bay Wildlife Sanctuary in 1964 (Bailey); at West Harwich (3) in 1974 (Nikula); in Marshfield from the 1970s irregularly to the present (VO); and in the salt marshes of Plum Island and Woodbridge Island, Newburyport, 29–30 June 1977 (Heil). Because reports of calling birds in suitable habitat have steadily declined during the past ten years, and because much of the habitat in which they previously bred is no longer suitable, it is possible that King Rails no longer breed in Massachusetts. *Egg dates:* Uncertain; most probably in late May and June.

**Nonbreeding:** King Rails occasionally appear during spring and fall migration in locations where they do not breed. Such records give some suggestion as to when these birds migrate. Spring records: 1, Springfield, 3–10 April 1954 (Phinney et al); 1 caught by a Northern Harrier, Orleans, 10 April 1977 (Nikula, Goodrich); 1, GMNWR, 21–23 April 1977 (Walton). Fall records: 1, Monomoy, 29 October 1967 (Bailey); 1, Monomoy, 1 September 1974 (Petersen); several records of single birds, 29 August–November.

Griscom and Snyder (1955) mention 7 specimens of King Rails from Cape Cod during winter in addition to the following records: 1, Cambridge, 30 December 1896 (Hill, MCZ #236948); 1 trapped, North Truro, February 1892 (Hill 1965); 1, Ellisville, 20 January 1903 (fide Griscom & Snyder 1955); 1, Sandwich, 14 February 1919 (Hill 1965); 1, Scituate, 28 January 1968 (Higginbotham); 1, North Eastham, 28 December 1968 (Alexander et al); 1, Cohasset, 30 December 1968 (Hancock et al); 1, Horn Pond, Woburn, 16 January 1971 (Petersen et al); 1, Plymouth, 20 February 1973 (Petersen, Sorrie, et al); 1, Plymouth, 23 February 1974 (Petersen, Sorrie, et al); 1, Fort Hill, Eastham, 30 January–16 February 1975 (Forster et al).

## Virginia Rail   *Rallus limicola*

**Range:** Nearctic and Neotropical; breeds, in North America, from southern British Columbia and Nova Scotia south to California and North Carolina. In the eastern United States, winters along the coast north to Massachusetts.

**Status:** Fairly common breeder; fairly common migrant and rare winter resident.

**Breeding:** Virginia Rails are patchily distributed in Massachusetts, according to the distribution of freshwater marshes. The only significant concentrations are in northeastern Essex County, the Sudbury River valley, and Berkshire County. Selected estimates of population size are as follows: 30–35 pairs, Berkshire County, 1977 (McNair 1978); 8 nests, Wayland, July 1955 (Morgan); 15 pairs, Concord, June 1959 (Gardler). In addition, there is probably a minimum of 75 pairs in Essex County, judging from the number of birds regularly heard calling at various locations there. Breeding has also been confirmed at Marshfield, Monomoy, and West Harwich, and there are scattered reports of single pairs elsewhere in the state. Virginia Rails are less specific in their habitat requirements than either King Rails or Soras—both of which require extensive and uninterrupted stands of cattails. *Egg dates:* 12 May–18 July.

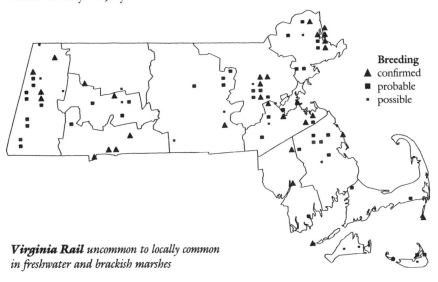

**Breeding**
▲ confirmed
■ probable
· possible

*Virginia Rail uncommon to locally common in freshwater and brackish marshes*

**Nonbreeding:** Reports of migrant Virginia Rails are uncommon away from known breeding localities. Nesting birds probably occasionally arrive on territory by late March—e.g., 2, Marshfield, 27 March 1976 (Petersen), although peak numbers are not recorded until late April. During September and October, Virginia Rails are occasionally seen in atypical locations— e.g., sand dunes, parking lots, flying in from the ocean, etc. The maximum fall count is: 26, Monomoy, 10–13 September 1966 (Baird). The population that winters on Cape Cod, Nantucket, and Martha's Vineyard arrives during October. *Winter maxima:* 17, Nantucket CBC, 3 January 1981; 14, West Harwich, December 1973 (Nikula); 4–5, South Peabody, 8–23 January 1978 (Heil). Winter survival until at least February has been proven several times at West Harwich, Nantucket, Cambridge, and South Peabody.

# Sora  *Porzana carolina*

**Range:** Nearctic; breeds from British Columbia and MacKenzie east to Nova Scotia and south to California and Maryland. Winters from the southeastern United States south to northern South America.

**Status:** Rare breeder and winter resident; common fall and uncommon spring migrant.

**Breeding:** The breeding population of Soras has decreased during the last several decades, concurrently with the deterioration of extensive cattail marshes. They are now largely restricted as breeders to Essex County (Plum Island, Lynnfield, Rowley), the Sudbury River valley (GMNWR, Sudbury River marshes), Marshfield (Cherry Hill Conservation Area), West Bridge-water (West Meadows Wildlife Management Area), and to the few other suitable cattail marshes remaining in the state. Calling birds were present at the south end of Monomoy during the summers of 1983 and 1984 (Nikula, Holt, et al), but breeding was not confirmed. *Egg dates:* 20 May–11 June.

**Nonbreeding:** The Sora is more northerly in its breeding distribution than the Virginia Rail and is more highly migratory. Soras generally arrive in Massachusetts by late April—earliest, 4, Sudbury, 26 March 1966 (Dalton)— with peak numbers in mid-May. *Spring maximum:* 20–25, Whitman, 15 May 1960 (Higginbotham). In fall, Soras gather in huge numbers in freshwater marshes during migration prior to their southward exodus in September. Until the early 1960s, the rice marshes along the Merrimack River in West Newbury supported vast aggregations of migrants in early fall. The conditions have changed there, so Soras no longer occur in such large numbers;

*While the draining and degradation of wetlands has precipitated the decline of several species of Massachusetts marsh birds, the **Virginia Rail** remains fairly common in suitable habitat.*  ▷

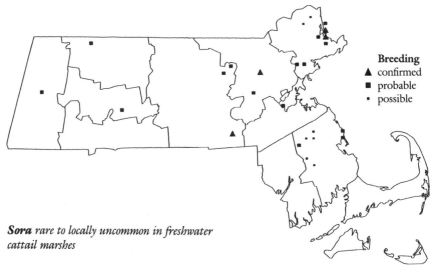

Breeding
▲ confirmed
■ probable
• possible

**Sora** *rare to locally uncommon in freshwater cattail marshes*

but smaller counts have been made along the North River in Hanover in recent years. **Fall maxima:** 1,500, West Newbury, 16 September 1958 (Gardler, Freeland); 1,000 +, West Newbury, 16–17 September 1961 (deWindt); 250, West Newbury, 10 September 1962 (deWindt); 50, Hanover, 9 September 1980 (Petersen); 30, GMNWR, 20 September 1980 (Stymeist).

Soras are less hardy than Virginia Rails, but individuals have occasionally survived the winter in Massachusetts in sections of marshes that remain unfrozen. Five were present in Harwich throughout January 1974 (Nikula), and single birds have been noted in midwinter a number of times at the Concord sewer bed outlet at GMNWR—e.g., 15 January 1978 (Walton)— and at a small, spring-fed marsh along Route 133 in Ipswich (VO).

## Purple Gallinule  *Porphyrula martinica*

**Range:** Nearctic and Neotropical; breeds, in North America, from southern Texas and southern Florida north to southwestern Tennessee and coastal South Carolina, with additional breeding sites in Kentucky, Maryland, and Delaware. Winters in peninsular Florida, southern Louisiana, and southern Texas.

**Status:** Rare visitor: at least 46 records.

**Occurrence:** The Purple Gallinule is the globe-trotter among North American rails, having occurred as far afield as Great Britain, South Georgia, Tristan da Cunha, South Africa (on twelve occasions), and Newfoundland. The specimens, photographs, and sight records from Massachusetts since 1955 are concentrated in April, May, and September, but birds have also occurred as late as January and February: e.g., 1, Pittsfield, 12 February 1964

(Kirchner, specimen to Berkshire Museum); 1, Morris Island, Chatham, 25 January 1979 (Reynolds).

The ages of the birds that occur in Massachusetts, adults in spring and immatures in fall, indicate that these birds derive from North American breeding populations. The possible future breeding of this species in Massachusetts should not be discounted. At least two different birds were present at Great Meadows National Wildlife Refuge in Concord during 1980–1983, and pairs have been recorded at Enfield (1888) and Boxford (1897) (Griscom & Snyder 1955).

## Common Moorhen   *Gallinula chloropus*

**Range:** Cosmopolitan; breeds, in eastern North America, from central Minnesota, southern Quebec, and Massachusetts south to Texas and Florida. Winters along the coast north to southern New Jersey, more rarely to Massachusetts.

**Status:** Uncommon to rare local breeder and fall migrant; rare in winter.

**Breeding:** Common Moorhens are restricted to cattail marshes bordering large freshwater ponds. Consequently, they are rather local and their numbers are decreasing in the state. Since 1970, breeding has been confirmed at Plum Island, Lynnfield, Peabody, Great Meadows National Wildlife Refuge in Concord, Wayland, Brookfield, Longmeadow, Pittsfield, South Egremont, West Harwich, and Nantucket. *Summer maxima:* 10 pairs, GMNWR, June 1959 (Gardler); 17 adults and 3 immatures, Plum Island, 4 August 1968 (Forster, Petersen). *Egg dates:* 22 May–17 July.

**Nonbreeding:** Moorhens are most numerous at such localities as Plum Island and Great Meadows National Wildlife Refuge during fall, when local breeding populations are augmented by migrants. *Fall maxima:* 60, Plum Island, 23 September 1973 (Petersen, Forster); 25, GMNWR, 21 September 1968 (Blodget); 19, Lynnfield, 5–11 September 1960 (Dillaway). *Winter maximum:* 6, Harwich, throughout January 1974 (and two still present 19 March) (Nikula). In recent years, a few moorhens have survived the winter on Nantucket and at West Harwich.

## American Coot   *Fulica americana*

**Range:** Nearctic; breeds throughout much of North America east to southeastern Quebec, western New Jersey, central Illinois, western Mississippi, and western Louisiana; also in southern Florida, with isolated breeding records on the Atlantic Coast northeast to Massachusetts. Winters in the southern United States, north to southeastern Massachusetts, Kentucky, Missouri, and Kansas.

**Status:** Has bred occasionally at Plum Island and in the Sudbury River valley. Local and irregularly abundant fall migrant and uncommon winter resident.

**Breeding:** Other than a pair of coots seen on Cheshire Reservoir, 21 June 1892 (McNair 1978), there is little evidence of coots breeding in Massachusetts until 1959. Since then, there are the following confirmed breeding records: 3 young and 5 eggs found, Concord, 16 May 1959 (Seamans, Bates); confirmed nesting at GMNWR annually from 1959 until 1966; 1 pair with 2 young, Sudbury, 27 May 1965 (Dalton). At Plum Island, 3 adults with 4 young were seen on 9 June 1968 (Powell, Argues), and nesting was confirmed annually there through 1978. Two adults were seen at Long Pond, Nantucket, 11 June 1969 (Petersen), and breeding was confirmed there at least once during the 1970s (Andrews, pers. comm.). *Egg date:* 16 May.

**Nonbreeding:** Coots are most numerous on the larger ponds of eastern and southeastern Massachusetts during late October and November. The number that remain to spend the winter depends on the amount of ice cover on the larger ponds. Numbers of fall migrants have declined considerably during the last fifteen to twenty years. *Maxima:* 2,000, Lakeville, 19 November 1975 (Maxim); 1,000, Cambridge, 5 November 1966 (BBC); 750, Fall River, 11 December 1975 (Athearn); 250, GMNWR, 22 November 1964 (Mazzarese); 240, Central Valley Lakes, Berkshire County, 7 November 1971 (Gagnon). *Winter maxima:* 268, Plymouth, 2 January 1988 (VO); 130, Eastham, 1 February 1976 (BBC, Baines); 125, Plymouth, 8 December 1985 (Petersen); 35, Lynn, 28 February 1978 (Heil).

# Sandhill Crane  *Grus canadensis*

**Range:** Nearctic; three disjunct breeding populations: *G. c. canadensis* of arctic Canada and Siberia; *G. c. tabida* of the interior; and *G. c. pratensis*, resident in peninsular Florida. The two migratory races winter mainly in California, Texas, and New Mexico.

**Status:** Rare visitor; increasing steadily since 1955.

**Occurrence:** The first Sandhill Crane to be recorded in Massachusetts this century appeared on outer Cape Cod, 1 September–24 October 1955 (Isleib, Smart, et al). Approximately half of the existing Sandhill Crane reports fall between September and October, and the rest are rather evenly scattered throughout the year. It is unclear from which of the populations (arctic or interior) the Massachusetts records derive, because both races have been collected in the Northeast (AOU 1957).

Selected records from 1975 to 1983 include: 1, Eastham, 6 January–early April 1975 (Campbell et al); 1, Nantucket, 9–24 April 1975 (Connor, Andrews); 1, South Plymouth, 29 May 1975 (Anderson); 1 immature, Bridgewater, 20 January 1977 (Timberlake et al); 1, Plymouth Beach, 28 May 1977 (MBO); 1, Katama, Martha's Vineyard, 25 July–8 August 1977 (Daniels); 1, Penikese Island, 26 August 1977 (Chambers); 1, Danvers, Middleton, and Beverly, 8 January–23 March 1979 (Heil et al); 1 immature, Nantucket, 8–22 October 1980 (Bennett, Andrews, Veit, et al); 1, Andover, Plum Island, 2–4 October 1982 (Kimball, Darling); 1, Chatham, 18–20 December 1983 (Laux, Goodrich, et al). The dates of some of these sightings suggest that the same bird may have been noted in more than one location. Since 1983, the Sandhill Crane has been of nearly annual occurrence in Massachusetts.

# Black-bellied Plover   *Pluvialis squatarola*

**Range:** Holarctic; in the New World, breeds in the high Arctic south to the Yukon River and Southampton Island and, in eastern North America, winters south along the coast from Massachusetts to Argentina and Chile.

**Status:** Locally abundant migrant on the coast; rare inland. One of the most regular of the summering nonbreeding shorebirds; occasionally survives the winter on the southeastern coastal plain.

**Occurrence:** The Black-bellied Plover is one of the most numerous shorebirds in Massachusetts and one whose status in the state has not changed appreciably since the 1930s. The species occurs in comparable abundance both on the mud flats of Essex County and on the sand flats of Cape Cod. The first spring arrivals appear in mid-April—e.g., 250, Eastham, 24 April 1960 (Fox, Smart). In this season some individuals may be local winterers or migrants from areas only a short distance farther south. The majority of migrants do not arrive until early May, with peak counts in the middle and last part of the month averaging between 2,000 and 3,000 birds. *Spring maxima:* 6,500+, Newburyport, 19 May 1976 (Moore & Light 1976); 4,100, Newburyport, 25 May 1977 (Veit, Perkins); 3,500, Monomoy, 21 May 1943 (Griscom et al). Usually a few yearling Black-bellied Plovers, mostly in first alternate plumage, spend the summer months in Massachusetts. In this season flocks seldom exceed 25 birds, so the following maxima at Monomoy are exceptional: 700, 27 June 1974 (Goodrich, Nikula); 125, 23 June 1975 (Bryant); 85, 25 June 1969 (Blodget).

Southward-moving adult Black-bellied Plovers reach peak concentrations during the second and third weeks of August, when counts at Newburyport and Monomoy average between 1,500 and 2,000 birds. A second and more extended peak consisting of both adults and juveniles occurs during the last half of September. *Fall maxima:* 4,000+, Monomoy, 21 September 1976 (Veit, Perkins); 3,000, North Beach, Chatham, 30 September 1950 (Bailey); 2,500, Monomoy, 2–7 September 1966 (Petersen).

The southeastern coastal plain of Massachusetts represents the normal northern limit of the winter range of this species, and a few individuals usually manage to survive the entire season—e.g., 30, North Chatham, 12 March 1960 (Mosher); 21, Chatham, 24 February 1973 (Nikula). *Winter maxima:* 80, Nauset, Eastham, 1 January 1978 (Goodrich); 52, Cape Cod CBC, 3 January 1960. The species is unusual in Essex County in winter.

Black-bellied Plovers are uncommon away from the immediate coast, and inland occurrences are chiefly confined to the peak migration periods. Ordinarily, only 1 to 3 birds are seen at interior locations, such as Great Meadows National Wildlife Refuge, along the Connecticut River, and at muddy sewer beds and reservoirs anywhere in the state. Inland spring records are less frequent than in fall, although the species is of almost annual occurrence in Worcester County and along the Connecticut River. *Spring maxima* (inland): 9, Lancaster, 12 May 1977 (Merriman); 8, Bolton, 17 May 1978 (Crompton); 8, Lancaster, 20 May 1979 (Carroll, Lynch); 5, Hadley, 17 May 1982 (Surner). *Fall maxima* (inland): 15, Clinton, 6 August 1971 (Blodget); 14, Onota Lake, Pittsfield, 2 November 1949 (Hendricks); 10, Onota Lake, Pittsfield, 25 October 1952 (Hendricks); 7, Sudbury, 18 September 1958 (Armstrong).

# Lesser Golden-Plover   *Pluvialis dominica*

**Range:** Nearctic; breeds across arctic Canada from Alaska to Devon Island south to Denali National Park, Alaska; Churchill, Manitoba; and southern Baffin Island; winters on the pampas of temperate South America.

**Status:** Rare but regular spring migrant. Irregularly fairly common to very common fall migrant, with largest numbers occurring during and after easterly winds accompanied by rain and fog.

**Occurrence:** Lesser Golden-Plovers and Eskimo Curlews were among the shorebirds that were most popular with New England sportsmen and market gunners during the latter part of the 19th century. Nantucket was one of the premier gunning localities on the Atlantic Coast. Its offshore location made it an ideal landfall for migrant plovers and curlews forced toward shore during easterly storms (Griscom & Folger 1948). Lesser Golden-Plovers periodically occurred abundantly there during the mid-1800s—e.g., 7,000–8,000 shot in one day, 29 August 1863; 500 shot, 28 August 1886 (Griscom & Folger op cit)—but, by 1898, the species seemed to be headed for extinction due mainly to overhunting, both on the East Coast in fall and in the Mississippi River valley in spring. With full protection, the species has now made a dramatic recovery.

In spring, golden-plovers migrate north through the Great Plains to the Arctic; whereas in fall they fly southeastward from their breeding grounds to the coasts of Labrador and Newfoundland, and then southeast over the Atlantic to South America. As a consequence of this migration strategy, many of the Lesser Golden-Plovers found in Massachusetts in fall are juveniles, which seem to follow the coastline more closely than the adults. When they do alight in Massachusetts, they prefer dry upland areas such as plowed fields, golf courses, and the uppermost reaches of sandy beaches, where they apparently feed upon crickets and other insects and vegetable matter, such as grass seeds and berries (Mackay 1891). Nearly every spring since 1955, one or two Lesser Golden-Plovers have been recorded at coastal locations between late March and early June. *Extreme dates:* 1, Newburyport, 14 March 1992 (Petersen); 1, Salisbury, 20 March 1980 (Merriman, VO); 1, Plum Island, 24 March 1979 (Clayton et al). In addition, there are several records for early summer of single birds, which are mostly nonbreeding yearlings—e.g., 1, Monomoy, 23 June 1965 (Bailey); 1, Plum Island, 25 June 1966 (Pertzoff); 1, Marblehead, 2 July 1967 (Leahy); 1 in full alternate plumage, Monomoy, 1 July 1970 (Harris); 1, Plymouth Beach, 29 June 1974 (Petersen).

In fall, single birds or small flocks of up to 15 or 20 are often seen flying overhead or roosting among flocks of Black-bellied Plovers. *Fall maxima:* 233, Hadley, 17 September 1969 (Yenlin); 112+, Edgartown, 7 September 1962 (Chalif, Sears); 100, Monomoy, 3 September 1972 (Donahue).

**Remarks:** The Greater Golden-Plover, *P. apricaria*, occurs with some regularity in spring in Newfoundland (see AB 35: 978–9). Although the species might reasonably be expected to occur in Massachusetts under similar circumstances, all spring golden-plovers, of recent years at least, have been carefully scrutinized and determined to be *P. dominica*.

# Wilson's Plover   *Charadrius wilsonia*

**Range:** Nearctic; breeds along the Gulf and Atlantic coasts of the United States north to southern New Jersey; rarely wanders north to Nova Scotia. Winters on the Gulf Coast and south to northern South America.

**Status:** Very rare, but almost annual visitor.

**Occurrence:** There are over twenty-five records of Wilson's Plovers in Massachusetts, spanning five months from: 1, South Dartmouth, 19 April 1976 (Veit) to 2, Plum Island, 21 September 1944 (Griscom). All records are from sandy beaches at the immediate coast, with records concentrated in late May and June or following hurricanes during August and September. Most records are of single birds, with the exception of the previously mentioned 1944 record and: 2, Menemsha Pond, Martha's Vineyard, 15 September 1949 (Wakeman). Since 1955, the majority of records have fallen in the period 20 May–10 June. The only fall occurrences that did not follow the passage of tropical storms are: 1, 25 August 1934 and 1, 28 August 1941, both at Chilmark, Martha's Vineyard (Emerson). Massachusetts specimens include: 1, Ipswich, 12 August 1873 (MCZ #291968); 1, Ipswich, 8 May 1904 (PMS #7464); 1, Truro, 26 June 1929 (MCZ #142165).

## Common Ringed Plover  *Charadrius hiaticula*

**Range:** Holarctic; breeds in North America in western Alaska and on Ellesmere, Bylot, and eastern Baffin islands. Winters from the British Isles and southern Eurasia south to southern Africa.

**Status:** Vagrant: one sight record.

**Occurrence:** The single Massachusetts record of this widespread Holarctic plover pertains to a bird in juvenal plumage at North Monomoy, 5 September 1990 (Perkins, Prescott, et al). Initially picked out and identified by its call notes, the bird was carefully observed, described, and photographed at close range (photos and written documentation on file at Massachusetts Audubon). Comparisons of photographs and field notes with museum specimens further reinforced details of facial and dorsal feather patterns that are probably species specific for birds in juvenal plumage (Perkins, ms in preparation).

## Semipalmated Plover  *Charadrius semipalmatus*

**Range:** Nearctic; breeds from the southern arctic tundra south to the Magdalen Islands and Nova Scotia on the Atlantic Coast; winters, on the East Coast, from South Carolina south to Argentina.

**Status:** Very common to abundant spring and very abundant fall migrant at favorable coastal localities. Uncommon but regular inland in both spring and fall.

**Occurrence:** Semipalmated Plovers are conspicuous and abundant migrants at favored stopover sites such as Newburyport Harbor, Scituate, and Monomoy. Early spring migrants include: 1, Eastham, 12 April 1955 (Hill, Petty); 1, Plum Island, 28 April 1979 (Heil); 2, Chatham, 30 April 1973 (Nikula). All early arrival records have been carefully screened to avoid possible confusion with either Piping Plovers or Killdeer. Spring maxima in mid-May usually peak at about 200 +, with the following exceptions being noteworthy: 550, Essex County, 4 June 1940 (Griscom); 500, Essex County, 13 May 1945 (Griscom). Inland, the species is found annually in spring—e.g., 12–15, Longmeadow, 25 May 1903 (Morris); 6–8, Bolton, 22 May 1983 (Lynch, Carroll).

Fall migration normally has peaks of 1,000 to 1,500 adult birds during the first week of August at the favored localities. *Fall maxima:* 5,000, Monomoy, 4 August 1955 (Smart, Griscom); 4,000, Quincy, 6–21 August 1954 (Higginbotham). Juveniles have a more protracted migration and are common from late August through September. Inland, the species is of regular occurrence in fall—i.e., 30, GMNWR, 1 September 1969 (Albee, VO); 22, Pittsfield Sewer Beds, 22 August 1938 (Hendricks); 17, Princeton, 19 August 1964 (McMenemy); 15, Quabbin, 27 August 1972 (Stone). In August of 1938, when conditions were said to be ideal, up to 25 per day were seen in the Sudbury River valley (Griscom). By mid-November most migrants have departed, but there are at least eight December records: e.g., 1, Eastham, 21 December 1980 (Clapp, Veit); 1, Manomet, 23 December 1975 (Sorrie); 2, Scituate CBC, 27 December 1967; 1, North Beach, Chatham, 28 December 1969 (Petersen).

## Piping Plover   *Charadrius melodus*

**Range:** Nearctic; breeds along the coast from the Gulf of St. Lawrence to Virginia and also along the shores of inland lakes west to central Alberta. Winters in the Greater Antilles and on the southeastern coast of the United States north to South Carolina.

**Status:** Locally uncommon and declining breeder at the coast; uncommon to common migrant.

**Breeding:** In Massachusetts, Piping Plovers breed on extensive sandy beaches, often in association with Least Terns. They are particularly susceptible to disturbance by off-road vehicles and other human activity, as well as to nest predation. Collectively, these factors are undoubtedly to blame for the population decrease since 1900. In 1986, the U. S. Fish and Wildlife

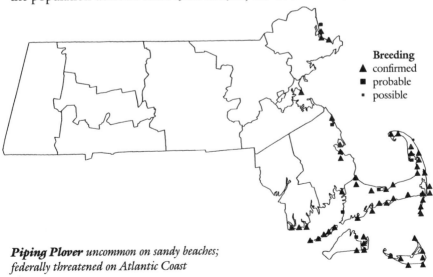

**Breeding**
▲ confirmed
■ probable
· possible

*Piping Plover uncommon on sandy beaches; federally threatened on Atlantic Coast*

Service listed the Piping Plover as a threatened species on the Atlantic Coast. Recent protective efforts as part of a recovery program have included the use of fences and signs to exclude humans and predators from nesting areas. Maximum counts of nesting birds include: 25 with 7 young, Monomoy, 3 June 1962 (Gardler); 25 with 6 young, New Island, Eastham, 7 July 1979 (Heil); 21, Plymouth Beach, 27 June 1972 (Gagnon); 20 +, Plum Island, 21 June 1971 (Dwelley), 13 pairs, Coast Guard Beach, Eastham, 1986. In 1991, the Massachusetts breeding population numbered 158 pairs (fide Blodget).

**Nonbreeding:** Breeding Piping Plovers usually arrive by late March. Early dates include: 1, Waquoit Bay, Mashpee, 13 March 1938 (Taber); 8, Chatham, 19 March 1959 (Wellman). A maximum of 50 +, North Beach, Chatham, 30 April 1973 (Nikula) undoubtedly included migrants bound for more distant breeding localities. Fall peak counts between mid-August and late September probably involve migrants from the interior, as well as from the coastal population. *Fall maxima:* 100, Nauset, Eastham, 19 July 1975 (Nikula); 75, Monomoy, 1 September 1976 (Veit, Moore); 70, Monomoy, 8 July 1972 (Martin, VO); 52 +, Monomoy, on the unusually late date of 30 September 1973 (Veit, Stymeist, Russell). Although Piping Plovers are very rare in winter, a handful of midwinter records suggests that a few occasionally survive the entire season in Massachusetts, much as they do on Long Island, New York (Buckley, pers. comm.). Selected records include: 2, Orleans, 2 January 1972 (Petersen); 2, North Beach, Chatham, 12 January 1971 (Bailey et al); 6, Chatham, 6 February 1954 (Binford); 3 collected, Orleans, 21 February 1954 (Morgan). In addition, there are at least five additional January and February records. The only inland record is: 1, GMNWR, Concord, 20 July 1975 (Forster).

# Killdeer   *Charadrius vociferus*

**Range:** Nearctic; breeds throughout temperate North America north, on the Atlantic Coast, to western Newfoundland; winters from southern New England (rarely) and Ohio south to the Greater Antilles, with the highest densities along the southern Atlantic and Gulf coasts.

**Status:** Uncommon and widespread local breeder on the mainland and Martha's Vineyard; uncommon on Cape Cod and Nantucket. Fairly common spring and common fall migrant.

**Breeding:** Killdeer nest in a variety of open habitats, especially airports, golf courses, agricultural fields, waste areas, and, with increasing frequency,

*As the battle for preeminence on barrier beaches rages, the resilient* **Piping Plover** *continues its struggle for survival, even in the face of ecological adversity. Fortunately, many conservation agencies are working together to ensure the survival of this gentle shorebird.*

flat gravel rooftops. The timing of the arrival of Killdeer in the spring seems to be influenced by weather conditions. In mild seasons, when there is little snow cover, they appear by late February, but in cold seasons the first arrivals may not be reported until a month later. *Summer maxima:* 146, Pittsfield, 20 July 1955 (Schumacher); 104, Worcester, 25 July 1974 (Mierzejewski); 96, Spencer, 25 July 1951 (Crompton); 48, Fitchburg, 3 July 1980 (Jenkins); 30 families, June 1961, Newburyport area (deWindt).

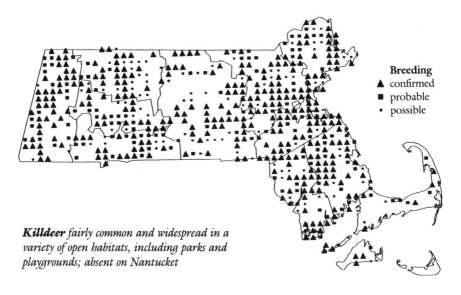

**Breeding**
▲ confirmed
■ probable
· possible

*Killdeer fairly common and widespread in a variety of open habitats, including parks and playgrounds; absent on Nantucket*

**Nonbreeding:** The first arrivals of spring usually appear during early March, but occasionally earlier, e.g., 1, Worcester, 18 February 1981 (Babbitt); 4, Pittsfield, 21 February 1954 (Schumacher). Ordinarily, maximum numbers of 25 to 40 are seen during the first two weeks of April. The highest Killdeer counts occur in fall, with peaks often occurring in October. *Fall maxima:* 250 +, Westport, 23 October, 1968 (Garrey); 200, East Bridgewater, 7 October 1978 (Petersen). Several counts of 100 to 150 during October exist from both the coast and the Connecticut River valley. On Nantucket, the highest recorded total is: 40, 15 October 1980 (Veit). Flocks of Killdeer occasionally arrive in Massachusetts during November, well after the local breeders have departed, and a great flight was reported on Cape Cod, 25–26 November 1888 (Chadbourne 1889), when hundreds were observed arriving from over the ocean.

During mild, snowless winters, many Killdeer remain late into the fall, and some actually survive the winter. The sum of January totals has ranged from zero in several seasons to 48 in 1977 (BOEM). Midwinter maximum: 6, Gloucester, 6 February 1972 (Weissberg, VO).

# Mountain Plover   *Charadrius montanus*

**Range:** Nearctic; breeds from southern Alberta, northern Montana, and northeastern North Dakota south through Wyoming, Colorado, and western Kansas to southeastern New Mexico and western Texas. Winters from central California and southern Arizona south to northern Mexico.

**Status:** Vagrant: one record.

**Occurrence:** The single Massachusetts specimen was fortuitously collected from a flock of Black-bellied Plovers at Chatham, 28 October 1916 (Crowell, see Brooks 1917).


# American Oystercatcher   *Haematopus palliatus*

**Range:** Nearctic and Neotropical; breeds along the Atlantic Coast of North America from Massachusetts to Louisiana and Texas and south through the Caribbean to northern South America. North American breeders winter mainly from southern Virginia to the Gulf Coast.

**Status:** Uncommon to fairly common, and steadily increasing, breeder; rare in winter.

**Breeding:** Regarded in 1955 as a rare vagrant from the south (Griscom & Snyder 1955) with only nine records during the 20th century. Since then, the breeding population of American Oystercatchers has steadily increased in Massachusetts as the species has expanded north from New Jersey through Long Island, New York (Bull 1964). On 29 June 1969, a nest with 3 eggs was found at Chappaquiddick, Martha's Vineyard, and a second nest was later found there in August (Schneider, Sears). These nestings represented the first 20th century breeding confirmations in Massachusetts. In 1970, 1 pair fledged 3 young at Monomoy (Bailey), and 2 adults were present all summer at Tuckernuck Island (Veit). Since that time, the American Oystercatcher population has expanded so that by 1990 over 50 pairs were breeding in Massachusetts, with the greatest concentrations on Monomoy and the Islands. By 1989, one to two pairs were nesting as far north as Boston Harbor.

American Oystercatchers usually nest on the open sand or on gravel ridges in salt marshes. Like Piping Plovers and Least Terns, oystercatchers are susceptible to disturbance by humans, spring storms, and predation by gulls, night-herons, and dogs. In spite of this, the species continues to increase within its known range and to expand northward.

**Nonbreeding:** The earliest arrival date is: 1, Muskeget Island, 10 March 1981 (Schurman). Occasionally, oystercatchers appear north of their known breeding range during spring, e.g., 2, Newburyport, 20 May 1979 (Petersen,

VO). Because American Oystercatchers do not currently breed north of Massachusetts, fall migrants from the north do not occur. Nonetheless, late summer gatherings of breeding adults and their young, usually on Monomoy, account for the largest counts of the year—e.g., 90, North Monomoy, 2 September 1990 (Nikula); 50 +, North Monomoy, 10 August 1986 (Nikula). Occasionally, lingering birds have occurred into early winter: 1, Nantucket, 13 January 1986 (Beattie); 1, Chatham, 28 December 1985 (Trull); 5, Orleans, 22 December 1985 (Forster).

## Black-necked Stilt  *Himantopus mexicanus*

**Range:** Nearctic and Neotropical; breeds in the western United States, in Central and South America, and locally along the southeast Atlantic Coast, north to Delaware. Winters from Florida south to northern South America.

**Status:** Vagrant: at least nineteen records.

**Occurrence:** Black-necked Stilts have appeared with increasing frequency in Massachusetts since 1970, with nearly all records occurring in May and June. In addition to two, old, undated specimens in the BMS (Griscom & Snyder 1955), the records include: 1, South Harwich, 27 May 1950 (Thompson, fide Bailey); 2, Plum Island, 5 June 1953 (Stanwood, Burnett); 2, Chilmark, Martha's Vineyard, 12 June 1954 (Bigelow); 1, Ipswich, 19–25 October 1969 (Garrett); 1, Newburyport, 7 June 1970 (Petersen); 1, Plum Island, 26 May–6 June 1972 (Forster, Conant); 2, Truro, 6 May 1973 (Bailey); 1, Martha's Vineyard, week of 1 September 1974 (Manwaring); 1, Nantucket, 12 June 1978 (Tiffney, Andrews); 1, Nantucket, 3–12 May 1979 (Andrews et al); 1, Ipswich, 24–29 May 1983 (Meyer); 2, Martha's Vineyard, 3–5 June 1983 (Laux); 1, East Boston, 25 May 1986 (Foley); 1, Nantucket, 21–29 June 1986 (Frost); 1, Nantucket, 16–31 May 1990 (Hayden); 1, Chatham, 27 May 1990 (Barlow); 1, Plum Island, 6–13 June 1990 (Zaremba, Hoye); 1, South Dartmouth, 8 July 1990 (Boucher).

## American Avocet  *Recurvirostra americana*

**Range:** Nearctic; breeds from British Columbia and Manitoba south to southern California and Texas; winters from California and Texas south to Guatemala, and also on the Atlantic Coast between North Carolina and Florida. Fall migrants are found along the Atlantic Coast from southern New Jersey to Florida.

**Status:** Rare but regular fall visitor; exceedingly rare in spring.

**Occurrence:** Prior to 1955, the American Avocet was recorded as a purely accidental straggler to New England. Griscom and Snyder (1955) and Bailey (1955) listed only five records for the state: 1 specimen, Lake Cochituate, Natick, 19 October 1880 (see Forbush 1925); 1 specimen, Salisbury, 23 May 1887 (Forbush op cit); 3 specimens, Ipswich, 13 September 1896 (in PMS); 1, Edgartown, 20 September 1933 (Edey); 1, Marshfield, 10 September 1935 (Hagar); 1 collected (believed to be the same bird), Sagamore, 11 September 1935 (Hagar 1936). Since that time, there have been numerous reports from such coastal localities as Newburyport, Eastham, and Wellfleet, primarily during August and September. This increase corresponds with a concurrent increase in the numbers of fall migrants noted on the southern Atlantic Coast. Unusually late sightings include: 1, Nauset, Eastham, 11–20 October 1976 (Butler et al); 1, Chatham, 27 October 1979 (Nikula, Heil); 1, Gay Head, Martha's Vineyard, 11–12 November 1967 (Petersen, Kenneally, Garrey).

There are only a few spring occurrences—e.g., 1, Newburyport, 11–15 May 1968 (Garrett et al); 1, Manomet, 18 May 1971 (Houghton et al); 1, Nantucket, 26 April 1977 (Andrews, Faunce); 1, South Dartmouth, 13 May 1987 (Lyons). The only inland record besides the Natick specimen cited above is: 1, Longmeadow, 18–24 August 1974 (Kellogg).

# Greater Yellowlegs   *Tringa melanoleuca*

**Range:** Nearctic; breeds in boreal Canada south to Quebec, Newfoundland, and northern Nova Scotia on the Atlantic Coast. Winters, on the Atlantic Coast, from Massachusetts (sporadically) and Long Island south to southern South America.

**Status:** Abundant migrant on the coast, and occasionally fairly common at suitable inland localities. Rare but regular in winter.

**Occurrence:** Greater Yellowlegs are primarily birds of mud flats and salt marshes. Peak numbers of spring migrants tend to occur during late April and early May. *Spring maxima* (all from Newburyport): 900, 16 May 1948 (fide Bailey); 800, 19 May 1946 (fide Bailey); 750, 15 May 1947 (fide Bailey); 600 +, 15 May 1974 (Veit); 500, 6 May 1980 (Heil). The first fall migrants appear in mid-July, but peak numbers are not reached until late August to late September at favored localities such as Newburyport Harbor, Eastham, and North Monomoy. *Fall maxima* (all from Newburyport): 1,000, 26 August 1944 (Snyder); 600, 26 September 1970 (Petersen). *Inland maxima:* 72, Bolton, 19 May 1967 (McMenemy); 61, Clinton, 16 August 1966 (Blodget); 33, Pittsfield, 8 October 1952 (Hendricks).

Greater Yellowlegs appear to move about continuously throughout the winter. Therefore, midwinter records of Greater Yellowlegs do not necessarily indicate that the birds spent the entire winter in any particular location.

Usually 1 or 2 birds per locality are reported during January, but by February the species is quite rare. *Winter maxima:* 19, eastern Massachusetts, January 1980 (including 4, Eastham, throughout February 1980) (VO); 25, Buzzards Bay CBC, 15 December 1979; 15, Cape Cod CBC, 16 December 1979. In severe winters, the laggards usually succumb or move farther south.

# Lesser Yellowlegs   *Tringa flavipes*

**Range:** Nearctic; breeds from central Alaska, northern Manitoba, northern Ontario, and central Quebec south to central British Columbia, central Saskatchewan, and southeastern Manitoba. Winters from the Gulf Coast states regularly north to coastal South Carolina and south to Chile and Argentina.

**Status:** Uncommon to fairly common spring and abundant fall migrant. Totals fluctuate considerably from year to year, especially in spring.

**Occurrence:** Lesser Yellowlegs prefer the uppermost reaches of salt marshes and are especially fond of marshes and salt meadows that are regularly mowed, such as those adjacent to Newburyport Harbor. They also routinely occur inland during spring and fall when suitable habitat conditions exist. In spring, most Lesser Yellowlegs migrate north through the Mississippi River valley and are thus rather scarce on the East Coast as far north as New England. In fall, they follow a southeasterly route over the Atlantic Ocean, in a manner similar to that of Lesser Golden-Plovers and Hudsonian Godwits. During the fall migration, Newburyport Harbor has historically been one of the most heavily used staging areas for this species on the eastern coast of North America.

Previous authors have suggested that progressively declining counts of migrant Lesser Yellowlegs from the northeastern United States during the 20th century reflect a population decline. Bull (1964) states that Lesser Yellowlegs have "slightly decreased within the last 25 years," and Hill (1965) speaks of a "decrease since 1942." They clearly suffered during the market gunning period (Stone 1937), but recovered afterward, and Forbush (1925–29) considered them "the most generally common of our shorebirds." Since the 1920s, the numbers of Lesser Yellowlegs seen in Massachusetts have varied considerably from year to year. Maximum counts of 2,000 to 5,000 adults were recorded in the Newburyport area during the late 1940s, the years 1955 to 1958, and in 1961. During those same years, however, much lower maxima were recorded in some years, e.g., 275, 29 July 1952 (Griscom). Recent maxima seem to have stabilized at about 1,000, usually during late July and early August. It is difficult to say whether this variation reflects changes in the Lesser Yellowlegs population size or changes in suitability of

Massachusetts habitats previously used by the birds. Extremely early spring arrivals are: 1, Newburyport, 12 March 1978 (Petersen); 1, South Hadley, 25 March 1964 (Hubley, VO); 1, Spencer, 27 March 1968 (McMenemy); 1, Truro, 28 March 1976 (Nikula). *Spring maxima:* 30 +, Newburyport, 1 May 1976 (Veit); 20, Newburyport, 10 May 1973 (Forster); 20 +, Wellfleet, 8 May 1976 (Goodrich); 5, Northampton, 12 May 1960 (Eliot). Rare on Cape Cod and the Islands in spring, despite a slight increase throughout the state since 1960.

*Fall maxima:* 4,000, Newburyport, 6 August 1947 (Griscom); 2,500, Newburyport, 18 July 1940 (Griscom); 2,500, Newburyport, 7 August 1941 (Griscom); 2,000, Newburyport, 4 August 1948 (Snyder); 1,300, Newburyport, 3 August 1976 (Veit, Moore); 1,100, Newburyport, 11 July 1977 (Veit); 960, Newburyport, 2 August 1980 (Forster). Lesser Yellowlegs are most common inland at sewer beds, flooded meadows, and plowed fields such as the Bolton Flats. Inland: 87, Worcester, 17 August 1948 (Crompton); 81, Worcester, 11 August 1974 (Mierzejewski); 64, Spencer, 16 September (Crompton); 47, Spencer, 5 September 1954 (Crompton); 45, Pittsfield, 25 July 1938 (Hendricks). Because the Worcester and Spencer sewer beds no longer operate, inland totals of Lesser Yellowlegs have decreased considerably.

## Spotted Redshank   *Tringa erythropus*

**Range:** Palearctic; breeds on the tundra of northern Eurasia; winters from the Mediterranean basin to eastern China. Regular vagrant to western Alaska; accidental elsewhere in North America.

**Status:** Vagrant: two records.

**Occurrence:** There are two records of this handsome tringid in Massachusetts, both photographically documented. The first record was an adult in prebasic molt at Plum Island, 28 July 1981 (Cloughley, photos at MAS). The second individual, also an adult in changing plumage, remained at the WBWS in South Wellfleet from 31 July to 19 August 1990 (Smith, Kaufman, VO) and was photographed by many individuals (AB 44: 1114).

## Solitary Sandpiper   *Tringa solitaria*

**Range:** Nearctic; breeds in boreal forests from Alaska to Labrador and south on the Atlantic Coast to south-central Labrador. Winters primarily in South America, although stragglers have been found along the Gulf Coast.

**Status:** Fairly common migrant; most numerous in fall.

**Occurrence:** The best habitat for Solitary Sandpipers is the muddy shores of ponds, reservoirs, streambeds, and sewage ponds. They are less common in coastal situations than inland and are notably uncommon at traditional shorebird areas such as Monomoy. Early spring arrivals are: 1, Northampton, 3 April 1969 (Gagnon); 1, Bolton, 4 April 1974 (Forster). Most migrants move through in the first half of May, and the species becomes decidedly uncommon after May 15. Records spanning the period 26 May to 16 June very likely represent nonbreeding individuals. *Spring maxima:* 67, Hudson, 14 May 1990 (Salmela); 62, Millis, 15 May 1985 (Cassie); 20 +, Middleton, 12 May 1979 (McClellan); 16, Spencer, 20 May 1956 (Fleming); 12, Sudbury River valley, 20 May 1984 (Forster). The earliest fall report is: 1, Concord, 28 June 1957 (Gardler), with most migrants passing between mid-July and early October. *Fall maxima:* 51, Spencer, 17 August 1959 (Freeland); 51, Pittsfield, 3 August 1973 (Goodrich); 44, Pittsfield, 1 August 1954 (Schumacher). It is unusual to record more than six birds per day near the coast. Late dates include: 1, Mt. Auburn Cemetery, Cambridge, 28 November 1895 (Robinson, fide Brewster); 1, Holyoke, 13–21 November 1971 (Gagnon, Goodrich); 1, Holyoke, 21 November 1971 (Albertine, Goodrich); 1, Deerfield, 19 November 1948 (fide Bailey); 1 dead, Eastham, 14 November 1941 (fide Bailey). There are no December records.

**Subspecies:** The nominate race, *T. s. solitaria*, is of regular occurrence, while the western race, *T. s. cinnamomea*, which breeds in eastern Manitoba, has been collected in Massachusetts once, in August of an unspecified year (Conover 1944).

# Willet   *Catoptrophorus semipalmatus*

**Range:** Nearctic; nominate *C. s. semipalmatus* breeds along the Atlantic Coast from Nova Scotia to Florida and Texas; also in the Greater Antilles. Winters from the Gulf Coast states south to northern South America. The western subspecies, *C. s. inornatus*, breeds in western North America from Oregon and Manitoba south to California and South Dakota and winters primarily on the Pacific Coast from California to Chile; a few migrate southeast to the Atlantic Coast and winter along the Gulf Coast.

**Status:** Fairly common local breeder; fairly common to common migrant.

**Breeding:** Before 1880, *C. s. semipalmatus* bred along the length of the Atlantic Coast from Nova Scotia to Florida and was presumably a common breeder in salt marshes at such localities as Plum Island, Cape Cod, and the Islands. Willets were known to nest in New Bedford in 1842 (Audubon) and on Muskeget until 1869 and Penikese Island until 1877 (Brewer). They also probably bred in Ipswich in 1887 (Townsend 1905). Egging and shooting drastically reduced the population so that by the early 20th century there were no nesting pairs between Nova Scotia and New Jersey. This gap has gradually closed during the last 80 years, and Willets now breed from Long Island, New York, to Maine.

In July 1976, an adult with chicks was discovered at Monomoy (Forster et al), establishing the first breeding record in Massachusetts since 1877. Between 1977 and 1981, two pairs almost certainly nested at Plum Island, where the species is now well established (Heil et al); in 1978, three territorial pairs summered at Monomoy (Heil); and, in 1980, twenty adults and one chick were found there (Petersen, Nikula). In addition, territorial birds have recently been observed in Duxbury and Barnstable. Because of an abundance of habitat that seems to be suitable, Willets are continuing to increase as breeders in Massachusetts.

**Nonbreeding:** In spring, migrating Willets bound for Nova Scotia are regularly seen on Cape Cod and the Islands in late April, especially when they are grounded by rain or fog. In this season they are much more uncommon north of Boston, where from 1 to 6 are occasionally seen per day. The earliest arrival is: 1, Chatham, 19 March 1959 (Wellman). *Spring maxima:* 122, Chatham, 24 April 1980 (Nikula); 45, Edgartown, 27 April 1968 (Petersen, Forster); 25, Nauset, Eastham, 4 May 1961 (Drury); 21, Nantucket, 30 April 1979 (Litchfield); 20, Muskeget Island, 27 April 1945 (Andrews). Inland records, where the species is very rare, are: 1, West Peabody, 14 May 1966 (Hill); 1, Northampton, 19 May 1979 (Surner). There is a single spring record of *C. s. inornatus*, a female in alternate plumage collected at Monomoy, 21 April 1933 (Smith).

In fall, peak counts of migrating Willets occur during the last two weeks of August, although they are seen regularly into late October, particularly on the outer Cape. It is likely that the majority of fall migrants are of the western race, *C. s. inornatus*. Of the extant fall Massachusetts specimens, *C. s. inornatus* outnumbers *C. s. semipalmatus* 33 to 6. *Fall maxima:* 30, Nantucket, 4 August 1962 (Andrews); 20, Monomoy, August 1979 (VO) and 1980 (Nikula); 5, identifiably *C. s. inornatus*, Newburyport, 9 September 1979 (Heil). Willets are rare after late September; however, there are at least seven December records, including: 1, Nantucket CBC, 31 December 1967; 1, Long Island, Boston, 30 December 1966 (Kearney, VO). There are only two fall records from inland localities: 1, Spencer, 20 August 1947 (Crompton); 1, Dana, 2 October 1970 (Clark).

# Wandering Tattler   *Heteroscelus incanus*

**Range:** Nearctic and eastern Palearctic; breeds, in North America, along the Pacific Coast from Alaska to the Yukon and northern British Columbia;

winters along the Pacific Coast from southern California to Ecuador. Vagrant to eastern North America.

**Status:** Vagrant: one record.

**Occurrence:** A Wandering Tattler in alternate plumage was discovered and photographed at the south end of Monomoy Island, 25 May 1968 (Bailey) and was subsequently seen by Petersen, Forster, Kenneally, and Fox (photo at MAS ). The bird remained until 30 May. There are no other records for the Atlantic Coast, although the species has been recorded twice in the Buffalo, New York, area.

## Spotted Sandpiper   *Actitis macularia*

**Range:** Nearctic; breeds throughout temperate North America and winters from the Gulf Coast states south through Central and South America to Chile.

**Status:** Fairly common, but declining, breeder throughout the state; common migrant.

**Breeding:** The Spotted Sandpiper nests around ponds, lakes, and streams, as well as on pebbly and sandy beaches on offshore islands or in grass at the upper borders of salt marshes. It is still a fairly common bird today, but not nearly so numerous as it was 100 years ago—e.g., 50 to 100 pairs, Monomoy, each season in the late 1800s (Cahoon 1888). By 1964, Hill (1965) stated that only 6 to 8 pairs could be found there. *Summer maxima:* 35, Monomoy, 4 July 1965 (Forster); 24, Worcester, 7 July 1974 (Mierzejewski); 21, Longmeadow, 1 August 1965 (Yenlin); 20 +, Wellfleet, 31 July 1967 (Nichols); 10 families, June 1961, Newbury area (deWindt).

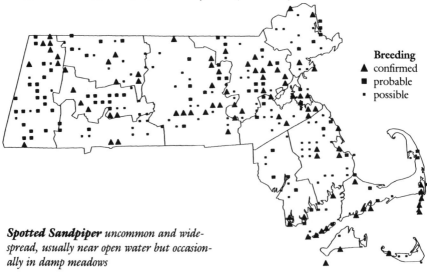

**Breeding**
▲ confirmed
■ probable
· possible

*Spotted Sandpiper uncommon and widespread, usually near open water but occasionally in damp meadows*

**Nonbreeding:** It is difficult to separate migrants from local breeders, but the bulk of the population arrives during the first week of May, with early dates including: 1, Andover, 27 March 1975 (Huyck); 1, South Easton, 4 April 1971 (Crane); 1, West Newbury, 5 April 1958 (Banes). *Spring maxima:* 99, North Scituate–Marshfield, 20 May 1982 (Cassie, Winkler); 70, Holyoke, 4 May 1954 (Eliot); 50, Plymouth, 1 June 1951 (Fox); 41, North Scituate, 22 May 1974 (Brown, Cornwell). In the fall, most Spotted Sandpipers have departed by late September. *Fall maximum:* 25, Spencer, 11 August 1964 (Gura). The latest date on record is: 1, Chatham, 3 January 1976 (Clem); however, there are definite December records from Gloucester, Woburn, Newburyport, and the Middlesex Fells.

## Terek Sandpiper   *Xenus cinereus*

**Range:** Palearctic; breeds from Finland, northern Russia, and northern Siberia south to central Russia. Winters from the Persian Gulf, the southern Red Sea, and Southeast Asia south to South Africa (along the coast of eastern Africa), India, New Guinea, and Australia.

**Status:** Vagrant: one sight record.

**Occurrence:** A Terek Sandpiper was discovered at Plum Island, 23 June 1990 (Stemple, Moore, Giriunas, Paine) and was meticulously described by Stemple et al (1990, 1991). A careful comparison of notes taken in the field with specimens at the Museum of Comparative Zoology confirmed that the bird was an adult in alternate plumage. This record apparently represents the first for eastern North America.

## Upland Sandpiper   *Bartramia longicauda*

**Range:** Nearctic; breeds from Alaska and Oregon southeast to the central eastern United States, from southern New Brunswick to Virginia. Winters in South America.

**Status:** Local and very uncommon breeder, greatly decreased since the 1800s; uncommon migrant.

**Breeding:** Upland Sandpipers probably reached their peak abundance during the early to mid-19th century, when the eastern United States was extensively used for agriculture. During the market gunning period in the latter part of the 19th century, Upland Sandpiper numbers were severely depleted by gunners because the species was favored for its superior taste. Attesting to their former abundance, Stone (1937) mentions that hundreds were shot during the 1860s near Long Branch, New Jersey, and they were likewise sought by Nantucket gunners—"49 shot in the years 1875–1889"

(Griscom and Folger 1948). They were also hunted on their winter range on the pampas of Argentina until the 1950s (Harrington, pers. comm.). Since the market gunning era, Upland Sandpipers in Massachusetts seem to have increased slowly. However, they have never regained their former abundance and the species is presently listed as endangered in the state by the Massachusetts Natural Heritage and Endangered Species Program.

Most breeders now are on short-grass fields surrounding military airfields, as well as Boston's Logan Airport, but a few still nest in grassy pastures in the Newbury area, as well as in Bridgewater, Middleboro, and the Connecticut River valley. During the mid-19th century, they bred commonly on Cape Cod and the Islands and specifically on Nantucket and Tuckernuck until the 1940s. None currently breed on the Islands, with the possible exception of 1 or 2 pairs at Katama, Martha's Vineyard. The discovery of Upland Sandpipers breeding at military airfields has been recent. *Maxima:* 100 + individuals (including 14 nesting pairs), Otis Air Force Base, Cape Cod, July 1985 (White); 10–15 pairs, Westover Air Force Base, Chicopee, July 1984 (fide Melvin); 12–15 individuals, Hanscom Field, Bedford, July 1985 (Heil). In 1990, the entire Massachusetts breeding population numbered approximately 35 to 50 pairs (Melvin, pers. comm.).

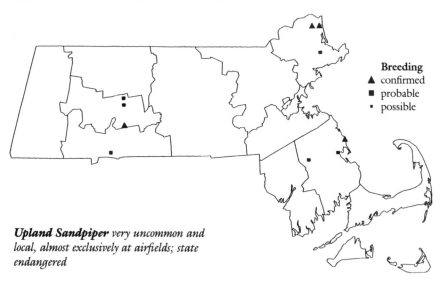

**Breeding**
▲ confirmed
■ probable
· possible

*Upland Sandpiper very uncommon and local, almost exclusively at airfields; state endangered*

**Nonbreeding:** Many spring records of Upland Sandpipers probably represent the arrival of local breeding birds. The general arrival is in mid-April; however, birds occasionally appear earlier: e.g., 1, Brewster, 31 March 1962 (Rich); 1, Halifax, 31 March 1989 (Kellogg); 1, Essex County, 3 April 1904 (Wilson); 3, Martha's Vineyard, 3 April 1984 (Laux); 1, Middleboro, 5 April 1973 (Briggs); 1, Ipswich, 8 April 1972 (Hale). The maximum count away from a known breeding locality is: 5, Bolton, 4 April 1974 (Forster). *Fall* *maxima:* 27, Plum Island, 1 September 1962 (Russell); 16, Marshfield, 4 August 1977 (Petersen); 13, Leicester, 26 August 1967 (Blodget); 12, outer Cape, 18 August 1978 (fide Nikula); 12, Westboro, 31 August 1946 (Kelly). The species is rare after early September—latest: 1, Northampton, 21 October 1926 (Eliot).

# Eskimo Curlew   *Numenius borealis*

**Range:** Nearctic; formerly bred in northwestern Mackenzie and wintered on the pampas of southern South America. Migrated north in spring through the Mississippi River valley and south in the fall over the Atlantic Ocean from Labrador and Newfoundland directly to South America. Recent evidence of continued survival of a small population.

**Status:** Formerly occurred as an erratic, occasionally abundant, fall migrant. Largest numbers occurred following the heavy rains of easterly gales.

**Occurrence:** Nantucket Island was one of the best places on the Atlantic Coast of the United States for hunting Eskimo Curlews. They alighted there only when periods of easterly winds and rain coincided with the dates of southward migration in late August and September. In the absence of such fall weather, Eskimo Curlews flew nonstop from Newfoundland and Labrador to South America. Griscom and Folger (1948) point out that the abundance of Eskimo Curlews as migrants along the eastern coast of North America has been exaggerated and list the following Nantucket counts from the late 19th century: "Last great flight in history anywhere on the Atlantic seaboard," 29 August 1869; 250, 27 August 1877 (Mackay); 8, 26 August 1897. During seasons in which no storms occurred in late August or September, few or none were seen. There have been no specimens collected and only one suggestive sight record of this species since 1913. The sight record was: 2, Black Point Pond, Chilmark, Martha's Vineyard, 6–7 August 1972 (Daniels). This report represents the most convincing recent Massachusetts sight record (AB 26: 907–8).

**Remarks:** In evaluating reports of this exceedingly rare species, it has become apparent that the Upland Sandpiper, particularly when seen out of the context of its nesting habitat, can be confused with the Eskimo Curlew. Both species are of similar shape and size and can occur in similar habitats in appropriate seasons. This resemblance seems not to have been properly emphasized in most of the more popular field guides.

# Whimbrel   *Numenius phaeopus*

**Range:** Holarctic; breeds, in North America, across boreal Canada south to western Hudson Bay; winters primarily in South America.

# Birds of Massachusetts

**Status:** Uncommon spring and common to locally abundant fall migrant on the coast; very rare inland.

**Occurrence:** In spring, Whimbrels are most frequently seen on the southeastern coastal plain during late April and again in late May, possibly representing individuals from different portions of the breeding range. The earliest record is: 1–2, Plum Island, 5 April 1974 (Johnson et al). *Spring maxima:* 19, outer Cape, 30 May 1948 (Bishop); 15, Monomoy, 30 May 1970 (Blodget); 7, Chatham, 21–25 April 1978 (Nikula); 6, West Dennis, 19 May 1979 (Trull); 5, Plum Island, 23 April 1960 (deWindt). There are at least a dozen June records, which undoubtedly include late spring migrants, early fall migrants, and nonbreeding subadult birds.

Before the market gunning period, Whimbrels were considered to be the least common of the three curlew species occurring in Massachusetts. However, G. H. Mackay kept careful records of the species' abundance on Nantucket during the 1800s (AK 9: 345–352), and he cites a gunner's report that states that some 1,500 Whimbrels were present on Tuckernuck and Nantucket islands during the summer of 1833. With the exception of this account, however, it seems clear that Whimbrels were uncommon migrants throughout New England during the early part of this century and that their numbers have steadily increased since then. Evening roost counts on North Monomoy reflect this increase—e.g., 750, 28 July 1990 (Harrington); 550+, 1 August 1987 (Nikula, Petersen, et al); 360+, 1 August 1979 (Heil, Nikula); 352, 27 July 1985 (Bailey et al); 290+, 31 July 1986 (Nikula). The average migration period is from mid-July to late September, with the peak flight of adults occurring in late July to early August and the peak of juveniles in September—e.g., 95, Monomoy, 17 September 1937 (Griscom). Most migratory flocks contain 15 to 40 birds, some of which are occasionally seen flying along the coast, or even some distance offshore. The latest migrants depart by the end of October.

The Whimbrel is a rare migrant inland—e.g., 1, North Orange, 16 July 1919 (fide Eliot); 1 undated specimen, Northampton, in Springfield Museum (fide Eliot); 1, Hardwick, 19 July 1972 (Gagnon, Orzulak); 1, Middleboro, 8 August 1978 (Petersen); 1, GMNWR, 25 August 1982 (Walton); 1, Whately, 3 October 1990 (Sorrie). Most unusual were: 9 seen flying south, Mt. Wachusett, 23 September 1983 (Kamp, Roberts, et al).

**Subspecies:** There are two subspecies from the Old World, both of which have been collected in North America: *N. p. phaeopus* of mainland Europe and *N. p. islandicus* of Iceland. Separation of the two, each of which

*Like other large shorebirds, the **Whimbrel** was heavily persecuted by market gunners prior to 1900. Always wary, the species escaped the plight of the smaller Eskimo Curlew, and numbers now occasionally reach the hundreds at evening roosts on Monomoy Island.*

176

possesses a white rump and a paler belly and underwings than *N. p. hudsonicus*, would be extremely difficult in the field. Whimbrels with white rumps of one or another subspecies have been reliably reported on at least seven occasions in Massachusetts: 1, Monomoy, 7–9 September 1951 (Bailey et al); 1 (judged to be the same individual that was at Monomoy), Great Island, Hyannis, 16 September 1951 (Coolidge); 1, Plum Island, 17 June 1972 (Petersen et al); 1, Duxbury, 11–12 November 1973 (Petersen, Forster, et al); 1, Plum Island, 1 September 1976 (Gardler); 1, Nantucket, 29–30 April 1979 (Litchfield); 1, Nantucket, 9–10 August 1984 (Harte).

# Eurasian Curlew  *Numenius arquata*

**Range:** Palearctic; breeds from southern Eurasia south to southern Europe. Winters south to southern Africa and southeast Asia. Vagrants have been recorded in Greenland, Iceland, New York (specimen), Massachusetts, Nova Scotia, and Bermuda.

**Status:** Vagrant: three Massachusetts records.

**Occurrence:** On 19 September 1976, a Eurasian Curlew was discovered at Monomoy (Veit, Perkins), where it remained until 16 October, was seen by many, and was identifiably photographed in color (AB 31: 232). On 18 February 1978, another Eurasian Curlew was discovered at Menemsha Pond, Martha's Vineyard (Sargent, Daniels, et al), where it remained until 18 March (AB 32: 310). The third occurrence involved a feather-worn adult seen at Tuckernuck Island and at Monomoy, 5 September–23 November 1984 (Veit, Braun, Nikula, Petersen).

During the late fall of 1977, a curlew with a white rump was observed on eastern Long Island, New York, and a Eurasian Curlew was identified near Halifax, Nova Scotia, in May of 1978. This accumulation of records suggests that a small irruption to North America may have occurred during the years 1976 to 1984.

# Long-billed Curlew  *Numenius americanus*

**Range:** Nearctic; breeds across the Great Plains from British Columbia and Manitoba south to Utah and Texas. Winters primarily from California and Texas south to Guatemala, with a few wintering in South Carolina and Florida.

**Status:** Vagrant: fewer than ten 20th-century records.

**Occurrence:** Before the market gunning period in the late 1800s, Long-billed Curlews were regular and at times fairly common migrants in Massachusetts (Hill 1964). Since the turn of the century, their breeding range has been considerably reduced, and between 1900 and 1987 there were only six records of migrants from Massachusetts: 2 collected, Ipswich, August 1900 (fide Griscom & Snyder 1955); 1 collected, Marshfield, 10 August 1909 (fide Griscom & Snyder 1955); 1 collected, Chatham, 15 June 1938, (Bishop, Griscom, BMS #18790); 1, Monomoy, 31 May 1979 (Nisbet); 1, Monomoy, 6–10 June 1984 (Nikula et al); 1, Nauset, Eastham, 8–12 June 1987 (Stabins, Everett, photo at MAS). Additional sight records published in RNEB, Bailey (1955), and Griscom and Emerson (1959) may include misidentified individuals, although three records from Martha's Vineyard—1, 30 August 1946 (Emerson); 3, early September 1951 (fide Griscom & Emerson 1959); 1, 9 September 1952 (Emerson, Brewer)—may be authentic.

# Black-tailed Godwit  *Limosa limosa*

**Range:** Palearctic; breeds across northern temperate Eurasia, including Iceland. Winters in southern temperate Eurasia.

**Status:** Vagrant: one record.

**Occurrence:** The second record for North America was discovered on 23 April 1967, when a Black-tailed Godwit in prealternate molt was found in the company of an Upland Sandpiper and a golden-plover at a farm pond in South Dartmouth (Fernandez, Baird). It was subsequently seen by about 50 people during its stay until 30 April and was clearly photographed in color by Severyn Dana (see Baird 1968, photo at MAS).

# Hudsonian Godwit  *Limosa haemastica*

**Range:** Nearctic; breeds in Alaska, northwestern Mackenzie, and along the western shores of Hudson and James bays; winters primarily in coastal Argentina.

**Status:** Very rare in spring and during all seasons inland. Fairly common to locally common fall migrant at a few specific coastal localities.

**Occurrence:** There are fewer than ten records of the Hudsonian Godwit in spring, all spanning the dates 18 May to 3 June, except for the early date of 29 April, cited without reference in Howe and Allen (1901). One is an inland record—i.e., 1 in first alternate plumage, Bolton, 25–26 May 1978 (Merriman, Blodget, Forster, et al)—and the other records are all from the Newburyport area and Monomoy. Monomoy Island is probably the most important traditional fall stopover area in North America for this transoceanic migrant, which typically flies nonstop from James Bay in Ontario to South America. The first migrants ordinarily show up at Monomoy during the first week of July: earliest, 22 June 1969 (Blodget). Peak counts of adults often reach

150. *Fall maxima* (at Monomoy): 200, 11 August 1976 (VO); 152, 8 August 1979 (Bailey); 146, 6 August 1977 (VO). The totals at Newburyport ordinarily range between 50 and 85 birds.

Larger numbers have occasionally been seen during and after severe northeasterly storms. *Storm-related maxima:* 400–500, Monomoy, 30–31 August 1935 (Hagar, Eldredge, see Hagar 1936); 200, Eastham, 2 September 1974 (Goodrich); 82, Nauset, Eastham, 30–31 August 1935 (Hagar, Eldredge, see Hagar 1936); 32, Tuckernuck Island, 20 August 1974 (Veit). The peak migration of juveniles occurs in September and October, when up to 55 individuals have been seen together. *Maxima* (for juveniles): 55, Barnstable, 24 September 1975 (Forster); 23, Newburyport, 22 October 1972 (Moore). The species is rare by late October, and the latest date on record is: 1, Nauset, Eastham, 21 November 1976 (VO).

Inland records of the Hudsonian Godwit are most unusual. Selected reports include: 1 juvenile, Concord, 12 October 1961 (Shaw); 1, Onota Lake, Pittsfield, 21–28 October 1963 (Hendricks); 2, East Brookfield, 10–16 October 1965 (Wetherbee); 1, GMNWR, 6–19 October 1971 (McClellan, Baird); 1, Westboro, 4–19 September 1981 (McMenemy et al); 40, Middleboro, 29 October 1989 (Petersen).

# Bar-tailed Godwit *Limosa lapponica*

**Range:** Palearctic; breeds from northern Scandinavia east to eastern Siberia and western Alaska. Winters from Britain and Iraq south to Africa and Ceylon, and from China and the Philippines south to Australia and New Zealand. Regular vagrant to both coasts of North America.

**Status:** Vagrant: at least fourteen records. Since 1972, there have been ten records, suggesting an increasing incidence of dispersal.

**Occurrence:** The records are: 1, Cape Cod, 17 September 1907 (MCZ #254872); 1, Nauset, Eastham, 26 July 1937 (Hagar, BMS x03–077); 1, Chappaquiddick Island, 26–31 August 1968 (Sears, Chalif); 1, Chatham, 9–16 September 1972 (Clem, Bailey, et al); 1, Newburyport, 15 May–1 June 1976 (Petersen et al); 1 adult in pre-basic molt, Plum Island, 4–7 September 1978 (Buckley et al); 1, Nantucket, 23 September–21 October 1978 (Petersen et al); 1, Monomoy, 4 July–31 August 1979 (Clem, Nikula, et al); 1, Plum Island, 7–10 August 1979 (Wiggin et al); 1, Revere, 12 April 1981 (Zendeh); 1, Chatham-Monomoy, 13–25 June 1984 (Holt, Lortie, et al); 1, Monomoy, 31 July–13 August 1988 (Nikula et al); 1, North Monomoy, 10 June–19 August 1990 (Nikula, VO); 1, North Monomoy, 11–14 August 1991 (Nikula et al). All those identified to subspecies were *L. l. lapponica* of the western Palearctic, except the 1988 record, which was clearly of the race *L. l. baueri* of Siberia and Alaska.

# Marbled Godwit  *Limosa fedoa*

**Range:** Nearctic; breeds on the Great Plains from central Alberta and northern Ontario south to the Dakotas; also breeding colonies were recently discovered at the southern end of James Bay (Morrison, Manning, Hagar 1976) and in southern Alaska. Winters primarily in the southern United States.

**Status:** Very rare spring and uncommon fall migrant on the coast. Very rare inland.

**Occurrence:** The statement by Osgood (1890), perpetuated by Howe and Allen (1901) and Griscom and Snyder (1955), that the Marbled Godwit "bred now and then on the Lynn Marsh in the 1840s" is highly improbable because the Marbled Godwit has otherwise never been known to breed east of Wisconsin (AOU 1983).

Marbled Godwits are restricted to extensive tidal flats during migration and thus occur most regularly at Monomoy, Eastham, and Newburyport. They have slowly regained their local status after a decline during the market gunning period. Most are seen in Massachusetts between late July and late September. There are, nonetheless, seven spring records spanning the period 14–29 May; all are from Newburyport except: 1, Brookline, May 1883 (BMS x03–162); 1, Chatham, 19 May 1885 (Whitcomb); 1, Revere, 16–17 May 1944 (Griscom et al). The only June records are: 2, Newburyport, 19 May–16 June 1964 (Barry); 1, Newburyport, 27 June 1972 (Baird). *Fall maxima:* 12, Nauset, Eastham, 16–17 September 1978 (VO); 11, Monomoy, 30 August 1975 (Harris). Usually only 1 to 6 birds are seen, and they are always less numerous in the Newburyport area than on Cape Cod. Winter records: 1, Ipswich, December 1960–February 1961 (VO); 1, North Beach, Chatham, 5 December 1970 (Petersen, Goodrich); 2, Chatham, 5 December 1971 (Stymeist et al); 1, Chatham, 29 December 1973–5 May 1974 (Goodrich, Nikula, et al); 1, Nauset, Eastham, 1–17 December 1975 (Goodrich); 1, East Boston, 2 December 1977 (Zendeh); 1, Tuckernuck Island, 31 December 1979 (Veit); 1, Marshfield, 31 January–21 February 1982 (Petersen).

There is a single sight record from the Connecticut River valley: 1, Hadley, 24–27 July 1977 (Gagnon et al).

# Ruddy Turnstone  *Arenaria interpres*

**Range:** Holarctic; breeds, in North America, from high arctic Canada south to Southampton Island. On the Atlantic Coast, winters from Massachusetts south to northern South America.

**Status:** Locally abundant migrant and locally uncommon in winter; very rare inland in any season.

**Occurrence:** Ruddy Turnstones are particular in their choice of habitat, selecting sandy and pebbly beaches rather than the extensive mud flats preferred by many other species of migrant shorebirds. Thus, turnstones are found in large numbers only at Monomoy and on the sod banks and sand flats at the mouth of the North River, Scituate. Spring totals of 300 to 600 typically occur during the last week of May at Monomoy. *Spring maxima* (at Monomoy): 2,000, 1 June 1957 (Griscom); 1,000, 27 May 1970 (Petersen); 900, 24 May 1959 (Nisbet); 600 + , 30 May 1976 (Petersen). Away from Monomoy, counts of over 50 in spring are unusual, and the species is notably uncommon in the Newburyport region—maximum: 15, 18 May 1967 (Forster).

In fall, the peak of southward-moving birds ordinarily reaches 200 to 500 at Monomoy and Scituate during early August, although higher counts are occasionally reported. *Fall maxima:* 1,500, Monomoy, 4 August 1955 (Smart); 1,000, Scituate, 12 August 1961 (Higginbotham).

Since the early 1960s, flocks of turnstones have successfully wintered in most years on the offshore rocks in the vicinity of Minot, North Scituate. This flock has numbered between 60 and 80 birds since 1972 (Moore, Higginbotham, Petersen, et al) and as such is anomalous because Bull (1964) considers a maximum count for the New York City area of 9 "an unusual number." Away from North Scituate, between 5 and 30 birds have wintered on the jetties at the entrance to Nantucket Harbor since at least 1950 (Andrews). Other midwinter records include: 13, Squaw Island, Hyannis, 27 January 1974 (Nikula); 4, Salem, 13 February 1978 (Blodget); 2, Beverly, 6 March 1957 (Kleber).

The Ruddy Turnstone is one of the rarer shorebird species at inland sites. McNair (1978) lists four spring (19 April–31 May) and eight fall (21 July–2 October) records for Berkshire County—maximum: 7, Pittsfield Sewer Beds, 28 July 1955 (Schumacher). In the Connecticut River valley, turnstones occur, on average, every other year during fall on sandbars in the Connecticut River—maximum: 6, South Deerfield, 28 May 1973 (Hebert). There are at least ten fall and two spring records from Worcester County— maximum: 4, Clinton, 29 August 1971 (Blodget).

# Red Knot   *Calidris canutus*

**Range:** Holarctic; breeds, in North America, from Northern Alaska east to Ellsmere and south to Victoria and Southampton islands. This population winters primarily in Argentina, but also along the coast of North America from Massachusetts to the Gulf of Mexico.

**Status:** Locally very common spring and locally abundant fall migrant. Sporadic, but occasionally common in winter. Very rare away from the immediate coast.

**Occurrence:** During migration, Red Knots are mainly found at five localities along our coast: Third Cliff, Scituate; Plymouth Beach; Duxbury Beach; Monomoy; and New Island, Eastham. These areas serve as major staging and stopover areas for the birds during their southward fall migration (Harrington & Morrison 1979). Before 1900, knots frequented a now-nonexistent sandbar that extended west from the western end of Tuckernuck Island (Mackay 1893) and at Billingsgate Shoal off Wellfleet. The birds return to their preferred areas with remarkable tenacity from year to year and are notably scarce at other locations.

Spring peak counts usually number 100 to 200 during the last week of May and the first week of June, almost invariably at Monomoy. Flocks of presumed nonbreeders include: 40, Monomoy, 13 June 1970 (Blodget); 20, Ipswich, 20 June 1971 (McClellan). In fall, the peak of adults, averaging 2,500 birds per site, occurs in the third to fourth week of July, after which most juveniles move through in late August and September—e.g., 170, New Island, Eastham, September 1974 (Veit, Stymeist, Perkins). *Fall maxima:* 5,000, Monomoy, 22 July 1954 (Griscom); 4,500, Monomoy, 30 July 1961 (Gardler); 3,000, Monomoy, 25 July 1976 (Goodrich); 2,500, Scituate, 27 July 1980 (Petersen); 1,100, New Island, Eastham, 13 August 1979 (Heil).

The number of knots that survive the winter in Massachusetts fluctuates widely. *Winter maxima:* 230, Revere Beach, 26 January 1974 (Veit, Perkins); 150, North Scituate, 5 January 1979 (Emery et al); 130, Revere Beach, 16 February 1974 (Petersen); 125, North Scituate, 18 March 1962 (SSBC). There have been several winters since 1955 when none were reported.

The Red Knot is one of the most unusual shorebird species to occur at inland localities in Massachusetts. The records include: 8 (also the maximum), Pittsfield, 27 August 1946 (Bailey et al); 1, Deerfield, 1 August 1976 (Goodwin); 1, Longmeadow, 2 August 1982 (Withgott et al); 1, Westboro, 27 August 1983 (Blodget, McMenemy, Kamp); 1, Longmeadow, 6 August 1985 (Withgott, Kellogg); 1, Richmond, 27 July 1986 (Goodrich); 1, Dana, East Quabbin, 21 August 1988 (Blodget). Griscom and Snyder (1955) mention that the species has been collected three times inland but list no dates or localities.

**Remarks:** An albino Red Knot was seen at Sandy Neck, Barnstable, 18 September 1977 (Petersen).

# Sanderling   *Calidris alba*

**Range:** Holarctic; breeds, in North America, in high arctic regions south and east to Southampton and the northern Baffin Islands; North American population winters on sandy beaches on both coasts of the Americas from Alaska and Massachusetts south to Tierra del Fuego.

**Status:** Very common to abundant migrant, common in winter, and uncommon in midsummer. Rare and irregular away from sandy beaches on the coast.

**Occurrence:** The recent history of the Sanderling in Massachusetts, like that of the Semipalmated Sandpiper, is particularly interesting in that marked variations in the number of migrants may reflect both changes in the preferred habitat at Monomoy, where Sanderlings have historically been most numerous in the state, and changes in the overall population. Peak counts of adults have always occurred in the last few days of May and again in late July and early August. Numbers of migrants at Monomoy peaked during the 1950s but have dropped considerably since then.

Hill (1965) describes the increase of migrating Sanderlings in the state following the market gunning period, and, in the 1950s, Griscom noted spring peak counts at Monomoy and North Beach, Chatham—e.g., 27,000, 30 May 1952; 20,000, 31 May 1954; 20,000, 31 May 1958. Peak fall counts, also at Monomoy, were: 10,000, 22 July 1954 (Griscom); 7,000, 4 August 1955 (Griscom). Since that time, peak counts of Sanderlings have averaged about 2,000 birds in both spring and fall, suggesting that the Monomoy flats may no longer be as attractive to Sanderlings as they once were. *Spring maxima:* 3,500, Monomoy, 16 May 1980 (Nikula); 1,800, Monomoy, 28 May 1978 (Petersen). *Fall maxima:* 3,000 +, Monomoy, 17 August 1976 (Nikula); 2,000, Monomoy, 31 July 1977 (Nikula); 2,000, Monomoy, 5 August 1978 (Petersen); 2,000, Monomoy, 6 September 1980 (Nikula). Peak counts of juveniles are always smaller.

Sanderlings winter on sandy beaches south of Boston and occasionally do so as far north as Essex County. Since 1955, Cape Cod CBC totals have ranged from 60 (1955, 1965) to 1,153 (1976). Other counts include: up to 300, Revere Beach, during most winters (BOEM), with 800 there, 16 December 1973 (Abbott, Finch, Veit); 500 +, Barnstable, 6 March 1976 (Petersen).

Sanderlings are uncommon to rare inland and tend to be more regular in fall (July–November) than spring. For spring, there are only three records since 1971: 1, Northampton, 24 May 1974 (Yenlin); 1, Worcester, 31 May 1975 (Jenkins); 1, Hadley, 26 May 1979 (Champeaux). Records inland in fall include: 17, Clinton, 5 November 1977 (Merriman); 9, Wayland, early November 1898 (Maynard); 3, Longmeadow, 10 September 1967 (Leshure). McNair (1978) states that 2 are the most that have ever been seen at one time in Berkshire County.

# Semipalmated Sandpiper   *Calidris pusilla*

**Range:** Nearctic; breeds from northern Alaska, central Baffin Island, and northern Labrador south to western Alaska, northeastern Manitoba, northern Quebec, and coastal Labrador. Winters in northern South America south to southern Brazil and northern Chile.

**Status:** Very common to locally very abundant migrant on the coast; uncommon but regular inland.

**Occurrence:** This species is the most numerous shorebird occurring in Massachusetts, where it is found primarily on extensive tidal flats. In spring, most peak accounts occur between mid-May and early June. *Spring maxima:* 8,000, Newburyport, 30 May 1973 (Petersen); 8,000, Monomoy, 24 May 1959 (Nisbet); 6,000, Newburyport, 28 May 1980 (Heil). Semipalmated Sandpipers are uncommon inland in spring, with counts of more than 5 birds being usual. A count of: 110, Hadley Cove on the Connecticut River, 31 May 1981 (Surner) is exceptional.

During fall, adults arrive in the first week of July and reach maximum abundance by the last week of that month. Juveniles appear by mid-August and peak by late August. *Fall maxima:* 23,500, Newburyport-Ipswich, 12 August 1962 (Snyder, Leahy); 12,000, Newburyport, 21 July 1974 (Petersen); 12,000, Newburyport, 26 July 1975 (Petersen).

During the late 1940s and 1950s, Griscom and others reported several counts of tens of thousands of Semipalmated Sandpipers in both spring and fall—e.g., 60,000, Newburyport, 15 August 1945; 60,000, Newburyport, 6 August 1947; 40,000, East Boston, 2 August 1948; 35,000, Monomoy, 1 June 1957. During the same period, exceptionally high numbers also occurred inland to Worcester County—e.g., 1,500, Spencer, 30 July 1952 (Wetherbee); 1,000 +, Spencer, 2 August 1954 (Wetherbee); 800 +, Spencer, 8 August 1953 (Wetherbee). Since 1960, the maximum count for Worcester County is: 150, Sterling, 31 July 1971 (Blodget).

Semipalmated Sandpipers have declined substantially as migrants in Massachusetts; peak totals have not exceeded 12,000 birds in fall or 8,000 in spring for 20 years. It is possible that a shift in migration routes, rather than a population decline, has occurred since Harrington and Morrison (1979) have pointed out that upwards of 3 to 4 million Semipalmated Sandpipers have been estimated during July along the shores of the Bay of Fundy in recent years.

*Extreme dates:* Early May–8 November 1888 (MCZ #219304). Specimens or photographs of unusually high quality are desirable for substantiating the occurrence of Semipalmated Sandpipers either before May or after October. Phillips (1975) has pointed out that all winter records of Semipalmated Sandpipers north of Florida prior to 1975 are based on misidentified Western Sandpipers. In light of Phillips' find, the following records are reported as *Calidris* sp.: 1, Rockport, 9 December 1959 (Smith); 1, Nahant, 15 December 1966 (Alexander); 1, Nauset, Eastham, 19 December 1975 (Bailey); 1, Barnstable, 24 December 1974 (Nikula); 2, Scituate CBC, 30 December 1967; 1, Orleans, 2 January 1966 (Fox, Morgan); 1, Chatham; 6, January 1974 (Laux); 1, Barnstable, 6 January 1974 (Laux).

Semipalmated Sandpipers are never as numerous as Least Sandpipers at inland locations. *Fall maxima* (inland): 400, Halifax, 7 August 1978 (Petersen); 275, Spencer, 6 August 1959 (Freeland, Gardler); 165, Pittsfield Sewer Beds, 28 July 1955 (Schumacher, Eliot); 90, Longmeadow, 25 July 1971 (Yenlin); 75, Lincoln, 28 July 1965 (Eldred).

**Remarks:** An albino Semipalmated Sandpiper was seen in Scituate, 6 September 1968 (M. and A. Argue).

# Western Sandpiper   *Calidris mauri*

**Range:** Nearctic; breeds in coastal arctic Alaska and extreme northeastern Siberia; winters coastally from California and the Carolinas south to South America. Regular on migration along the Atlantic Coast north to Maine.

**Status:** Variously uncommon to occasionally very common fall migrant at preferred coastal sites; very rare in spring. Rare, but perhaps overlooked, inland.

**Occurrence:** In Massachusetts, Western Sandpipers are almost invariably found among flocks of Semipalmated Sandpipers. In spring, there are at least ten records spanning the period 3 April to 24 June, with most occurring in the latter two weeks of May. These include a specimen from Marblehead, 3 April 1889 (MCZ #301667), a most unusual occurrence this far north so early in the spring.

In fall, Western Sandpipers migrate somewhat later than Semipalmateds, so that peak counts of Westerns, mostly juveniles, occur in early to mid-September. Adult Western Sandpipers, which are less numerous than juveniles in Massachusetts, appear by the end of July and are most common during early August. *Fall maxima:* 150 +, Nauset, Eastham, 13 September 1980 (Heil); 100, Marshfield, 6 September 1944 (Griscom); 100, Plum Island, 12 September 1973 (Alden); 5, Pittsfield, 12 October 1969 (Hendricks); 3, Sheffield, 20 September 1955 (Saunders).

*Extreme dates:* Western Sandpipers occasionally linger into November, and there are convincing sight records into December, including: 1, Orleans, 1–7 December 1974 (Nikula); 1, Duxbury, 7 December 1980 (Petersen); 1, Orleans, 21 December 1975 (Gardler); 1, Chilmark, Martha's Vineyard, 29–30 December 1985 (Nikula, Petersen); 1, Orleans, 2 January 1966 (Fox, Morgan).

# Rufous-necked Stint   *Calidris ruficollis*

**Range:** Chiefly eastern Palearctic; breeds in northeastern Siberia and western Alaska; winters from China to Australia and New Zealand. Of occasional occurrence on the Pacific Coast of North America. Vagrant on the Atlantic Coast.

**Status:** Vagrant: two records.

**Occurrence:** There are two records of this species for Massachusetts, both in 1980: 1 in first alternate plumage, seen in direct comparison with a Little Stint, Monomoy, 24–28 June (Laux, Veit, Nikula, Heil, Trull); 1 adult in alternate plumage, Scituate, 17–24 July (Petersen et al, see Veit & Petersen 1982). A photo in AB 35: 158 purporting to be the Scituate Rufous-necked Stint is in reality a Sanderling.

## Little Stint  *Calidris minuta*

**Range:** Palearctic; breeds from northern Scandinavia to western Siberia; winters primarily in Africa and India. Vagrant to North America.

**Status:** Vagrant: five records

**Occurrence:** Massachusetts Little Stint records include: 1 alternate plumaged adult, Monomoy, 19–25 June 1980 (Nikula, Heil, Petersen, Forster, Goodrich, et al; see Nikula 1980); 1 alternate plumaged adult, Third Cliff, Scituate, 25 July–5 August 1985 (Petersen et al 1985); 1 molting adult, Duxbury Beach, 6–14 August 1986 (Petersen et al); 1 adult, Plum Island, 19 August 1989 (Abrams, Perkins, Petersen, et al); 1 adult, Squantum, 28 July–5 August 1990 (Abrams, Cameron). Some of these individuals were identifiably photographed (photos at MAS).

## Least Sandpiper  *Calidris minutilla*

**Range:** Nearctic; breeds across boreal North America, from western Alaska and northern Labrador south to British Columbia and Nova Scotia (including Sable Island). Winters coastally from Oregon and North Carolina south to central South America.

**Status:** One extralimital nesting record for Monomoy Island. Locally abundant spring and very common fall migrant on the coast; common in both seasons inland.

**Breeding:** A first breeding record for the lower 48 United States was established when a freshly dead downy chick was found at Monomoy, on "a drier portion of the salt marsh," 12 July 1979 (Anderson et al). The specific identity of the chick was confirmed by J. R. Jehl, Jr., and the specimen is currently at the MCZ (#330877) (AB 34: 867). As startling as the discovery was at the time, the record may not be that surprising in that Least Sandpipers breed commonly as close as southeastern Nova Scotia (Godfrey 1966) and on Sable Island, where the habitat is strikingly similar to that of Monomoy. In addition, nonbreeding Least Sandpipers have frequently been recorded summering at Monomoy, so future salt-marsh breeding could possibly be anticipated.

**Nonbreeding:** Least Sandpipers, like Semipalmated Sandpipers, occur in large flocks on extensive tidal flats during migration. Due to their habit of feeding at the borders of salt marshes in fall, they are particularly difficult to count at that time of year. During spring, they are inclined to feed on open mud flats in places such as Newburyport Harbor. Although they are less numerous as migrants in Massachusetts than Semipalmated Sandpipers, they tend to occur earlier in both spring and fall. The species is rare before late April—earliest, 1, Newburyport, 11 April 1981 (Heil). *Spring maxima:* 4,500+, Newburyport, 12 May 1974 (Petersen); 4,000, Newburyport, 12 May 1972 (Donahue); 4,000, Newburyport, 9 May 1979 (Heil); 3,500, Newburyport, 17 May 1975 (Forster). Inland, peak spring counts seem to occur somewhat later in May—e.g., 130, Spencer, 24 May 1981 (Meservey); 70, Spencer, 18 May 1955 (Wetherbee); 60+, Granby, 20 May 1970 (Yenlin); 55, Concord, 16 May 1982 (Forster); 30, Hadley, 16 May 1971 (Yenlin); 11, Lancaster, 21 May 1977 (Merriman). During the fall migration, Least Sandpipers are among the first shorebird species to appear in early July, with peak counts usually occurring during the last half of the month. *Fall maxima:* 1,500, Monomoy, 18 July 1954 (Griscom); 1,400, North Monomoy, 19 July 1984 (Nikula); 1,200, North Monomoy, 27 July 1990 (Nikula). Inland: 300, GMNWR, 24 July 1975 (Forster); 110+, Westboro, 16 July 1981 (Blodget); 100+, Spencer, 8 August 1953 (Wetherbee); 74, Spencer, 20 July 1969 (Yenlin); 64, Pittsfield Sewer Beds, 9 September 1934 (Hendricks). The Least Sandpiper is rare after September, so the following records are most unusual: 1, West Falmouth, 14 December 1974 (Donahue, Veit, Stymeist); 1, Harwich, 4 December 1982 (Nikula); 3, Westboro, 12 November 1973 (Kamp).

# White-rumped Sandpiper  *Calidris fuscicollis*

**Range:** Nearctic; breeds in arctic North America from northern Alaska and Bathurst Island south to northwestern Hudson Bay and southern Baffin Island. Winters in South America south to Tierra del Fuego.

**Status:** Variously uncommon to occasionally very common spring migrant; fairly common to occasionally abundant fall migrant.

**Occurrence:** Market gunners referred to this species as one of the "grass birds"; however, it is not nearly as restricted to grassy habitats as are the Pectoral and Least sandpipers. White-rumped Sandpipers are found in a wide variety of habitats in the state, including sandy and pebbly beaches, mud flats, and salt pannes, where they frequently associate with roosting Semipalmated Sandpipers and Dunlins. Their abundance fluctuates considerably from year to year, but there is no evidence from Massachusetts records of a general decline since the early part of the 20th century (cf Bull 1964).

Most White-rumped Sandpipers are recorded between mid-May and early June and again from late July to late October. ***Spring maxima:*** 250, Newburyport, 14 May 1978 (Heil); 150, Monomoy, 11 May 1978 (Nikula); 100 +, Newburyport, 25 May 1961 (Willmann, Harte); 32, Chatham, 3 June 1941 (Hill). In some seasons—e.g., 1956, 1957—fewer than six individuals were reported during the entire spring. Rare before May—e.g., 1, Monomoy, 29 April 1984 (Nikula)—but late migrants and nonbreeders occur into June— e.g., 9, Plum Island, 28 June 1961 (Snyder). Very rare inland—e.g., 1, Hadley, 24 May 1933 (Bagg, Eliot); 1, Hadley, 17 May 1936 (Bagg, Eliot, Griscom); 1, Spencer, 22 May 1954 (Crompton); 1, Bolton, 25 May 1981 (Blodget).

In fall, the maximum counts of White-rumped Sandpipers average 200 birds. Juveniles are rare before mid-September but regularly occur until late November. ***Fall maxima:*** 235, Monomoy, 9 September 1942 (Mason); 200, Ipswich, 27 August 1955 (Bailey); 200, Monomoy, 8 September 1968 (Petersen); 200, Monomoy, 22 October 1969 (Bailey et al). Two exceptional counts, the latter of which was associated with a storm, include: 2,000, Newburyport, 23 September 1950 (Snyder); 800, Plum Island, 14 September 1986 (VO). ***Inland maxima:*** 50, Halifax, 22 October 1989 (Petersen); 10, Pittsfield, 1 November 1969 (Wetherbee, Foison); 8, Longmeadow Flats, 25 September 1972 (Willard, Leshure); 5, Pittsfield, 13 August 1955 (Schumacher, Hendricks).

There are at least seven December records—latest, 1, Newburyport, 23 December 1979, (Petersen, Nikula, Anderson). There is one January record: 1, Marshfield CBC, 1 January 1972.

# Baird's Sandpiper *Calidris bairdii*

**Range:** Nearctic; breeds in arctic Alaska and Canada south and east to southwestern Baffin Island. Migrates mainly through the Mississippi River valley in spring; more widespread in fall, occurring regularly in small numbers on both coasts of North America. Winters in the Andes from Ecuador to Argentina and on the coast of Argentina south to Tierra del Fuego.

**Status:** Uncommon fall migrant on the coast; rare inland.

**Occurrence:** In Massachusetts, the Baird's Sandpiper is the least gregarious of the "peeps" and is frequently found apart from other shorebirds at such localities as the impounded pools at Plum Island, around the ponds at South Monomoy, and occasionally inland at sewer beds and along the shores of reservoirs. It appears to be less common on Nantucket and Martha's Vineyard than it was formerly, possibly due to the disappearance of plowed fields. Adult Baird's Sandpipers are rare in the Northeast, but the following early records clearly represent adult birds: 1, Plymouth Beach, 8 July 1976 (Moore); 1, Nauset, Eastham, 13 July 1976 (Nikula); 1, Plum Island, 23 July 1981 (Heil). The only records of adults inland are: 1, Marlboro, 27 July 1967 (Argue); 2, GMNWR, 24 July 1975 (Forster, Baird).

The average migration period for juveniles is from late August to late September, when ordinarily 1 to 4 birds are seen. *Fall maxima:* 9, Monomoy, 7 September 1980 (Harrington); 8, Plum Island, 27 September 1977 (Perkins, Vickery); 6, Monomoy, 31 August 1965 (Chandler). Inland: 1, Pittsfield Sewer Beds (first Berkshire County record), 16 August–7 October 1933 (Eliot). Elsewhere inland the Baird's Sandpiper occurs when conditions are suitable—e.g., 3, GMNWR, 2 September 1975 (Brown); 1 collected, Sudbury River meadows, 2 September 1930 (Maynard). Overall seasonal totals average 15 to 20 birds, and the only change in status seems to have occurred inland where a decline results from changes in sewage treatment techniques. Baird's Sandpipers are rare by late October, with the latest records being: 1, Newbury, 17 November 1991 (Leukering); 1, Plum Island, 15–16 November 1968 (Forster, Willmann); 1, Newburyport, 12 November 1972 (Gardler).

## Pectoral Sandpiper   *Calidris melanotos*

**Range:** Primarily Nearctic; breeds from eastern Siberia east through arctic Canada to Southampton Island and south locally to the south coast of Hudson Bay. Winters in southern South America.

**Status:** Locally common to uncommon spring migrant, except on the southeastern coastal plain, where rare. Locally common to very common fall migrant.

**Occurrence:** Pectoral Sandpipers are especially fond of mowed salt marshes and wet, grassy or muddy fields. In spring, they migrate north through the Mississippi River valley and then fly southeastward over the Atlantic Ocean to their South American wintering grounds in fall. They tend to be rather uncommon in spring in Massachusetts and usually occur in largest numbers in fall following stormy or rainy weather.

Pectoral Sandpipers occur most frequently and in largest numbers either at Newburyport or inland in flooded fields during spring migration. Ordinarily, flocks of 20 to 50 are seen, although occasionally many more appear. *Spring maxima:* 85, Newburyport, 20 April 1977 (Gardler); 46, Marshfield, 2 April 1977 (Petersen); 44, Bolton, 17 April 1977 (Merriman). In the spring of 1981, unprecedented numbers were seen in the Northeast, from coastal

Massachusetts and Connecticut west to central New York. Peak counts for Massachusetts were: 1,000 +, Newburyport, 20 April (Heil et al); 360, Marshfield, 11 April (Veit, Litchfield); 68, Concord, 27 April (Walton); 43, Topsfield, 11 April (Heil). The causes of this major eastward displacement are unclear. Pectoral Sandpipers are scarce before April and after early May. *Extreme dates:* 1, Newburyport, 12 March 1978 (Petersen); 5, Hardwick, 16 March 1971 (Clark).

Occasionally, Pectoral Sandpipers are reported in Massachusetts during the summer—e.g., 1, Rowley, 6 June 1964 (Emery et al); 1, WBWS, 12 June 1973 (Harris); 2, Monomoy, 12 June 1980 (Nikula); 1, Plymouth Beach, 17 June 1967 (D'Entremont); 1, Monomoy, 12–30 June 1980 (Petersen). The fall migration is very protracted, normally extending from the third week of July to late October. *Fall maxima:* "hundreds," Ipswich, early October 1899 (fide Townsend); 205, "after northeast storm," Nantucket, 8 August 1956 (Dennis); 200 +, Monomoy, 30 September 1962 (Copeland); 200, Nauset, Eastham, 27 September 1975 (VO); 175 +, Monomoy, 27 September 1979 (Nikula). Inland: 200, Halifax, 27 October 1984 (Petersen); 119, Worcester, 8 October 1954 (Crompton, Eliot); 70, Halifax, 21 September 1985 (Petersen); 65, Halifax, 8 August 1978 (Petersen); 50, GMNWR, 27 September 1980 (Petersen); 42, Pittsfield, 9 October 1948 (Eliot et al); 40–50, Lancaster, 27 September 1975 (Merriman). The latest date is: 2, 28 November 1978, Wellfleet (Nikula).

## Sharp-tailed Sandpiper    *Calidris acuminata*

**Range:** Eastern Palearctic; breeds in northeastern Siberia; winters in the southwest Pacific from New Guinea and the Tonga Islands south to Australia. Regular in fall along the western coast of North America.

**Status:** Vagrant: three records.

**Occurrence:** There are three records of the Sharp-tailed Sandpiper in Massachusetts. The first record was a remarkable spring occurrence, when Karsten Hartel discovered an adult in vivid, unworn alternate plumage at Plymouth Beach on 30 June 1971. It was collected later the same day by Hagar; specimen currently at the MCZ (#329444). The two fall records are: 1 juvenile, Newburyport Harbor, 3–5 November 1973 (Petersen, Forster, Emery, et al); 1 juvenile, Newburyport, 15 October 1989 (McMenemy, VO).

## Cox's Sandpiper    *Calidris paramelanotos*

**Range:** Uncertain; all existing specimens and previous sight records are from Australia during the period September to March (Hayman et al 1986).

**Status:** Vagrant: one record.

**Occurrence:** Possibly the most intriguing and enigmatic bird to ever appear in Massachusetts was a juvenile calidrid sandpiper that was captured, banded, photographed, and released by a shorebird banding team from the Manomet Bird Observatory at Duxbury Beach, 15 September 1987 (Kasprzyk et al). Although ambiguous in plumage characteristics and bill length, the bird was initially identified as a Pectoral Sandpiper. Upon subsequent examination of photos taken of the bird in hand, the original identification was questioned and opinion swung toward the possibility that the bird was a Sharp-tailed Sandpiper. Between 18 and 21 September, Mark Kasprzyk, Richard Forster, Peter Vickery, Davis Finch, and a number of other observers again located the mysterious sandpiper, photographed it, and took copious notes on its appearance (Vickery et al 1987, Forster 1987b). By 19 September, a number of experienced observers expressed the opinion that the bird showed many of the characteristics of the recently described Cox's Sandpiper (Parker 1982). Unfortunately, the sandpiper evaded further attempts to recapture it before its disappearance on 21 September.

Opinions regarding the precise taxonomic status of the Cox's Sandpiper remain controversial. Some argue that it represents a hybrid between the Curlew Sandpiper and either the Sharp-tailed Sandpiper or the Pectoral Sandpiper (Kasprzyk et al 1987, Morimoto 1987) while others support the notion that it is a distinct species with an undescribed breeding range somewhere in eastern Eurasia. In either case, its appearance has analogues in other eastern Paleartic shorebirds that have occurred in Massachusetts (e.g., Terek Sandpiper, Rufous-necked Stint, Sharp-tailed Sandpiper). While the precise identity and taxonomic standing of this interesting sandpiper await final determination, its well-documented occurrence in Massachusetts cannot be denied.

# Purple Sandpiper  *Calidris maritima*

**Range:** Holarctic; breeds, in North America, on islands in the Canadian Arctic south to the east shore of Hudson Bay; winters along rocky coasts from Newfoundland to Virginia.

**Status:** Locally very common winter resident; rare elsewhere.

**Occurrence:** The Purple Sandpiper is the most numerous and regular of the wintering shorebirds in mainland Massachusetts, where it is confined to rocky coasts. It is most common along the North Shore, on the outer islands of Boston Harbor, and in the Cohasset-Scituate area; however, flocks of more than 10 birds are unusual on Cape Cod and the Islands. The first migrants of fall usually arrive by early October, although maximum concentrations occur between early November and late March. In recent years, sizeable flocks have lingered until late May—e.g., 150, Nahant, 22 May 1979

(Stymeist); 125+, North Scituate, 21 May 1977 (Petersen); 120, Lynn, 21 May 1977 (Veit). *Maxima:* Up to 800 birds in flock, North Scituate, since the early 1960s (VO); 400, Nahant, 30 April 1972, (Petersen). Summer records: 2 collected, Beverly, 30 July 1897 (Clark); 3, Tuckernuck Island, 31 July 1977 (Veit, Litchfield); 1, Plymouth Beach, 8 August 1975 (B. Harrington); 1, Plymouth Beach, 11 August 1970 (Petersen, Hartel); 1, Acoaxet, 12 August 1954 (Proctor, Hentershee); 2, Manomet, 17 August 1977 (Houghton); 1, Salem, 20 August 1979 (Alden). The only inland records are: 1, Onota Lake, Pittsfield, 25 October 1953 (not 1954 as stated by Griscom and Snyder 1955) (Hendricks); 1, Onota Lake, Pittsfield, 28 October 1963 (Hendricks).

# Dunlin   *Calidris alpina*

**Range:** Holarctic; the North American race, *C. a. pacifica*, breeds in arctic North America from northern Alaska and Somerset Island south to the south coast of Hudson Bay. Winters along the Gulf Coast, the Pacific Coast, and the Atlantic Coast from Massachusetts to Florida.

**Status:** Abundant to locally very abundant spring and fall migrant on the coast; rare inland. Locally common winterer, mainly south of Boston.

**Occurrence:** The Dunlin is one of the most numerous and familiar sandpipers in the Northern Hemisphere and one of the most frequently encountered species on local tidal flats in fall and winter. In spring there seem to be two separate peaks of migrants, the largest occurring during the first two weeks in May, with a secondary wave taking place in late May. Large counts during April are assumed to be congregations of birds that have wintered locally or just to the south of Massachusetts—e.g., 1,000, South Wellfleet, 20 April 1963 (Bailey); 1,000, Outer Cape, 12 April 1955 (Hill, Petty); 300, Duxbury Beach, 18 April 1981 (Petersen). Normally, peak counts in May average fewer than 1,000 birds at Newburyport and Cape Cod. *Spring maxima:* 3,500, Monomoy, 16 May 1980 (Nikula); 1,600, Chatham, 3 May 1945 (Griscom). Inland counts are usually of single birds—maximum: 30, Onota Lake, Pittsfield, 15 May 1976 (VO). Nonbreeding stragglers are rare but regular in June and July.

The average fall migration period is from late August to late November, with peak counts usually occurring in October or early November. *Fall maxima:* 5,000, Nauset, Eastham, 31 October 1981 (Petersen); 4,200, outer Cape, 25–28 November 1960 (Smart et al); 4,000+, Monomoy, 17 October 1976 (Veit et al); 4,000, Barnstable, 24 October 1977 (Pease); 3,500+, Duxbury, throughout November 1976 (Moore). Inland, usually 1 to 10 birds are seen, but occasionally much higher counts occur—e.g., 85, GMNWR, 14 October 1969 (Alden); 70+, Petersham, 22 October 1972 (Racik, McGuirk); 35, Sudbury River valley, 18 October 1946 (Snyder); 15, Sudbury River valley,

12 October 1897 (Paine, fide Griscom). Cape Cod Christmas Bird Count totals have ranged from 244 to 3,000 during the years 1954 to 1980 and have averaged about 1,000. *Winter maxima:* 2,000 +, Nauset, Eastham, 21 January 1971 (Petersen); 1,000, Eastham, 11 February 1978 (Petersen); 1,000, Hull-Scituate, 15 January 1978 (Litchfield); 200, Revere, 26 January 1974 (Veit). Several hundred birds often winter in the vicinity of Cohasset and Scituate.

**Subspecies:** Additional races of the Dunlin have been collected in Massachusetts as follows: 1, *C. a. alpina*, Monomoy, 8 August 1936 (Griscom 1937a); 1, *C. a. arctica*, Monomoy, 11 August 1900 (Cochrane, Griscom 1937a).

**Remarks:** An albino Dunlin was observed at Plum Island, 26 November 1968 (Leahy).

## Curlew Sandpiper   *Calidris ferruginea*

**Range:** Palearctic; breeds in northeastern Siberia, east to Alaska (rarely). Winters in the Old World south to southern Africa, Australia, and New Zealand.

**Status:** Rare but regular migrant in late spring and early fall.

**Occurrence:** The Curlew Sandpiper is a Eurasian species whose frequent occurrence on the East Coast of North America has been hypothetically explained in three different ways (see Bull 1964). In Massachusetts, this sandpiper has been found most frequently at Newburyport, Squantum, Plymouth Beach, Monomoy, and Nauset, Eastham. Since 1954, there have been over twenty spring records spanning the period 15 May to 20 June, with over half of these between 20 and 30 May. There are at least twenty-nine published fall sight records, distributed as follows: July, 8; August, 10; September, 5; and October, 2. Records of juveniles should be carefully examined because, to date, there are only two such confirmed Massachusetts records: 1, Ipswich, 21–22 September 1985 (Nielsen, VO); 1, Squantum, 5–20 September 1991 (Donovan, VO). In addition to the localities listed above, there are two records from the Islands: 1, West Tisbury, "about" 9 July 1967 (Chalif); 1, Nantucket, 4–5 August 1979 (Harte, Litchfield).

**Remarks:** Of all the fall specimens of Curlew Sandpipers from New England, only one, from Pine Point, Maine, 15 September 1881 (BMS #XOI–164) was a juvenile. It is unlikely that many juveniles have been overlooked because juvenile Curlew Sandpipers are quite distinctive. If Nisbet's hypothesis that Curlew Sandpipers cross the Atlantic directly east to west during fall migration (BB 52: 205–15) is correct, then we should expect to see at least as many juveniles as adults here in Massachusetts. Thus, one would be more inclined, on the basis of Massachusetts records, to accept Eisenmann's view (BB 53: 136–40) that the birds cross the tropical Atlantic during the fall migration and then migrate north the following spring with the New World shorebirds. This would account for the numerous spring records on the East Coast, as well as the lack of records of juveniles here in the fall. Curiously, however, juvenile Curlew Sandpipers have occurred with some regularity in the New York area (Davis, pers. comm.) during fall.

## Stilt Sandpiper  *Calidris himantopus*

**Range:** Nearctic; breeds from northern Alaska and Victoria Island, south and east to northern Ontario; winters in central South America.

**Status:** Rare but regular in spring; variously uncommon to locally common fall migrant.

**Occurrence:** Stilt Sandpipers migrate north in spring mainly through the Mississippi River valley, but in fall they occur regularly on the Atlantic Coast from Massachusetts south. In Massachusetts, Stilt Sandpipers are found in greatest numbers at the salt pannes on Plum Island, at the ponds on South Monomoy, and occasionally at inland sewer beds.

Although both Griscom and Snyder (1955) and Hill (1964) suggested that the Stilt Sandpiper was unrecorded in Massachusetts prior to about 1870, Brewer (1876, quoted in Townsend 1905) clearly states that "nearly 200 individuals were secured by members of the Phillips family . . . in Swampscott . . . about the year 1860." Considering that 215 individuals were shot near the Chatham Beach Hotel from 1897 to 1904, including 103 in 1901 (see Griscom & Snyder 1955, Hill 1964), it seems likely that, prior to the market gunning period, the Stilt Sandpiper was a regular, but overlooked, fall migrant in Massachusetts.

Since 1955, when flocks of 20 to 30 represented maximum fall counts and there were only two acceptable spring reports, the Stilt Sandpiper has markedly increased in Massachusetts. There have been at least nineteen spring sight records of Stilt Sandpipers since 1954, and flocks of over 50 birds are not unusual in late July and early August. Most of these spring records are from the Newburyport area during the last three weeks of May. Early dates include: 1, Salisbury, 7 April 1984 (Bennett et al); 1 clearly photographed, Newburyport, 10–30 April 1977 (Veit, Litchfield); 1, Ipswich, 13 April 1990 (Richards, Bieda); 2, Plum Island, 28–30 April 1971 (Garrey, Donahue). There are four spring records from Cape Cod: 1, Monomoy, 26 May 1951 (Griscom, Eliot, et al); 1, Monomoy, 31 May 1975 (Nisbet, Howard); 1, Wellfleet, 8 May 1976 (Nikula); 1, Monomoy, 28 May 1976 (Bailey). Also, 1, Marshfield, 11 May 1980 (Petersen). The species has been reported almost annually in spring since 1964. Fall migrants regularly arrive during the first week of July, the earliest being: 1, Plum Island, 30 June 1986 (Petersen). *Fall maxima:* 81, Plum Island, 4 August 1974 (Forster); 78, Monomoy, 30 July 1974 (Harrington); 70, Monomoy, 22 July 1975 (Goodrich); 70, Plum Island, 15 August 1976 (Forster). The majority of these birds were adults; juvenile Stilt Sandpipers are uncommon to rare in Massachusetts and occur mainly between mid-August and October. *Inland maxima:* 35 after a heavy rain, Wayland, 3 September 1955 (Morgan, Stackpole); 12, Westboro, 9 September 1981 (Jenkins); 11, Spencer, 10 August 1946 (Kraus); 10, GMNWR, 6 September 1978 (Albee, Forster).

Away from Plum Island and Monomoy, Stilt Sandpipers are ordinarily rare, with "no more than two reported daily" from Berkshire County (McNair 1978). Stilt Sandpipers are rare in Massachusetts after September, although there are at least ten October and five November records since 1956, the latest being: 4, Rowley, 12 November 1979 (Petersen).


# Buff-breasted Sandpiper  *Tryngites subruficollis*

**Range:** Nearctic; breeds in Alaska and northwestern Canada east to Devon and Victoria islands; winters in Patagonia. Most migrate through the Mississippi River valley, although some juveniles migrate along the Atlantic Coast in fall.

**Status:** Uncommon fall migrant on the coast; rare inland.

**Occurrence:** Although Buff-breasted Sandpipers have never been numerous in Massachusetts, they became especially rare following the market gunning period at the turn of the century. They have subsequently increased, especially during the last 40 years. Buff-breasted Sandpipers are most often found in plowed areas or fields with short grass; also occasionally on the uppermost reaches of tidal flats, where they associate with Lesser Golden-Plovers or Baird's Sandpipers. There are only two spring sight records in Massachusetts: 1, Newburyport, 12–13 May 1971 (Fray, Scott, Emery, Claybourne); 1, Bolton, 28 April 1984 (Carroll, Lynch). The species is rare before the third week of August—e.g., 1, Sterling, 5 August 1971 (McMenemy)—and after late September. Massachusetts fall totals have ranged from a few individuals to as many as twenty-six (1973). Typical counts range from 1 to 6 birds. *Maximum:* 18, Plum Island, 2 September 1971 (Forster, Baird). The latest date on record is: 1, Nantucket, 1 December 1980 (Veit). Most Buff-breasted Sandpipers are seen on the coast, but they are occasionally recorded inland where conditions are suitable. There are seven Worcester County records between 1958 and 1982, spanning the period 5 August 1971 to 2 October 1977 (fide *The Chickadee*). In Berkshire County, there are three records of single birds from the Pittsfield Sewer Beds: 27 August 1970; 8 September 1974; and 10–11 September 1959 (McNair 1978).

# Ruff   *Philomachus pugnax*

**Range:** Chiefly Palearctic; breeds from Britain and Scandinavia east to northeastern Siberia and, occasionally, western Alaska. Winters from Africa and Britain to Australasia. Rare but regular migrant virtually throughout North America.

**Status:** Rare but regular migrant.

**Occurrence:** The Ruff is the Palearctic shorebird most frequently encountered in North America, and it occurs in Newburyport Harbor almost as frequently as at any other locality on the Atlantic Coast. For instance, between 1955 and 1981, there were sixty-nine spring and eighty-one fall reports, mostly from Newburyport and Monomoy, but also including eleven records from inland sites.

In spring, there is a concentration of records from mid-April to mid-May, but the fall migratory period is less clearly defined. There is a slight preponderance of records in early July, mostly pertaining to adult males, and all records of juveniles have occurred during September. Early records include: 1, Plympton, 3–4 April 1969 (Pratt, VO); 1, East Boston, 5 April 1981 (Zendeh). *Maximum:* 4, Newburyport, 29 April–14 May 1978 (VO). There are no records of more than 2 birds together at any one place in fall, but as many as 7 have been reported in Massachusetts during the course of a single fall migration (e.g., 1974 [BOEM]). The only Berkshire County record is: 1, Ashley Falls, 23 May 1970 (Parker et al). The latest date on record is: 1, Nantucket, 28 November 1953 (Heywood).

**Remarks:** Unlike Curlew Sandpipers, there are at least eight substantiated records of juvenile Ruffs from New England, all seen in September, including a specimen from Chatham, 15 September 1880 (PMS #7726), and, more recently: 1, Plum Island, 8–22 September 1974 (Petersen, Forster).

# Short-billed Dowitcher   *Limnodromus griseus*

**Range:** Nearctic; breeds in coastal southern Alaska and in Canada from southeastern Yukon and northeastern Manitoba south to central British Columbia and Saskatchewan; also on the Ungava Peninsula. Winters from central California, the Gulf Coast, and South Carolina south to Peru and Brazil.

**Status:** Very common spring and abundant fall migrant on the coast; occasionally very common inland.

**Occurrence:** Short-billed Dowitchers are among the more conspicuous of the migrant shorebirds in Massachusetts. Because they prefer to feed on extensive sand and mud flats, they are numerous in Essex County and on Cape Cod. The first migrants arrive in Massachusetts during the last few days of April, but the peak of northward-moving birds occurs between 14 and 25 May, with maximum counts consistently numbering between 250 and 400 birds at Newburyport and Cape Cod. Definite early records have occurred as follows: 1, Plum Island, 23 March 1978 (Kasprzyk, Heil); 3, Marshfield, 4 April 1954 (May). *Spring maxima:* 1,400+, Newburyport, 23 May 1976 (Veit); 700, Newburyport, 27 May 1977 (Veit). Flocks of inland migrating dowitchers are occasionally forced to land due to rainy weather—e.g., 250+, Bolton, 18 May 1978 (Salmela); 150, Ashley Falls, 20 May 1970 (Conant); 134, Granby, 20 May 1970 (Yenlin); 101, Pittsfield, 24 May 1970 (Goodrich). On 22 May 1979, 235 were counted flying northeast over South Hanson (Petersen).

Though there are several records of summering birds, migrating adult dowitchers do not appear until early July, with peak counts occurring the third or fourth week; juveniles follow in August and September. Short-billed Dowitchers are rare after September. *Fall maxima:* 6,000, Monomoy, 25 July 1958 (MacLary); 5,000, Monomoy, 22 July 1954 (Griscom); 2,300, Monomoy, 18–21 July 1979 (Heil); 2,200, Newburyport, 18 July 1978 (Petersen). Exceptionally late fall migrants include: 1, Menemsha Pond, Martha's Vineyard, 2 December 1979 (Laux, Nikula, Trull); 2, WBWS, 27 October 1979 (Heil, Nikula); 1, Eastham, 24 October 1976 (Petersen). Virtually all December dowitchers in Massachusetts have proven to be *L. scolopaceus*. Inland, Short-billed Dowitchers are uncommon, with maxima of: 22, South Egremont, 28 July 1955 (Eliot); 15, Bolton, 5 July 1967 (Jenkins, Blodget); 9, GMNWR, 24 July 1975 (Forster); 2, GMNWR, 3 October 1978 (Walton, Forster).

**Subspecies:** Two races of the Short-billed Dowitcher, *L. g. griseus*, which breeds in northern Quebec and Labrador, and *L. g. hendersoni*, which breeds in inland Canada to the west of Hudson Bay, occur in the state. The vast majority of spring Short-billed Dowitchers in Massachusetts are of the nominate race; indeed, *L. g. hendersoni* remains to be positively recorded in Massachusetts in spring. Heil (in litt.) found that at Newburyport, *L. g. griseus* outnumbered *L. g. hendersoni* by about 100 to 1 in fall (cf Jehl 1963) and that the two races appear to have similar migratory schedules. In Plymouth, Harrington (in litt.) found that most *L. g. hendersoni* occur in July and that this race comprises less than 5 percent of the Short-billed Dowitchers seen at that locality. For a discussion of the field identification of the dowitchers, see Pitelka (1950) and Prater et al (1977).

# Long-billed Dowitcher   *Limnodromus scolopaceus*

**Range:** Primarily Nearctic; breeds along the north and west coasts of Alaska east to northern Mackenzie and in northeastern Siberia; winters from

California and Virginia south to northern South America. In fall, migrants reach the Atlantic Coast from Maine (rarely) to Florida.

**Status:** Very rare in spring; uncommon to fairly common local fall migrant.

**Occurrence:** Long-billed Dowitchers have a strong preference for freshwater habitats near the coast, especially the impoundments and salt pannes at Plum Island. They are uncommon to rare on Cape Cod and the Islands. This species, like the Stilt and Western sandpiper, migrates northwestward toward Alaska at about the latitude of southern New Jersey and is therefore rare along the coast north of that region in spring. A sampling of spring records includes: 1 in alternate plumage, Newburyport, 4 May 1974 (Petersen, Forster); 1 in alternate plumage, Newburyport, 18–24 May 1975 (Petersen, Forster); 1, Monomoy, 31 May 1975 (Nisbet, Howard); 1 in alternate plumage, Newburyport, 11 May 1982 (Forster). The following records almost certainly involve birds that wintered nearby because they appeared four to six weeks before the usual migration period: 1, Nantucket, 15 March 1981 (Perkins); 1, East Boston, 6 April 1980 (Perkins, Veit); 1, Chatham, 13 April 1980 (Nikula); 2, Newburyport, 15–24 April 1978 (Petersen); 1, Newburyport, 19 April 1981 (Perkins).

Since the early 1970s, fall migrating Long-billed Dowitchers have occurred not only in increased numbers, but also earlier in the fall than ever before. Currently, it is not unusual to see the vanguard of adults by mid-July—e.g., 5, Plum Island, 10 July 1981 (Heil); 30, Plum Island, 26 July 1981 (Heil). The majority of adults (frequently 30 to 50 birds) arrive between mid-August and early September, but maximum counts usually occur from late September to early October. The abundance of this species in any given year is contingent upon the suitability of conditions within its preferred habitat. For example, during July 1981 (see above counts), the water level in the Plum Island impoundments was lowered considerably, thereby creating ideal conditions for Long-billed Dowitchers. This species consistently occurs much later in fall than the Short-billed Dowitcher, often remaining common at Plum Island until mid-October, by which time most Short-billeds have departed. *Fall maxima:* 120, Plum Island–Newburyport, 17 October 1976 (Veit, Litchfield); 85 +, Plum Island, 4 September 1985 (Heil). *Extreme dates:* There is an increasing number of December records, the latest of which are: 1, Duxbury, 16 January 1980 (Cutler); 5, Newburyport, 26 December 1977 (Petersen). There are, in addition, several December records of unidentified dowitchers.

Inland, the status of the Long-billed Dowitcher is indeterminate, but the species is probably regular in suitable habitat. Griscom (1949) states that "flocks of up to ten" dowitchers have been recorded in the Sudbury River valley during the period 24 August–18 September, the dates suggesting that either species could be involved. Single Long-billeds have been identified in Worcester, 24 September 1950 (Crompton) and at Sterling, 26–29 Sep-

tember 1971 (Blodget). There are also two records of Long-billeds from
Berkshire County: 1, Pittsfield Sewer Beds, 8–11 September 1943 (Snyder); 1,
Pittsfield Sewer Beds, 25 September 1977 (McNair).

## Common Snipe    *Gallinago gallinago*

**Range:** Holarctic species; the race *G. g. delicata* breeds in boreal and
temperate North America south on the East Coast to northern New Jersey.
Winters from southern British Columbia east through the central United
States, north on the Atlantic Coast to Massachusetts, and south to northern
South America.

**Status:** Rare and local breeder. Common, at times very common, migrant;
rare but regular in winter.

**Breeding:** Common Snipe are rare and local as breeders in Massachusetts,
which lies at the southern periphery of their breeding range. There is,
however, evidence that the species may have been more widespread as a
breeder before the turn of the century (Forbush 1916, Townsend 1905,
Brewster 1906, Griscom 1949).

Six nests were found in Berkshire County between 1976 and 1979 (McNair
1978). Locations there included Pittsfield, Lenox, Windsor, and Stockbridge. In Plymouth County, a pair probably bred at East Bridgewater in
1978 and 1979, although no nest could be located (Petersen et al). Nesting
was confirmed at Bolton in 1980, when a recently fledged chick was found
on 4 July (McMenemy), and at Rutland, 26 May 1983, when 4 downy young
were photographed (Klunk). In addition, single birds have been seen between June and early August in Newburyport, Concord, Spencer, Gloucester, South Hanson, Rowley, and Cambridge.

**Nonbreeding:** Numbers of migrant snipe vary considerably from year to
year, depending on the suitability of the local habitat. The largest numbers
are found when heavy rainfall floods cornfields and grassy meadows. The
statement by Forbush (1912) that the species is more numerous in spring
than in fall due to an overwater migration in fall seems unlikely. It is much
more probable that reduced rainfall and denser vegetation in late summer
result in snipe failing to concentrate to the extent that they do in spring.
Brewster (1906) mentions an enormous flight of snipe that occurred in
September 1875, when four or five hundred snipe were flushed from a rain-
soaked field in Belmont. Such a concentration supports the notion that
Common Snipe congregate whenever the conditions are particularly suitable, without respect to season.

Ordinarily in spring, counts of 30 to 50 are made during the peak of
migration, which typically occurs very near 15 April. Snipes are rare away
from nesting localities after April, and the species is always uncommon on

Cape Cod and the Islands in spring. ***Spring maxima:*** 300, West Bridgewater, 16 April 1982 (Petersen); 225+, Rowley-Newbury, 17 April 1972 (Petersen); 200, Sudbury River valley, 9 April 1972 (Howard); 130+, Bolton, 14 April 1978 (Blodget); 130+, Bolton, 24 April 1980 (Merriman); 80, Pittsfield, 17 April 1965 (McNair).

During the fall, peak migration is ill defined; maximum counts, which range from 30 to 50 in most instances, occur from mid-September to early November. Rare after late December. During midwinter, snipe are rare but rather evenly distributed throughout the state wherever wet places remain unfrozen. January totals for Massachusetts since 1954 have ranged from 1 (1961) to 46 (1974). ***Winter maxima:*** 16, Buttermilk Bay, Wareham, 18 December 1971 (Petersen); 12 survived the winter, North Adams, 1977–1978 (McNair).

# American Woodcock   *Scolopax minor*

**Range:** Nearctic; breeds in eastern North America from southern Newfoundland and southern Ontario south to the Gulf states and southern Florida; winters in the southeastern United States north occasionally to Massachusetts.

**Status:** Locally fairly common breeder and fairly common migrant; rare but regular in winter.

**Breeding:** Woodcocks breed throughout the state wherever there are low, wet thickets and bogs adjacent to fields or clearings. The population is declining, however, mainly due to habitat destruction. ***Egg dates:*** 11 April to 6 May.

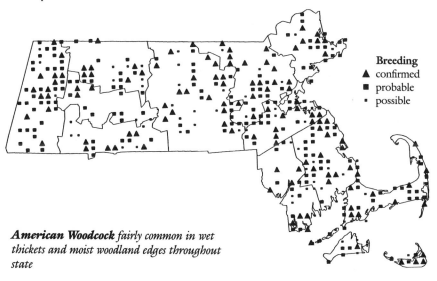

**Breeding**
▲ confirmed
■ probable
· possible

*American Woodcock fairly common in wet thickets and moist woodland edges throughout state*

**Nonbreeding:** Woodcocks generally arrive on their nesting grounds shortly after the first spell of mild weather any time after late February. The general arrival occurs during the second week of March. *Spring maxima:* 49, Martha's Vineyard, 4 April 1962 (Keith); 30, Milton, 25 April 1956 (O'Reagan); 22, Norwood-Milton, 21 April 1980 (Brown).

Due to their secretive behavior, it is difficult to determine the peak of fall migration for woodcocks, and there may well be a separation of age classes as there is with most other shorebird species. During late September and early October, woodcocks are frequently observed flying south just above tree level at dusk. A traditional place to observe this is from the Mid-Cape Highway (Route 6) along the 10-mile stretch to the east of the Sagamore Bridge. During migration, woodcocks often turn up in unlikely places, such as in populated urban areas or on ships at sea.

Cumulative Christmas Bird Count totals probably do not represent the true wintering population, but counts have ranged from 0 (1973) to 13 (1976). *Winter maxima:* 9, Cape Cod CBC, 2 January 1971; 8, Cape Ann CBC, 22 December 1974. Latest inland record: 1, Great Barrington, 31 January 1965 (Smith, Otsch).

**Remarks:** Although voluminous notes have been published on the behavior of American Woodcocks, the following observations are of particular interest because they relate to winter survival. In February 1965, 2 birds were seen feeding upon a mixture of suet and seeds in Mansfield (Emery); and on 18 February 1980, following a deep freeze, Veit, Stymeist, and Litchfield observed a woodcock feeding on a tidal mud flat in Falmouth. The bird was drumming with its feet on the mud in typical woodcock fashion and then extracting polychaete worms after probing the length of its bill into the mud.

# Wilson's Phalarope  *Phalaropus tricolor*

**Range:** Nearctic; breeds from British Columbia and southern Ontario south to California and Texas. There are recent breeding records for Massachusetts, and courting birds have been seen during summer elsewhere on the East Coast. Winters in western South America.

**Status:** Rare breeder. Rare but regular spring and uncommon fall migrant.

**Breeding:** Primarily western in distribution, Wilson's Phalaropes have steadily increased on the East Coast, primarily as fall migrants, since the 1920s. During the 1970s, evidence suggestive of breeding was observed in upstate New York (Montezuma Refuge), Delaware (Little Creek Refuge), New Brunswick (Tantramar Marshes), New York (Jamaica Bay Wildlife Refuge), New Jersey (Hackensack Meadows), and Plum Island, Massachusetts. Between 17 and 21 June 1953, a pair was present at Plum Island (Emilio,

Griscom); after a lapse of ten years, birds were again noted during June at Plum Island from the early 1960s until the present, and, on 22 June 1979, Heil found a nest with three eggs in the Plum Island marshes. Another nest, also with three eggs, was found and photographed at Monomoy, 7 June 1980 (Petersen). Since 1980, occasional breeding has been suspected at one or both localities every summer.

**Nonbreeding:** Aside from the presence of suspected breeding birds, most spring migrants occur in mid-May. *Spring maxima:* 8, Plum Island, 18 May 1977 (VO); 6, Monomoy, 17 May 1977 (Nikula, Goodrich, Bailey); 3, GMNWR, 28 May 1979 (BBC); 2, Bolton, 28 May 1976 (Salmela et al). During fall migration, adult birds arrive in mid-July, and juveniles arrive by early August. Peak numbers normally occur in August, most often at Plum Island and on outer Cape Cod. *Fall maximum:* 12, Plum Island, 2 September 1971 (VO). The species is rare after September. An exceptionally late bird was recorded at Plum Island, 24 November 1966 (Petersen, Forster). Inland, Wilson's Phalaropes are rare, but regular, at localities such as GMNWR, the Bolton Flats, and various sewer beds whenever conditions are suitable. The species was unrecorded in Worcester County until: 1, Spencer, 19–20 September 1947 (Crompton). *Inland maxima:* 2, Pittsfield Sewer Beds, 1 September 1974 (Mineci); 2, GMNWR, 21 August 1977 (Forster).

# Red-necked Phalarope    *Phalaropus lobatus*

**Range:** Holarctic; breeds, in North America, from northern Alaska and southern Baffin Island south to northwestern British Columbia, northern Ontario, and Labrador. Winters at sea, primarily off Peru and western Africa (Senegal).

**Status:** Very common migrant offshore. More frequently seen from land than the Red Phalarope, due to its less pelagic distribution, but outnumbered by the latter species during storms.

**Occurrence:** Red-necked Phalaropes seem to have a shorter migration period than Red Phalaropes, usually arriving somewhat later in spring and departing much earlier in fall. They are occasionally seen from shore at such places as Monomoy and Plum Island; boat trips to Stellwagen Bank and Jeffrey's Ledge often record 1 to 50 birds, with peak numbers in May and from late August through September.

*Spring maxima:* 3,000, North Beach, Chatham, 19 May 1963 (fide Bailey); 2,000, Nahant, 18 May 1978 (Kasprzyk); 1,000, Monomoy, 25 May 1969 (Bailey); 1,000, Plymouth Beach, 11 May 1977 (MBO staff). *Fall maxima:* 10,000, Provincetown Harbor, 9 September 1963 (fide Bailey); 2,000, Rockport to Isles of Shoals, 14 August 1965 (BBC); "thousands," Salisbury, 9

September 1965 (Nichols); 2,000, Ipswich, 3 September 1949 (fide Griscom); 1,500 +, Rockport, 6 August 1968 (Leahy); 1,000, Nauset, Eastham, 7 August 1953 (Snyder). Recent maxima much lower—e.g., 300 +, First Encounter Beach, Eastham, 31 August 1975 (Petersen); 235, off Rockport, 11 August 1973 (Jodrey et al). The latest definitive record is: 1 shot, Plum Island, 4 December 1971 (specimen at MAS).

All inland spring records are from May, and fall records span the dates 25 July-November. *Spring maxima* (inland): 4, Bolton, 26 May 1979 (Blodget, McCaig); 3, Andover, 15 May 1904 (fide Townsend); three Berkshire County records, all mid-May. *Fall maxima* (inland): 5, Pittsfield Sewer Beds, 17–18 August 1947 (Hendricks); 4, Spencer, 25 August 1963 (Crompton). The latest inland date is: 1, Pittsfield Sewer Beds, 7 November 1970 (Weigand).

# Red Phalarope   *Phalaropus fulicaria*

**Range:** Holarctic; breeds, in North America, from Ellesmere Island south to northern Quebec and northern Labrador; winters at sea near the continental slopes of western Africa and western South America.

**Status:** Very abundant migrant near the continental slope; occasionally large numbers are seen from shore, usually during storms. Rare in winter.

**Occurrence:** Red Phalaropes migrate north and south from their arctic breeding grounds along the continental slope off New England, where they feed upon fish eggs (mainly of cod and cusk), which are especially abundant on the surface in that area (Powers 1983). Flocks of many thousands may occasionally be seen during migration by those fortunate enough to travel to slope waters in appropriate seasons. The birds are apparently present off New England from mid-April—earliest, 1, Monomoy, 26–28 March 1966 (Bailey)—to early June, and then again from early September to mid-December. Such an extended stay suggests that the waters of the New England continental slope provide substantial food resources. Major coastal storms with gale-force easterly winds sometimes drive large numbers of these birds within sight of coastal vantage points. During such storms, most phalaropes are usually seen from Cape Cod and the Islands, although, occasionally, major fall flights have been witnessed at Cape Ann.

*Maxima:* 2,416, south edge of Georges Bank, 28 May 1977 (MBO staff); 2,000, Nantucket Lightship, 30 April 1954 (Crompton); 1,500, Great Round Shoal, 13 May 1959 (Crompton); 1,440, south edge of Georges Bank, 27 May 1977 (MBO staff). From land: 25,000, Rockport, 15 November 1957 (Burnett); 7,500, Rockport, 10 November 1962 (Drury); 4,500, Nauset, Eastham, 1 December 1957 (Armstrong et al); 3,000, off Monomoy, 10 May 1969 (Bailey); 2,500, Cape Cod CBC, 22 December 1975; 1,100 +, First Encounter Beach, Eastham, 13 November 1968 (Forster). Tremendous flights also occurred during the fall of 1957, 1962, 1968, and 1992. On the inshore fishing banks, such as Stellwagen Bank, Red Phalaropes are rare before October, and it is unusual to see more than 25 birds per day.

Red Phalaropes occur irregularly into January—e.g., 200, Rockport, 4 January 1958 (Emery et al); 50, First Encounter Beach, Eastham, 21 January 1978 (Nikula, Goodrich); 1, 60 miles northeast of Provincetown, 5 February 1978 (Nikula). Occasionally, they are recorded far inland, and there are six records spanning the dates 8 May to 15 June, from Wellesley, Greenfield, Springfield, Rowley, Lakeville, Lynnfield, and Concord. *Fall maxima:* 2, Chicopee, 30 September 1893 (in Springfield Museum); 1 specimen, Medfield, 16 October 1888 (MCZ #25648); 1, Sudbury River valley, 9 October 1896 (Maynard); 1, Spencer, 22 September 1947 (Crompton); 1, Pittsfield Sewer Beds, 10 October 1959 (Bates); 1, Lake Waban, Wellesley, 29 September 1962 (Gulick); 1, Hadley, 4 September 1968 (Cavanaugh); 1, GMNWR, 27 September 1980 (Petersen); 1, Southboro, 6 November 1983 (Blodget, Meservey, Merriman); 1, GMNWR, 15 October 1988 (Bennett). Some of these birds were storm driven, but others were not, which therefore suggests that at least some overland migration occurs.

## Pomarine Jaeger   *Stercorarius pomarinus*

**Range:** Holarctic; breeds, in North America, along the immediate coast from Alaska and Devon Island south to northern Quebec and southern Baffin Island. Winters at sea in tropical latitudes.

**Status:** Uncommon spring and fairly common fall pelagic migrant. More pelagic and usually less numerous than the Parasitic Jaeger.

**Occurrence:** The relative abundance of the two large jaeger species in Massachusetts is confused by problems of field identification, particularly of immatures in fall. Because many subadults differ between species only with respect to the relative proportions of the body, head, bill, and wings, correct identification requires considerable firsthand experience. Puzzling inconsistencies between years and even between different locations on the same day suggest that specific identification of jaegers should never be based upon probability due to date or location.

Two generalizations seem to be true, especially with the resurgence of interest in oceanic birds during the last ten years. First, while in Massachusetts waters, Pomarine Jaegers are certainly more pelagic than Parasitic Jaegers. Consequently, they are less frequently seen from land, except during easterly storms. Jaegers seen beyond 30 miles from shore are mostly Pomarines. It seems probable that Parasitic Jaegers closely follow large flocks of migrating terns during fall migration, and most of them remain close to shore while in Massachusetts waters. Typically, in Massachusetts, Pomarine

Jaegers are never reported in the large numbers that Parasitic Jaegers are (except see 1991 maxima). Second, jaeger reproductive success apparently varies considerably from year to year, due largely to fluctuations in microtine rodent populations on their breeding grounds. In lean rodent years, adult jaegers occasionally depart from their tundra nesting areas in June without even attempting to nest (Maher 1974). Consequently, migration dates, as well as local numbers in our area, may vary considerably from year to year.

The variation from year to year in local jaeger numbers seems also to be related to the size of schooling fish populations in coastal waters. For instance, in 1981 unprecedented numbers of seabirds were present from September through December in the waters off Cape Cod and Nantucket. Many seabirds were observed feeding upon sand lances (*Ammodytes* sp.), which were so enormously abundant in the littoral zone that thousands of their carcasses could be found strewn along the eastern shores of Nantucket and Cape Cod. Particularly large numbers of both Parasitic and Pomarine jaegers were recorded throughout that period. A similar situation involving "sea herring" (*Clupea* sp.) was recorded in September–November 1886 (Baird 1887), when exceptional numbers of Cory's Shearwaters and jaegers were seen and collected in Buzzards Bay. Extant specimens from that flight year include 2 Pomarine (USNM #109661, #109537), a Parasitic, and a Long-tailed Jaeger, all collected between September and December 1886 by Vinal G. Edwards. All are juveniles or immatures. A jaeger influx of somewhat smaller magnitude occurred during the fall of 1977, when sand lances were again especially abundant in inshore waters.

The earliest spring record is: 2, Martha's Vineyard, 4 May 1947 (Griscom, Emerson). *Spring maxima:* 20 + (mostly immature birds, no Parasitics seen), Georges Bank, 1–14 June 1977 (Veit); 14, off Monomoy, 4 June 1978 (BBC, D'Entremont); 11, Georges Bank, 30 May 1977 (MBO staff). Immatures are of regular occurrence far offshore all summer, and there are five to six records of single birds seen from shore between late June and early August.

Pomarine Jaegers are rare inshore before September; peak counts in recent years have usually occurred in October and November, and most November jaegers have proven to be Pomarines, although Parasitics occasionally occur at that time of year as well. *Fall maxima:* 1,100 during storm, First Encounter Beach, Eastham, 31 October 1991 (Nikula, Perkins, et al, Nikula 1992); 400 during storm, Sandy Neck, Barnstable, 30 October 1991 (Abrams, Cameron); 300 during storm, First Encounter Beach, Eastham, 11 November 1991 (Perkins et al); 50 +, First Encounter Beach, Eastham, 21 September 1977 (Nikula); 53 (3 dark), western Georges Bank, 11–17 September 1979 (Heil); 38 (2 dark), Nantucket Shoals, 20–30 November 1979 (Veit); 30, 30 miles east of Cape Cod, 6 November 1977 (MBO staff); 25, Nantucket, week of 22 September 1974 (Jodrey, Soucy); 25 immatures, North

Beach, Chathem, 11 November 1981 (Petersen, Veit, Nikula, Comeau); 12, Nantucket Sound, 27 November 1981 (Bailey et al); 10+ (mostly light adults), First Encounter Beach, Eastham, 10 December 1978 (Nikula, Bailey); 10+ adults, First Encounter Beach, Eastham, 10 December 1978 (Nikula, Bailey); 8 (2 adults, 5 subadults, 1 dark subadult), First Encounter Beach, Eastham, 31 August 1975 (Forster, Petersen, et al). Very late records include: 1, Nantucket CBC, 1 January 1984 (Brown, D'Entremont); 1, Nauset, Eastham, 26 December 1981 (Nikula); 1 subadult, Cape Cod CBC, Eastham, 20 December 1981 (Petersen). There are also the following December records of unidentified immature jaegers: 1, Revere, 16 December 1978 (Veit); 1 dark, Tuckernuck Island, 13–15 December 1975 (Veit); 2–4, First Encounter Beach, Eastham, 10 December 1978 (Nikula, Bailey); 1, Rockport, 9 December 1978 (Veit). The latest local specimens are: 1 collected out of a flock of 25, off Boston Light, 20 November 1909 (MCZ #180003); 1 (light) subadult collected, Woods Hole, 9 December 1891 (Edwards, USNM #128586).

The Pomarine appears to be the least likely jaeger species to occur inland. The only report is: 1 (dark) following Hurricane David, Lake Quabog, East Brookfield, 6 September 1979 (Jenkins).

## Parasitic Jaeger   *Stercorarius parasiticus*

**Range:** Holarctic; in North America breeds from northern Alaska and southern Ellesmere Island south to the south shore of Hudson Bay and northern Labrador. Winters at sea off both coasts of southern South America and off western Africa between Senegal and South Africa.

**Status:** Uncommon spring and uncommon to occasionally very common fall migrant; uncommon to rare in midsummer. Abundance varies considerably from year to year.

**Occurrence:** During migration, Parasitic Jaegers, unlike Pomarines, are found in coastal waters, rarely farther than 25 miles from shore. In fall, this distribution may be influenced by the coastal gathering of Common and Roseate terns, which they regularly parasitize for food. Parasitic Jaegers are encountered most frequently at major tern staging areas, such as Stellwagen Bank, Monomoy, and Nantucket. This distribution suggests that the jaeger's southward migratory path has evolved to follow the migrating terns and may explain their consistently earlier departure in fall than that of Pomarine Jaegers.

The peak of spring migration is ill defined, and it is possible that Parasitic Jaegers stay farther offshore in spring than they do in fall. The earliest spring records are: 1–2, Stellwagen Bank, 3 May 1980 (Petersen); 2, Manomet, 5 May 1977 (MBO staff). *Spring maxima:* 20 adults during a storm,

Cape Cod Bay, 11 June 1977 (Petersen); 10, North Beach, Chatham, 17 May 1970 (Bailey); 9, Sandy Neck, Barnstable, 14 May 1978 (Pease); total of 9 light adults, Muskeget Island, 9–28 May 1981 (Heil); 6, Monomoy, 29 May 1955 (Griscom). In summer, scattered singles are reported in late June and early July. *Summer maxima:* 20 during a storm, Sandy Neck, Barnstable, 30 June 1975 (Pease); 11, Tuckernuck Island, 30 July 1975 (Veit); 8, Monomoy, 28 July 1964 (Bailey).

A pronounced peak of southward-moving birds occurs in late September, although Parasitics occur regularly from August through early October, occasionally remaining into late November. *Fall maxima:* 100, First Encounter Beach, Eastham, 21 September 1977 (Nikula); 85–100 (90 percent light adults), Provincetown, 25 September 1977 (Veit, Perkins, Vickery); 80, off Chatham, 21 August 1954 (Griscom); 80 (2 dark adults), Manomet, 20 September 1977 (Petersen); 80, Sandy Neck, Barnstable, 21 September 1977 (Forster); 70, Stellwagen Bank, 13 September and 20 October 1980 (Hallowell, Stemple); 60, Provincetown, 23 September 1979 (Nikula); 50 +, First Encounter Beach, Eastham, 11 October 1972 (Gardler, Stymeist). The following November records are considered correct: 25–30, First Encounter Beach, Eastham, 13 November 1968 (Forster); 18, First Encounter Beach, Eastham, 3 December 1974 (Goodrich); 10, First Encounter Beach, Eastham, 5 December 1970 (Donahue); 5–6, First Encounter Beach, Eastham, 26 November 1971 (Petersen).

The alleged winter occurrence of the Parasitic Jaeger north to Maine (AOU 1983) seems to be based on a vague statement in Palmer (1949) of birds reported by fishermen in midwinter. The latest Maine record for any jaeger that Palmer specifically mentions is a single bird seen on 30 December 1898, and he suggests that the bird was not identified to species. The extensive seabird distribution survey conducted by the Manomet Bird Observatory never detected any jaegers in winter in New England waters. Inland records: 1, Canton, 13 September 1907 (specimen in BMS); 1, Lake Pontoosuc, Pittsfield, 17–20 September 1970 (Shampang et al).

# Long-tailed Jaeger  *Stercorarius longicaudus*

**Range:** Holarctic; in North America, breeds on the tundra from western Alaska and Ellesmere Island south to northern Quebec and the west shore of Hudson Bay. Atlantic migrants winter off the coast of Argentina and off southwestern Africa.

**Status:** Rare migrant offshore, particularly near the continental slope. Exceedingly rare within sight of land.

**Occurrence:** Long-tailed Jaegers apparently migrate to their wintering grounds off South America via the mid-Atlantic Ocean (Wynne-Edwards

1935), and they do not ordinarily occur close enough to our coast to be influenced by storms, which regularly drive other seabirds close to shore. Recent sight records made from ships (Powers 1983) suggest that a few Long-tailed Jaegers occur regularly during migration near the continental slope off Massachusetts. Although this species at least occasionally travels across the North American continent during migration, as is evidenced by numerous sight records and specimens from the Great Lakes (e.g., Godfrey 1966), there is only one inland record from Massachusetts—i.e., 1 dark juvenile, Massapoag Lake, Sharon, 20 September 1880 (MCZ #29104).

Long-tailed Jaegers have occurred in Massachusetts primarily from late May through mid-June, and again from mid-August through late September. Specimens: 1 juvenile, Gloucester, 23 August 1878 (USNM #75207); 1 subadult, Dorchester Bay, 13 June 1903 (MCZ #18007); 1 subadult, five miles off Cape Ann, 28 July 1910 (MCZ #328069); 1 juvenile shot while "flying over his [Pitman's] decoys in the salt marsh," Eagle Hill, Ipswich, 24 August 1901 (Pitman, see Townsend 1905) (PMS #7471); 1 juvenile, Woods Hole, September 1886 (USNM #109450).

There are thirteen spring sight records since 1940, spanning the dates 24 May to 20 June, four of these from Georges Bank, including: 1 adult clearly photographed, 8 June 1977 (Veit). In fall, there are at least twenty reports since 1954, mainly of single birds, spanning the dates 16 August to 10 November. *Fall maxima:* 6 adults, Monomoy, 21 September 1941 (Griscom); 4 adults, Monomoy, 9 September 1941 (Griscom); 3, Monomoy, 29 August 1954 (Griscom). Since then, all records are of single birds, except: 3 juveniles, near Hydrographer Canyon, 2 September 1982 (Russell, Veit, Powers, et al).

# Great Skua   *Catharacta skua*

**Range:** Palearctic in northern hemisphere; nominate race, *C. s. skua*, breeds in Iceland and on the Faeroe and Shetland islands and disperses widely over the North Atlantic in winter. The other three races all breed in the Southern Hemisphere and have not yet been proven to disperse north of the equator (Devillers 1977).

**Status:** Rare to uncommon, but regular, visitor to Georges Bank and Nantucket Shoals. Occasionally seen from land during storms, especially from October to December.

**Occurrence:** In Massachusetts, skuas are found over the open ocean and, perhaps due to their powerful flying capability, are only rarely seen from land during storms. Skuas occur most frequently around the perimeter of Georges Bank and on the Nantucket Shoals, and most concentrations that have been observed were associated with commercial fishing operations. At these rich food sources, they have been observed feeding mostly by scavenging rather than by kleptoparasitic behavior.

Since at least 1870, skuas of one form or another have been recorded in New England waters in every month of the year, with a clustering of records during November to February and again during June and July (Collins 1884b). It is suspected that most of the winter records pertain to this species, whereas most of the summer birds are clearly South Polar Skuas. Because skuas do not breed until they are five years old (Cramp et al 1974), it is possible that some immature Great Skuas are resident off the New England coast all year. **Maxima** (offshore): Unless otherwise indicated, all the following records pertain to Great Skuas: 10, Georges Bank, 20–30 October 1976 (Lloyd-Evans); 10 unidentified skuas, Great South Channel and Northeast Peak, Georges Bank, 1–30 November 1977 (MBO); 4–6, 75 miles south of Martha's Vineyard, 4 February 1978 (Nikula); 3, Eastham, 31 October 1991 (Perkins, Nikula, VO). Between 1972 and 1986, there were nine records of skuas from First Encounter Beach, Eastham, between 28 August and 16 December (Nikula, Goodrich, Bailey, Petersen, et al); 1, Milk Island, Rockport, 19 February 1930 (Griscom); 1, Rockport, 28 December 1973 (Leahy); 1, Provincetown, 19 September 1976 (Bailey). There are two records for summer: 1, 40° 53′N, 70° 21′W, or 20 miles south of Nantucket, 17 June 1979 (Nickerson); 1 collected, south of Martha's Vineyard, July 1980 (Nickerson for MBO). There are three records of Great Skuas from Massachusetts waters that were banded in Britain: 1 found dead, Swampscott, 4 February 1940 (Garrison 1940, BMS #X03–153); the July 1980 specimen previously mentioned; 1 picked up dead, Duxbury, 1 November 1981 (fide Forster), which had been banded as a chick at Foula, Shetland Islands, 1976.

# South Polar Skua  *Catharacta maccormicki*

**Range:** Antarctic; breeds on the Antarctic continent and north to the South Shetland and Balleny islands. In southern winter, north to the North Pacific and North Atlantic oceans.

**Status:** Rare to uncommon, but regular, summer (May–September) visitor or resident.

**Occurrence:** Prior to Devillers' (1977) clarification of the taxonomy and distribution of the various forms of *Catharacta*, *C. maccormicki* was not recognized as occurring anywhere in the Northern Hemisphere. In that work, Devillers concentrated on the identification of the skuas that are regularly recorded in the North Pacific Ocean, showed that every specimen collected there was, in fact, *C. maccormicki*, and suggested that this form is the only transequatorial migrant of the group.

More recently, Salomonsen (1976), Veit (1978), and Lee and Booth (1979) have shown that *C. maccormicki* also occurs in the North Atlantic between May and September. In Massachusetts, the first definite record of a South Polar Skua was from Georges Bank, June 1977, when Veit (op cit) identified at least 8 to 10 individuals out of 25 skuas that were feeding in the vicinity of a Soviet fishing fleet roughly 175 miles east southeast of Nantucket. In 1978, 5 to 6 South Polar Skuas were identified between 7 and 13 June at various points on Georges Bank (Veit), and a single individual was seen 15 September 1979 on Georges Bank (Heil).

Two specimens of South Polar Skuas have recently been taken in Massachusetts waters: 1, 73 miles southeast of Nantucket, 18 August 1978 (Nickerson for MBO); 1 dark-morph adult, Hydrographer Canyon, 25 May 1981 (Backus for MBO, USNM #582499). Powers (1983) demonstrated that all the recent sightings of South Polar Skuas off the Massachusetts coast have occurred between April and October, with peak numbers in May and June. Peak numbers of unidentified skuas, however, occur in July. These sightings are probably mostly South Polar Skuas but may also include a few Great Skuas.

The discovery of South Polar Skuas off the New England coast prompted a reexamination of the extant specimens of skuas from New England waters. Two specimens (BMS #20803, #20804) collected 18 miles east of Chatham, 11 August 1957 (Kleber) are *C. maccormicki*, 1 adult female and 1 immature male. A male collected on the Northeast Peak of Georges Bank, 4 August 1877 (MCZ #35991) is either *C. maccormicki* or possibly a *C. maccormicki* x *C. s. lonnbergi* hybrid (Watson, in litt.).

# Laughing Gull   *Larus atricilla*

**Range:** Nearctic; breeds along the Atlantic Coast from Nova Scotia south to Florida, along the Gulf Coast, in the Caribbean, and in the Salton Sea of southern California. Atlantic birds winter from North Carolina and the Gulf Coast south to Panama.

**Status:** Very common to abundant local breeder; locally very common spring and common to abundant fall migrant. Very rare in midwinter on the coast and rare inland in any season.

**Breeding:** Laughing Gulls were almost extirpated from New England due to persecution for the millinery trade in the latter portion of the 19th century. Following a protection program initiated largely through the efforts of George H. Mackay, the traditional colony at Muskeget Island increased steadily until the 1940s, when an estimated 20,000 pairs bred there (Drury 1973a, 1974; Nisbet 1971). From then until 1972, the colony steadily decreased, concurrent with the arrival and subsequent massive increase of Herring and Great Black-backed gulls. Nisbet (1971) acknowledged that the nature of the competition between the Laughing Gull and the larger species was unclear, but suggested that the Herring and Great Black-backed gulls simply arrived earlier in the season and usurped the space that would otherwise have been available for Laughing Gulls. In 1972, Laughing Gulls disappeared entirely from Muskeget following Hurricane Agnes, but 42 nests and 200 adult birds were found on Monomoy later in the same season (Nisbet 1976a). The Monomoy colony then increased to 1,000 nesting pairs by 1981 (Nisbet). During recent years, most birds from Monomoy have shifted to New Island, Eastham, where Hecker reported 956 nesting pairs in 1990.

A very recently fledged young bird was found at Salem, 6 July 1945 (Walcott), and Nisbet (1971) cites records of up to 700 adults seen at Nahant during May and June in the years 1940 to 1952, so it is possible that Laughing Gulls nested on one of the offshore islands between Cape Ann and Boston during that period. *Egg dates:* 21 May–12 July.

**Nonbreeding:** In spring, single birds or small flocks of up to ten birds are seen moving north along the coast between mid-April and mid-May. Earliest arrivals are: 1, Brewster, Acoaxet, 22 March 1958 (Gardler, Anderson); 1, Martha's Vineyard, 25 March 1923 (Foster); 6, Nahant, 8 April 1945 (Griscom). *Spring maxima:* 800 +, Chatham, 7 May 1980 (Heil); 700, Nahant, 14 May 1945 (Griscom). Inland records include: 1, Blackstone, 9 March 1950 (Crompton); 2, Wachusett Reservoir, 12–13 May 1979 (Blodget); 2, Boylston, 13 May 1979 (Blodget); 1, Holyoke, 27 April 1954 (Eliot). *Fall maxima:* 2,500 +, Menemsha Pond, Martha's Vineyard, 28 October 1979 (Laux et al); 2,300 +, Monomoy, 18 August 1980 (Petersen et al); 1,500, Quincy, 12 August 1951 (Higginbotham); 1,000, Quincy, 2 September 1957 (Higginbotham). Inland: 4 after a hurricane, Pittsfield, 16 October 1954 (Hendricks); 1, Lake Pontoosuc, Pittsfield, 8 November 1959 (Eliot); 2, Lakeville, 24 August 1980 (Petersen); 1, Northampton, 21 August 1935 (Eliot et al); 1, Northampton, 7 August 1954 (Eliot); 1, Concord, 8 October 1972 (Agush). In recent years, up to 20 have been seen daily in late summer on ponds two to three miles inland in Lynn and Peabody.

In November, after the bulk of locally nesting Laughing Gulls have departed, large flocks of the young of the year congregate at staging areas in Winthrop, Nahant, on Wollaston Beach, and occasionally off Martha's Vineyard. It is unclear whether these are birds of more southerly origin that disperse northward following the breeding season or locally raised birds that have lingered undetected until they aggregate at these staging areas. *Maxima:* 600 +, Menemsha Pond, Martha's Vineyard, 2 December 1979 (Laux et al); 300, Boston Harbor, 11 November 1973 (Brown); 226, Wollaston, 2 December 1948 (fide Bailey); 175, Wollaston, 24 November 1956 (Higginbotham).

Of the existing records, the following are most indicative of local wintering: 1, Nantucket, 3 March 1954 (Crompton); 1, Chatham, "throughout February" 1955 (Mosher); 1, Gay Head, Martha's Vineyard, 4 February and 29 March 1968 (Hancock); 1, Plymouth, 27 February 1974 (Briggs); 1, Revere-Lynn, 8–14 February 1976 (Komar, Veit).

**Remarks:** Banding returns indicate that at least some Monomoy breeders winter in Central America (Nisbet, pers. comm.).

## Franklin's Gull  *Larus pipixcan*

**Range:** Nearctic; breeds from southeastern Alberta and southwestern Manitoba south to eastern Oregon and northwestern Iowa. Winters primarily along the Pacific Coast of South America south to Tierra del Fuego. Vagrant to the East Coast of North America and to western Europe.

**Status:** Very rare spring and rare fall migrant.

**Occurrence:** The first Massachusetts specimen of a Franklin's Gull was an immature in first basic plumage collected in Salem, 28 October 1885 (PMS #6240). It was not until 1941 that another was recorded in the state; then, between 1941 and 1983, fifteen records were established as follows: 8 during the limited period 1–11 September; 4 in May; 3 in October; and 1 each in July, August, and December. The clustering of records in early September contrasts with the October–November occurrence of juveniles at the Niagara River on the New York–Ontario border (Beardslee & Mitchell 1965, Bull 1974). This pattern may result from a differential migration of the age classes because most of the Massachusetts records from September pertain to adult birds. Since 1985, Franklin's Gulls have become of nearly annual occurrence in Massachusetts. Among the convincing spring occurrences in Massachusetts are: 1 adult, Monomoy, 30 May 1946 (Griscom); 1 adult, Monomoy, 23 June 1946 (fide Bailey); 1 adult, 10 miles east of Boston, 25 May 1981 (Petersen et al); 1 adult, Nantucket, 9–10 June 1982 (Farrell, Andrews, Perkins); 1 adult color photographed, Monomoy, 28 May 1983 (Petersen); 1 adult, Newburyport, 25 April 1988 (Perkins et al). Additional non-September records include: 1 adult, Ipswich, 30 July 1952 (Snyder, Searle); 1 adult, Newburyport, 4–26 August 1961 (deWindt, Snyder, et al); 1 immature, Newburyport, 30 October–4 November 1952 (Searle, deWindt, collected by Morgan, PMS #7279); 1 immature, Newburyport, 4 October 1970 (Forster); 1 adult, Vineyard Sound, 10 October 1977 (Nickerson 1978); 1 adult, Monomoy, 7 December 1978 (Clem).

## Little Gull  *Larus minutus*

**Range:** Mainly Palearctic; breeds from Sweden, Denmark, and Holland east to Lake Baikal. Since 1962, the Little Gull has nested around the Great

Lakes and, in 1981, at Churchill, Manitoba. Winters, in North America, on the Great Lakes and along the Atlantic Coast from Massachusetts to Virginia.

**Status:** Rare to locally uncommon migrant at the coast. One inland record.

**Occurrence:** Unlike Common Black-headed Gulls, Little Gulls are usually found among flocks of Bonaparte's Gulls but are also occasionally found singly. Although they have been recorded during every month of the year, Little Gulls appear to have ill-defined migratory peaks in April and May, and again in August. As with the Bonaparte's Gull, they normally depart following spells of very cold winter weather. The first Little Gulls ever recorded in Massachusetts occurred when Griscom found single birds at Nahant, 7 June 1934, and at Plum Island, 28 July–31 August 1935. The first specimen collected was: 1 adult, Newburyport, 3–4 September 1941 (Griscom PMS #6243). The species first appeared on Cape Cod when one sick individual appeared at North Beach, Chatham, 3 September–30 December 1957 (Griscom, Fox, Rich, Morgan). *Maxima:* 15, Newburyport, 17 October 1973 (Gardler); 13 (2 adults, 11 subadults), Newburyport, 14 August 1980 (Heil); 11 adults, Newburyport, 10 April 1976 (Veit); 10 + immatures, Newburyport, 30 May 1973 (Finch, Abbott); 7, Nantucket, 29 December 1979–28 January 1980 (Andrews, Veit); 5 (4 adults, 1 immature), Truro, 1 December 1974 (Nikula). A Little Gull at Onota Lake, Pittsfield, 20–21 April 1946 (Griscom) is the only inland record for Massachusetts.

**Remarks:** Heil observed a juvenile Little Gull begging for food from an adult at Newburyport Harbor, 20 September 1980, and a seemingly territorial pair (1 adult and 1 one-year-old) was present at Woodbridge Island, Newburyport, in June and July 1982 (Heil).

# Common Black-headed Gull  *Larus ridibundus*

**Range:** Primarily Palearctic; rare breeder and uncommon migrant in North America. Breeds in Iceland and across northern temperate Eurasia; winters south to Africa and eastern China and, in North America, along the Atlantic Coast from Newfoundland to Long Island, New York. Breeds at the Magdalen Islands off Nova Scotia and in Newfoundland (Finch 1978, Montevecchi et al 1987).

**Status:** One unsuccessful breeding attempt at Monomoy in 1984 (Holt et al). Uncommon to locally fairly common winter resident; rare but regular in summer.

**Breeding:** In 1983, a single adult Common Black-headed Gull established a territory in a Laughing Gull colony on North Monomoy Island, but it was eventually displaced by Laughing Gulls. The following season, a pair of black-headed gulls appeared in the same location, and, on 21 May 1986, a nest with two eggs was discovered, thus representing the first breeding attempt in the United States (Holt et al 1986). Unfortunately, following hatching of the eggs, the chicks died of exposure to heavy rains. No further breeding attempts have been documented.

**Nonbreeding:** The first specimen of a Common Black-headed Gull for North America was collected at Newburyport Harbor, 27 January 1930 (Emilio & Griscom 1930), although specimens had previously been obtained at Barbados and at Vera Cruz, Mexico, in 1911 and 1912 respectively (Lincoln 1925). The second Massachusetts occurrence was an adult that appeared at Newburyport in 1936, spent three winters there, and was last seen in January 1941 (Griscom). Three additional specimens were taken from Newburyport Harbor between 21 September 1952 and 12 April 1953 (Drury). Since that time, Common Black-headed Gulls have steadily increased in North America, reaching peak abundance in the early 1970s but with a local decline since. The recent decrease in the size of wintering Common Black-headed Gull flocks in Massachusetts is possibly due to the refinement of sewage treatment techniques, and the general cleaning up of Boston and Newburyport harbors.

The largest numbers of Common Black-headed Gulls in Massachusetts have occurred in Newburyport and Boston harbors and on Cape Cod during the period from December to late April. The species has, however, been recorded in every month of the year, with 1–3 birds representing maximum counts for the period May to October. *Maxima:* 26, Wollaston, 17 December 1972 (Brown, Higginbotham); 17, Newburyport, 25 March 1975 (Gardler); 10, Chatham, 7 December 1979 (Goodrich et al); 5, Nantucket, 3–4 January 1982 (Veit, Boyle, Heil, et al).

# Bonaparte's Gull  *Larus philadelphia*

**Range:** Nearctic; breeds from western Alaska and northern Manitoba south to southern British Columbia and central Ontario. Winters along both coasts; on the Atlantic Coast from Massachusetts to Florida.

**Status:** Variously common to abundant migrant and winter resident. Locally common in midsummer; rare but regular migrant inland.

**Occurrence:** Flocks of Bonaparte's Gulls seasonally congregate at sewage outfalls and near tidal rips at Newburyport Harbor, Nahant, Boston Harbor, Chatham, and Nantucket. The birds move about continuously during the nonbreeding season, seemingly in response to the localized availability of food. Bonaparte's Gulls also appear to spend considerable time at sea. At both Newburyport and Nantucket, flocks have been observed flying directly out to sea following a change in the tide, only to return from beyond the range of visibility when inshore conditions become appropriate again.

Whether they spend the time at sea feeding or roosting is open to question, although Rowlett (1980) described a "feeding flock of 300, 44 kilometers east of Ocean City, Maryland, 4 December 1976." *Spring maxima:* 600 Newburyport, 3 May 1975 (Forster); 400, Newburyport, 14 May 1960 (VO). *Inland maxima:* 16 (after blizzard), Onota Lake, Pittsfield, 10 May 1977 (Goodrich); 8 and 5, Cheshire Reservoir and Onota Lake, Pittsfield, 14 April 1971 (Weigand, HBC); 6, Onota Lake, Pittsfield, 17 May 1970 (HBC); 2, GMNWR, 15 April 1974 (Robinson). Flocks of 100 to 300 one-year-old nonbreeders regularly spend the summer at Newburyport Harbor and Revere Beach, but the species is rare elsewhere from early June to early August.

In late fall and winter, maximum numbers of Bonaparte's Gulls occur at Newburyport, Nahant, Boston, and Chatham, where they remain until they are driven out by ice or intense cold. Some of the largest counts recorded in Massachusetts have come from Nantucket, although these flocks often do not arrive until midwinter. *Winter maxima:* 7,600 feeding on sand lances (*Ammodytes* sp.), off Falmouth, 17 December 1983 (Forster, Nikula); 4,000+, Nantucket, 26 January 1980 (Andrews et al); 3,000+, Chatham, 7 December 1979 (Goodrich); 2,500+, Nantucket, 10 December 1976 (Andrews et al); 2,000–3,000, Acoaxet, 27 November 1961 (Proctor, Hentershee); 2,000, Nahant, 29 November 1975 (Buckley, Forster); 1,000, Chatham, 21 December 1937 (Griscom).

Inland, Bonaparte's Gulls are less numerous in fall than during spring, and there are no midwinter records. Fall inland records are usually of 1 to 2 birds and span the dates 31 July 1976, GMNWR (Forster), to 29 November 1968, Quabbin (Goodrich, Forster); except, 7, Lake Pontoosuc, Pittsfield, November 1893 (McNair 1978); 10, Lakeville, 1 November 1981 (Petersen).

# Mew Gull  *Larus canus*

**Range:** Holarctic; three disjunct breeding populations. Breeds, in North America, from Alaska east to southern Yukon, south to Vancouver Island and central Saskatchewan; also throughout northern Eurasia. Winters in North America south along the Pacific Coast to Baja California.

**Status:** Vagrant, primarily in late March and April; also from August through the winter.

**Occurrence:** The records of Massachusetts Mew Gulls fall into two distinct seasonal categories: over twenty records, including two specimens of European *L. c. canus*, exist for the period 1 January to the first week in May; and five records, two of which were identifiably of the North American race, *L. c. brachyrhynchus*, have occurred between 6 August and 10 October.

Of the more than twenty winter and spring occurrences, more than half are from Newburyport Harbor (incorporating an unknown amount of duplication due to the possible return of single individuals in successive years), plus: 1 adult, East Bridgewater, 1 April 1979 (Petersen); 1 adult, Hull, 13 April 1980 (Petersen); 1 adult, Revere Beach, 9 May 1980 (Zendeh); 1 adult, Provincetown, 15 January 1984 (Nikula); 1 adult, Provincetown, January 1985 (Petersen). Specimens collected during the winter season have been conclusively identified as *L. c. canus*, including: 1 first winter plumage, photographed but not collected, Nantucket, 3–30 January 1981 (Veit et al).

The five fall occurrences are as follows: 1 adult, Nauset, Monomoy, 2 and 4 September 1945 (Griscom et al); 1 adult, Newburyport, 6 August–24 September 1947 (Curtis, VO); 1 adult, Monomoy, 17–18 August 1976 (Goodrich, Nikula); 1 *L. c. brachyrhynchus* in first basic plumage, Nantucket Harbor, 10 October 1980 (Veit, Perkins); 1 *L. c. brachyrhynchus* in first basic plumage, Nantucket, 28–29 September 1981 (Perkins).

Recent records suggest that the Mew Gull may be increasing in Massachusetts, and the species may actually be of annual occurrence in the state— e.g., 4, eastern Massachusetts, February 1991 (BOEM).

**Remarks:** Although the adults of the two races are extremely difficult to identify in the field, birds in first basic plumage have distinctly different tail patterns and body plumage (Lauro & Spencer 1980).

# Ring-billed Gull   *Larus delawarensis*

**Range:** Nearctic; breeds from British Columbia and northeastern California east, locally, to Lake Ontario; Lake Champlain, New York; Lake Umbagog, New Hampshire; Maine; New Brunswick; and Newfoundland. Steadily increasing and expanding its range. On the East Coast of North America, winters primarily from Massachusetts to Florida.

**Status:** Abundant migrant and locally very common winterer on the coast; uncommon migrant and rare inland in winter. Large numbers of nonbreeding immatures summer in Newburyport Harbor and regularly elsewhere. Generally increasing in abundance.

**Occurrence:** Ring-billed Gulls are most common at localities such as Revere Beach, Newburyport Harbor, and Plymouth Harbor, as well as in plowed fields in southeastern Massachusetts. Although common on Cape Cod, the species is scarce at Nantucket, and it is rarely seen at sea. After heavy rains, large numbers alight to feed on earthworms in plowed inland fields. *Spring maxima:* 860, Revere Beach, 8 May 1980 (Zendeh); 800, Newburyport, 25 March 1978 (Petersen); 800, Newburyport, 8 April 1979 (Heil); 350 +, Clinton, 6–12 April 1975 (Blodget); 86, Longmeadow, 31 March 1972 (Weigand); 35, Pittsfield, 9 May 1977 (Goodrich); 25 +, North

Adams, 9 May 1977 (fide McNair). *Summer maxima:* 1,350 immatures, Newburyport, 8 June 1980 (Heil). Ordinarily, 100 to 200 are found in the summer in the Newburyport area, and numbers will probably increase concurrent with the recent expansion of the breeding range. Evidence of possible nesting should be sought at localities such as Wachusett and Quabbin reservoirs, and even at Plum Island. *Fall maxima:* 2,500, Middleboro, 1 December 1985 (Petersen); 1,800, Bridgewater-Halifax, 3 November 1985 (Petersen); 800, Newburyport, 2 August 1980 (Stymeist); 600, Middleboro, 22 November 1975 (Higginbotham et al); 122, Agawam, 27 August 1972 (Yenlin); 77, Northampton, 30 November 1972 (Gagnon); 23, Pittsfield, 7 August 1978 (McNair); 15, Pittsfield, 18 October 1972 (Goodrich). Ring-billed Gulls are rare in winter away from the coast, and they are almost invariably forced out as inland bodies of water freeze over. Ring-billed Gulls were first recorded wintering on Cape Cod around 1900 and in Essex County in 1909 (fide Griscom & Snyder 1955). *Winter maxima:* 3,586, Greater Boston CBC, 16 December 1990; 400 + , Westport, 19 January 1980 (Heil); 220, Flax Pond, Lynn, 20 January 1982 (Heil); 200, Newburyport, 15 January 1972 (Harrington et al).

## California Gull   *Larus californicus*

**Range:** Nearctic; breeds from southern Mackenzie south through eastern Alberta, Saskatchewan, southwestern Manitoba, central Montana, and central North Dakota to central Colorado west to southern British Columbia and south to northeastern California, western Nevada and northern Utah. Winters from southern Washington and eastern Idaho south, mostly along the Pacific coast, to Baja California and Mexico.

**Status:** Vagrant: one sight record.

**Occurrence:** A California Gull in third summer plumage was carefully identified at Newburyport, 24 April 1988 (Forster). The bird was studied at close range in comparison with Herring and Ring-billed gulls so that its dark eyes, greenish yellow legs, slightly darker mantle, and intermediate size all made it stand out from its nearby congeners. Written details of this record are on file at Massachusetts Audubon.

## Herring Gull   *Larus argentatus*

**Range:** Holarctic; widespread and abundant virtually throughout the northern temperate region. Breeds in eastern North America from southern Baffin Island and northern Quebec south to the Great Lakes and, on the Atlantic Coast, to South Carolina. On the Atlantic Coast winters from Newfoundland south to Mexico and the Caribbean.

**Status:** Locally very abundant breeder, migrant, and winterer; less numerous inland with increasing distance from the coast but still a common migrant in Berkshire County.

**Breeding:** Before 1900, Herring Gulls were not known to breed south of eastern Maine (Drury 1973a, 1974). In the summer of 1912, the first nesting in Massachusetts was recorded by Allan Keniston on the south side of Edgartown Great Pond, Martha's Vineyard, and, between 1919 and 1921, 20 pairs were found breeding on an ephemeral sandbar called Skiffs Island off the southern end of Chappaquiddick Island (Forbush 1925—note, however, that the photograph of "young Herring Gulls" at Skiffs Island, facing p. 78, actually depicts chicks of the Common Tern). At the time, the prospects seemed so remote that Herring Gulls could ever establish themselves in Massachusetts in the face of the expanding human population that Forbush was prompted to state, "It is improbable that the Herring Gull can long maintain itself anywhere on the coast of southern New England." Defying Forbush's prediction, the Herring Gull underwent one of the most remarkable population expansions of any New England bird. The growth of the population between 1930 and 1970 (Kadlec & Drury 1968, Drury 1973a, 1973b, 1974) was almost exponential until about 1965, when it leveled off. The slackening in the rate of increase may have been due to the refinement of garbage disposal, sewage treatment, and fish-processing practices because the space for nest sites does not seem to be a limiting factor.

In 1980, the U.S. Fish and Wildlife Service and the Massachusetts Audubon Society conducted two of the most thorough censuses to date of the Monomoy gull colony. They recorded totals of 14,500 (USFWS) and 14,550 (MAS) nesting pairs of Herring Gulls, respectively. A more comprehensive effort was undertaken in 1984–1985, when the U. S. Fish and Wildlife Service conducted a census of all waterbird colonies between Maine and Virginia (Andrews 1990) and found 35,421 pairs of Herring Gulls nesting along the Massachusetts coast.

The dramatic increase of nesting Herring Gulls at Monomoy occurred during the late 1970s, several years after a decline at Muskeget between 1965 and 1972, so it is unclear whether or not the Muskeget birds shifted to Monomoy.

The only documented nesting of Herring Gulls inland in Massachusetts has been at Wachusett Reservoir. They were first proven to breed at Cunningham Ledge, a small island in the reservoir, in 1966, when 100 nests were found on 19 June, and 100 juveniles were seen on 4 July. The population peaked at 500 pairs in 1967, at which point a control program was instituted by the MDC to prevent contamination of the water supply. By 1976, only 30 nests remained, and it seems now that the colony has been almost completely eradicated (Blodget 1976). *Egg dates:* 24 April–26 July.

**Nonbreeding:** Kadlec and Drury (1968) found that most first-year Herring Gulls winter along the Gulf Coast, while the adults winter from New York to North Carolina (see also Gross 1940). Before 1975, Herring Gulls were most abundant in Massachusetts during winter around large garbage dumps, such as those in the Lynn-Revere area. Since the larger dumps have been closed, the maximum winter counts of Herring Gulls in the state have been made at Cape Cod and Nantucket during winters when schooling fish, mainly sand lances (*Ammodytes* sp.), are exceptionally abundant. For example, during the winter of 1981–82, enormous schools of sand lances were present in a more or less uninterrupted swarm extending from Stellwagen Bank south to Nantucket. Between October and early January, an estimated 140,000 ( ± 10 percent) Herring Gulls were observed feeding on the fish in the surf along the eastern shores of Cape Cod and Nantucket (Nikula, Veit, et al). Such a high count obviously includes an influx of migrants from other colonies to the north (or possibly south) of Massachusetts. At that time, Herring Gulls outnumbered Great Black-backeds by at least 100 to 1, and, by December, first-year Herring Gulls comprised less than 1 percent of the total Herring Gulls at Nantucket (Veit). Similarly, in November 1976, Bailey estimated 40,000 large gulls, mostly Herrings, feeding upon a "wreck" of beached squid on the bay side of Cape Cod. Other high counts include: 48,000, Hull (Quincy CBC), 23 December 1950 (Harrington); and 25,000, Nahant, November 1948 (Griscom). *Inland maxima* (steadily increasing since the turn of the century): 2,984, Worcester CBC, 17 December 1983; 2,340 +, Wachusett Reservoir, 31 December 1978 (Blodget).

**Subspecies:** *L. a. smithsonianus* is the only subspecies recognized as occurring in eastern North America. However, specimens of birds in first winter plumage resembling *L. a. argentatus* of the British Isles have been observed and collected at Nantucket (Veit, Perkins MCZ #331162). Further collecting may reveal that European Herring Gulls regularly cross the Atlantic, as apparently do Lesser Black-backed Gulls.

**Remarks:** An almost pure white Herring Gull was color photographed in Weymouth, 25 July 1981 (Petersen). The existence of such leucistic individuals should serve as a cautionary note when identifying summer "white-winged" gulls.

# Thayer's Gull   *Larus thayeri*

**Range:** Nearctic; breeds in arctic Canada, south to northeastern Mackenzie and southern Baffin Island. Winters primarily on the Pacific Coast from British Columbia to California, but apparently of regular occurrence on the East Coast of North America during winter in recent years.

**Status:** Rare winter visitant; possibly overlooked in the past.

**Occurrence:** Due to complicated systematic and identification problems with gulls in the Herring-Iceland-Thayer's complex, extralimital records of the Thayer's Gull have been open to question for many years. The specimen referred to by Griscom and Snyder (1955, BMS #18875) has been redetermined to be *L. glaucoides* by Veit. There is one definite specimen record of a bird showing the characteristics of a Thayer's Gull from Massachusetts: 1 female in first prenuptial molt collected, off the north end of Plum Island, 23 March 1982 (Veit, Hatch, Heil, MCZ #331163); its identity was confirmed by J. R. Jehl, Jr. In addition, there are five other records that probably pertain to this species: 1 color photographed in first basic plumage, Newburyport Harbor, 9 March 1975 (Buckley et al); 1 color photographed in first basic plumage, Nantucket, 26 December 1980–27 February 1981 (Veit et al); 1 color photographed in first winter plumage, Stellwagen Bank, 25 April 1981 (Petersen et al); 1 in first winter plumage, Newburyport, 22 April 1982 (Heil); 1 color photographed in first winter plumage, Chatham, 1–23 February 1986 (Nikula, VO).

# Iceland Gull  *Larus glaucoides*

**Range:** Nearctic; breeds on southern Baffin Island and in northwestern Quebec; also in Greenland, Iceland, and Jan Mayen. In North America, winters along the coast from Newfoundland south to Massachusetts, and more rarely to Virginia.

**Status:** Locally uncommon to fairly common winter resident. Rare during summer and in any season away from the immediate coast.

**Occurrence:** Iceland Gulls concentrate in winter at the north end of Plum Island, around Gloucester Harbor, in Provincetown Harbor, and off the east shore of Nantucket. They have steadily increased in Massachusetts since first being collected in Boston, 31 January 1880 (Bangs). They presently greatly outnumber Glaucous Gulls in Massachusetts.

As is the case with Glaucous Gulls, Iceland Gulls are not particularly common at garbage dumps, tending to be found instead at commercial fishery operations, both in harbors and at sea, and along the southeast shore of Nantucket, where they feed over schools of sand lances (*Ammodytes* sp.). The majority of local wintering birds are either in adult or first winter plumage. *Maxima* (coastal): 150 +, Nantucket, January 1981 (Veit et al); 140 +, Gloucester, February 1981 (Heil); 120, Plum Island, 1 March 1981 (Veit); 32, Eastern Point, Gloucester, 24 December 1917 (Brainerd, fide Forbush). Inland, Iceland Gulls occur rarely but regularly at garbage dumps, along rivers, and on frozen lakes. Iceland Gulls are rare before late October and after April; however, there are at least ten coastal records of single birds in the period mid-June to mid-August.

**Remarks:** The AOU (1957) recognized two subspecies of the Iceland Gull: *L. g. glaucoides* of Greenland, which is characterized by a relatively small size and pure white primaries, and *L. g. kumlieni* of the eastern Canadian Arctic, which is somewhat larger and has a variable amount of gray pigment in the wing tips. Smith (1966) stated that 30 percent of the North American Iceland Gulls actually have pure white primaries, which suggests that the characteristics used to separate these subspecies are not definitive. In any case, the vast majority of Iceland Gulls in Massachusetts have some gray in the wing tips.

# Lesser Black-backed Gull  *Larus fuscus*

**Range:** Western Palearctic; the race *L. f. graellsii* breeds in Iceland, the Faeroes, the British Isles, and along the northern coast of France. Winters south along the coast to Nigeria. Regular visitor to the New World, primarily along the coast from Cape Cod to Florida and the Caribbean, but also north to northern Canada and southwest to central California and the Pacific Coast of Panama and Costa Rica.

**Status:** Rare but regular migrant and winter resident. Most numerous at Nantucket and Cape Cod.

**Occurrence:** Despite a marked increase of sightings in the New York City area during the 1940s and 1950s (Bull 1964), the Lesser Black-backed Gull was not recorded with certainty in Massachusetts until 14 September 1971, when an adult was seen at Monomoy (Clem, Bailey, Harrington). From 1973 to 1979, at least fourteen occurrences were documented from Cape Cod and the Islands, all involving birds three years old or older, during the period August to February. The first spring record was: 1 adult, Nantucket, 22 April 1978 (Perkins). Since then, Lesser Black-backed Gulls have been reported annually and in every month of the year, with a peak between late November and early January. *Maxima:* 12, Nantucket, November 1980–January 1981 (Veit); 8, Nantucket, 3–4 January 1982 (Veit, Heil, et al). The only individuals in first winter plumage reported were: 1, 20 miles south of Nantucket, 30 November 1979 (Veit); 1 photographed, Nantucket, throughout January 1981 (Veit, Andrews, Litchfield). Away from Nantucket and Cape Cod, the species has been seen at a number of localities—e.g., 1, Lake Congamond, Southwick, 4–5 January 1975 (Kellogg); 1, Chicopee, 20 December 1975 (Cavanaugh, Longley); 1, on the Connecticut River between Miller's Falls and Hadley, 19 March–2 April 1976 (fide Kellogg); 1, Scituate, 27 July 1980 (Petersen); 1, Newburyport, 2–9 August 1980 (Forster, Hamilton, Stymeist, et al); 1, Plymouth Beach, 30 December 1981 (Heil et al); 1, Gloucester, 15–21 November 1981 (Heil); 1, Flax Pond, Lynn, 11 December 1981 (Heil); 1, Plymouth Beach, 15–30 May 1982 (Petersen); 2, Scituate, 1 August 1982

(Petersen); 1, Wareham, 18 December 1982 (Petersen); 1, Clinton, 29 September–29 October 1982 (Crompton, Babbitt); 1, Stellwagen Bank, 2 June 1985 (Petersen et al).

# Glaucous Gull   *Larus hyperboreus*

**Range:** Holarctic; breeds, in North America, from northern Alaska and northern Ellesmere Island south to southern Baffin Island and central Labrador. Winters south regularly to coastal North Carolina, but most abundantly in Newfoundland and Labrador.

**Status:** Uncommon and somewhat local winter resident; very rare in summer.

**Occurrence:** Glaucous Gulls are most often found in winter among large flocks of Herring, Great Black-backed, and Iceland gulls. Localities frequented include the jetties at the north end of Plum Island, Gloucester Harbor, Provincetown Harbor, and the eastern shore of Nantucket. Unlike Iceland Gulls, Glaucous Gulls have not increased dramatically since 1940, although the two species are much more regular on Cape Cod, and especially Nantucket, than they were during the 1960s and 1970s. Unlike the situation in the New York City area, Glaucous Gulls are not found in greatest abundance at garbage dumps; rather, they are attracted by commercial fisheries operations in Essex County, whereas at Nantucket they join the multitudes of other seabirds feeding upon the massive concentrations of sand lances (*Ammodytes* sp.) that periodically occur off the eastern shore of the island. *Maxima* (coastal): 12, Cape Ann, 14 January 1979 (Kasprzyk, Heil); 10, Nantucket, January 1981 (Veit, Andrews). Inland: 10, Danvers, 17 February 1964 (Drury); 3, West Concord, 17 January 1960 (Alden); 3, Longmeadow, 13 January 1962 (Magee); 3, Sudbury, 1 January 1972 (Alden); 1, Lenox, 19–29 April 1969 (Dunbar).

Since 1954, there have been fewer than twenty records from the period June to August, all from coastal areas. The species is rare before November and after early May.

# Great Black-backed Gull   *Larus marinus*

**Range:** Holarctic; restricted to the North Atlantic Ocean. In North America, breeds along the coast from southern Greenland south to North Carolina and, in increasing numbers, inland at Lake Ontario and Lake Huron. Winters from Newfoundland south to North Carolina and more rarely to Florida.

**Status:** Locally abundant breeder and even more numerous in late summer, fall, and winter on the coast. Locally very common, and increasing, both inland as well as on the coast.

**Breeding:** Before 1930, Great Black-backed Gulls occurred primarily as winter residents, with scattered summer stragglers reported from 1890 on (Griscom & Snyder 1955). The first nest in Massachusetts was found in Salem, 7 July 1931 (Eaton), and the species first nested on Cape Cod in 1941 (Griscom & Snyder 1955). Since then, the nesting population has increased from 9 pairs in 1941 to 51 in 1943, 60 in 1950, 2,575 in 1965, and 3,175 in 1972 (Drury 1973a, 1974). In the past, the largest colonies were always on Muskeget Island and on islands in Massachusetts Bay north of Boston. Erwin and Korschgen (1979) recorded 4,670 nesting pairs of Great Black-backed Gulls from fifty colonies in Massachusetts (1977), the largest being Monomoy (920 pairs), Milk Island in Massachusetts Bay (600 pairs), and Coatue Beach, Nantucket (550 pairs). In the summer of 1980, both the U.S. Fish and Wildlife Service and the Massachusetts Audubon Society censused the gulls at Monomoy (see under Herring Gull) and found 3,300 (USFWS) and 2,500 to 3,000 (MAS) pairs. In the same summer, Muskeget Island was carefully censused and found to contain 600 breeding pairs (Heil). By 1984–1985, an extensive coastal census conducted by the USFWS (Andrews 1990) produced a total of 10,577 pairs breeding in Massachusetts.

It would seem that following the massive population increase during the period 1940 to 1970, the rate of increase has slowed. Nisbet (in litt) suggested that in 1982 the Massachusetts population exceeded 7,000 pairs. Despite the fact that Great Black-backed Gull chicks hatch some two weeks earlier than Herring Gull chicks, and that the two species invariably nest in mixed colonies, there is no unambiguous evidence that the increase of Great Black-backeds has been at the expense of the Herring Gull. At Muskeget, however, Great Black-backed Gulls increased in proportion to Herring Gulls from a few pairs in the early 1950s to over 65 percent of the total in 1980. This proportional increase may reflect a subtle difference in nesting site or dietary preference between the two species. Breeders usually arrive at colonies in mid-March, but occasionally much earlier in mild seasons. There are no records of Great Black-backed Gulls nesting away from the immediate coast in Massachusetts. *Egg dates:* 15 April–3 July.

**Nonbreeding:** Peak counts of Great Black-backed Gulls come from Monomoy and the Islands in late summer and fall. *Maxima:* 10,000 +, Monomoy, 30 August 1975 (Petersen, Forster, Harrington); 8,425, Cape Cod CBC, 17 December 1978; 8,000 +, Tuckernuck Island, 1 December 1974 (Veit). Inland, the highest counts are usually from Christmas Bird Counts—e.g., 401, Wachusett Reservoir, 10 January 1984 (Blodget); 389, Worcester, 1983; 208, Concord, 1980. In Berkshire County, most are reported during spring and fall—maximum, 4, Pittsfield, 20 April 1978 (McNair). There are very few inland winter records—e.g., 1, Pittsfield, 23 January 1968 (Robinson, Purdy).

Immature birds from a few months to three years of age disperse widely over the open ocean and are commoner farther offshore than Herring Gulls. It is routine to see up to 500 young Great Black-backed Gulls following a single fishing trawler within 30 miles of shore, and the species is not uncommon even along the continental slope east to the southeast part of Georges Bank, 175 miles from shore. Closer to shore, recently fledged Great Black-backeds are abundant in late summer and fall at Jeffrey's Ledge and Stellwagen Bank, where they usually greatly outnumber Herring Gulls.

**Remarks:** At least four probable Great Black-backed Gull x Herring Gull hybrids, all adults, have been described in Massachusetts—e.g., 1, Eel Point, Nantucket, 18 October 1979 (Veit, Litchfield); 1, Muskeget Island, May–July 1982 (Heil 1983b); 1, Plum Island, 25 August 1982 (Forster, Raymond, et al); 1, North Monomoy, 31 July 1985 (Petersen, Veit, Forster, Nikula).

# Black-legged Kittiwake   *Rissa tridactyla*

**Range:** Holarctic; breeds, in North America, from northern Baffin Island and northern Labrador south to islands in the Gulf of St. Lawrence, Newfoundland, and the Bird Rocks off Cape Breton, Nova Scotia. Winters at sea in the western North Atlantic from Newfoundland south to North Carolina.

**Status:** Abundant migrant and winter resident offshore. Occasionally very abundant within sight of land. Occasionally, small numbers of summering nonbreeders have occurred on Cape Cod.

**Occurrence:** Kittiwakes are among the most numerous and widespread winter seabirds in the Gulf of Maine and on Georges Bank. Ordinarily they are pelagic, not approaching within sight of land unless they are driven there by onshore winds or are attracted by a superabundance of food. Thus, high counts of migrants seen from shore are to a certain extent biased by the timing of storms. The largest numbers of kittiwakes are ordinarily seen between mid-November and late December, and then again in March. Apparently, the bulk of the population winters south of Massachusetts.

In typical years, kittiwakes arrive in October, so the following records are exceptional: 1, Provincetown, 25 August 1891 (fide Hill 1965); 15, Eastham, 31 August 1975 (Laux et al); 10, Eastham, 3 September 1972 (Harrington et al). *Fall maxima:* 15,000, Nauset, Eastham, 30 November 1957 (Smart, Fox); 15,000, off Orleans, 16 December 1979 (Goodrich); 11,000, Rockport, 1 January 1953 (Snyder); 5,000 +, First Encounter Beach, Eastham, 10 December 1978 (Nikula); 2,500, 17 miles east southeast of Monomoy, 16 December 1979 (MBO). During the late 1970s and early 1980s, an unprecedented abundance of sand lances (*Ammodytes* sp.) in coastal waters attracted enormous numbers of kittiwakes very close to shore. In the fall of 1981, for example, tens of thousands could be seen off the eastern coast of Cape Cod and Nantucket daily between late October and January—e.g., 50,000, outer Cape, 22 November (Nikula); 18,000 +, Eastham-Chatham, 31 October (Petersen et al); 10,000, Nantucket, 28–29 November (Veit et al)—after which time both the fish and birds disappeared. On 17 December 1983, 9,500 were observed actively feeding upon sand lances in Nantucket Sound along the Falmouth shore (Nikula, Forster), and, the following day, 29,000 were counted along the eastern shore of Cape Cod between Eastham and Chatham (Petersen, Goodrich, et al). Even more impressively, between 13–15 December 1984, a careful estimate of kittiwakes feeding along the east and south shores of Nantucket indicated that 50,000 to 100,000 were present (Veit, Braun) that month. *Winter maxima:* 15,000, Provincetown, 28 January 1979 (Nikula); 4,500, Rockport, 25 February 1979 (Veit, Stymeist); 750 in one hour, Rockport, 17 January 1959 (Snyder).

In spring, kittiwakes generally disappear from Massachusetts inshore waters by mid-April, so the following spring counts are noteworthy: 275, Rockport, 15 May 1978 (Stymeist); 100, First Encounter Beach, Eastham, 5 April 1975 (Goodrich, Nikula); 85 during a storm, Cape Cod Bay, 9 May 1977 (Petersen, Forster, Anderson).

In recent years, varying numbers of one-year-old Black-legged Kittiwakes have spent portions of the summer months at Monomoy and Provincetown, and other individuals have turned up at various beaches around the state, primarily on the Outer Cape and Islands. This phenomenon was virtually unrecorded before 1955, although a kittiwake in first summer plumage was collected at Chatham, 30 May 1957 (BMS #20801). Clearly, the following counts are suggestive of a recent change in the summer distribution of nonbreeding kittiwakes: 630, Provincetown, 23 June 1980 (Heil); 400, Provincetown, 4 June 1978 (Goodrich); 132, off Chatham, 4 June 1978 (BBC); 85, Monomoy, 4 June 1978 (Veit, Litchfield); 80, Provincetown, 10 June 1978 (Nikula); 60, Provincetown, 3 August 1980 (Heil, Nikula). A number of these summering birds have been found dead of aspergillosis (Nisbet, pers. comm.). The only inland record is: 1 shot, Bridgewater, 13 November 1909 (MAS #2385).

# Ross' Gull   *Rhodostethia rosea*

**Range:** Holarctic; breeds in northern Siberia and in North America near Bathurst Island, at Churchill, Manitoba (Chartier & Cooke 1980), and at Disko Bay, Greenland. Probably winters at sea in open arctic waters. Re-

*The dramatic appearance of a **Ross' Gull** in Newburyport in 1975 marked the first such occurrence in the lower 48 United States. The ultimate vagrant, the gull triggered a pilgrimage that brought birders by the hundreds to the banks of the Merrimack River.*

▷

corded as a vagrant at widely separated localities in North America, with an apparent increase during the 1980s. It is also of increasingly frequent occurrence in the British Isles (O'Sullivan 1977).

**Status:** Vagrant: four records.

**Occurrence:** No doubt, the most sensational vagrant ever to occur in Massachusetts was an adult Ross' Gull that was present in Newburyport Harbor from at least 12 January (possibly as early as 7 December 1974) to 9 May 1975. Although the bird was first definitely seen by Parsons and Weissberg in January, news of the bird's presence was not disclosed until it was conclusively identified on 2 March (Miliotis & Buckley 1975, BOEM 3: 12–16). Other records: 1 adult, Newburyport, 26 April 1981 (Nash, Argues, Wiggin); 1 adult, Newburyport, 3 December 1984 (Tingley, Bloss, et al); 1 adult, East Gloucester, 1–13 February 1990 (Forster et al).

Miliotis and Buckley (op cit) and Gibson (AB 29: 646) expressed the opinion that the 1975 bird most likely arrived at Newburyport via the British Isles, as suggested by the recent increase of the species in Great Britain. Also, the precedent for other European vagrant gulls recorded at Newburyport lends support to this hypothesis. However, the recent discovery of Ross' Gulls breeding in Canada, coupled with various recent inland occurrences, suggests the possibility of a Canadian origin to both the American and British occurrences.

# Sabine's Gull  *Xema sabini*

**Range:** Holarctic; breeds, in North America, from northern Alaska and Banks Island south and east to Southampton and Coats islands and southwestern Baffin Island. Winters at sea off Peru and off western South Africa.

**Status:** Very rare spring and rare, but regular, fall migrant.

**Occurrence:** Sabine's Gulls are rare in spring, but this may be due in part to less frequent pelagic coverage in late May, when they seem most likely to occur. Seven of the eleven spring records have been from the north end of Monomoy, and all have occurred between 15 May and 16 June: 1, Monomoy, 26 May 1942 (Griscom); 1, Monomoy, 20 May 1944 (Griscom); 1, Nauset, Eastham, 30 May 1950 (Mason); 1 immature, Chatham, 2 June 1957 (Bowen, Griscom); 1, Monomoy, 22 May 1968 (Bailey); 1, two miles north of Graves Ledge, 16 June 1968 (Walters); 1, Monomoy, 31 May 1975 (Nisbet, Howard); 1, Sandy Neck, Barnstable, 15 May 1978 (Pease); 1, Monomoy, 1 June 1979 (Nisbet, Welton); 1, Chatham, 25 May 1979 (Nisbet, Trull); 1, Monomoy, 19–22 May 1980 (Clapp, Forster, et al).

The fall migration of Sabine's Gulls over the Atlantic Ocean remains somewhat of a mystery. Although they are abundant in winter off western South Africa, Sabine's Gulls have never been encountered in large numbers in the North Atlantic. It is possible that they migrate far out to sea, beyond the continental slope, where they would likely escape detection. It is very unusual to ever see more than one Sabine's Gull in a day in Massachusetts waters, although the species is apparently more frequently recorded off Massachusetts than anywhere else along the East Coast of North America. There are at least seventy-five fall records of Sabine's Gulls in Massachusetts, with over fifty since 1955. Most of these fall between the dates 20 August and 8 October, as do the seven specimens collected prior to 1954, which span the dates 21 August–29 September. Definite early records are: 1 adult, Monomoy, 27 July 1941 (Griscom et al); 1 adult, Monomoy, 25 July 1972 (Forster, Goodrich).

Usually only single birds are seen, either from shore during easterly storms, on the coastal fishing banks, or occasionally among the massive flocks of aggregating terns at Monomoy or Nantucket. Only three records are not from the Cape and Islands or Stellwagen Bank: 1 adult, Boston Harbor, 27 September 1874 (Diamond, MCZ); 1 adult, Newburyport, 19 August 1952 (Griscom); 1 adult, Newburyport, 6 September–10 October 1976 (Veit, Petersen). Of approximately 66 birds reported since 1874, only 14 were identified as immature, and, with one exception (1, Monomoy, 28 August 1955, [Griscom]), these seem to occur later in fall than adults—i.e., 18 September–18 November. *Fall maxima:* 9 birds reported (including 3 adults, Manomet Point, 20 September [Petersen, Harrington]), coastal Massachusetts, 18–21 September 1977 (BOEM); 5 (1 adult, 4 immatures), Eastham, 7 October 1962 (Bailey); 3, Eastham, 21 September 1977 (Nikula); 2 collected, Chatham, 2 September 1912 (Hersey 1913). The latest definitive record is: 1 immature, at sea in Massachusetts Bay, 18 November 1976 (Lloyd-Evans).

# Ivory Gull  *Pagophila eburnea*

**Range:** Holarctic; breeds, in North America, in the high Arctic south to northern Baffin Island; winters in the Arctic Ocean and south to northern Newfoundland (Strait of Belle Isle), rarely to New York and New Jersey.

**Status:** Very rare winter visitor.

**Occurrence:** There are a total of nine documented occurrences of Ivory Gulls in Massachusetts, including two 19th-century records: 1 shot, Swampscott, mid-1800s (fide Townsend 1905); 1 shot, Monomoy, 1 December 1886 (fide Cahoon, in Hill 1965). Apparently, there was a major flight to the Northeast in 1940, when an immature was seen during a northeast storm at Newburyport Harbor, 14 January (VO), and 2 or 3 were found the same day at Cape Ann (Eaton, Curtis). Other records include: 1 adult found dying

from internal parasites, Gloucester, 27 January 1946 (Bailey); 1 oiled immature, Newburyport, 27 January–13 February 1949 (Parsons, VO); 1 immature,
Salisbury, 22 December–5 March 1976 (Strickland, VO); 1 immature, Rockport and Gloucester, 10 December 1976–10 January 1977 (Crofoot, Grugan,
photographed by Veit).

# Gull-billed Tern  *Sterna nilotica*

**Range:** Cosmopolitan in tropical and warmer temperate regions; the race
*S. n. aranea* breeds along the Gulf Coast, in the Caribbean, and along the
Atlantic Coast from Long Island, New York (1975 on), to Florida. Winters
along the Gulf Coast south through the Caribbean to Surinam.

**Status:** Rare but nearly annual summer visitor.

**Occurrence:** Through 1985, there were forty published Massachusetts
records of this southern tern, spanning the dates 1 May to 27 September.
They are distributed by month as follows: May, 5; June, 5; July, 19; August,
9; September, 11. A number of the earlier records involved birds seen after
hurricanes; however, most of the May and early summer records were not
associated with storms. Since 1985, Gull-billed Terns have appeared nearly
every summer in Massachusetts, most often at Plum Island, Plymouth
Beach, and outer Cape Cod.

Prior to 1955, Gull-billed Terns occurred mainly in August and September,
and there were no reports earlier than July. Since 1975, however, there has
been one April report—1, Nantucket, 16 April 1982 (Perkins)—and there
have been four reports of birds in May, which may reflect the recent
northward extension of the species' breeding range to Long Island (Buckley
et al 1975). The possibility of Massachusetts breeding attempts should not be
overlooked in the future. A reference in William Brewster's journals to the
nesting of Gull-billed Terns on Nantucket in the 1800s suggests that they
may actually be recolonizing a former breeding area (Nisbet, pers. comm.).
*Maxima:* 6 birds, Provincetown, Scituate, Martha's Vineyard, Monomoy, 2–
19 September 1954 (RNEB); 6 birds, Wollaston, Manomet, Chilmark,
Hingham, 13–18 September 1960 (RNEB); 3, Monomoy, 28 May 1979 (Nisbet). The majority of other reports are of single birds. The only inland
record for Massachusetts is: 1 after Hurricane Bob, Wachusett Reservoir,
Clinton, 20 August 1991 (Bradbury).

**Remarks:** A reexamination of a specimen alleged to be a Gull-billed x
Forster's Tern hybrid (MCZ #271643) collected at Nauset, Eastham, 6
September 1941 (Griscom, see Hill 1965), proved to be a juvenile Forster's
Tern, based both on plumage characteristics and measurements (Veit).

# Caspian Tern *Sterna caspia*

**Range:** Cosmopolitan; eastern North American birds breed in three disjunct areas: around lakes and in marshes from northeastern Alberta south and east to northwestern Pennsylvania and southeastern Quebec; on islands along the north shore of the Gulf of St. Lawrence; and along the Gulf and Atlantic coasts of the United States locally from Virginia to Louisiana and Texas. Along the Atlantic Coast, winters from North Carolina south to Florida; also through the western Caribbean and Gulf of Mexico to southern Mexico.

**Status:** Uncommon spring and occasionally fairly common fall migrant on the coast; rare but regular inland during spring and fall.

**Occurrence:** The Caspian Terns that occur in Massachusetts are migrants to and from more northerly or westerly breeding grounds. Spring migrants are mainly seen between late April and mid-May, and fall migrants occur between mid-September and mid-October. The species occurs inland more frequently in spring than in fall, and coastal records are widely distributed, the largest numbers usually occurring at Plum Island, Monomoy, and Nantucket.

Griscom and Snyder (1955) suggest that Caspian Terns decreased in numbers during the early part of the 20th century; but, because they breed primarily at inland locations, they did not suffer from the plume trade to nearly the extent that the coastal-nesting species did.

Migrating Caspian Terns fly quickly and directly to their breeding grounds and do not usually remain in Massachusetts for long. The earliest spring record is: 1, Sagamore, 19 April 1955 (Hill). Reports after mid-May are rare—e.g., 1, Nauset, Eastham, 5 June 1972 (Wait); 2, Plymouth, 9 June 1982 (Forster). *Spring maxima:* 6, Marshfield, 1 May 1976 (Castle); 3, Turners Falls, 29 April 1956 (Weeks, Eliot); 3, Newburyport, 29–30 April 1972 (D'Entremont, Petersen). *Fall maxima:* 16, Ipswich, 3 October 1955 (Cottrell); 16, Monomoy, 12 October 1976 (Bailey); 15, Salisbury, 30 September 1978 (Hale); 11, Monomoy, 8 October 1975 (Bailey); 10, Edgartown, 30 September 1978 (Laux). The latest record is: 5, Plum Island, 5 November 1977 (Garrett et al). Late inland records include: 1, Northampton, 22 September 1944 (Bracewell); 1, Longmeadow, 22 September 1963 (Blackshaw).

Whereas the records cited above are undoubtedly of migrants from either inland or Gulf of St. Lawrence colonies, records of birds following hurricanes or during midsummer probably derive from colonies on the southeastern coast of the United States. Twelve Caspian Terns were seen along the Massachusetts coast after hurricanes in 1954, and 7 were seen after a hurricane in 1960. Many records between late June and early September are suspect due to probable confusion with Royal Terns, which occur primarily during that period, although the following sample of records is presumed to be correct: 3, Eastham, 21 August 1954 (Buckley); 1, Newburyport, 11–28 July 1946 (fide Griscom & Snyder 1955); 1, Plum Island, 11 July 1977 (Heil). Five were seen between 3 and 28 June 1982 at Plymouth, Monomoy, and Plum Island (BOEM).

# Royal Tern  *Sterna maxima*

**Range:** Primarily southern Nearctic; breeds along the Atlantic Coast from Maryland to Georgia; also along the Gulf Coasts of Texas and Louisiana, in Baja California, and in the West Indies. Atlantic birds winter from North Carolina south to central Argentina.

**Status:** Regular visitor, primarily in midsummer or after hurricanes in early fall.

**Occurrence:** Royal Terns have increased in their frequency of occurrence in Massachusetts since 1950, concurrent with their population increase and northward range expansion on the middle and southern Atlantic Coast (Griscom & Snyder 1955, Bull 1964). Between 1874 and 1950, Bailey (1955) listed only eleven records of Royal Terns from the state; more recently, from ten to fifteen have been recorded in a single year. Most individuals occur on Cape Cod and the Islands between late June and mid-August, with a peak in mid-July. Since about 1970, there has been an increase in reports in late May; the earliest are: 1, Martha's Vineyard, 17 May 1979 (Laux); 1, Plymouth Beach, 20 May 1979 (MBO staff). The maximum counts north of Boston are: 4, Plum Island, 28 July 1975 (Heil); 3, Revere Beach, 3 August 1977 (Zendeh). *Maximum:* 9, Monomoy, 10 July 1971 (VO).

Large numbers of Royal Terns have historically been recorded following hurricanes. For example, between 1 and 19 September 1954, 23 coastal reports included one as far north as Plum Island, and, between 13 and 27 September 1960, 125 coastal occurrences were recorded, including 50 at Nantucket, 22 at Martha's Vineyard, and 17 at Monomoy. During the same storm, 300 were estimated along the south shore of Long Island, New York—the largest flight ever recorded there (Bull 1964). Ordinarily, Royal Terns are rare after early September, and September and October records are often suspect because of possible confusion with Caspian Terns. Nonetheless, the following constitute bona fide records for November: 1–2, Eastham, 25–27 November 1979 (Finch, Russell, et al); 1, Nauset, Eastham, 22 November 1954 (Griscom); 1, Nantucket, 12–15 November 1960 (Seeler, Andrews); 1, Sandy Neck, Barnstable, 9 November 1972 (Rhome, Petersen, et al).

# Sandwich Tern  *Sterna sandvicensis*

**Range:** Eastern Nearctic and western Palearctic; breeds, in North America, along the Atlantic Coast in Virginia and North and South Carolina, along the Gulf Coast of Louisiana and Texas, on islands off the Yucatan Peninsula, in the Bahamas, and in the Virgin Islands. Winters from Louisiana and Florida south to Colombia and on the Pacific Coast from southern Mexico to Panama.

**Status:** Rare but increasingly regular summer visitor.

**Occurrence:** Sandwich Terns associate very closely with Royal Terns throughout their North American range. They typically nest in mixed colonies with that species, except on the Gulf Coast, where large pure colonies occur. Consequently, it is not surprising that the pattern and recent increase in frequency of occurrence of the Sandwich Tern in Massachusetts parallels closely that of the Royal Tern. Practically all records are from the southeastern coastal plain, with only a few exceptions—e.g., 1 collected, Lynn, 1870 (fide Griscom & Snyder 1955); 1 after Hurricane Agnes, Newburyport, 28 June 1972 (Forster). All of the records since 1950 fall in the months of May through October, with most individuals appearing in July and September. Most exceptional was a minimum total of 75 Sandwich Terns seen at Martha's Vineyard and Nantucket in the wake of Hurricane Gloria, 28–29 September 1985 (VO). As is the case with the Royal Tern, all May records have been recent—e.g., 1, Monomoy, 28 May 1979 (Petersen); 1, Muskeget Island, 27 May 1981 (Heil); 1, Plymouth Beach, 30 May 1981 (D'Entremont). The latest date on record is: 1, 2 October 1979, Nantucket (Veit, Litchfield).

# Roseate Tern  *Sterna dougallii*

**Range:** Cosmopolitan, although local, primarily in tropical and subtropical sections of the Caribbean Sea and the western Pacific and Indian oceans. In the North Atlantic, breeds from Nova Scotia to New York and from northeastern Britain to northwestern France. Ninety percent of the North American population breeds in the Cape Cod–Long Island area. These individuals apparently winter along the northern coast of South America.

**Status:** Locally abundant breeder and migrant but decreasing. The population of northeastern North America was listed as endangered by the United States Fish and Wildlife Service in 1987 (USFWS 1987). About half of this population breeds in Massachusetts.

**Breeding:** Prior to the persecution of terns during the plume trade (1870–1900), the status of Roseate Terns in Massachusetts was obscure, although

Brewster implied that they were abundant breeders among colonies of the more numerous Common Terns at Nantucket and Muskeget islands. Nisbet (1980, 1983) estimated that the population reached a low of roughly 2,000 pairs, mostly at Muskeget and Penikese islands, during the 1880s. Following protection, Roseate Terns steadily increased to a peak of about 7,500 pairs in 1940. The colonies were progressively overrun by Herring Gulls between 1936 and 1972 (Nisbet 1973, 1980). They reached another low of about 1,500 pairs in the mid-1970s but have remained fairly stable since. In 1991, 1,776 pairs were counted: 1,728 pairs, Bird Island, Marion; 25 pairs, New Island, Orleans; 16 pairs, Long Beach, Plymouth; 7 pairs, Gray's Beach, Yarmouthport. Roseate Terns invariably nest in mixed colonies with Common Terns but select nest sites that are more protected by vegetation, and they typically lay two, rather than three, eggs. *Egg dates:* 12 May–late July; most from 21 May–15 June.

Roseate Terns were listed as endangered by the USFWS primarily because the population of northeastern North America has become dangerously concentrated into a few colony sites (USFWS 1989). In Massachusetts, this occurred because Herring Gulls displaced the terns from offshore colonies to inshore sites, thus making the birds subject to more predation by Great Horned Owls, Black-crowned Night-Herons, and other predators. Bird Island, Marion, is the only site in Massachusetts where the terns have been relatively secure from significant predation, and it now supports about half the entire population of northeastern North America (USFWS 1989). Nisbet (1981–1989) has reported that Roseate Terns have been consistently productive (raising 1.0 to 1.5 chicks per pair to fledging each year) since at least 1930. In spite of this, the species declined rapidly in the 1970s and failed to recover during the 1980s. Human persecution in the winter quarters may be the factor responsible for this (USFWS 1989). Western European populations similarly declined in the same period, apparently because of human predation in West Africa (Dunn 1981).

**Nonbreeding:** In spring, Roseate Terns arrive at their breeding colonies a week or so later than Common Terns, usually during the first week of May. Earliest records are: 12, Bird Island, Marion, 26 April 1980 (Nisbet); 3, Bird Island, 27 April 1991 (Nisbet); 3, Martha's Vineyard, 28 April 1979 (Laux). In 1981, Heil spent the month of May on Muskeget Island and observed hundreds of migrant Roseate Terns (maximum 350, 19 May). During late July to early September, the local breeding population is augmented by birds dispersing from other colonies throughout the Northeast, as determined by color banding (Nisbet, pers. comm.). These birds concentrate in August and September along the outer beaches of Cape Cod and the Islands. *Fall maxima:* 10,000, 28 August 1961, Nauset, Eastham (Bailey); 7,000, 22 August 1954, Monomoy (Griscom); 4,000 +, Provincetown, 21–31 August 1980 (Nikula, Heil); 2,000, Monomoy, 30 August 1978 (VO); 2,000, Nauset, Eastham, 1 September 1981 (Nikula); 1,500, Monomoy, 1 September

1974 (Petersen). By the end of September, most birds have departed; the latest dates are: 1, Chatham, 20 November 1965 (Bailey, photographed by Clem); 1, Provincetown, 11 November 1982 (Nikula).

Most inland reports of Roseate Terns are more likely to be misidentified individuals of some other species, although 10 to 15 birds among 475 Common Terns in Andover, following Hurricane Carol, 31 August 1954 (Smith, Root), are believed to have been correctly identified.

## Common Tern  *Sterna hirundo*

**Range:** Holarctic; breeds, in North America, from northeastern Alberta and southern Mackenzie east, sporadically, to southeastern Labrador and south along the Atlantic Coast to North Carolina; very local in the Caribbean Sea. In New England, the only inland breeding site is on Lake Champlain. Atlantic populations winter from South Carolina and Florida south to northern Argentina.

**Status:** Locally abundant breeder (but with numbers variable over decades) and abundant migrant at the coast; rare and irregular inland and very rare in winter.

**Breeding:** The histories of Common, Roseate, Arctic, and Least terns as breeding species in Massachusetts have been summarized in detail by Nisbet (1973, 1978) and Kress et al (1983). The Common Tern was, prior to 1870, a very abundant nesting species on the islands south of Cape Cod, with estimates from Muskeget Island and Coatue Beach, Nantucket, running as high as hundreds of thousands of pairs. Beginning about 1870, the numbers of all the species breeding in the state were severely depressed by plume hunters so that their combined breeding populations were probably reduced to about 5,000 to 10,000 pairs in the 1890s, most of which survived only at Muskeget and Penikese islands.

After protection was initiated between 1900 and 1910, the population of Common Terns steadily increased to a maximum of 30,000 pairs in Massachusetts by 1920. From then until the 1970s, the population decreased again, due largely to the massive expansion of the Herring Gull population. The population reached a low of about 5,000 to 6,000 pairs in the mid-1970s but increased steadily during the 1980s to its present level of about 10,000 pairs as a result of efforts to protect them from disturbances and predation (Nisbet, pers. comm.). In 1991, 9,822 nests were counted at 21 sites, including 3,222 pairs at New Island, Orleans; 2,308 pairs at Long Beach, Plymouth; and 1,780 pairs at Bird Island, Marion (fide Blodget). In recent years the population has been increasingly concentrated at these three sites because the offshore sites have been occupied by gulls and most inshore sites are subject to predation (see comments under Roseate Tern).

Herring and Great Black-backed gulls, which return to nesting islands at least six weeks earlier in spring than terns, usurp nesting space previously occupied by terns. This displacement has forced the terns to move from safer, more remote insular sites, such as Muskeget Island, to islands closer to shore, or coastal localities such as Monomoy, Nauset in Eastham, Gray's Beach in Yarmouth, West Dennis, Craigville, and Dead Neck–Sampson's Island in Osterville. In these more coastal locations, the chicks occasionally suffer heavy predation from Black-crowned Night-Herons and Great Horned Owls.

At some colonies, such as Monomoy, adult terns regularly desert their nests at night, apparently to avoid predation, thus leaving the chicks defenseless against herons and owls and also vulnerable to the weather. This problem does not auger well for the future of certain colonies. Trull (1983) found a fisherman in Guyana who was trapping large numbers of terns for food during the fall and early winter. Because so many banded birds from Massachusetts have been trapped and killed there, it would appear that winter mortality may have a substantial effect on the species. *Egg dates:* 4 May–5 August.

**Nonbreeding:** In spring, Common Terns usually arrive at their nesting colonies during the last few days of April, and northward migration continues until at least the end of May. The simultaneous arrival of large flocks of Common Terns has occasionally been witnessed at Chatham—e.g., 8,000 arriving at sunset, 13 May 1952 (Hill); 2,000 at noon, 8 May 1962 (Bailey).

Inland, Common Terns occur in spring over large bodies of water following storms or periods of heavy rain—e.g., 11, Quabbin, 27 April 1965 (Robillard); 20, Boylston, 17 May 1978 (Merriman); 10, Lancaster, 20 May 1979 (FBC). All inland terns should be carefully scrutinized because Arctic Terns have also appeared inland during mid- to late May.

During fall, large numbers of terns congregate to feed on bait fish at localities such as Nantucket, Monomoy, Barnstable, and Stellwagen Bank before leaving for the south (Nisbet 1976b). Among these flocks, color-banded birds from Great Gull Island in Long Island Sound are regularly seen, and it seems likely that terns from even more distant colonies may often assemble at Cape Cod in fall to exploit the food supply there. *Fall Maxima:* 10,000, Nauset, Eastham, 13 August 1959 (Bailey); 10,000, Nantucket, 11–24 September 1978 (Soucy, Veit); 10,000, Stellwagen Bank, 21–31 August 1980 (Petersen, Nikula); 3,600, Nantucket, 23 September 1981 (Stymeist). On 21 September 1978, a single flock of 10,000 + terns was observed circling high into the air at dusk at Nantucket and finally departing to the southwest (Petersen, Veit).

Although the bulk of the tern population has ordinarily left by the third week of September, in some years sizeable flocks remain into November, especially between Provincetown and Truro and at Nantucket—e.g., 600,

Barnstable, 26 October 1978 (Petersen); 500+, Provincetown, 8 November 1981 (Heil, VO); 400, Provincetown, 1 November 1980 (Heil, VO); 200, Chatham, 3 November 1956 (Harrington); 20, Rockport, 23 November 1958 (Bailey). Inland, the largest numbers occur following hurricanes and other coastal storms—e.g., 400+, Andover, 31 August 1954 (Smith); 200, Wayland, 31 August 1954 (Stackpole). More typically, 1 to 5 birds are seen, which rarely remain for longer than one day—e.g., 9, Turners Falls, 9 August 1954 (Harrington); 7, Richmond Pond, 25 August 1978 (Goodrich, McNair); 5+, Boylston, 15 October 1977 (Merriman, Blodget). They occur less regularly inland in fall than spring.

Mackay (1895) reported two midwinter specimens of Common Terns from Woods Hole, collected by Edwards, 20 February 1891 and 17 January 1894. Since that time, there have been only two sight records later than the first few days of January, despite the considerable increase in observers during this century—e.g., 1, Rockport, 23 January 1971 (Sanborn et al); 1, Cohasset, 11 January 1975 (Fox). Common Terns regularly remain in Massachusetts until late December and early January, and there have been at least nine records during that period since 1954. *Winter maximum:* 5, Chatham, 4 January 1954 (Hill, Barry).

# Arctic Tern    *Sterna paradisaea*

**Range:** Circumpolar; breeds, in North America, throughout arctic Canada and south on the Atlantic Coast to Maine and Massachusetts. Migrates to the eastern Atlantic and then south to wintering grounds at the edge of the Antarctic pack ice.

**Status:** Very uncommon, local, and decreasing breeder. Regular, and possibly fairly common, migrant far offshore but rare within sight of land. Very rare south of New England on the Atlantic Coast but detected with increasing frequency, mainly in spring since the 1970s. Large flocks of one-year-old birds have occurred in recent years during June and July on Cape Cod and Nantucket.

**Breeding:** The status of the Arctic Tern as a breeding species in Massachusetts prior to 1870, when the other tern species were most abundant, is unclear due to difficulties in field identification. However, it was almost certainly the least common of the three larger breeding species, and the population was probably reduced to a mere handful by 1890. Following protective measures, this species recovered more slowly than either Common or Roseate terns. The population reached a peak density during the period 1945 to 1947, when approximately 400 pairs nested in the state. Most of these were on Cape Cod and the offshore islands (Nisbet 1973). The breeding population has steadily decreased since that time so that, by 1991, only 17 pairs remained—e.g., 8, New Island, Orleans; 6, Plymouth Beach; 1, North Monomoy; 1, Race Point, Provincetown; 1, Nashawena Island (fide Blodget). Arctic Terns nest on open sand or gravelly substrates with Least Terns or on the edges of Common Tern colonies. *Egg dates:* 21 May–12 July; much later than Common Terns (Nisbet, pers. comm.).

**Nonbreeding:** Unlike one-year-old Common Terns, a few one-year-old Arctic Terns are regularly seen at breeding colonies during their first summer (Hatch, pers. comm.). Curiously, between the years 1975 and 1980, exceptionally large numbers of these immature birds were seen at Monomoy (Forster 1980)—e.g., 550 +, June 1976 (Forster, Nisbet); 300 +, 25 June 1977 (Nisbet); 800 +, 6 July 1979 (Nikula, Heil); 200, June 1980 (Heil). There are also occasional reports of smaller numbers from other sites—e.g., Provincetown (up to 50), Nauset, Eastham (up to 60), No Mans Land (up to 12), and Plymouth (up to 10). Three MCZ specimens dating back to 1938 suggest that the occurrence of Arctic Terns in first summer plumage in Massachusetts during summer has historical precedence. Obviously, birds of this age class are much too numerous to derive from the Massachusetts colonies alone. Considering that immature Arctic Terns occur in greatest numbers at certain Maine colonies during July (Hatch, pers. comm.), it is possible that the Massachusetts birds move north after first congregating here in June.

During the fall, Arctic Terns are very rarely detected as migrants in Massachusetts because the bulk of the population migrates east to Europe before heading south to wintering grounds in Antarctica—a fact substantiated by banding records (Godfrey 1966). Adults invariably leave the breeding colonies and head north or east by early August, and there are only three acceptable Massachusetts records of this species later than the second week of August. Cahoon collected three adults in alternate plumage on Cape Cod, 22 September, 24 September, and 24 October, 1886 (MCZ #12770, 12769, 250555). More recently, single juveniles were identified at Monomoy, 12 September 1981 (Petersen, Harrington, et al) and Pamet River, Truro, 12 October 1973 (P. and F. Buckley, Warner).

There is evidence that during spring at least some Arctic Terns migrate north along the continental slope of North America during mid- to late May. They have definitely been recorded at that time off North Carolina (Lee & Booth 1979), New Jersey, and Maryland (Rowlett 1980). At the continental slope off Georges Bank, loose flocks of 5 to 10 birds, totaling 83 individuals, were seen flying steadily north between 4 and 13 June 1977 (Veit), and 31 were seen near 41° 47′N, 67° 00′W on 7–10 June 1978 (Veit). During an unseasonal spring snowstorm, 10 May 1977, 200 Arctic Terns were seen in Cape Cod Bay (Petersen, Forster, Anderson); otherwise, the only reports of spring migrants seen from shore are: 2, Newburyport, 15–17 May 1975 (Gardler, Petersen); 2, Muskeget Island, 20 May 1981 (Heil). There is evidence that some Arctic Terns migrate over land to reach their breeding grounds in the Canadian Arctic (Godfrey 1973), so the following records could possibly be indicative of that passage: 16, Heard's Pond, Wayland, 20 May 1979 (Forster); 1, Walden Pond, Concord, 7 June 1989 (Sorrie). Other records of birds seen inland but identified as other species may properly belong here.

# Forster's Tern   *Sterna forsteri*

**Range:** Nearctic; breeds from southeastern British Columbia and central Saskatchewan south to southern California and along the Gulf Coast from central Mexico to Louisiana, and, disjunctly, along the Atlantic Coast from Long Island (1981) to North Carolina. Winters from North Carolina south to Guatemala.

**Status:** Rare breeder; one nesting record. Uncommon to locally common fall migrant at the coast; occasional inland after hurricanes. Rare, but increasingly frequent, in spring.

**Breeding:** An apparently mated pair of Forster's Terns was discovered at Plum Island, 24 June 1990 (Perkins, Heil), although no further evidence of breeding was observed. The following season, a nest containing two eggs was located in a small salt-marsh colony of Common Terns, 10 June 1991 (Rimmer, Hopping 1991). This nesting represents the northernmost breeding location on the Atlantic Coast of the United States.

**Nonbreeding:** Prior to 1940, the status of Forster's Tern in Massachusetts was somewhat clouded due to problems of field identification. Griscom and Snyder (1955) felt that it was "a regular fall transient . . . in flocks of 15–24" on Cape Cod, and "rarer in Essex County," which probably indicates no significant change in status since 1879, when Brewster (1879) stated that Forster's Terns occurred far too frequently to be termed accidental. Since 1973, however, there has been a marked increase in the number of fall migrants reported. It remains unclear whether these derive from inland or southern coastal populations, so a juvenile Forster's Tern found dying at Hampton, New Hampshire, 20 July 1968, which had been banded as a chick in Worcester County, Maryland, 20 May 1968 (Anderson, Smart; Anderson 1968), is particularly interesting.

There has also been a slight increase in spring records. Birds in this season are mostly in basic plumage, suggesting that they are subadult individuals. Spring records include: 1, Plymouth Beach, 8 June 1969 (Hartel, Blakeslee); 1, Newburyport, 13 May 1975 (Leahy); 1, Newburyport, 10–30 April 1976 (VO); 1, Newburyport, 12 March 1977 (Grugan); 1, Falmouth, 19 March 1978 (Coskren); 1, Chatham, 30 March 1978 (Nikula, Rich); 1–2, Monomoy, 23 May–late July 1980 (Nikula, Petersen, et al); 1, Newburyport, 16 May and 13 June 1981 (Gove); 1, Monomoy, 2 June and 23–29 June 1981 (Nikula, Trull); 1

collected, Monomoy, 24 June 1982 (Veit). The only inland spring records are: 1 in breeding plumage, Concord, 16 April 1990 (Perkins, Forster); 1 in breeding plumage, Northampton, 13 May 1990 (Gagnon). The highest counts of the year always occur in the fall. *Maxima:* 200 +, Wellfleet Bay, 27 October 1979 (Heil, Nikula, Trull); 200 +, Nauset Bay, Eastham, 13 September 1980 (Heil, Nikula); 52, Nauset, Eastham, 12 October 1973 (Bailey, Goodrich).

Forster's Terns regularly linger into late fall; the latest reports on record are: 1, Menemsha Pond, Martha's Vineyard, 21 January 1979 (Laux); 1, Nantucket, 28 December 1979 (Buckley, Able). Inland, following the first hurricane of 1954, 20 Forster's Terns were seen at Longmeadow, 31 August–9 September (Eliot et al). Another inland sighting, 1, Onota Lake, Pittsfield, 16 October 1954 (E. and A. Fitz), was probably hurricane driven as well. There are at least five additional sight records of Forster's Terns from the Connecticut River valley, including counts of: 34, Longmeadow, 4 October 1964 (Yacavone, Cavanaugh); 8, South Quabbin, 16 September 1965 (Gura). Additional inland records include: 1, Lakeville, 24 August 1980 (Petersen); 1 after hurricane, Lakeville, 29 September 1985 (Petersen).

## Least Tern *Sterna antillarum*

**Range:** Nearctic; breeds on the Pacific Coast, in the Mississippi River valley, and along the Atlantic Coast from southern Maine to Florida and west along the Gulf Coast to Texas; winters off South America from Colombia east to Brazil.

**Status:** Locally abundant breeder on sandy beaches.

**Breeding:** Unlike Common, Arctic, and Roseate terns, Least Terns rarely nest on small offshore islands but are instead distributed along the beaches of the mainland or on large barrier islands. They most often select places such as the ends of sand spits, where winter storms maintain open sand or gravel conditions for breeding. They experience frequent disturbance, and colonies often shift from one site to another when they are disrupted by storms or human activity. For this reason, they are particularly difficult to census, with total counts for the state being strongly influenced by the date on which they are conducted. Nisbet (1973) indicated that the Massachusetts Least Tern population reached a peak of 1,500 pairs during the period 1945 to 1952, after a low point of about 250 pairs near the turn of the century. The population began to slowly increase again about 1980, and, by 1988, 2,681 pairs were breeding in Massachusetts (fide Blodget).

Since the early 1970s, the larger colonies have been fenced and posted, which has generally afforded effective protection. The annual statewide tern surveys since 1972 indicated an increase to about 2,000 breeding pairs by

1981, which reflects both a real increase as well as more thorough censusing techniques. In 1991, the largest colonies were: 605 pairs, Nauset Heights, Orleans; 257 pairs, Dunbar Point, Barnstable; 185 pairs, West Dennis Beach, Dennis; 145 pairs, Plymouth Beach. There were an additional 161 pairs in Essex County, 40 + pairs on the South Shore, and 34 pairs in the Dartmouth area. Pairs elsewhere in Massachusetts brought the state total to 2,356 (fide Blodget). *Egg dates:* 20 May–23 August.

**Nonbreeding:** Flocks of up to 500 Least Terns have been reported at such areas as Nauset, Eastham, and Monomoy between late May and mid-August and have mostly departed by early September. Early dates are: 1, Chappaquiddick, Martha's Vineyard, 27 April 1968 (Petersen, Forster); 1, Martha's Vineyard, 27 April 1979 (Laux). Reports after mid-September are rare, the latest being: 3, North Chatham, 29 September 1955 (Mosher). There are no inland records of Least Terns in Massachusetts except for a few localities in Plymouth and Barnstable counties, where the species regularly forages in freshwater ponds within several miles of the coast.

# Bridled Tern  *Sterna anaethetus*

**Range:** Pantropical; in the Atlantic, breeds off Mauritania, and in the Antilles, north to and including the Bahamas. Wanders regularly (mostly nonbreeders) in the Gulf Stream north at least to Cape Hatteras, North Carolina. In winter, individuals have been recorded north to Newfoundland and south to Tierra del Fuego, but most apparently disperse at sea between the Caribbean and western Africa.

**Status:** Vagrant: eleven records.

**Occurrence:** Bridled Terns are recorded far less frequently after hurricanes in eastern North American than Sooty Terns. However, they regularly occur at least as far north as North Carolina, especially in August and September. So it seems curious that they do not occur more frequently north to Massachusetts. They appear to feed exclusively in tropical waters, often near floating mats of gulf weed (*Sargassum* sp.).

Hurricane-related reports of Bridled Terns in Massachusetts include: 2 following Hurricane Donna, Harwichport, 12 September 1960 (Smart); 2, Manomet Point, 13 September 1960 (Ernst); 3 following Hurricane Bob, Martha's Vineyard, 19 August 1991 (Keith, Whiting); 2, First Encounter Beach, Eastham, 19 August 1991 (Cassie). In addition, a dead immature Bridled Tern was found at Monomoy, 14 September 1960 (Barry, Hill 1965).

The only other reports of Bridled Terns in Massachusetts are: 1 oiled immature, Monomoy, 16 September 1934 (Griscom et al); 1, Nantucket, 8 September 1952 (Elkins, Smart); 1, Monomoy, 30 August 1953 (Rich, Griscom); 1, First Encounter Beach, Eastham, 31 August 1975 (Petersen, Forster,

Harrington, et al); 1, Sandy Neck, East Sandwich, 12 August 1979 (Heil); 1, 7 miles east of Gloucester, 25 August 1984 (Ellison et al). These sightings correspond to the period of maximum abundance of Bridled Terns off Cape Hatteras, North Carolina (Lee & Booth 1979), and all but the 1984 record pertain to immature birds.

## Sooty Tern  *Sterna fuscata*

**Range:** Pantropical; breeds, in the Atlantic Ocean, in the Greater and Lesser Antilles; on islands off the Yucatan Peninsula, Texas, and Louisiana; and on the Dry Tortugas, Florida, and elsewhere in the tropical Atlantic. Disperses eastward to tropical Africa in winter. Vagrant, principally after hurricanes, to eastern North America, north to Nova Scotia.

**Status:** Irregular visitor, primarily but not exclusively after tropical storms and hurricanes.

**Occurrence:** Sooty Terns breed in enormous colonies in the Caribbean from April to August, after which they disperse widely over the tropical oceans, the immatures traveling as far as the coast of western Africa (Robertson 1969). This highly pelagic distribution during fall, coupled with the species' reluctance to alight on the water (Watson 1910), make Sooty Terns prime subjects for vagrancy during hurricanes. Bull's (1964) statement that Sooty Terns are more regularly reported after hurricanes than any other tropical bird species on Long Island, New York, applies to Massachusetts as well.

The largest numbers of Sooty Terns recorded locally have followed hurricanes in 1876, 1878, 1954, 1960, and 1979, as enumerated below. *1876:* 1 picked up dead, Williamstown, 18 September (Tenney); 1, collected on the Merrimack River, Lawrence, 29 October (Ruthven); and others reported elsewhere in New England. *1878:* 2 collected, Holyoke, mid-September (Lamb, Bennett); the latter bird, collected by Bennett, was erroneously reported as being collected on Cape Cod (Bailey 1955). *1954:* 11 seen, 31 August–6 September, following Hurricane Carol, including: 4, Nantucket; 2, Provincetown; 2, Andover; 1, Plum Island; 1, Sagamore; 1, Scituate (RNEB). Oddly, no Sooty Terns were seen on Long Island following this storm, despite the occurrence of numerous other southern species there. *1960:* Following Hurricane Donna, which passed over Massachusetts 12 September, 40 Sooty Terns were recorded, all but one (at Newburyport) on the southeastern coastal plain. The largest concentrations recorded following Hurricane Donna were: 25 (18 adults, 7 immatures) seen "struggling against the wind in tight formation," Swansea (Bowen, RNEB 16: 9); 12 (and 6 found dead the next day), Nantucket, 13 September (Andrews). *1979:* Following Hurricane David, which reached Massachusetts 6 September, at least 85 Sooty Terns were recorded in the state, the large total in part reflecting the preparedness and mobility of observers who anticipated the birds' arrival. Interestingly, the first individuals were seen inland: 1, Lake Quabog, Brookfield; 1, Holyoke; 1, Longmeadow. Also, 3, Nantucket; 8, Gloucester; 3, Lakeville; 5, Buzzards Bay (BNWM, BOEM). On the next day, observers covered the coast and noted the terns heading rapidly south, with the following maxima: 19, Nantucket; 13, First Encounter Beach, Eastham. As is often the case with storm-driven birds, fewer than 20 percent of the individuals seen were immatures.

Non-storm-related records include: 3, Chatham, September 1877 (Jeffries); 1 adult, First Encounter Beach, Eastham, 18 October 1970 (Bailey); 1 adult, Monomoy, 3 July 1971 (Harris); 1 adult, Bird Island, Marion, 29 June 1974 (Hatch); 1 adult, Nauset, Eastham, 10 July 1974 (Nisbet); 1 adult photographed, North Monomoy, 21 June 1985 (Humphrey, MacIvor).

# White-winged Tern   *Chlidonias leucopterus*

**Range:** Palearctic; breeds from Belgium and Germany east to eastern Siberia. Winters in Africa. Vagrant to the British Isles, Scandinavia, and North America.

**Status:** Vagrant: one record.

**Occurrence:** Two White-winged Terns, including an adult in alternate plumage, were closely studied over Musquashicut Pond, Scituate, 25–27 May 1954 (May, VO, see Griscom & Snyder 1955). As the incidence of White-winged Terns in Britain and North America has increased over the last 10 to 15 years, future records from Massachusetts should be optimistically expected.

# Black Tern   *Chlidonias niger*

**Range:** Holarctic; breeds, in North America, from British Columbia and California east to Maine and Vermont and south to central California, central Illinois, and western New York. Eastern North American birds winter in South America south to Surinam.

**Status:** Fairly common spring and common to occasionally very common fall migrant.

**Occurrence:** In spring, the majority of Black Terns migrate north to their breeding grounds over land. Consequently, in Massachusetts they are seen mainly between mid-May and mid-June following periods of rainy weather, which forces the birds down over inland bodies of water, including lakes, reservoirs, marshes, and rivers. If no rain occurs during the appropriate season, Black Terns apparently fly high enough so as not to be detected, although single birds or small groups are regularly recorded near coastal colonies of other terns during May and June.

The earliest spring record is: 3, Chatham, 3 May 1956 (fide Bailey). *Spring maxima* (inland): 30, Hadley, 15 May 1967 (Goodrich); 25, Littleton, 15 May 1967 (Baird); 16, Sudbury River valley, 12 May 1956 (Morgan); 12, Wayland, 8 May 1980 (Forster); 7, Boylston, 19 May 1968 (McMenemy). Coastal: 13, Newburyport, 19 May 1973 (BOEM); 9, Nauset, Eastham, 22 May 1973 (Nikula). Although the species is rare in midsummer, from 2 to 5 individuals are usually present each year near Bird Island, Marion, and at Monomoy and Nauset, Eastham, between late May and mid-July.

During the fall, migrant Black Terns are most numerous on the sandbars around tidal rips off Cape Cod and the Islands, and occasionally they are quite numerous offshore. In this season, they are rare and irregular inland. The peak period of abundance is usually between the last week of August and the first week of September. *Fall maxima* (coastal): 500, Monomoy, 1–3 September 1948 (Maclay); 400, off Chatham, 10–11 September 1949 (MAS); 300, Monomoy, 9 September 1955 (Goodell et al); 200 +, Monomoy, 1 September 1967 (Forster); 60 +, First Encounter Beach, Eastham, 3 September 1972 (Harrington et al); 60, First Encounter Beach, Eastham, 16 August 1986 (Petersen). Inland: 9, Clinton, 22 August 1974 (Blodget); 7 after hurricane, Auburn, 29 August 1971 (McMenemy); 6, Ludlow, 29 August 1935 (Leshure); 2 after hurricane, North Andover, 31 August 1954 (Root); 1 (late date), Wachusett Reservoir, 12 October 1950 (Nutting). The species is rare after early October—e.g., 1 juvenile caught in midair by a Northern Harrier, Nantucket, 18 December 1980 (Veit, Andrews); 1, Nantucket, 6 December 1981 (Perkins); 5, Nantucket, 7 October 1979 (Veit, Litchfield).

# Brown Noddy *Anous stolidus*

**Range:** Pantropical; in the Atlantic Ocean, breeds on oceanic islands northwest to the Bahamas and the Dry Tortugas, Florida. Disperses widely over tropical seas during winter.

**Status:** Vagrant: two records.

**Occurrence:** After Hurricane Carol, 31 August 1954 (not the "second" hurricane as stated in Griscom and Snyder 1955), a dead noddy, presumably this species, was found on the beach at Martha's Vineyard, 3 September (Hornblower) but was not preserved. More surprising was the discovery of a Brown Noddy at Smith Point, Nantucket, 27 August 1957 (P. and B. Heywood) following a mild tropical disturbance (Mason & Robertson 1965). The bird—an immature in the opinion of Mason and Robertson, who examined the photographs—remained until 3 September, was seen by Edith Andrews, and was clearly photographed in color.

Unlike Bridled Terns, and to a certain extent Sooty Terns, Brown Noddies do not ordinarily disperse northward in Gulf Stream waters.

## Black Skimmer   *Rynchops niger*

**Range:** Primarily eastern Nearctic; breeds, on the Atlantic Coast, from Massachusetts south to Florida and along the Gulf Coast to Texas; also in Mexico and South America. Winters from North Carolina south to the Gulf of Mexico.

**Status:** Rare, local, and irregular breeder; regular summer and fall visitant, occasionally abundant after hurricanes.

**Breeding:** Forbush (1925) summarized the history of the Black Skimmer as a breeding species in Massachusetts, including a citation of Champlain's (1605) detailed description of skimmers at Cape Cod. Black Skimmers apparently bred as recently as 1830 at Muskeget Island (Purdie 1882) but were not subsequently found nesting in Massachusetts for over 100 years. In 1934, Black Skimmers first recolonized Long Island, New York (Bull 1964), and, by 1946, 2 or 3 nests were found at Plymouth Beach (Hagar 1946). Since then, 1 to 3 pairs of skimmers have nested at Plymouth Beach (1959, 1960, 1961, 1966), Monomoy (1966, 1968, 1969, 1977, 1984, 1986, 1987, 1990), Cotuit (1956), Tern Island, Chatham (1971), and New Island, Orleans (1988, 1989, 1990). It is surprising that a population has never really taken hold in Massachusetts, considering the species' current abundance as a breeder on Long Island—e.g., 339–495 pairs at 10–13 sites, 1974–1978 (Buckley, pers. comm.).

**Nonbreeding:** Large numbers of Black Skimmers are often displaced northward along the coast by storms, and there is even a specimen from Springfield, 29 August 1893, after a hurricane (Griscom & Snyder 1955). The largest numbers of Black Skimmers recorded in Massachusetts were in 1879, 1924, 1944, 1954, and 1968. Forbush (1925) describes the meteorological characteristics of a storm in 1879 that produced "the famous skimmer invasion" to Massachusetts but does not say how many skimmers were found in Massachusetts. The 1944, 1954, and 1968 storms were documented in more detail (fide RNEB). *1944:* 400, Newburyport, 21 September; 386, Nauset, Eastham, 23 September; 1, Newburyport, as late as 8 November. *1954:* 1,050 following Hurricane Carol, 31 August, reported along the entire length of the coast during the month of September; 453+ birds still present in October, with a maximum of 250+, Chatham, 2 October. *1968:* A coastal storm (not a tropical storm) in late October displaced 220+ to Massachusetts between 1 and 28 November, including: 76, Wingaersheek Beach, Gloucester, 8 November; 5, Plymouth Beach, as late as 8 December.

Unlike tropical terns, Black Skimmers almost invariably remain in Massachusetts for considerable periods of time before returning south following their northward displacement. It is curious that the hurricanes of 1960 and 1979 (cf Sooty Tern) brought very few skimmers to Massachusetts. *Non-storm-related maximum:* 19 (16 immatures), Monomoy, 4 September 1970 (Bailey et al). *Extreme dates:* 1, found moribund during blizzard, Auburn, 14 March 1993 (Grocia, fide Blodget); 2, Monomoy, 5 May 1970 (Blodget); to 1, Squantum, 20 December 1970 (Brown).

# Dovekie  *Alle alle*

**Range:** Holarctic; breeds in the high Arctic south to central Greenland, Jan Mayen, and Spitzbergen. Winters at sea from the breeding range south, commonly, to Newfoundland and, irregularly, along the continental slope to Maryland.

**Status:** Irruptive; irregular late fall and winter visitor; at times abundant.

**Occurrence:** Although it has generally been supposed that flights of Dovekies to the Northeast are caused by storms, the data from Massachusetts suggests that this is not true. Because some flights have occurred in the absense of storms, and many storms have yielded no Dovekies, it is clear that large Dovekie flights represent major southward incursions. On occasion, particularly during November, large numbers of Dovekies are blown ashore by coastal storms. Major Dovekie "wrecks" have been documented in Massachusetts in 1871, 1932, 1950, 1957, 1959, 1962, and 1969, with others of lesser magnitude recorded during the intervening years. The last flight of any sizeable proportions occurred in 1974, and Dovekies have been relatively scarce since then.

Curiously, large flights of Dovekies do not occur in the same years as large flights of other alcids. An enumeration of the largest flights follows. *1871:* Brewster found hundreds on Fresh Pond, Cambridge, on 15 November. Examination of the stomachs of some of these birds revealed that they had been eating alewives, which were then abundant in Fresh Pond (Brewster 1906). *1932:* Two northeasterly storms, 7–10 and 19–20 November, brought the most southerly extending Dovekie flight on record, with literally thousands of birds recorded in Florida and eight specimens taken in Cuba (Murphy & Vogt 1933). During both storms, Dovekies were reported inland to Athol, Holyoke, Huntington, Springfield, Westborough, Westfield, and Worcester. Of all the records enumerated from the East Coast by Murphy and Vogt (op cit), none occurred farther than 100 miles inland. *1957:* 18,000 counted flying past Halibut Point in two hours, 30 November (Kieran), and 10,000 there, 27 December (Gardler). None recorded on Cape Cod. *1962:* Northeasterly storms on 4 November and again on 6–8 December stranded large numbers of Dovekies far inland. Counts from coastal vantage points did not exceed 3,000 birds; however, at least 150 Dovekies were picked up inland following the December storm, including individuals as far from the coast as Ashby, Fitchburg, and Hudson. *1969:* 12,000 estimated during a southeasterly storm, North Beach, Chatham, 2 November (Petersen, Goodrich). Many dropped exhausted upon the beach, where they were quickly grabbed and eaten by Great Black-backed Gulls. Also, 2,724 were counted passing Manomet Point between 1 and 10 November (MBO staff), and several other counts of hundreds of birds were reported along the length of the Massachusetts coastline. Nearly 150 that were picked up exhausted inland in the eastern portion of the state—all east of Route 495—were reported to Massachusetts Audubon.

Several anomalous flights have occurred during fair weather and under conditions that seemed to be inappropriate for driving birds to shore. The most notable of these flights took place 7 November 1950, when 14,000 Dovekies were carefully estimated passing Halibut Point in one hour and forty minutes (Snyder 1953). The most unusual aspect of this particular flight was the conditions, which Snyder described as: "sunny and mild, mid-60's, wind SW-WSW, 10–12 mph." On 25 November of that same year, a major storm did occur, and 2,500 Dovekies were counted at Cape Ann. Numerous incapacitated birds were found at inland localities—e.g., Williamstown, Adams, and North Adams, all in Berkshire County, 27–30 November. There is only one additional Berkshire County record: 1, Otis, 26 November 1972 (fide Sanborn). The only other flight not obviously associated with a storm was on 10–18 November 1948, when 1,000 were seen each day from Halibut Point, Rockport, during fair weather (fide Griscom & Snyder 1955).

Other flights of lesser magnitude, generally involving fewer than 2,000 birds per day per locality, were recorded in 1958, 1959, 1963, 1966, 1968, 1970, 1972, and 1974. Dovekies have always been rare within sight of land after early January, and many midwinter sight records are suspect. There have been no large flights of Dovekies since 1974, despite the occurrence of coastal storms in the appropriate season. This invites speculation on the causes of these massive historic "wrecks." *Extreme dates:* 1, Manomet, 25 September 1977 (Hartel); 1, Rockport, 2 October 1976 (Veit, Litchfield); 1 found freshly dead, Orleans, 24 April 1989 (Williams). Rare before November and after December. There are several June records, the latest being: 1 oiled individual, Monomoy, 16 June 1940 (Karplus 1947).

# Common Murre *Uria aalge*

**Range:** Holarctic; in the western North Atlantic, breeds from southern Greenland to the Gulf of St. Lawrence, with the center of abundance in eastern Newfoundland; winters at sea primarily between the Grand Banks off Newfoundland and Georges Bank off New England.

**Status:** Rare but regular winter resident on the Nantucket Shoals and Georges Bank. Much rarer within sight of land than the Thick-billed Murre.

**Occurrence:** Before 1970 most records of Common Murres involved oiled individuals washed ashore, but the studies by the Manomet Bird Observatory (1976–1982) revealed a frequent presence offshore. The species' pelagic distribution in the vicinity of shipping lanes likely predisposes Common Murres to oiling. For example, in December 1976, when Thick-billed Murres were present in exceptional numbers off Massachusetts (see under Thick-billed Murre), 9 oiled Common Murres, but no Thick-billed Murres or Razorbills, were found washed ashore on Nantucket following the sinking of the tanker *Argo Merchant* on the Nantucket Shoals.

Unoiled Common Murres are occasionally seen off Cape Cod and Cape Ann, but the species is ordinarily rare within sight of land in Massachusetts, even after severe storms when other species of alcids are occasionally numerous. *Maxima:* 6, southwest of Martha's Vineyard, 4 February 1980 (MBO staff); 3–4, Provincetown, 6–17 December 1976 (Bailey et al); 3, Nantucket Shoals, 12 February 1977 (MBO staff); 2, Provincetown, 16 January 1977 (Veit, Litchfield). Oiled birds: 11, outer Cape, 20–26 February 1980 (Reynolds); 9, Nantucket, 1 January 1961 (Heywood); 9, outer Cape, January 1977 (Reynolds); 5, outer Cape, 5–25 February 1961 (fide Bailey).

In addition to the records above, there are approximately fifty records of single Common Murres seen since 1955 between late December and mid-April. ***Extreme dates:*** 1, Penikese Island, 29 June 1913 (Cobb, BMS #16290); 1 oiled, Westport, 24 June 1959 (Freeland); 1, Plum Island, 24 May 1975 (Petersen, Forster, et al); 1 oiled, Nantucket, 11 May 1969 (Brown); 1, Cape Cod Bay, 18 April 1981 (Nikula); 1, Chatham, 2–18 April 1976 (Clem et al).

# Thick-billed Murre    *Uria lomvia*

**Range:** Holarctic; breeds from Ellesmere Island and northern Greenland south to the Gulf of St. Lawrence, with the center of abundance largely north of 70° N (Brown et al 1975). Winters on unfrozen waters within breeding range south to Hudson Bay and New England, occasionally farther south.

**Status:** Rare to uncommon but regular winter resident and migrant; occasionally much more numerous. Occurs inland after storms more frequently than either Razorbills or Common Murres.

**Occurrence:** Although Thick-billed Murres are vastly outnumbered as breeders by Common Murres in Newfoundland, they move farther south in larger numbers during the winter, thus possibly making them the most common winter alcid in the Gulf of Maine (Finch et al 1978). They also appear to have a less pelagic distribution off Massachusetts than the Common Murre and are, therefore, more frequently seen from land. Because of their preference for rocky shores, Thick-billed Murres are generally outnumbered by Razorbills off the sandy shores of Cape Cod and the Islands.

Most often, between 1 and 20 birds are seen from vantage points at Cape Ann following northeasterly storms between mid-November and mid-January. An influx of entirely unprecedented proportions occurred in December 1976 and January 1977, when thousands of Thick-billed Murres were seen along the Massachusetts coast. The flight began on the evening of 16 December as a major storm approached from the south. As the winds increased from the northeast during the late afternoon, loose flocks of Thick-billed Murres began flying south past Halibut Point, Rockport. Before sunset, 450 were tallied (Veit, Litchfield). The next day by 10:00 a.m., amid heavy snow and 10-knot northeast winds, the same observers counted 2,300 + Thick-billed Murres (and 45 to 50 Razorbills) and estimated that 3,000 to 5,000 birds must have actually been involved. All of the birds passed the point within easy identification range. On the same day, 3,000 were seen in Cape Cod Bay (Bailey et al). Following another storm, 16 January, 4,000 Thick-billed Murres and 800 Razorbills were seen from Race Point, Provincetown (Veit, Litchfield). During this same incursion, counts of up to 53 Razorbills, but only one Thick-billed Murre, were reported off Maryland (Rowlett 1980).

Tuck (1961) has suggested that southward irruptions of murres are triggered by two factors: a freezing over of the northern portions of their winter range, which induces them to migrate, and major storms centered over the northwest Atlantic in which northeasterly winds drive the birds farther south and closer to land than is normally the case. It is possible that localized food abundance, such as an increased abundance of sand lances, around Cape Cod encouraged the murres to remain once they arrived in 1976–1977 because few were found dead or stranded along the beaches.

*Other maxima:* 190, Wellfleet Bay, 10 November 1959 (Bailey); 45 +, scattered along the coast from Plum Island to Nantucket, early January 1972 (fide Emery); 40, Manomet Point, 25 November 1975 (Harrington); 32, Rockport, 27 January 1952 (Griscom); 12, Manomet, 20 February 1972 (Youngstrom). *Maxima* (inland): 2, Lenox, 17 to 20 December 1932 (Pell); singles, Milton, Wayland, Westwood, 7 March 1962 (RNEB); singles, Billerica, Framingham, 3 November 1969 (RNEB); 1 collected, Longmeadow, 30 November 1899 (Morris). There are fewer than ten records before mid-November and after mid-March: e.g., 1, Provincetown Harbor, 8 October 1973 (Bailey, Veit); 1, Rockport, 29 October 1960 (Forster); to 1, off Monomoy, 9 April 1958 (Crompton). Summer records: 1, Newburyport Harbor, 21 July 1962 (Banes, Nash); 1, Monomoy, 30 July 1964 (Harrington); 1, Wellfleet, 6 August 1966 (Haskell).

# Razorbill    *Alca torda*

**Range:** Holarctic; breeds from Maine and western Greenland east to Iceland, the Faeroes, and the British Isles, and south to northern France. Western Atlantic birds winter at sea from the Grand Banks off Newfoundland south, regularly in small numbers, to Maryland and Virginia, with a concentration off southern New England.

**Status:** Variously uncommon to abundant migrant and winter resident offshore. Occasionally abundant within sight of land after storms.

**Occurrence:** In winter, Razorbills feed primarily in waters of less than 30 fathoms, shallower than those preferred by most other alcids. Because of this, they are most abundant at localities such as the Nantucket Shoals and Georges Bank. The other species are commoner farther offshore. As with other alcids, the winter distribution of the Razorbill varies considerably from year to year (cf Rowlett 1980), and it is probably dependent upon both food supply and weather conditions. In Massachusetts, peak numbers occur from late November—earliest, 2, First Encounter Beach, Eastham, 8 October 1972 (Stymeist)—to early January and again in March and April, suggesting that a substantial number ordinarily move farther south in late winter, only to return in midspring. A few seem to be present throughout the winter at Nantucket and off the eastern shores of Cape Cod, but they are scarce farther north in late winter.

A substantial influx to Nantucket waters has been apparent during March in recent years. *Spring maxima:* 330, Nantucket, 14 March 1981 (Perkins); 82, Nantucket, 18 April 1980 (Perkins). There are at least thirteen summer records of Razorbills since 1955, largely of sick, oiled, or freshly dead birds spanning the dates 15 May–1 September. *Fall and winter maxima:* 4,700 +, Provincetown, 22 January 1984 (Nikula); 4,363, Cape Cod CBC, 20 December 1987; 2,920, Cape Cod CBC, 18 December 1983; 1,500, Nantucket, 2 January 1984 (Andrews et al); 1,020, Sandy Neck, Barnstable, 4 December 1979 (Pease); 800, Provincetown, 16 January 1977 (Veit, Petersen); 500, Orleans, 15 January 1977 (Veit, Petersen); 400, Wellfleet Bay, 16 November 1959 (Bailey); 316 in two hours, Rockport, 18 December 1960 (Snyder, Leahy); 300–400, First Encounter Beach, Eastham, 16 January 1980 (Petersen); 250 +, off Provincetown, 15 January 1978 (Veit); 185 +, Rockport, 16 December 1976 (Veit). Small numbers of oiled Razorbills are routinely reported each winter, particularly around Nantucket. *Maximum* (oiled): 53 reported to the Cape Cod Museum of Natural History, from the outer Cape, 20–26 February 1980 (fide Reynolds). Unlike murres and Dovekies, Razorbills are very rarely reported inland after storms.

# Black Guillemot    *Cepphus grylle*

**Range:** Holarctic; breeds, in North America, in northern Alaska and from northern Hudson Bay, northern Labrador, and northern Greenland south to the Isles of Shoals off New Hampshire. Winters within the breeding range and south to Massachusetts; rarely farther south.

**Status:** Locally fairly common winter resident.

**Occurrence:** Prior to 1955, the Black Guillemot wintered almost exclusively off rocky coasts and was rare and irregular south of Cape Ann. Within the last three decades, however, they have increased dramatically as winter residents off Provincetown and the southeastern corner of Nantucket and have also become more frequent at Minot Ledge off North Scituate. Black Guillemots feed exclusively in inshore waters and have not been recorded out of sight of land in Massachusetts. They normally arrive in Massachusetts during late October, and most have departed by early May. *Maxima:* 267, Provincetown, 17 January 1984 (Brown); 70, Provincetown, 20 March 1983 (Nikula); 42, off Cape Ann, 18 February 1940 (Griscom et al); 32, Marblehead, 10 February 1981 (Heil); 30, Nantucket, 14 March 1981 (Perkins); 17, North Scituate, 13 January 1980 (Veit). There are at least eleven records of Black Guillemots, including three juveniles, between June and August, occurring between Salisbury and Nantucket. These may derive entirely from breeding areas to the north of Massachusetts, but breeding could conceivably occur in the future on one of the rocky islands off Cape Ann or in Boston Harbor. A helicopter survey on 15 June 1982 revealed no such evidence of breeding (Hatch, Veit). Inland, there are two records: 1, Quabbin Dike, 29 December 1971 (Albertine); 1 specimen, Fall River, 19 November 1899 (BMS #1510).

# Marbled Murrelet   *Brachyramphus marmoratus*

**Range:** Primarily western Nearctic; *B. m. perdix* breeds in northeastern Siberia and *B. m. marmoratus* along the west coast of North America from the Aleutian Islands south to central California. Winters south to Japan and California. *B. m. perdix* has occurred at least six times in North America (Anderson 1982).

**Status:** Vagrant: one record.

**Occurrence:** A dead Marbled Murrelet of the Siberian race, *B. m. perdix*, was brought by a cat to the home of the Harrisons in Middleboro, 17 September 1982 (Anderson 1982). The bird was in alternate plumage but had almost completed a molt of its primaries. Interestingly, a second Asiatic Marbled Murrelet was photographed on a Colorado reservoir during October 1982 (Anderson op cit).

# Atlantic Puffin   *Fratercula arctica*

**Range:** Holarctic; in North America, breeds from Maine and Newfoundland east to western Greenland and Iceland. The center of abundance of the western Atlantic population is in Newfoundland and on islands in the Gulf of St. Lawrence. In winter, disperses widely at sea, with a concentration along the continental slope as far south as the Chesapeake Bight.

**Status:** Rare but regular winter visitor; more numerous far offshore.

**Occurrence:** The winter distribution of Atlantic Puffins has been somewhat of a mystery until recent investigations by Manomet Bird Observatory revealed them to be widely distributed over the open ocean, with a pronounced concentration of sightings in the vicinity of the continental slope and along the northern edge of Georges Bank. Rowlett (1980) has suggested that Atlantic Puffins drift southward during fall and winter along the continental slope with the prevailing surface currents. Unlike most other Atlantic alcids, puffins are often solitary during winter. Their pelagic distribution and solitary habits mean they are among the rarer seabirds to occur within sight of land in Massachusetts, where they are usually only seen after major storms between late October and April.

There was a pronounced increase of sightings during the mid-1970s, probably due in part to an increase in interest in pelagic birding, but a rash of sightings of immature birds in October from Cape Cod Bay may involve individuals recently stocked at Eastern Egg Rock in Maine. Earliest records are: 1, Sandy Neck, Barnstable, 7 September 1974 (Petersen); 1, Stellwagen Bank, 6 October 1979 (Petersen, Heil, et al). *Maxima* (from land): 8, First Encounter Beach, Eastham, 8 January 1977 (Nikula, Goodrich); 8, Rockport, 26 November 1977 (Forster); 6 observed swimming and diving together, Coast Guard Beach, Eastham, 4 and 11 February 1978 (Petersen); 3, Nauset, Eastham, 17 January 1960 (Bailey). It is unusual to see more than 1 to 3 birds per day, and rarely are flocks of puffins seen, even at sea. *Maxima* (at sea): 16, Georges Bank, 17–26 April 1977 (Nickerson); 14 immatures (a most unusual concentration for any inshore locality south of Newfoundland), between the Isles of Shoals and Jeffrey's Ledge, 12 November 1972 (ASNH, Finch, Phinney, et al); 11, Stellwagen Bank, 28 October 1984 (BBC); 7, northern edge of Georges Bank, 19 February 1980 (MBO); 6, 15 miles southeast of Monomoy, 16 December 1979 (MBO). A number of Atlantic Puffins have been picked up oiled on the outer beaches during winter (maximum, 3, outer Cape Cod beaches, 22–24 February 1980 [fide Reynolds]). Summer records: 3, Stellwagen Bank, 1 May 1981 (Prescott); 1 found entangled in a fishing net, Sandwich, 5 June 1924 (fide Forbush 1925); 1 seen standing on the beach, Monomoy, 16 July 1969 (Blodget et al); 1 banded immature found dead (from Eastern Egg Rock, Maine), Scituate, summer of 1980 (fide Forster).

There is a remarkable inland record of an Atlantic Puffin from Lee, Berkshire County, 8 November 1970 (Stiles, Smith, Hendricks 1970), which represents the only inland occurrence for Massachusetts.

# Rock Dove   *Columba livia*

**Range:** Originally Palearctic; now introduced and resident, mainly in urban areas, throughout the New World.

**Status:** Abundant resident; most numerous around the larger cities.

**Breeding:** Pigeons nest abundantly on city buildings, under bridges, and occasionally at such "ancestral" sites as the sea cliffs at Nahant. They feed on refuse at dumps and beaches, on seeds and other vegetable material in agricultural fields, and on vast quantities of bird seed at artificial feeding stations, where they aggressively drive other birds away. Rock Doves reported migrating are probably trained carrier or racing pigeons, which are quite frequently observed at various locations in the state. *Egg dates:* throughout the year; most often from March–June and again from August–November.

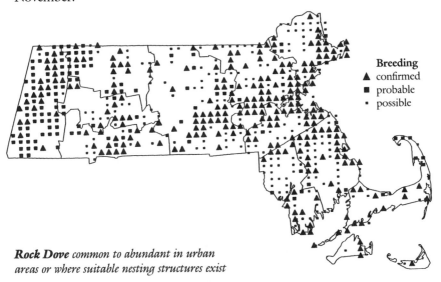

**Breeding**
▲ confirmed
■ probable
· possible

*Rock Dove common to abundant in urban areas or where suitable nesting structures exist*

**Nonbreeding:** Recent sample CBC totals in 1990 include: 3,318, Greater Boston CBC; 1,945, Northampton CBC; 1,046, Cape Ann CBC; 170, Central Berkshire CBC; 62, Nantucket CBC; 42, Cape Cod CBC.

# White-winged Dove   *Zenaida asiatica*

**Range:** Primarily Neotropical; breeds, in North America, from southern Texas south to Costa Rica; also in the Bahamas and Greater Antilles, with a recently established population in southern Florida. Some northern birds migrate south to Central America during winter.

**Status:** Vagrant: at least fourteen records.

**Occurrence:** White-winged Doves have been recorded rather frequently as vagrants in eastern North America north to Ontario, New Brunswick, and Nova Scotia. Many of these birds occur in late June and July and are probably young of the year, which typically fledge by the middle of June (Bent 1932). Massachusetts records are as follows: 1 banded and photographed, Nantucket, 18–20 June 1961 (van Duyne, Depue, Andrews); 1 photographed, Chilmark, 29 July 1965 (Epstein, Chalif); 1, Rockport, 19 November 1967 (Petersen, Forster); 1 (died), Holyoke "late June" 1969 (Bozzo); 1, Chatham, 5–8 May 1973 (Rich); 1, Truro, 25 May 1974 (Nikula, Saunders, Goodrich); 1, South Wellfleet, 4 July 1974 (Laux); 1, Nantucket, 9–12 June 1978 (Henning); 1, South Wellfleet, 2–4 July 1980 (Bailey); 1, Sandy Neck, Barnstable, 16 November 1981 (Pease); 1, Chatham, 16 November 1985 (Vass); 1, Chatham, 8–10 August 1986 (T. and M. Vose, photo in BOEM 14: 307); 1, Nantucket, 19–21 June 1987 (Vigneau): 1, Nantucket, 2–13 November 1991 (Vigneau et al). A recently established and thriving population in southern Florida might account in part for the increased incidence of this species in the Northeast, which could be supported or refuted through the subspecific identification in the hand of future individuals.

# Mourning Dove   *Zenaida macroura*

**Range:** Nearctic and northern Neotropical; breeds throughout most of the United States and southern Canada south to Panama. Portions of the northeastern population migrate south to the southeastern United States in winter.

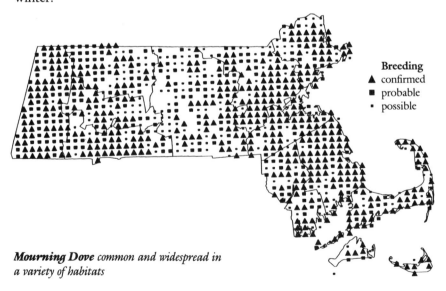

**Breeding**
▲ confirmed
■ probable
• possible

*Mourning Dove common and widespread in a variety of habitats*

**Status:** Widespread and common breeder; very common migrant. Greatly increased as a winter resident in recent years.

**Breeding:** At the turn of the century, Mourning Doves were considered rare summer residents, being restricted as breeders to the coastal plain and lower portions of the river valleys (Howe & Allen 1901). Their scarcity at that time possibly resulted from hunting pressure during the previous century because abundant suitable habitat existed at that time. Since 1900, Mourning Doves have dramatically increased, no doubt partly due to an increase in winter bird-feeding stations. Mourning Doves regularly survive the entire season, even as far inland as Berkshire County. *Egg dates:* 17 April–27 July.

**Nonbreeding:** Spring migrants begin arriving in mid-March, but they never congregate in spring in the large flocks typically seen during late summer and fall. The largest numbers of doves are seen between August and November, when the local population is augmented by migrants from more northerly localities. The birds congregate in agricultural fields throughout the state, but large flocks of migrants are also seen on outer Cape Cod and the Islands. *Fall maxima:* 500 +, Nantucket, 27 November 1980 (Veit); 500 +, Halifax, 15 November 1980 (Petersen); 450 +, Nantucket, 15 October 1980 (Veit); 400 +, Race Point, Provincetown, 1 October 1977 (Stymeist, Veit, et al). Flocks of 200 to 300 are typical in October at lower elevations in the interior of the state. The largest numbers of wintering birds are in agricultural fields in the Connecticut River valley and on the southeastern coastal plain. *Winter maxima:* 2,245, Northampton CBC, 16 December 1980; 1,370, Concord CBC, 31 December 1980; 310, Worcester CBC, 17 December 1989; 174, Central Berkshire CBC, 16 December 1989.

# Common Ground-Dove   *Columbina passerina*

**Range:** Southern Nearctic and Neotropical; breeds, in eastern North America, on the Gulf and Atlantic coasts north to South Carolina. Has occurred as a vagrant north to Illinois, New York, and Massachusetts.

**Status:** Vagrant: one record.

**Occurrence:** A Common Ground-Dove was discovered at the north end of Monomoy Island, 7 October 1973, by T. Howell and more than a hundred other observers on an AOU annual meeting field trip. Although the possibility of the bird being transported artificially to the area was immediately raised, the date and locality are perfectly appropriate for a bona fide vagrant, and the species has been documented to stray quite far from its normal range (AOU 1983).

# Common Cuckoo  *Cuculus canorus*

**Range:** Palearctic; breeds throughout much of temperate Eurasia. Winters from Africa to Indonesia. Vagrant to the New World; although apparently regular in the western Aleutians between May and July (Roberson 1980), and there is one record from Barbados, West Indies, 5 November 1958 (Bond 1980).

**Status:** Vagrant: one record.

**Occurrence:** On 3 May 1981, a Common Cuckoo was discovered by Arnold Brown in his backyard in Vineyard Haven, Martha's Vineyard. V. Laux managed to observe it the same afternoon, and, by the next day, a group from the Manomet Bird Observatory (Lloyd-Evans, Veit, Petersen, Nikula, Anderson, et al) succeeded in relocating and mist-netting the bird. Photographs and measurements taken in the hand confirmed the bird's specific identity, thus distinguishing it from the strikingly similar Oriental Cuckoo (*C. saturatus*).

# Black-billed Cuckoo  *Coccyzus erythropthalmus*

**Range:** Eastern Nearctic; breeds from central Alberta, central Ontario, New Brunswick, and Nova Scotia south to southeastern Wyoming, Nebraska, and South Carolina. Winters in northwestern South America.

**Status:** Uncommon but widespread breeder; uncommon to occasionally fairly common migrant.

**Breeding:** This species is more widespread than the Yellow-billed Cuckoo, occurring at higher elevations in the inland portions of the state and

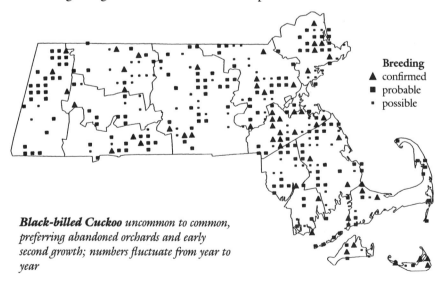

Breeding
▲ confirmed
■ probable
∙ possible

*Black-billed Cuckoo uncommon to common, preferring abandoned orchards and early second growth; numbers fluctuate from year to year*

breeding commonly in the Scrub Oak forests of Cape Cod and the Islands, where Yellow-billed Cuckoos are uncommon. The comments under the following species concerning the relationship between caterpillar abundance and cuckoo population size apply to this species as well. *Summer maxima:* 13 pairs, Newburyport area, June 1956 (deWindt); 12, Newburyport BBS, 15 June 1980; 12, Greater Boston BBS, 14 June 1980; 6, southern Berkshire County, 16–17 June 1962 (Forster). *Egg dates:* 20 May–29 August.

**Nonbreeding:** Black-billed Cuckoos arrive somewhat earlier in spring than Yellow-billeds, usually during the first week of May, and migrants have been recorded at MBO as late as the second week of June. Ordinarily, 1 to 4 birds are seen per day per locality. As with the Yellow-billed Cuckoo, a few Black-billeds have been recorded in April, usually immediately following coastal storms—e.g., 2, Harwich and Eastham, 4 April 1973 (Walsh); 1 dead, Newbury, 7 April 1973 (Goldberg); 1 dead, Orleans, 16 April 1961 (Fox); 1, Sandwich, 29 April 1973 (Pease). Fall migrants are mostly reported between late August and early October. *Fall maxima:* 37, throughout Massachusetts, October 1954 (RNEB); 32, eastern Massachusetts (including 25 from Cape Cod and the Islands), October 1979 (BOEM); 10, Monomoy, 22 September 1955 (Goodale); 8, outer Cape, 24 August 1958 (Bowen); 5, Monomoy, 23 September 1968 (Forster); 5 banded, MBO, 11 September 1974. Very late records include: 1, Duxbury, week of 20 November 1955 (Marsh); 1, Nantucket, 15 November 1969 (Petersen); 1, Ipswich River Wildlife Sanctuary, Topsfield, 9 November 1961 (Foye). Rare before early May and after September.

# Yellow-billed Cuckoo  *Coccyzus americanus*

**Range:** Nearctic; breeds from California, northern Utah, Minnesota, and southern New Brunswick south throughout the United States into Mexico and the Greater Antilles. Winters in tropical South America.

**Status:** Uncommon but widespread breeder; variably abundant from year to year and scarce on the coastal plain. Variously rare to occasionally fairly common migrant; usually more numerous in fall.

**Breeding:** Yellow-billed Cuckoos are most numerous in deciduous second-growth woodlands that contain scattered clearings. In Massachusetts, they are especially common in the lowlands between Boston and Providence and to a lesser extent in the major river valleys. Although ordinarily uncommon on Cape Cod, Yellow-billed Cuckoos were apparently relatively numerous in the Hyannis area in 1944 (fide Griscom and Snyder 1955), and single calling birds have recently been reported in Wellfleet, Truro, Chatham, and Orleans in midsummer. *Egg dates:* 20 May–30 June.

Although the relationship has not been rigorously demonstrated, it appears that Yellow-billed Cuckoos are particularly numerous in years when caterpillars, particularly those of Gypsy Moths (*Porthetria dispar*) and Eastern Tent Caterpillars (*Malacosoma americana*), are very abundant; however, Griscom (1949) pointed out that the relationship between caterpillar and cuckoo abundance is complicated, and he suggested, "The erratic fluctuation in the numbers of cuckoos is not wholly proportional to the incidence of tent caterpillars." For instance, Tent Caterpillars and Gypsy Moths have pupated by late June, before young cuckoos ordinarily fledge. Furthermore, large flights of Yellow-billed Cuckoos in the fall may involve reverse migrants from the south, thus potentially obscuring the relative abundance of locally hatched birds. It is likely, however, that adult cuckoos arriving in spring "determine" whether or not to breed based upon the local abundance of caterpillars. During years of high caterpillar abundance, they are undoubtedly able to raise more young.

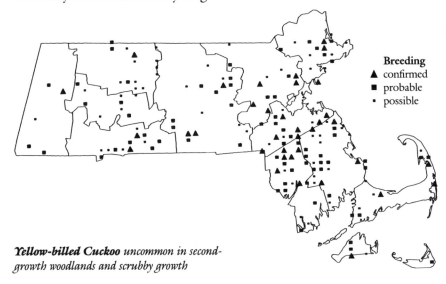

**Breeding**
▲ confirmed
■ probable
· possible

*Yellow-billed Cuckoo uncommon in second-growth woodlands and scrubby growth*

**Nonbreeding:** In spring, most Yellow-billed Cuckoos appear between mid-May and early June, with birds often arriving in the Connecticut River valley a few days earlier than in the eastern part of the state. *Spring maxima:* 6, Littleton, 31 May 1964 (Bolton); 3, Plymouth, 2 June 1973 (Donahue). Unusually early migrants are occasionally reported after coastal storms in April (cf Indigo Bunting)—e.g., 1, Chathamport, 17 April 1956 (Mayo); 1, Nantucket, 17 April 1961 (van Duyne, Depue); 1 banded, MBO, 18 April 1980; 1, Wellesley Hills, 23 April 1958 (Smith); 1, Chappaquiddick Island, 27 April 1980 (Laux).

During the fall, most migrants are found between late August and early October, and 1 to 3 birds are usually seen per day per locality. In some years, most especially 1954, exceptionally large flights of Yellow-billed Cuckoos have occurred. In each case, unusually large numbers of other species, such as Indigo Buntings and southern warblers, have been similarly observed, suggesting that reverse migrants from the south, rather than locally raised birds, were involved. In 1954, following the passage of three hurricanes through New England (Carol, 31 August; Edna, 11 September; and Hazel, 16 October), enormous numbers of Yellow-billed Cuckoos were seen in New England, the largest counts occurring from mid-September to mid-October. During October, at least 300 were reported, 245 of these from the eastern part of the state. Many were very tame and appeared to be starving; some were said to have been "flushed from roadside weed patches like quail," and many were picked up either incapacitated or dead (Griscom 1955).

Roy Latham, veteran ornithologist of Orient Point, Long Island, New York, reported 1,000 cuckoos (two-thirds of which were Black-billed) passing through Orient Point per day during the peak of the flight between 23 September and late October (Nichols 1955). At least 250 were seen in Maine, and 3 birds were recorded as far north as Newfoundland. Because the 1954 flight of cuckoos to the Northeast occurred during a fall dominated climatologically by three hurricanes, it is tempting to propose a causal relationship between hurricanes and northward displacement of cuckoos. However, as Griscom (op cit) has pointed out, most of the cuckoos were seen between 23 September and 15 October, and the hurricanes passed through on 31 August, 11 September, and 16 October.

In 1953, the Northeast experienced one of the most severe infestations of Gypsy Moths ever recorded. Therefore, it seems possible that the high counts of migrants in 1954 were the result of elevated reproductive success the previous season. No other flight remotely comparable in magnitude to that of 1954 has occurred, despite some severe infestations of Gypsy Moths in 1962, 1974, 1977, and 1979. *Fall maxima* (other than in 1954): 45 +, eastern Massachusetts (including 12 + on Nantucket [Veit, Litchfield]), October 1979 (BOEM); a total of 27, eastern Massachusetts (13 of these from Nantucket), 7–23 October 1980 (BOEM). Ordinarily, it is very unusual to see more than 5 birds per day per locality. Latest records are: 1, Martha's Vineyard, 21 November 1954 (Willey, fide Worden); 1, Sandwich, 16 November 1975 (Pease); 1, Gloucester, 13 November 1968 (Jodrey).

# Barn Owl   *Tyto alba*

**Range:** Nearly cosmopolitan; in eastern North America, breeds north to southern New Hampshire and Vermont. North and southward dispersal, probably of immature birds, in fall and winter.

**Status:** Rare to uncommon and local breeder; locally uncommon in winter roosts.

**Breeding:** Howe and Allen (1901) described the Barn Owl as an "accidental straggler from the south" and listed five specimens from the state. Subsequent to 1900, Barn Owls increased in Massachusetts; Forbush (1925) cited eleven additional records between 1900 and 1920. The species was first discovered breeding on Martha's Vineyard in 1928—where 1–6 nests were found annually from 1932–1960 (Keith 1964)—and in Springfield in 1931 (Griscom & Snyder 1955). By 1955, ten additional breeding locations were discovered: Cambridge, Lincoln, Concord, South Hadley, Belchertown, Hingham, Seekonk, North Chatham, Ipswich, and Pittsfield (Griscom & Snyder 1955). Recent breeding areas have also included Martha's Vineyard (13 nests, 1989), the Boston Harbor Islands (1974 on), and Newburyport (irregularly since 1979). Pairs were found nesting in Berkshire County in 1945 and 1952 (McNair 1978) but not since then.

Barn Owls usually nest in human-made structures at lower elevations in the state, mainly in river valleys and on the southeastern coastal plain. On Martha's Vineyard, as on Block Island, Rhode Island, they have been found nesting naturally in holes in bluffs facing the sea, as well as in owl boxes. They are undoubtedly overlooked more than other owls because of their comparatively infrequent vocalizations; however, observers familiar with their rasping calls have occasionally heard them at night hunting over open fields and salt marshes. Barn Owls apparently decreased in Massachusetts during the 1960s, possibly due to the effects of winter mortality and pesticides. Keith (1964) has shown that the Martha's Vineyard Barn Owl population crashed following the severely cold winter of 1960–61, and he states that "more than ten owls were picked up dead in barns where they had sought warmth or shelter." Apparently, unusually cold weather may be as influential as pesticides as a limiting factor for Barn Owl populations in New England. Numbers seem to be increasing again following the decline in the 1960s. *Egg dates:* 29 February–early July.

**Nonbreeding:** Like other owls, Barn Owls often congregate in winter roosts, usually in dense groves of conifers. They are comparatively intolerant of extremely cold weather, and they are routinely found dead following cold spells in midwinter. *Winter maxima:* 8 (including 5 on Martha's Vineyard), eastern Massachusetts, December 1974 (BOEM); 3, Martha's Vineyard, 17–26 February 1978 (Sargent et al); 3, Nantucket, most winters from 1973–1979 (VO). Most unusual was the observation of a Barn Owl feeding during daylight hours over the Salisbury marshes, 27 December 1980 (Forster, Hamilton, Petersen).

# Eastern Screech-Owl  *Otus asio*

**Range:** Eastern Nearctic; resident from southern Manitoba east to southwestern Maine south to Texas and Florida.

**Status:** Fairly common resident at lower elevations; uncommon on Cape Cod and virtually absent from Nantucket and from most higher elevations. Possibly the most numerous breeding raptor in Massachusetts.

**Breeding:** Screech-owls breed in open deciduous woodlands, woodlots bordering fields or marshes, farmlands, and city parks. They nest in cavities and are readily attracted to human-made bird houses. They seem to be particularly numerous in the Connecticut River valley, Sudbury River valley, and the Taunton River watershed region of southeastern Massachusetts. They are common on Martha's Vineyard, where 6 to 8 are often recorded on the Christmas Bird Count. The abundance of this species appears to decline rather abruptly in southern New Hampshire near the northern border of Essex County.

Most remarkable was the discovery in June 1944 of four fledgling screech-owls on a porch in Siasconset, Nantucket, where a screech-owl had been heard calling in the center of town in April of the same year (Folger). Vocalizing is most frequent between August and March, and nesting occurs from March to June. *Maxima*: 8 nests, Andover area, May 1959 (Holt). *Egg dates:* 7 April–5 May.

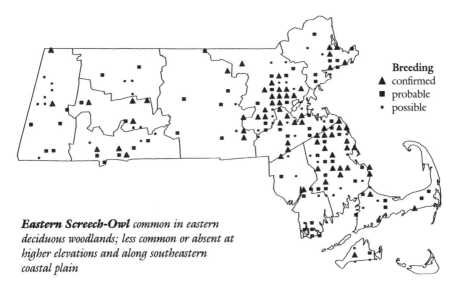

Breeding
▲ confirmed
■ probable
• possible

*Eastern Screech-Owl common in eastern deciduous woodlands; less common or absent at higher elevations and along southeastern coastal plain*

**Nonbreeding:** Many of the highest counts of Eastern Screech-Owls are made during the Christmas Bird Count period. Samples include: 65, Concord CBC, 29 December 1985; 44, Millis CBC, 19 December 1987; 34, Newburyport CBC, 23 December 1979; 29, Northampton CBC, 27 December 1970; 25, Concord CBC, 2 January 1978.

# Great Horned Owl   *Bubo virginianus*

**Range:** Nearctic and Neotropical; one of the most widespread American birds, breeding from the tree limit in Canada south to Tierra del Fuego. *B. v. virginianus* breeds from Minnesota and Nova Scotia south to the Gulf Coast and Florida.

**Status:** Uncommon to fairly common resident throughout the state, but absent on Nantucket and other smaller islands; only irregularly migratory.

**Breeding:** Great Horned Owls begin nesting in February, usually selecting abandoned nests of other large birds such as Red-tailed Hawks, Ospreys, and Great Blue Herons. They are voracious predators, mainly taking small mammals, but occasionally preying on nesting terns at Cape Cod tern colonies. *Egg dates:* 17 February–20 April.

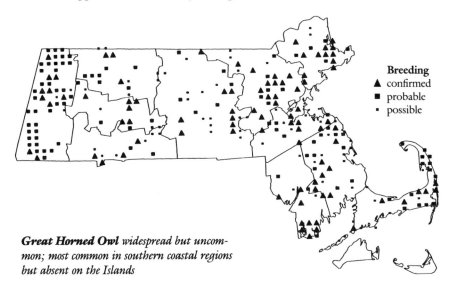

**Breeding**
▲ confirmed
■ probable
• possible

*Great Horned Owl widespread but uncommon; most common in southern coastal regions but absent on the Islands*

**Nonbreeding:** The highest counts of Great Horned Owls are usually made in December and January. This reflects increased observer effort on Christmas Bird Counts, increased vocalizing prior to the breeding season, and, possibly, an influx of birds from more northerly localities (see under "Subspecies"). Great Horned Owls are regularly reported at coastal localities, such as Plum Island and Monomoy, mainly in late summer and fall; these birds may represent migrants or locally raised immatures. *Maxima:* 62, Newburyport CBC, 28 December 1986; 22, Plymouth-Carver, 18 December 1972 (Petersen, Goodrich); 20, Sheffield CBC, 26 December 1959; 15, Newburyport CBC, 23 December 1979; 12, Cape Cod CBC, 3 January 1954; 12, Cape Cod CBC, 29 December 1974.

**Subspecies:** Houston (1981) has shown that the northerly populations of Great Horned Owls are irregularly migratory or irruptive. Occasional fluctuations in the food supply in the north seem to cause these massive irruptions into southern regions. Thus, it is not especially surprising that three extralimital subspecies have been recorded in Massachusetts. *B. v. wapacuthu* breeds in northern Canada southeast to northeastern Ontario. This very pale form has been collected twice in Massachusetts: 1, Cambridge, 4 December 1917 (BMS #12434); 1, Somerville, 26 November 1918 (BMS #12435). In the latter year, there was a major incursion of this form into the Northeast (Bull 1964). *B. v. occidentalis* breeds in western North America from southern Alberta and Minnesota south to northern California and Kansas. A specimen of this race was collected in Waltham, 30 November 1867 (BMS #12195), and a second was collected in Barre, 13 December 1892 (BMS #15676). *B. v. heterocnemis* breeds in Newfoundland, Labrador, and northern Quebec. This very dark form was collected in Marshfield, 22 December 1917 (MCZ #328075) and in South Braintree, 2 April 1892 (MCZ #244749).

## Snowy Owl   *Nyctea scandiaca*

**Range:** Holarctic; in North America, breeds on the tundra south to western Alaska, northeastern Manitoba, northern Quebec, northern Labrador, and northern Greenland. Moves south at irregular intervals in winter to the United States; has been recorded as far south as South Carolina, Louisiana, Texas, and southern California.

**Status:** Irregular winter resident; in some years fairly common in preferred habitat.

**Occurrence:** Snowy Owls are diurnal predators of open country. When they migrate as far south as Massachusetts, they are found most commonly in the salt marshes around Plum Island and Salisbury and on the islands and marshes of Boston Harbor. Smaller numbers occur on Cape Cod and the Islands and in farmlands of the interior.

   Major incursions have occurred in the following winters: 1876–77, 1882–83, 1889–90, 1901–02, 1905–06, 1922–23, 1926–27, 1941–42, 1945–46, 1949–50, 1960–61, 1964–65, 1967–68, 1971–72, 1980–81, and 1986–87, the largest of which are enumerated below. *1876–77:* "Some of the New England taxidermists had from 50–150 birds each." (Forbush 1925). *1901–02:* "at least 1,000 killed in Ontario," and "many killed in New England" (Forbush, op cit). *1926–27:* 2,363 recorded within the United States, 1,000 in New England and 294 in Massachusetts alone. R. W. Wood, the keeper at No Man's Land, "shot 38 and captured 9 alive during the first week that the owls appeared" (Gross 1927). *1949–50:* About 65 reported in RNEB for December, with maxima of 20 at Plum Island, 10 in the Rowley-Ipswich area, 5 in the Connecticut River valley, and 3 on Martha's Vineyard. *1960–61:* At least 50 birds reported during November, 27 of these in the Plum Island–Salisbury area (fide Emery). As in other flights, daily totals gradually diminished during the course of the winter. *1964–65:* 69 reported during November, including 23 in the Plum Island–Salisbury area, 3 on Cape Cod, 3 in the Connecticut River valley, and 2 in Berkshire County (fide Emery). *1971–72:* 23 reported in December, 3 of these in the Connecticut River valley (fide Emery). *1980–81:* 16 reported in December (BOEM). *1986–87:* Very large invasion; i.e., from late November through early April, N. Smith banded 43 birds at Logan Airport, Boston. Most banded during the first half of the winter were immatures, and a number during the last half were adults (see Nikula, AB 1987).

Although the flights in recent years have been rather unimpressive compared to the great flight of 1926–27, it is unlikely that the Snowy Owl population has been adversely affected in any permanent way. Because Snowy Owls ordinarily lay five to seven or eight eggs (Bent 1938) and are able to successfully raise that many young in years of high lemming or hare abundance, they should clearly be able to recover from excessive mortality, such as that sustained during several of the early southward irruptions. Therefore, another major irruption at some point in the future would not be unlikely (cf Great Gray Owl). When present in Massachusetts, Snowy Owls feed primarily upon rats, Meadow Voles, and other small mammals and have regularly been seen taking a wide variety of bird species (Smith, pers. comm.). *Extreme dates:* 1, Shirley Center, 7 October 1961 (fide RPE); 1, Logan Airport, Boston, 7 July 1990 (Smith); 1, Harvard Field, Cambridge, 10 June 1968 (Petersen, Forster); 1, Plum Island, 22 May 1974 (Forster, Emery). Rare before early November and after March.

# Northern Hawk Owl  *Surnia ulula*

**Range:** Holarctic; breeds, in North America, from central Alaska east to northern Quebec and Newfoundland south to central Alberta, southern Ontario, and southern Quebec. Migrates in winter irregularly south to New England.

**Status:** Vagrant. Five documented records since 1900; formerly of more frequent occurrence.

**Occurrence:** Griscom and Snyder (1955) knew of twenty-four specimens of Northern Hawk Owls collected in Massachusetts, all before 1890, the major-

*Although **Snowy Owl** numbers south of arctic Canada are highly variable from year to year, Boston's Logan International Airport hosts as many owls annually as any other area in the Northeast.* ▷

ity during the pronounced flight year of 1867–68, and also during the five-year period 1884–1888. The documented records since 1900 are as follows: 1 specimen, Ipswich, 28 November 1927 (PMS #7088); 1 specimen, Wakefield, 19 November 1927 (BMS #17411); 1 dead, Dennis, February 1941 (Finley, fide Hill 1965); 1, Concord, 28 November 1958 to 21 January 1959 (when found dead)(Holden and hundreds of observers); 1 banded and photographed, Hinsdale, 17 January to 3 March 1965 (Fitzes et al). Additional sight records that are presumed to be correct include: 1, Greenfield, 16–22 February 1942 (Bagg); 1, West Peabody, 7–23 February 1946 (RNEB); 1, Chatham, 9 March 1958 (Mosher); 1, Chatham, 13 February 1962 (Drake); 1, South Wellfleet, 11 February 1970 (Bailey). Several other published sight records lack substantiation. Because Northern Hawk Owls continue to occur regularly in northern New England, the species should be expected to appear again in Massachusetts at any time.

## Burrowing Owl   *Athene cunicularia*

**Range:** Nearctic and Neotropical; breeds on the Great Plains from southern British Columbia and southern Manitoba south to Baja California, central Texas, and Louisiana; winters south to Panama. Also resident in peninsular Florida and the Bahamas.

**Status:** Vagrant: seven records.

**Occurrence:** The single Massachusetts specimen of a Burrowing Owl is of the migratory western subspecies, *A. c. hypugaea*. It was taken at Newburyport, 17 May 1875 (Deane BMS #12186). Additional records include: 1 (which followed a slight incursion to the Northeast the previous fall), Amesbury, 13 February 1964 (Rich); 1, Plymouth Beach, 13 May 1980 (Harrington); 1, Monomoy, 6 June 1980 (Bailey, Goodrich); 1, Katama, Martha's Vineyard, 12 July–1 October 1980 (Laux et al); 1, Northampton, 4 May 1982 (Gagnon et al); 1, Katama, Martha's Vineyard, 17 July–30 September 1986 (Vickery, VO). Although the largely nonmigratory subspecies *A. c. floridana* has been recently recorded on Long Island, New York (AB 31: 314), in North Carolina (Sykes 1974), and in Connecticut (AB 34: 254), most vagrant Burrowing Owls in the Northeast have either proven to be *A. c. hypugaea*, or they have remained subspecifically unidentified.

## Barred Owl   *Strix varia*

**Range:** Nearctic; resident from eastern Washington and southern British Columbia, east through the wooded portions of southern Canada to the Gaspé Peninsula and Nova Scotia, and throughout the United States east of the Great Plains.

**Status:** Locally uncommon to fairly common resident.

**Breeding:** Barred Owls breed in moist woodlands, similar to habitats occupied by the Red-shouldered Hawk. In Massachusetts, they are particularly numerous in the central and western parts of the state. Other established localities include swampy woodlands in interior southeastern Massachusetts and the Boxford State Forest in Essex County. They are absent from Cape Cod, the Islands, and the sandier portions of the southeastern coastal plain. *Egg dates:* late February–10 May, with most in late March.

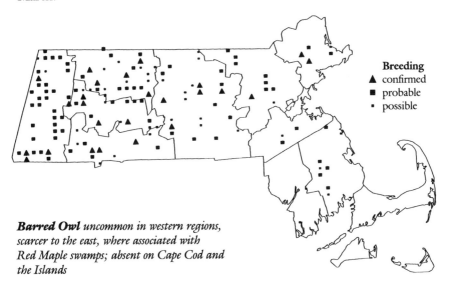

Breeding
▲ confirmed
■ probable
• possible

*Barred Owl uncommon in western regions, scarcer to the east, where associated with Red Maple swamps; absent on Cape Cod and the Islands*

**Nonbreeding:** As with other owls, the largest numbers of Barred Owls are reported between November and May, probably due to an influx of birds from northern areas; increased vocalizations prior to the breeding season in April and May; and increased "owling" activity by birders at the time of the Christmas Bird Counts. Following periods of heavy snow in the Northeast, Barred Owls are frequently seen in urban parks in downtown Boston or in such unlikely localities as a rock crevice on the Salisbury jetty, 27 December 1975 (VO) and on a ledge on the fifth floor of an office building in downtown Boston, 31 October 1979 (Holt). During such stressful conditions, they are occasionally seen feeding over fields or marshes during daylight hours, particularly during overcast weather. *Maxima:* "invasion" into backyards and city parks (with 15 reported in the Connecticut River valley, December 1961 [fide Emery]); 10, Northampton CBC, 1 January 1966; 7, Prescott Peninsula, Quabbin Reservoir, 19 November 1972 (Gagnon, D'Entremont); 2–3 pairs, Lakeville, 26 May 1980 (Petersen); 4–5, Boxford State Forest, most springs (April–May) since at least 1970 (VO); 4, Greater

Boston CBC, 18 December 1977; 2–3, MIT Campus, Cambridge, 2–28 January 1977 (VO). Coastal plain records: 1, Morris Island, Chatham, 2 January 1956 (Cape Cod CBC); 2, West Dennis, 21–28 February 1965 (Dunn, Sprong, Aikens); 1, Falmouth, 9 October 1984 (Sorrie). Many reports of Barred Owls from Cape Cod probably pertain to misidentified immature Great Horned Owls.

## Great Gray Owl  *Strix nebulosa*

**Range:** Holarctic; breeds in northwestern Canada and Alaska southeast to northern Ontario; also in the Sierra Nevada of California. During irregular southward emigrations in winter, has occurred south to southern New England, Long Island, New York, and New Jersey.

**Status:** Very rare and irregular winter visitor.

**Occurrence:** During the 19th century, when most northern raptors were apparently more numerous, some twenty-five specimens of Great Gray Owls were collected in Massachusetts. There were two major flights recorded during that period, one during the winter of 1842–43, when seven Great Gray Owls were collected in Massachusetts, and one during the winter of 1890–91, when 2 were taken. Single specimens were also obtained in 1831, 1835, 1839, 1847, 1859, 1864, 1866, 1872, 1882, and 1896.

Between 1900 and 1978, no flights of Great Gray Owls reached Massachusetts, although single specimens were obtained in the Sudbury River valley in 1906 and 1910 (R. and N. Howe), and there are also two published sight records: 1, Lincoln, 27 March 1942 (Maynard); 1, West Becket, 9 January 1952 (Morse). From then until 1973, Great Gray Owls were unrecorded in the state, despite the occurrence of several individuals in northern New England and northern New York.

On 22 January 1973, a Great Gray Owl was discovered in Gill (Vose, VO), on the eastern floodplain of the Connecticut River. It remained in that area until late March, during which time it was observed by hundreds of birders and was color photographed by many people. Another Great Gray Owl was seen briefly in Andover, 5–6 January 1977 (Kellogg, Miliotis, Forster, Veit), and a number were found during the winter of 1978–79, when the first incursion of the 20th century reached Massachusetts. Between 28 January and 28 March, 17 different Great Gray Owls were found in the state: Topsfield, Amesbury, Amherst, Hatfield (2), Stockbridge, Lexington (dead), Marlboro, Thorndike, Magnolia, Bernardston, West Boxford, Brookline, Concord, Carlisle, Wayland, West Roxbury, Sutton, and Canton. Vickery and Yunick (1979) have shown that 79 additional Great Gray Owls were reported elsewhere in New England during that winter and have pointed out that this flight was not apparent anywhere west of Michigan, suggesting that the birds might have originated in northern Quebec or Ontario—areas where the species has never been proven to breed. The most recent Massachusetts records are: 1, Oakham, 29 January–1 March 1980 (Blodget et al); 1, Hadley, 10 February–25 March 1984 (Clark, VO).

When Great Gray Owls appear in Massachusetts, they tend to favor large, moist open fields surrounded by patches of woodland sufficiently vegetated to provide cover for roosting. Such situations are typical of river valleys, especially the agricultural fields in the Connecticut River valley. The owls frequently hunt during daylight hours, particularly if the sky is overcast, and feed primarily on Meadow Voles (*Microtus pennsylvanicus*). Some owls were observed to take 8 to 9 voles during the course of a morning during the 1979 flight year. The hunting behavior of the Massachusetts birds is very similar to that described by Nero (1980) in that the owls course low over the fields, pounce on the snow when a prey item is sighted, and then continue the pursuit on foot through the snow.

# Long-eared Owl   *Asio otus*

**Range:** Holarctic: breeds, in North America, from eastern British Columbia, central Ontario, New Brunswick, and Nova Scotia south to Oklahoma, Arkansas, Pennsylvania and Virginia. Winters from southern Canada south to the Gulf Coast and casually to Florida.

**Status:** Rare breeder. Rare, but probably overlooked, migrant; variously uncommon to occasionally fairly common in winter roosts.

**Breeding:** It is exceedingly difficult to find conclusive evidence of Long-eared Owls breeding in Massachusetts. Among the localities where nests or recently fledged young have been positively found since 1955 are Cohasset, Weston, Newbury, Cambridge, Barnstable, Bridgewater, Westwood, Nantucket, and Chatham. Calling birds have been reported from a number of localities in the state during midsummer, but observers are cautioned that Long-eared Owls produce a number of vocalizations easily confused with those of other owl species. On Nantucket, for example, where Northern Saw-whet and Long-eared owls both breed, saw-whet owls often produce an extraordinary variety of catlike and doglike calls, very similar to the vocalizations usually ascribed to the Long-eared Owl. *Egg dates:* 15 March–14 May.

**Nonbreeding:** Long-eared Owls are rarely detected during migration due to their retiring nature, but there are concentrations of records in April and from October to early December in areas where the species is not known to breed. *Maxima:* 6, Ipswich, 11 December 1955 (Norton); 4, Martha's Vineyard, 28 October 1979 (Laux, Heil); 4, Nantucket, 16 November 1980 (Barrera, Veit, et al); 3, Ipswich, 17 November 1956 (Earle). Long-eared

Owls seem to migrate more regularly than most of the larger owls, and influxes to Massachusetts of varying magnitude are recorded almost every winter. In this season, the birds often roost communally in dense groves of evergreens adjacent to open fields, over which they hunt at night. *Winter maxima:* 22, East Lexington, 10 January 1981 (Andrews 1982); 10, Amherst, 28 January–16 February 1959 (Westcott); 9, Beverly, 2 March 1960 (Gedney); 7, Nantucket, 17–23 March 1980 (Barrera, Veit, et al); 6, Oak Bluffs, Martha's Vineyard, 31 December 1966 (CBC).

# Short-eared Owl   *Asio flammeus*

**Range:** Cosmopolitan, except absent from Australia; breeds, in North America, from Alaska east to northern Quebec and Newfoundland south to California, southern Illinois, and New Jersey. Northern breeders migrate south in winter to the Gulf Coast and Florida; also to Mexico.

**Status:** Very uncommon breeder on the islands off Cape Cod; fairly common late fall migrant and winter resident.

**Breeding:** Although one or more pairs of Short-eared Owls bred at Longmeadow until 1935, and an egg was reportedly collected in Danvers in 1878 (Townsend 1905), the species is now restricted as a breeder to islands off Cape Cod. The population fluctuates from year to year, but a 1985 estimate indicated that a total of 20 to 25 pairs bred on Monomoy, Nantucket, Tuckernuck, Muskeget, Martha's Vineyard, and Pochet Marsh, Orleans (Holt 1986). *Egg dates:* late May–mid-June.

**Nonbreeding:** Short-eared Owls vary considerably in abundance from year to year, presumably depending upon the availability of their preferred prey items in the north. In Massachusetts, they are normally found between late September and early April, with the highest numbers in December. They are most common at Plum Island, in marshes around Boston Harbor, in open farmlands in the Middleboro area, and on Cape Cod and the Islands. A few also occur in the Connecticut River valley. Major flights occurred in the winters of 1961–62, 1978–79, and 1981–82. *Maxima:* 43, throughout Massachusetts, December 1961 (fide Emery); 30, eastern Massachusetts, December 1978 (BOEM); 8, Salisbury, February 1979 (VO). Of eleven records for Berkshire County, only three are from midwinter: 1, Pittsfield, 8 January 1964 (Sanborn); 1, Pittsfield, 16 January 1976 (Burg); 1, Richmond, 14 January 1979 (Nixon, Blair).

In late spring and early fall, it is difficult to distinguish migrants from birds nesting locally, but the following records are from localities where Short-eared Owls are not known to breed: 1, Plum Island, 21 August 1954 (Emery); 1, Bridgewater, 11 May 1960 (Briggs, Pratt).

# Boreal Owl   *Aegolius funereus*

**Range:** Holarctic; breeds, in North America, in Alaska and boreal Canada from the tree limit south to central Alberta, northern Minnesota, western Ontario, and once, after a major flight to the Northeast, at Grand Manan Island, New Brunswick. During irregular winter irruptions has occurred south on the East Coast to southern New England, New Jersey, and Pennsylvania.

**Status:** Very rare and irregular winter visitor.

**Occurrence:** Like other northern owls, Boreal Owls were recorded more frequently during the 19th century than they are today. Eighteen specimens were taken between 1859 and 1905, with slight flights apparent in 1863, 1884–85, 1888–89, and 1902–03. The largest incursion on record occurred during the winter of 1922–23, when 26 specimens were received by a single taxidermist in Jaffrey, New Hampshire; 30 were brought to another taxidermist in Bangor, Maine (Townsend, in Bent 1938); and 30 were apparently taken in Massachusetts (Griscom & Snyder 1955). Of the Massachusetts records, individuals were reported south and east to Cohasset, Sandwich, and Seekonk, and Herbert Maynard saw 5 or 6 and shot 2 in the Sudbury River valley. Interestingly, during the following summer, a nest was found at Grand Manan Island, New Brunswick, and a single bird was seen on General Stark Mountain, Vermont (Townsend, op cit). Since that time there was but one additional sight record of a Boreal Owl in Massachusetts—i.e., 1, Belmont, 15 February 1942 (Elkins)—until 1978.

The most recent records of this inconspicuous northern owl in Massachusetts are: 1 photographed while it was roosting in a small pine grove, Salisbury State Reservation, 31 December 1978 (Atwood); 1 photographed in color, Back Bay, Boston, 2–8 November 1983 (Thayer, photographs at MAS); 1 picked up injured (and later taken to the New Bedford Zoo, where it was color photographed by Petersen), Chatham, 16 January 1984 (fide Turner, Anderson). A major "flight" occurred in 1991–1992, with six Massachusetts records as follows: 1, Long Island, Boston; 30–31 October (Donovan, Petersen); 1 captured alive, Plymouth, 5 November (fide Litchfield); 1, South Boston, 6 November (Donovan); 1 captured and released, Dedham, 8 November (fide Pokras); 1 captured and released, Brookline, 19 November (Nordquist, Petersen, Perkins); 1 banded, Canton, 27 December (Smith).

# Northern Saw-whet Owl   *Aegolius acadicus*

**Range:** Nearctic; breeds from Alaska, central Saskatchewan, southern Manitoba, and Nova Scotia south to southern California, Veracruz, Mexico, West Virginia, and Maryland. On the Atlantic Coast, Cape Cod is the southern boundary of the regular breeding range of the Northern Saw-whet Owl. Winters from the breeding range south to the Gulf Coast. Northern breeders are migratory.

**Status:** Uncommon resident and migrant; most numerous in late fall.

**Breeding:** In Massachusetts, saw-whet owls breed in Pitch Pine barrens; White Pine plantations; cedar swamps on Cape Cod, Nantucket, and Martha's Vineyard; and dense stands of conifers in mature forests on the mainland. They are uncommon and local in their distribution. Many of the unusually high counts of calling birds in Massachusetts undoubtedly include migrants from farther north. This was particularly true during the major flight year of 1958–1959. At least four pairs regularly breed on Nantucket, where one or two pairs have occasionally nested in artificial nest boxes placed in a White Pine plantation. Saw-whet owls have also been heard calling in a Red Maple swamp on Nantucket, suggesting that they may breed in that habitat as well. On the mainland, definite nesting localities since 1955 have included Middleboro, Amherst, North Andover, Wellesley, Mt. Greylock, Adams, Springfield, Lenox, Rutland, Middleton, West Newbury, Scituate, Topsfield, and Ipswich. *Maxima:* 10 calling, Rutland, March–April 1981 (Kleber); 10 (including adults and young), West Newbury, 25 June 1974 (Poore); up to 4 heard calling, Nickerson State Park, Brewster, in several different years. *Egg dates:* 4 April–31 May.

**Nonbreeding:** Spring migrant saw-whet owls are rarely detected, but the following records undoubtedly refer to migrants: 1, Prudential Building, Boston, 23 March 1976 (Palmer); 1 dropped into the water and eaten by Herring Gulls, 10 miles northeast of the Nantucket Lightship, 10 April 1958 (Crompton); 3, Brookline-Boston, 1–25 April 1960 (RNEB). They are much more conspicuous during fall migration, probably due to the increased incidence of immature birds that seem to become disoriented and reach coastal areas. Banding data indicates that the peak migration period is in the last week of October. *Maxima* (major flight in 1958–59): 39 found during an intensive owl survey, North Andover, Andover, and Boxford, 8–30 November 1958 (Holt); 8, West Boxford, 12 January 1959 (Holt). On 20 and 21 October 1965, 3 saw-whet owls landed on board a ship at Jeffrey's Ledge, and "several others were seen" (Couture, fide Robbins). Other counts are: 5, Littleton, 27 October 1969 (Baird); 5 banded at night, MBO, 22–26 October 1977; 5 calling, Nantucket, 2–4 November 1979 (Veit); 5 banded at night, MBO, 10–16 October 1980.

As is the case with other owls, numbers of Northern Saw-whets vary considerably from year to year, presumably in response to the variation in availability of food in the north. *Winter maxima:* 42, Quabbin CBC, 28 December 1991; 7 reported (3 dead), throughout Massachusetts, 2–30 January 1967 (fide Emery); 7 reported, urban sections of eastern Massachusetts, January 1977 (BOEM).

# Common Nighthawk  *Chordeiles minor*

**Range:** Nearctic and Neotropical; breeds virtually throughout North America north to the tree limit; winters in South America, south to central Argentina.

**Status:** Uncommon and local breeder; common spring and occasionally abundant fall migrant.

**Breeding:** Common Nighthawks were originally ground nesters in Massachusetts. During the 20th century, however, they gradually adapted to nesting on gravel rooftops (Townsend 1905), which is presently where most Massachusetts nesting attempts occur, mainly in the Boston area and in the southern Connecticut River valley. Nonetheless, in 1978, 3 nests were found on the ground in Pitch Pines at the Myles Standish State Forest in Plymouth (Hiam & Sutherland 1979), and at least 4 pairs were found breeding there in 1982 (Lloyd-Evans). Representative breeding counts: 4 pairs, Cambridge, June 1973 (Stymeist); 6 pairs, Cambridge-Waltham, June 1978 (Stymeist); 8–9 pairs, Cambridge-Brookline, June 1981 (Stymeist). Common Nighthawks are apparently absent as breeders from Cape Cod and the Islands, but there are recent summer records from those areas: e.g., 1, Nantucket, 13 July 1980 (Litchfield); 2, Eastham, 21 July 1980 (Forster); 1, Mashpee, 15 June 1982 (Petersen). *Egg dates:* 5–15 July.

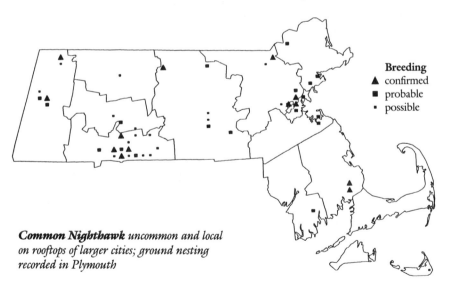

**Breeding**
▲ confirmed
■ probable
• possible

*Common Nighthawk uncommon and local on rooftops of larger cities; ground nesting recorded in Plymouth*

**Nonbreeding:** The majority of northward-moving nighthawks pass through during May and early June—e.g., 356, Squantum, 17 May 1974 (Brown); 61, Littleton, 1 June 1967 (Baird); 52, Springfield, 1 June 1967 (Bates); 48, Wellesley, 1 June 1967 (Forster); 35 in one-half hour, Littleton,

30 May 1973 (Baird). This species is occasionally detected much earlier in spring. Forbush (1927) describes in detail five reports of Common Nighthawks from New England and Nova Scotia between 14 and 29 March 1925, following a coastal storm, and Bagg and Eliot (1937) describe additional records that occurred under similar circumstances: e.g., 1, Amherst, 18 March 1871 (Stearns); 1, Connecticut River valley, 26 March 1886 (Kuwada). There were also three reports of single birds from Massachusetts, Connecticut, and New Jersey in March 1920 (Bagg & Eliot 1937). Griscom and Snyder (1955) unaccountably dismissed these records, despite the lengthy discussions by both Forbush and Bagg and Eliot. Since that time, only two March occurrences have been noted: 1, West Newbury, 14 March 1966 (Haack); 1, Brookline, 27 March 1966 (Wade). April occurrences are only slightly more frequent.

The fall migration of the Common Nighthawk through Massachusetts is one of the state's more spectacular ornithological phenomena. During the last week of August and the first week of September, hundreds, and occasionally thousands, of nighthawks are seen flying south at dusk, singly and in loose flocks. The largest numbers are always seen in the Connecticut River valley, with the counts decreasing steadily eastward. They are rare on Cape Cod and the Islands. Reverse migration is a common occurrence with nighthawks, and occasionally large numbers have been counted flying north in fall. As with passerines, this may well reflect the tendency of migrants to fly downwind (Able 1973). *Fall maxima:* 3,674, Northampton, 22 August 1991 (Gagnon); 2,756, Southwick, 28 August 1983 (Kellogg); 2,182, Florence, 26–31 August 1969 (Gagnon); 2,047, Southwick, 31 August 1982 (Kellogg); 1,424, Florence, 29 August 1971 (Gagnon); 1,365, Willimansett, 29 August 1971 (Yenlin); 1,180, Wellesley, 30 August 1978 (Cassie); 1,094 flying north, Florence, 28 August 1970 (Gagnon). Most daily totals east of the Connecticut River valley do not exceed 300 birds, but Stymeist and Heywood counted a total of 2,006 flying over Brookline between 20 August and 7 September 1983.

Common Nighthawks occasionally appear unusually late in fall. Most of these late records are presumably of reverse migrants rather than lingerers. *Extreme dates:* 1, Eastham, 25 October 1977 (Olmstead); 6, Eastham, 22 October 1979 (Nikula); 1, Chatham, 22 October 1978 (Petersen, Forster); 7, MBO, 7 October 1976; 10, Longmeadow, 3 October 1969 (McCrillis). Curiously, Chimney Swifts have been reported late in the fall under similar conditions—i.e., on the same dates—as these late Common Nighthawks.

# Chuck-will's-widow   *Caprimulgus carolinensis*

**Range:** Southeastern Nearctic; breeds, from eastern Kansas, Ontario (Point Pelee), and Long Island, New York, south to the Gulf Coast and Florida;

winters in the West Indies and northern South America north to Louisiana and Florida.

**Status:** Rare but regular visitor, primarily in spring.

**Occurrence:** Chuck-will's-widows have been expanding their breeding range steadily northward for the last 30 years and have recently nested on Long Island, New York (1975). However, despite the presence of summering birds on Martha's Vineyard and Nantucket intermittently since 1971, breeding has not yet been confirmed. Prior to 1955, there were only four records from Massachusetts: 1 killed by a cat, Revere, October 1884 (BMS #12205); 1 collected, East Boston, 13 October 1915 (Brooks, BMS #12189); 1, Nahant, 26 May 1945 (Griscom et al); 1, Mt. Auburn Cemetery, Cambridge, 11–13 May 1952 (Elkins, Cottrell, VO).

Since 1956, there have been numerous records of migrant birds from coastal areas (plus, 1, North Amherst, 10 May 1971 [fide Willmann]) between 9 May and 10 June, and single calling birds were recorded on Nantucket between 1971 and 1975 and on Chappaquiddick almost annually since 1971, with three there between 1980 and 1983. The Nantucket bird inhabited Scrub Oaks adjacent to a field from early June until late August, and those on Chappaquiddick were found in mixed Scrub Oak and Pitch Pine forests. Individuals have also been banded at MBO, 26 May 1971, 17 May 1974, and 18 May 1982, and one was heard calling for three nights in the Middlesex Fells Reservation, Medford, 19–21 June 1979 (Zendeh, Roberts). Most remarkable was a female Chuck-will's-widow that came aboard a whale-watching boat approximately 20 miles east of Boston, 16 May 1981 (Bird & Payne 1981). The bird was taken to MBO, where it was later banded and released.

Fall records of Chuck-will's-widows are rare, undoubtedly due to their silence in that season and the absence of breeders north of Massachusetts. Fall records include: 1 calling, Fowl Meadow, Canton, 6 October 1972 (Brown); 1 found dead in a driveway, Dartmouth, 15 November 1975 (Fernandez).

# Whip-poor-will *Caprimulgus vociferus*

**Range:** Eastern Nearctic; breeds from central Saskatchewan, central Ontario, and Nova Scotia south to southeastern South Dakota, northern Georgia, and east-central North Carolina; also in the Southwest. Winters along the Gulf Coast and in Central America south to El Salvador and Honduras.

**Status:** Locally fairly common breeder, but decreasing. Uncommon and very inconspicuous migrant.

**Breeding:** The Whip-poor-will breeds in deciduous and mixed forests adjacent to large clearings. It has markedly decreased as a nesting species in many areas of Massachusetts, especially during the last 30 years and is now absent from many areas where it previously bred (cf Forbush 1929). In Berkshire County, Whip-poor-wills were fairly common breeders until about 1960, but they have since disappeared. Currently, they breed commonly on outer Cape Cod, Nantucket, and Martha's Vineyard, and they are especially common in the Plymouth pine barrens—e.g., 55 calling, Myles Standish State Forest, Plymouth, 22 June 1989 (D'Entremont). They have apparently held their own in relatively undeveloped areas—e.g., 22 calling, West Newbury, 15 June 1980 (Stymeist, Veit)—and have declined most dramatically in heavily developed and urbanized areas, which suggests that urbanization, including the attendant increase in predators such as cats and Raccoons, may be especially influential in contributing to the decline of this species. Brewster (1906) implied that Whip-poor-wills were entirely extirpated from the area currently bounded by Route 128 as early as 1900—a situation that is still largely the case.

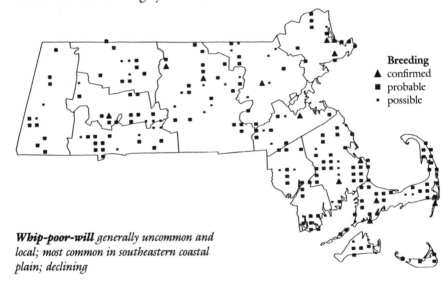

**Breeding**
▲ confirmed
■ probable
· possible

***Whip-poor-will*** *generally uncommon and local; most common in southeastern coastal plain; declining*

**Nonbreeding:** Although Whip-poor-wills are rarely observed during migration, they do occasionally turn up at such places as Mt. Auburn Cemetery, Cambridge, Nahant Thicket, and banding stations such as MBO. Spring birds typically arrive between the third week of April and late May, and fall migrants are most often noted from August to late September. ***Spring maxima:*** 40 calling, Dunstable, 30 May 1968 (Elkins); 35 calling, Rowley–West Newbury, 21 May 1977 (Stymeist, Veit); 16, Martha's Vineyard, 23–26 May 1980 (BBC, Drummond). ***Fall maxima:*** 6 banded, MBO, 15–22 August 1970; 3–4, Nantucket, 4 September 1975 (Perkins). ***Extreme dates:*** 1, Newbury, 12 April 1957 (deWindt); 1, Martha's Vineyard, 13 April 1975 (Griswold); 1, West Newbury, 15 April 1965 (deWindt); 1, Muskeget Island, 1

June 1981 (Heil); 1, Granby, 28 October 1935 (Schurr, fide Bagg & Eliot 1937); 1, Rockport, 27 October 1962 (Johnson, Jodrey); 1, Pembroke, 26 October 1974 (Clancy).

## Chimney Swift   *Chaetura pelagica*

**Range:** Eastern Nearctic; breeds throughout eastern North America from southern Manitoba, New Brunswick, and Newfoundland south to the Gulf Coast and south central Florida. Winters in the upper portion of the Amazon drainage in Peru, Chile, and Brazil.

**Status:** Common breeder; common spring and occasionally abundant fall migrant; most numerous inland.

**Breeding:** Chimney Swifts have nested almost exclusively in chimneys throughout the historical period. There is no evidence that any but a small fraction of Massachusetts swifts nest in hollow trees today. There has been no apparent change in abundance of Chimney Swifts in Massachusetts, although massive die-offs apparently occurred following periods of exceptionally heavy rain in June 1903 (Forbush 1927), June 1959, and June 1982. Such disasters appear to have no permanent effect upon the population as a whole. *Egg dates:* 5 June–July.

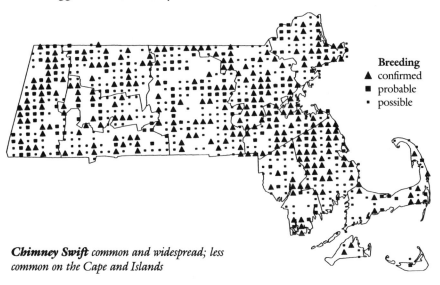

Breeding
▲ confirmed
■ probable
• possible

*Chimney Swift common and widespread; less common on the Cape and Islands*

**Nonbreeding:** The migration pattern of Chimney Swifts is strikingly similar to that of the Common Nighthawk, both in terms of average arrival and departure dates and in the occurrence of unseasonal reverse migrants. Typically, spring migrants appear by the last week in April, and the fall migration is normally over by late September. *Spring maxima:* 5,000 forced down from a high diurnal migration for 25 minutes during a heavy rain, Springfield, 18 May 1952 (Griscom); 1,000, Northampton, 21–22 May 1960 (BNWM); 200, Mt. Auburn Cemetery, Cambridge, 18 May 1967 (Stymeist); 200, West Newbury, 18 May 1968 (Emery). *Fall maxima:* 1,420, Northampton, 1 September 1955 (Eliot); 1,160, Northampton, 27 August 1955 (Eliot); 727, Framingham, 16 September 1975 (Taylor). These fall totals are of birds counted flying into chimney roosts (see Taylor 1975).

*Extreme dates:* 2, Southboro, 5 April 1945 (Marshall); 2, Longmeadow, 5 April 1962 (McCrillis); 1, Plum Island, 11 November 1977 (Soucy); 1, East Brewster, 7 November 1968 (Lund); 1, Bridgewater, 5–6 November 1983 (Petersen). In the fall, there are about twenty records later than the first week of October, with a major flight occurring in 1977, when 11 were reported during the period 18–22 October, including: 3, Nantucket, 20 October (Andrews); 4, WBWS, 21 October (Goodrich, Nikula).

# Ruby-throated Hummingbird   *Archilochus colubris*

**Range:** Eastern Nearctic; breeds from central Alberta, southern Manitoba, and Nova Scotia south to Texas and Florida. Winters from Florida and the Gulf Coast south, through Mexico, to Costa Rica.

**Status:** Uncommon but widespread breeder; uncommon to occasionally common migrant.

**Breeding:** Ruby-throated Hummingbirds are sparsely distributed as breeders in the state, although congregations of up to 15 to 20 birds are occasionally seen during the summer around fruit orchards or cultivated flower gardens. They have decreased as breeders in the eastern part of the state over the past 30 years. *Egg dates:* 24 May–22 July.

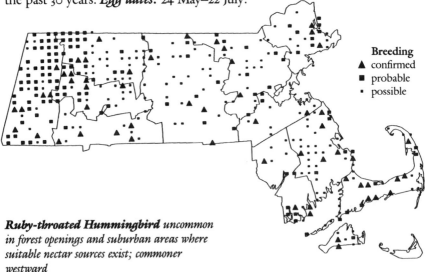

**Breeding**
▲ confirmed
■ probable
· possible

*Ruby-throated Hummingbird uncommon in forest openings and suburban areas where suitable nectar sources exist; commoner westward*

**Nonbreeding:** In spring most hummingbirds move through Massachusetts in May, and on good flight days they may be seen flying rapidly northward along the outer coast (less commonly on outer Cape Cod and the Islands), and they are regularly seen from boats at sea during both spring and fall migration. *Spring maxima:* 87 throughout Massachusetts, 20 May 1967 (RNEB); 60 banded, 6–31 May 1974 (MBO); 20, Plum Island, 24 May 1980 (BOEM). There are at least sixteen records of hummingbirds earlier than 20 April (which could possibly involve species other than the Ruby-throated). The earliest are: 1, Sudbury, 18 March 1973 (fide Baird); 1, Chatham, 26 March 1969 (Fuller, fide Baird). During the fall, most pass through the state between late August and late September, although there are eleven November records. *Fall maxima:* 24, Ludlow, 12 September 1965 (Soja); 17, West Newbury, 8 September 1956 (deWindt); 14, MNWS, 22 September 1976 (Anderson). Included is a list of the latest hummingbird records from Massachusetts, but it should be emphasized that their specific identity remains uncertain, particularly in light of the documented occurrence of other species in the state. *Extreme dates:* 1, Swampscott, 20 November 1950 (Gardner); 1, Nantucket, 17 November 1978 (fide Andrews); 1, Chatham, 14 November 1958 (Norman); 1, Beverly, 13 November 1977 (Gardner).

# Black-chinned Hummingbird  *Archilochus alexandri*

**Range:** Western Nearctic; breeds from British Columbia and Montana south to Baja California and Texas. Winters from southern California south to Mexico.

**Status:** Vagrant: one record.

**Occurrence:** A hummingbird that appeared in a greenhouse in Cohasset, 25 November 1979, was eventually collected 10 December and, on the basis of bill length and the shape of the remiges and rectrices, was determined to be *A. alexandri* (Petersen, Sorrie, MCZ #330896). A. R. Phillips (in litt.) further ascertained that the specimen is *A. a. alexandri*, the migratory northern subspecies. Although this represents the first confirmed record for the East Coast, Newfield states (in litt.) that in Louisiana in winter *A. alexandri* outnumbers *A. colubris* by a margin of 10 to 1, thus suggesting that any November records of *Archilochus* hummingbirds could possibly pertain to *A. alexandri*.

Heil (1981) discussed the meteorological conditions that preceded this sighting and the occurrence of a number of other unseasonal migrants in Massachusetts during the same time period.

# Allen's Hummingbird  *Selasphorus sasin*

**Range:** Nearctic; breeds from southwestern Oregon south through coastal California. Winters in Baja California and Mexico.

**Status:** Vagrant: one record.

**Occurrence:** The only Massachusetts record of Allen's Hummingbird, and the first in eastern North America away from the Gulf Coast, occurred when a bird was mist-netted at Nantucket, 26 August 1988 (Bennett [see Bennett 1989], Andrews). Unfortunately, the hummingbird expired in captivity; however, it serendipitously made possible definitive identification in the hand. The specimen was subsequently sent for confirmation to Dr. William Baltosser at the University of New Mexico and Dr. Allan R. Phillips at the Denver Museum. The specimen presently rests at the MCZ (#332830).

Obviously, the occurrence of such an improbable vagrant in Massachusetts clearly raises questions over the specific identity of other indeterminate *Selasphorus* hummingbirds in the eastern United States. For example, in Massachusetts, a male *Selasphorus* hummingbird with a complete gorget appeared in a Newton backyard, 15–17 April 1978, where it was photographed in color by Allison McGowan. The color slides were mailed to V. Remsen, L. Binford, and B. Sorrie for their opinions on the bird's specific identity. The conclusion, based upon the collective authorities' comments on plumage characteristics, as well as upon geographical probability, is that the bird was probably a male Rufous Hummingbird in its first alternate plumage; however, the possibility of its being an Allen's Hummingbird could not be ruled out with total certainty. The photos and correspondence are on file at Massachusetts Audubon.

A second record of an indeterminate *Selasphorus* hummingbird was established when an immature male appeared at feeders at the Massachusetts Audubon Wellfleet Bay Wildlife Sanctuary, South Wellfleet, 27–29 August 1986 (Reynolds, photographed in color by Petersen and Forster, photos at MAS).

# Belted Kingfisher   *Ceryle alcyon*

**Range:** Nearctic; breeds, in eastern North America, from southern Hudson Bay and Labrador south to the Gulf Coast and Florida. Winters from British Columbia, Washington, and California east to New England and south to northern South America.

**Status:** Uncommon but widespread breeder; fairly common migrant.

**Breeding:** Belted Kingfishers are largely resident at lower elevations around lakes, rivers, and reservoirs at inland locations, but they are driven south or toward the coast during midwinter. They nest in excavated burrows in river banks or gravel pits, sometimes near colonies of Bank Swallows and not infrequently in bluffs facing the ocean on Cape Cod and the Islands. *Egg dates:* 14 May–6 June.

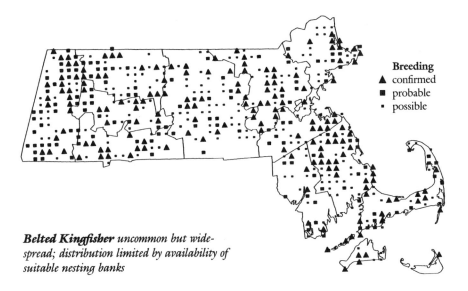

*Belted Kingfisher uncommon but widespread; distribution limited by availability of suitable nesting banks*

Breeding
▲ confirmed
■ probable
• possible

**Nonbreeding:** An observer afield can expect to find up to 5 birds a day in almost any season; however, the highest numbers are usually recorded from April to November. McNair (1978) states that in winter, "The Hoosic River valley from Adams to Williamstown has recorded as many as four in recent years." The total of wintering birds that survive fluctuates according to the relative severity of the weather. Most wintering birds occur along the coast. *Winter maxima:* 35, Cape Cod CBC, 16 December 1984; 31, Martha's Vineyard CBC, December 30, 1984; 29, Buzzards Bay CBC, 15 December 1984.

## Lewis' Woodpecker  *Melanerpes lewis*

**Range:** Western Nearctic; breeds from southern British Columbia to western Nebraska south to southern California, southern New Mexico, and eastern Colorado. Winters southeast to western Texas and northern Mexico.

**Status:** Vagrant: two records.

**Occurrence:** This distinctive western woodpecker has occurred twice in Massachusetts. The first was seen on Naushon Island, 2–23 May 1966 (Frothingham, later shown to Garrey and Bailey). A clear color photograph taken by W. Bailey is on file at Massachusetts Audubon. The second record was: 1, West Newbury, 2–4 June 1969 (Nason, Kenneally, Fox). Although Lewis' Woodpeckers have been recorded east of their normal range on several occasions (see Peterson 1980), the only other New England record is: 1 collected, near Providence, Rhode Island, 16 November 1928 (Bryant 1929).

# Red-headed Woodpecker   *Melanerpes erythrocephalus*

**Range:** Eastern Nearctic; breeds from southern Saskatchewan, southern Manitoba, southern New Hampshire, and New Brunswick south to Texas and Florida. Winters within the southern portion of the breeding range, occasionally north to Massachusetts.

**Status:** Rare, local, and irregular breeder. Variously uncommon to rare but regular migrant; occasionally winters.

**Breeding:** Although Red-headed Woodpeckers have always been highly irregular in their local occurrence, they were clearly much more numerous prior to 1900 than they have been since. During the fall of 1881, they "literally swarmed about Cambridge and Boston" (Brewster 1906); were "abundant in many parts of Massachusetts" (Forbush 1927); and, on 24 September of 1881, "several hundred were counted before 10:00 a.m. at Miller Place, Long Island, N.Y." (Bull 1964). In the early fall of 1894, a flock of 50 spent several weeks in the Springfield area (Forbush, op cit).

These flights were, however, very unusual even at that time, because all authorities who wrote prior to 1930 agreed that Red-headed Woodpeckers were irregular in their occurrence in Massachusetts. Forbush (op cit) knew of only eighteen breeding records widely distributed about the state east to Cambridge and Essex County, with none from Cape Cod or the Islands. Brewster refers to a pair that attempted to breed in Cambridge in 1883, but, "They had so seriously disturbed the meditations of Father O'Brian, the resident priest at St. Peter's church, by their incessant drumming, that he had them shot" (Brewster, op cit). The pronounced general decline of Red-headed Woodpeckers throughout the Northeast during the early 1900s may have been due in part to their frequent fatal encounters with automobiles, as well as the usurpation of suitable nesting holes by European Starlings, which appeared about 1890.

In recent years, Red-headed Woodpeckers have definitely been found nesting in Wilbraham, Hadley, Amherst, Northfield, Williamstown, Sherburn, Holbrook, and Lynn, where they have used dead trees in open deciduous forests bordering on fields. Two or more pairs have been resident on Martha's Vineyard since the late 1970s (Laux). Considering that Forbush's eighteen breeding records were collected over a period of 40 years (1880–1920), the decrease of breeding records in Massachusetts since that time is not nearly so pronounced as is the decrease of migrants. *Egg dates:* 28 May–17 June.

**Nonbreeding:** The distribution of Red-headed Woodpeckers in the Northeast has always been marked by extreme variation from year to year. *Spring maxima:* 11, eastern Massachusetts, May 1964 (fide Emery); 9 reported, throughout the state, 7–29 May 1955 (RNEB); 7, eastern Massachusetts, May 1971 (fide Emery). During fall migration, Red-headed Woodpeckers, especially immatures, are frequently encountered on the outer coast, and an active observer can expect to occasionally see one during late September and October. *Fall maxima:* 15 immatures reported, throughout Massachusetts, November 1968 (RNEB); 4, Cuttyhunk Island, 30 September 1966 (Higginbotham); 3, Nantucket, 13–16 October 1979 (Veit, Litchfield). Single birds are more frequently reported throughout the state during fall, with some occasionally surviving the winter.

Red-headed Woodpeckers sporadically winter at diverse locations in the state. They are rare only at higher elevations in Berkshire County, although "single birds have occasionally wintered successfully since the late 1960s, most often in Williamstown, and have usually departed in May" (McNair 1978). They usually depend on beech mast and acorns for food—except when visiting bird feeders—during winter, and they are likely to be absent when these crops fail. *Winter maxima:* 6 (1 each in Woburn, Dover, Yarmouth, and Littleton; 2 in Rockport), January 1974 (BOEM); 5, 1 each in Gloucester, Hopkinton, Spencer, Dover, Harwichport, January–February 1978 (BOEM).

# Red-bellied Woodpecker   *Melanerpes carolinus*

**Range:** Southeastern Nearctic; resident from Minnesota and Massachusetts south to Texas and Florida.

**Status:** Rare to very uncommon and local, but increasing, resident. Rare to uncommon but regular migrant.

**Breeding:** Prior to 1955, Red-bellied Woodpeckers were considered rare vagrants from the south by Griscom and Snyder (1955), who listed only fifteen records. During the late 1950s and early 1960s, they began extending their range northward. This was most evident in the New York area during the winter of 1960–61 (Bull 1964), and during 1962 in Massachusetts. Between 1960 and 1976, at least fifty additional sightings accumulated from widely scattered locations in the state, but with most coming from the coastal plain and the Connecticut River valley. Robinson (1977) summarized all of the records of Red-bellied Woodpeckers in Massachusetts through 1977.

In 1977, the first Red-bellied Woodpeckers were confirmed breeding in the state: 1 pair feeding recently fledged young, South Natick, 20 June (Robinson, op cit); 1 nest found, North Attleboro, 3 July (Forster). Those sites have been intermittently used since then, and another was found at West Tisbury, Martha's Vineyard, May 1982 (Laux, Brown, Veit). Red-bellied Woodpeckers are now locally established breeders in the southeastern portion of the state, in Worcester County and the Connecticut River valley (e.g., resident in Southwick since 1976). Martha's Vineyard presently holds the only significant colony of Red-bellied Woodpeckers in Massachusetts. Since the first confirmed nesting on the island in 1982, the population has increased significantly, possibly to as many as 40 pairs (Laux, pers. comm.). *Egg dates:* no data; probably May and June.

**Nonbreeding:** Scattered reports throughout the year in Massachusetts suggest that Red-bellied Woodpeckers are more or less resident. There is, however, an influx of reports during early winter when birds seem to be attracted to bird feeders. *Maxima:* 15, Martha's Vineyard CBC, 3 January 1989; 12, eastern Massachusetts, December 1979–February 1980 (BOEM); 8, Martha's Vineyard CBC, 30 December 1984; 7, Martha's Vineyard CBC, 28 December 1986; 3, Martha's Vineyard, 9–12 October 1979 (Laux); 2, Nantucket, 5–27 October 1979 (Veit, Litchfield).

# Yellow-bellied Sapsucker *Sphyrapicus varius*

**Range:** Nearctic; breeds across much of southern Canada, east to southern Labrador and Newfoundland, and, in the East, south in the mountains to northwestern Connecticut and, locally, to western North Carolina. Winters in the southern United States south to the Caribbean and northern South America, occasionally north to Massachusetts.

**Status:** Fairly common breeder west of the Connecticut River. Uncommon to fairly common migrant; rare and irregular in winter.

**Breeding:** In deciduous and mixed forests of Berkshire County east to the Connecticut River valley, Yellow-bellied Sapsuckers are fairly common breeders—e.g., 48 counted along a 25-mile Breeding Bird Survey route,

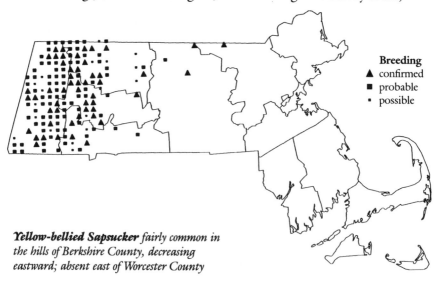

**Breeding**
▲ confirmed
■ probable
• possible

*Yellow-bellied Sapsucker fairly common in the hills of Berkshire County, decreasing eastward; absent east of Worcester County*

Chesterfield to Heath, 30 June 1971 (Goodrich, Petersen)—but they are surprisingly scarce east of that area despite the presence of apparently suitable habitat. The easternmost nesting record known is: a pair feeding young, Mt. Watatic, Ashburnham, 25 June 1977 (Roberts). *Egg dates:* 15 May–June.

**Nonbreeding:** In spring, most migrant sapsuckers pass through the state between mid-April and early May. *Spring maxima:* 25, Mt. Tom, 22 April 1972 (Petersen et al); 20, Rockport, 19 April 1965 (Hooper); 14, Mt. Auburn Cemetery, Cambridge, 17 April 1970 (Stymeist); 12, Plum Island, 3 May 1973 (Swaebe). They are rare after mid-May in eastern Massachusetts. During the fall, sapsuckers are sometimes fairly numerous at coastal land-bird traps during major flights of passerines, but they have never, for some curious reason, been recorded in this state in the huge numbers that are frequently recorded at Monhegan Island, Maine, or Block Island, Rhode Island. *Fall maxima:* 19, WBWS, 30 September 1968 (Bailey); 17, Chatham, 27 September 1968 (Forster); 16, Monomoy, 19 September 1965 (Bailey). In eastern Massachusetts, sapsuckers are rare before September, and they are rare anywhere in the state after October.

A few sapsuckers seem to survive each winter in the state, apparently by subsisting on bark beetle larvae—e.g., 6, eastern Massachusetts, 1–23 January 1976 (BOEM). Records from January and February during the past 30 years are uniformly distributed and are not exclusively concentrated near the climatologically milder coast, and there are at least eight winter records from west of the Connecticut River later than 25 December. March records are usually impossible to separate into overwintering birds and early migrants, but the following possibly fall into the latter category: 1, Boston, 18 March 1961 (Keith); 1, Newton, 18 March 1964 (Stoeger).

# Downy Woodpecker   *Picoides pubescens*

**Range:** Nearctic; resident throughout much of the wooded portions of North America.

**Status:** Common resident and irregular, but occasionally fairly common, migrant.

**Breeding:** Downy Woodpeckers are numerous and widespread in deciduous and mixed woodlands throughout Massachusetts. They are also found in secondary growth and Scrub Oak forests, whereas Hairy Woodpeckers are generally restricted to more mature woodlands. Daily spring and summer totals of 10 to 15 are typical, except: 91, Wellesley, 6 May 1961 (Leverett et al). *Egg dates:* 20 May–21 June.

**Breeding**
▲ confirmed
■ probable
• possible

***Downy Woodpecker*** *common in deciduous
and mixed woodlands*

**Nonbreeding:** Although present year-round throughout the state, at least some Downy Woodpeckers regularly migrate—e.g., 18 banded, MBO, 1–13 October 1966—and *P. p. nelsoni,* the breeding subspecies of northwestern Canada, has been collected many times in eastern Massachusetts (Griscom & Snyder 1955). Most birds reported from areas where they do not breed probably represent postbreeding dispersal of immatures rather than true migrants from farther north. *Maxima:* 568, Concord CBC, 1 January 1989; 479, Concord CBC, 31 December 1989; 268, Millis CBC, 17 December 1987; 200, Newburyport CBC, 23 December 1989.

# Hairy Woodpecker   *Picoides villosus*

**Range:** Nearctic and Neotropical; resident throughout the forested portions of North America, south in mountains to Panama, and also in the Bahamas.

**Status:** Fairly common resident throughout the state, although less numerous on the outer Cape than on the mainland and rare on Nantucket. Migrants are occasionally detected at coastal localities.

**Breeding:** Hairy Woodpeckers are generally less common in Massachusetts than Downy Woodpeckers, and they tend to prefer more mature deciduous woodlands than that species. In late May and early June, the noisy begging calls of fledgling Hairy Woodpeckers is often a giveaway to their presence. *Egg dates:* 22 April–30 May.

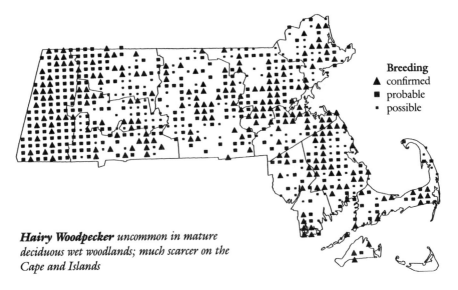

***Hairy Woodpecker*** *uncommon in mature deciduous wet woodlands; much scarcer on the Cape and Islands*

**Breeding**
▲ confirmed
■ probable
▪ possible

**Nonbreeding:** Christmas Bird Count totals for Massachusetts indicate that the Massachusetts population of Hairy Woodpeckers fluctuates considerably from year to year. This fluctuation is probably influenced to a certain extent by an influx of birds from more northerly areas, as is evidenced by the collection of the northern subspecies, *P. v. septentrionalis*, at Nahant, 23 October 1946, by Griscom (PMS #6307), and by the occurrence during fall of migrants at localities where the species does not breed—e.g., 6, Plum Island, 17 October 1965 (Forster); 3, Nantucket, 1–30 November 1980 (Veit); 1, Tuckernuck Island, 5–9 November 1980 (Veit); "a definite influx of migrants in spring and fall" in Berkshire County (McNair 1978). ***Maxima:*** 136, Concord CBC, 1 January 1989; 103, Concord CBC, 27 December 1987; 68, Northampton CBC, 16 December 1990.

# Three-toed Woodpecker   *Picoides tridactylus*

**Range:** Holarctic; resident in North America from northwestern Alaska, central MacKenzie, northern Manitoba, northern Ontario, northern Quebec, northern Labrador, and Newfoundland south, in the East, to northern New England and the Adirondack Mountains in New York. Has occurred as far south as Massachusetts, Rhode Island, Delaware, and Pennsylvania during winter irruptions.

**Status:** Very rare and irregular winter visitor.

**Occurrence:** Like the Black-backed Woodpecker, this species may occur in Massachusetts following massive population outbreaks of bark beetles in Canada. If so, it is possible that during great Black-backed Woodpecker invasions, Three-toed Woodpeckers may have been overlooked in the past. The following records are believed to be correct: 1, Mt. Tom, 29 April 1940 (Merrick, Reidel); 2, Horseneck Beach, Westport, 21–23 February 1942 (Bowen, Clement, Drury, Emerson, Littlefield); 1, Rowley, 28 January to 31 March 1957 (deWindt, VO); 1, Savoy State Forest, 15 December 1959 (Bailey); 1, Harvard, 15 January to 27 April 1975 (Perry et al, photograph in BOEM 3: 27); 1, Amherst, 4–10 November 1981 (Berkel).

McNair (1978) listed five satisfactory records from Berkshire County but suggests that there are also a number of unsubstantiated reports. The most intriguing Berkshire County record is an account of a pair feeding two young at Mt. Greylock, August 1919 (Cartwright, Forbush 1925).

It seems likely that many records of this species have been overlooked because of the irregularity of its movements and its reclusive nature. Given the pattern of occurrence of the Black-backed Woodpecker in Massachusetts, Three-toed Woodpeckers were possibly more numerous in New England in past years than they are today.

# Black-backed Woodpecker   *Picoides arcticus*

**Range:** Nearctic; resident from Alaska east across boreal Canada to Labrador south, in eastern North America, to southern Ontario and the Adirondack Mountains and northern New England. Moves south irregularly in winter to New Jersey and Delaware.

**Status:** Rare to very uncommon and irregular winter visitor.

**Occurrence:** Both species of northern *Picoides* woodpeckers feed upon boring insects that infest dead and dying spruce trees, typically in boggy habitats. Periodically, following periods of especially high food abundance, large numbers of Black-backed Woodpeckers move considerably farther south than their normal wintering range and then frequently feed on insects in dead deciduous trees, especially elms. In the Northeast, Black-backed Woodpeckers occur much more frequently than Three-toed Woodpeckers. Southward incursions of Black-backed Woodpeckers have occurred in clusters, with most flights taking place during a series of consecutive winters, often followed by extended periods with few or no flights. Van Tyne (1926) has pointed out a relationship between spruce budworm infestations in northern spruce-fir forests and southward incursions of Black-backed Woodpeckers.

Major flights to Massachusetts were recorded during the following years. *1860–61:* Black-backed Woodpeckers were said to be locally numerous, although the only published numbers that Forbush was aware of were 6 to 8 per day in Lynn in "fire-killed pine timber" (Forbush 1927). *1923–24:* About 31 were recorded throughout Massachusetts, southeast to Nantucket. The first specimen for New Jersey was also collected during this flight (Griscom, AK 41: 343–344). The general arrival of the birds was noted during the third and fourth weeks of October, and a few were still present in May. Van Tyne (op cit) points out that between 1909 and 1914, a severe infestation of spruce budworm resulted in the death of "three-fourths of the balsam in the southern part of the Province of Quebec . . . New Brunswick, and Maine." Between 1922 and 1924, the populations of certain bark beetles "bred in inconceivable abundance," so that woodpeckers would have had "an almost inexhaustible supply of the very best food." Presumably, the large surplus of young that were produced then dispersed southward. *1924–26:* Comparatively minor flights occurred in these two winters. There is no indication of the actual number of birds recorded, but Griscom and Snyder (1955) list four collected specimens. Black-backed Woodpeckers were reported during the summer in the following years, including: 1, Pelham, 30 June 1921 (Nice); 1, Winchendon, 11 June 1926 (Capen, AK 43: 545–546); 1, Newton, 12 June 1924 (Kennard).

Griscom and Snyder (1955) categorically dismissed the possibility that these summering birds may have bred; however, there is enough suitable breeding habitat in Berkshire County—e.g., Savoy State Forest, Mt. Grey-lock—that it seems plausible that they may have either bred in Massachusetts in the past or could conceivably do so following future incursions. Other irruptive species have frequently been documented breeding far outside their normal ranges following irruptions—e.g., Boreal Owl, Pine Siskin, and Red and White-winged crossbills.

Following this period, Black-backed Woodpeckers became scarce, with only nine individual records between 1926 and 1954. *1956–57:* Twelve reported between 6 and 31 October, thirteen reported during December, and singles seen as late as 5 and 7 May. Allowing for some duplication, at least twenty birds occurred in the state during that winter (RNEB). *1957–58:* Total of nine sightings, south to Eastham, Falmouth, and Martha's Vineyard (RNEB). *1958–59:* Eight reported, 7 and 28 October, probably an additional fifteen to twenty until 9 May (RNEB). *1959–60:* Only five reported (RNEB). *1960–61:* Ten in October; thirteen in November, probably a total of thirty for the whole winter, with a maximum of five at the Newton-Wellesley Hospital through most of the winter. Six seen in May (fide Emery). *1961–62:* Fifteen to twenty seen between 2 October and June (1, Topsfield) (fide Emery). One was reported from Newburyport, 18–25 August 1961 (de-Windt). *1963–64:* Sixteen reported, including one southeast to Wellfleet in February (fide Emery). *1964–65:* Eight reported, the earliest from Martha's Vineyard, 6 October, Chatham, Milton, and Nantucket (RNEB). *1965–66:* Eleven reported, including one from Chatham, 20 August; otherwise none until November (RNEB). *1974–75:* Thirteen reports between 19 October, Pocasset, and 14 May, Wellesley (BOEM).

There have been no major flights since 1975, and no more than three to four individuals have been reported in any winter. However, the boreal forests of Maine and New Brunswick are routinely infested by spruce budworm caterpillars, so a future incursion of Black-backed Woodpeckers would not be surprising. Most reports of this species are between October and March, except in the flight years previously noted.

## Northern Flicker *Colaptes auratus*

**Range:** Nearctic; the race *C. a. auratus* breeds from eastern Alaska southeast to James Bay, southern Labrador, and Newfoundland and south, east of the Great Plains, to the Gulf Coast. The migratory populations winter north of Mexico to southern Canada.

**Status:** Common breeder; common spring and very common fall migrant. Fairly common in winter on the coast, but rare inland in that season.

**Breeding:** Northern Flickers breed practically throughout Massachusetts wherever there are dead or dying trees that are of sufficient size and that contain suitable cavities for nesting. There is at least one known record of ground nesting in the state: 1, Attleboro, 1–9 June 1964 (Kinsey). *Egg dates:* 29 April–14 June.

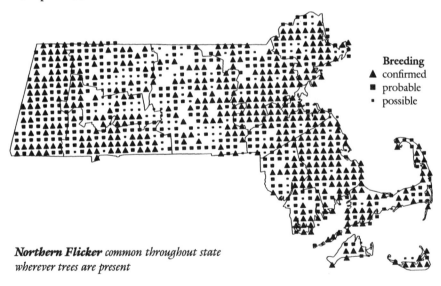

Breeding
▲ confirmed
■ probable
· possible

*Northern Flicker common throughout state wherever trees are present*

**Nonbreeding:** Northern Flickers are among the most conspicuous migrant land birds in the state, particularly along the coast during the fall. In spring, the first migrants arrive by late March, with peak numbers occurring in mid-April. Ordinarily, between 20 and 50 may be seen during a day in late April. *Spring maxima:* 400, Mt. Tom, 19 April 1972 (fide Emery); 250, Holyoke, 19

April 1972 (fide Emery). During the peak of the fall flight in late September, daily totals along the coast are occasionally punctuated by explosive flights following frontal passages from the north. *Fall maxima:* 300, Monomoy, 25 September 1966 (Bailey); 250, Cuttyhunk Island, 28 September 1975 (Petersen); 250, Cuttyhunk Island, 27 September 1966 (Higginbotham); 175, Essex County, 17 September 1964 (Forster).

Due to the relative severity of most Massachusetts winters, the majority of Northern Flickers leave the inland portions of the state in midwinter. For example, in Berkshire County, only singles have been recorded and they are not reported annually (McNair 1978). However, varying numbers routinely survive the entire winter on the coastal plain—e.g., 40, Orleans, 26 February 1978 (Grugan); 30, Nantucket, 14–16 February 1976 (Jackson et al); 22, North Beach, Orleans, 21 January 1968 (Forster, Goodrich).

**Remarks:** Intergrades between *C. a. auratus* ("Yellow-shafted Flicker") and *C. a. cafer* ("Red-shafted Flicker") occur infrequently in Massachusetts, primarily during fall. The Manomet Bird Observatory investigated the ratio of intergrades to "pure" (i.e., no trace of red pigment on·the underface of remiges or rectrices) *C. a. auratus* caught during the course of their banding operations during the years 1978 to 1981. They found no intergrades among 42 birds trapped in spring, but 22 intergrades out of 91 (or 24 percent) flickers trapped during fall. This suggests that either the intergrades usually don't survive the winter, or there are relatively few intergrades breeding near the Atlantic Coast and that those caught at Manomet have traveled east during fall (cf Short 1965). There are, nonetheless, at least four records of intergrades during spring, and one was found dead in Lincoln, 4 July 1964 (MAS collection). There are no Massachusetts records of "pure" *C. a. cafer*.

# Pileated Woodpecker  *Dryocopus pileatus*

**Range:** Nearctic; resident from British Columbia, central Ontario, southern Quebec, and Nova Scotia south to northern California, the eastern Dakotas, central Texas, the Gulf Coast, and Florida.

**Status:** Uncommon resident; local east of Worcester County and virtually absent from Cape Cod and the Islands.

**Breeding:** Because Pileated Woodpeckers inhabit extensive tracts of large timber, they declined markedly in Massachusetts as land was cleared during the 18th and 19th centuries. Howe and Allen (1901) considered the Pileated Woodpecker to be a "very rare permanent resident in Berkshire, Hampden and northern Worcester counties"; however, with the gradual reforestation of the state, Pileated Woodpeckers have steadily increased eastward. They are currently widespread residents through Middlesex County, and there are a number of breeding pairs in Essex and Norfolk counties as well. *Egg dates:* 11–28 May.

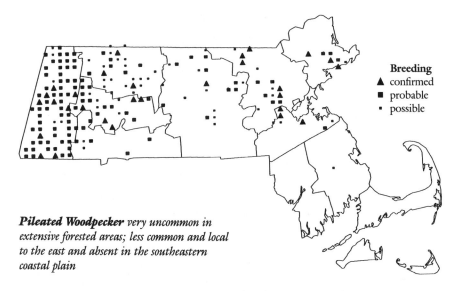

*Pileated Woodpecker very uncommon in extensive forested areas; less common and local to the east and absent in the southeastern coastal plain*

**Breeding**
▲ confirmed
■ probable
• possible

**Nonbreeding:** Occasionally, Pileated Woodpeckers appear in unlikely places where they are not known to breed: e.g., 1, Mt. Auburn Cemetery, Cambridge, 15 May 1971 (fide Emery); 1, Mt. Auburn Cemetery, Cambridge, 19 April 1980 (Hill); 1, Great Island, Yarmouth, 12–20 June 1982 (Trimble, CCBC). A particularly unusual record is: 1, Siasconset, Nantucket, 26 December 1954 (Heywood). The following summer, 20 August 1955, Whittles observed what was presumably the same bird at the Moth Ball Pines.

# Olive-sided Flycatcher  *Contopus borealis*

**Range:** Nearctic; breeds, in eastern North America, from northern Ontario, southern Labrador, and Newfoundland south to northern Michigan, northern New York, and western Massachusetts, and south in the Appalachian Mountains to Tennessee and North Carolina. Winters in tropical South America.

**Status:** Very uncommon and local breeder in Berkshire County and east at high elevations to Worcester County; uncommon migrant.

**Breeding:** The history of the Olive-sided Flycatcher as a breeding bird in Massachusetts is particularly erratic. Prior to about 1870, it was widely distributed, breeding in every county except Nantucket, and even nesting in Mt. Auburn Cemetery, Cambridge (Brewster 1906). By 1927, it had entirely disappeared from the Boston area but still bred regularly, although uncommonly, in two disjunct areas: in coniferous forests surrounding bogs at higher elevations from Worcester County west and in Pitch Pine barrens of the southeastern coastal plain, including Cape Cod. Currently, the species is restricted to a few sites in Berkshire and Worcester counties and has entirely abandoned the Pitch Pine forests of the coastal plain, despite the persistence of this habitat in the past 50 years. A single bird heard singing continually through June 1981 in Scituate (Bartlett et al) gave no further indication of breeding. *Egg dates:* 5 June–1 July.

**Nonbreeding:** In spring, Olive-sided Flycatchers are among the last passerine species to arrive; they are decidedly rare before the third week of May, and migrants are frequently encountered into the second week of June. Ordinarily, only 1 to 3 birds are seen per day. *Spring maxima:* 9, Plum Island, 30 May 1973 (Petersen); 5, Mt. Auburn Cemetery, Cambridge, 28 May 1974 (Leverich); 4, Annisquam, 31 May 1980 (Wiggin). The fall migration is early and rapid with most migrants passing in late August and early September. *Fall maxima:* 6, Gloucester, 25 August 1966 (Wiggin et al); 5, Nantucket, 12 September 1976 (Soucy, Jodrey); 2–3, MNWS, 31 August 1962 (Leahy). Olive-sided Flycatchers are rare after mid-September, with only six records for October since 1955, and two for November, as follows: 1, Brewster, 25 November 1956 (Smart et al); 1, Martha's Vineyard, 15 November 1957 (Rogers et al).

# Western Wood-Pewee   *Contopus sordidulus*

**Range:** Primarily western Nearctic; breeds from southeastern Alaska and south-central Manitoba south to southern California, Texas, and, in mountains, to Guatemala. Winters from Colombia and Venezuela south to Peru and Bolivia.

**Status:** Vagrant: four records.

**Occurrence:** Two Western Wood-Pewees were fortuitously mist-netted and collected at Monomoy, 29 August and 11 September 1966 (Baird). Their specific identity was confirmed by W. Lanyon at the American Museum of Natural History, but the specimens, which were deposited in the collection of the Massachusetts Audubon Society, were, unfortunately, destroyed by beetles. Two sight records of birds uttering their species-specific song are believed to be correct: 1, Monomoy, 28 May 1976 (Goodrich, Bailey); 1, Morris Island, Chatham, 23 May 1980 (Bailey).

# Eastern Wood-Pewee   *Contopus virens*

**Range:** Eastern Nearctic; breeds from southeastern Saskatchewan, Manitoba, New Brunswick, and Nova Scotia south to southeastern Texas and northern Florida. Winters from Colombia and Venezuela south to Peru and western Brazil.

**Status:** Uncommon to common breeder; fairly common spring and un-common fall migrant.

**Breeding:** Eastern Wood-Pewees are ubiquitous in the state, breeding mainly in hardwood forests, but also commonly in Pitch Pines on the coastal plain. *Maxima:* 33, NBBC, 15 June 1980; 18 pairs, Wellesley, July 1954 (Freeland); 17, Truro-Wellfleet, 10 June 1960 (Tudor). *Egg dates:* 10 June–25 July.

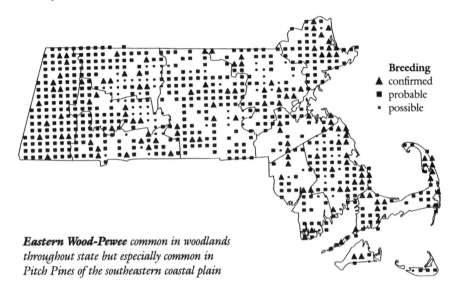

**Breeding**
▲ confirmed
■ probable
• possible

*Eastern Wood-Pewee common in woodlands throughout state but especially common in Pitch Pines of the southeastern coastal plain*

**Nonbreeding:** Eastern Wood-Pewees ordinarily arrive during the first big passerine wave in mid-May, but the highest counts are usually recorded during the third week of that month. *Spring maxima:* 10, Plum Island, 27 May 1970 (Argues); 10, Mt. Auburn Cemetery, Cambridge, 24 May 1974 (Stymeist). During the fall, migrant wood-pewees are seen anytime between late August and early October, at which time it is unusual to see more than 5 in one day. *Fall maxima:* 11, West Worthington, 28 August 1969 (Wei-gand); 5, Plum Island, 12 September 1967 (Petersen); 5, Plum Island, 24 September 1970 (fide Emery). Eastern Wood-Pewees occur regularly in Massachusetts as late as mid-October, but birds present later than this in fall should be examined carefully to determine whether they are possibly West-ern Wood-Pewees. Pewees have the convenient habit of uttering a subsong during fall migration, which can often be an aid to positive identification. *Extreme dates:* 1, Chilmark, 30 April 1969 (Pough, fide Petersen); to 1, Edgartown, 11 November 1961 (Keith); 1, WBWS, 1 November 1979 (Bailey). There are at least six additional records for the last two weeks in October.

# Yellow-bellied Flycatcher  *Empidonax flaviventris*

**Range:** Eastern Nearctic; breeds from northern British Columbia east to southern Labrador and Newfoundland, south to northern New England, and the Adirondack Mountains, New York. Winters in Central America.

**Status:** Uncommon to fairly common migrant; breeding suspected on Mt. Greylock, but never confirmed.

**Occurrence:** The Yellow-bellied Flycatcher has never been proven to breed in Massachusetts; however, a long history of summer occurrences on Mt. Greylock are suggestive of possible nesting—e.g., 1 pair, 28 June 1883 (Brewster); 1, 1 July 1908 (Peters); 1, 17–24 July 1933 (Bailey); 1, 9 July 1944 (Snyder); 2, 23–25 June 1961 (Jameson); 1, 6–26 June 1972 (Gagnon); 1 to 2 more or less regularly throughout June, 1980s (VO). Reports during mid-summer in eastern Massachusetts undoubtedly pertain to late migrants or other species of flycatchers.

Spring-migrant Yellow-bellied Flycatchers are found very precisely during the last week of May and the first two weeks of June. Ordinarily, 1 to 6 birds are seen during a day's field trip along the coast. *Spring maxima:* 31 banded, MBO, 1–12 June 1973; 20, Plum Island, 27 May 1957 (Elkins); 11 banded, MBO, 3 June 1980; 10, Springfield, 31 May 1967 (Cavanaugh); 8, Nahant to Plum Island, 27 May 1977 (Veit, Perkins). In fall, most migrants pass through Massachusetts during the last week of August and the first week of September. *Fall maxima:* 15 +, Chatham, 19–31 August 1975 (fide Nikula); 12, Monomoy, 14 September 1968 (Harris); 8, Nantucket, 21 September 1955 (Dennis, Andrews); 7, Monomoy, 7 September 1970 (Forster); 7 banded, Monomoy, 26–31 August 1968 (Baird); 6 dead, Mt. Greylock Tower, 6 August 1959 (Stone); 6 banded, MBO, 30 August 1971. Although this species is rare after September, the following records certainly do not pertain to any other eastern species of flycatcher, but the possibility of certain western *Empidonax* species cannot be eliminated: 1, Nantucket, 5 October 1956 (Dennis); 1, Duxbury, 5 October 1958 (Whiting); 1, MBO, 7 October 1974; 1, Nantucket, 14 October 1980 (Veit, Stymeist); 1, Truro, 19 October 1976 (Veit); 1, MNWS, 23 October 1960 (Forster); 1, Winchester, 26 October 1969 (Donahue, Everett).

# Acadian Flycatcher  *Empidonax virescens*

**Range:** Southeastern Nearctic; breeds from southern South Dakota, southern Ontario, and Massachusetts south to the Gulf Coast and central Florida; winters from southern Mexico to western Panama.

**Status:** Rare and local but steadily increasing breeder. Rare to uncommon, but regular spring migrant; at least five fall records, but probably overlooked.

**Breeding:** An Acadian Flycatcher nest with 3 eggs was collected in Hyde Park during June 1888 (Hill, MCZ #245093), after which the species was unrecorded in Massachusetts until the early 1960s, when the following records were established: 1 singing, Newburyport, during June 1961 (de-Windt); 1 singing, Marblehead Neck, 8 June 1962 (Smith, Snyder, Ingalls); 1, collected, Monomoy, 30 May 1966 (Baird, MCZ #328610). For the next ten years, spring reports of Acadian Flycatchers steadily increased: e.g., 3 banded, MBO, 6–8 June 1971; 4 banded, MBO, 1–14 June 1974. Between 1 and 14 June 1975, 8, including 3 birds banded, were reported from Manomet, Wellfleet, Dover, and Cohasset. On 26 June 1977, a nest containing 3 eggs was discovered in Middleboro (Petersen 1977), and a second nest, also with 3 eggs, was found in Scituate, 15 June 1979 (B. and M. Litchfield), but the eggs and adults disappeared shortly thereafter. By 1980 and 1981, 10–12 pairs were determined to be breeding in the southern Connecticut River valley and at Quabbin Reservoir (Kellogg et al). It now appears that the Acadian Flycatcher has established itself as a breeding species in the southeastern portion of the state—e.g., 1 nest, Plymouth, 18 June 1987 (Petersen)—in the southern Connecticut River valley, and in Berkshire County—1 nest, Savoy, 29 June 1990 (Rancatti). *Egg dates:* 15, 26 June.

**Nonbreeding:** Since about 1980, it has not been unusual to encounter 1 to 3 birds during a day afield in the first week of June; however, there are only a few definite fall records, all of which refer to banded birds—e.g., 1, MBO, 23 August 1972; 1, MBO, 25 August 1972; 1, MBO, 25 August 1977; 1, MBO, 26 August 1980; 1, Nantucket, 4 September 1984 (Andrews).

# Alder Flycatcher   *Empidonax alnorum*

**Range:** Nearctic; breeds from central Alaska, northern Alberta, northern Ontario, central Quebec, southern Labrador, and Newfoundland south to Minnesota, northern Michigan, northern Virginia, New York, and Massachusetts. Winters ("Traill's" Flycatcher) in South America south to northern Argentina.

**Status:** Locally uncommon to fairly common breeder, mainly in the western part of the state. Probably a fairly common migrant, but identification in fall is often difficult or impossible.

**Breeding:** Following the separation of *E. traillii* into two sibling species, *E. alnorum* (Alder Flycatcher, or "we-bee-o" song type) and *E. traillii* (Willow Flycatcher, or "fitz-bew" song type), much attention has focused on delineating the ranges and habitat preferences of these two species in Massachusetts (see Sorrie 1975a). Although the Willow Flycatcher has been steadily increasing in the Northeast and expanding its range elsewhere in recent years, the Alder Flycatcher is still the more common breeding species at higher elevations west of the Connecticut River—e.g., 23 breeding pairs, Hinsdale Flats, 1978 (McNair). Alder Flycatchers are scarce east of that area, probably because large tracts of alder thickets and forested bogs are lacking (cf Stein 1963). *Egg dates:* 19 June–3 July.

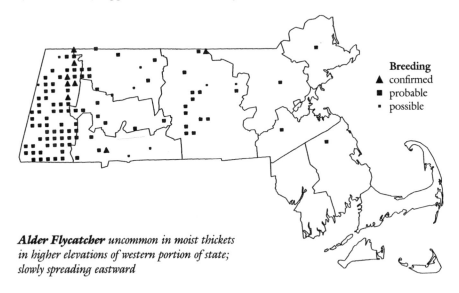

**Breeding**
▲ confirmed
■ probable
• possible

*Alder Flycatcher uncommon in moist thickets in higher elevations of western portion of state; slowly spreading eastward*

**Nonbreeding:** It has not yet been determined how to safely separate Willow from Alder flycatchers in the hand, but "Traill's" Flycatchers, in the inclusive sense, migrate north in spring during late May and June and migrate south during late August and early September. *Spring maxima:* 57 banded, MBO, 1–13 June 1971 (29 of these between 4–9 June); 38 banded, MBO, June 1975; 31 banded, MBO, 1–12 June 1974; 8 banded, MBO 4–8 June 1972; 8 *E. alnorum*, eastern Massachusetts, 2–13 June 1981 (BOEM); 3 *E. alnorum*, Plum Island, 2 June 1979 (Forster). *Fall maxima:* 11 banded, Monomoy, 26–31 August 1968 (Baird); 9 banded, Monomoy, 27–29 August 1966 (Baird); 8 banded, Monomoy, 2–13 September 1966 (Baird); 6 banded, Monomoy, 1–3 September 1967 (Baird). Because the Alder Flycatcher is more numerous as a breeder than *E. traillii* throughout northern New England and the Canadian Maritime Provinces, it is more likely to outnumber that species in Massachusetts during fall migration. *Extreme date:* 1 netted and measured, WBWS, 28 November–5 December 1992 (Jones, Reid, Perkins, Petersen, Forster).

# Willow Flycatcher  *Empidonax traillii*

**Range:** Nearctic; breeds virtually throughout the western and northeastern United States. In northeastern North America, breeds from southern Ontario, the Gaspé Peninsula, and New Brunswick south on the coast to Maryland and inland to western North Carolina; expanding its breeding range northward. Apparently winters in northern South America, but separation from *E. alnorum* in this season is difficult.

**Status:** Locally fairly common breeder and spring migrant. Presumably a regular fall migrant, but problems of identification preclude a determination of precise status in that season.

**Breeding:** Willow Flycatchers are widespread and increasing as breeders in the state, particularly in lowland areas. They are especially numerous in grassy or cattail marshes interspersed with low shrubs; along river banks, such as those of the Sudbury and Neponset rivers; and around the periphery of extensive marshes, such as those in Lynnfield. There have been numerous occasions when both Willow and Alder flycatchers have been heard singing in close proximity to one another. Such areas probably comprise habitats intermediate between the preferred types for each species. Willow Flycatchers seem to be increasing in Massachusetts at the expense of Alder Flycatchers, possibly due to subtle changes in habitat, but the exact relationship is not yet fully understood. *Egg dates:* 2, 7 July.

*Spring maxima:* See under Alder Flycatcher for banding totals; 10, GMNWR, 31 May 1976 (Clayton). *Summer maxima* (counts probably include some migrants): 25, NBBC, 15 June 1980; 16, GBBBC, 17 June 1978; 14, Wayland, 13 June 1981 (Forster); 11, Plum Island, 2 June 1979 (Forster); 10, Plum Island, 2 June 1972 (Forster).

**Nonbreeding:** See comments under Alder Flycatcher.

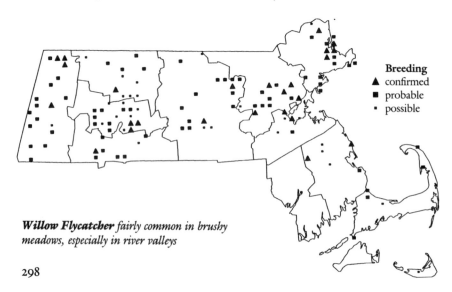

**Breeding**
▲ confirmed
■ probable
• possible

*Willow Flycatcher fairly common in brushy meadows, especially in river valleys*

# Least Flycatcher   *Empidonax minimus*

**Range:** Eastern Nearctic; breeds from southern Yukon and southern Mackenzie, central Manitoba, northern Ontario, central Quebec, and Nova Scotia south to southern North Dakota, northern Illinois, Pennsylvania, and New Jersey, south in the Appalachian Mountains to Georgia. Winters from central Mexico south to Honduras and Nicaragua.

**Status:** Fairly common breeder, but rare on Cape Cod and the Islands and generally declining in eastern Massachusetts; fairly common to common migrant.

**Breeding:** Least Flycatchers breed in open woods, farmland, and suburban areas—habitats that are currently very prevalent in Massachusetts. Griscom and Snyder (1955) suggested that the abundance of Least Flycatchers has varied considerably since colonial times. The species was scarce and local when the state was largely covered with mature forests; then by about 1900 the population increased to a maximum density during the agricultural boom. The species then gradually declined through the early part of the 20th century as farmland was replaced by shopping malls and housing developments, and old fields were replaced by forests. Similar fluctuations on a smaller scale have continued in recent years. In the late 1970s, many observers in eastern Massachusetts and New Hampshire commented upon the decline of the Least Flycatcher, during both the breeding season and on migration (Holmes, Sherry & Sturges 1986). Presently, Least Flycatchers are fairly common from Worcester County west but are increasingly uncommon farther east. They are currently absent from Cape Cod and the Islands as breeders. *Summer maxima:* 27, Wayland, 13 June 1959 (Freeland); 23, Little-

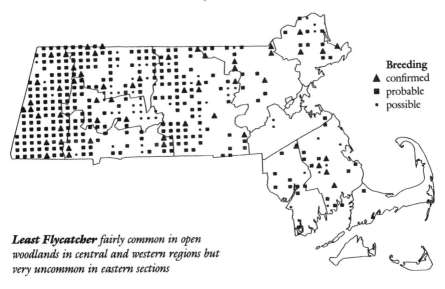

**Breeding**
▲ confirmed
■ probable
• possible

*Least Flycatcher fairly common in open woodlands in central and western regions but very uncommon in eastern sections*

ton, June 1960 (Bolton). By the 1970s, it was unusual to find more than five territorial males during a day in the field in eastern Massachusetts. *Egg dates:* 20 May–late July.

**Nonbreeding:** *Spring maxima:* 50 (assumed to be Leasts), Plum Island, 25 May 1974 (Drummond); 45 *Empidonax* (assumed to be mostly Leasts), North Scituate, 25 May 1974 (Emery); 18, Plum Island, 18 May 1967 (Forster); 12, Mt. Auburn Cemetery, Cambridge, 27 May 1974 (Stymeist). Least Flycatchers ordinarily appear in peak numbers 11 to 14 days earlier (fide MBO data 1966–1974) than the other species of *Empidonax*, and they are even occasionally reported in April—e.g., 10 (accompanying a large variety of other early migrants, especially Indigo Buntings) in eastern Massachusetts, 19–23 April 1954 (RNEB).

Griscom and Snyder (1955) assumed that the majority of migrant *Empidonax* flycatchers seen in Massachusetts during late August and early September were Least Flycatchers; James Baird's banding data refutes this, however, and indicates that "Traill's" and Yellow-bellied flycatchers are just as numerous in that season. Because of this fact, it is reasonable to suspect that Griscom's reported maximum of 50 + Least Flycatchers on Monomoy, 22 August 1954, may have included a substantial proportion of "Traill's" Flycatchers. Similarly, Forster's count of 55 *Empidonax*, Monomoy, 7 September 1970, definitely included 7 Yellow-bellied Flycatchers the same day. *Fall maxima:* 13 banded, Monomoy, 26–31 August 1968 (Baird); 7 banded, MBO, 18–31 August 1975; 4 banded, Monomoy, 27–30 August 1966 (Baird); 4 banded, Monomoy, 1–8 September 1966 (Baird). The following high counts of *Empidonax*, although in many cases reported specifically as one or another species, are conservatively treated here as *Empidonax* sp.: 15, including one singing Least, MNWS, 2 September 1982 (Heil); 14, Monomoy, 7 September 1962 (Forster); 12, Monomoy, 14 September 1968 (Forster); 10, Nantucket, 21 September 1955 (Heywood); 10, MNWS, 1 September 1977 (Heil). *Extreme dates:* An *Empidonax* found freshly dead after having struck the window of Thelma Coffin's house on Tuckernuck Island, 27 November 1977 (Veit, Litchfield) was identified by Lanyon as *E. minimus* and is currently in the collection at the American Museum of Natural History in New York. The following records could pertain to any one of a number of species: 1, Salem, 3 December 1977 (Heil); 1, MNWS, 8 November 1964 (Snyder); 1, Orleans, 7 November 1976 (Goodrich, Nikula); 1, Lincoln, 2 November 1983 (Forster).

# Hammond's Flycatcher  *Empidonax hammondii*

**Range:** Nearctic; breeds from central Alaska, northern British Columbia, south-central Montana, and northwestern Wyoming south to southeastern Alaska, and through British Columbia and the Pacific states to central

California, central Utah, western Colorado, and northern New Mexico. Winters from southeastern Arizona south through Mexico to Honduras and Nicaragua.

**Status:** Vagrant: one record.

**Occurrence:** An *Empidonax* flycatcher that was discovered in a suburban backyard in Wellesley, 19–29 December 1988 (Winkler [see Winkler 1988], VO) was captured, banded, videotape recorded, and released. Confirmation on the identity of the bird as a Hammond's Flycatcher was made possible by several authorities who were able to hear and see the bird on videotape.

# Gray Flycatcher  *Empidonax wrightii*

**Range:** Southwestern Nearctic; breeds from south-central Washington and central Colorado south to eastern California and central western New Mexico. Winters in the southwestern United States and Mexico.

**Status:** Vagrant: one record.

**Occurrence:** The first recorded instance of a Gray Flycatcher on the East Coast of North America occurred when James Baird mist-netted and collected a bird in his backyard in Littleton, 31 October 1969. The specimen was examined by Wesley Lanyon, who confirmed that it was *E. wrightii*. The specimen is now in the collection at the American Museum of Natural History. A large pale *Empidonax* seen in Salem, 11 September 1981 (Heil), on the same day that Canada's first Gray Flycatcher was banded at Toronto (AB 36: 173), may quite possibly also have been this species.

# Eastern Phoebe  *Sayornis phoebe*

**Range:** Nearctic; breeds from northeastern British Columbia east to southern Quebec and Nova Scotia south to southern Alberta, central Texas, and western South Carolina. Winters mainly in the southeastern United States and in Mexico, north on the East Coast to Virginia.

**Status:** Common and widespread breeder; common migrant. Occasionally overwinters in very mild seasons.

**Breeding:** Eastern Phoebes are familiar birds of suburban areas and farmlands, frequently nesting in portions of human-made structures, such as under bridges, eaves of houses, and outbuildings, and often close to open water, where flying insects are abundant. They are largely absent from the highest elevations of the state, although one was seen at 2,100 feet on Mt. Greylock, 16–17 June 1962 (Petersen). *Maxima:* 37 pairs, Wellesley, June 1954 (Freeland); 35, Greater Springfield Census, 20 May 1972. *Egg dates:* 27 April–15 August.

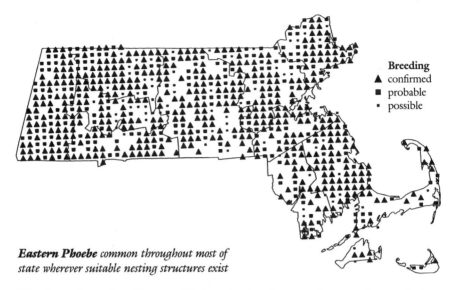

Breeding
▲ confirmed
■ probable
• possible

***Eastern Phoebe*** *common throughout most of state wherever suitable nesting structures exist*

**Nonbreeding:** As with many bird species that do not migrate to the tropics in winter, the first arrival of Eastern Phoebes in spring usually reflects the relative mildness of the season and the occurrence of weather conducive to migration. Usually, the first migrants are seen during the first week of March, but in some years they may not arrive until late in the month. Reports in late February probably involve birds that wintered close to Massachusetts. ***Spring maxima:*** 50, Plum Island, 13 April 1971 (Frothingham); 40+, Connecticut River valley, 18 April 1965 (Wiggin); 35–40, Wayland, 8 April 1956 (Drury).

The fall migration of Eastern Phoebes generally reaches a peak in late September or early October, but phoebes are regularly seen through November, and 1 or 2 are reported most years on a CBC, particularly on the southeastern coastal plain—e.g., singles at Cambridge, Chatham, Topsfield, and Ware, 21–30 December 1967 (RNEB); singles at Plymouth, Martha's Vineyard, and East Middleboro, 22–29 December 1979 (BOEM). ***Fall maxima:*** 80, Weston, 29 September 1975 (Hines); 60+, Cuttyhunk Island, 28 September 1975 (Petersen, Sorrie). These counts are exceptional because ordinarily a daily total of over 20 Eastern Phoebes in fall is unusual.

There are more than thirty reports since 1955 of Eastern Phoebes lingering into January and February, and it is difficult to determine to what extent these birds move about during those months. ***Winter maxima:*** 7 in Massachusetts west to Athol, 1–27 February 1956 (RNEB); 3, Middleboro, throughout January 1973 (fide Briggs).

## Say's Phoebe   *Sayornis saya*

**Range:** Western Nearctic; breeds from central Alaska, northwestern Mackenzie, central Alberta, and southwestern Manitoba south to southern

California and east to the central Dakotas, central Kansas, and northern Texas; also breeds in Mexico. Winters from northern California southeast to Texas and south to Mexico.

**Status:** Rare, but increasingly frequent, fall migrant.

**Occurrence:** There are at least eighteen Massachusetts records of this common and highly migratory western flycatcher, with a maximum of four birds occurring in 1977. The records are: 1 collected, North Truro, 30 September 1889 (Miller); 1 collected, Ipswich, 13 October 1920 (not 1930, as listed in Bailey 1955) (Emilio, PMS #6320); 1, North Chatham, 1 January 1949 (Griscom et al); 1, Plum Island, 2 September 1957 (Hooper, Harrington); 1, Chatham, 6 September 1957 (Bailey, Witty); 1, Plum Island, 1–2 October 1967 (D'Entremont, Argues, Parsons, et al); 1, Monomoy, 18–19 September 1968 (Forster, Bailey); 1, West Tisbury, 27 September 1974 (Clarke); 1, South Wellfleet, 4–7 October 1974 (Bailey et al); 1, Monomoy, 6 September 1976 (Bailey); 1, off Martha's Vineyard near Cox's Ledge, 30 September 1977 (Forster, Vickery, et al); 1, Nauset Beach, Eastham, 1 October 1977 (Waldren, see BOEM 6(1): 26); 1, Nantucket, 1–8 October 1977 (Jodrey et al); 1, South Wellfleet, 23–25 October 1977 (Bailey); 1, Plum Island, 8 September 1979 (Leverich, Stymeist); 1, Nantucket, 24 September 1980 (Seibert, Andrews, Ellis); 1, Littleton, 2 January 1983 (Baird); 1, Monomoy, 14 October 1989 (Nikula).

# Vermilion Flycatcher   *Pyrocephalus rubinus*

**Range:** Neotropical and southern Nearctic; breeds, in North America, north to southern Nevada, central Arizona, and western Oklahoma. Winters throughout much of the breeding range and south to Mexico. Vagrant to eastern North America.

**Status:** Vagrant: two sight reports.

**Occurrence:** A Vermilion Flycatcher, judged to be an immature male based upon the limited extent of red on the underparts, was independently reported by two groups of observers as the bird perched on a wire at Plum Island, 22 October 1954 (Kellogg, Shute, Hale, Williams, Vickery). That such a distinctive species should have been coincidentally reported the same day at the same locality strongly suggests that this record was valid. A second report with less supporting information pertains to a bird seen at Barnstable, 7 October 1961 (Austin, Davis, fide Hill 1965).

# Ash-throated Flycatcher   *Myiarchus cinerascens*

**Range:** Western Nearctic; breeds from Oregon and southern Idaho south to southern California and central Texas; winters from southeastern California and central Arizona south to El Salvador.

**Status:** Vagrant: eight records.

**Occurrence:** The Massachusetts records are: 1 clearly photographed, Eastern Point, Gloucester, 25 November–2 December 1972 (Harty, Jodrey, Soucy, et al, photo at MAS); 1, Orleans, 22 November 1975 (Laux, Goodrich); 1 photographed, Cambridge–Belmont line, 1–9 December 1979 (Taylor, Stymeist, Forster, et al); 1, Acoaxet, 15 December 1979–January 1980 (Emerson et al); 1, Rowley, 18–24 May 1980 (Blaisdell, Giriunas, Stymeist); 1, Wellesley, 11–12 November 1980 (Winkler, Cassie); 1, Gay Head, Martha's Vineyard, 5 November 1989 (Daniels, Keith); 1, WBWS, 1 November–9 December 1991 (Ensor, VO, video and photos at MAS). Bohlen (1975) has shown that the Ash-throated Flycatcher is of rather frequent occurrence east of the Mississippi River; combining his citations with more recent ones from *American Birds*, there are over twenty-five eastern records, all but six from the period September to December. Thus, some of the late fall records listed under *M. crinitus* may actually refer to this, or possibly other species of *Myiarchus*—e.g., *M. tyrannulus, M. tuberculifer*).

# Great Crested Flycatcher  *Myiarchus crinitus*

**Range:** Eastern Nearctic; breeds throughout eastern North America, north to southern Ontario and southern Nova Scotia. Winters mainly in southern Central America and northern South America; also in Florida and Cuba.

**Status:** Fairly common breeder throughout the state (not absent from Nantucket, as stated by Griscom and Snyder [1955]); uncommon to fairly common migrant, more numerous in spring.

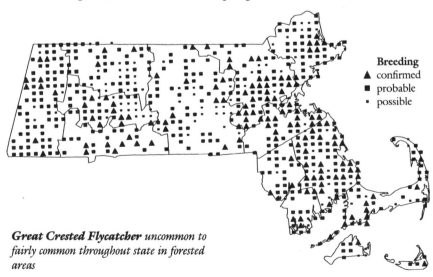

Breeding
▲ confirmed
■ probable
· possible

*Great Crested Flycatcher uncommon to fairly common throughout state in forested areas*

**Breeding:** Great Crested Flycatchers are cavity nesters, breeding in a rather wide variety of habitats throughout the state, including wooded swamps, mature deciduous woodlands, and dry Pitch Pine barrens. Nantucket breeding birds nest in Red Maple swamps. *Maxima:* 48, GBBBC, 17 June 1979; 17 pairs, Wellesley, June 1954 (Freeland); 32, Greater Springfield area census, 9 May 1970; 28, NBBC, 15 June 1980; 15 +, Westport-Acoaxet, 2 June 1966 (Petersen); 8 pairs, July 1975, Nantucket (Veit). *Egg dates:* 27 May–13 June.

**Nonbreeding:** The first arrivals of spring are typically found during the last week of April, while peak counts, including some residents, usually occur during mid-May. *Spring maxima:* 25, Wellesley, 16 May 1964 (Leverett et al); 23, Sudbury River valley, 14 May 1949 (Griscom); 25, Concord, 18 May 1968 (Seamans). In fall, single migrants are regularly seen until mid-October, especially at the immediate coast, and there are at least thirteen records from November. *Fall maxima:* 6, Annisquam, 16 August 1961 (Wiggin); 3, Monomoy, 10 September 1969 (Bailey); 3, Scituate, 20 September 1958 (Fox). Some of the late reports raise suspicions as to their specific identity. Positively identified *M. crinitus* have occurred as late as: 1, Marion, 15 December 1973 (Anderson, Lloyd-Evans); 1, Rockport, 23 November 1975 (Heil); 1, Martha's Vineyard, 17 November 1969 (specimen at MAS). There are ten additional records of *Myiarchus* flycatchers reported as this species later than 15 November—latest: 1, Taunton-Middleboro CBC, 21 December 1975.

# Sulphur-bellied Flycatcher  *Myiodynastes luteiventris*

**Range:** Mainly Neotropical; breeds from southeastern Arizona and Mexico south to central Costa Rica; winters in northern South America.

**Status:** Vagrant: one record.

**Occurrence:** The only Massachusetts record of a Sulphur-bellied Flycatcher is of an individual found near Squibnocket Pond, Martha's Vineyard, 12 November 1983 (Manter). It was seen the following day by Laux and several other observers but could not be subsequently relocated. Critical examination of photographs of the flycatcher by Ridgely, Forster, and Veit ruled out the possibility that the bird might have been the similar Streaked Flycatcher (*Myiodynastes maculatus*) of Central and South America.

# Cassin's Kingbird  *Tyrannus vociferans*

**Range:** Southwestern Nearctic; breeds from Central California, northern Arizona, southeastern Montana, and western Texas south to central Mexico. Winters from the southwesternmost portions of the United States south to Guatemala.

**Status:** Vagrant: two records.

**Occurrence:** The first Cassin's Kingbird recorded in Massachusetts was discovered behind the Eastham Town Hall in the presence of four Western Kingbirds, 21 October 1962 (Bailey), and was collected the next day by Clem. The specimen, an immature, is currently at the MCZ (#331367). A second individual was carefully identified by James Baird at the south end of Monomoy, 9 October 1965, but it did not remain for other observers to see.

# Western Kingbird  *Tyrannus verticalis*

**Range:** Primarily western Nearctic; breeds from southern British Columbia and western Minnesota south to northern Mexico and south-central Texas; sporadically eastward to southern Ontario, Illinois, and Ohio. Regular fall migrant along the Atlantic coast from Nova Scotia to Florida. Winters primarily in Central America, but also along the East Coast between Florida and South Carolina.

**Status:** Uncommon fall migrant on the coast; rare and irregular inland. Two spring records.

**Occurrence:** The first Western Kingbird recorded in Massachusetts was collected at Hyannis, 3 October 1887 (Cory), but since then the species has occurred with increasing frequency. Griscom and Snyder (1955) considered it, "a regular fall transient (up to 6 in one day)," by 1930. Since 1954, there have been well over five hundred Western Kingbirds reported in the state, roughly distributed by month as follows: August-15; September-176; October-129; November-157; December-44; and January-4. The overwhelming majority of reports are from the immediate coast, with fewer than twenty-five records for the inland portions of the state, west to include Berkshire County—e.g., 1, Ashley Falls, 5 September 1955 (Bailey, Mazzeo); 1, Ashley Falls, 1–3 November 1959 (Bailey); 1, Sheffield, 10 October 1974 (McGee). *Fall maxima:* 6, Martha's Vineyard, 16–18 September 1955 (BBC, Jameson); 6, Nantucket, 26 October 1956 (Andrews); 6, Chatham, 12 November 1956 (Sands); 5, Nantucket, 28 October 1979 (Veit, Litchfield).

Seasonal totals have ranged from 4 (1976, 1978 [BOEM]) to 42 (1955 [RNEB]) and 41 (1961 [fide Emery]), although these totals may involve some duplication. Similar to Western Tanagers, Western Kingbirds occurred more frequently in Massachusetts in the late 1950s than they seem to today. *Extreme dates:* 1, Gloucester, 22 August 1971 (Wiggin); 1, Nantucket, 26 August 1955 (Heywoods); 1, Nantucket, 2 January 1967 (Willmann); 1, Chatham, 2 January 1981 (fide Nikula); 1, Plymouth, 1 January 1980 (Petersen, Sorrie). In 1953, two survived until 28 February at a North Tisbury feeder (fide Griscom & Emerson 1959). Rare before mid-September and after November. Spring records: In light of their frequent incidence in the fall, it is surprising how extremely rare Western Kingbirds are during spring in the Northeast. There are only two spring records for Massachusetts: 1 carefully studied for possible confusion with other species of *Tyrannus*, Plum Island, 14–15 May 1971 (Forster, Miliotis); 1, Chatham, 30 June 1986 (Trull, Bailey).

# Eastern Kingbird   *Tyrannus tyrannus*

**Range:** Nearctic; breeds from central British Columbia, northern Saskatchewan, southern Quebec, and Nova Scotia to southwestern Washington and Florida. Winters in tropical South America.

**Status:** Common and widespread breeder; very common migrant, particularly in fall.

**Breeding:** Eastern Kingbirds are among the more conspicuous and pugnacious of our nesting land birds, usually building ragged, bulky nests in trees and also occasionally on utility poles. They are common in second-growth habitats and in suburbia and often nest over water. They breed throughout the state except at the highest elevations and in the densest forests. *Maxima:* 89, NBBC, 16 June 1979; 84, GBBBC, 17 June 1978. *Egg dates:* 30 May–4 July.

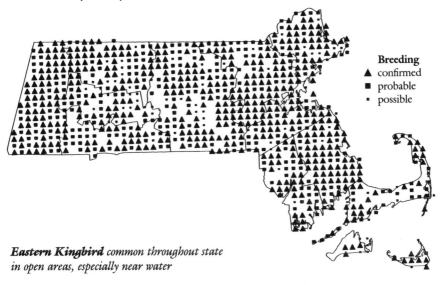

Breeding
▲ confirmed
■ probable
• possible

*Eastern Kingbird common throughout state in open areas, especially near water*

**Nonbreeding:** Eastern Kingbirds generally arrive from the south during the first week of May, although there are at least fifteen records prior to 25 April. *Spring maxima:* 50, Plum Island, 30 May 1973 (Petersen); 42, Wellesley, 16 May 1964 (Leverett et al). In fall, Eastern Kingbirds begin congregating on the outer coast by late July, and migrants are continually detected from then until mid-September. Ordinarily rare after September. *Fall maxima:* 240, Newbury, 14 August 1957 (deWindt); 197, Norfolk, 26 August 1989 (Cassie); 125, Longmeadow, 25 August 1962 (Magee); 85 +, Plum Island, 6 September 1975 (Drummond). *Extreme dates:* 1, Littleton, 5 April 1969 (Sprong); 1, Truro, 12 April 1960 (SSBC); 1, Westport, 12 April 1970 (Stymeist); to 1 most exceptionally late and carefully studied, Falmouth, 8 December 1973 (Laux); 1, Truro, 31 October 1983 (SSBC).

## Gray Kingbird  *Tyrannus dominicensis*

**Range:** Neotropical and southeastern Nearctic; breeds virtually throughout the West Indies, in Florida, and along the North American Atlantic and Gulf coasts sparingly to Mississippi and South Carolina. North American breeders migrate to the West Indies during winter.

**Status:** Vagrant: three records.

**Occurrence:** Gray Kingbirds have been collected twice in Massachusetts, and both specimens are extant: 1, Lynn, 23 October 1869 (Goodale, BMS #17432); 1, West Newbury, 22 November 1931 (Griscom, PMS #6315). A recent additional sight record is: 1 photographed, Squibnocket, Martha's Vineyard, 9 September 1988 (Manter, Laux, photograph at MAS).

## Scissor-tailed Flycatcher  *Tyrannus forficatus*

**Range:** Nearctic and Neotropical; breeds in the south-central United States, north to South Dakota and east to western Arkansas and Louisiana. Winters mainly in southern Central America, but also along the Gulf Coast and in Florida.

**Status:** Rare but regular spring and irregular fall visitor.

**Occurrence:** Unlike other vagrants to Massachusetts from the western or southwestern parts of North America, most Scissor-tailed Flycatchers appear during spring and early summer. The more than twenty-five spring records span the period between April and June—e.g., 1, Harwichport, 21 April 1968 (Dickey) to 1, Rockport, 26–27 June 1981 (Stangel). At least eighteen of these reports are from eastern Massachusetts, but there are also four definite Connecticut River valley records. Two recent summer records are: 1, Plum Island, 6–8 July 1984 (Heil); 1, Chatham, 14–15 July 1984 (BBC, Drummond). Fall occurrences include: 1, Gloucester, 16 August 1942 (Seymour); 1, Martha's Vineyard, 4–9 November 1942 (Leigh et al); 1, Plum Island, 26–28 September 1965 (Keenan et al); 1, Martha's Vineyard, 16 November 1969 (Wheeler et al); 1, North Hadley, 23–28 October 1971 (Bartlett, Emery, Stymeist); 1, South Monomoy, 21 October 1984 (Stabins);

1, Martha's Vineyard, 14 November 1985 (Manter); 1, Nantucket, 9 November–7 December 1986 (Fusoro, Litchfield, VO).


## Fork-tailed Flycatcher   *Tyrannus savana*

**Range:** Neotropical; breeds in Argentina, southern Bolivia, Paraguay, and southern Brazil; migrates north for the southern winter to Columbia, Venezuela, Trinidad and Tobago, Guyana, and northeastern Brazil.

**Status:** Vagrant: at least eleven records.

**Occurrence:** The Massachusetts records of this highly migratory South American flycatcher are: 1, Gay Head, Martha's Vineyard, 22 October 1916 (Foster 1917); 1, Oak Bluffs, Martha's Vineyard, 26–27 September 1961 (VO, see AFN 16: 10); 1, Plum Island, 4–8 May 1968 (Harrington, Burbank, Brown, et al); 1, Chatham, 22 September–4 October 1980 (Vickery et al); 1 (a different, much longer-tailed bird), Orleans, 27 September–7 October 1980 (Swift, Doll, et al); 1, Chatham, 22–27 September 1981 (Bailey et al); 1, Nantucket, 16–18 September 1982 (Holt, fide Andrews); 1, East Boston, 11–12 October 1985 (Thomas et al); 1, Marshfield, 20–21 June 1987 (Shapiro, SSBC); 1 Falmouth, 13 June 1987 (Griffis, Bouchard); 1, Concord, 2–3 May 1990 (Handley et al).

Monroe and Barron (1980) have summarized the North American records of the Fork-tailed Flycatcher through 1978 and point out two things. First, all extant specimens are assignable to the migratory nominate subspecies (*T. s. savana*), and, second, the majority of North American records are from the period July to November, the season when these populations generally migrate *south.*


## Horned Lark   *Eremophila alpestris*

**Range:** Holarctic; breeds virtually throughout North America except absent from the Gulf Coast and Florida; the northernmost populations are migratory.

**Status:** Locally uncommon to common breeder; very common, but local, migrant and winter resident.

**Breeding:** The race *E. a. praticola*, originally termed "Prairie" Horned Lark, is presently an uncommon breeder in Massachusetts in suitable habitat, particularly on Cape Cod and the Islands. Before 1850, *E. a. praticola* was restricted to the Great Plains, but the gradual clearing of the forests in eastern North America allowed eastward expansion of this population. This expansion has been documented in detail by Forbush (1927). Horned Larks are among the earliest passerine migrants to arrive in Massachusetts, routinely appearing in early February and then departing by November. **Maxima:** 350+ (including an unknown number of *E. a. alpestris*), Hadley, 21 March 1971 (Yenlin); 60, Monomoy, throughout July 1965 (Forster); 50 "white-browed" birds, Salisbury, 2 March 1958 (Parker). **Egg dates:** March–16 July.

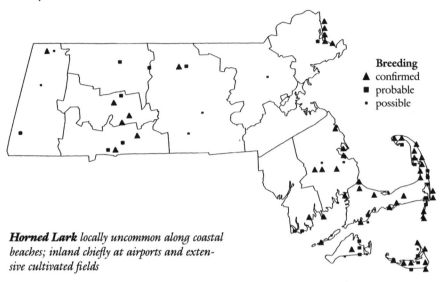

**Breeding**
▲ confirmed
■ probable
• possible

*Horned Lark locally uncommon along coastal beaches; inland chiefly at airports and extensive cultivated fields*

**Nonbreeding:** Nominate *E. a. alpestris*, which breeds in northeastern Canada south to Newfoundland and winters south to South Carolina, is an abundant spring and fall migrant and is occasionally a common winter resident in Massachusetts, particularly during snowless winters. It is most numerous between November and March in open areas such as agricultural fields, airports, and beaches. **Maxima:** 1,000, East Hadley, 19–21 February 1956 (Saunders); 500, Hadley-Amherst, 25 February 1959 (Goodrich); 400, Eastham, 22 February 1967 (Rhome); 300, Truro, 4 November 1979 (Petersen). Higher counts in February may include an unknown number of the breeding subspecies or other "white-browed" races.

## Purple Martin   *Progne subis*

**Range:** Nearctic; breeds throughout the United States and south-central Canada, although absent from the higher mountains in the West. Winters in

*The striking **Fork-tailed Flycatcher** is one of the few vagrants from South America that regularly reaches the Atlantic Coast of the United States. Although it is most frequent in fall, there are also a number of spring records.*

▷

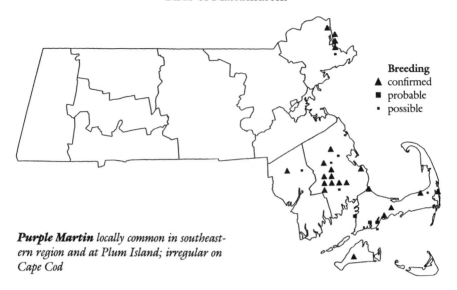

**Breeding**
▲ confirmed
■ probable
• possible

***Purple Martin*** *locally common in southeastern region and at Plum Island; irregular on Cape Cod*

northern South America from Colombia and Venezuela south to Bolivia and southeastern Brazil.

**Status:** Uncommon to common local breeder in widely separated colonies, primarily in eastern Massachusetts; uncommon to rare migrant elsewhere.

**Breeding:** Griscom and Snyder (1955) state that the Purple Martin was "formerly a locally common summer resident throughout the state . . . [but was] virtually exterminated by prolonged cold rains in June 1903." The inclement weather of that summer also severely decimated all swallow populations in the state, most of which quickly recovered. According to Forbush (1929), Purple Martins inhabited ancestral tree cavity nesting sites as recently as the late 1800s; since that time, however, they seem to have become entirely dependent upon artificial martin houses provided by people. Because other species of swallow recovered quickly from the cold and rainy summer of 1903, it seems likely that competition from European Starlings may have been a major factor preventing the rapid recovery of Purple Martins.

Purple Martins are presently established in two major areas: Parker River National Wildlife Refuge and nearby Ipswich and at scattered sites in interior Plymouth County—e.g., Middleboro, Lakeville, South Carver, Marshfield, Hanson, Kingston. In addition, small colonies have been irregularly present in recent years in Centerville, Marstons Mills, Brewster, and East Orleans. Nikula (pers. comm.) states, "There are probably at least a couple of active colonies on the Cape every year, though locations change periodically." In Middleboro, as many as 210 pairs nested until 1959, when heavy rains in June killed many adults and young. Since then, combined totals from the Middleboro and South Carver colonies have fluctuated between 100 and 160 pairs, and the maximum total for that area, including adults and young, was 800 during August of 1971 (Briggs et al). The Plum Island colony held approximately a dozen pairs until the late 1960s, but, since about 1970, 75 to 100 pairs have nested there continually. After the breeding season, Purple Martins abruptly depart in late August, and it is unusual to see migrants away from the immediate vicinity of the colonies after that time.

**Nonbreeding:** In spring, most Purple Martins arrive during late April and early May; however, small numbers are routinely seen in early April—e.g., 6, Middleboro, 1 April 1974 (Maxim); 4, Chappaquiddick, Martha's Vineyard, 4–5 April 1970 (Potter). Occasionally, exceptionally early reports have followed periods of strong southwest winds in March—e.g., 1, Chatham, 10 March 1979 (Perkins); 1, Chatham, 11 March 1983 (Bailey); 1 dead, Orleans, 12 March 1963 (Bailey). During the fall, the only reports of significant numbers of martins away from the colonies are: 250, Ipswich, 7 September 1987 (Berry); 70, Ipswich, 3 September 1988 (Forster); 6, Hanson, 20 September 1950 (Higginbotham). Latest dates are: 1, Weston, 23 September 1956 (Gardler); 1, Chatham, 5 October 1974 (Goodrich, Nikula); 1, Nantucket, 5 October 1980 (SSBC, Veit).

# Brown-chested Martin  *Phaeoprogne tapera*

**Range:** Neotropical; breeds from Colombia, Venezuela, and Guyana south, east of the Andes to eastern Peru, northern Argentina, and Uruguay. The migratory southern race, *P. t. fusca*, spends the austral winter, from mid-April to late September, in northern South America and Panama.

**Status:** Vagrant: one record.

**Occurrence:** The first Brown-chested Martin ever to occur in North America was discovered near the lighthouse at the south end of Monomoy, 12 June 1983 (Petersen, Nikula, Holt). The bird was photographed in color (AB 37: 969) before it succumbed later the same day. The specimen (U.S. National Museum of Natural History #699678) was confirmed by Richard Banks as a hatching year individual of the southern migratory race *P. t. fusca*.

# Tree Swallow  *Tachycineta bicolor*

**Range:** Widespread Nearctic species; breeds from Alaska and central Labrador south to southern California and central Maryland. Winters, in the East, along the coast from Virginia to Florida; also in Cuba and northern Central America.

**Status:** Locally common breeder. Very common spring migrant and very abundant fall migrant, especially along the immediate coast. Rare and irregular in early winter on Cape Cod.

**Breeding:** The Tree Swallow has benefited greatly from the erection of human-made bird houses, despite the fact that most pairs still breed in cavities in dead trees in wooded swamps, Beaver ponds, and cranberry-bog reservoirs. These habitats are particularly prevalent in the western and southeastern parts of the state. During April and May, heavy rains or periods of protracted cold weather occasionally kill large numbers of Tree Swallows, as in 1959 and 1982. Fortunately, these periodic decimations appear to have little lasting effect on the population as a whole. *Egg dates:* 19 April–15 June.

Breeding
▲ confirmed
■ probable
• possible

*Tree Swallow locally common throughout state, especially near water*

**Nonbreeding:** The general arrival of Tree Swallows in spring is usually recorded during the first week of April, but there are a few instances when birds have actually arrived during the first week of March. The earliest arrival date that clearly does not pertain to a local wintering bird is: 1, Wayland, 28 February 1954 (Stackpole). *Spring maxima:* 3,000 +, Plum Island, 7 May 1954 (RNEB); 1,500, Berkshire County, 20 April 1946 (Griscom); 1,000, Mt. Holyoke, 22 April 1972 (Petersen).

One of the most striking phenomena of the fall migration in Massachusetts is the vast number of Tree Swallows that congregate at the outer coast to feed on ripening bayberries and swarms of flying insects during late August and September. Tens of thousands of individuals may regularly be seen at such localities as Plum Island, Duxbury Beach, the outer Cape, and over the extensive open fields in the Halifax–Middleboro area. *Fall maxima:*

300,000, Plum Island, 5 August 1989 (Heil); 100,000, Duxbury, 22 September 1962 (Kellogg); 90,000 +, Sandy Neck, Barnstable, 21 September 1978 (Pease); 75,000, Plum Island, 22 September 1973 (Emery); 50,000, Plum Island, 17 August 1981 (BOEM). Well after most Tree Swallows have normally departed in late September, occasional large flocks are recorded—e.g., 6,000, Monomoy, 9 October 1971 (Stymeist); 2,000 +, Monomoy, 9 November 1975 (Goodrich); 1,000 +, Tuckernuck Island, 11 November 1975 (Veit); 200, Scituate, 11 November 1969 (Bartlett). There are fewer than fifteen early winter records for the past 35 years—e.g., 50, Eastham, 15 December 1991 (Petersen); 4, Plymouth, 23 December 1977 (MBO staff); 5, Eastham, 11 January 1992 (Petersen). Overwintering on Cape Cod was definitely recorded in 1924 and 1944, but not since.

# Northern Rough-winged Swallow   *Stelgidopteryx serripennis*

**Range:** Nearctic; breeds throughout the United States, north, on the East Coast, to southern Maine. Winters from southern Louisiana south to Panama.

**Status:** Uncommon breeder; occasionally fairly common spring and rare fall migrant.

**Breeding:** Prior to 1850, Northern Rough-winged Swallows were unrecorded in New England. They first invaded the western part of the state in the late 1800s, and a nesting pair was collected in North Adams in 1895 (Brewster, BMS #14499). By 1927 they were sparsely distributed as breeders

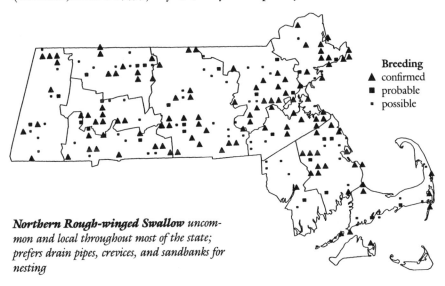

Breeding
▲ confirmed
■ probable
• possible

*Northern Rough-winged Swallow uncommon and local throughout most of the state; prefers drain pipes, crevices, and sandbanks for nesting*

west of the Connecticut River. The first sight record for Essex County was: 1, 21 May 1916 (Brewster), and Brewster (1906) also provided an accurate description of two seen in Belmont, 24 May 1884. Northern Rough-winged Swallows first bred in the Connecticut River valley in 1903 (Morris 1906), in Essex County in 1930 (Emilio), in Concord in 1936 (fide Griscom 1949), and in Harwich (2 pairs) in 1937 (Bishop). Currently, this species breeds in small numbers throughout the state, usually preferring to nest singly or only in very small colonies. The most frequently chosen nest sites are under bridges crossing streams, in pipes and culverts, and in excavated holes in sand or clay banks. *Egg dates:* 7 May–8 June.

**Nonbreeding:** In spring, Northern Rough-winged Swallows regularly arrive by mid-April, and maximum counts usually occur shortly thereafter. Earliest dates are: 1, MNWS, 23 March 1962 (Snyder); 1, Middleboro, 4 April 1972 (Briggs). *Spring maxima:* 66, Hingham, 7 May 1966 (SSBC); 55, Weston, 27 April 1975 (Robinson); 21 +, Holyoke, 25 April 1967 (Yenlin); 20, Falmouth, 29 April 1977 (Clarke). Reports of more than one or two Northern Rough-winged Swallows together in fall likely pertain to immature Tree Swallows because most Rough-wingeds leave immediately following breeding in late July or early August. Especially late records are: 2, South Egremont, 24 September 1954 (Saunders); 3, Harwich, 12 September 1981 (Heil); 3, Nantucket, 8 September 1955 (Dennis, Whittles).

# Bank Swallow  *Riparia riparia*

**Range:** Holarctic; breeds, in North America, from central Alaska, northern Manitoba, southern Labrador, and Newfoundland south to southern California, New Mexico, Tennessee, and Virginia. Winters in South America south to Peru and Argentina.

**Status:** Locally common to occasionally abundant breeder in dense colonies; common to very common migrant.

**Breeding:** Bank Swallows breed in colonies in ocean bluffs, sandbanks, and gravel pits—habitats that are often transitory—so the precise location of nesting colonies is apt to shift frequently. In spite of this, they breed throughout the state wherever suitable habitat exists, and there has been no apparent long-term change in their status during the historical period. *Maxima:* 800 nests, Plum Island, 28 June 1964 (Wiggin); 760 nests, Plum Island, 4 July 1959 (Wiggin); 130 nests, Millis, May 1980 (Cassie); 700 individuals, Hadley, 26 July 1969 (Yenlin); 200 pairs, Rowley, July 1974 (Argues); 100 pairs, Middleboro, 20 June 1981 (Petersen). *Egg dates:* 28 May–17 June.

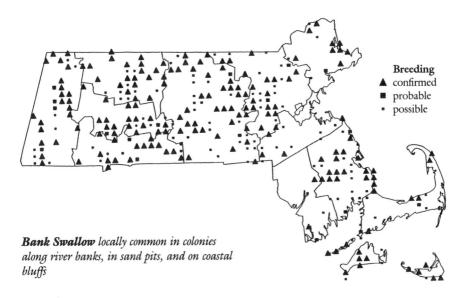

**Bank Swallow** *locally common in colonies along river banks, in sand pits, and on coastal bluffs*

Breeding
▲ confirmed
■ probable
• possible

**Nonbreeding:** Bank Swallows regularly arrive in spring during the second week of April—earliest: 1, South Carver, 5 April 1980 (Petersen)—although peak counts, which include some local breeding birds, do not occur until mid-May. *Spring maxima:* 1,200 + (while this count far exceeds any other migratory total for the state, Bank Swallows are abundant breeders in Nova Scotia and New Brunswick; so such totals could presumably occur more frequently), Newburyport, 28 May 1980 (Heil); 200, Plum Island, 5 May 1967 (Wiggin); 100, Littleton, 4 May 1974 (Baird). The fall migration of the Bank Swallow is far less protracted than that of the Tree Swallow, and the species is notably rare after mid-September. *Fall maxima:* 500, Plum Island, 2 September 1966 (Gardner); 400, Plum Island, 9 August 1980 (D'Entremont); 300 +, Nantucket, 8 September 1954 (Whittles); 250, Hadley, 17 August 1969 (Yenlin). *Extreme dates:* 1, Manomet, 30 November 1979 (Anderson); 2, Martha's Vineyard, 29 November 1953 (Emerson).

## Cliff Swallow  *Hirundo pyrrhonota*

**Range:** Nearctic; breeds, in eastern North America, from southern Ontario, southern Quebec, Anticosti Island, and Nova Scotia south, on the East Coast, to Delaware. Winters in South America from Paraguay and central Brazil south to central Argentina.

**Status:** Fairly common breeder west of Worcester County; uncommon and local in eastern Massachusetts. Uncommon migrant; occasionally more numerous.

**Breeding:** Forbush (1929) effectively summarized the history and the decline of the Cliff Swallow in New England. He indicated that, with the clearing of land in the Northeast for agricultural purposes, Cliff Swallows gradually altered their ancestral breeding sites on cliffs to include nesting under the eaves of buildings and beneath highway bridges, and it appears that they reached a peak in Massachusetts by about 1870. At about the same time, House Sparrows, which competed with the swallows for nesting sites and which killed their young, were introduced from Europe. Furthermore, because the mud nests of Cliff Swallows will not adhere to freshly painted wood, a further decrease was precipitated by the growing custom of painting barns—a tradition not practiced before the 20th century.

Since the turn of the century, as agricultural land has gradually been replaced by forests and suburbia, Cliff Swallows have steadily declined, and they are currently numerous only in the western part of Massachusetts, where they still can find suitable nest sites. The further decline of the Cliff Swallow as a breeding species since the 1950s is reflected by the fact that between 1956 and 1960 about eighty-five nesting pairs were reported from Newbury, Rockport, Lakeville, and Marshfield, whereas, by 1982, there were fewer than thirty known nesting pairs in eastern Massachusetts. The most current large colony is in Marshfield, where, on 14 June 1991, 33 pairs were counted nesting on a barn adjacent to the Marshfield Airport (fide Clapp). *Egg dates:* 25 May–20 July.

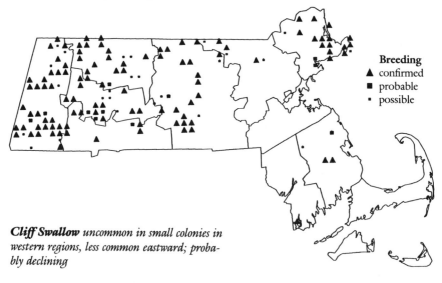

**Breeding**
▲ confirmed
■ probable
▪ possible

*Cliff Swallow uncommon in small colonies in western regions, less common eastward; probably declining*

**Nonbreeding:** Cliff Swallows are ordinarily the last swallows to arrive in numbers in Massachusetts in the spring, the bulk of them not appearing until the last week of April. The largest counts (presumably including many local residents) normally occur in western Massachusetts. Exceptionally early dates are: 1, Falmouth, 9 March 1991 (Evell); 1, Brookfield, 29 March 1960 (Crompton); 1, West Harwich, 31 March 1979 (Nikula, Trull). *Spring maxima:* 500, Stockbridge, 18 April 1942 (Hanson); 40–50, Plum Island, 10 May 1969 (Miliotis); 35–50, Provincetown, 2 May 1972 (O'Regan); 9, Harwich, 25 May 1974 (Nikula). Cliff Swallows are notably uncommon on Cape Cod and the Islands in any season, although stragglers occasionally appear in summer—e.g., 1, Chilmark, 28 July 1962 (Keith); 1–2, Monomoy, 26 June 1967 (Petersen); 2, Monomoy, 21 July 1972 (Pease); 1, Nantucket, 8 June 1974 (Veit); 1, Wellfleet, 20 July 1974 (Blodget).

In fall, this species is much less numerous in eastern Massachusetts than it is in the Connecticut River valley and the Berkshires, and in eastern Massachusetts it is currently unusual to see more than 10 in a day in fall away from breeding localities. *Fall maxima:* 800, Sheffield, 30 August 1978 (McNair); 300 + , Williamsburg, 21 August 1969 (Gagnon et al); 35, Plymouth, 19 September 1959 (Fox); 33, Nauset, Eastham, 13 September 1958 (Gardler). Latest dates include: 1, South Hanson, 1 October 1981 (Petersen); 4, Waltham, 2 October 1981 (Hines); 1, Northampton, 4 October 1971 (Gagnon); 2, Provincetown, 15 October 1977 (Veit); 1, Plum Island, 4 November 1961 (Earle); 3, Nantucket, 24 November 1953 (Heywood).

## Barn Swallow *Hirundo rustica*

**Range:** Cosmopolitan; breeds nearly throughout North America, north to southeastern Alaska, central Manitoba, southern Quebec, and southern Newfoundland. Winters from Mexico south to South America; also in the Caribbean.

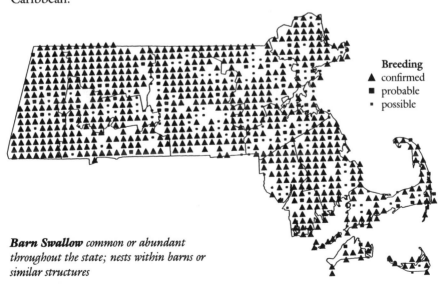

**Breeding**
▲ confirmed
■ probable
• possible

*Barn Swallow common or abundant throughout the state; nests within barns or similar structures*

**Status:** Very common and conspicuous breeder throughout the state; very common to abundant migrant, especially along the coast.

**Breeding:** The Barn Swallow is one of the most widespread nesting birds in the state. Evidence of its adaptability to human artifacts includes the presence of 56 nests at an abandoned Coast Guard station at the southern end of Monomoy in June 1962 (Bailey); nesting in abandoned artillery bunkers on the Brewster Islands in outer Boston Harbor (fide Hatch); and former nesting on the partially sunken *Pendleton* shipwreck off Monomoy until the hull was totally submerged (fide Petersen). *Egg dates:* 18 May–12 July.

**Nonbreeding:** The first Barn Swallows of spring ordinarily arrive during mid-April, with peak counts of migrants occurring in May. They are rare before the second week of April, so the following March records are exceptional: 1, Swampscott, 4 March 1956 (Green); 1, Dedham, 6 March 1951 (Marsh); 2, Chatham, 28 March 1956 (Mosher); 1, GMNWR, 29 March 1976 (Evans); 2, Taunton, 31 March 1975 (Delger). *Spring maxima:* 4,000, Essex County, 12 May 1946 (Griscom); 800, Plum Island, 26 May 1960 (deWindt). More recent counts tend to be lower—e.g., 400 +, Plum Island, 11 May 1974 (Petersen, Forster). High counts for the year are recorded in August, and migration is mostly over by early October. *Fall maxima:* 700, GMNWR, 18 August 1959 (Freeland); 600, Plum Island, 10 August 1974 (Berry); 360 in one hour, Littleton, 18 August 1968 (Baird).

The Barn Swallow, more than almost any other Massachusetts land bird, regularly appears along the coast following extended periods of southwesterly winds during November. Maxima for this late fall period: 40 +, Rockport, 31 October 1973 (McClellan); 26 reported, 3–22 November 1981 (24 of these on Cape Cod and Martha's Vineyard) (BOEM); 19 reported, eastern Massachusetts, 4–12 November 1978 (BOEM); 13, Nantucket, 3 November 1955 (Dennis); 11 reported, eastern Massachusetts, 14–17 November 1974 (BOEM); 10 reported, eastern Massachusetts, 9–23 November 1975 (BOEM). Records outside the November period described above are: 1, Concord, 6 December 1953 (Wellman); 1, Plum Island, 29 November 1986 (Petersen); 1, Rockport, 28 November 1954 (deWindt); 1, Plum Island, 24 November 1979 (Jodrey). A most astounding and unaccountable record is that of a Barn Swallow clearly seen at Plum Island, 31 January 1974 (Lewis, Parsons, Jodrey).

# Gray Jay  *Perisoreus canadensis*

**Range:** Northern Nearctic; breeds from Alaska to northern Quebec and Newfoundland south, in eastern North America, to northern New York, northern New England, New Brunswick, and Nova Scotia. Winters south irregularly to southern New England.

**Status:** Very rare winter visitor; occasionally more numerous during southward irruptions.

**Occurrence:** Like a number of boreal species, Gray Jays, which are usually sedentary, occasionally move south of their breeding range during winter. Recent records suggest that a few Gray Jays may irregularly occur in winter in Massachusetts' remote forested areas, such as those surrounding Quabbin Reservoir. In some years, minor flights have even been reported; the most notable was during the winter of 1965–1966, when at least fourteen birds were reported in Massachusetts between 15 October and late March, southeast to Weymouth, Norwell, Scituate, and Carver (RNEB). Other winters during which more than one was reported include: 1917–1918, 2 (fide Bailey 1955); 1921–1922, 4 (op cit); 1960–1961, 3 (fide Emery); 1968–1969, 2 (RNEB); 1972–1973, 3 (BOEM). Griscom and Snyder's (1955) statement that Gray Jays had "greatly decreased in the past fifty years" seems unwarranted because Howe and Allen (1901) considered the Gray Jay to be "accidental from the north," and Forbush (1927) listed only seven records for the state. Bailey (1955) listed fourteen records between 1900 and 1954, one of these an extant specimen and another (1954) seen and amply confirmed by many observers.

It is appropriate to list all the reports of Gray Jays since 1970 because they accurately reflect its current (and probably historic) status: 1, Gate 5, Quabbin, December 1971 (Seitz); 1, Monson, 14 March 1972 (Lewing); 1–2, Prescott Peninsula, Quabbin Reservoir, 22–29 October 1972 (Gagnon); 1, Springfield, 24 October 1972 (Shanley); 1–2, Pelham, 4 November 1972–early March 1973 (BNWM); 1, Longmeadow, 6 January 1973 (Simicovitz); 1, South New Salem, 13 January 1973 (Gagnon); 1, Hardwick, 12 January 1975 (Dzwonkoski); 1, Athol, 14–15 March 1976 (French); 2, Dana, 23 October–20 November 1976 (Blodget); 1, Byfield, 23–24 December 1976 (fide Stymeist); 1, New Marlboro, 29 January–2 February 1977 (Schwartz); 1, Quabbin, 29 October 1978 (Deyo); 1, Williamsburg, 18–25 November 1978 (Graves, Kellogg); 1, Pittsfield, 18–28 December 1978 (Valiask); 1, Becket, 16 January–8 March 1983 (Lambert); 1, Petersham, 17 December 1983 (Hood); 1, Quabbin, 15 March 1985 (Johnson); 1, Prescott Peninsula and East Quabbin, 24–29 October 1989 (Davis, Johnstone).

# Blue Jay  *Cyanocitta cristata*

**Range:** Nearctic; breeds throughout eastern and central North America north to central Alberta, central Manitoba, southern Quebec, and Newfoundland. Northern populations are regularly migratory, others irregularly, but all winter within North America.

**Status:** Common and widespread breeder and common to occasionally abundant migrant. Variously uncommon to common winter resident.

**Breeding:** Blue Jays are widespread, common, and conspicuous residents throughout the state, preferring to nest in conifers if they are available. *Egg dates:* 28 April–18 June.

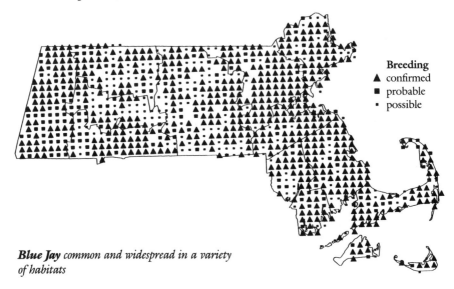

Breeding
▲ confirmed
■ probable
• possible

*Blue Jay common and widespread in a variety of habitats*

**Nonbreeding:** The greatest annual concentrations of Blue Jays are usually noted during late May and between September and November. During these seasons, obvious migrants may be seen along the outer coast, as well as inland as far west as Berkshire County. *Spring maxima:* 1,500 in one hour, North Scituate, 22 May 1980 (Flaherty et al); 1,178 migrants counted, Connecticut River valley, 5–29 May 1971 (maximum 302, 7 May [fide Bates]); 1,000+, North Scituate, 21 May 1968 (Gardner et al); 500, Chatham, 27 May 1970 (Petersen); 300, Plum Island, 1 June 1958 (Gardler). Although omnivorous during the breeding season, Blue Jays largely depend upon acorns and other nuts for sustenance during winter. Consequently, massive migratory movements during September are occasionally triggered by a failure of the acorn supply. *Fall maxima:* 2,393 recorded migrating south, Manomet, 1–26 October 1967 (maximum 1,000, 1 October [MBO]); 1,150, Mt. Tom, 28 September 1972 (Gagnon); 1,064, Quabbin, 3 October 1968 (Eliot); 758, Provincetown, 1 October 1977 (Stymeist, Veit, et al). Prior to the winter of 1978–1979, when the Blue Jay population in Massachusetts was especially low, a massive southward movement was noted at Lighthouse Point, New Haven, Connecticut, and 2,875 were counted flying south over Fobes Hill, Windsor, 28 September 1977 (McNair). In this case, the massive southward exodus was probably caused by a localized failure of the acorn crop; oaks were severely damaged by an unseasonal snowstorm in May 1977 and were thus unable to produce a normal acorn crop in 1977 and 1978.

# Black-billed Magpie   *Pica pica*

**Range:** Holarctic; mainly resident, in North America, from southern Alaska, south central Saskatchewan, and western Ontario south to central eastern California and western Oklahoma. Wanders irregularly east to the Atlantic Coast.

**Status:** Irregular visitor; precise status uncertain.

**Occurrence:** There are approximately fifteen reports of Black-billed Magpies for Massachusetts, most of which have in the past been summarily dismissed as escaped cage birds. However, twelve of these occurred during the years 1959 to 1961, a period when magpies were also reported elsewhere well east of their normal range, in Ohio, Tennessee, North Carolina, and New York. See Bull (1974) for a discussion of the evaluation of extralimital records of this species. Among the more recent Massachusetts records are: 1, Salisbury, throughout July 1959 (deWindt); 3, North Andover, 17 August 1959 (Ashburn); 1, Acoaxet, 7 June 1960 (Claflin, Elkins); 1, Norwood, 5 July 1960 (Gould); 1, Plum Island, 11 March 1961 (Gulick); 1, Waltham, 13 May 1961 (Patterson); 1, Marblehead, 10–20 October 1961 (Hawkes, Snyder, et al); 1, Rockport, 25–26 October 1961 (Kieran et al); 1, South Lincoln, 28 May 1964 (Gropius); 1, Medford, 3 December 1965 (Glassberg); 1, Petersham, 4 March 1966 (Swedberg); 1, Mattapoisett, 25 April–4 May 1992 (Mock, Thompson). A bird in Belchertown, early May 1981, was proven to be an escapee from a nearby wild animal farm (fide Petersen).

# American Crow   *Corvus brachyrhynchos*

**Range:** Nearctic; breeds from British Columbia, northern Ontario, and Newfoundland south to central Arizona and southern Florida. Northern populations are migratory, but all winter within North America.

**Status:** Very common resident and occasionally abundant migrant. Fairly common in winter.

**Breeding:** Crows nest commonly throughout the state, but they are most numerous where there is a mixture of open country and woodlands. *Egg dates:* 5 May–13 June.

**Nonbreeding:** Maximum numbers of migrant American Crows are recorded during the months of March and October; however, few systematic counts have ever been made. During fall, large numbers are occasionally counted by hawk watchers as the birds move south along inland ridges in late October. Regrettably, these counts are somewhat sporadic and incidental. *Spring maxima:* 700+, Dartmouth, 23 March 1958 (Gardler); 600+ flying north, Salisbury–Plum Island, 15 March 1982 (Veit, Litchfield); 250+, North Amherst, 27 March 1961 (Elkins, Claflin). *Fall maxima:* 2,268, west-

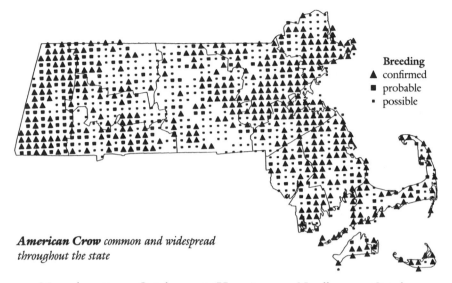

**Breeding**
▲ confirmed
■ probable
· possible

*American Crow common and widespread throughout the state*

ern Massachusetts, 29 October 1938 (Hagar); 1,500, Needham, 30 October 1979 (Malland); 1,175, Ashburnham, 27 October 1979 (Petersen); 1,000 +, Berkshire County, 22 October 1950 (Minneci).

In winter American Crows are usually most numerous on the coast and in agricultural areas inland. Massachusetts CBC totals indicate a fairly stable winter population since the late 1950s. Although Griscom and Snyder (1955) suggested that crows were declining in the state due to the destruction of their winter roosting sites, current records for the largest known roosts reflect no particular continued decline—e.g., 1,414, West Roxbury, 3 January 1978 (Butler); 2,800, Framingham, throughout February 1978 (Taylor); 5,000–6,000, Waltham, 19 February 1978 (Stymeist, Robinson); 4,100 +, Framingham, 9 December 1981 (Forster, Hamilton); 10,000 Framingham, January and February 1990 (Taylor). These high counts may simply indicate that American Crows are either currently more concentrated in winter roosts than they were formerly (prior to 1935) or that roosts are being more systematically monitored than was previously the case. In either situation, recent high counts may not truly reflect a population increase.

## Fish Crow  *Corvus ossifragus*

**Range:** Southeastern Nearctic; mainly resident along the immediate coast and in major river valleys from Massachusetts to Georgia, throughout peninsular Florida, along the Gulf Coast to eastern Texas, and north along the Mississippi River drainage to southern Illinois.

**Status:** Uncommon and local resident.

**Breeding:** Fish Crows have an interesting distribution and history of occurrence in Massachusetts. The first record for the state was of a bird seen being pursued by American Crows and heard calling in Cambridge, 16 May 1875 (Brewster). Shortly thereafter, two local specimens were obtained: 1 pair collected, Wareham, 16 July 1884 (not 1887 as listed by Griscom & Snyder 1955, BMS #17618); 1, Springfield, 9 June 1896 (BMS #17618). Between 27 March and 30 May 1905, Forbush and Farley found several Fish Crows— maximum, 17, 7 May—around Buzzards Bay but could find no evidence of breeding (op cit). By 1955, Griscom and Snyder claimed that Fish Crows were "occasionally reported in spring in southeastern Massachusetts along the coast from Cambridge south, and at Longmeadow in the Connecticut River valley."

Fish Crows have markedly increased since that time, and presently they have either been proven to breed or are presumed to be breeding at a number of localities in eastern Massachusetts—e.g., 2 nests (first record), West Roxbury, 13 June 1973 (Atwood 1975); 1 nest building, Myles Standish State Forest, Plymouth, 10 April 1978 (MBO staff); 4 nests, Mt. Auburn Cemetery, Cambridge, May 1990 (Stymeist). The first presumed breeding of Fish Crows in the Connecticut River valley took place in 1986 in Forest Park, Springfield, where 2 pairs were found (Cavanaugh). *Egg dates:* (Connecticut) 5 May–6 June.

**Nonbreeding:** The spring arrival and fall departure, or dispersal, of Massachusetts Fish Crows is somewhat mysterious. In spring, the birds begin to punctually appear near known breeding areas in eastern and southeastern Massachusetts during March and April. This movement appears to coincide with their departure from the dumps and roosts west of Boston where they occur in winter. In this season, counts typically range from 1 to 5, although occasionally much larger concentrations are recorded—e.g., 75, Rehoboth, 25 March 1955 (Hill); 25, Marshfield, 26 April 1980 (Petersen).

A general withdrawal from the nesting areas takes place in September, and, by midfall, Fish Crows are almost rare away from traditional wintering quarters, where the highest counts of the year are recorded. *Maxima:* 1,000 + (roosting), Framingham, 6 January 1990 (Hamilton, Morrier); 400 +, West Roxbury, 9 March 1971 (Petersen, Goodrich); 394, Concord CBC, 30 December 1990; 200, West Hanover, 9–30 September 1986 (d'Entremont); 175, Middleboro, 16 September 1989 (Petersen); 45, North Attleboro, 20 September 1984 (Sorrie); 35, Wayland, 16 November 1980 (Forster). Somewhat surprisingly, Fish Crows have only recently begun to appear on Cape Cod—e.g., 2, Provincetown, 16–18 May 1982 (Nikula); 11, Truro, 3 May 1989 (Nikula); 1, mid-Cape Cod CBC, 28 December 1989—and they are very uncommon as far north as northern Essex County in any season—e.g., 1, Salisbury, 11 October 1971 (Forster); 2, Rowley, 16 April 1964 (Petersen).

## Common Raven   *Corvus corax*

**Range:** Holarctic; widespread resident in western North America, but restricted to boreal forests of northern latitudes and high mountains in eastern North America, where it breeds south to western Massachusetts and locally in the Appalachian Mountains to Georgia. Some southward migration of northern populations occurs in winter, but the species is still rare anywhere outside of its breeding range.

**Status:** Very uncommon and local breeder from Worcester County westward; generally uncommon and local during migration and in winter. Rare in eastern Massachusetts.

**Breeding:** Forbush (1927) cites Wood (1634) and Josselyn (1674) in stating that Common Ravens were numerous on Cape Cod at the time when the Pilgrims settled there, but that the birds were quickly eradicated by shooting and by the clearing of the forests. Forbush (op cit) also states that, "[The Common Raven] is said to have bred formerly on an inaccessible cliff on the side of Ragged Mountain in the town of Adams, Massachusetts." Two specimens from Williamstown, one collected in 1877 (Sandborn) and the other undated, currently in the collection at Williams College, may have derived from that nesting locality.

On 12 April 1980, 2 ravens were observed in courtship flight near Mt. Watatic (Komar, Sytmeist, Veit), and, by 1982, they were presumably breeding at three different sites in Massachusetts. In April, a pair of adults was seen on the Prescott Peninsula, Quabbin Reservoir, visiting a ledge formerly used as an aerie by Peregrine Falcons; and, throughout June of that year, a pair with recently fledged young was observed in the vicinity (Gagnon et al). The other instances of breeding in 1982 are based upon the presence of family groups—e.g., 5, Mt. Greylock, throughout June; 5–6, Shelburne, 21 June (fide Kellogg). By 1990, at least fourteen active nest sites were known from western Massachusetts (fide French). *Egg dates:* 26 March–20 April.

**Nonbreeding:** Common Ravens were of rare or irregular occurrence in Massachusetts from the historical period until the 1970s. Griscom and Snyder (1955) and Bailey (1955) together cite a total of seventeen records for Massachusetts up until 1954. These include nine vaguely labeled specimens from Tyngsboro, Springfield, Dedham, Williamstown, Northampton, and Methuen, with dates spanning the period from 22 May to July. Sight records since then, which are believed to pertain to correctly identified wild birds, include: 1, Hadley, 11 December 1954 (Ballman); 1, Hardwick, 25 October 1958 (Eliot, Stone); 1, Quabbin, 14 February 1971 (Gagnon, D'Entremont); 1, Quabbin, 8 November 1971 (Brown); 1, Milton, early November 1971 (Veit); 1, Rockport, 4 December 1971 (Forster); 2, Savoy State Forest, 29 May 1977 (Ferren, McNair, Sanborn).

ı    Since about 1980, spring and fall hawk watches have regularly recorded ravens at sites such as Wachusett Mountain, Mount Watatic, and at several locations in the Berkshires—e.g., 25, Pittsfield, 4 November 1989 (Perkins); 17, Wachusett Mountain, 15 September 1990 (Taylor). By midwinter, peak numbers of birds tend to concentrate at Quabbin Reservoir, where an abundance of carrion is able to readily sustain them. Typically, from 1 to 10 are encountered in that season, but the overall numbers present are undoubtedly much greater—e.g., 28, Quabbin CBC, 30 December 1989.

## Jackdaw    *Corvus monedula*

**Range:** Palearctic; widespread and mostly resident in temperate Eurasia west to Ireland and Norway. Range recently expanding and species increasing in abundance in recent years.

**Status:** Vagrant: one record.

**Occurrence:** A Jackdaw was discovered on the beach near Tom Nevers Head, Nantucket, 28 November 1982 (Perkins, Stymeist, Heywood), where it remained until 9 July 1984, when it was joined by a second individual (Jenks-Jay, VO). From then on, 1 to 2 Jackdaws were present on the island until 1 individual was last reported, 8 December 1986 (Bouchard et al). Jackdaws have been expanding their range in western Europe during the recent past, and because of a well-documented "fall-out" of Jackdaws in eastern Canada in 1984 (AB 39: 149), it seems likely that the Nantucket birds were bona fide vagrants.

## Black-capped Chickadee    *Parus atricapillus*

**Range:** Nearctic; breeds from Alaska and Newfoundland south in eastern North America to central Kansas and central New Jersey, and locally in the Appalachian Mountains to Tennessee. Northern populations are irregularly migratory but generally unrecorded south of the species' breeding range in winter.

**Status:** Common resident throughout the state and common to occasionally abundant migrant.

**Breeding:** Black-capped Chickadees breed in a variety of wooded habitats throughout the state in either cavities or artificial bird boxes. During the summer, they are most often encountered in pairs or in small family groups. *Egg dates:* 4 May–12 July.

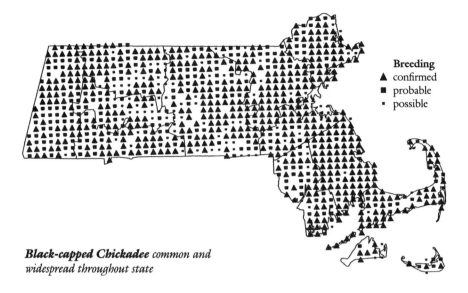

**Breeding**
▲ confirmed
■ probable
· possible

***Black-capped Chickadee*** *common and*
*widespread throughout state*

**Nonbreeding:** The spring migration of Black-capped Chickadees is not
nearly so pronounced as that which sometimes occurs in fall, and spring
migrants frequently go undetected. However, during April 1981 (following a
major fall flight in 1980), the Manomet Bird Observatory banded 149 chickadees, which they termed "an unprecedented spring movement." In Lloyd-
Evans' opinion (1981), most of the young birds involved in the fall flights
eventually perish from starvation, thus accounting for the usual lack of
migrants the following spring. He also describes one immature chickadee
"banded at MBO 16 September 1976, a normal fall migrant, which vanished
for a year and a half and then turned up in Madsen, Ontario, in May 1978."
This further suggests that young appearing on the coast in fall may migrate
farther inland during the following spring.

The most remarkable aspect of the Black-capped Chickadee population in
New England is the irregular occurrence of massive southward fall migrations involving, for the most part, immature birds. Bagg (1969), in analyzing such a flight during the fall of 1969, pointed out that chickadees that
breed in northern New England feed on conifer seeds and insects associated
with the flowering parts of these trees. Because conifers (mainly spruces
and firs) produce cone crops every other year, and especially heavy crops at
irregular intervals, chickadees seem to move south in response to changing
food availability. Migrating during daylight hours, small flocks are frequently encountered along the outer coast. Sorrie (1975b) and Lloyd-Evans
(op cit) have summarized data from the Manomet Bird Observatory, which
clearly indicates the variation from year to year in the number of chickadees
banded at the station and shows that major flights occurred in 1961, 1968,
1971, and 1980. Eighty to eighty-five percent of the chickadees banded at

MBO were immatures (i.e., birds of the year). Sorrie and Lloyd-Evans' papers provide seasonal banding totals from MBO. Other selected single-day, single-locality maxima for the state include: hundreds, Chatham, 1 November 1954 (Fuller); 334, Quabbin, 9 October 1971 (Yenlin); 126 migrating, Littleton, 9 October 1969 (Baird). Because chickadees are reluctant to cross large expanses of open water, they are notably uncommon at Nantucket.

Massachusetts CBC data indicates that the winter population of Black-capped Chickadees fluctuates considerably from year to year. Curiously, high winter density is not necessarily correlated with major fall flights. Thus, it appears that migrants usually move to locales farther south than our area in winter, and chickadee density in Massachusetts in winter is presumably controlled by local food abundance and weather. *Winter maxima:* 4,066 (all-time national high for CBC count), Millis CBC, 21 December 1985; 3,651, Concord CBC, 30 December 1990; 3,414, Millis CBC, 20 December 1986.

# Boreal Chickadee  *Parus hudsonicus*

**Range:** Nearctic; largely resident in boreal forests of North America south in eastern North America to eastern Maine, northern New Hampshire, and northern Vermont. Irregularly migrates south in winter to New Jersey, Maryland, and Pennsylvania.

**Status:** Rare and irregular migrant and winter resident.

**Occurrence:** Sorrie (1975b) has shown that every flight of Boreal Chickadees into Massachusetts has occurred during a major southward movement of Black-capped Chickadees, suggesting that both species are dependent upon the same cyclically abundant food source to the north. However, it should be emphasized that Boreal Chickadees have not been recorded during every flight of Black-capped Chickadees. Although migrant Boreal Chickadees have been reported widely throughout Massachusetts (except from the outer Islands) and from a diversity of habitats, those that spend the winter are almost always found in dense spruce and fir groves.

Christmas Bird Count data accurately reflects the largest flights recorded in Massachusetts since 1954. An enumeration of this and other data follows. *1954–55:* at least 19 reported, 11 October–5 May, with maxima of: 6, Newburyport, throughout January; 4–5, Arnold Arboretum, Jamaica Plain, 21 November (RNEB). *1959–60:* at least 31 reported from 16 locations, 30 September–late April, with a maximum of: 6, Ashby, 11 November (RNEB). *1961–62:* at least 75 reported (54 + in November), 14 October–12 May. Maxima: 12, Northampton CBC, 30 December 1961; 10, Rockport, 26 October; 8–10, Arnold Arboretum, Jamaica Plain, throughout November

(RNEB). *1968–69:* An accurate record was not kept for the early part of
1969, but at least 75 were recorded during October 1968 (RNEB), including
24 banded, MBO; and 15 banded, Littleton (Baird). A single count of 25 +
was reported at the Middlesex Fells Reservation in January (Everett), and
6 northbound migrants were seen at North Scituate, 11 May 1969 (King).
*1971–72:* at least 25 recorded, 1 October–22 April (fide Emery), including: 12
banded, MBO, throughout October; and 7, East Quabbin, 30 October
(Yenlin). *1975–76:* at least 40 reported, 4 October–19 April, including 7,
Arnold Arboretum, Jamaica Plain, and 9, Hamilton, throughout January
(BOEM). *1980–81:* at least 14 recorded, 16 October–late April (BOEM),
including: 3, Salisbury, 2 November (Forster).

Less well-documented flights occurred in earlier years, but the numbers
and extreme dates do not exceed those recorded since 1955. There are still no
records from Nantucket and Martha's Vineyard. ***Extreme dates:*** 1, Lanesboro, 18 September 1975 (Minneci), to 1, Plum Island, 2 June 1962 (Conant,
Snyder).

## Tufted Titmouse *Parus bicolor*

**Range:** Eastern Nearctic; largely resident from southeastern Minnesota,
central New York, southern Vermont, New Hampshire, and Maine south to
the Gulf Coast and southern Florida. Recently expanding range northward.

**Status:** Locally fairly common resident in deciduous forests across the
state.

**Breeding:** Tufted Titmice are currently widespread as breeders in Massachusetts, although they are notably absent from the offshore islands and
from forested areas at higher elevations in the interior. Tufted Titmice have
recently undergone a major northward range expansion; Griscom and
Snyder (1955) listed the species as "hypothetical" in Massachusetts, and
Bailey (1955) listed only seventeen sight records between 1912 and 1954. The
first and second nests in the state were found in Waban in 1958 and 1959
(Appleton). In 1961, 1 pair with 4 young was seen in Fitchburg (Marble),
and, during the fall of 1961, a major influx was reported, with numerous
individuals reported at feeding stations at widely scattered localities in the
state. By 1962, 14 nesting pairs were reported between eastern Massachusetts
and the Connecticut River valley, and, in January 1963, 60 were reported
from 23 locations (fide Emery). The first Berkshire County nesting record
was established in Pittsfield, 18–29 June 1964 (Kelton).

Massachusetts CBC data suggests that the population had saturated the
state by the early 1970s, although banding totals at MBO continued to
increase through 1981. It appears that the increase of the Tufted Titmouse in
Massachusetts correlates with the gradual warming trend that has character-

ized New England winters over the past 25 years, as well as with the increase in winter bird feeding. Almost all Tufted Titmice in winter are found in close proximity to feeders. The first record for Martha's Vineyard was: 2, Chilmark, 22 January 1949 (Butler); however, the species continues to be rare on the island—e.g., 1, Martha's Vineyard CBC, 30 December 1978. *Egg dates:* May–June.

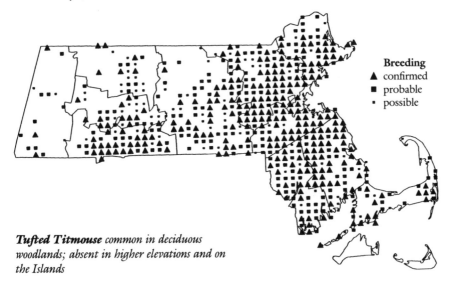

Breeding
▲ confirmed
■ probable
• possible

*Tufted Titmouse common in deciduous woodlands; absent in higher elevations and on the Islands*

**Nonbreeding:** Tufted Titmice seem to be among the more sedentary land birds in Massachusetts; however, noticeable concentrations away from known breeding localities in fall suggest that at least some dispersal occurs—e.g., 74 banded, MBO, fall 1974. As an indication of the species' current abundance in the state, the following CBC counts are exemplary: 1,017, Concord CBC, 30 December 1990; 970, Concord CBC, 31 December 1989; 604, Millis CBC, 15 December 1990.

**Remarks:** A "Black-crested Titmouse" (*P. b. atricristatus*) was reported from a feeder in Weymouth during November and December 1965 (Sylvester, O'Regan, VO). Although the AOU (1983) has included this record, it is here treated as unacceptable due to a lack of photographs or other fully convincing documentation.

# Red-breasted Nuthatch  *Sitta canadensis*

**Range:** Nearctic; breeds, in eastern North America, from central Manitoba and northern Michigan east to southern Labrador, Long Island, and New

Jersey, south in the Appalachian Mountains to western North Carolina. Irregularly migratory, with some birds reaching the Gulf Coast in winter after major flights.

**Status:** Uncommon and local breeder; uncommon spring and variously uncommon to very common fall migrant and winter resident.

**Breeding:** Red-breasted Nuthatches breed exclusively in coniferous forests (or patches of conifers in mixed forests), including cedar swamps and pine groves of the southeastern coastal plain. Although they breed regularly at higher elevations in the western part of the state, their nesting in eastern Massachusetts is markedly irregular, with most nesting records following major flights the previous fall. Recent evidence suggests that they nest more frequently in White Cedar swamps and White Pine groves in the eastern and southeastern parts of the state than was previously realized. They have even occasionally nested in ornamental conifers at localities such as Mt. Auburn Cemetery, Cambridge. *Egg dates:* 18 May–10 June.

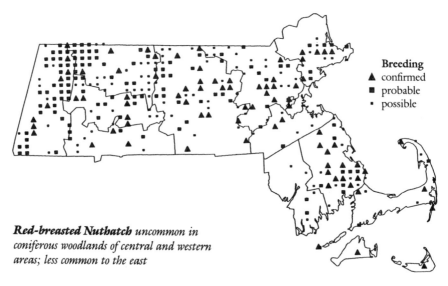

Breeding
▲ confirmed
■ probable
• possible

*Red-breasted Nuthatch uncommon in coniferous woodlands of central and western areas; less common to the east*

**Nonbreeding:** In spring, Red-breasted Nuthatches are uncommon migrants, with only a slight peak occurring in late April or early May in some years—e.g., 8, Plum Island, 26 April 1958 (Conant); 8, Nantucket, 6–13 May 1958 (Larsen); 8, Plum Island, 22 April 1961 (Conant). During fall migration, they vary considerably in their abundance from year to year; in some years none are recorded whereas in others (i.e., 1977, 1980) major flights occur throughout the Northeast (Bock & Lepthien 1972). Fall migrants are reported between late July and December, and peak numbers are usually recorded in October and November. *Fall maxima:* 220, throughout eastern Massachusetts, November 1977 (BOEM); 200, Weston, 26 December 1977

(Robinson); 35 +, Nantucket, 14–18 October 1980 (Stymeist, Veit, Laux, et al). Unlike the fall flights of the Black-capped Chickadee, Red-breasted Nuthatch irruptions are often followed by a high winter density because the birds apparently remain in Massachusetts for the winter—e.g., 158, Worcester CBC, 17 December 1977; 142, Concord CBC, 2 January 1978; 127, Greater Boston CBC, 18 December 1977.

# White-breasted Nuthatch   *Sitta carolinensis*

**Range:** Nearctic; resident from British Columbia, Montana, southern Quebec, northern Maine, and central Nova Scotia south to southern Baja California and southern Florida; absent from the Great Plains.

**Status:** Uncommon to fairly common resident, most numerous during fall and early winter.

**Breeding:** White-breasted Nuthatches breed in mature deciduous forests, using tree cavities and occasionally bird boxes for nest sites. They are widespread on the mainland and are increasing on the outer Cape, yet they remain rare on Nantucket. They are seldom reported in large numbers, except occasionally during migration and early winter, when they are concentrated around feeding stations. *Egg dates:* 3 April–1 May.

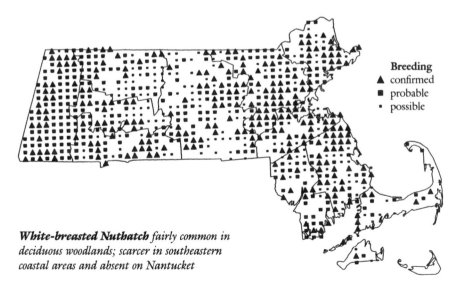

Breeding
▲ confirmed
■ probable
· possible

*White-breasted Nuthatch fairly common in deciduous woodlands; scarcer in southeastern coastal areas and absent on Nantucket*

**Nonbreeding:** Most White-breasted Nuthatches are resident in Massachusetts, but birds do appear at places where they do not breed, usually in April and from September to November—e.g., 15, Nahant, 20 April 1947 (Kelly);

3, Monomoy, 10 April 1955 (Goodell); 4, Nantucket, 25 April 1961 (Depue, Van Duyne); 6, Nantucket, 25 October 1980 (Veit).

The largest counts of White-breasted Nuthatches are generally recorded in early winter, when local populations are augmented by migrants from the north, and the birds concentrate at feeding stations, where CBCs monitor their numbers. *Winter maxima:* 521, Concord CBC, 30 December 1990; 494, Concord CBC, 1 January 1989; 411, Concord CBC, 26 December 1971; 39, Cape Cod CBC, 30 December 1981.

## Brown Creeper *Certhia americana*

**Range:** Nearctic; breeds, in eastern North America, from central Manitoba and Newfoundland south to northern Michigan and Long Island, and in the Appalachian Mountains south to western North Carolina. Winters south to the Gulf Coast and central Florida.

**Status:** Uncommon resident; variously uncommon to common migrant.

**Breeding:** Brown Creepers tend to breed in mature forests and seem to be partial to wet, swampy areas, including cedar and maple swamps in the southeastern part of the state. The nest is typically lodged behind a loose flap of bark, and less frequently it is placed in a cavity. Although the species is never found at a high density in summer, "seven pairs were found along two miles of back country roads and paths bordering hemlock-deciduous swamps in Sheffield in 1978" (McNair 1978). *Egg dates:* 6–23 May.

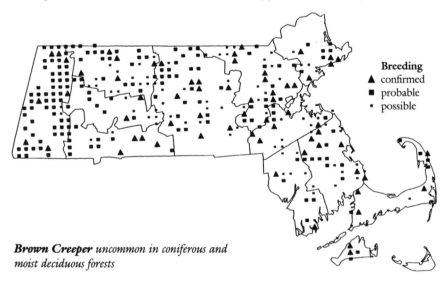

**Breeding**
▲ confirmed
■ probable
• possible

*Brown Creeper uncommon in coniferous and moist deciduous forests*

**Nonbreeding:** Creepers are generally less common in spring than fall. Residents commence singing in late March, but peak counts of migrants usually don't occur until late April and early May. ***Spring maxima:*** 25, Plum Island, 21 April 1961 (deWindt); 25, Provincetown, 28–29 April 1979 (Nikula, Trull); 24, Nahant, 30 April 1962 (Alexander et al); 20–30, Chappaquiddick, 6–20 April 1964 (Potter).

The number of Brown Creepers seen during fall migration varies from year to year. These variations probably reflect local weather conditions more than anything else. ***Fall maxima:*** 50, Nantucket, 28–30 September 1968 (Soucy); 40, Plum Island, 17 September 1964 (Forster); 25, East Orleans, 30 September 1973 (Forster); 20, Lynn Woods, 13 November 1980 (Heil).

Brown Creepers move into the woods during midwinter and are not generally attracted to feeding stations. Therefore, the number encountered on a given day is probably more reflective of the time spent in suitable habitat than of actual winter abundance. Counts of more than five individuals in winter are unusual, although the species is regularly present every year. ***Winter maxima:*** 65, Quabbin CBC, 30 December 1989; 54, Concord CBC, 30 December 1990; 44, Concord CBC, 27 December 1991.

# Rock Wren   *Salpinctes obsoletus*

**Range:** Western Nearctic and northern Neotropical; breeds from southern British Columbia east to western North Dakota and southern South Dakota south to southern Arizona and southern Texas; also in Central America to Costa Rica. Winters from northern California, southern Utah, and north-central Texas south through the southern portions of the breeding range.

**Status:** Vagrant: two records.

**Occurrence:** The first Rock Wren to occur in Massachusetts was discovered at Andrews Point, Rockport, 19 December 1965 (Nichols, Forster, Petersen, Proctor), where it remained until 25 January 1966, was seen by many observers, and was clearly photographed in color (photo at MAS). The second occurrence was: 1, South Orleans, 2 November 1991–mid-February 1992 (Thompson, VO, photo in AB 45: 65). The suggestion by the AOU (1983) that Rock Wrens in the East may have been "transported accidentally in railroad boxcars" is tenuous at best, particularly because most eastern records are from the period October to December, the season when many vagrants from the West typically occur.

# Carolina Wren   *Thryothorus ludovicianus*

**Range:** Nearctic; resident throughout southeastern North America, north to southeastern Wisconsin, southern Michigan, southern Ontario, and Massachusetts.

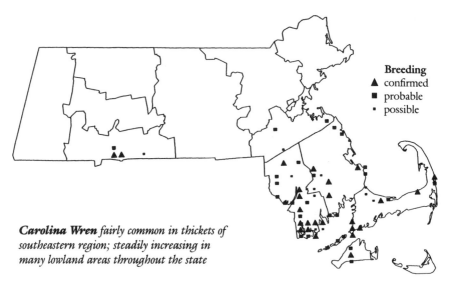

**Breeding**
▲ confirmed
■ probable
• possible

*Carolina Wren fairly common in thickets of southeastern region; steadily increasing in many lowland areas throughout the state*

**Status:** Locally fairly common resident, but historically subject to periodic fluctuations from year to year.

**Breeding:** Carolina Wrens require dense, swampy thickets and relatively mild winter weather for year-round survival and are thus most common in the southeastern parts of the state, most notably in Bristol, Plymouth, and Barnstable counties, along with Martha's Vineyard and the Elizabeth Islands.

Since they were first found nesting in Massachusetts at Naushon Island in 1901 (Brewster), Carolina Wrens have slowly, but erratically, increased, despite the fact that the entire population is occasionally eliminated by severe winters, such as in 1911–1912 and 1928–1929. Christmas Bird Count totals for Carolina Wrens suggest that their numbers appear to be largely correlated with the relative severity of winter weather. Typically, reestablishment has quickly followed each of these decimations. It is also possible that the increased amount of food provided by artificial feeding stations in recent years may be contributing to their gradual increase.

Away from the southeastern coast of the state, Carolina Wrens are uncommon and local residents. There are definitely two breeding records for Berkshire County (Stockbridge, 1955 and North Adams, 1975 [fide McNair 1978]), and, until recently, the species bred only rarely and erratically in the southern Connecticut River valley beginning about 1970 (Kellogg, pers. comm.). Since that time, it has slowly and steadily increased in a number of areas in central and western Massachusetts. Griscom and Snyder (1955) refer to an early nesting record from Essex County but give no details; however, the species definitely bred in Ipswich, July 1989 (Berry). Pairs of Carolina Wrens were present all summer in Worcester in 1975 and Carlisle in 1981 and

*Wrens*

1982, but nesting was not confirmed. By the 1980s, however, Carolina Wrens reached an all-time population high in Massachusetts (see CBC data that follows). *Maxima:* 20, Martha's Vineyard, 27–29 May 1978 (SSBC, Kenneally); 18, Naushon Island, June 1950 (fide Griscom & Snyder 1955); 10 +, Acoaxet, 18 May 1987 (Lynch); 10, Westport, 28 May 1990 (Stymeist); 7, Cuttyhunk Island, 22 July 1959 (Freeland). *Egg dates:* 8–10 June.

**Nonbreeding:** Although normally sedentary, Carolina Wrens regularly exhibit evidence of some migration or dispersal, as reflected by their appearance away from known breeding areas—e.g., 1, Nantucket, 24 May 1957 (Van Duyne, Depue); 1, MNWS, 23 October 1971 (Snyder); 3, Nantucket, 13 October 1979 (Veit, Litchfield). The highest counts of the year consistently occur in late fall and winter, when Carolina Wrens are tallied on CBCs or when they are attracted to feeding stations in residential areas. *Winter maxima:* 128, Buzzards Bay CBC, 15 December 1990; 120, Buzzards Bay CBC, 17 December 1988; 112, Taunton-Middleboro CBC, 23 December 1989; 76, Martha's Vineyard CBC, 3 January 1989; 58, Cape Cod CBC, 16 December 1990.

## Bewick's Wren *Thryomanes bewickii*

**Range:** Nearctic; resident through much of southern temperate North America but absent from the eastern coastal plain. Breeds regularly northeast to central Pennsylvania and southeastern New York but declining in eastern part of range.

**Status:** Vagrant: three, convincing, recent sight records.

**Occurrence:** The three convincing sight records of Bewick's Wren from Massachusetts are: 1, Cuttyhunk Island, 27 September 1975 (Petersen, Sorrie); 1, Monomoy, 12 October 1976 (Goodrich, Bailey); 1, Chatham, 14 September 1986 (Bailey, Goodrich). Other earlier sight records—e.g., 1, Southampton, 18–31 July 1933 (Graves); 1, Old Deerfield, 12 August 1951 (Bagg); 1, Sheffield, 17 October 1951 (Mazzeo)—mainly from western Massachusetts at improbable times of year, while possibly correct, lack sufficient details, making evaluation difficult.

## House Wren *Troglodytes aedon*

**Range:** Nearctic; breeds, in eastern North America, from southern Manitoba and northwestern New Brunswick south to northern Oklahoma and eastern North Carolina. Eastern birds winter in the southeastern United States northward to coastal Maryland.

**Status:** Uncommon to fairly common breeder on the mainland; uncommon on Cape Cod and the Islands. Uncommon to fairly common migrant away from breeding localities. Rare but regular in early winter, particularly during mild seasons, but not proven to survive the entire season.

**Breeding:** The nesting population of House Wrens in our area was severely depressed following the introduction of House Sparrows from Europe (1868 in Boston). Forbush (1929) states, "The disappearance of House Wrens was progressive from about 1875 to 1883, and after that they became rare and local. A few still remained in isolated old orchards." However, according to Griscom and Snyder (1955), House Wrens had regained their former abundance by 1930, after which time House Sparrows decreased from their period of maximum abundance around the turn of the century. There is no evidence of any noticeable change in the status of the House Wren since then. Today, they are common and familiar backyard birds, nesting in almost any suitable cavity, artificial or natural, from which they aggressively drive away other potentially competing species. Sample breeding counts include: 58, GBBC, 14 June 1980; 18 pairs, Breakheart Reservation, Saugus, 23 June 1974 (Stymeist); 30, NBBC, 15 June 1980. They are less common on the outer Cape and Islands—e.g., 5 pairs, Chatham, 3 June 1967 (Earle). House Wrens frequently raise at least two broods in a season. *Egg dates:* 25 May–1 August.

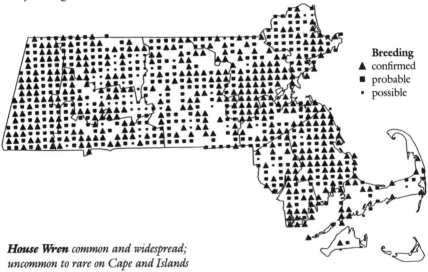

Breeding
▲ confirmed
■ probable
• possible

*House Wren common and widespread; uncommon to rare on Cape and Islands*

**Nonbreeding:** In spring, House Wrens usually arrive during the third or fourth week of April, and peak counts generally occur during mid-May. The earliest reliable date is: 1 banded, MBO, 16 April 1981; however, there are at least six reports earlier than 10 April, some of which undoubtedly pertain to misidentified Winter Wrens. *Spring maxima:* 46, Wellesley, 6 May 1961

(Leverett et al); 40, Essex County, 12 May 1946 (Griscom); 32, Wellesley, 15 May 1965 (Leverett et al). Most locally breeding House Wrens have departed by mid-September, but migrants are regular through early October. *Fall maxima:* 24, Northampton, 15 September 1972 (Yenlin); 18, Sharon, 6 September 1980 (Clapp); 17 banded, MBO, 9–30 August 1969; 9, Nantucket, 11 October 1979 (Veit, Litchfield). Stragglers routinely occur into December— e.g., 6 reported from the southeastern coastal plain following a mild fall, December 1977 (BOEM). A sample of midwinter records includes: 1, Falmouth, 9 February 1980 (Heil, Nikula); 1, Falmouth, 29 January 1972 (Gardler); 1, Falmouth, 25–26 January 1967 (Proctor, Forster).

# Winter Wren  *Troglodytes troglodytes*

**Range:** Holarctic; breeds, in eastern North America, from central Manitoba, eastern Quebec, and Newfoundland south to northern Michigan, southern New York, and Connecticut, and in the Appalachian Mountains to western North Carolina. Winters from southern New England and eastern Nebraska south to the Gulf Coast and Florida.

**Status:** Uncommon and local breeder; uncommon migrant. Very uncommon and irregular in winter.

**Breeding:** Winter Wrens typically breed in deep coniferous forests, especially near water. They are fairly common breeders on Mt. Greylock (McNair 1978)—e.g., 12, 24 June 1956 (Jameson)—but are rather local east of the higher Berkshire Hills due to habitat limitations. In the eastern part of the state, they breed irregularly in cool cedar and maple swamps, but they have never nested on Cape Cod or the Islands. *Egg dates:* (Maine) 20 May–8 August.

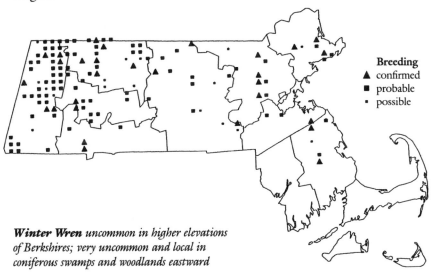

**Breeding**
▲ confirmed
■ probable
· possible

*Winter Wren uncommon in higher elevations of Berkshires; very uncommon and local in coniferous swamps and woodlands eastward*

**Nonbreeding:** Most spring migrant Winter Wrens are recorded between mid-April and mid-May, although, following a severe winter, active field observers often fail to record a single spring migrant. *Spring maxima:* 4, Fowl Meadow, Milton, 27 April 1977 (Veit, Litchfield); 3, Plum Island, 17 April 1976 (Grinley); 3, MNWS, 18 April 1977 (Kasprzyk); 3, Nahant, 29 April 1979 (Perkins); 3, MNWS, 19–29 April 1979 (Kasprzyk, VO). Fall migrants are recorded from early October through December, and some occasionally attempt to winter at coastal localities. *Fall maxima:* 19, Worcester, 8 October 1974 (Quinlan); 12, Sandy Neck, Barnstable, 20 October 1974 (Laux); 6, Plum Island, 8 October 1977 (Stymeist).

Some Winter Wrens successfully survive the entire winter in Massachusetts in mild seasons. Contrary to Bailey (1955), winter records are not always concentrated near the coastal plain. A substantial proportion of overwintering birds survive inland, frequently near breeding areas, but also in low thickets in the river valleys. A coastal maximum of: 15, Plymouth CBC, 21 December 1974, probably represents straggling migrants, most of which probably did not survive the winter. *Winter maxima:* 9 reports (6 in eastern Massachusetts), January 1968 (RNEB); 4, Concord CBC, 28 December 1975; 1, Marblehead, 1, North Andover, 1, Concord, and 1, South Hadley, February 1959 (RNEB); 1, Plymouth, 1, Manomet, 1, Sandwich, and 3, Bridgewater, February 1975 (BOEM); 1, Lincoln, 1, South Lincoln, 1, Mt. Tom, 1, Quincy, and 1, Concord, February 1962 (fide Emery). During severe winters, many either perish or, possibly, migrate farther south in midwinter.

# Sedge Wren   *Cistothorus platensis*

**Range:** Nearctic and Neotropical; several disjunct populations between southern Canada and Tierra del Fuego. Breeds, in North America, from central Manitoba and southern Quebec south to northern Arkansas and West Virginia; also on the Delmarva Peninsula and, erratically and very locally, in southern New England, New York, and New Brunswick. Winters from Maryland and Tennessee south to northeastern Mexico and east to Florida.

**Status:** Rare and irregular breeder and rare migrant; most frequently reported in fall.

**Breeding:** Sedge Wrens, unlike Marsh Wrens, do not breed in cattail marshes, but rather seem to prefer damp fields with dense growths of grasses and sedges, frequently with scattered low shrubs. Such habitats are now scarce in New England because many such fields are periodically mowed, have become overgrown, or have been spoiled by development. Currently, Sedge Wrens are among the state's rarest nesting passerines and are markedly erratic in their occurrence, frequently not even appearing at breeding stations until late June or July, and then often not returning to known breeding sites in successive years. Prior to 1940, at a time when there were many more fields suitable for nesting in Massachusetts (especially in northeastern Essex County and in the Connecticut River valley), Sedge Wrens were considered common summer residents, but the severe winter of 1940–1941 apparently decimated the population, which as of 1955 had "by no means yet recovered" (Griscom & Snyder 1955).

Nonetheless, during the summers of 1954 and 1955 (RNEB), Sedge Wrens were noted breeding at West Newbury–Newburyport (14 pairs), New Braintree (1 pair), South Egremont (1–2 pairs), Ashfield (1 pair), Williamsburg (2 pairs), Sheffield (1 pair), and Pittsfield (1 pair). The Essex County birds, located in the "Common Pastures" of Newburyport, Newbury, and West Newbury, declined to 9 pairs by 1961, 3 pairs by 1962 (fide Emery), and had entirely disappeared by 1965. They have not been recorded at that locality since. That habitat is no longer suitable for nesting due to human development. Since 1970, Sedge Wrens have been very scarce and erratic in their occurrence. In 1971, 6 birds were present in Dana, along the shores of Quabbin Reservoir, 6 June–26 August (Gardler, Stone, et al). They also bred in the Hadley-Amherst area in: 1973 (Gagnon); 1977 (2 pairs seen feeding young and removing egg shells from the nests, 26 June [Veit, Litchfield]); 1989 (VO). Additional singing individuals seen during the breeding season include: 1, Tewksbury, 27–28 June 1978 (Veit); 1, Framingham, 7–22 June 1980 (Forster); 1, Westboro, 26 July 1980 (Lynch, Carroll). *Egg dates:* 25 May–7 July.

**Nonbreeding:** The Sedge Wren is very rare as a spring migrant away from known or suspected nesting areas. Credible records since 1960 are: 1, Wellesley, 15–17 May 1965 (Petersen, Forster); 1, Moon Island, Boston Harbor, 17 May 1972 (Brown); 1, Prudential Building, Boston, 25 May 1974 (Wiggin et al). Since 1960, there have been a few acceptable fall sight records spanning the dates 6 September–23 October, with the majority coming from the outer coast, but including two found at the base of the Prudential Building in Boston. *Extreme dates:* 1, Amherst, 27–29 April 1960 (Hawks et al); to 1, Orleans, 29 December 1957 (CBC); 1, Eastham, 16 December 1979 (Petersen). One bird that was first seen on Nantucket, 17 November 1980, remained until 3 January 1981, after which it is believed to have died following a sudden cold snap (Veit, Andrews, et al).

# Marsh Wren  *Cistothorus palustris*

**Range:** Nearctic; breeds throughout most of the northern and central United States and southern Canada. *C. p. dissaeptus* breeds from northern North Dakota, southern Manitoba, southern Ontario, and New Brunswick south to eastern Kansas, southern Indiana, central New York, Massachusetts, and eastern West Virginia. Winters mainly along the Gulf Coast from Texas to Florida, occasionally north along the coast to Massachusetts.

**Status:** Locally common breeder and fairly common migrant. Some birds overwinter during mild seasons.

**Breeding:** In Massachusetts, Marsh Wrens breed in extensive cattail marshes at such localities as Plum Island, Lynnfield, Marshfield, Great Meadows National Wildlife Refuge in Concord, Brookfield, West Harwich, along the uppermost reaches of the salt marshes in northeastern Essex County, and in river meadows such as those that occur along the Sudbury and North rivers. The largest Massachusetts colony may be the one along the North River between Hanover and Marshfield (Petersen, pers. comm.). They are rare and local in the western part of the state due to lack of suitable habitat. *Maxima:* 135+, North River between Hanover and Marshfield, 7 June 1987 (Petersen); 100, GMNWR, 22 June 1967 (BBC); 50+, Plum Island, 1–6 June 1981 (BBC); 18 pairs, Charles River between Needham and Dedham, 7 July 1961 (Gardler); 16 pairs, West Harwich, 24 June 1973 (Blodget); 25+, Wayland, 13 July 1981 (Hines). *Egg dates:* 5 June–1 August.

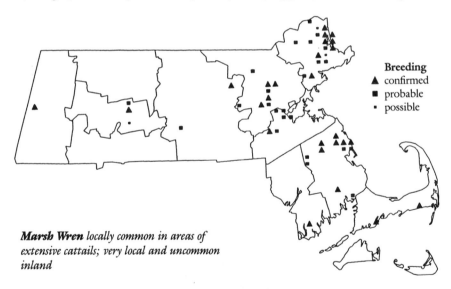

**Breeding**
▲ confirmed
■ probable
· possible

*Marsh Wren locally common in areas of extensive cattails; very local and uncommon inland*

**Nonbreeding:** The first Marsh Wrens of spring usually arrive by late April (8 records earlier than 20 April), and maximum counts from breeding colonies are recorded from mid-May on. Away from known breeding localities, Marsh Wrens are rarely recorded in spring—e.g., 1, Hadley, 8 April 1959 (Keith); 1, Monomoy, 29 May 1960 (Bailey); 1, Littleton, 28 May 1960 (Bolton); 1, Mt. Auburn Cemetery, Cambridge, 14 May 1971 (Stymeist); 1, Prudential Building, Boston, 25 May 1971 (Wiggin, Keenan); 1, Lancaster, 20 May 1975 (Merriman); 1, Nantucket, 20 April 1980 (Perkins). In fall, it is frequently difficult to separate migrant Marsh Wrens from local breeders, but some counts clearly represent influxes after the breeding population has departed (usually by early September)—e.g., 35, GMNWR, 21 September 1959 (Freeland); 42, South River, Marshfield, 17 September 1977 (Petersen).

Marsh Wrens are also rather frequently found in late fall and early winter in areas where they do not breed. For example, on Nantucket, where they are not known to nest, they are commonest in November—e.g., 20, Quaise, 20 November 1980 (Veit)—and December, usually remaining until heavy snows or severe cold drives them out. *Winter maxima:* 22, West Harwich, throughout December 1973 (Nikula); 4, GMNWR, 1 January 1966 (Corey). Although Marsh Wrens regularly survive into late December, even at inland locations, they are apparently gradually killed off by progressively worsening weather conditions and depleted food supplies, or else they migrate farther south in midwinter. Records of probable survivors include: 3, West Harwich, 19 March 1974 (Nikula); 1, South Peabody, 20 February 1980 (Heil); 1, Concord, 16–21 February 1960 (Gardler); 1, Wayland, 28 January 1962 (Petersen).

# Golden-crowned Kinglet  *Regulus satrapa*

**Range:** Nearctic; breeds, in eastern North America, from northern Manitoba, central Quebec, and Newfoundland south to northern Wisconsin and southern New York, and in the Appalachian Mountains to western North Carolina. Winters mainly in the southeastern United States, but many northeastern populations (north to Newfoundland) are resident or only partially migratory.

**Status:** Uncommon and local breeder; variously uncommon to very common migrant and winter resident.

**Breeding:** Golden-crowned Kinglets are restricted as breeders to dense stands of spruce and fir. In Massachusetts they nest on the higher mountains in Berkshire and Worcester counties as well as in exotic spruce plantations at several eastern localities. They were apparently more widespread in the early 1800s before many large conifer stands were cut. In Berkshire County, they are "very uncommon to uncommon and local" as nesters (McNair 1978), and, for the most part, are restricted to the northern sections of that region (McNair 1978). Griscom and Snyder (1955) stated that 15 pairs nested at Mt. Greylock, but counts there have been somewhat lower in recent years. Blodget and Clark found 3 pairs nesting at Mt. Watatic, Ashburnham, 2 July 1971, and estimated that during that season 20 pairs bred in northern Worcester County. On 26 June 1977, 3 territorial males were found in a spruce plantation in Lakeville, where adults were seen feeding young on 9 July (Petersen, Anderson). They have bred there more or less continuously since, as well as sporadically at one or two other locations elsewhere in Plymouth County. In a spruce plantation on Hog Island, Essex, 13 birds were heard singing, and at least one "nesting family" was found, 30 June 1979 (Berry). A pair nested in Falmouth for a first Cape Cod record in 1979 (fide Forster) and at Martha's Vineyard in 1983 (Keith). *Egg dates:* late May–29 June.

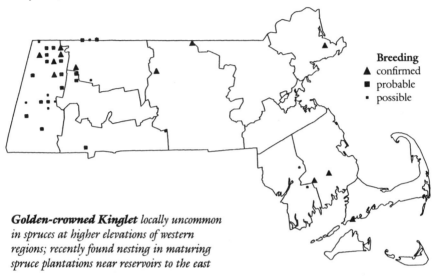

**Breeding**
▲ confirmed
■ probable
• possible

*Golden-crowned Kinglet locally uncommon in spruces at higher elevations of western regions; recently found nesting in maturing spruce plantations near reservoirs to the east*

**Nonbreeding:** The number of Golden-crowned Kinglets seen each year during spring and fall migration in Massachusetts is extremely variable. This variation seems to be dependent upon winter mortality in the south, variation in food supply in the north (cf Black-capped Chickadee), and in fall, upon suitable weather conditions for grounding large numbers of migrants. *Spring maxima:* 30, Mt. Auburn Cemetery, Cambridge, 6 April 1980 (Stymeist). *Fall maxima:* 200 +, Nantucket, 11 October 1976 (Veit, Perkins, Litchfield); 200, Plum Island, 7 October 1967 (Wiggin); 160, Pochet Island, Orleans, 30 September 1973 (Forster). The number of Golden-crowned Kinglets that spend the winter in Massachusetts appears to depend on a number of factors, including the relative severity of the weather and availability of food, both locally and to the north of Massachusetts where many local winterers originate. *Winter maxima:* 225, Buzzards Bay CBC, 14 December 1974; 222, Newburyport CBC, 27 December 1987; 221, Quabbin CBC, 30 December 1989; 111, Cape Cod CBC, 30 December 1967; 60, Lynn Woods, 19 January 1976 (Heil).

# Ruby-crowned Kinglet   *Regulus calendula*

**Range:** Northern Nearctic; breeds, in eastern North America, from northern Manitoba and central Labrador south to northeastern Minnesota, northeastern New York, and northern and eastern Maine, rarely to Massachusetts. Winters in the southeastern United States, north occasionally to Long Island and southeastern Massachusetts.

**Status:** Two confirmed nesting records. Variously common to occasionally abundant migrant; rare and irregular in midwinter.

**Breeding:** The first confirmed breeding of the Ruby-crowned Kinglet in Massachusetts occurred when an adult with a recently fledged young was seen at Borden Mountain, Savoy, 3 July 1932 (Bagg 1932). More recently, singing males, and occasionally pairs, have been seen on Mt. Greylock and in Savoy in 1973, 1975, 1976, and 1977, but the only evidence of recent nesting was the observation of a fledged young pursuing an adult at Savoy, 27 July 1976 (Quinlan). An anomalous sighting is that of two birds in dense spruce forest on Hog Island, Essex, 18 June 1977 (Berry). It would be most remarkable to find evidence of breeding there.

**Nonbreeding:** Ruby-crowned Kinglets are among the earliest songbird migrants to arrive in the state in spring, usually appearing during the first two weeks of April. They are normally rare before April and after mid-May. *Spring maxima:* 150, Mt. Tom, 23 April 1972 (Petersen); 125+, Provincetown, 28–29 April 1979 (Nikula); 100, Mt. Auburn Cemetery, Cambridge, 24 April 1979 (Perkins). During fall, peak numbers occur in early October, when the variation in numbers seen from year to year is perhaps most directly dependent upon proximal weather conditions. *Fall maxima:* 300+, Plum Island, 5 October 1975 (Veit); 150, Duxbury Beach, 7 October 1967 (Drury); 120, lower Cape Cod, 10 October 1981 (Heywood, Stymeist).

Although Ruby-crowned Kinglets regularly linger into early January, particularly in the Connecticut River valley and along the southeastern coastal plain, they rarely survive the entire season. *Winter maxima:* 35, throughout Massachusetts (including 15 on the Springfield CBC), January 1965 (RNEB); 33, eastern Massachusetts CBCs, December 1979; 12, Cape Ann CBC, 23 December 1961; 8, Buzzards Bay CBC, 15 December 1990; 6 (2 in the Connecticut River valley and 4 on the southeastern coastal plain), February 1972 (fide Emery).

# Blue-gray Gnatcatcher  *Polioptila caerulea*

**Range:** Primarily southern Nearctic; breeds, in the East, north to central Wisconsin, central Michigan, northern New York, and central Maine, and expanding northward. Winters from the Gulf Coast north to Virginia and south to Guatemala, Cuba, and the Bahamas.

**Status:** Increasingly widespread and locally fairly common breeder; uncommon to fairly common migrant.

**Breeding:** At the turn of the century, Blue-gray Gnatcatchers were regarded as accidental stragglers from the south (Howe & Allen 1901); however, they have expanded their range steadily northeastward since that time. Aside from a unique breeding record from Maine sometime prior to 1929 (Forbush 1929), gnatcatchers did not breed in New England until the late 1950s. Following a steady increase in the number of migrants reported in both spring and fall during the 1940s and 1950s (Ernst 1948)—e.g., 67 reported during 1953 (RNEB)—Blue-gray Gnatcatchers were first recorded nesting in Hingham, 1961 (fide Emery); Milton, 1965 (Keitt); Sheffield, 1968 (Fitz); Northampton, 1969 (fide Emery); Dunstable and Quabbin Reservoir, 1971 (fide Emery). They now breed practically throughout the state at scattered localities in both mature and secondary-growth deciduous forests, usually near water. *Maximum:* 13 singing males and 4 nests found along the Ipswich River, Essex County, 16 June 1979 (Heil). *Egg dates:* Data incomplete; probably mid-May–mid-June.

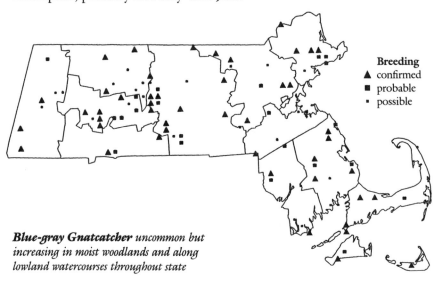

Breeding
▲ confirmed
■ probable
• possible

*Blue-gray Gnatcatcher uncommon but increasing in moist woodlands and along lowland watercourses throughout state*

**Nonbreeding:** The numbers of migrant gnatcatchers in Massachusetts have increased concurrently with their increase as breeders. They are rare before mid-April—earliest, 1, Mt. Auburn Cemetery, Cambridge, 10 April 1981 (Scott et al)—and after early October. *Spring maxima:* 20, Manomet, late April 1974 (Sorrie); 20, Harwich to Wellfleet, 20–30 April 1975 (Nikula); 20, Provincetown, 5 May 1979 (Nikula). In May 1984, Nikula observed a total of 66 gnatcatchers at Provincetown, with a maximum of 12 +, 12 May. *Fall maxima:* 10, Chatham, 14 September 1958 (Gardler); 8, Manomet, 26 August 1970 (Petersen); 6, Manomet, 3 September 1971 (Wait). *Extreme dates:* 10 during record-breaking, mild weather, CBCs (including: 2, Marshfield CBC), December 1984; 1, Manomet, 7 December 1978 (MBO staff); 1, Boston Public Garden, 4 December 1910 (Wright); 1, Manomet, 4 December 1975 (Kelley).

# Northern Wheatear   *Oenanthe oenanthe*

**Range:** Holarctic; two subspecies occur in North America. *O. o. leucorhoa* breeds in Greenland, southern Ellesmere Island, Baffin Island, northern Devon Island, northern Quebec, and coastal Labrador; vagrant to the East Coast of North America. *O. o. oenanthe* breeds in Alaska, Yukon, and western Mackenzie. Both populations migrate back to the Old World tropics in winter.

**Status:** Vagrant, or very rare migrant. Approximately thirty-five records; most frequent in fall.

**Occurrence:** The first Massachusetts record for the Northern Wheatear was: 1, Pigeon Cove, Rockport, 17 September 1910 (Lamb). The range of dates for subsequent occurrences is: 1, Duxbury Beach, 23 August 1976 (Walton et al), to 1, Rockport, 13 November 1966 (Bolte, Fowler). All but one of these records have occurred since 1954, with a maximum of seven different birds seen during the fall of 1976 (BOEM). Nearly all have appeared in coastal regions, with one exception: 1, Quabbin, 6 September 1978 (Gagnon et al). One bird found dead at Nauset, Eastham, 1 October 1976 (fide Bailey), proved to be of the race *O. o. leucorhoa*. In addition to these fall occurrences, there are four spring records from Massachusetts: 1, Plymouth Beach, 17 June 1964 (Bolton, Armstrong); 1, Osterville, 21 May 1980 (Proctor); 1, Chatham, 23 May 1980 (Nikula); 1, Newbury, 6 June 1980 (Soucy et al).

# Eastern Bluebird   *Sialia sialis*

**Range:** Eastern Nearctic; breeds throughout eastern North America northeast to southern Quebec, New Brunswick, and Nova Scotia, south to Nicaragua. Mainly winters in the southeastern United States northeast to southern New England.

**Status:** Uncommon, but slowly increasing, breeder and migrant; rare to very uncommon winter resident.

**Breeding:** Eastern Bluebirds nest in three distinct habitats in Massachusetts: in bird boxes and natural cavities adjacent to open fields and farmlands; in cavities in dead trees in secluded Beaver ponds; and in cavities in Pitch Pines of newly burned areas in the pine barrens of southeastern Massachusetts. Those nesting in the latter two habitats have maintained a more or less stable population over the historical period, whereas those in the first habitat listed seriously and steadily declined until the mid-1980s, when a slow recovery began.

Bull (1974) suggested that this decline was not the result of occasional heavy mortality during severe winters or periods of heavy rain in spring;

bluebird populations appear to recover from such losses quickly, often within 2 to 3 years. Instead, the decline of the Eastern Bluebird population seems to be attributable to four factors: usurpation of nesting sites by House Sparrows, with a decline especially apparent following the introduction of House Sparrows during the 1870s (Forbush 1929); a similar problem caused by European Starlings, which did not become common in Massachusetts until the 1920s; a destruction of rural habitats required by bluebirds during the last 20 years, particularly in eastern Massachusetts; and the heavy use of pesticides during the 1950s and 1960s.

On a more optimistic note, the increase in the Beaver population in Massachusetts over the past 75 years has led to an increase in the number of Beaver ponds at which bluebirds can nest. Additionally, bluebirds have shown modest increases in areas where the erection of many bird boxes has provided sufficient nesting spots to allow the bluebirds to successfully compete with more aggressive cavity-nesting species—e.g., 17 pairs fledged 123 young, High Ridge Wildlife Management Area, Westminster, June 1989 (Blodget).

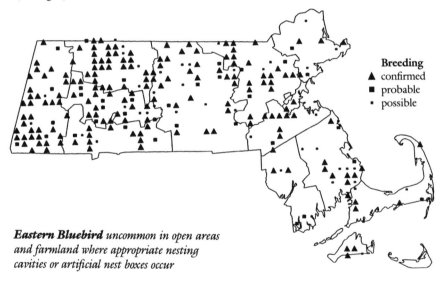

**Breeding**
▲ confirmed
■ probable
▪ possible

*Eastern Bluebird uncommon in open areas and farmland where appropriate nesting cavities or artificial nest boxes occur*

**Nonbreeding:** Spring migrants usually arrive in late February or March, and fall migrants may be found in October and November, including at coastal localities where they do not breed. Bluebirds on Cape Cod arrive in late fall, where they occasionally remain for the winter. If the ground remains open in winter, some bluebirds remain on their breeding territories throughout the year, where they subsist primarily on berries and seeds. *Spring maxima:* 100, New Marlboro, 9 February 1976 (Wilson, Morse); 14, Sharon, 23 March 1976 (Clapp). In eastern Massachusetts, counts at single localities have rarely exceeded 6 to 8 birds in the last 20 years, while counts of 25 to 40 are still occasionally reported in the Connecticut River valley and in Berkshire County. The timing of their arrival is directly dependent upon the local weather conditions, especially lingering snow cover and local temperature. *Fall maxima:* 200, Topsfield, 26 October 1947 (Kelly); 200, outer Cape Cod, 11–12 November 1950 (Snyder); 20, South Carver, 15 October 1980 (Davison); 14, Sharon, 12 October 1980 (Clapp). Large counts on Cape Cod seem to be a thing of the past. Winter numbers of bluebirds have varied considerably along with the overall change in the species' status in Massachusetts. Changes reflected by the Cape Cod CBC are exemplary— e.g., 236, Cape Cod CBC, 3 January 1954; 36, Cape Cod CBC, 3 January 1965; 11, Cape Cod CBC, 21 December 1975; 4, Cape Cod CBC, 16 December 1979. Other midwinter counts include: 12, Chatham, throughout February 1978 (Nikula); 10, Nantucket CBC, 2 January 1977; 7, Eastham, throughout February 1978 (Nikula).

## Mountain Bluebird   *Sialia currucoides*

**Range:** Western Nearctic; breeds from central Alaska, southern Yukon, and western Manitoba south to southern California and southern New Mexico. Winters south to northern Mexico. Vagrant to the East Coast.

**Status:** Vagrant: one record.

**Occurrence:** A Mountain Bluebird, judged by its plumage characteristics to be a male in first prenuptial molt (Lloyd-Evans, pers. comm.), was captured alive on a ship 70 miles south-southeast of Nantucket (40° 08′N, 69° 34′W), 28 April 1980 (Cherry). When it died, the specimen was deposited at the MCZ (#330895).

## Townsend's Solitaire   *Myadestes townsendi*

**Range:** Western Nearctic; breeds from central Alaska and southern Mackenzie east to the eastern foothills of the Rocky Mountains south to central Arizona and New Mexico; also in northern Mexico. Winters south to southern Mexico.

**Status:** Vagrant: four records.

**Occurrence:** This peculiar thrush of the Rocky Mountains and the Pacific Coast has occurred four times in Massachusetts. The first two occurrences were in the same year, i.e., 1, West Gloucester, 3 December 1957 (Viator 1958); 1, Worcester, 25 December 1957 (Heywood). Other records are: 1 photographed, West Tisbury, Martha's Vineyard, 1 December 1981–10 February 1982 (Whiting, Laux, Petersen, photos at MAS); 1, Leyden (Greenfield CBC), 31 December 1990 (Potter, Morrissey, Fairbrother).

## Veery  *Catharus fuscescens*

**Range:** Nearctic; breeds, in eastern North America, from southwestern Ontario, southeastern Quebec, and southwestern Newfoundland south to northern Illinois, southern Pennsylvania, and northern New Jersey; also south in the Appalachian Mountains to northern Georgia. Winters in tropical South America south to central Brazil.

**Status:** Common breeder and spring migrant; uncommon in fall.

**Breeding:** Veeries breed in moist deciduous forests throughout the mainland portions of the state but are particularly numerous in Red Maple swamps east of Worcester County. They are largely absent as breeders from Cape Cod and the Islands, with the notable exception of Naushon Island, where they are common in the island's beech forest. Griscom and Snyder (1955) indicate that in June, over 100 could be heard in a day at Naushon; however, the species seems to have declined since then. In general, there is no direct evidence indicating that Veeries have significantly changed in overall abundance during the historical period. *Maxima:* 57, Middleboro, 15 June 1985 (SSBC); 39, NBBC, 15 June 1980; 22, East Quabbin, 12 June 1971 (Yenlin); 22 banded, Easton, 5–6 July 1967 (Anderson). *Egg dates:* 20 May– 30 June.

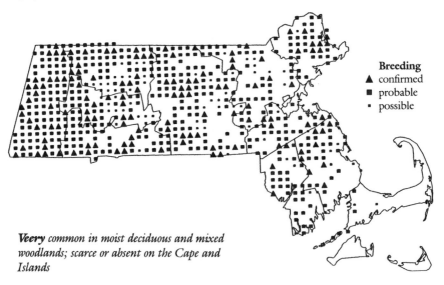

Breeding
▲ confirmed
■ probable
• possible

*Veery common in moist deciduous and mixed woodlands; scarce or absent on the Cape and Islands*

**Nonbreeding:** Veeries normally migrate earlier in both spring and fall than Gray-cheeked and Swainson's thrushes, with peaks most often occurring in early May and late August. Aside from counts of calling nocturnal migrants, it is unusual to record more than 10 to 15 Veeries per day per locality in spring. *Spring maxima:* 400 night calls, Cambridge, 11 May 1959 (Nisbet);

114 + night calls (3:52–4:30 a.m.), Amherst, 10 May 1961 (Simmers); 60, Springfield area (including many local breeders), 22 May 1971 (ABC); 30, Provincetown, 25 May 1981 (Nikula); 22, Plum Island, 18 May 1967 (Forster); 16, MNWS, 27 April 1983 (Heil). Ordinarily, Veeries are rare after the third week of May away from known breeding areas. *Fall maxima:* 85 night calls, Cambridge, 6 September 1959 (Simmers); 19 banded, Raynham, 6–27 August 1968 (Anderson); 14 banded, MBO, 1–9 September 1973; 11, Chatham, 29 August 1982 (Forster); 10, MNWS, 1 September 1982 (Heil); 6, Monomoy, 30 August 1965 (Forster). *Extreme dates:* 1, MNWS, 23 April 1977 (Stymeist, Leverich); to 1, Nantucket, 17 October 1979 (Veit).

# Gray-cheeked Thrush  *Catharus minimus*

**Range:** Northern Nearctic (and extreme eastern Paleactic); breeds from eastern Siberia east to northern Quebec and northern Labrador, south sporadically to northern Nova Scotia and (*C. m. bicknelli*) in the Appalachian Mountains of central Maine, northern Vermont, New Hampshire, and extreme northeastern New York. Winters in the West Indies—especially Hispaniola (*C. m. bicknelli*)—and tropical South America.

**Status:** Generally very uncommon migrant; largest numbers are heard calling at night during migration. Formerly bred near the summit of Mt. Greylock.

**Breeding:** Gray-cheeked Thrushes (*C. m. bicknelli*) were first detected breeding at the summit of Mt. Greylock in 1888 (Faxon 1889) and were then present somewhat erratically until 1972, with 6 to 11 pairs estimated breeding consistently from 1934 to 1960 (VO). From about 1960 on, they gradually dwindled to 1 to 2 pairs in 1972 (Gagnon), and none have been seen or heard there since then. McNair (1978) expressed the opinion that their disappearance from Mt. Greylock may be due to increased human disturbance near the summit since 1973. *Egg dates:* 18 June 1948 (Snyder, Tousey).

**Nonbreeding:** An active observer may expect to see 1 to 10 Gray-cheeked Thrushes during either spring or fall migration in Massachusetts, although larger numbers are occasionally heard calling overhead at night. The call uttered by nocturnally migrating Gray-cheeked Thrushes is very similar to that of the Veery and the Rose-breasted Grosbeak, so reports of night-calling migrants must be evaluated with caution. In spring, most migrants are seen during late May to early June and in fall from late September to mid-October. These migration periods are supported by banding data from the Manomet Bird Observatory. *Spring maxima:* 80 calling overhead in one hour at night, Cambridge, 11–12 May 1959 (Nisbet); 40 calling overhead in one-half hour (1:30–2:00 a.m.), Wellesley, 16 May 1965 (Forster); 8 +, Provincetown, 25 May 1981 (Nikula); 6, Plum Island–Newburyport, 2 June 1967

(Forster); 6 banded, Plum Island, 25–26 May 1957 (Goodridge). *Fall maxima:* 34 calling overhead at night, Cambridge, 19–20 September 1958 (Simmers); 22, Nantucket, 30 September 1957 (Heywoods); 19 banded, MBO, 1–19 October 1968; 12 calling overhead at night, South Peabody, 3–4 September 1981 (Heil); 5, Monomoy, 23 September 1968 (Forster); 5, Sandy Neck, Barnstable, 29 September 1973 (Petersen). *Extreme dates:* 1, MNWS, 27 April 1983 (Heil); 1, Salem, 29–30 April 1928 (PMS #6372); to 1 dead, Prudential Building, Boston, 18 August 1975 (Wiggin); 1 banded, MBO, 10 November, 1977.

# Swainson's Thrush   *Catharus ustulatus*

**Range:** Nearctic; the race *C. u. swainsoni* breeds from Central British Columbia, Central Quebec, and southern Labrador south, in eastern North America, to northern Minnesota, southern Ontario, southern Quebec, central New England, and in the Appalachians to West Virginia. Winters from central Mexico south to central Brazil and northern Argentina.

**Status:** Uncommon and declining breeder in Berkshire County; common to abundant migrant (mainly evidenced by calling birds at night).

**Breeding:** Swainson's Thrushes breed only in the dense boreal spruce and fir forests of the Berkshires. McNair (1978) estimated a total of 40 to 50 pairs there; however, the species has apparently declined considerably since that time. According to Griscom and Snyder (1955), they formerly bred in northern Franklin and Worcester counties but were gradually extirpated as the spruce woods were cut. *Egg dates:* 29 May–early July.

**Nonbreeding:** Swainson's Thrush is a convenient species for contrasting counts of migrants heard at night with numbers seen on the ground the following day. During some nights, particularly those that are foggy or rainy, very large numbers of Swainson's Thrushes are heard as they migrate low overhead. Totals of thousands of birds have occasionally been counted at night during May and September. Observers on the ground, however, seldom see more than 10 Swainson's Thrushes in a day in either spring or fall, although occasionally many more are found. The largest ground counts usually correlate to local weather conditions, such as fog and rain, which tend to put the migrants down. *Spring maxima:* 4,700 night calls, Boston, 21 May 1975 (Leverich); 2,000 night calls in two hours, Cambridge, 11–12 May 1959 (Nisbet); 100, Monomoy, 24 May 1974 (Harris); 80, Essex County, 25 May 1974 (Petersen); 45, Provincetown, 25 May 1981 (Bailey). Migrants

*The "Bicknell's" race of the **Gray-cheeked Thrush** was first discovered nesting near the southern limit of its range on the summit of Mt. Greylock in 1888. Since that time, its numbers have slowly diminished, and by 1972 the species was extirpated in Massachusetts.*   ▷

are regularly recorded into mid-June—e.g., 11 banded, MBO, 1–12 June 1973; 27, Plum Island, 2 June 1967 (Petersen, Forster ). *Fall maxima:* 2,700 night calls, Cambridge, 19–20 September 1958 (Willman); 600 + night calls, South Peabody, 3–4 September 1981 (Heil); 500 during daylight hours on the ground (a most extraordinary concentration), Monomoy, 23 September 1968 (Bailey, Forster); 200, Nahant, 13 October 1958 (Harte). That Swainson's Thrushes regularly occur through mid-October is attested to by banding totals at MBO: e.g., 67, 1–11 October 1968; 42, 2–14 October 1966. Fall migrants are occasionally detected near the coast as early as August—e.g., 3, Plum Island and West Newbury, 9 August 1983 (Petersen). *Extreme dates:* 1, Mt. Auburn Cemetery, Cambridge, 22 April 1970 (Stymeist); to 1, Littleton, 1 January 1972 (Baird); 1, Norfolk, 15 December 1979 (Fuller, CBC); 1, Falmouth, 15 December 1979 (J. and R. Baird, Forster, CBC). Rare before early May and after October. Many late fall and winter reports of this species have been rejected because of proven confusion with the Hermit Thrush.

# Hermit Thrush  *Catharus guttatus*

**Range:** Widespread Nearctic species; the race *C. g. faxoni* breeds from central Yukon, eastern Saskatchewan, northern Ontario, and southern Labrador south on the East Coast to southern New England and northern New Jersey. Winters in the southeastern United States northeast to southern New England and south to Guatemala and El Salvador.

**Status:** Fairly common local breeder; fairly common migrant. Rare to uncommon, but regular, during all but the most severe winters.

**Breeding:** Hermit Thrushes are restricted as breeders to coniferous forests, including stands of hemlock and White Pine in the interior and pine-oak woodlands in the southeastern parts of the state. At inland sites, they seem to be particularly numerous in areas that are regenerating following logging operations. Although they have probably declined over the last 80 years due to habitat destruction, locally, there is little data to support this.

Hermit Thrushes are decidedly local in the eastern part of the state and appear to be common only in the Myles Standish State Forest in Plymouth and in areas of similar habitat elsewhere in Plymouth County and on Cape Cod. They have declined on Cape Cod in recent years as Pitch Pine forests have succeeded to oak. *Maxima:* 30 + , MSSF, 20 June 1979 (Heil); 14, Wellfleet, 23–24 May 1969 (Donahue). Most nesting-season counts from the eastern part of the state are of 1 to 3 pairs per locality, and McNair (1978) considered them uncommon nesters in Berkshire County. *Egg dates:* 17 May–14 June.

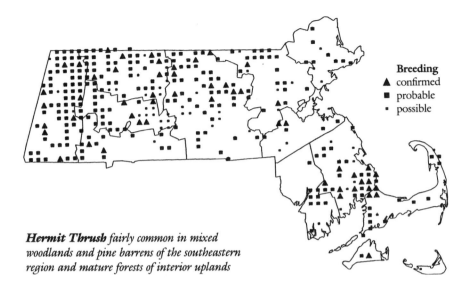

**Hermit Thrush** *fairly common in mixed woodlands and pine barrens of the southeastern region and mature forests of interior uplands*

Breeding
▲ confirmed
■ probable
· possible

**Nonbreeding:** Hermit Thrushes arrive earlier in spring and depart later in fall than other Massachusetts thrushes, possibly as a result of the close proximity of their winter quarters. Because most winter within the United States, they are occasionally susceptible to population fluctuations due to heavy mortality during severe winters. In spring, peak numbers of Hermit Thrushes are recorded during the second and third weeks of April, and migrants are rare after mid-May. *Spring maxima:* 45 (5 dead), Prudential Building, 18 April 1972 (Wiggin); 40+, Mt. Tom, 22 April 1972 (Petersen); 35, Dorchester, 16 April 1976 (Murphy); 30+, Plum Island, 29 April 1956 (Sands et al); 30, MNWS, 29 April 1956 (Jodrey); 27, Mt. Auburn Cemetery, Cambridge, 19 April 1972 (Stymeist).

The fall migration of Hermit Thrushes is particularly protracted. Although peak counts have usually occurred in the last week of October, they are fairly common from early October through early December. *Fall maxima:* 52, Salisbury and Plum Island, 30 October 1976 (Forster, Hamilton); 31, Lynn, 22 October 1980 (Heil); 30, Provincetown, 27 October 1976 (Nikula); 27, Mt. Tom, 15 October 1969 (Gagnon). In winter, most Hermit Thrushes are recorded on the CBCs in late December and early January. From the published records, there is little evidence that individuals often survive the entire winter in Massachusetts; however, it is probable that few observers search for this shy and retiring species later in winter than the CBC period. Nonetheless, one present at Strongwater Brook, Salem, 5 January–16 February 1981 (Heil) may have survived the winter, and McNair (1978) listed twelve records for January and February in Berkshire County. *Winter maxima:* 23, Buzzards Bay CBC, 17 December 1988; 20, total from all eastern Massachusetts CBCs, 15–31 December 1979; 18, Cape Cod CBC, 19

December 1976; 16, Buzzards Bay CBC, 14 December 1991; 9, North Falmouth, 20 December 1975 (Veit).

## Wood Thrush  *Hylocichla mustelina*

**Range:** Eastern Nearctic; breeds from southeastern South Dakota, northern Michigan, southern Quebec, central Maine, and Nova Scotia south to eastern Texas and northern Florida. Winters from southern Texas to Panama.

**Status:** Common but declining breeder and fairly common spring migrant; uncommon in fall. Very rare in early winter.

**Breeding:** Wood Thrushes breed in mature deciduous forests, frequently near low, wet areas. In the eastern United States, they have extended their breeding range northeastward over the last 75 years, and Griscom and Snyder (1955) stated: "It is now common on the eastern coast and on Naushon Island (since 1902), local on Martha's Vineyard (since 1919), slowly spreading east on Cape Cod, abundant in the Connecticut Valley and common in the Housatonic Valley, often nesting in residential areas of cities." McNair (1978) considered Wood Thrushes to be "common to very common nesters" throughout Berkshire County. In the eastern part of the state, however, their breeding status and abundance seem to have undergone a noticeable decline since about 1980. *Maxima* (recent): 43, NBBC, 15 June 1980; 41 pairs, Wellesley, June 1956 (Freeland); 32, GBBBC, 13 June 1981. *Egg dates:* 25 May–26 June.

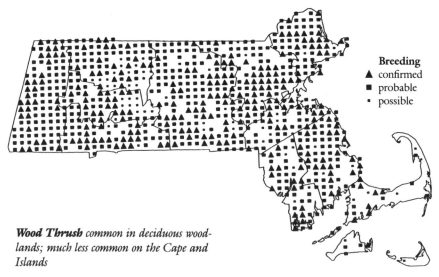

Breeding
▲ confirmed
■ probable
▪ possible

*Wood Thrush common in deciduous woodlands; much less common on the Cape and Islands*

**Nonbreeding:** Most Wood Thrushes breed south of New England, so relatively few migrants pass through our area from the north, unlike the

*Catharus* thrushes. There has, however, been an increase in the numbers of spring migrants reported over the last 50 years. In that season, the first Wood Thrushes arrive at breeding sites during the last few days of April and the first week of May. Ordinarily, it is unusual to see more than six migrants in a day. *Spring maxima:* 60, Wellesley, 9 May 1959 (Leverett et al); 20 (including some residents), Westport area, 20 May 1979 (BBC). During the fall, Wood Thrushes gradually depart in late August and September, and it is unusual to see more than two or three during a day at coastal migrant traps. Stragglers are frequent into late October, and there are at least six November records since 1955. *Fall maxima:* 18, Easthampton, 15 September 1955 (Reidel); 5 banded, MBO, 3–14 October 1966. *Extreme dates:* 1, Concord CBC, 26 December 1971–6 January 1972 (Bemis et al); 1 clearly photographed, Millis CBC, 21 December 1980; 1 freshly dead, Milton, 3 December 1976 (Wachman).

# Fieldfare   *Turdus pilaris*

**Range:** Palearctic; breeds from southern Greenland and Scandinavia east to northern Siberia and south to central Europe, central Russia, and southern Siberia. Winters from Iceland, the British Isles, southern Scandinavia, and central Europe south to the Mediterranean regions, Asia Minor, and northwestern India; casual in North America.

**Status:** Vagrant: one record.

**Occurrence:** The single state record of this highly migratory Palearctic thrush occurred when a bird appeared at Nine Acre Corner, West Concord, 6–14 April 1986 (Richards [see Richards 1986], VO, Arvidson 1986). During the period of its stay, it consorted with American Robins and was observed by carloads of birders who came from all over the Northeast to enjoy it.

# American Robin   *Turdus migratorius*

**Range:** Nearctic; breeds, in eastern North America, from northern Manitoba and Labrador south to central Florida and Texas. Winters north to southern New England, coastal Nova Scotia, southern Ontario, and central Michigan.

**Status:** Very common breeder; abundant migrant and locally common winter resident.

**Breeding:** American Robins are among the state's most widespread and numerous nesting birds, breeding from offshore islands to the summits of the highest mountains in Berkshire County. They are most common in suburban areas and in open areas interspersed with patches of forest, and families of robin fledglings are a frequent sight on suburban front lawns during late June, July, and August (Howard 1966, 1967, 1968). Ancestrally, robins were retiring birds of deep forests, and a few still breed in these habitats in Massachusetts. **Maximum:** 523, GBBBC, 14 June 1980. **Egg dates:** 12 April–25 July; 2–3 broods yearly.

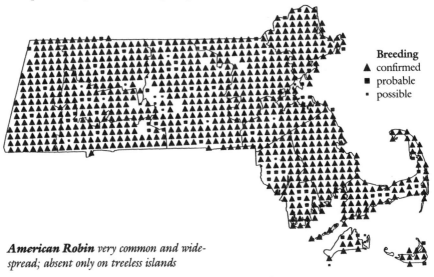

Breeding
▲ confirmed
■ probable
• possible

**American Robin** *very common and widespread; absent only on treeless islands*

**Nonbreeding:** Flocks of diurnally migrating American Robins are among the state's most conspicuous birds during both the spring and fall migration seasons. Groups may be seen passing overhead or, in late summer and fall, entering large communal evening roosts (Andrews 1981). Although the peak of migration occurs in mid-April and late October, robins occasionally move about en masse during midwinter, depending upon local weather conditions and food supply. **Spring maxima:** 3,000, Boxford, Georgetown, and West Newbury, 14 April 1957 (Argues); 2,500, Newburyport–West Newbury, 19 April 1965 (Kearney et al); 2,000 +, West Newbury, 14 April 1974 (Petersen); 1,080, Hadley, 19 April 1967 (Yenlin); 865, Littleton, 19 April 1967 (Baird). **Fall maxima:** 5,500 migrating, Littleton, 21 October 1967 (Baird); 4,200 flying to roost, West Roxbury, 15 October 1972 (Atwood); 2,000, Williamsburg, 19 October 1955 (Graves); 1,500–2,000, West Chop, Martha's Vineyard, 17 October 1961 (Bagg).

Robin numbers in winter are determined by food abundance and snow cover. Large flocks occasionally appear suddenly on the outer coast in the aftermath of midwinter snowstorms or after periods of unseasonably mild weather. In mild seasons, robins successfully survive, usually subsisting upon the fruits of ornamental and agricultural trees and shrubs. The berries of Red Cedar and American Holly form a substantial portion of the natural diet of robins in southeastern Massachusetts. In severe winters, virtually all robins disappear from the state. *Winter maxima:* 3,095, Mid-Cape Cod CBC, 27 December 1988; 1,655, Cape Cod CBC, 18 December 1988; 1,000 +, Wellfleet, 7 January 1979 (Nikula); 1,000, Conway, 28 February 1954 (Rockwood); 960, Quincy CBC, 19 December 1976.

**Subspecies:** American Robins breeding in Massachusetts are of the race *T. m. migratorius*. In addition, the well-marked race, *T. m. nigrideus* ("Blackbacked" or "Newfoundland" Robin), the breeding form of Newfoundland, Labrador, and eastern Quebec, is of regular occurrence in Massachusetts during spring and fall, as has been proven by the collection of about twenty-five specimens in both spring and fall. One winter specimen—Cambridge, 17 February 1873—suggests that they may occasionally winter here (Griscom & Snyder 1955).

# Varied Thrush  *Ixoreus naevius*

**Range:** Western Nearctic; breeds from north-central Alaska and northwestern Mackenzie south to northwestern California and northwestern Montana. Winters south to northern Baja California. The two Massachusetts specimens are *I. n. meruloides*, the more easterly subspecies, as are all other East Coast specimens.

**Status:** Rare but increasingly frequent late fall and winter visitor since 1961.

**Occurrence:** The first Varied Thrush specimen for Massachusetts was collected in Ipswich, 12 December 1864 (Maynard). Almost a century elapsed before another was recorded—i.e., 1, Rockport, 23 November 1961 (Geddes, Murphy, Kieran, Jodrey). Since then, there has been a continuous increase in the number of sightings, primarily of individuals coming to feeders between November and April. Varied Thrushes have occurred in marked flights, occasionally with several birds reported in one winter, or with none seen in other years. Eastward vagrancy in this species is thought to be triggered by heavy snows in the Rocky Mountains, which drive numbers of the birds to lower altitudes and latitudes in search of food (Keith 1968). Significant winter flights occurred in the following years. *1962–63:* 1, Groton, 24 December (Harrington); 1, Hubbardston, 5 January–1 March (fide Emery); 1, Hamilton, 28 February–7 March (fide Emery). *1967–68:* 1 killed, Woods Hole, 29 October (Gardield); 1, Andover, 5 December–4 March (Stevens); 1, Dartmouth, 25 December–14 January (Lees). *1969–70:* 5 reported, North Eastham, Waban, Rockport, Holliston, and Westhampton, between 17 November and 25 March (fide Emery). *1971–72:* 7 reported, Northampton, Great Barrington, Attleboro, Blandford, South Egremont (2), and Holbrook, 29 November–19 April (fide Emery). *1977–78:* 7 reported, Brewster, Bedford, Melrose, Ipswich, West Concord, Wayland,

and North Eastham, 5 December–early February. After a lapse of six weeks, 8 additional birds were seen in late March and early April, all in eastern Massachusetts (BOEM). *1981–82:* 4 reported, Framingham, Manomet, Eastham, and Dennis, 24 December–23 January (BOEM). *1983–84:* 3 reported, South New Salem, Buckland, Pittsfield, December–5 April (BNWM). *1987:* 1 dead, Concord, 26 December (fide Clayton, MCZ #332829).

## Gray Catbird   *Dumetella carolinensis*

**Range:** Nearctic; breeds from southern British Columbia east to southern Quebec and Nova Scotia south to central New Mexico, the central Gulf states, and northern Florida. Winters along the southeastern coast from Massachusetts (rarely) to northeastern Mexico and also in the Mississippi River valley north to southern Illinois.

**Status:** Very common breeder throughout the state and very common to abundant migrant. Rare but regular in winter, mainly on the southeastern coastal plain.

**Breeding:** For nesting, Gray Catbirds prefer moist thickets and swampy woods with dense secondary growth and are thus most numerous on the coastal plain, in shrubby swamps of southeastern Massachusetts, and at lower altitudes in the interior river valleys. They are also often conspicuous in well-planted suburban areas. *Maxima:* 244, GBBBC, 14 June 1980; 195, (MVBBC), 22–25 May 1981; 180, NBBC, 15 June 1980; 175, Wellesley, June 1959 (Freeland); 126, MCCBBC, 20 June 1982; 50, Littleton, June 1960 (Bolton). *Egg dates:* 22 May–10 August.

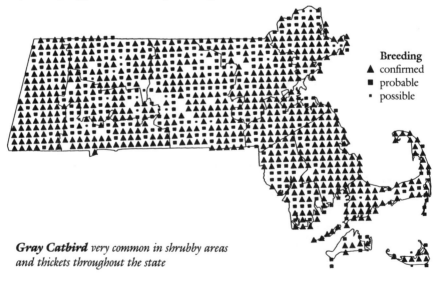

Breeding
▲ confirmed
■ probable
• possible

*Gray Catbird very common in shrubby areas and thickets throughout the state*

**Nonbreeding:** The majority of the resident Massachusetts catbirds arrive during early May, with early arrivals routinely reported during the fourth week of April. Sightings earlier than mid-April probably pertain to birds that overwintered in Massachusetts. *Spring maxima:* 135 banded, MBO, May 1981; 100+, Nahant, 10 May 1961 (Argue); 75, Mt. Auburn Cemetery, Cambridge, 13 May 1964 (Argue); 45, Boston Public Garden, 19 May 1967 (Emery). In the fall, the gradual departure of local breeders during September is often obscured by influxes of migrants from farther north. *Fall maxima:* 900 banded, MBO, August–November 1981; 200, Plum Island, 6 September 1975 (Drummond et al).

Gray Catbirds often survive the winter in coastal southeastern Massachusetts, and there are at least five records of proven winter survival in Berkshire County. *Winter maxima:* 55 on all CBCs in eastern Massachusetts, 15–31 December 1979 (an especially mild fall); 50, Westport CBC, 17 December 1988; 41, Martha's Vineyard CBC, 3 January 1989; 23, Mid-Cape Cod CBC, 27 December 1988. Usually from one to four birds survive the entire winter in Massachusetts—e.g., 6 singles during March 1960 and 1962 (RNEB).

# Northern Mockingbird   *Mimus polyglottos*

**Range:** Southern and south-central Nearctic; mainly resident from central California, central New England, and Nova Scotia south to Baja California, the Isthmus of Tehuantepec, and southern Florida; also in the Greater Antilles east to the Virgin Islands.

**Status:** Common resident; most numerous on the outer coast during late fall and winter. Some migrants are noted in spring and fall.

**Breeding:** Howe and Allen (1901) considered the mockingbird to be a "very rare summer resident: breeding at Chatham, Springfield, Marshfield, Groton. . . ," while Forbush (1929) stated that they were "resident the entire year, but most commonly observed in coastal regions from November–April." All authorities concurred that, although mockingbirds gradually increased in Massachusetts from about 1870 until 1955, they were notably erratic. They typically showed up at widely scattered locations in the state, usually around feeding stations with nearby dense shrubbery and mainly during the winter season. Single birds did, however, appear in midsummer on a number of occasions (see map in Forbush, op cit), and nesting was confirmed prior to 1900 at Nantucket, Springfield, Northampton, Northfield, Groton, Arlington, and "possibly" at Hyannis and North Truro.

The adverse influence of severe winters upon mockingbirds was evident to Forbush and to Griscom and Snyder (1955), who pointed out that very few reports followed the winters of 1888–1889, 1919–1920, and 1947–1948. It is likely that the mockingbirds that attempted to overwinter in those years died from starvation or freezing. A second pronounced increase in the Massachusetts mockingbird population began in the early 1960s and reached a peak in the late 1970s, but it seems to have leveled off since then. There appears to be a relationship between the increase of mockingbirds and the amelioration of the winter climate in Massachusetts. The gradual warming trend in New England winters since 1955 correlates closely with the observed population increase. They have also unquestionably benefited from the tremendous increase in suburban plantings (especially *Rosa multiflora*), which has taken place since the 1950s.

Mockingbirds are absent from the most heavily forested portions of the state in Worcester County and in the Berkshires. They breed most frequently in suburban habitats, which provide dense shrubbery and ornamental conifers for nesting, tall perches for singing males, and plenty of food for winter sustenance, primarily in the form of fruits on ornamental plantings. *Egg dates:* 3 June–19 August.

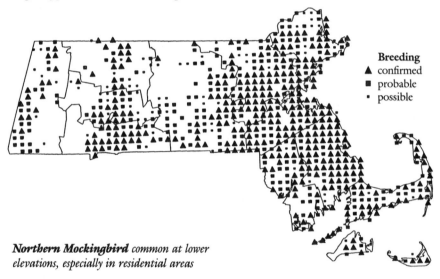

**Breeding**
▲ confirmed
■ probable
• possible

*Northern Mockingbird common at lower elevations, especially in residential areas*

**Nonbreeding:** It is not known to what extent the mockingbirds that nest in Massachusetts migrate, but small flocks are occasionally seen migrating south overhead—e.g., 3 together, Plum Island, 15 September 1974 (Forster); 1 with Blue Jays, Framingham, 26 September 1981 (Forster). Otherwise, migrants are difficult to separate from local residents. The largest totals of mockingbirds in Massachusetts have been recorded during the CBCs, both because of the mockingbird's greater abundance and concentration around suburbia at that time and because of the comparative lack of reporting in other seasons. *Winter maxima:* 314, Concord CBC, 28 December 1980; 285, Concord CBC, 30 December 1990; 282, Concord CBC, 1 January 1989; 187, Buzzards Bay CBC, 20 December 1980; 171, Concord CBC, 20 December 1978.

# Sage Thrasher  *Oreoscoptes montanus*

**Range:** Western Nearctic; breeds from southern British Columbia and Montana south to northern California, southern Nevada, northern New Mexico, and western Oklahoma. Winters southeast to extreme southern Texas. Vagrant east of the Mississippi River.

**Status:** Vagrant: one record.

**Occurrence:** The only occurrence of a Sage Thrasher in Massachusetts pertains to a bird discovered and photographed at Plum Island, 26 October 1965 (French, photos at MAS). The majority of other East Coast records are also during the month of October.

# Brown Thrasher  *Toxostoma rufum*

**Range:** Eastern Nearctic; breeds from southeastern Alberta, southern Ontario, southwestern Quebec, and New Brunswich south to eastern Texas, the Gulf Coast, and Florida. Winters in the southeastern United States north on the Atlantic Coast to Massachusetts.

**Status:** Uncommon to fairly common breeder and migrant. Rare but regular in winter east of the Berkshires.

**Breeding:** Brown Thrashers breed in dry secondary growth, along power line cuts, in dry forests bordering fields, and in coastal thickets. They are less likely than Gray Catbirds to nest close to human habitation. In Massachusetts, they are most numerous as breeders on the coastal plain, such as in the pine barrens of Myles Standish State Forest, Plymouth, and in the interior river valleys. They are absent from the higher mountains. *Maxima:* 40, GBBBC, 17 June 1979; 18 pairs, Wellesley, June 1956 (Freeland); 14, Littleton, June 1960 (Bolton). *Egg dates:* 9 May–21 June.

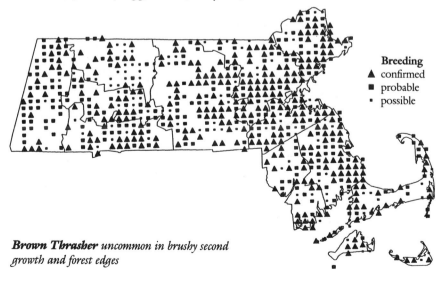

Breeding
▲ confirmed
■ probable
▪ possible

*Brown Thrasher uncommon in brushy second growth and forest edges*

363

**Nonbreeding:** As with Gray Catbirds, resident Brown Thrashers arrive gradually during spring and depart gradually during fall, thus making the numbers of true migrants difficult to determine. In spring, the first residents begin to appear on their nesting territories during the third and fourth weeks of April, but the largest numbers are typically recorded during the first half of May. *Spring maxima:* 65, Wellesley, 15 May 1965 (Leverett et al); 60, Plum Island, 7 May 1949 (Griscom); 40, East Longmeadow, 3 May 1969 (Weigand). During the fall, peak counts of 10 to 15 birds are frequently reported from late August to late September, primarily along the immediate coast. *Fall maxima:* 18, Plum Island, 27 August 1988 (Lynch); 13 Plum Island, 13 August 1990 (Delorey).

Brown Thrashers regularly survive the entire winter in Massachusetts but usually only in the vicinity of feeding stations or in coastal thickets with an abundance of berries. They are widespread, but less numerous, than Gray Catbirds during the winter, and they seem to be as frequent inland in eastern Massachusetts and in the Connecticut River valley as they are on the southeastern coastal plain. There are, however, no proven instances of winter survival in Berkshire County. *Winter maxima:* 22, eastern Massachusetts, February 1967 (RNEB); 18, eastern Massachusetts and Connecticut River valley, February 1966 (RNEB); 5, Connecticut River valley, February 1972 (BNWM).

# American Pipit   *Anthus spinoletta*

**Range:** Holarctic; breeds in arctic North America and in the Rocky Mountains south, in the East, to Newfoundland, with peripheral populations on the Gaspé Peninsula and at Mt. Katahdin, Maine, and Mt. Washington, New Hampshire. Winters in the southern United States, north occasionally to Massachusetts on the East Coast.

**Status:** Locally common to very common migrant, more numerous in fall. Rare and irregular in winter.

**Occurrence:** Migrant American Pipits are most frequently found in open areas such as agricultural fields, airports, beaches, and salt marshes. The species is highly gregarious, and the largest flocks are usually found in agricultural fields in the Connecticut River valley. During the protracted spring migration from late March to mid-May, 1 to 50 birds are ordinarily observed, with peak counts usually occurring in April. *Spring maxima:* 250, Hadley, 26 April 1969 (Yenlin, Gagnon); 200, Hadley, 24 April 1954 (Eliot). During the fall, the highest counts occur in October. *Fall maxima:* 750 +, eastern Massachusetts, 11–24 October 1976 (BOEM); 400 +, Hadley, 25 October 1969 (Yenlin); 300 +, Hadley, 1 November 1970 (Yenlin); 250 +, Lincoln, 28 October 1967 (Petersen). At the outer coast, flocks of 50 to 100 are more typical.

American Pipits are very unusual after early winter—e.g., 1, Deerfield, 17–

20 February 1955 (Boyden et al); 1, Gloucester, 11–18 February 1967 (BBC); 1, Truro, 10–13 February 1973 (Forster). *Extreme dates:* 1, Nantucket, 6–28 June 1951 (Heywood); 1, South Wellfleet, 25 June 1963 (fide Bailey); 2 (with male giving flight song), summit of Mt. Greylock, 5–6 June 1953 (Snyder et al); 1, Provincetown, 3 June 1977 (Forster).

## Sprague's Pipit  *Anthus spragueii*

**Range:** Nearctic; breeds from northern Alberta east to central Manitoba south to Montana, North Dakota, and northwestern Minnesota. Winters from southern Arizona and southern New Mexico east to northwestern Mississippi and southern Louisiana south through Mexico.

**Status:** Vagrant: two records.

**Occurrence:** The first Sprague's Pipit ever recorded in Massachusetts was discovered at the Provincetown airport during the Stellwagen Bank CBC, 17 December 1988 (Smith, Heil). During the weeks that followed, the bird was seen by dozens of observers and definitively photographed (see BOEM 17: 139) before its disappearance on 12 February. The second record was established when one was found at the Wachusett Reservoir, Clinton, 26 October–2 November 1991 (Blodget, VO). In addition to being recognizably photographed, the bird gave distinctive call notes that were heard on various occasions.

## Bohemian Waxwing  *Bombycilla garrulus*

**Range:** Holarctic; breeds, in North America, from Alaska east to northern Manitoba and south to central Washington and southern Alberta. Highly erratic in winter; found most regularly in the northwestern United States and southwestern Canada (north to southeastern Alaska) but wanders eastward with increasing regularity to central Maine and much more rarely to New Brunswick and Nova Scotia.

**Status:** Highly erratic rare winter visitor; increasingly frequent since 1955.

**Occurrence:** Griscom and Snyder (1955), in their harsh critical review of the records of Bohemian Waxwings from Massachusetts, may have obscured any major irruptions that occurred prior to 1955, so this species' historical status is unclear. Bohemian Waxwings were undoubtedly rarer in New England before 1960 than they are at present, and many reports of Bohemian Waxwings then, as now, probably involved misidentified Cedar Waxwings. Nonetheless, Bull (1974) showed that pronounced eastward incursions occurred in the winters of 1879–1880 and 1919–1920, and Wright (1921) describes in detail a flight that brought 21 Bohemian Waxwings to eight localities in Massachusetts between February and April 1919 (not 1920 as stated by Griscom and Snyder 1955).

A definite increase has occurred since 1955, with major irruptions into New England recorded in 1961–1962 and 1968–1969. During the winter of 1961–1962, 33 were recorded in Massachusetts, with the largest single flock being: 20, Ipswich, 26 February (Lunt). In 1968–1969, the largest flight to reach New England in recorded history (Finch 1969) brought 330 + birds to Massachusetts, including: 235, Worcester Airport, 18 February (Blodget); 75, Pittsfield, 9 February (Purdy et al); 20, Wellfleet (first Cape Cod record), 12 February (Bailey). This Massachusetts flight spanned the dates 24 December 1968 (Andover) to 26 May 1969 (Amherst).

Although no other Massachusetts flights approaching the magnitude of the one in 1968–1969 have been recorded, the species has been reported nearly every winter since 1970–1971, with a number of coastal reports in late fall and early winter—e.g., 4, North Scituate, 1 November 1975 (Sorrie et al); 2, Truro, 2 November 1980 (Petersen); 1, Tuckernuck Island CBC, 1 January 1981; 1, Nantucket, 28–29 November 1981 (Veit et al). *Maxima* (since 1969): 50, New Marlboro, 9 January 1980 (Bailey); 13, Athol, 28 December 1975 (Coyle).

## Cedar Waxwing  *Bombycilla cedrorum*

**Range:** Nearctic; breeds across most of the northern United States and southern Canada, and in eastern North America from central Manitoba and Newfoundland south on the coast to southern New Jersey and in the mountains to northern Georgia. Moves about erratically during migration

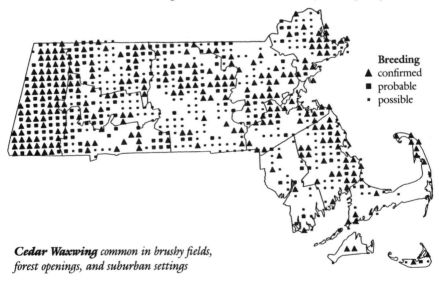

*Cedar Waxwing common in brushy fields, forest openings, and suburban settings*

and winter; recorded from New England south to Mexico and the Greater Antilles in midwinter.

**Status:** Common breeder and migrant; variously rare to locally fairly common in winter, especially near the coast. Highly erratic in abundance and in timing of migration.

**Breeding:** Cedar Waxwings have one of the most protracted breeding seasons of any Massachusetts passerine. The birds appear to settle down and nest wherever berries and fruit are abundant, most often in orchards or secondary growth near open fields. Throughout the rest of the year, they wander about in nomadic flocks. Their status has changed little since 1900, although they now breed on Cape Cod and the Islands (cf Griscom & Snyder 1955) in varying numbers. *Egg dates:* 30 May–late August; one record of eggs hatching on 19 September.

**Nonbreeding:** Peak numbers of migrating Cedar Waxwings are seen in late May and early June, and again during August and September. In addition, nomadic flocks are reported throughout the year, their erratic movements apparently governed by localized food abundance. *Spring maxima* (including nomadic flocks): 400, Waltham, 11 March 1947 (Griscom & Snyder 1955); 160, Framingham, 24 May 1980 (Forster); 150 +, Beverly, 27 April 1957 (Jameson et al); 150, East Longmeadow, 14 April 1965 (LeFave). *Summer maxima:* 200, Annisquam, 31 July 1945 (Griscom & Snyder 1955); 70, NBBC, 15 June 1980; 17 pairs Newburyport, June–July 1956 (deWindt). *Fall maxima:* 300, Nantucket, 2–5 September 1977 (BBC, Drummond); 250, Nantucket, 30 August 1953 (Griscom & Snyder 1955); 200, Pittsfield, early November 1971 (Goodrich); 180 +, Tuckernuck Island, 28 August 1974 (Veit).

The distribution of Cedar Waxwings in winter is greatly influenced by the presence or abundance of fruits and berries. *Winter maxima:* 1,090, Buzzards Bay CBC, 15 December 1984; 654, Concord CBC, 29 December 1985; 521, Millis CBC, 17 December 1988; 150, Chatham, 31 January 1982 (Nikula); 110, Pittsfield, 27 February 1962 (fide McNair). Griscom and Snyder (op cit) state that coastal reports of 200 are not uncommon, although counts of that magnitude since 1955 are unusual.

# Phainopepla  *Phainopepla nitens*

**Range:** Southwestern Nearctic; mainly resident north to central California, southern Nevada, and southern Utah.

**Status:** Vagrant: two sight records.

**Occurrence:** On 7 October 1977, Margaret LaFarge carefully studied a bird feeding on viburnum berries and flycatching from a perch atop a small juniper on Tuckernuck Island. Her convincing, detailed, written description left little doubt that the bird was an immature male Phainopepla, an identification that she later confirmed against a series of specimens at the Peabody Museum at Yale University. The date and location are entirely appropriate for a bona fide vagrant, and there is precedent for the species in New England as evidenced by the occurrence of a Phainopepla at Block Island, Rhode Island, 14 November 1975 (AOU 1983). Curiously, the Tuckernuck observation brought to light a previously unpublished record of a Phainopepla, apparently an adult male, which was present at a feeder on Nantucket in February 1973 (Andrews et al). At the time, the bird was assumed to be an escaped cage bird, but in light of the above records that conclusion seems highly improbable.

# Northern Shrike  *Lanius excubitor*

**Range:** Holarctic; breeds, in North America, from northern Alaska east to central Labrador south to southern Alaska, northern Quebec, and southern Labrador. Winters, in eastern North America, regularly south to southern New England and in major flight years to Virginia and Maryland.

**Status:** Irregular; variously rare to fairly common migrant and winter resident.

**Occurrence:** The Northern Shrike is an irruptive species. The extent and magnitude of the bird's southward migrations appear to be determined by the availability of rodents and small birds on their boreal breeding grounds and the number of young shrikes produced during the previous season. Although some authors (i.e., Bent and Brewster) have suggested that these southward incursions occur at four-year intervals, Massachusetts data suggests that these flights occur at more irregular intervals. Flight years appear to occur in clusters, with "echo" incursions following the heaviest flights, as in the winters of 1978–1979 and 1979–1980. Griscom and Snyder (1955) cite an incursion in 1949–1950, when 12 were seen in one day at Nantucket; however, in recent decades, the largest flight occurred in 1978–1979, when a minimum of 100 birds was reported from eastern Massachusetts alone (BOEM).

In flight years, the first migrants are ordinarily seen during the last week of October—earliest, 6 October (Griscom & Snyder 1955)—with peak counts occurring in December and January. Most birds have departed by early April, the latest report being 1 May (Griscom & Snyder 1955). Northern Shrikes are most prevalent in open country where abundant supplies of rodents exist, such as on Cape Cod and the Islands, in the Plum Island–Salisbury area, and in the Connecticut River valley. They also occasionally hunt small passerines around bird feeders. *Maxima:* 18, Nantucket CBC, 31 December 1978; 10, Concord CBC, 30 December 1978.

**Remarks:** It seems ironic to note that shortly after House Sparrows were introduced to Boston, a warden was hired to shoot Northern Shrikes on the

Boston Common in order to protect the House Sparrows. The warden shot upwards of 50 shrikes in one winter on the Boston Common (probably circa 1878–1879, Brewster 1906). Such a figure not only documents the abundance of Northern Shrikes during that winter, but also suggests that some individuals must move about considerably during the course of the winter.

## Loggerhead Shrike  *Lanius ludovicianus*

**Range:** Nearctic; breeds throughout most of the United States and north to central Saskatchewan and southern Manitoba but has disappeared from much of the Northeast during the past 50 years. Winters in the southern part of the breeding range, very rarely north to southern New England.

**Status:** Rare migrant and very rare winter resident. Extirpated breeder.

**Breeding:** Historically, Loggerhead Shrikes bred in Berkshire County (late 1800s) and in the Connecticut River valley (Greenfield in 1901 [Griscom & Snyder 1955]); however, the species has always been a rare nester in Massachusetts, and nesting attempts have traditionally been sporadic. The most recent breeding records include: 4 young fledged, Newburyport, 8 July 1956 (deWindt); 4 young fledged, Danvers, 9–11 June 1956 (Grayce); 1 young fledged, Berlin, 11 June 1956 (Crompton et al); 5 (including young), Newburyport, August 1957 (deWindt); 1 pair nesting, Danvers, June 1957 (VO, RNEB); 1 pair and 3 fledged young, Newbury, 2 May–early June 1971 (Forster, VO). There is no evidence that Loggerhead Shrikes have bred anywhere in Massachusetts since 1971, although there are two recent summer records of solitary adults: 1, Plymouth, 27 July 1974 (Stymeist); 1, Newbury, 8–9 June 1991 (Weissberg).

**Nonbreeding:** As recently as the 1960s, Loggerhead Shrikes were uncommon but regular migrants in Massachusetts during April and from late August to early October, with as many as ten reported per season. They have always been most numerous in fall. Since 1975, only 1 to 2 shrikes have been reported in spring and fall, most often inland in the spring and on Cape Cod and the Islands in fall.

Although they are very rare, there are a few convincing records of Loggerhead Shrikes in winter—e.g., 1, Salisbury, 20 September 1975–25 January 1976 (Moore et al); 1, Barnstable, 1 February 1976 (Pease); 1, Martha's Vineyard, 14–15 February 1976 (Daniels); 1, Concord, 2 January 1977 (Kenneally et al).

## European Starling  *Sturnus vulgaris*

**Range:** Originally Palearctic; introduced to North America in the late 1880s. Now breeds virtually throughout North America, in the East, north to central Ontario, central Quebec, and southern Labrador. Retreats from northernmost portions of the breeding range in winter.

**Status:** Very common breeder; abundant migrant and winter resident.

**Breeding:** The history of the introduction of European Starlings into the Northeast is well documented by Forbush (1927), who showed that they became abundant and widespread by 1920, although they were susceptible to heavy winter mortality in severe seasons. Griscom and Snyder (1955) state, "Maximum numbers were reached from 1928–1933, when flocks of half a million were reported. It has been steadily decreasing since then, with winter killing and hurricanes as the chief known causes."

They are currently among the most widespread and numerous nesting birds in the state, being absent only from the most extensive forests. They nest in both natural and artificial cavities and frequently usurp nesting sites that would otherwise be used by Purple Martins, Eastern Bluebirds, Eastern Screech-Owls, and woodpeckers. *Egg dates:* early April–July.

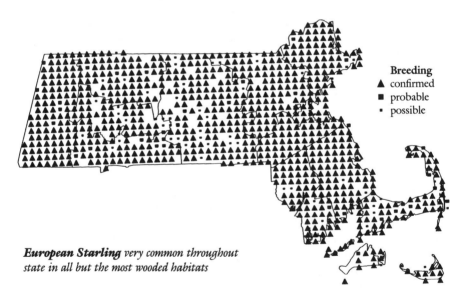

Breeding
▲ confirmed
■ probable
• possible

*European Starling very common throughout state in all but the most wooded habitats*

**Nonbreeding:** Starlings are regularly migratory, as is suggested by the flocks of 5,000 to 10,000 birds that are regularly seen on coastal salt marshes and in coastal thickets between October and December.

Maximum counts for the year are obtained by counting birds flying into two of the largest known winter roosts in the state: the Mystic River Bridge in Everett and the Fore River Bridge in Quincy. Combined CBC totals for these two roosts obtained on the Greater Boston and Quincy CBCs have ranged between 180,000 and 210,000 since 1960; also, 193,668, Greater Boston CBC, 18 December 1988.

# White-eyed Vireo  *Vireo griseus*

**Range:** Southeastern Nearctic; breeds from central Iowa, southeastern Pennsylvania, and eastern Massachusetts south to the Gulf Coast. Winters in the Gulf Coast states south to northern Honduras and Cuba.

**Status:** Locally uncommon breeder; uncommon to rare migrant.

**Breeding:** Prior to 1880, White-eyed Vireos were widespread breeders in Massachusetts. Brewster (1906) stated, "Up to about 1880, White-eyed Vireos bred regularly and rather commonly in a dozen or more localities within the Cambridge region." Townsend (1905) reported that they bred commonly in Swampscott in the 1870s and 1880s and implied that he knew of other nesting records for Essex County. According to McNair (1978), the only nests found in Berkshire County were in the Housatonic Valley, in Williamstown sometime prior to 1858, and in Sheffield in 1888 and 1896. Forbush (1929) suggested that White-eyed Vireos bred frequently in Bristol County and that there were a few nesting records from the Connecticut River valley and, possibly, Worcester County, all during the period before 1880. In summary, it seems that White-eyed Vireos were widespread and locally fairly common breeders in Massachusetts during the mid- to late 1800s.

Between 1880 and 1930, White-eyed Vireos all but disappeared as nesting birds in Massachusetts. Griscom and Snyder (1955) implied that they did not breed at all during that period and that they occurred only in the Westport area as rare stragglers in spring migration. This decline could have been due to exceptionally heavy winter mortality in the south because the breeding habitat required by the species in Massachusetts did not change substantially during those years.

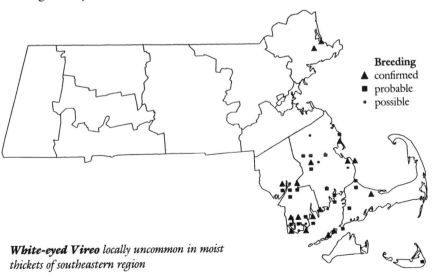

**Breeding**
▲ confirmed
■ probable
. possible

*White-eyed Vireo locally uncommon in moist thickets of southeastern region*

Since about 1940, White-eyed Vireos have been gradually increasing, first as spring migrants and eventually as breeding birds. By 1950, 21 migrants were reported in May, and Griscom and Snyder (1955) reported a possible nesting record from Essex County in 1953. By the 1960s, the species was a fairly common breeder in the Westport region—e.g., 14 singing males, 2 June 1966 (Petersen, Forster), and they have gradually extended their breeding range since then. However, there are no recent breeding records from either the Housatonic or Connecticut river valleys, but territorial birds were reported in Worcester County in 1971 and 1978 (*The Chickadee*). During the Massachusetts Breeding Bird Atlas Project, several pairs were located in eastern Massachusetts (north to Plum Island), and they continue to breed fairly commonly on the southeastern coastal plain—e.g., Plymouth, Marshfield, Falmouth, Westport, Naushon Island, Martha's Vineyard. *Egg dates:* 22 May–18 June.

**Nonbreeding:** The White-eyed Vireo is rare in Massachusetts before late April and after October. In spring, there are usually not more than 1 or 2 per day per locality, mostly in May. *Spring maxima:* 5 (probably mostly local breeders), Plymouth, 30 May 1973 (Sorrie). *Fall maxima:* 12 banded, MBO, 29 August 1974; 9, Plymouth, 20 September 1975 (SSBC, Harrington). *Extreme dates:* 1, Acoaxet, 9 April 1989 (D'Entremont); 1, Chatham, 13 April 1973 (Bailey); to 1, East Falmouth, 15 December 1979 (Nikula, Heil). There are also four records for November.

## Solitary Vireo   *Vireo solitarius*

**Range:** Nearctic; the race *V. s. solitarius* breeds from northeastern British Columbia east to northern Ontario, northern Quebec, and Newfoundland and south on the East Coast to northern New Jersey. Winters from the Gulf Coast states south to Guatemala.

**Status:** Fairly common breeder from Worcester County west; rare and local in eastern Massachusetts and absent from Cape Cod and the Islands. Fairly common migrant.

**Breeding:** Solitary Vireos prefer extensive mixed forests that contain stands of White Pines or hemlocks. Brewster (1906) remarked, "[They] suffered severely from cold and starvation in the South in the winter of 1894–1895, and since then they have not revisited eastern Massachusetts in anything like its [sic] former numbers." Griscom and Snyder (1955) point out that the Solitary Vireo population was again depressed following the hurricane of 1938, "which blew down many stands of White Pine." In the western part of the state, where there are still extensive tracts of forest, Solitary Vireos may possibly be as numerous as they were during the mid-1800s, but they have remained rare and local east of Worcester County since the early 1900s, presumably due to the progressive alteration and destruction of their habitat. *Egg dates:* 13 May–26 June.

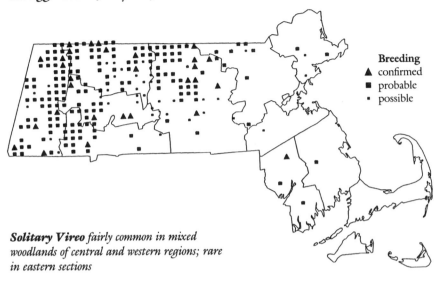

**Breeding**
▲ confirmed
■ probable
▪ possible

*Solitary Vireo fairly common in mixed woodlands of central and western regions; rare in eastern sections*

**Nonbreeding:** The Solitary Vireo is the earliest vireo to arrive in spring and usually the last to depart in fall. After the Red-eyed Vireo, it is the most abundant vireo to occur on migration in Massachusetts. General arrival occurs in mid-April, and by mid-May Solitary Vireos are rare away from known breeding localities. The fall migration extends from early September to mid-October. *Spring maxima:* 15, Nahant, 12 May 1974 (Leahy); 14, Newburyport, 15 May 1955 (deWindt); 14, Nahant, 10 April 1961 (Argue). *Fall maxima:* 12, Holyoke, 26 September 1970 (Yenlin); 12, Orleans, 5 October 1974 (Goodrich); 10, Chatham, 9 October 1981 (Nikula). *Extreme dates:* 1, Harwich, 9 April 1962 (Walsh); to 1, Nantucket, 30 December 1978 (Surner, Yaukey, Smart); 1, North Falmouth, 16 December 1978 (Stymeist et al). There are six additional November records.

**Subspecies:** *V. s. plumbeus*, which breeds east to southwestern South Dakota and northeastern Nebraska, has been reported once in Massachusetts: 1, MNWS, 29 September 1961 (Snyder, Searles). The field description stressed "the smooth gray from bill to end of tail . . . with no break at neck . . . pure, clean white below, with not a touch of yellow."

# Yellow-throated Vireo   *Vireo flavifrons*

**Range:** Eastern Nearctic; breeds from southeastern Manitoba and southeastern Quebec south to Texas and central Florida. Winters mainly from Mexico to northern South America.

**Status:** Uncommon and local breeder and rare migrant.

**Breeding:** Prior to 1900, Yellow-throated Vireos were widespread and fairly common breeders in Massachusetts, although they have always been absent from Cape Cod and the Islands. Griscom and Snyder (1955) reported that Yellow-throated Vireos had greatly decreased by 1955, but a decrease between 1875 and 1901 was already apparent to Brewster (1906). Their status has not changed appreciably since 1955. They are local in their distribution, being most numerous and widespread in the Connecticut River valley and in western Berkshire County. There are also scattered pairs breeding in eastern Massachusetts.

They nest in shade trees and orchards in rural settings, even in the centers of small towns, as well as in undisturbed mixed forests, such as at Quabbin Reservoir and occasionally the Boxford State Forest. In western Worcester County, and in the eastern foothills of Berkshire County, Yellow-throated Vireos appear to breed in rural habitats similar to those occupied by Warbling Vireos in eastern Massachusetts. *Egg dates:* 24 May–17 June.

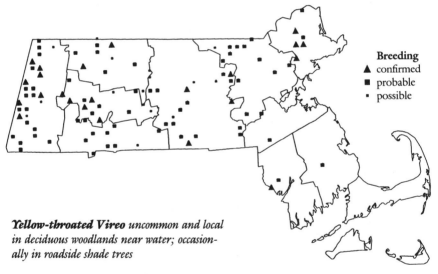

**Breeding**
▲ confirmed
■ probable
• possible

*Yellow-throated Vireo uncommon and local in deciduous woodlands near water; occasionally in roadside shade trees*

**Nonbreeding:** Yellow-throated Vireos are only rarely encountered during migration away from known breeding localities. Most migrants are reported from mid- to late May and from late August through September. It is rare to find more than one a day during migration—e.g., 3, Mt. Auburn Cemetery, Cambridge, 16 May 1973 (Martin). *Extreme dates:* 1, Provincetown, 1 May 1980 (Nikula); to 1 banded, MBO, 13 October 1967.

# Warbling Vireo  *Vireo gilvus*

**Range:** Nearctic; breeds from southeastern Alaska, southern Manitoba, southern Quebec, central Maine, and central Nova Scotia south to Baja

California, central northern Mexico, southern Louisiana, and the coastal plain of Virginia. Winters from Mexico to Guatemala and El Salvador.

**Status:** Fairly common local breeder and uncommon migrant.

**Breeding:** Warbling Vireos are entirely absent as breeders from mature forests. Instead, breeding birds are restricted to open rural and suburban areas with scattered shade trees, often near water. They are particularly numerous in northeastern Essex County, in the outlying western suburbs of Boston, in the Sudbury River valley, and in the Connecticut River valley. They have always been rare on the southeastern coastal plain and absent from Cape Cod, although there is one nesting record for Nantucket (in a tall Sycamore in town), June 1974 (Perkins, Andrews).

Brewster (1906) and Griscom and Snyder (1955) concurred that Warbling Vireos greatly decreased after the mid-1880s, when they were common summer residents. Both authors cite the introduction of the House Sparrow, the spraying of insecticides, and the increased use of the automobile as causes for the decline. It is difficult to understand how each of these factors could have so drastically affected the Warbling Vireo population, especially considering that Warbling Vireos are still fairly common in portions of Cambridge where Brewster found them nesting nearly 100 years ago—e.g., 3 pairs nesting, Hell's Half Acre, Cambridge, 19 May 1973 (D'Entremont); 20 (including four or five family groups), Fresh Pond, Cambridge, 2 August 1976 (Veit). It seems more plausible to think that Warbling Vireos may be suffering from habitat modification, both locally and on their wintering grounds. *Summer maxima:* 48, GBBBC, 14 June 1980; 44, Greater Springfield Area Survey, 22 May 1971 (ABC); 26 singing males, Wayland, 20 May 1965 (Forster); 20, NBBC, 15 June 1980. One of the very few summer records for Cape Cod is: 3, Provincetown, throughout June 1978 (Nikula, Goodrich). *Egg dates:* 30 May–11 June.

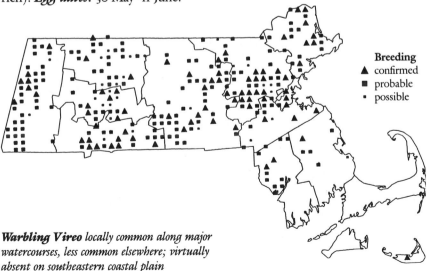

Breeding
▲ confirmed
■ probable
· possible

*Warbling Vireo locally common along major watercourses, less common elsewhere; virtually absent on southeastern coastal plain*

**Nonbreeding:** In spring, migrant Warbling Vireos are difficult to distinguish from local residents. Nonetheless, single birds are regularly reported in May from coastal thickets, where they do not breed. Residents generally arrive on territory during the first week of May. In fall, resident birds gradually withdraw during September. At that time they are decidedly uncommon on the outer coast. *Fall maxima:* 4, Plum Island, 25 September 1956 (Goodridge); 3 banded, Monomoy, 11–16 September 1966 (Baird); 3, Plum Island, 6 September 1980 (Forster). *Extreme dates:* 1, Lynnfield, 28 April 1957 (Griscom); 3, Wayland, 28 April 1961 (Garrey); to 1 banded, MBO, 11 November 1982; 1, Chatham, 19–24 October 1976 (Veit); 1, Cambridge, 21 October 1966 (Raabe).

# Philadelphia Vireo   *Vireo philadelphicus*

**Range:** Nearctic; breeds from northeastern British Columbia and North Dakota east to central Quebec, New Brunswick, and southwestern Newfoundland, and in the Appalachian Mountains of northern New York, New Hampshire, northern Vermont, and central Maine. Winters from Guatemala to northwestern Colombia.

**Status:** Rare spring and uncommon fall migrant.

**Occurrence:** In spring, Philadelphia Vireos most frequently appear during large warbler waves in late May, especially at coastal migrant traps in Essex County. They are always rare in that season with no reports of more than 2 birds at any one locality in a day. Spring seasonal totals since 1954 have ranged from 2 to 12 (1971 [fide Emery]) birds. In fall, the vast majority of Philadelphia Vireos are seen at the immediate coast during September and early October. Under appropriate conditions, an active observer can expect to see from 1 to 4 per day at that time at such favored localities as Nahant, Marblehead, and Monomoy. *Fall maxima:* 11, Plum Island, 4 September 1979 (BOEM); 8, Chatham, 13 September 1981 (Nikula); 8, Pochet Island, East Orleans, 11 September 1971 (Petersen). Away from the immediate coast, it is unusual to see more than one or two Philadelphia Vireos per day per locality. *Extreme dates:* 1, Monomoy, 8 August 1965 (Forster); to 1 banded, MBO, 5 November 1979.

# Red-eyed Vireo   *Vireo olivaceus*

**Range:** Nearctic; breeds from northern British Columbia, southern Mackenzie, central Ontario, southern Quebec, and Nova Scotia south to Oregon, eastern Colorado, eastern Texas, the Gulf Coast, and Florida. Winters in northern South America east of the Andes.

**Status:** Common breeder, although less numerous on Cape Cod and absent from the smaller islands; common migrant.

**Breeding:** Robbins et al (1966) state that the Red-eyed Vireo is the most abundant bird in eastern deciduous forests. In Massachusetts, the species is most numerous in mature deciduous forests, and it is notably less common in the Scrub Oak forests of the coastal plain. Overall, it is one of the most common and widespread nesting songbirds in Massachusetts. *Summer maxima:* 121 (including an unknown number of migrants), Petersham, 30 May 1960 (Hunt); 88, NBBC, 15 June 1980; 76, GBBBC, 17 June 1978. From Cape Cod, Hill (1965) lists "densities of 10 to 12 pairs per 100 acres at Brewster, 6 to 8 pairs per 100 acres at Sagamore, 5 pairs at Provincetown, 12 to 15 pairs per 100 acres at Woods Hole, etc.," but gives no dates for these estimates. *Egg dates:* 25 May–20 July.

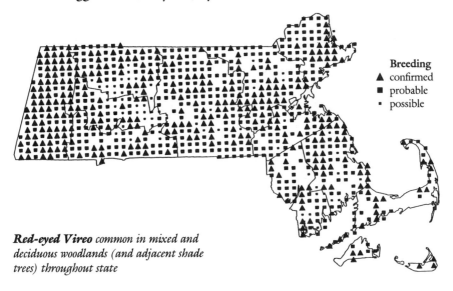

Breeding
▲ confirmed
■ probable
▪ possible

*Red-eyed Vireo common in mixed and deciduous woodlands (and adjacent shade trees) throughout state*

**Nonbreeding:** This is by far the most abundant vireo during migration in Massachusetts, a fact readily confirmed by MBO banding data. Most spring migrants pass through Massachusetts during mid-May. *Spring maxima:* 112, Concord, 16 May 1964 (Seamans et al); 93, Springfield Area Census, 22 May 1971. At least some Red-eyed Vireos continue migrating north as late as mid-June—e.g., 24 banded, MBO, 1–12 June 1973. In fall, most migrants occur in September and early October. *Fall maxima:* 60, Chatham, 17 September 1970 (Rich); 50 +, Chatham, 8 September 1976 (Nikula); 50, MNWS, 8 September 1982 (Heil); 37, North Scituate, 19 September 1970 (Higginbotham); 24, Williamstown, 16 September 1970 (Weigand). Selected banding totals from MBO in 1967 and 1968 reveal that considerable numbers of Red-eyed Vireos migrate as late as mid-October—e.g., 34 banded, 1–23

October 1967; 51 banded, 1–24 October 1968. *Extreme dates:* 1, Province-
town, 13 April 1980 (Nikula); to 1, North Middleboro, 29 November 1957
(Romaine); 1, Chatham, 27 November 1969 (Copeland); 1 banded, MBO, 18
November 1974.

## Blue-winged Warbler    *Vermivora pinus*

**Range:** Eastern Nearctic; breeds from eastern Nebraska and central Iowa
east locally to southern New England and south to Arkansas, northern
Georgia, and Delaware. Winters from southern Mexico to Panama.

**Status:** Locally fairly common breeder and increasing; uncommon migrant
away from known breeding localities.

**Breeding:** Blue-winged Warblers breed in brushy, overgrown pastures and
at the edges of dense secondary growth. They are especially numerous in the
Connecticut River valley (where they first colonized Massachusetts in the
early 1900s), in northeastern Essex County, and in the second-growth
lowlands between Boston and Providence. They are scarce on Cape Cod
and the Islands and have not been recorded at elevations above 1,700 feet in
Berkshire County. Once considered accidental from the south by Howe and
Allen (1901), Blue-winged Warblers have gradually increased and have displaced Golden-winged Warblers from areas where the latter species was
formerly numerically dominant. It is difficult to separate residents from
migrants in late May, so the following counts undoubtedly include many
breeding birds: 70, Greater Springfield Census, 22 May 1971 (ABC); 38,
South Groveland, 8 June 1991 (Stymeist, VO); 29, South Groveland, 10 June
1990 (Stymeist, VO); 17 (and only 3 Golden-wingeds), West Newbury, 9–
30 May 1981 (Stymeist, Heil, et al); 16 (and 1 Golden-winged), Wrentham-
Medfield, 7–8 June 1979 (Forster). *Egg dates:* 29 May–6 June.

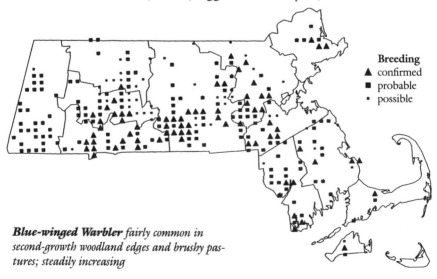

Breeding
▲ confirmed
■ probable
· possible

*Blue-winged Warbler fairly common in
second-growth woodland edges and brushy pastures; steadily increasing*

**Nonbreeding:** Blue-winged Warblers arrive somewhat earlier in spring than Golden-winged Warblers, usually during the first week of May, and most have departed by late August or early September. *Spring maxima:* 18, Sharon, 13 May 1979 (Clapp); 12, MNWS, 9 May 1964 (Perry); 4, Mt. Auburn Cemetery, Cambridge, 10 May 1970 (Stymeist). *Fall maxima:* 30, Martha's Vineyard, 21 August 1979 (Laux); 9, MNWS, 16 August 1982 (Heil); 7, Chatham, 23 August 1964 (Harrington); 6, Chatham, 1 September 1962 (Gardler). *Extreme dates:* 1, Woods Hole, 21 April 1969 (Kaan); to 1, Medford, 29 October 1969 (Payson).

**Remarks:** Although hybrids and intergrades between *V. pinus* and *V. chrysoptera* are continuously variable, the regulation of the face pattern appears to be under the control of a single gene (Short 1963). Thus, field observers have, under the influence of the field guides, categorized "hybrid" individuals as "Brewster's" Warblers if they lacked a black throat and "Lawrence's" if they had it. As such, there have been nearly five times the number of reports of "Brewster's" Warblers than of "Lawrence's" Warblers in Massachusetts since 1954. However, the incidence of "Lawrence's" Warblers has increased in proportion to that of "Brewster's" Warblers in recent years, suggesting that there is increasing introgression of *pinus* genes into the population. For example, before 1970, 114 "Brewster's" Warblers and 21 "Lawrence's" Warblers were reported from Massachusetts, but between 1970 and 1980, 19 "Brewster's" and 8 "Lawrence's" were noted.

# Golden-winged Warbler   *Vermivora chrysoptera*

**Range:** Northeastern Nearctic; breeds locally from northeastern North Dakota and southeastern Iowa east to western New York and Massachusetts and south on the coast to Maryland and in the Appalachian Mountains to Georgia. Winters from Guatemala to Colombia.

**Status:** Very uncommon, local, and decreasing breeder. Rare migrant away from known breeding locations.

**Breeding:** Brewster (1906) found several pairs of Golden-winged Warblers nesting in Waltham in 1874. In his opinion, these were the first known to breed in the Cambridge region, if not in Massachusetts. Both Brewster and Townsend (1905) agreed that from 1874 until the early 1900s, Golden-winged Warblers steadily increased. Apparently, they reached a maximum density in the state in the early 1940s—e.g., 40, Essex County, 17 May 1942 (Haydock); 8, Sheffield-Monterey, Berkshire County, 22 May 1941 (fide McNair). Since that time, the species has steadily decreased, due, it seems, to competition with the increasingly numerous Blue-winged Warbler.

Confer and Knapp (1981) have shown a significant difference in habitat preference between these two species. Golden-wingeds are habitat specialists, requiring open fields in early successional stages, whereas Blue-wingeds are more generalized, breeding in both early and late successional deciduous forests. Gill (1980) agrees and feels that the regeneration of abandoned fields in New England has provided Blue-winged Warblers with a competitive advantage over Golden-winged Warblers.

Short (1963) and Gill (op cit) show a progressive introgression of Blue-winged Warbler genetic characteristics into the Golden-winged Warbler population as a result of cross breeding, beginning as early as the late 1800s in southern New England. Gill also demonstrated that a period of 50 years elapsed in Connecticut between the first arrival of Blue-winged Warblers and the extirpation of Golden-wingeds from the colony. Thus, the future of Golden-winged Warblers in Massachusetts seems perilous. *Maximum* (recent): 9, NBBC, 15 June 1980. *Egg dates:* 20 May–20 June.

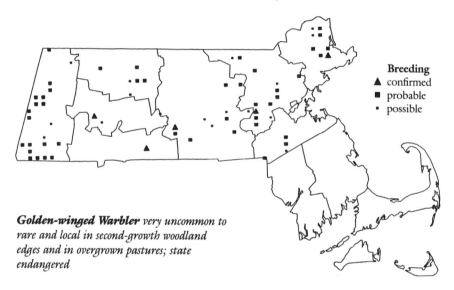

**Breeding**
▲ confirmed
■ probable
• possible

*Golden-winged Warbler very uncommon to rare and local in second-growth woodland edges and in overgrown pastures; state endangered*

**Nonbreeding:** Concurrent with their decrease as breeders, Golden-winged Warblers have become especially rare as migrants in Massachusetts. Breeders arrive during early May and gradually depart between late July and September. There are few recent observations of more than one individual per day per locality during migration, and the species is especially rare at the outer coast. *Spring maxima:* 20, Great Barrington, 17 May 1965 (Parker); 12, MNWS, 9 May 1964 (Perry); 4, Mt. Auburn Cemetery, Cambridge, 8 May 1965 (PBC). *Fall maximum:* 2, MNWS, 1 September 1979 (Forster). Increas-

> *The **Golden-winged Warbler** (bottom) is a steadily disappearing summer resident of woodland edges and regenerating old pastures. Changing ecology and interbreeding with the northward-expanding and genetically similar **Blue-winged Warbler** (top) may spell eventual doom for this lovely parulid.*

▷

ingly unreported in fall in recent years. *Extreme dates:* Singles, Wayland and Needham, 28 April 1957 (MAS, Sargent); to 1, West Newbury, 13 November 1955 (Drury).

# Tennessee Warbler   *Vermivora peregrina*

**Range:** Nearctic; breeds from southeastern Alaska, northern Manitoba, central Labrador, and western Newfoundland south to northern Minnesota, northern Michigan, and northern New England. Winters from Mexico to Colombia and Venezuela.

**Status:** Variously uncommon to very common migrant; most conspicuous in spring.

**Occurrence:** Tennessee Warblers breed in boreal deciduous and mixed forests and appear to vary in abundance in relation to outbreaks of the Spruce Budworm in those areas. Because of this, their occurrence in Massachusetts has been historically erratic and they continue to fluctuate considerably in abundance from year to year. Spring migrants normally arrive during the second week of May (earliest 27 April, fide Griscom & Snyder 1955), but their numbers are always variable. *Spring maxima:* 500, Hoosic River valley, 18 May 1977 (McNair); 100, Sudbury, 23 May 1975 (Forster); 50, Provincetown, 24 May 1974 (Bailey).

Singing males have occasionally been reported during midsummer at various locations in the state, but no evidence of breeding has been obtained. Summer records include: 1, South Orleans, 4 July 1962 (Earle); 1, Mt. Greylock, 22–23 June 1969 (BBC, Jameson); 1, Canton, 2 July 1978 (Litchfield); 1, Lexington, 8 July 1978 (Baird); 1, Wellfleet, 8 July 1979 (Heil). The protracted fall migration, which begins in August—e.g., 1, West Newbury, 6 August 1983 (Petersen)—normally reaches a peak in late September and early October. *Fall maxima:* 50, Northampton, 1 October 1955 (Eliot); 30 + , West Boylston, 18 September 1978 (Baird); 15, Lynn, 2 October 1981 (Heil); 14, Rockport, 3 October 1981 (Heil); 10, Monomoy, 1 October 1974 (Bailey et al). *Extreme date:* 1, Avon, 2 December 1965 (Baird). There are, in addition, at least seven records for November.

# Orange-crowned Warbler   *Vermivora celata*

**Range:** Nearctic; the race *V. c. celata* breeds from central Alaska east to central Quebec and southern Labrador south, in the East, to central Ontario and western Newfoundland. Winters from the southern United States south to Guatemala.

**Status:** Rare spring and uncommon fall migrant. Rare but regular in winter.

**Occurrence:** Orange-crowned Warblers are rare in spring and most often occur among large waves of other migrant land birds, primarily in eastern Massachusetts during the last half of May. It is unusual to see more than one in a day during spring. *Spring maxima:* 4, Newburyport, 20 May 1978 (Weissberg et al). In fall, the Orange-crowned is among the latest migrant warblers to ordinarily occur in Massachusetts; it is most often recorded during October and November. In this season, they are typically found near the coast, especially in weedy areas with lots of goldenrod.

As an indication of their scarcity inland, only one was banded during 15,174 net hours over a five-year fall period (1962–1966) at Round Hill, Sudbury (Howard 1967b). McNair (1978) considered the Orange-crowned Warbler to be very rare in Berkshire County. By contrast, the active observer at the outer coast can expect to see from 1 to 2 birds per day in late October and November and up to 10 during the course of a season. *Fall maxima:* 10, Orleans, 19 October 1974 (Goodrich); total of 21 reported, eastern Massachusetts, October 1974 (BOEM); 7, Nantucket, 11–28 October 1979 (Veit, Litchfield).

Orange-crowned Warblers occasionally appear at feeding stations that provide suet during midwinter. Although the majority of records are from the southeastern coastal plain, there are a number of instances in which Orange-crowned Warblers have survived the entire season at inland localities. *Winter maxima:* 5, Orleans, 25 January 1957 (Keith); 5, Greater Boston CBC, 15 December 1991; 4, Brewster, 2 January 1972 (Goodrich et al). Three survived the winter of 1966–1967 in eastern Massachusetts (RNEB).

# Nashville Warbler   *Vermivora ruficapilla*

**Range:** Nearctic; breeds from southern British Columbia, central Ontario, and Nova Scotia south to central California, northern Illinois, and northeastern West Virginia. Winters from Mexico to central Honduras.

**Status:** Fairly common breeder and uncommon to fairly common migrant.

**Breeding:** Nashville Warblers were virtually unknown in Massachusetts prior to 1830, but they rapidly increased and were fairly common by 1842 (Griscom & Snyder 1955). The species apparently reached maximum densities by about 1900 but has declined gradually since then. Nashville Warblers prefer to breed near the edges of deciduous second-growth forests and in suitable forest clearings. They are most numerous from Worcester County west, but scattered pairs also nest in eastern Massachusetts. They are especially numerous in regenerating burned areas in Plymouth County. *Egg dates:* 21 May–21 June.

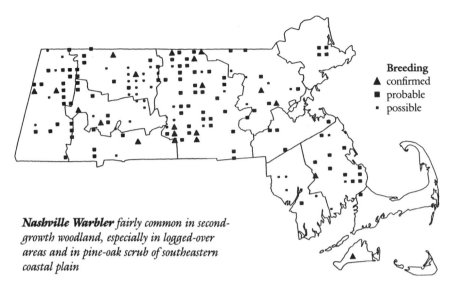

*Nashville Warbler fairly common in second-growth woodland, especially in logged-over areas and in pine-oak scrub of southeastern coastal plain*

**Breeding**
▲ confirmed
■ probable
• possible

**Nonbreeding:** The first arrivals of spring appear in early May, and peak counts for the year occur shortly thereafter. *Spring maxima:* 48, Greater Springfield Census, 9 May 1970; 25, Cambridge, 13 May 1956 (Keenan et al); 23, Mt. Auburn Cemetery, Cambridge, 15 May 1967 (Forster); 20, MNWS, 6 May 1977 (Kasprzyk). During fall, Nashville Warblers are never especially numerous, but they nonetheless occur regularly from late August until the end of October. *Fall maxima:* 8, Littleton, 6 September 1978 (Baird); 20, Monomoy, 26 September 1981 (Nikula); 8, South Peabody, 17 September 1981 (Heil). *Extreme dates:* 1, Mt. Tom, 18 April 1964 (Coolidge); 1, Littleton, 24 April 1976 (Baird); to 1, Swampscott, 31 January 1890 (fide Griscom & Snyder 1955); 1, Woods Hole, 29 December 1973 (Veit); 1, Arlington, 20–21 December 1981 (Alden et al).

## Lucy's Warbler    *Vermivora luciae*

**Range:** Nearctic and Neotropical; breeds in the southwestern United States north to southern Nevada and east to western Texas. Winters in western Mexico.

**Status:** Vagrant: one record.

**Occurrence:** A Lucy's Warbler was discovered at Clark's Pond, Ipswich, 1 December 1979 (Heil). The bird was seen by numerous observers and identifiably photographed in color by Kasprzyk (photo on file at MAS). Heil (1981) described this occurrence in detail, along with the occurrence of several other southwestern species in the northeastern United States during the late fall of 1979.

# Northern Parula   *Parula americana*

**Range:** Eastern Nearctic; breeds from southern Canada south to Florida and Texas but very local in the northeastern United States. Winters in the West Indies and in Central America from Mexico to Nicaragua.

**Status:** Rare and local breeder; common migrant.

**Breeding:** Northern Parulas build their nests largely of *Usnea* sp. lichen, and, therefore, seem to be restricted as breeders to areas where *Usnea* is present. Because *Usnea* has disappeared from many woodlands in the Northeast, parulas have steadily decreased and are currently restricted as breeders to a few localities on Cape Cod (e.g., Mashpee, Harwich), Naushon Island, and, possibly, Martha's Vineyard. The presence of 2 singing males at Hog Island, Essex, 10 June 1982 (Heil) suggests that they may also have attempted to breed there. *Egg dates:* 30 May–5 July.

**Nonbreeding:** Northern Parulas arrive during the last days of April and the first week of May and reach peak numbers during the third week of May. *Spring maxima:* 103, Greater Springfield Census, 9 May 1970; 60, Mt. Auburn Cemetery, Cambridge, 7 May 1972 (Emery et al); 55, West Newbury, 19 May 1967 (Forster); 50, MNWS, 21 May 1955 (Snyder); 45, Plum Island, 12 May 1991 (Perkins). In the fall, most migrants pass through the state in September, when peak numbers are usually recorded midmonth. By early October, the migration is normally over. *Fall maxima:* 24, Hingham, 25 September 1956 (Raymond et al); 22, Lynn, 1 October 1981 (Heil); 17, Holyoke, 26 September 1970 (Yenlin); 15, Littleton, 6 September 1978 (Baird). *Extreme dates:* 1 dead, Westport, 1 April 1978 (Leddy); 1, MNWS, 14 April 1977 (Kasprzyk); 1, Manomet, 20 December 1973 (Anderson); to 1, Williamstown, 8–14 December 1969 (Goodell et al).

# Yellow Warbler   *Dendroica petechia*

**Range:** Nearctic; breeds from Alaska, northern Manitoba, and Newfoundland south, in eastern North America, to central Georgia and Alabama and, on the coast, to Virginia. Winters from Mexico and the West Indies south to northern South America.

**Status:** Common and widespread breeder and common migrant.

**Breeding:** Yellow Warblers breed in low, wet areas, especially in scrubby growth near ponds, marshes, swamps, and wet meadows. They are particularly common at localities such as Plum Island, Great Meadows National Wildlife Refuge in Concord, and in all the major river valleys. They are absent from densely forested areas. *Summer maxima:* 100 +, Plum Island, 4 June 1967 (Argues); 37 pairs, Wellesley, June 1955 (Freeland); 41, MCCBBC, 20 June 1982. *Egg dates:* 20 May–20 June.

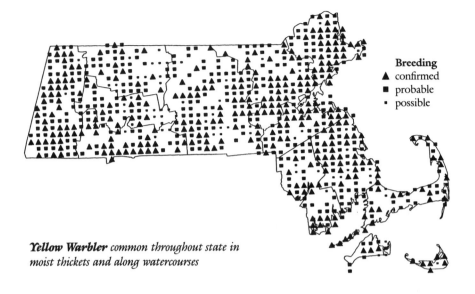

**Breeding**
▲ confirmed
■ probable
• possible

*Yellow Warbler common throughout state in moist thickets and along watercourses*

**Nonbreeding:** Resident Yellow Warblers frequently arrive on territory by late April and are thus difficult to separate from migrants. *Spring maxima:* 270, Greater Springfield Census, 9 May 1970; 200, Plum Island, 25 May 1966 (Forster); 140, Plum Island, 18 May 1992 (Heil); 78, Wellesley, 15 May 1965 (Petersen et al). After nesting, resident birds quickly depart in late July and early August, and many fall migrants frequently go undetected because observers do not ordinarily check coastal thickets in midsummer. *Fall maxima:* 40, MNWS, 10 August 1982 (Heil); 25, Marblehead-Nahant, 3 August 1982 (Heil). *Extreme dates:* 1, Edgartown, 6 April 1962 (Keith, Goodale, Hancock); 1, Sudbury, 17 April 1976 (Irish); to 1, Ipswich, 1 December 1979 (Heil); 1, Ipswich, 12 November 1972 (Gardler).

**Subspecies:** Griscom and Snyder (1955) list specimens of *D. p. amnicola* and *D. p. rubiginosa* from Massachusetts, including a record of one of each subspecies collected the same day at Monomoy, 9 September 1941 (Griscom 1941a). *D. p. amnicola* breeds across northern Canada from north-central Alaska to Newfoundland and must occur routinely during migration in Massachusetts. On the other hand, *D. p. rubiginosa* is restricted as a breeder to southeastern Alaska and British Columbia. Griscom claimed that four specimens assignable to *D. p. rubiginosa* have been collected in Massachusetts, but the information currently available is insufficient to prove that these dingy greenish Yellow Warblers are not simply *D. p. amnicola*. It is clear, however, that the specimens to which Griscom refers are much darker (greener) than the immature Yellow Warblers that breed in Massachusetts.

386

# Chestnut-sided Warbler   *Dendroica pensylvanica*

**Range:** Nearctic; breeds from east-central Alberta and Nova Scotia south to southern Michigan, Pennsylvania, and New Jersey, and in the Appalachian Mountains to northern Georgia. Winters from southern Mexico to Panama.

**Status:** Uncommon to fairly common breeder throughout the state, except rare on the southeastern coastal plain. Fairly common migrant.

**Breeding:** Chestnut-sided Warblers breed in brushy forest clearings and disturbed areas with an abundance of low deciduous shrubbery, such as along power-line cuts. They are rather inexplicably absent from areas with apparently suitable habitat in the southeastern part of the state. Prior to about 1835, they were very rare (Griscom & Snyder 1955), but they increased gradually as farmland became overgrown with saplings. Currently, they are most numerous in Worcester County, the Connecticut River valley, and Berkshire County.

Sample densities from the Wellesley-Weston area in the 1950s—i.e., 34 pairs, Wellesley, June 1954 (Freeland); 34 pairs, Weston, June 1954 (Freeland); 41 singing males, Wellesley, June 1959 (Freeland)—suggest that in those areas, at least, the species has declined considerably over the last 25 years (fide Petersen). Hill (1965) mentions breeding pairs at Harwich and Brewster on Cape Cod, and, more recently, breeding has been confirmed in Falmouth and Sandwich. *Egg dates:* 22 May–5 June.

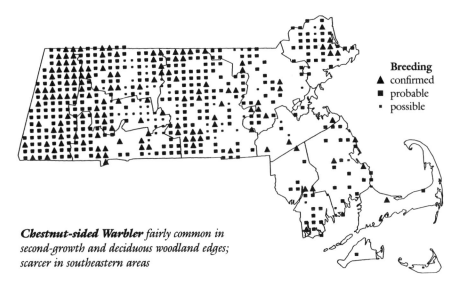

**Breeding**
▲ confirmed
■ probable
• possible

*Chestnut-sided Warbler fairly common in second-growth and deciduous woodland edges; scarcer in southeastern areas*

**Nonbreeding:** Resident Chestnut-sided Warblers arrive during the first week of May, and most migrants have passed through the state by the end of the month. *Spring maxima:* 30+, MNWS, 17 May 1968 (Ingalls); 30,

Newburyport, 30 May 1956 (deWindt). Fall records suggest that most adult Chestnut-sided Warblers depart in August and early September and that by early October the migration is over. *Fall maximum:* 10, Chatham, 31 August 1976 (Nikula). *Extreme dates:* 1, Milton, 22 April 1954 (Higginbotham); to 1, Cambridge, 4 November 1974 (Raabe); 1, Florence, 3 November 1972 (Gagnon); 1, Truro, 2 November 1974 (Nikula).

## Magnolia Warbler  *Dendroica magnolia*

**Range:** Nearctic; breeds from northeastern British Columbia to southern Newfoundland and south to northeastern Minnesota, northern New England and in the Appalachian Mountains south to western Virginia. Winters in the West Indies and from Mexico south to Panama.

**Status:** Locally common breeder and common to occasionally very common migrant, most numerous in spring.

**Breeding:** Magnolia Warblers nest in stands of spruce or fir and are therefore restricted as breeders to the higher elevations of western Massachusetts and northern Worcester County. Breeders at elevations lower than 2,000 feet tend to be associated with artificial plantations of evergreens, such as Norway or White Spruce. McNair (1978) claimed that, "At least 30 pairs nest on Mt. Greylock, and numbers there have remained constant since the 1940s." *Egg dates:* 15–24 June.

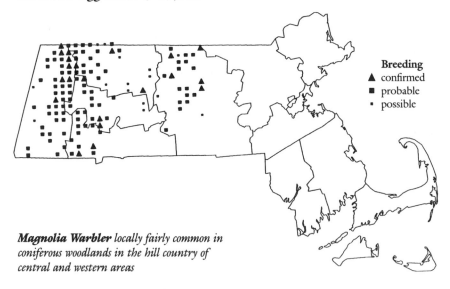

**Breeding**
▲ confirmed
■ probable
· possible

*Magnolia Warbler locally fairly common in coniferous woodlands in the hill country of central and western areas*

**Nonbreeding:** Magnolia Warblers are rare before early May, but most spring migrants have ordinarily arrived by the second week of the month.

Griscom and Snyder (1955) claimed that up "to 300 in a spring day" have been recorded; however, since 1955, counts have generally been smaller. *Spring maxima:* 200 +, Provincetown, 24 May 1974 (Bailey); 200, Nahant–Plum Island, 21 May 1961 (Argue); 100, MNWS, 12 May 1959 (Argue). Late migrants are occasionally recorded into mid-June—e.g., 1, Middlesex Fells Reservation, 14 June 1975 (Payson). Most southbound migrants occur in late August and September, and the species is rare after early October. *Fall maxima:* 30, Monomoy, 9 September 1968 (RNEB); 30, MNWS, 27 September 1964 (Nichols). *Extreme dates:* 1, Weston, 18 April 1976 (Robinson); to 1, Wayland, 27 November 1970 (Moon).

# Cape May Warbler  *Dendroica tigrina*

**Range:** Nearctic; breeds from northeastern British Columbia east to southern Quebec and Nova Scotia and south to northeastern Minnesota and northern New England. Winters primarily in the Greater Antilles.

**Status:** Variously uncommon to fairly common spring and uncommon to occasionally very common fall migrant.

**Occurrence:** Cape May Warblers breed in the spruce forests of northern New England and the Canadian Maritime Provinces, where they opportunistically congregate at infestations of Spruce Budworm (*Choristoneura fumiferana*). Periodically, massive flights of Cape May Warblers reach coastal Massachusetts during fall and probably reflect especially high reproductive success following such infestations. Griscom and Snyder (1955) state that the Cape May Warbler has "exactly the same fluctuating history as the Tennessee Warbler," and Tyler (1915) and Morse (1978) have pointed out the close association between budworm infestations and the enhanced reproductive success of Tennessee, Cape May, and Bay-breasted warblers.

As spring migrants, Cape May Warblers have always been notoriously scarce in Massachusetts, suggesting that the bulk of the population passes west of the state at this time of year. *Spring maxima:* 40, Provincetown, 17 May 1980 (Nikula); 36, Greater Springfield Census, 9 May 1970 (ABC); 25, Williamstown, 15 May 1971 (Weigand); 13, South Peabody, 16 May 1979 (Heil). The largest counts of the year of Cape May Warblers typically occur on the outer Cape and Islands during late August and early September. In this season, they are frequently the most conspicuous warbler migrant. *Fall maxima:* 500, Monomoy, 8–10 September 1976 (Bailey); 400, Chatham, 20 August 1975 (Goodrich, Nikula); 400, Chatham, 26 August 1977 (Goodrich, Nikula).

Even allowing for year-to-year fluctuations in the numbers of Cape May Warblers, they have steadily increased since 1955, when Griscom and Snyder (1955) determined that 35 birds per day per locality was the highest total published at the time. As an example, Nikula (BOEM 5: 179), extrapolating from his own counts, estimated that 100,000 to 150,000 warblers, 80 percent of which were Bay-breasted and Cape Mays, arrived on the outer Cape on 26 August 1977. This figure, based upon an estimate of "4–5 birds per acre x approximately 30,000 suitable acres," although astonishing at first glance, lends intriguing insight into the usual disparity existing between published field records and the actual size of migratory bird populations. *Extreme dates:* 1, Chatham, 28 April 1973 (Nikula); 1, West Tisbury, Martha's Vineyard, 15 June 1968 (Daniels); to 2, South Wellfleet, 29 December 1975 (Bailey).

## Black-throated Blue Warbler   *Dendroica caerulescens*

**Range:** Primarily eastern Nearctic; breeds from western Ontario east to southern Quebec and Nova Scotia and south to northern Wisconsin, northern New England, and in the Appalachian Mountains to northern Georgia. Winters primarily in the Greater Antilles and Bahama Islands.

**Status:** Fairly common breeder from Worcester County west; uncommon to fairly common migrant.

**Breeding:** Black-throated Blue Warblers breed in mountainous, northern hardwood forest areas, often where there is an understory of Mountain Laurel. Thus, they are restricted as breeders in Massachusetts to the hills of Worcester County and western Massachusetts. They are fairly common in suitable habitat—e.g., 12, Mt. Greylock, 16–17 June 1962 (Petersen)—and have not appeared to appreciably change their status during the historical period. *Egg dates:* 23 May–10 June.

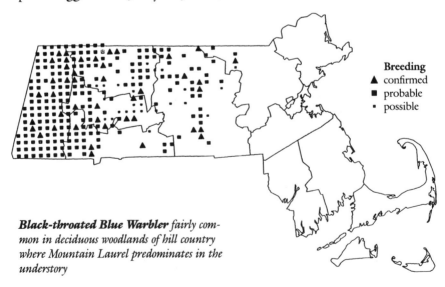

**Breeding**
▲ confirmed
■ probable
• possible

*Black-throated Blue Warbler fairly common in deciduous woodlands of hill country where Mountain Laurel predominates in the understory*

**Nonbreeding:** The first Black-throated Blue Warblers of spring normally appear in early May, with peak counts occurring midmonth. In fall, migration takes place between late August and mid-October. *Spring maxima:* 76, Greater Springfield Census, 9 May 1970 (ABC); 50, Mt. Auburn Cemetery, Cambridge, 9 May 1991 (Ferguson); 35, Gloucester, 14 May 1989 (Nove, BBC); 25, MNWS, 12 May 1954 (Sargent); 20, Provincetown, 19 May 1977 (Stymeist et al). *Fall maxima:* 18, MNWS, 7 September 1955 (Snyder); 14, Nantucket, 10 October 1968 (PBC); 12 banded, MBO, 5 October 1968. *Extreme dates:* 1, Newburyport, 23 April 1960 (deWindt); to 1, Northampton CBC, 16 December 1979.

# Yellow-rumped Warbler   *Dendroica coronata*

**Range:** Nearctic; the race *D. c. coronata* breeds from Alaska east across Canada and south to the north-central United States, New York, and New England. *D. c. coronata* winters from Massachusetts and the central United States south to Panama and also in the Greater Antilles.

**Status:** Locally fairly common breeder, mainly at higher elevations in the western part of the state. Very common to occasionally abundant migrant; very common to abundant winter resident on Cape Cod and the Islands.

**Breeding:** Yellow-rumped Warblers breed most commonly in coniferous forests at higher elevations in central and western Massachusetts; however, they also nest locally in mature White Pines near the southeastern coastal plain.

McNair (1978) described this species as an uncommon to common nester in Berkshire County, and that status is equally applicable to sections of

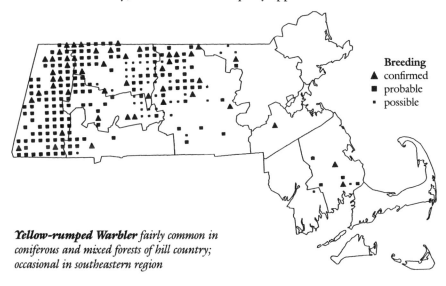

**Breeding**
▲ confirmed
■ probable
▪ possible

*Yellow-rumped Warbler fairly common in coniferous and mixed forests of hill country; occasional in southeastern region*

Worcester County where there is suitable habitat—e.g., East Quabbin, Mt. Wachusett, and Mt. Watatic. In eastern Massachusetts in recent years, Yellow-rumped Warblers have nested in Plympton (nest found, 19 June 1977 [O'Neill et al]), Plymouth (Myles Standish State Forest), and Lakeville. According to Griscom and Snyder (1955) and Forbush (1929), this species was formerly more numerous and widespread as a breeder when stands of White Pines were more extensive. *Egg dates:* 23 May–5 June.

**Nonbreeding:** Yellow-rumped Warblers are among the most numerous migrant warblers, usually arriving earlier in spring and departing later in fall than most other Massachusetts warbler species. From mid-April to early May, large numbers of migrant Yellow-rumped Warblers are regularly found congregating in low woods and around ponds or swamps where flying insects are abundant. *Spring maxima:* 600, Provincetown, 28 April 1979 (Nikula); 450 +, South Peabody, 7 May 1976 (Heil); 350, Mt. Auburn Cemetery, Cambridge, 14 May 1964 (Stymeist et al); 300, Quabbin, 13 May 1967 (Gura). Rare in eastern Massachusetts after mid-May.

In fall, southbound migrants usually do not arrive in any numbers until mid- or late September, and many remain on the outer coast all winter. Inland, however, most Yellow-rumps have departed by late November. "Myrtle" Yellow-rumped Warblers are distinctive in that they regularly shift their diet from insects to bayberries during the winter. By so doing, they are usually able to survive the entire winter season along the coast, their numbers varying depending upon the severity of the weather and the supply of bayberries. *Fall maxima:* 2,000, Monomoy, 16 October 1964 (fide Bailey); 1,500, Monomoy, 12 October 1956 (Gendall et al); 1,000 +, Plum Island, 8 October 1977 (Stymeist); 1,000, Monomoy, 9 October 1960 (Bailey); 500 departing in a northwesterly direction, Nantucket, 18 October 1979 (Veit).

*Winter maxima* (coastal): 3,128, Nantucket CBC, 29 December 1979; 1,943, Cape Cod CBC, 2 January 1954. By late winter, maximum counts are considerably lower—e.g., 300, Sandwich, 4 March 1973 (Brown); 130 +, Truro, 2 February 1975 (Petersen). An interesting exercise would be to repeat certain coastal CBCs during late February to better determine the actual extent of winter survival.

Inland, winter survival has been recorded west to Berkshire County: e.g., 1, Dalton, 16 December 1972–16 April 1973 (Shampang). Other inland wintering records include: 1, Springfield, 11 January 1965 (Maher); 1, South Hadley, 8 March 1966 (RNEB); 1, Framingham, throughout February 1968 (Weir); 2, Wayland, 16 and 28 February 1980 (Entin, Forster); 20, Bridgewater, 29 January 1983 (Petersen). *Extreme dates* (restricted to localities where they do not breed): 1, Nantucket, 11 June 1955 (Andrews); to 1, Plum Island, 4 August 1957 (Argue).

**Subspecies:** There are approximately ten records of the western subspecies, *D. c. auduboni*, from Massachusetts—e.g., 1 specimen, Watertown, 16 November 1876 (BMS #12977); 1 dead, Ipswich, 2 January 1939 (Emilio, PMS #6424); 1, Ipswich, 1–12 April 1959 (Wade, Root, Hunt, et al); 1, Nahant, 17–21 November 1964 (Ingalls, Batchelder, et al); 1, Chatham, 13 December 1977 (Bailey, specimen to MAS); 1, Greenfield CBC, 26 December 1988.

## Black-throated Gray Warbler  *Dendroica nigrescens*

**Range:** Western Nearctic; breeds from southwestern British Columbia and southern Wyoming south to southeastern Arizona and southern New Mexico. Winters in western Mexico.

**Status:** Vagrant: ten records.

**Occurrence:** This common western warbler has occurred in Massachusetts as follows: 1 collected, Lenox, 8 December 1923 (Voorhees, BMS #16344); 1, Springfield, 23 October 1955 (Keltz); 1 male collected, Chatham, 25–26 September 1962 (Bailey, Tudor, Clem, specimen at MAS); 1 male, Winchester, 20–30 November 1962 (Boone, Baird, VO); 1 female, Plum Island, 10 October 1964 (Conant); 1, Winchester, 11 October 1970 (Everett); 1 male photographed, South Peabody, 18 October–23 November 1977 (Heil, VO, see photo in AB 32: 179); 1, Scituate, 21–23 October 1987 (Leggett); 1, Chatham, 9–13 September 1987 (Guthrie); 1 male, Chatham, 4–5 September 1989 (Talin, Tuttle). Several sight records lacking convincing details have been omitted.

## Townsend's Warbler  *Dendroica townsendi*

**Range:** Western Nearctic; breeds from central coastal Alaska and southwestern Alberta south to northern Idaho. Winters from southern California south to Costa Rica.

**Status:** Vagrant: three records.

**Occurrence:** The only documented occurrences of this western warbler in Massachusetts are: 1 male, Mt. Auburn Cemetery, Cambridge, 4 May 1978 (Vaughan, later shown to many other observers and clearly photographed in color by Simon Perkins, photo at MAS); 1 photographed at feeder, Framingham, 16–30 December 1987 (Holmes, photo at MAS); 1, Falmouth, 1–12 December 1991 (d'Entremont, VO, see photo in BOEM 20: 98).

## Hermit Warbler  *Dendroica occidentalis*

**Range:** Western Nearctic; breeds from southwestern Washington south to east-central California. Winters from Mexico south to Nicaragua.

**Status:** Vagrant: one record.

**Occurrence:** A singing male Hermit Warbler was first discovered at Mt. Auburn Cemetery, Cambridge, 16 May 1964 (Earle). The bird was later seen by S. and R. Higginbotham, Emery, and dozens of other observers, several of whom were previously familiar with the species in California. This was the first record for eastern North America.

## Black-throated Green Warbler  *Dendroica virens*

**Range:** Nearctic; breeds from eastern British Columbia east to southern Labrador and Newfoundland and south to the north-central United States; also on the coastal plain from Virginia to South Carolina and in the Appalachian Mountains to northern Georgia. Winters from southern Florida and Texas to Panama and the Greater Antilles.

**Status:** Fairly common breeder throughout the state, except uncommon on the southeastern coastal plain; common migrant.

**Breeding:** Black-throated Green Warblers breed wherever stands of White Pine or hemlock are interspersed with mature deciduous forest, especially in central and western Massachusetts. There has been a marked decline in this species in southeastern Massachusetts since 1955, and it apparently no longer nests on Cape Cod. Nesting records from Martha's Vineyard are from White Pine plantations. *Summer maxima:* 18, Hawley, 29 June 1991 (Lynch, Carroll); 14, Becket, 1 July 1991 (Laubach); 13, East Quabbin, 15 July 1989 (Lynch). *Egg dates:* 30 May–18 June.

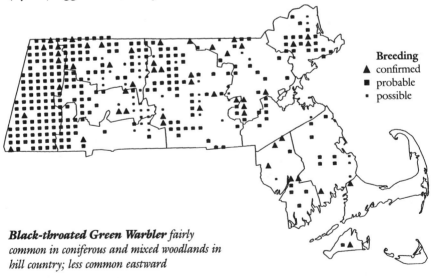

Breeding
▲ confirmed
■ probable
· possible

*Black-throated Green Warbler fairly common in coniferous and mixed woodlands in hill country; less common eastward*

**Nonbreeding:** In the spring, Black-throated Green Warblers are common migrants, usually arriving in warbler waves during the first half of May, when their distinctive song often makes them particularly conspicuous. *Spring maxima:* 119, Greater Springfield Census, 9 May 1970 (ABC); 50, Mt. Auburn Cemetery, Cambridge, 21 May 1965 (Hartel); 35, Mt. Auburn Cemetery, Cambridge, 13 May 1975 (Barton); 30, Newburyport, 14 May 1989 (Griffis, BBC). Of the fall migration in Berkshire County, McNair (1978) states, "September migrants may dominate a day's warbler flight, sometimes accounting for one-half of the numbers seen." Although this is one of the commoner migrants in eastern Massachusetts as well, it is usually outnumbered in recent fall flights by species such as Bay-breasted, Cape May, and Blackpoll warblers. *Fall maxima:* 58, Quabbin, 6 September 1972 (Yenlin); 50, Magnolia, 10 September 1954 (fide Griscom); 50, Duxbury Beach, 7 October 1967 (Drury); 44, Holyoke, 26 September 1970 (Yenlin); 40, Chatham, 26 September 1981 (Nikula). *Extreme dates:* 1, WBWS, 25 March 1966 (Bailey); 1, Marshfield, 15 April 1974 (Litchfield); to 1 dead, Scituate, 15 December 1945 (fide Griscom); 1, Manchester, 9 December 1962 (deWindt). There are at least nineteen November records since 1954.

# Blackburnian Warbler   *Dendroica fusca*

**Range:** Nearctic; breeds from Saskatchewan east to Nova Scotia and south to central Minnesota and Michigan, Pennsylvania, and Massachusetts, and in the Appalachian Mountains south to Georgia. Winters from Guatemala south to northern South America.

**Status:** Uncommon breeder from Worcester County west and locally eastward to Essex and Middlesex counties. Fairly common to common spring and uncommon fall migrant.

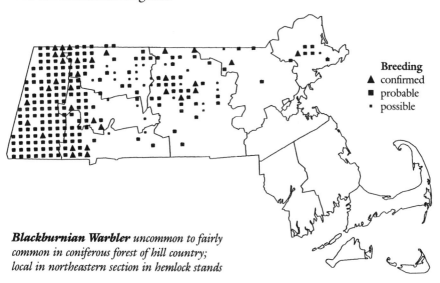

Breeding
▲ confirmed
■ probable
• possible

***Blackburnian Warbler*** *uncommon to fairly common in coniferous forest of hill country; local in northeastern section in hemlock stands*

**Breeding:** Blackburnian Warblers breed in mature stands of spruce, hemlock, and White Pine. They are widespread in the higher hills of the interior but in the east are restricted to large, mature forests (e.g., Boxford State Forest). *Summer maxima:* 50, Mt. Greylock, 18 June 1966 (BBC); 21, Mt. Greylock, 15 June 1991 (Gagnon); 17, Savoy, 20 June 1990 (Rancatti). There has been no demonstrable change in the status of this species during the historical period, although its local numbers were said to have been diminished after many large evergreens were toppled by the 1938 hurricane (Griscom & Snyder 1955). *Egg dates:* 6–26 June.

**Nonbreeding:** Blackburnian Warblers are occasionally common during large warbler waves in mid-May but are usually widely dispersed and seldom encountered in any numbers during fall. Local residents usually arrive during the first few days of May and depart by mid-August. *Spring maxima:* 234 reported, throughout Massachusetts, May 1968 (RNEB)—with a peak of 50, MNWS, 22 May (Leahy); 40 + , Provincetown, 25 May 1983 (Nikula); 35 + , Boxford, 21 May 1967 (Petersen); 24, Plum Island, 26 May 1957 (Argue). Recent totals have generally been considerably lower. *Fall maxima:* 10, Plum Island, 22 August 1964 (BBC); 6, Plum Island, 8 September 1990 (Moore, BBC); most reports are of single birds, occasionally 2 or 3. *Extreme dates:* 1, Baldwinville, 17 April 1977 (O'Regan); 1, Lincoln, 20 April 1964 (Powell); 1, Plum Island, 22 July 1962 (Chevone); to 1, Martha's Vineyard, 4 November 1979 (Laux).

# Yellow-throated Warbler  *Dendroica dominica*

**Range:** Eastern Nearctic; breeds from southern Wisconsin, northern Ohio, and central New Jersey south to Texas, the Gulf Coast states, and central Florida. Winters from the Gulf Coast to Costa Rica and the Greater Antilles.

**Status:** Rare but regular visitor in spring and fall.

**Occurrence:** Yellow-throated Warblers, like other southern warblers, occur in Massachusetts during April and early May, often after coastal storms, but also among large flocks of early migrating Yellow-rumped Warblers. Since 1954, there have been over fifty spring records, spanning the dates: 1 ("feeding on insects over seaweed on sand"), Sandy Neck, Barnstable, 28 March 1969 (Terry, fide Emery); to 1, Wareham, 16 June 1984 (Robinson). At least ten of these records are from April, and all are of single birds. During late June 1965, two separate male Yellow-throated Warblers were found in Holyoke, one of which remained until 7 July (Yenlin). Otherwise, there have been no records of summering birds in Massachusetts.

Fall records of Yellow-throated Warblers since 1954 span the period from late July to early November—e.g., 1, Plum Island, 28 July 1968 (Emery,

Argue), and 1, Naushon Island, 29 July 1982 (Litchfield, Hatch); to 1, Nantucket, 24 November 1957 (Andrews, Heywood). Virtually all of the fall records are from the immediate coast. In fact, all are from the southeastern coastal plain except: 1, Plum Island, 4 October 1967 (Stymeist); 1, Annisquam, 26 August 1977 (Wiggin); 1, MNWS, 28 September 1982 (Heil). Aside from 4 following Hurricane Edna, Morris Island, Chatham, 12 September 1954 (Emery et al), all reports are of single birds. Of the November records, one bird survived at Vineyard Haven until 3 December 1956 (Rogers, Goodale). Four remarkable winter records of birds at feeders are: 1, Harwich, 9 December 1985–2 January 1986 (Comeau); 1, Falmouth, 19 December 1987 (Buzzards Bay CBC); 1, Duxbury, 3–23 January 1990 (Richmond, VO); 1, Essex, 15 December 1991–31 January 1992 (Gentleman, VO).

**Subspecies:** Griscom and Snyder (1955) list specimens of both the southeastern coastal subspecies, *D. d. dominica*, which breeds north to Cape May, New Jersey, and *D. d. albilora*, which breeds northeast to the Delaware River valley in New Jersey. Due to difficulties in field identification of these races (Parkes 1953, Baird 1958), it is difficult to positively determine the relative frequency of each form in Massachusetts.

# Pine Warbler   *Dendroica pinus*

**Range:** Primarily eastern Nearctic; breeds from southern Manitoba, central Ontario, and central Maine south to Texas, the Gulf Coast, and Florida, and also on Hispaniola and in the Bahama Islands. Winters in the southeastern United States and Mexico.

**Status:** Common breeder on the southeastern coastal plain; uncommon and local elsewhere on the mainland. Very uncommon migrant away from breeding localities; very uncommon to rare in winter on the coastal plain.

**Breeding:** Pine Warblers commonly breed in Pitch Pine forests on the southeastern coastal plain and are uncommon and local in Red Pine and White Pine groves at inland sites. In the pine barrens of Plymouth County and Cape Cod, it is one of the most numerous songbirds during the summer. However, Griscom and Snyder (1955) and Hill (1965) have appropriately pointed out that, because extensive tracts of Pitch Pine are progressively changing to oak forest on Cape Cod, Pine Warblers have been gradually declining as breeders in that area since a peak of abundance in the 1940s and 1950s. Bull (1964) points out a similar decline for the breeding population of Long Island, New York. There is little precise data available on the breeding density of Pine Warblers on Cape Cod since the 1940s, but the numbers of fall migrants reported have greatly decreased during the last 40 years. *Egg dates:* 8 May–late July.

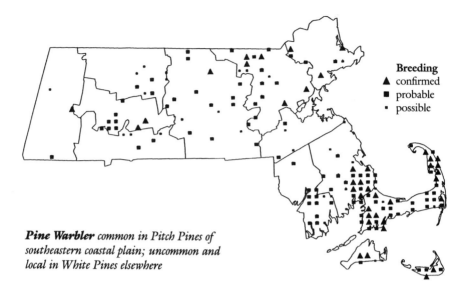

*Pine Warbler* common in Pitch Pines of southeastern coastal plain; uncommon and local in White Pines elsewhere

**Nonbreeding:** Because a few Pine Warblers regularly spend the winter in Massachusetts, it is difficult to distinguish recently arrived migrants from winter residents. Brightly plumaged males have been reported singing as early as late February at inland locations following spells of unseasonably warm weather—e.g., 1, Holyoke, 28 February 1973 (Forster). Most migrants, however, apparently arrive from mid-April to early May. *Spring maxima:* 30 +, Provincetown, 13 April 1980 (Nikula); 20 singing males, Martha's Vineyard, 15 April 1955 (Bagg); 15, Quabbin, 18 April 1966 (Clark); 10 migrants, Provincetown, Beech Forest, 5 May 1979 (Nikula, Veit).

In the fall, during the 1940s and early 1950s, large flocks of Pine Warblers were regularly found on Cape Cod and Nantucket in mid-September—e.g., 150 reported on several occasions, outer Cape: 12 September 1941 (Griscom); 10 September 1945 (Griscom); 9–11 September 1949 (MAS Campout); 8 September 1951 (Highley, Bryant); also 40, Nantucket, 4 September 1952 (Heywood). From 50 to 100 birds were counted during roughly the same dates on a number of occasions by experienced observers who reported smaller numbers of both Blackpoll and Bay-breasted warblers on the same days. Thus, it is clear that Griscom and others carefully identified these birds as Pine Warblers and noted that a decline was apparent as early as 1955. It seems reasonable to assume that much of the recent decline in the Pine Warbler population on Cape Cod and Nantucket is attributable to the gradual disappearance of extensive, pure stands of Pitch Pine. In recent years, it is unusual to see more than 5 Pine Warblers per day in fall, even on Cape Cod and Nantucket. *Fall maxima:* 30 +, WBWS, 22 August 1979 (Heil); 4, Plum Island, 11 November 1975 (Lawrence); 4, South Peabody, 11 November 1976 (Heil). *Winter maxima:* 15 +, Middleboro, 21 January

1989 (Petersen); 12, Plymouth CBC, 30 December 1987; 9, Nantucket CBC, 28 December 1991; 8, Lakeville, Bridgewater, and Middleboro, 2 January 1971 (Taunton-Middleboro CBC); 7, Wareham, 15 December 1975 (Petersen et al). One survived at Longmeadow until at least 26 February 1967 (Williams et al).

# Prairie Warbler   *Dendroica discolor*

**Range:** Eastern Nearctic; breeds from eastern Nebraska and southern Ontario and Massachusetts south to east Texas, northern Louisiana, and Florida. Winters in south Florida and throughout the West Indies.

**Status:** Locally common breeder; uncommon to common migrant.

**Breeding:** Prairie Warblers breed commonly on the southeastern coastal plain in Scrub Oak and Pitch Pine barrens, especially those that are periodically burned. Away from the coastal plain, they are especially numerous in disturbed areas with heavy secondary growth, such as in clearings beneath high-tension lines, in overgrown pastures, and near brushy gravel pits. *Summer maxima:* 50 pairs, Middlesex Fells Reservation, 9 July 1972 (Payson); 71 singing males, North Andover and Andover, 8–19 June 1951 (Root); 42, Truro-Wellfleet, 10 June 1960 (Tudor); 40 pairs, Lawrence, 10 June 1954 (Smith); 42, Groveland, 8 June 1991 (Stymeist). *Egg dates:* 28 May–18 June.

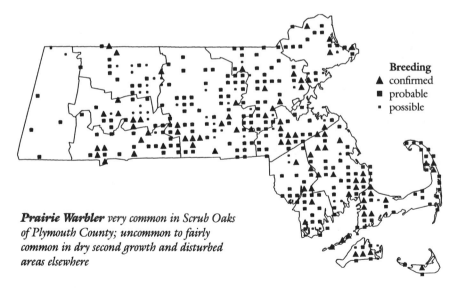

**Breeding**
▲ confirmed
■ probable
▪ possible

*Prairie Warbler very common in Scrub Oaks of Plymouth County; uncommon to fairly common in dry second growth and disturbed areas elsewhere*

**Nonbreeding:** Because Massachusetts lies close to the northeastern periphery of the breeding range of the Prairie Warbler, observers here witness an arrival of residents during early May at breeding areas, but migrants away from known nesting localities are uncommon. It is unusual to see more than 5 individuals in a day at such localities as Mt. Auburn Cemetery, Cambridge, for instance. In the fall, Prairie Warblers have one of the more protracted migrations of the warblers occurring in Massachusetts. Residents begin to depart by early July—e.g., 2, Monomoy, 5 July 1970 (Blodget). They are routinely seen through October, and there are approximately ten December records and at least one record of a bird that survived until January—i.e., 1 collected, South Yarmouth, 2 January 1909 (McKechnie, AK 26: 195).

Griscom and Snyder (1955) called the Prairie Warbler "an abundant transient," with up to 75 a day on Monomoy (e.g., 11 September 1948) and 67, Marblehead Neck, 15–22 September 1951. No counts remotely approaching these have been recorded since. This may reflect a gradual decline in the nesting population as clearings either grow into mature forests or are disturbed by development. *Fall maxima:* 30 +, Chatham, 9 September 1968 (RNEB). *Extreme dates:* 1, Westport, 13 April 1974 (O'Hara); 3, North Quabbin, 18 April 1966 (Clark); to 1, Orleans, 29 December 1973 (Baird, Forster); 1, Nantucket, 29 December 1979 (Buckley, Freeman).

## Palm Warbler   *Dendroica palmarum*

**Range:** Nearctic; breeds from northern Alberta, northern Ontario, southern Labrador, and Newfoundland south to northern Wisconsin and northern Maine. Winters in the southern United States, in Mexico, and in the Bahamas and Greater Antilles.

**Status:** Common to occasionally very common migrant; rare in winter.

**Occurrence:** Next to the Pine Warbler, the Palm Warbler is the earliest migratory warbler to pass through Massachusetts in the spring. Peak counts are usually recorded during late April, and, until about 1979, they were infrequently reported on the southeastern coastal plain, undoubtedly due to lack of observer coverage in that area in that season. *Spring maxima:* 150, Andover, 18 April 1954 (Kleber); 150, Granby, 24 April 1956 (Ballman); 100 +, Hingham, 21 April 1961 (Nelson); 100 +, Hingham, 24 April 1962 (Nelson); 89, Northampton, 25 April 1972 (Gagnon); 60 +, Provincetown, 28–29 April 1979 (Nikula).

Unlike the situation in spring, Palm Warblers in fall are much more numerous at the coast than they are inland. *Fall maxima:* 300, Plum Island, 18 October 1964 (Jodrey); 140, Monomoy, 29 September 1968 (Forster); 100, Monomoy, 22 September 1973 (Goodrich). Palm Warblers occasionally remain common at the immediate coast until late December—e.g., 60, Nantucket, 31 December 1978 (Heil), but they rarely survive the entire season—e.g., 1, South Attleboro, 23 February 1986 (Hallett). *Winter maxima:* 46, Buzzards Bay CBC, 14 December 1991; 30, Nantucket CBC, 1

January 1989; 27, Mid-Cape Cod CBC, 22 December 1991; 14, Eastham, 19 January 1975 (Laux); 4–5, Bridgewater, entire winter of 1977–1978 (Petersen). There are no midwinter records from inland portions of the state. **Extreme dates** (for migrants): 1, Mt. Auburn Cemetery, Cambridge, 21 March 1973 (Robinson); to 1, Chappaquiddick, 16 August 1974 (Chalif).

**Subspecies:** Most spring migrants are of the eastern breeding subspecies, *D. p. hypochrysea* ("Yellow" Palm Warbler). *D. p. palmarum* ("Western" Palm Warbler) is rare in spring; the only recent published records are: 1 with 75 *D. p. hypochrysea*, Swampscott, 8 May 1962 (Ingalls, Snyder); 1, IRWS, 27 April 1982 (Heil). Most fall migrant Palm Warblers in Massachusetts, on the coast at least, are *D. p. palmarum*, although an undetermined number of dull-plumaged immature *D. p. hypochrysea*, which usually migrate inland in this season, may occur. Nonetheless, it is not unusual to see a few clearly marked *D. p. hypochrysea* among large flocks of Palm Warblers in fall.

# Bay-breasted Warbler   *Dendroica castanea*

**Range:** Primarily eastern Nearctic; breeds from southwestern MacKenzie, northern Ontario, and Nova Scotia south to northern Minnesota and northern New England. Winters in Panama and northern South America.

**Status:** Uncommon to fairly common spring and uncommon to occasionally very common fall migrant.

**Occurrence:** Bay-breasted Warblers breed in coniferous and mixed boreal forests. As migrants through Massachusetts during both spring and fall, their abundance fluctuates considerably from year to year. The earliest spring arrival date is: 2, Holyoke, 3 May 1970 (Yenlin), with a peak normally occurring during the third week of May. An exceptionally late wanderer appeared in Dover, 2 July 1962 (Wood, Reynolds, Lade). **Spring maxima:** 50, Andover, 26 May 1956 (Smith); 40, Plum Island, 26 May 1957 (Emery et al); 30, Mt. Auburn Cemetery, Cambridge, 23 May 1978 (Stymeist); 30, Mt. Auburn Cemetery, Cambridge, 18 May 1980 (Stymeist); 28 +, Nantucket, 15–20 May 1974 (Veit).

In a typical fall, the first migrants regularly appear in the third week of August, with the peak occurring during the last week of the month and the first week in September. By far, the largest numbers ever recorded occurred during the period between mid-August and late September of 1975 to 1979 and mostly involved birds on outer Cape Cod and Nantucket. Because Bay-breasted Warblers opportunistically feed upon larvae of the Spruce Budworm (*Choristoneura fumerifana*) (Morse 1978), an insect species that underwent a major "outbreak" or infestation in northern New England between 1974 and 1982, it seems likely that the large numbers of Bay-breasted Warblers in Massachusetts during that period reflect the species' high reproductive success in northern New England. Morse (op cit) found that bud-worm numbers at a study site in Maine were "far in excess of the food demands of these warblers," which suggests that the warblers may have successfully raised unusually large numbers of young during such infestations. *Fall maxima:* 400, Chatham, 26 August 1976 (Goodrich, Nikula); 100, Chatham, 20 August 1975 (Petersen); 25, Plum Island, 8 September 1990 (Moore, BBC). Prior to 1975, maximum counts were on the order of 15 to 20 birds per day per locality. There are five November records, the latest being: 1, Hamilton, 26 November 1969 (Nash).

## Blackpoll Warbler   *Dendroica striata*

**Range:** Nearctic; breeds from Alaska east to northern Ontario, northern Labrador, and Newfoundland south to central Manitoba, central Ontario, central Quebec, and, locally, at high elevations, to western Massachusetts. Winters in northern South America.

**Status:** Uncommon breeder near the summit of Mt. Greylock; very common to occasionally abundant migrant.

**Breeding:** Blackpoll Warblers were first confirmed breeding in the spruce forest near the summit of Mt. Greylock during the summer of 1934 (Bagg & Eliot 1937), although breeding was suspected as early as 1878 by Brewer, who believed he observed locally fledged young there. Snyder felt that 20 to 25 pairs were breeding there during the 1940s, but McNair (1978) stated that "Counts in the past decade [1970s], based on singing males and pairs seen, indicate that 12–14 pairs are now present." *Egg dates:* 15 June–early July (Maine).

**Nonbreeding:** This species and the Yellow-rumped Warbler are the two most abundant warblers to occur during migration in Massachusetts. In spring, the Blackpoll is one of the latest warblers to arrive, and the majority of migrants do not appear until late in the second week of May, although single birds are routinely seen during the first few days of the month. *Spring maximum:* 300, Plum Island, 26 May 1957 (Argue). There are five records of singing males from Cape Cod and Plymouth between the dates 8 June and 29 July, including one that spent the entire summer at Wellfleet Bay Wildlife Sanctuary in 1967 (Rhome et al). There are also records of singing males in July—e.g., Sudbury, Boston, Plum Island, and Marblehead Neck Wildlife Sanctuary.

Nisbet (1970a, 1970b) has shown that in fall, Blackpoll Warblers migrate southeastward across Canada to the Atlantic Coast between Nova Scotia and Virginia, and from there embark on a nonstop transoceanic flight to the West Indies and mainland South America. The bulk of the migrants pass through New England from mid-September to mid-October. During spring, they disperse more widely across eastern North America; and many are recorded in that season in the Mississippi Valley (cf Lowery 1974).

The abundance of Blackpoll Warblers in Massachusetts during the fall can be exemplified by the banding totals from Round Hill, Sudbury, by Howard and Baird: during September 1964, 899 were banded in 3,978 net hours; and in September 1966, 1,538 were banded in 1,736 net hours. Of these, 39.9 percent were adults; comparable banding records from the outer coast indicate that most of the individuals (80 to 90 percent) trapped there are immatures. On the coast, large numbers of Blackpoll Warblers occur only at irregular intervals, during or immediately following periods of rain or fog. For example, on 23 to 25 September 1952, Whittles counted 100 + in a half-acre patch of Pitch Pine on Nantucket and estimated that thousands must have been present on the island. Similarly, on 9 October 1979, after a period of heavy rain, 700 + Blackpoll Warblers were estimated around a ship 20 miles south of Martha's Vineyard by Manomet Bird Observatory staff. *Fall maxima:* 1,350, Belmont, 17 September 1940 (Robbins, Nash, Davis); 700 flying west, Littleton, 12–13 September 1968 (Baird); 300, Hadley, 23 September 1962 (Gardler). *Extreme dates:* 1, Hadley, 26 April 1969 (ABC); to 1, Eastham, 13 December 1979 (Goodrich). Blackpoll Warblers are regularly reported into late November, especially on the Cape and Islands.

## Cerulean Warbler  *Dendroica cerulea*

**Range:** Eastern Nearctic; breeds from southeastern Minnesota, southern Ontario, and Vermont south to northern Louisiana, Alabama, and North Carolina. Winters in northern South America.

**Status:** Rare and local breeder; rare but regular visitor or migrant, more numerous in spring.

**Breeding:** Over the years, singing male Cerulean Warblers have been reported in suitable breeding habitat on several occasions—e.g., 1, Lenox, 8–10 June 1956 (MAS campout); 1, Shelburne Falls, 23 May–8 July 1977 (Barnard); 1, Boxford, 1–14 June 1988 (Drummond); 1, Princeton, 14–29 June 1988 (Sferra). However, the species was not confirmed as a breeder in Massachusetts until 2 males were discovered feeding young at Quabbin Reservoir, Petersham, July 2–9, 1989 (Brownrigg, Petersen, VO), and up to 3 birds were present at Ware the same year. Breeding has seemingly been more or less continuous at Quabbin since that time, but the total Massachusetts breeding population probably does not exceed 5 to 10 pairs. The colonization of Massachusetts by Cerulean Warblers is consistent with the species' gradual increase throughout the Northeast (see Bull 1974).

**Nonbreeding:** There were 108 spring records of Cerulean Warblers during the years 1954 to 1981 and spanning the dates 20 April 1976 (Mt. Auburn

Cemetery, Cambridge [Stymeist et al]) to early June. Since 1981, spring reports of this species have increased to the point that it is now annually reported during major flights of commoner warblers in mid-May. The records are rather evenly distributed throughout the mainland portion of the state, including a number of records from Berkshire County. Cerulean Warblers have been reported more frequently from Mt. Auburn Cemetery, Cambridge, than any other single locality in the state, which is undoubtedly due to the enormous concentration of observers there in spring. Most reports are of single birds, except: 3, Newburyport Cemetery, 22 May 1983 (Grugan).

Cerulean Warblers are much rarer in fall than in spring, with the records spanning the dates: 1, Monomoy, 10 August 1961 (Harrington); to 1 banded, MBO, 29 September 1969. Nearly all of the fall records are from the southeastern coastal plain, except: 1 that flew on board ship, Georges Bank, 20 August 1985 (Petersen, VO).

# Black-and-white Warbler   *Mniotilta varia*

**Range:** Primarily eastern Nearctic; breeds from southwestern Mackenzie, central Manitoba, and Newfoundland south to eastern Texas and eastern North Carolina. Winters from coastal South Carolina and Texas south to northern South America.

**Status:** Uncommon to fairly common breeder and migrant. Very rare in winter.

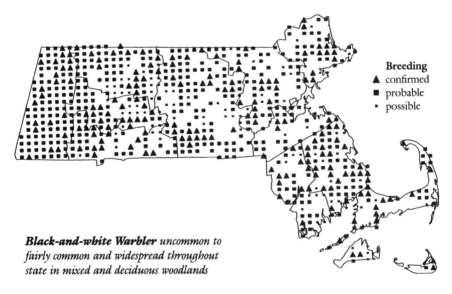

Breeding
▲ confirmed
■ probable
· possible

*Black-and-white Warbler uncommon to fairly common and widespread throughout state in mixed and deciduous woodlands*

**Breeding:** Black-and-white Warblers are widespread breeders in both deciduous and mixed forests throughout most of Massachusetts. They are only absent from intensely urbanized areas and from the highest elevations. *Summer maxima:* 32 pairs, West Newbury, June 1955 (deWindt); 47, Rocky Gutter Wildlife Management Area, South Middleboro, 15 June 1985 (SSBC); 36, East Quabbin, 12 June 1971 (Yenlin); 30, Wachusett Meadow Wildlife Sanctuary, Princeton, 14 June 1964 (FBC); 17, MCCBBC, 20 June 1982. *Egg dates:* 18–30 May.

**Nonbreeding:** This is one of the earlier warbler migrants of spring, routinely appearing in numbers in the last few days of April, with peak counts in early May. *Spring maxima:* 175, Nahant, 10 May 1948 (Griscom); other totals much lower—e.g., 60, Newburyport, 14 May 1989 (Griffis, BBC); 42, Mt. Auburn Cemetery, Cambridge, 13 May 1975 (fide Stymeist); 40+, Provincetown, 14 May 1980 (Nikula); 40, Winchester, 9 May 1975 (McClellan).

During fall migration, most birds occur between mid-August and late September. *Fall maxima:* 25, Chatham, 8 September 1976 (Nikula); 25, Chatham, 29 August 1982 (Nikula); 21, MNWS, 2 September 1982 (Heil). Despite their usual early departure from New England in fall, Black-and-white Warblers have been reported on at least a dozen occasions in December during the past 25 years, and there are even a few records later than December—e.g., 1, Norwell, 24 February 1960 (Merritt); 1, Hingham, 22 February 1960 (Hanley); 1, Milton, 10 January 1971 (MacDonald); 1, Norwell, 10 January 1971 (Litchfield). These midwinter records are most unusual. *Extreme dates* (aside from winter records): 2, North Easton, 1 April 1968 (Harris); 1, Manomet, 4 April 1973 (MBO staff).

# American Redstart   *Setophaga ruticilla*

**Range:** Nearctic; breeds from southeastern Alaska, northern Ontario, and Newfoundland south to northern Utah, southern Louisiana, and central Georgia. Winters from southern Florida, the Bahamas, and Mexico south to northern South America.

**Status:** Fairly common to very common breeder; common to very common migrant.

**Breeding:** The American Redstart is one of the commonest warblers to occur in Massachusetts, both as a breeding species and as a migrant. The species is a widespread breeder throughout most upland portions of the state, particularly where mature deciduous forests exist. East of Worcester County, redstarts are less common, and they are virtually absent from the pine barrens of the coastal plain. *Egg dates:* 29 May–21 June.

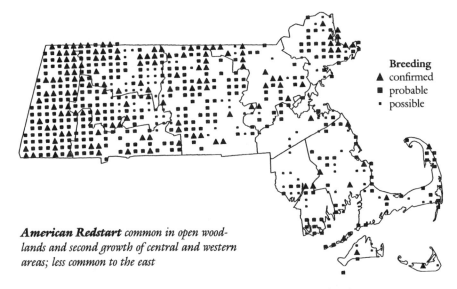

Breeding
▲ confirmed
■ probable
• possible

*American Redstart common in open wood-
lands and second growth of central and western
areas; less common to the east*

**Nonbreeding:** The American Redstart may sometimes be the most common migrant passerine in Massachusetts during late May, when many of the
birds that are seen are recognizable as one-year-old males. Arrival of local
breeders takes place in mid-May. *Spring maxima:* 600, Connecticut River
valley, 20 May 1948 (Griscom); 400 +, Plum Island, 2 June 1967 (Forster);
300 +, Plum Island, 30 May 1973 (Petersen); 250 +, Plum Island, 31 May 1977
(Veit). During fall, the majority of migrants pass through during late
August and September, but there are at least twenty records later than 15
November since 1954. *Fall maxima:* 150, Chatham, 29 August 1982 (Nikula);
75, Monomoy, 28 August 1981 (Goodrich); 68 banded, Sudbury, 2–17 September 1966 (Baird); 60, Cuttyhunk, 27 September 1968 (Higginbotham); 53
banded, Manomet, 14–24 September 1966 (Anderson); 50, Monomoy, 10
September 1971 (Bailey). *Extreme dates:* 1, Avon, 22 April 1962 (Crane); to 1,
Sandwich, 6 December 1978 (Pease).

## Prothonotary Warbler  *Protonotaria citrea*

**Range:** Southeastern Nearctic; breeds from western Iowa, southwestern
Minnesota, southwestern Ontario, and Long Island, New York, south
to eastern Texas and central Florida. Absent from high elevations. Winters
from Mexico south and east to Venezuela.

**Status:** One definite and two probable breeding records. Rare but regular
spring and fall visitor.

**Breeding:** On 9 May 1886, Brewster collected a male Prothonotary Warbler
along the Sudbury River in Concord. On 17 August, he collected a female

and a juvenile, which he had found the previous day, and, on 23 August, he finally collected a second male. The presence of a juvenile bird on 16 August is evidence that the birds bred very close to that locality, although Brewster himself was "convinced that he had missed establishing a definite breeding record" (Griscom 1949). In 1979, a female Prothonotary Warbler built a nest in a garage in Hawley between 18 May–11 June (fide Kellogg) but was apparently never joined by a male. Most conclusively, a pair of Prothonotary Warblers built a nest in Sharon (Shannon et al) in 1982; however, the eggs were apparently destroyed by a House Wren, after which time the warblers disappeared.

There have also been instances in which apparently territorial male Prothonotary Warblers have been recorded singing in suitable habitat through early summer in Massachusetts. Kennard found a singing male along the Charles River in Auburndale, 19 June 1890, and collected it the next day. Other records include: 1 male singing daily along the Ipswich River, Topsfield, 18 May–1 June 1974 (McClellan et al); 1 apparently injured male singing along a stretch of the Charles River, Needham, 11 May–26 June 1980 (Pickup et al); 1 male present intermittently, Heard's Pond, Wayland, 12–17 June 1984 (Forster); 1 singing male, GMNWR, Concord, 29 May–July 1991 (Petersen, VO). *Egg dates:* June.

**Nonbreeding:** An average of 3 to 4 Prothonotary Warblers have been recorded each spring season since 1955. They may be found in April following coastal storms, most often in dense thickets near water on the Cape and Islands, and also during major warbler waves in May, when they are seen at scattered localities throughout the state, nearly always in swamps and wet thickets. *Spring maxima:* 2, Eastern Point, Gloucester, 14 May 1961 (Leahy); 2, Stoughton, 22 May 1961 (Keith). The highest seasonal total is: 8 reported, 26 April–11 May 1979 (BOEM).

As an example of the relative seasonal status of the Prothonotary Warbler, during the 26-year period from 1954 to 1979, the species was recorded only slightly more frequently in fall than in spring in Massachusetts (78 versus 68 records). Fall records are rather evenly distributed from late August to early October, with a slight concentration on Cape Cod during early September. *Fall maxima:* At least 10 (and possibly 14) in southeastern Massachusetts after Hurricane Edna, 10–11 September 1954 (RNEB). Usually only 1 to 3 birds are reported per season, and very rarely more than one per day per locality—e.g., 2, Chatham, 27 August 1964 (Harrington). The maximum seasonal total since 1954 is of seven birds on Cape Cod and the Islands (and one bird captured at sea in the Great South Channel), 18 August–11 October 1979 (BOEM). *Extreme dates:* 1, Chatham, 22 March 1983 (Bailey); 1, Martha's Vineyard, 22 March 1983 (Laux); 1, Dennis, 31 March 1981 (Stenberg, fide Nikula); to 1, Bolton, 14 November 1962 (Donovan, fide Kleber); 1, Nantucket, 21 October 1954 (Andrews). Inland, most occurrences are from the Connecticut and Sudbury River valleys, and only rarely from Berkshire County—e.g., 1, Pleasant Valley Wildlife Sanctuary, Lenox, 14 May 1945 (Bailey, Derby); 1, Pittsfield, 4–8 May 1954 (Noble); 1, Pittsfield, 1 September 1954 (Schumacher).

## Worm-eating Warbler   *Helmitheros vermivorus*

**Range:** Eastern Nearctic; breeds from northeastern Kansas and northeastern Texas northeast to southeastern New York and southern New England. Winters from southern Florida and Mexico south to the West Indies and Panama.

**Status:** Rare and local breeder; rare but regular migrant.

**Breeding:** Worm-eating Warblers breed in dense understory in ravines and on dry wooded hillsides. The first indication of possible breeding in Massachusetts occurred in 1923, when a singing male was found 24 June at Bash Bish Falls, Mt. Washington (Schmidt). Since then, the species has been recorded at three or more localities in southern Berkshire County, including the discovery of the first nest in the state at South Egremont, 19 June 1949 (McCarthy, Minneci). Singing Worm-eating Warblers were first found at Mt. Tom, Holyoke, in 1952 (Griscom & Snyder 1955), and as many as 12 have been heard singing there in a single day—e.g., 26 May 1968 (Gagnon). Mt. Tom continues to have the highest breeding density of the species in Massachusetts, although no more than two pairs per year have ever actually been proven to nest there.

In 1962, a nest of Worm-eating Warblers containing 5 well-grown young was found at Doublet Hill, Weston (Burt, Fitzpatrick). The nest was said to be "typical . . . lined with stems of *Polytrichium*, and built on the ground beneath an overhanging lowbush blueberry . . . on a southwest slope in open deciduous woods, about six feet from a sheer rock face," (Smith 1964). Since then, Worm-eating Warblers have been confirmed breeding at Dover (1975 on) and Weston (more or less continuously since 1962), and territorial males have been reported in Southwick (1975–present), Uxbridge (June–July 1978), Southbridge (1979), Upton (1981), and the Blue Hills Reservation, Norfolk County (1984 on). *Egg dates:* 18–19 June.

**Nonbreeding:** There has been a steady increase in reports of migrant Worm-eating Warblers since the turn of the century, but this may simply be a reflection of an increased number of observers. The pattern of occurrence of this species during migration is quite similar to that of the Prothonotary Warbler, although Worm-eating Warblers are generally scarce away from known breeding localities. The maximum number recorded during any spring is seventeen, including thirteen migrants at eastern Massachusetts coastal localities between 23 April–27 May 1979 (BOEM). Like Prothonotary

Warblers, Worm-eating Warblers occasionally appear in Massachusetts following coastal storms in April—e.g., 1, Salem, 16 April 1902 (PMS #6405).

The maximum seasonal total for a fall season is five singles between 5–26 September 1971 and five singles during September 1962 (fide Emery). *Fall maximum:* 3, Chatham, 1 September 1963 (Forster). *Extreme dates:* 1, Salem, 16 April 1902 (PMS #6405); to 1, Sandwich, 6 December 1975 (Nikula, Laux); 1, Orleans, 29 November 1968 (Smart et al).

# Swainson's Warbler  *Limnothlypis swainsonii*

**Range:** Southeastern Nearctic; breeds from northwestern Arkansas, southern Indiana, southern Ohio, and coastal Maryland south to southern Louisiana and northern Florida. Winters in the Bahamas, the Greater Antilles, and on the Yucatan Peninsula.

**Status:** Vagrant: one, or possibly two, records.

**Occurrence:** A Swainson's Warbler that appeared at the Beech Forest, Provincetown, 4 May 1982 (Young) remained until 6 May, during which time it occasionally was seen by numerous observers (Nikula, Bailey, Petersen, Forster, et al) and was color-photographed by Nikula (photos on file at MAS). A second sight record of a Swainson's Warbler in Massachusetts, not previously published anywhere other than *Bird News of Western Massachusetts* (8: 37), seems likely to have been correct. The bird was seen at Sandy Beach, Hadley, 30 April 1968 (Reese, Strom), during an early wave of passerine migrants.

# Ovenbird  *Seiurus aurocapillus*

**Range:** Nearctic; breeds from northeastern British Columbia, central Quebec, southern Labrador, and Newfoundland south to Arkansas and northern Georgia. Winters from Texas and South Carolina south to Panama and northern South America, and also in the West Indies.

**Status:** Common breeder, except on the outer Islands. Variously uncommon to common migrant; very rare in winter.

**Breeding:** Ovenbirds breed commonly in deciduous and mixed woodlands throughout the state, although their apparent abundance relative to many other species is somewhat exaggerated by their loud and distinctive song. Sample densities: 131, Rocky Gutter Wildlife Management Area, South Middleboro, 15 June 1985 (SSBC); 91, Petersham, 30 May 1960 (Hunt); 48, Littleton, June 1960 (Bolton); 20, MCCBBC, 20 June 1982. *Egg dates:* 17 May–8 July.

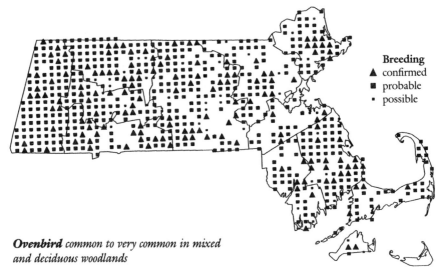

**Breeding**
▲ confirmed
■ probable
· possible

***Ovenbird*** *common to very common in mixed and deciduous woodlands*

**Nonbreeding:** Ovenbirds that breed in Massachusetts are usually singing on territory by the last week of April—earliest, 1, Topsfield, 15 April 1973 (Webster)—but peak counts of migrants do not usually occur until the second week of May. ***Spring maxima*** (major "flights" in 1946 and 1948): 350, Nahant, 17 May 1946 (Argue); 260, Nahant, 10 May 1948 (Kelley); 100, Connecticut River valley, 20 May 1948 (Griscom). Counts such as these appear staggeringly high by recent standards—e.g., 88, Greater Springfield Census, 9 May 1970 (ABC); 40, Mt. Auburn Cemetery, Cambridge, 13 May 1964 (Argue); 25 dead and 15 alive, Prudential Center, Boston, 9 May 1969 (Wiggin); 22, MNWS, 17 May 1977 (Heil). The high totals from 1946 and 1948 were attributed to peculiar weather conditions at the time. Heavy rains on the nights before the observations apparently grounded many migrants.

Ovenbirds are much less numerous during fall migration than in spring, and it is unusual to see more than 5 at any locality on a single day. This is apparently only partly due to their inconspicuousness in that season, evidenced by the fact that the Manomet Bird Observatory, for example, bands about twice as many Ovenbirds during spring than fall. ***Fall maxima:*** 18 banded, August 1973 (MBO); 15 banded, Plymouth, August 1973 (Anderson); 12, MNWS, 23 September 1956 (Argues); 6, Eastern Point, Gloucester, 17 September 1978 (Veit).

Unlike most other species of warblers, Ovenbirds are reported rather frequently in late fall and winter. Since 1957, there have been nearly 20 December records, along with several midwinter records—e.g., 1, Montague, 17 December 1940–30 January 1941 (Bagg); 1, Framingham, 3 January 1976 (Quinlan, Forster); 1, Abington, 1–30 January 1975 (Pillsbury); 1, Sherborn, 1 February–3 March 1975 (Taylor et al); 1, Sandwich, 10–17 February 1974 (Pease et al); 1, Falmouth, 14 February 1958 (Walker).

# Northern Waterthrush   *Seiurus noveboracensis*

**Range:** Nearctic; breeds from central Alaska east to northern Ontario, central Labrador, and Newfoundland and south to southern Ontario, Pennsylvania, and Massachusetts. Winters from Florida and Texas south through Central America and the West Indies to Peru and Ecuador.

**Status:** Uncommon and local breeder; common migrant.

**Breeding:** Northern Waterthrushes were first discovered breeding in Massachusetts when Thayer (1905) found a nest in Lancaster during the summer of 1905. They have steadily increased since then, being first found in Berkshire County in 1937 (McNair 1978), and in Red Maple swamps in Bedford and Lincoln in 1942 (Griscom 1949). Anderson and Maxfield (1962), referring to Pine Swamp in Raynham, reported that Northern Waterthrushes were "probably . . . the commonest breeding warbler" in this southeastern Massachusetts swamp. Currently, Northern Waterthrushes have "occupied most conceivable nesting localities" in Berkshire County (McNair 1978) and are found in a number of wooded swamps, east locally to Essex County and the Sudbury River valley. They have also been proven to breed in most White Cedar and Red Maple swamps in the southeastern part of the state; however, breeding on Cape Cod and the Islands remains to be proven. *Egg dates:* 21 May–15 June; one brood yearly.

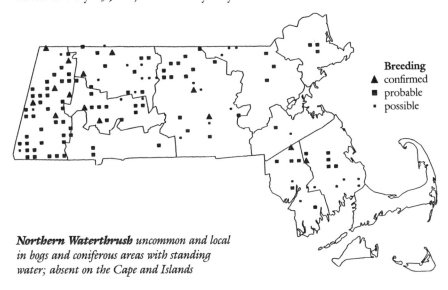

**Breeding**
▲ confirmed
■ probable
· possible

*Northern Waterthrush uncommon and local in bogs and coniferous areas with standing water; absent on the Cape and Islands*

**Nonbreeding:** Northern Waterthrushes arrive on their breeding territories in Massachusetts by the last few days of April. Peak counts of migrants, however, are not usually recorded until the second week of May. Under most circumstances, it is unusual to see more than 10 to 15 during a big spring flight of passerines, but under exceptional conditions, when large numbers of migrants are grounded, many more may be encountered. **Spring maxima:** 110, Connecticut River valley, 20 May 1948 (Griscom); 75+, Plum Island, 26 May 1955 (Griscom); 75, Nahant, 19 May 1946 (Baird); 20, Provincetown, 13 and 17 May 1980 (Nikula, Goodrich). Massachusetts breeders begin departing during late July, although migrants are commonly seen, particularly at the outer coast, until early October. **Fall maxima:** 14 banded, Nantucket, 3 September 1958 (Heywood, Andrews); 13 banded, Nantucket, 12 September 1958 (Willmann et al); 11, MNWS, 2 September 1979 (Stymeist); 11, South Wellfleet, 30 July 1965 (Forster). **Extreme dates:** 1, Orleans, 18 April 1974 (Goodrich); 1, Plum Island, 6 June 1965 (Forster); to 1, Topsfield, 6 January 1974 (Thomas); 1, Concord CBC, 16 December 1973.

## Louisiana Waterthrush   *Seiurus motacilla*

**Range:** Eastern Nearctic; breeds from eastern Nebraska, central Wisconsin, and southern New England south to northern Arkansas and northern Georgia. Winters from Mexico and the West Indies south to northern South America.

**Status:** Uncommon and local breeder; very uncommon migrant.

**Breeding:** Massachusetts lies within the rather limited region of sympatry between this species and Northern Waterthrush. Typically, there is a distinct difference between the nesting ecology of the two species; Northerns prefer wooded swamps with stagnant water, and Louisianas favor swiftly flowing streams through rich woodlands. Somewhat atypically, Louisiana Waterthrushes have been recorded nesting in Massachusetts around woodland

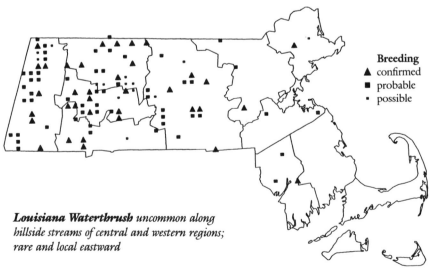

**Breeding**
▲ confirmed
■ probable
• possible

*Louisiana Waterthrush uncommon along hillside streams of central and western regions; rare and local eastward*

ponds in Berkshire County (McNair 1978), as well as in the Boxford State Forest and the Blue Hills Reservation in Milton. In 1981, a singing Louisiana Waterthrush was present all summer in a Red Maple swamp in Lakeville (Hill, Petersen, see Forbes & O'Regan 1970) in a habitat similar to that inhabited by this species on Long Island, New York (Bull 1974). Because Louisiana Waterthrushes have been known to breed in the Connecticut River valley since 1869, in Berkshire County since 1902, and in Essex County since 1948, it appears that the Northern Waterthrush may be the more recent arrival in Massachusetts. McNair (1978) actually suggested that Louisianas may have initially expanded their range to occupy habitats later usurped by Northerns. Sample densities: 14, Granville, 7 June–17 July 1989 (Kellogg); 8, Mt. Tom, 23 April 1971 (Petersen); 2–3 pairs, Boxford State Forest, since at least the mid–1960s (VO). *Egg date:* 23 May.

**Nonbreeding:** Louisiana Waterthrushes are infrequently detected as migrants away from breeding localities. A few are seen at localities such as Mt. Auburn Cemetery, Cambridge, Nahant, and Marblehead Neck during mid-April, but there are very few records from the outer coast between early July and mid-September. *Extreme dates:* 1, Sunderland Fish Hatchery, 31 March 1972 (Seitz); to 1, Tuckernuck Island, 12 September 1973 (Veit).

# Kentucky Warbler   *Oporornis formosus*

**Range:** Eastern Nearctic; breeds from southeastern Nebraska, northern Illinois, southeastern New York, and southwestern Connecticut south to Texas, Louisiana, and central Georgia. Winters from Mexico to northern South America.

**Status:** Rare but regular spring and fall migrant.

**Occurrence:** There has been a pronounced increase in the frequency of occurrence of this southern warbler in Massachusetts since 1955, at which time Griscom and Snyder knew of only six sight records and one specimen. Since 1954, more than 100 Kentucky Warblers have occurred in Massachusetts, the majority of which have appeared during major flights of other warblers between the dates 10 and 30 May. Among the largest seasonal totals are (fide BOEM): 10, 14–31 May 1977; 9, 13–24 May 1973; and 8, 6–21 May 1976. Most reports come from traditional migrant traps such as Mt. Auburn Cemetery, Cambridge; Nahant; and Marblehead Neck; but a few regularly appear in wooded swamps some distance inland—e.g., Milton, Dover, Weston, Holliston, Carlisle, Newton. The only record from Berkshire County is: 1 singing male, Richmond, 7 May 1976 (Goodrich et al). Other far inland records include: 1, Lunenburg, 22 May 1965 (Hayes); 1, Petersham, 15 May and 14 June 1971 (Clark, fide Blodget); 1, Bramanville, 24 May 1973 (Quinlan); 1, Uxbridge, 16 May 1980 (Wheelock, Muller).

Unlike other southern warblers, Kentucky Warblers do not frequently appear in April after southerly storms, and there is apparently only one such record: 1 dead, Eastern Point, Gloucester, 17 April 1961 (Morris). The presence of birds in summer suggests the possibility that this species may occasionally attempt to nest in Massachusetts, although definitive evidence is lacking. Possible nesting attempts include: 2 immature males (1 banded and photographed), Pine Swamp, Raynham, 17–18 August 1965 (Anderson, see RNEB, August 1965); 1 male, near Edgartown, Martha's Vineyard, spent the "summer" (until 21 August) of 1919 (Worden); 1 singing male, Carlisle, continuously present from 16 May through July 1982 (Harte et al); 1, Westminster, continuously present from 30 May–23 July 1987 (Quinlan).

There are nearly fifty fall records of Kentucky Warblers since 1954, but none previous to that time. Most fall reports occur between the dates 20 August and 10 September. Several inland fall records following hurricanes are: 1, Northampton, 29 August 1954 (Eliot); 1, Worcester, 1 September 1954 (Mills); 1, Pittsfield, 18 September 1954 (Schumacher). Other fall records include: 1, Waltham, 5 October 1959 (Lothrop); 1, Lincoln, 1 October 1974 (Nisbet). There are no reports in either spring or fall of more than two birds per day per locality. *Extreme dates:* 1 dead, South Wellfleet, 17 November 1969 (Bailey).

# Connecticut Warbler    *Oporornis agilis*

**Range:** Nearctic; breeds from eastern British Columbia, northern Ontario, and northwestern Quebec south to northern Minnesota and northern Michigan. Winters from northeastern Colombia south to central Brazil.

**Status:** Rare but regular fall migrant: two spring records.

**Occurrence:** Connecticut Warblers were much more common as migrants prior to 1900 than they are today. Brewster (1906) speaks of collecting 60 individuals between 10–30 September 1870 in Cambridge, and an even larger number in 1871. He felt that this collecting had little adverse effect upon the population and claimed, "Indeed I have never known them to be more abundant here than they were in September, 1881, and very many were noted during the following autumn also. We used to find Connecticut Warblers oftenest among thickets of clethra, *Andromeda ligustrina*, shad-bush, and black alder, which formed a dense undergrowth beneath the large maples that shaded the wooded islands of this swamp, and in the beds of touch-me-not (*Impatiens*) that covered some of its wettest portions." By 1955, Griscom and Snyder stated, "Recent high counts are 12 in a season and 5 at Marblehead Neck, 15–22 September 1951."

Currently, the Connecticut Warbler is one of the rarest migrant passerines to occur regularly in Massachusetts. Griscom and Snyder's implication that this species was more common than the Mourning Warbler in fall, coupled with the widely accepted, but seemingly fallacious, notion that Connecticut Warblers occur most frequently at the outer coast, has led to confusion among observers as to the relative abundance of Connecticut and Mourning warblers in Massachusetts. Connecticut Warblers are most often reported in precisely the habitat described by Brewster—inland Red Maple swamps containing lots of moist undergrowth.

The Manomet Bird Observatory banded seventy-one Mourning and forty-six Connecticut warblers during fall in the 9-year period 1966–1974, and extensive field experience suggests that, on the coast, Mourning Warblers may outnumber Connecticuts in fall by an even wider margin. In summary, banding data and field observations suggest that most *Oporornis* warblers seen from mid-August to mid-September in coastal thickets are Mournings, whereas a somewhat higher percentage of Connecticut Warblers occur between mid-September and early October at more inland locations. Totals since 1970 have averaged ten to fifteen reports per season. ***Fall maxima:*** 37, throughout Massachusetts—including 9 banded in Littleton (Baird), 5 banded at MBO, 4 in the Connecticut River valley—6 September–23 October 1968 (RNEB). ***Extreme dates:*** 1 collected, Readville, 24 May 1883 (Blaney, MCZ #291271); 1 male observed and heard singing, Mt. Auburn Cemetery, Cambridge, 31 May 1976 (Quinlan, McNair); to 1 banded, Petersham, 23 August 1991 (Baird).

# Mourning Warbler    *Oporornis philadelphia*

**Range:** Nearctic; breeds from central Alberta, northern Ontario, and Newfoundland south to northern Wisconsin, central Michigan, and western Massachusetts. Winters from Nicaragua south to northern South America.

**Status:** Very uncommon local breeder in Berkshire county; uncommon spring and fall migrant.

**Breeding:** In 1883, Brewster first discovered Mourning Warblers nesting abundantly in Massachusetts at Mt. Greylock, and Faxon and Hoffman (1900) similarly found them there in considerable numbers. As the forests on Greylock's upper slopes were allowed to mature, the numbers of breeding Mourning Warblers undoubtedly declined over the years. McNair (1978) suggested that during the 1960s and 1970s, 2 to 4 pairs probably nested on Mt. Greylock, but, by 1978, three additional localities were found at Hancock, Cheshire, and Dalton. By 1990, over fifty singing male Mourning Warblers were located in northern Berkshire and Franklin counties in June and July (Rancatti, Quinlan, fide Kellogg). Early successional brushy clearings and power-line cuts are essential to the successful breeding of this species. The only Worcester County breeding record occurred in Princeton in 1940 (Eliot 1941).

Birds of Massachusetts

**Nonbreeding:** The Mourning Warbler is the latest migrant warbler to arrive in Massachusetts; the bulk of the birds pass through during the last week of May and the first two weeks of June. During a heavy passerine migration between 20 May and 15 June, an active observer can expect to see 4 to 6 Mourning Warblers in a day, either at the coast or in the Connecticut River valley, but elsewhere it is unusual to see more than 1 or 2 per day. *Spring maxima:* 18, coastal Massachusetts, 17 May to 15 June 1975 (BOEM); 50 banded at MBO during this same time period, 44 of these between 1–11 June.

During the fall, Mourning Warblers, unlike Connecticut Warblers, are most frequently found in dense thickets at the immediate coast. Localities such as Plum Island, Nahant, Monomoy, and the offshore Islands are among the best places to observe this species, although small numbers are also regularly encountered inland. Most birds occur between mid-August and mid-September. *Fall maxima:* 24 reported, September 1976 (BOEM); 7, Nantucket, 20–21 September 1981 (Veit et al); 5+, Monomoy, 23 September 1978 (Nikula, Goodrich, et al). Inland, it is unusual to see more than 1 or 2 birds in a day. *Extreme dates:* 1 male dead, Hingham, 12 May 1965 (Terry); 1, Saugus, 18 June 1977 (Zendeh, Jackson); to 1, Beverly, 13–14 July 1957 (Snyder); 1 banded, MBO, 18 October 1976.

An *Oporornis* found dead in a snowbank in Manchester, 20 December 1972 (Hotz, specimen to PMS), was considered "probably *O. philadelphia*" by W. E. Lanyon.

# MacGillivray's Warbler  *Oporornis tolmiei*

**Range:** Western Nearctic; breeds from southern Alaska and southwestern Saskatchewan south to central California and central New Mexico. Winters from Mexico to Panama.

**Status:** Vagrant: four, possibly five, records.

**Occurrence:** The first indication of the possible presence of MacGillivray's Warbler in Massachusetts occurred when an indeterminate *Oporornis* was discovered at the Bergstrom's feeder in Waltham, 2 February 1939. The bird survived until 18 May, was seen by many people, including Griscom, but was not collected. Bergstrom reported that by April it had developed a partial white eye-ring, suggesting that it was probably *O. tolmiei*. Another *Oporornis* discovered at East Lexington, 13–29 November 1977 (Martin, Stymeist), was mist-netted, measured, and photographed on 15 November and was determined conclusively to be *O. tolmiei* (Stymeist 1978). A third individual carefully studied on Nantucket, 23 November 1978 (Veit, Litchfield, Perkins) was identified as *O. tolmiei* on the basis of its bright white eye crescents; pronounced gray hood, which was sharply demarcated from the yellow breast; and diffusely streaked grayish, rather than yellowish, throat. A fourth convincing sight record involved a bird carefully identified in South Peabody, 12–14 October 1990 (Heil et al). The most recent record was: 1 banded, MBO, 21 October 1991.

# Common Yellowthroat   *Geothlypis trichas*

**Range:** Nearctic; breeds from southeastern Alaska, northern Alberta, Quebec, and southeastern Newfoundland south to northern Mexico and southern Florida. Winters from California, the Gulf Coast, and South Carolina south to the Greater Antilles, Panama and Colombia.

**Status:** Common to very common breeder; very common migrant. Occasional in midwinter.

**Breeding:** The Common Yellowthroat is one of the most numerous and widespread nesting warblers in Massachusetts. The species is especially abundant on Cape Cod and the Islands—e.g., 118, MCCBBC, 20 June 1982. They are also very common in second growth, moist thickets, and marshes on the mainland—e.g., 72, South Groveland, 10 June 1990 (Stymeist); 65, Littleton, June 1960 (Bolton); 56, Wachusett Meadow Wildlife Sanctuary, Princeton, 14 June 1964 (FBC); 44, Rocky Gutter Wildlife Management Area, South Middleboro, 15 June 1985 (SSBC). *Egg dates:* 24 May–17 June.

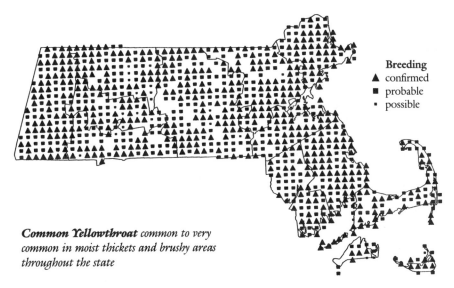

Breeding
▲ confirmed
■ probable
· possible

*Common Yellowthroat common to very common in moist thickets and brushy areas throughout the state*

**Nonbreeding:** The first arrivals of spring generally appear during the first week of May, but maximum counts are usually not recorded until mid-May. Griscom recorded some extraordinarily high counts during the 1940s following massive groundings of migrants by heavy rains; however, recent maxima have been much lower. *Spring maxima:* 525, Essex County, 29 May 1941 (Griscom); 300, Nahant, 10 May 1948 (Griscom); 225, Nahant, 17 May 1946 (Griscom); 150, Connecticut River valley, 20 May 1948 (Griscom). Recent counts include: 230, Plum Island, 19 May 1967 (Forster); 150+, Plum Island, 30 May 1973 (Petersen); 91, Wellesley, 15 May 1965 (Leverett et al).

In the fall, Common Yellowthroats gradually depart from Massachusetts during late August and September, thus making it difficult to detect pulses of migrants from farther north. *Fall maxima:* 129 banded, MBO, 7–31 August 1969; 72 banded, Monomoy, 26–31 August 1966 (Baird); 62 banded, Nantucket, September 1989 (Andrews): 60, Nantucket, 2–5 September 1977 (BBC, Drummond). Common Yellowthroats often linger until mid- or late December on the southeastern coastal plain and more rarely inland; however, most birds rarely survive the winter. *Winter maxima:* 8, Greater Boston CBC, 16 December 1979; 4, GMNWR, 2 January 1972 (Stymeist, Alden).

# Hooded Warbler   *Wilsonia citrina*

**Range:** Eastern Nearctic; breeds from southeastern Nebraska, southern Ontario, and southern New England south to northern Florida and the Gulf Coast states. Winters from southern Mexico to Costa Rica.

**Status:** Rare, local, and erratic breeder; uncommon to rare but regular visitor or migrant.

**Breeding:** Hooded Warblers were first recorded nesting in Massachusetts in 1954, when Hill observed a female feeding young in Fall River on 2 July. Apparently territorial singing males were recorded in the Westport-Acoaxet area from 1958 until 1974—a maximum of 5, 6 June 1966 (Petersen, Forster)—and two nests were found in Westport in 1968 (Barrowclough, Fernandez), one of which contained 3 young on 19 June. This peripheral population seems to have been quickly extirpated. The only other suggestion of breeding in Massachusetts was the observation of 2 young in Raynham, 23 July 1959 (Anderson), and the presence of a singing male in Southampton in the Connecticut River valley, 25–28 June 1959, and throughout June 1971 (Stone). Several additional scattered records of singing males in June gave no further evidence of nesting. *Egg dates:* 29 May–24 June (Connecticut).

**Nonbreeding:** Hooded Warblers are the most frequent of the southern warblers to occur in Massachusetts. Spring birds occur from late April to late May, sometimes following spring storms, while fall migrants occur from mid-August to mid-October. *Spring maxima:* 11–12 reported, 3–28 May 1959 (RNEB); 11 reported in eastern Massachusetts, 4–22 May 1977 (BOEM).

*Fall maxima:* 8 reported, throughout Massachusetts, 5–28 September 1959 (RNEB); 8 reported, eastern Massachusetts, 21 August–27 October 1974 (BOEM). The majority of reports are of single birds, most often along the immediate coast. *Extreme dates:* 1, Cohasset, 8 April 1970 (fide Emery); 1, MBO, 12 April 1989; to 1, Tuckernuck Island, 6 August 1977 (Veit et al); 1, Nantucket, 7 November 1969 (Reyes).

## Wilson's Warbler   *Wilsonia pusilla*

**Range:** Nearctic; breeds from northern Alaska, northern Ontario, central Labrador, and Newfoundland south to southern California, northern Mexico, northern Minnesota, and northern New England. Winters from Mexico to western Panama.

**Status:** Fairly common spring and fall migrant.

**Occurrence:** In Massachusetts, spring migrant Wilson's Warblers tend to be most common near the coast, often reaching their peak numbers during the last week of May. They are uncommon in the Connecticut River valley, in Berkshire County, and on Cape Cod in spring. *Spring maxima:* 50, Plum Island, 28 May 1957 (Smart); 38, North Scituate, 22 May 1974 (Brown); 30 +, Plum Island, 30 May 1973 (Petersen). In fall, the bulk of Wilson's Warblers migrate south through Massachusetts in late August and September, but there have been at least twelve November and four December records since 1954. *Fall maxima:* 20 +, Chatham, 30 August 1976 (Nikula); 20, Chatham, 12 September 1976 (Nikula); 17 banded, MBO, 27–30 August 1969; 17, Monomoy, 7 September 1967 (Forster); 16, Plum Island, 15 September 1974 (Petersen); 12 banded, Nantucket, 9–13 September 1989 (Andrews). *Extreme dates:* 1, 3 May (fide Griscom & Snyder 1955); to 1, Chatham, 12–31 December 1978 (Clem); 1, Forest Hills, Boston, 16–17 December 1979 (CBC, D'Entremont et al).

## Canada Warbler   *Wilsonia canadensis*

**Range:** Nearctic; breeds from central Alberta, southern Quebec, and Nova Scotia south to central Minnesota, northern Ohio, New Jersey, and Long Island, and in the Appalachian Mountains to northern Georgia. Winters in northern South America.

**Status:** Fairly common breeder east to Essex County; local on the southeastern coastal plain. Common to occasionally very common migrant.

**Breeding:** Canada Warblers breed in moist, swampy woodlands that contain a dense shrub understory. Sample density: 28, 6 June 1952, Mt. Greylock

(Snyder); 26, Granville, 7 June–17 July 1989 (Kellogg); 16 singing males, "along seven miles of the Old Appalachian Trail in Dalton and Cheshire," 22 June 1978 (McNair); 13, South Middleboro, 15 June 1985 (SSBC). *Egg dates:* 9–26 June; one brood yearly.

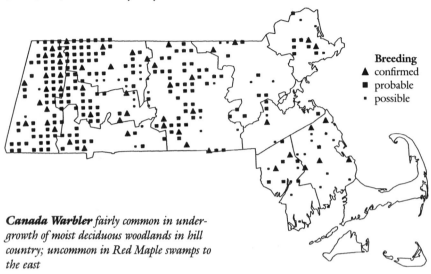

**Breeding**
▲ confirmed
■ probable
• possible

*Canada Warbler fairly common in under-growth of moist deciduous woodlands in hill country; uncommon in Red Maple swamps to the east*

**Nonbreeding:** In spring, breeding Canada Warblers arrive on territory by mid-May, but peak counts of migrants are usually recorded late in the month. *Spring maxima:* 300, Provincetown, 24 May 1974 (Bailey); 250, Connecticut River valley, 20 May 1948 (Griscom); 100, Provincetown, 25 May 1981 (Bailey); 75 +, Plum Island, 30 May 1973 (Petersen et al); 75, Chatham, 25 May 1981 (Nikula); 70, Andover, 26 May 1956 (Root). Canada Warblers depart rather early in fall and are rare after September. *Fall maxima:* 25 banded, MBO, 12–30 August 1969; 25, Chatham, 30 August 1976 (Nikula); 12, Eastern Point, Gloucester, 28 August 1977 (Veit). *Extreme dates:* 1, Middlesex County, 10 April 1878 (MCZ, fide Griscom and Snyder 1955); 1, Mt. Auburn Cemetery, Cambridge, 3 May 1977 (Earle); to 1, Worcester, 31 October 1960 (Crompton).

## Painted Redstart  *Myioborus pictus*

**Range:** Primarily Neotropical; breeds from northwestern Arizona and western Texas south to northern Nicaragua. United States breeders migrate south to Central America in winter.

**Status:** Vagrant: one record.

**Occurrence:** A Painted Redstart discovered at the Marblehead Neck Wildlife Sanctuary, 18 October 1947 (deWindt, Searle), represented the first record for eastern North America at the time. It was first identified by Herbert Caswell, and, on 19 October, it was seen by over 50 observers and photographed in color (fide Griscom & Snyder 1955).

## Yellow-breasted Chat  *Icteria virens*

**Range:** Nearctic; breeds from southern British Columbia, southern Minnesota, and southern Vermont south to northern Florida and Mexico. Winters mainly from southern Texas and Florida to Panama, and regularly in small numbers in the United States north to New England.

**Status:** Rare and local breeder; uncommon to very uncommon migrant. Rare but regular in winter, occasionally surviving in mild seasons.

**Breeding:** Yellow-breasted Chats have always been rare, local, and erratic in their breeding distribution in Massachusetts. They prefer open fields with scattered shrubs and patches of dense undergrowth for nesting. Breeding birds have most frequently been found in the Connecticut and Housatonic river valleys, in Bristol County, and in the Common Pastures around Newburyport.

During the period 1955–1970, chats were found breeding at the following locations (fide BNWM, RNEB, BOEM). *Berkshire County:* South Egremont (1955, 1957, 1962); Sheffield (1966); Hancock (1966). *Connecticut River valley:* four singing birds (1954); Longmeadow (1961); Westfield (1967). *Worcester County:* West Boylston (1958, 1961). *Essex County:* Newbury (1954, 1956, 1961 [2 pairs]); MNWS (1955); Ipswich (1962). *Southeastern Coastal Plain:* Acoaxet (1955, 1959, 1966); Chatham (1957, 1964); South Somerset (1959); South Dartmouth (1962); Middleboro (1962). In some cases, these records simply represent pairs of birds present in suitable breeding habitat throughout the summer, with no other conclusive evidence of nesting. It is probable, however, that nesting was attempted in each case.

Since 1970, chats have presumably nested at Southwick (1970), South Egremont (1971), Orleans (1971), Sandwich (1973 [Sorrie 1974]), Manomet (1973, 1977), Leicester (1974), Middleboro (1975), Dartmouth (1976), Fowl Meadow, Milton (1979), and Northampton (1983–1984). *Egg dates:* 18 May– 18 June.

**Nonbreeding:** Yellow-breasted Chats are rare to uncommon during spring migration in Massachusetts and are most often found in May during major flights of other passerines. *Spring maxima:* 9, throughout Massachusetts, 8–31 May 1991 (BOEM, BNWM); 8, throughout Massachusetts, 8–30 May 1968 (RNEB); 7, throughout Massachusetts, 5–29 May 1971 (fide Emery). There has been a slight decrease in the number of spring sightings since the late 1950s.

One of the more perplexing mysteries of fall passerine migration in

Massachusetts is the seemingly disproportionate number of Yellow-breasted Chats reported during fall migration at the outer coast, particularly compared to the frequency with which other southern species occur there. It has been suggested that the preponderance of fruiting shrubs along the New England coast in early fall may be a contributing factor in this seemingly anomalous abundance because chats apparently feed largely on fruit at that time of year (Lloyd-Evans, pers. comm.). *Fall maxima:* 58 banded, August–October 1974 (MBO); 41 banded, 12 August–26 September 1979 (MBO); 34 banded, Nantucket, 10 August–30 October 1957 (Dennis et al); 20 banded, Nantucket, September 1981 (Andrews); 11 banded, Nantucket, 2–27 September 1991 (Andrews). Despite these rather impressive banding totals, it is unusual for an observer to see more than 2 to 3 chats in a day in fall, even at ideal locations such as South Monomoy and Nantucket. Away from the immediate coast, Yellow-breasted Chats are decidedly uncommon—e.g., seasonal totals from the Connecticut River valley rarely exceed four.

Chats are hardy birds that routinely survive the winter at feeding stations, even at inland localities, as well as on the southeastern coastal plain where dense cover and abundant fruits and berries favor their survival. *Winter maxima:* 16 reported on CBCs (including 9, Cape Cod CBC), December 1991 (BOEM); 13 reported, eastern Massachusetts, January 1954 (RNEB); 3, Falmouth, 9 February 1980 (Nikula, Heil).

**Subspecies:** A Yellow-breasted Chat that spent the winter of 1944–1945 in Cambridge, surviving on berries and frozen bees, was found dead on 3 March 1945. Griscom determined the specimen to be *I. v. auricollis* of western North America on the basis of measurements (Griscom & Snyder, 1955). All other specimens from Massachusetts are apparently *I. v. virens*.

## Summer Tanager  *Piranga rubra*

**Range:** Primarily Nearctic; breeds from southeastern California, central Oklahoma, central Indiana, and southern New Jersey south to the Gulf States and southern Florida. Winters from central Mexico to central South America.

**Status:** Rare migrant; most numerous in spring.

**Occurrence:** Summer Tanagers appear in Massachusetts in numbers that vary considerably from year to year. Most individuals occur on Cape Cod and the Islands, principally in April and May and late September and October. It is possible that the factors that account for many of the April occurrences parallel those accounting for similarly early occurrences of Indigo Buntings (see that species account). Ordinarily, no more than one bird is seen per day per locality. *Spring maxima:* 29, throughout Massachusetts, 2 April–22 May 1961 (fide Emery); 12, eastern Massachusetts, 4–29 May

1979 (BOEM). The several summer records probably represent wandering lingerers from the spring migration—e.g., 1, Hingham, 5 July 1954 (Keenan); 1, Weymouth, 25 June 1963 (McWade); 1, Plum Island, 14 June 1974 (Clancy); 1, Middleboro, 15 June 1985 (Petersen). *Fall maxima:* 8, eastern Massachusetts, 5–9 October 1968 (RNEB); 5, coastal Massachusetts, 3–17 September 1969 (fide Emery). *Extreme dates:* 1, Nantucket, 2 April 1961 (Ferreira); to 1, North Scituate, 21–28 November 1964 (Bailey, Litchfield).

## Scarlet Tanager  *Piranga olivacea*

**Range:** Eastern Nearctic; breeds from southeastern Manitoba, southern Ontario, southern Quebec, and New Brunswick south to southeastern Oklahoma, central Arkansas, northern Georgia, and Maryland. Winters from Panama to Bolivia.

**Status:** Uncommon to common breeder; uncommon to fairly common migrant.

**Breeding:** Scarlet Tanagers are relatively common and conspicuous birds in mature deciduous and mixed forests. Their avoidance of Pitch Pines contributes to their scarcity on outer Cape Cod; however, they do routinely breed in the pine-oak woodlands of southeastern Massachusetts. Sample densities: 36, Newburyport Breeding Bird Census, 15 June 1980; 34 singing males, Wellesley, 12 June 1959 (Freeland); 21, GBBBC, 14 June 1980; 16, South Middleboro, 15 June 1985 (SSBC); 6 singing males, Brewster, 8 July 1955 (Smart). *Egg dates:* 2–17 June.

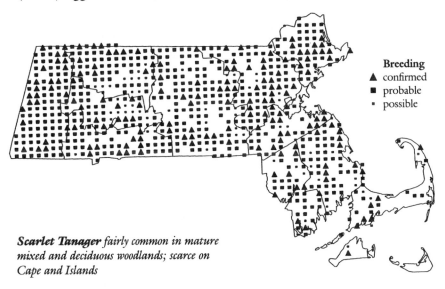

Breeding
▲ confirmed
■ probable
· possible

*Scarlet Tanager fairly common in mature mixed and deciduous woodlands; scarce on Cape and Islands*

**Nonbreeding:** Scarlet Tanagers seem to be more common as migrants during spring than fall, partly because they are more conspicuous in spring and partly because the fall migration is more protracted. Occasionally, they appear following April storms, long before the majority of regular migrants arrive—e.g., 6 individuals from Nantucket, Martha's Vineyard, and Quisset, 17–18 April 1961 (fide Emery). *Spring maximum:* 75, Essex County, 20 May 1967 (Hill). *Fall maxima:* 30 together after a hurricane, Needham, 12 September 1954 (Sargent et al); 22, Worthington, 5 September 1970 (Weigand); 8, Mt. Auburn Cemetery, Cambridge, 7 October 1970 (Stymeist). *Extreme dates:* 1, Chappaquiddick, Martha's Vineyard, 8 April 1958 (Worden); 1, North Chatham, 8 April 1958 (Mosher); to 1, Dover, 26 November 1955 (Bagg); 1, Avon, 26 November 1962 (Crane).

# Western Tanager  *Piranga ludoviciana*

**Range:** Western Nearctic; breeds from southern Alaska, northeastern Alberta, and central Saskatchewan south to southern California, southeastern Arizona, and west Texas. Winters from northern Mexico to northwestern Costa Rica.

**Status:** Rare migrant or visitor; recorded nearly annually in fall, much less frequently in spring.

**Occurrence:** Western Tanagers are among the more frequent vagrants to Massachusetts from western North America. They most often appear at feeding stations between mid-November and late December, but there is considerable variation in the number reported each year in Massachusetts. The largest statewide totals occurred during the late 1950s and early 1960s, as was also the case on Long Island, New York (Bull 1964)—e.g., 13, 25 September–16 December 1956 (RNEB); 12, 31 August–18 December 1957 (RNEB); 6, 14 August 1960–21 January 1961 (fide Emery). Since then, annual totals have been lower—e.g., 3, 20–31 December 1973 (BOEM); 3, 4–27 December 1977 (BOEM).

Western Tanagers are much rarer during spring than fall, there being fewer than ten reliable sight records—e.g., 1 male, Mt. Auburn Cemetery, Cambridge, 31 May 1961 (Claflin, fide Emery); 1 male, Barnstable, 10 May 1962 (Lyon); 1 male, Provincetown, 15 May 1967 (Bell, Bailey); 1, Chatham, 4 May 1970 (Copeland); 1, Duxbury, 29 May 1971 (Lund); 1 male, Scituate, 17 May 1976 (Flaherty); 1, Rowley, 21 May 1979 (Alexander).

**Remarks:** Spring male Western Tanagers should be identified with care because molting male Summer and Scarlet tanagers may have red heads, yellowish bodies, and dark wings in that season.

# Northern Cardinal  *Cardinalis cardinalis*

**Range:** Primarily eastern Nearctic; mainly resident from eastern South Dakota, central Minnesota, southern Ontario, and central Maine south to Baja California, central Texas, the Gulf States, and Florida.

**Status:** Common and widespread resident.

**Breeding:** Northern Cardinals occurred erratically in Massachusetts from 1835 (Griscom & Snyder 1955) until the 1940s. Many of the earlier reports may have involved escaped cage birds because cardinals were at one time popular as pets and were frequently imported from the South. Beginning about 1930, this species began a northward range extension that was apparently most rapid in the years between 1950 and 1970. There can be little doubt that the great increase in winter bird feeding has greatly enhanced their northward spread.

Cardinals first bred in Massachusetts in 1961, when a nest with 2 eggs was found in Wellesley, 29 May (Chandler, Petersen). Two nests were also found in Pittsfield during July 1961 (Hendricks et al). Throughout the 1960s, the species rapidly colonized the entire state, and, by 1970, cardinals nested in every county, being most numerous in the lowlands of the Connecticut River valley, in Berkshire County, and in the shore communities surrounding Buzzards Bay. In these areas, cardinals prefer to nest in dense thickets where there are lots of fruiting shrubs nearby. *Egg dates:* late April–late June.

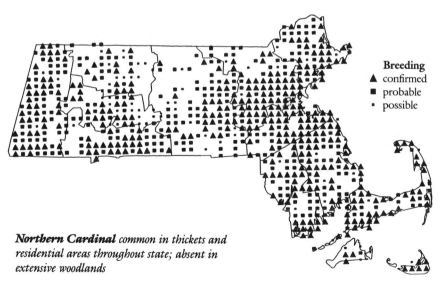

Breeding
▲ confirmed
■ probable
· possible

*Northern Cardinal common in thickets and residential areas throughout state; absent in extensive woodlands*

**Nonbreeding:** Cardinals are among the least migratory land birds in Massachusetts, and it is difficult to say at what time of year most dispersal occurs—e.g., a female was noted arriving at Muskeget Island, 18 June 1981 (Heil). *Maxima* (CBC): 567, Concord, 27 December 1991; 502, Northampton, 16 December 1990; 386, Concord, 27 December 1981; 300, Northampton, 20 December 1991; 299, Buzzards Bay, 14 December 1991.

## Rose-breasted Grosbeak   *Pheucticus ludovicianus*

**Range:** Primarily eastern Nearctic; breeds from northeastern British Columbia, southern Manitoba, southwestern Quebec, and Nova Scotia south to eastern Nebraska, northern Oklahoma, northern Ohio, and Maryland south in the Appalachian Mountains to northern Georgia. Winters from Mexico to northern South America.

**Status:** Fairly common breeder; uncommon to common migrant.

**Breeding:** Rose-breasted Grosbeaks are most numerous in the extensive broadleaf forests of the inland portions of Massachusetts, often in habitats similar to those preferred by Scarlet Tanagers. Unlike Scarlet Tanagers, however, they tend to avoid the dry pine-oak woodlands of southeastern Massachusetts, are rare breeders on Cape Cod, and seem to be absent from Martha's Vineyard and Nantucket. Sample densities: 23 males, Wellesley, June 1959 (Freeland); 29, GBBBC, 14 June 1980; 28, Newburyport Breeding Bird Census, 15 June 1980; 18, South Groveland, 10 June 1990 (Stymeist, VO); 10 pairs, Weston, June 1964 (Smith). *Egg dates:* 23 May–15 June.

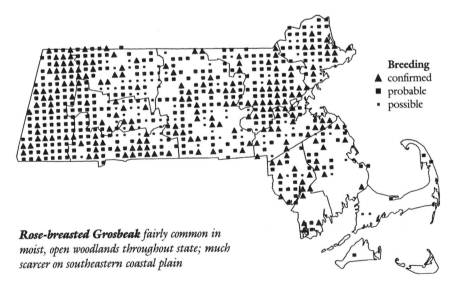

**Breeding**
▲ confirmed
■ probable
· possible

*Rose-breasted Grosbeak fairly common in moist, open woodlands throughout state; much scarcer on southeastern coastal plain*

**Nonbreeding:** Rose-breasted Grosbeaks are most numerous during spring and fall migration, with the highest counts usually occurring in spring. In that season, they are recorded in mid- to late May, but some occasionally occur in April after southerly storms. *Spring maxima:* 56, Wellesley, 21 May 1983 (Winkler); 50 +, Provincetown, 25 May 1983 (Nikula, Taylor); 22, Mt. Auburn Cemetery, Cambridge, 21 May 1975 (Stymeist et al); 20, Milton, 14 May 1980 (Veit); 20, Provincetown, 14 May 1980 (Nikula). In fall, most migrant Rose-breasted Grosbeaks are seen during September. *Fall maxima:* 21, Peabody, 8 September 1981 (Heil); 21, Princeton, 17 September 1977 (Stymeist); 15, Hadley, 17 September 1961 (Forster et al); 12, Nantucket, 5–25 October 1979 (Veit, Litchfield).

There are at least a dozen December and six January Massachusetts Rose-breasted Grosbeak records, including several specimens—e.g., 1 adult male, Salisbury, throughout the winter of 1961–1962 (deWindt); 1 adult male, Wellesley, 21 January–2 February 1982 (Cournoyer, Forster, et al). *Extreme dates:* 1, Northampton, 10 March 1968 (Hebert); 1, Springfield, 12 March 1968 (Cassidy); 1, Hopkinton, 19 March 1990 (Phipps); 1, Weston, 21–26 March 1968 (Davidson).

# Black-headed Grosbeak  *Pheucticus melanocephalus*

**Range:** Western Nearctic; breeds from southeastern British Columbia, southern Saskatchewan, and northwestern North Dakota south to eastern California, southeastern Arizona, west Texas, and central Kansas. Winters in Mexico.

**Status:** Rare late fall and winter visitor; approximately twenty records since 1970.

**Occurrence:** Many Black-headed Grosbeak reports in Massachusetts have not been accompanied by satisfactory documentation, which renders their evaluation difficult. However, there are enough detailed reports accompanied by clear color photographs to indicate that this species periodically occurs in the state. Records include: 1 immature male, Pittsfield, 2–4 May 1953 (Keith, Hendricks); 1 female, Annisquam, 16 January–23 April 1954 (Adams, Snyder, et al); 1 immature male, Barnstable, 28 October 1954–18 April 1955 (Lyons); 1, Ipswich, 4 December 1954–15 January 1955 (Gallant, VO); 1, Nantucket, 3–23 January 1956 (Blackshaw, Andrews, et al); 1, Beverly, late November 1957–9 May 1958 (Strickland et al); 1, Orleans, 1 January–1 May 1961 (fide Bailey); 1, Orleans, 19 November 1962–31 March 1963 (Lund et al); 1 immature male trapped and banded, Weston, 6–8 December 1962 (Baird et al); 1 immature male, Wellfleet, late December 1970 to 31 March 1971 (Martin, Bailey, et al); 1 male, Florence, 26 April 1971 (Clark, fide Stone); 1, Stockbridge, 3 January 1972 (Hendricks); 1 male, Scituate, early January–26 March 1974 (Litchfield, VO); 1 male, Worcester, 2 November 1974–21 March 1975 (Quinlan, Blodget); 1, Concord CBC, 15 December

1974–17 February 1975; 1, Littleton 22–28 December 1975 (Baird); 1 immature, Lexington, 2–6 February 1979 (Smith et al); 1 female, Nantucket, 27 October 1979 (Veit, Litchfield); 1 male, Walpole, December 1980–27 February 1981 (Colburn, fide Langley); 1, Felix Neck Wildlife Sanctuary, Martha's Vineyard, 3 December 1988–26 February 1989 (Small, VO).

## Blue Grosbeak  *Guiraca caerulea*

**Range:** Nearctic and Neotropical; breeds from central California, southern Colorado, central Illinois, and southeastern New York south to northern Florida, and in Central America to Costa Rica. Winters from Mexico to western Panama.

**Status:** Regular, but rare to very uncommon spring and fall visitor, mainly in eastern Massachusetts.

**Occurrence:** Since about 1930, Blue Grosbeaks have been gradually increasing in the East and have recently extended their breeding range north to southern New York. In Massachusetts they occur primarily during April and May and again from early September to mid-October, when they are most commonly found in weedy fields and overgrown vegetable gardens on Cape Cod and the Islands. There appear to be no records for Berkshire County, but Blue Grosbeaks do occasionally appear in the Connecticut River valley. There was apparently a major flight in eastern Massachusetts in 1973, with 8 reported in April (including 2 inland at Ashland and Mansfield); and 23 in May (with 2 inland at Mansfield and Franklin) (BOEM). Similarly, in April 1956, 6 were found along the coast and 2 were reported inland in Lincoln (RNEB). *Fall maxima:* 14 + , Nantucket, 1–16 October 1980 (Veit, Heil, et al); 11, Truro, 20–26 September 1981 (BOEM). The occurrence of Blue Grosbeaks at inland localities seems to invariably be related to the prevalence of optimum habitat. *Extreme dates:* 1, Westport, 21 March 1962 (Chase, fide Emery); 1 singing male, Worcester, 23 May–27 July 1991 (McMenemy, VO); to 1, Acoaxet, 1 February 1970 (Petersen, Goodrich); 1, Lakeville, 23 December 1989 (Taunton-Middleboro CBC, Kricher, Cassie); 1, West Tisbury, 13 November 1969 (Hancock).

## Indigo Bunting  *Passerina cyanea*

**Range:** Primarily eastern Nearctic; breeds from southeastern Saskatchewan, northern Minnesota, southern Ontario, southern Quebec, and southern New Brunswick south to central Texas, southern Alabama, and northern Florida. Winters from southern Mexico to Panama and also in the Greater Antilles.

**Status:** Common breeder and fairly common migrant. Very rare and irregular in winter.

**Breeding:** Indigo Buntings are fairly common and widespread breeders throughout the state, usually preferring disturbed habitats for nesting. Clearings below power lines, brushy gravel pits, and overgrown pastures are typical habitats for this species. They are less common on Cape Cod than elsewhere in the state and are unrecorded as breeders on Nantucket. Sample densities: 49, GBBBC, 14 June 1980; 39 males, Millis, throughout June 1985 (Cassie); 30, South Groveland, 10 June 1990 (Stymeist, VO); 27 males, Weston, June 1959 (Freeland); 10 pairs, West Roxbury, June 1973 (Atwood); 12, Newburyport Breeding Bird Census, 15 June 1980; 11 males, Wellesley, June 1959 (Freeland). A nest was found near the summit of Mt. Greylock, 16–17 June 1962 (Petersen). *Egg dates:* 3–22 June.

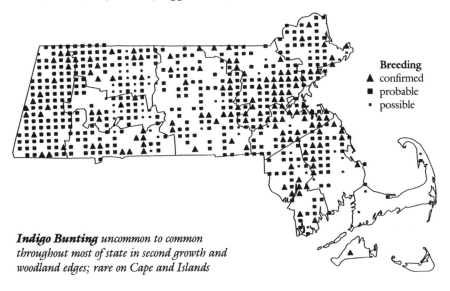

Breeding
▲ confirmed
■ probable
• possible

*Indigo Bunting uncommon to common throughout most of state in second growth and woodland edges; rare on Cape and Islands*

**Nonbreeding:** In Massachusetts, resident Indigo Buntings are present from mid-May until late September. Early spring migrants are occasionally seen during mid-April, most often following periods of sustained southwesterly air flow. The evidence suggests that these early birds may periodically encounter cold fronts while in flight during their trans-Gulf of Mexico migration from the Yucatan Peninsula to the Gulf Coast of North America. When this occurs, their migration may be deflected eastward, across northern Florida, and out over the Atlantic Ocean. Once over the ocean, the birds continue flying north, carried by southwesterly air flows that will eventually bring them to their first landfalls, such as Cape Cod, the coastal islands off New England, and the Canadian Maritime Provinces (Bagg 1955). The earliest of these April migrants arrive two to three weeks before most residents ordinarily appear. These same weather conditions also seem to account for the premature arrival of Prothonotary Warblers, Summer Tanagers, Blue Grosbeaks, and several other Central American winterers. Most of these early migrants appear in suburban yards on Cape Cod and the Islands or at feeders in eastern Massachusetts. During May, daily counts of migrants average 10 to 12 per locality. *Spring maxima:* 86, eastern Massachusetts, 8–30 April 1956 (RNEB); 41, eastern Massachusetts, 10–25 April 1961 (fide Emery).

In fall it is unusual to see more than 10 to 15 per day and, by late October, most birds have left. *Fall maxima:* 54, Nantucket, 11 October 1979 (Veit, Litchfield, Perkins); 30, Truro, 14 October 1979 (Nikula). Winter records: 1, Billerica, 22 February–14 April 1953 (Davis); 1 molting male, Lincoln, 22–27 January 1955 (Armstrong); 1 immature male, MNWS, 6 December 1961–8 March 1962 (Perry, Snyder); 1 molting male, Nantucket, 18 December 1977–February 1978 (Depue, van Duyne, Andrews).

# Painted Bunting  *Passerina ciris*

**Range:** Nearctic and Neotropical; breeds from southern New Mexico, southern Missouri, southwestern Tennessee, and southeastern North Carolina south to central Florida, the Gulf Coast states, and central Mexico. Winters from southern Louisiana and central Florida south to western Panama and the Greater Antilles.

**Status:** Rare visitor; most frequent in spring.

**Occurrence:** Although many of the early records of Painted Buntings were rejected by Griscom and Snyder (1955) on the grounds that the reports may have involved escaped cage birds, the current pattern of records suggests that wild birds were more likely to have been involved. Spring occurrences, which constitute the majority of records, range from: 1, Nantucket, 17–25 April 1961 (Magid, Andrews); to 1, Morris Island, Chatham, 30 May 1968 (Petersen, Forster). Fall reports, which are much less frequent, have occurred from: 1 collected, Monomoy, 30 August 1967 (Baird), to 1, North Falmouth, 10–14 December 1990 (McCloskey et al). There are also several remarkable winter records of birds at feeding stations—e.g., 1, Falmouth, 15 January–15 March 1957 (Collins, Athearn, et al); 1, Barre, 31 December 1971–6 January 1972 (Dorsey, Emery, Argue); 1, Hyannis, 20 January–28 February 1978 (Mycock).

# Dickcissel  *Spiza americana*

**Range:** Nearctic; breeds from eastern Montana, southern Manitoba, central Wisconsin, southern Ontario, and central New York south to western Texas, central Alabama, and northern Georgia. Winters from Mexico to northern South America and, in small numbers, in the United States, north to New England.

**Status:** Rare spring and uncommon fall migrant; rare winter resident.

**Occurrence:** Dickcissels have had an exceptionally varied history in Massachusetts (Gross 1956). They bred in the state during the period from 1835 to 1877 but then disappeared and were only recorded as rare stragglers until about 1918. Since then, Dickcissels have gradually increased; now they regularly occur at the outer coast during fall (mid-August to December) and more rarely in spring (April and May). Gross (op cit) found that between 1948 and 1955, 489 Dickcissels were reported in Massachusetts, most of these from September to December, but also during every month except June and July. Between the late 1950s and the mid-1970s, they occurred as fairly common migrants, particularly in fall, but they seem to have decreased somewhat since then—e.g., only 10 reported in eastern Massachusetts from September to November 1983 (BOEM).

During the fall, Dickcissels frequent weedy fields, whereas during winter and spring they are most often seen at feeders, where they tend to closely associate with House Sparrows. Since 1973, there have been approximately ten records of single birds during April and May, some of which undoubtedly represent undetected wintering individuals. In fall, migrant Dickcissels occasionally appear as early as the first week of August—e.g., 1, Nantucket, 2 August 1978 (Perkins); 1, Whitman, 5 August 1983 (Petersen). Reports earlier than this probably refer to wandering individuals following failed nesting attempts in the Midwest. For instance, both a male and a female were seen in Annisquam during the third week of July 1984 (Wiggin). Considering the historical status of Dickcissels on the East Coast during the 19th century, the possibility of future breeding in Massachusetts should not be ruled out. *Fall maxima:* 20–25 (including a flock of 6 on 9 October), Nantucket, 3–30 October 1979 (Veit, Litchfield); 8–10, Truro-Orleans, 22 October 1978 (Nikula). *Winter maximum:* 7, eastern Massachusetts, throughout January 1977 (BOEM).

# Green-tailed Towhee *Pipilo chlorurus*

**Range:** Western Nearctic; breeds from central Oregon, southern Idaho, and central Wyoming south in the mountains to southern California, central Arizona, and western Texas. Winters from southern California and Texas south to central Mexico.

**Status:** Vagrant: at least nine records.

**Occurrence:** The records indicate that the Green-tailed Towhee is most likely to occur in Massachusetts at bird feeders during fall and early winter.

The records include: 1, Northampton, 31 December 1946–26 April 1947 (Eliot, Shaub, VO); 1 banded, Weston, 9 October 1951 (Paine); 1, Bradford, 5 March–6 May 1953 (Tate, Root, VO); 1, Magnolia, January–March 1963 (AFN 17: 312); 1, Westport, December 1970–10 April 1971 (Kirkaldy, VO); 1, Scituate, 25 November–20 December 1973 (Kennedy, Swaabe, VO); 1, Wenham, November 1976–February 1977 (Whipple, VO); 1, South Peabody, 17 October–4 November 1979 (Heil); 1, East Orleans, 16 December 1979 (J. Baird, R. Baird, Forster).

# Rufous-sided Towhee   *Pipilo erythrophthalmus*

**Range:** Primarily Nearctic; breeds throughout most of the United States north to southern British Columbia, central Saskatchewan, northern Minnesota, southern Ontario, and northern New England and south to Guatemala. Winters from southern British Columbia, Colorado, Iowa, Ohio, and southern New England southward.

**Status:** Common to very common breeder, especially on the southeastern coastal plain; common migrant and uncommon but regular in winter.

**Breeding:** Rufous-sided Towhees are among the most numerous and conspicuous land birds in the Scrub Oak and second-growth forests of Plymouth, Cape Cod, and the Islands. They are particularly numerous in areas where moorland is succeeding to Scrub Oak barrens; however, as the oaks mature, towhee numbers decline. Elsewhere, the species is a common breeder throughout the state wherever there is secondary growth or forest openings. Sample densities: 300, Martha's Vineyard, 23–26 May 1980 (BBC, Drummond); 125, Martha's Vineyard, 17 July 1967 (Forster); 65 pairs, West

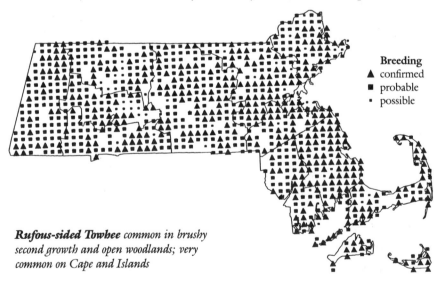

**Breeding**
▲ confirmed
■ probable
• possible

*Rufous-sided Towhee common in brushy second growth and open woodlands; very common on Cape and Islands*

Roxbury, May 1973 (Atwood); 55 pairs, Millis, June 1983 (Cassie); 90, Rocky Gutter Wildlife Management Area, South Middleboro, 15 June 1985 (SSBC, Anderson).

**Nonbreeding:** Rufous-sided Towhees migrate through Massachusetts in good numbers in late April and early May and again in September. In spring, it is often difficult to distinguish between true transients and arriving summer residents. *Fall maxima:* 200 +, Cuttyhunk Island, 27–28 September 1975 (Sorrie, Petersen); 120, Martha's Vineyard, 16 September 1980 (Laux). A few towhees regularly survive the entire winter in Massachusetts, especially in the dense thickets near Buzzards Bay and on Cape Cod and the Islands. *Winter maxima:* 50, Buzzards Bay CBC, 15 December 1979; 41, eastern Massachusetts, January 1974 (BOEM); 32, Martha's Vineyard CBC, 1 January 1989; 24, Martha's Vineyard CBC, 22 December 1989; 20, Cape Ann CBC, 18 December 1988.

**Subspecies:** There are at least three records of the western form *P. e. maculatus* from Massachusetts: 1, Monomoy, 12 October 1957 (Bailey); 1 male, North Scituate, 27 December 1987–January 1988 (Abrams, Petersen, et al); 1 female, Acton, January 1988 (fide Perkins). The last two records were confirmed by photographs now on file at Massachusetts Audubon.

# American Tree Sparrow  *Spizella arborea*

**Range:** Nearctic; breeds from northern Alaska across central Canada to Labrador and south to northern British Columbia, northern Saskatchewan, and northern Quebec. Winters from southern Canada south to northern California, central Arizona, central Texas, Tennessee, and North Carolina.

**Status:** Common to very common migrant and winter resident.

**Occurrence:** American Tree Sparrows are numerous in Massachusetts (except on the Islands, where they are comparatively scarce) between late October and late March, when they frequent weedy fields, brushy pastures, and grassy river meadows. Spring migrants from farther south largely pass through Massachusetts undetected, and most wintering birds have departed by late April. *Spring maximum:* 220, Truro, 13 April 1974 (Veit, Perkins, Hamlen). Fall migrants typically occur in the same sorts of weedy fields preferred by other migrant sparrows. *Fall maximum:* 150, Truro, 29 October 1976 (Veit).

In midwinter, when peak counts of tree sparrows are recorded, if snow buries weed seeds, the birds often retire to low swampy woodlands, where they feed on the seeds of birches and alders (see Brewster 1906). They also regularly visit suburban bird feeders in small numbers. *Winter maxima:* 1,486, Concord CBC, 28 December 1980; 1,076, Concord CBC, 1 January 1989; 810, Osterville, 3 January 1956 (Johnson); 300–400, Marion, throughout January 1974 (Harlow); 300, North Scituate, 10 January 1954 (Higginbotham). **Extreme dates:** 1, Truro, 25 September 1976 (Coolidge); to 1 banded, Andover, 20 May 1978 (Root).

# Chipping Sparrow    *Spizella passerina*

**Range:** Primarily Nearctic; breeds from eastern Alaska, northern Manitoba, southern Quebec, and southwestern Newfoundland south to Nicaragua, the Gulf Coast states, and northern Florida. Winters from central California, central New Mexico, Tennessee, and Maryland south through the rest of the breeding range.

**Status:** Common breeder and common migrant; rare but increasing winter resident.

**Breeding:** Chipping Sparrows are among the more conspicuous Massachusetts breeding birds because they frequent both suburban and rural habitats, nest in ornamental plantings, and sing incessantly throughout the day. They are most numerous in open habitats and are totally absent from mature forests. Because much formerly cleared land has succeeded to forests, Chipping Sparrows have declined in many areas since the 19th century. Brewster (1906) considered the Chipping Sparrow to be one of the commonest nesting birds in the Cambridge region but also felt that competition with House Sparrows contributed to their gradual disappearance from that area. Since the 1950s, they have appeared to benefit from the suburban planting of ornamental conifers, which they seem to particularly like for nest building. Sample densities: 62 pairs, Wellesley, June–July 1955 (Freeland); 50, Littleton, June 1960 (Bolton); 27, Gate 40, Quabbin, 14 July 1990 (Lynch); 14 singing, WBWS, 16 June 1968 (Blodget). **Egg dates:** 12 May–26 June.

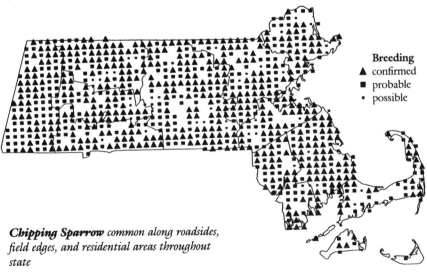

Breeding
▲ confirmed
■ probable
• possible

*Chipping Sparrow common along roadsides, field edges, and residential areas throughout state*

**Nonbreeding:** In spring, migrants occur in April and early May. *Spring maximum:* 44, Mt. Auburn Cemetery, Cambridge, 3 May 1973 (Stymeist). In fall, Chipping Sparrows are commonly encountered in flocks during late September and October and are most often found in weedy fields and suburban backyards, where they seem to especially relish the seeds of Crab Grass. *Fall maxima:* 300, Eastham, 11 September 1949 (fide Bailey); 170 +, Truro, 6 October 1974 (Veit et al). Chipping Sparrows were formerly very unusual after November, but more recently they seem to occur with much greater frequency into early winter—e.g., 20–25, Martha's Vineyard, January–February 1980 (Laux); 13, North Falmouth, 16 December 1978 (Brown); 5, Mid-Cape Cod CBC, 27 December 1988.

## Clay-colored Sparrow   *Spizella pallida*

**Range:** Nearctic; breeds from northeastern British Columbia, northern Manitoba, northern Michigan, central Ontario, and western New York (rarely) south to southeastern Wyoming, southern Nebraska, and southern Wisconsin. Winters from southern Texas south to southern Mexico and occasionally in the United States northeast to Massachusetts.

**Status:** Rare fall migrant; occasional in spring and winter.

**Occurrence:** Clay-colored Sparrows have become increasingly frequent in their occurrence on the East Coast during the last 25 years. Most individuals appear during the fall in weed fields near the coast and in open areas adjacent to coastal thickets. Most spring records occur in May—e.g., 1 singing male, South Carver, 23 May–1 August 1964 (Shaw, Anderson); 1 singing male, South Peabody, 27 May–1 June 1976 (Heil); singles banded at MBO, 16 May 1984 (MBO staff), and Rockport, 16 May 1984 (Norris)—and, since 1980, the species has become nearly annual at inland localities. These spring records, along with an intriguing record of an apparent pair that behaved as though they were defending territory at Fort Devens, Ayer, 6–10 June 1988 (Marshall), suggest that the breeding of this species in Massachusetts should be confidently expected.

In fall, most Clay-colored Sparrows appear in September and October, often in mixed flocks of other sparrows, but occasionally as solitary individuals. *Fall maxima:* 20, eastern Massachusetts, 16 September–4 November 1979 (BOEM); 7, outer Cape, 20 September–11 October 1978 (fide Nikula); 3, Truro, 1 October 1977 (Kasprzyk, Heil, Veit). A sample of winter records includes: 1, Dover, 18 December 1957 (Bagg); 1, Scituate, 11 February–1 May 1967 (Foley 1967); 1, Topsfield, 25 December 1969–23 March 1970 (Cyr et al); 1, Lincoln, 5 January 1971 (Forster); 1, Sudbury, 26 December 1971–1 January 1972 (Forster); 1, Orleans, 29 December 1973 (Baird, Forster, Nikula); 1, Rockport, 1 December 1981 (Norris); 1, Martha's Vineyard, 11–14 December 1981 (Laux); 1, Middleboro, 15 January–13 February 1989 (Petersen).

## Brewer's Sparrow   *Spizella breweri*

**Range:** Western Nearctic; breeds from southwestern Yukon, northwestern British Columbia, southwestern Saskatchewan, and southwestern North Dakota south to central Arizona and northwestern New Mexico. Winters from southern California, central Arizona, and central Texas to northern Mexico.

**Status:** Vagrant: one record.

**Occurrence:** The single Massachusetts record for a Brewer's Sparrow is an immature male that was collected in Watertown, 15 December 1873, by William Stone (MCZ #291121). Despite two October sight records from Long Island (Bull 1964), the AOU (1983) has cited this as the only record for the Atlantic Coast.

## Field Sparrow   *Spizella pusilla*

**Range:** Nearctic; breeds from northwestern Montana, central Minnesota, southern Ontario, and southern New Brunswick south to central Texas, southern Mississippi, and southern Georgia. Winters from Kansas, Ohio, and Massachusetts south to central Florida and northeastern Mexico.

**Status:** Fairly common breeder; common migrant and locally common winter resident.

**Breeding:** For nesting, Field Sparrows prefer lightly overgrown pastures, often with a scattering of Red Cedars—a habitat becoming increasingly scarce in Massachusetts. As a result, Field Sparrows are much less numerous

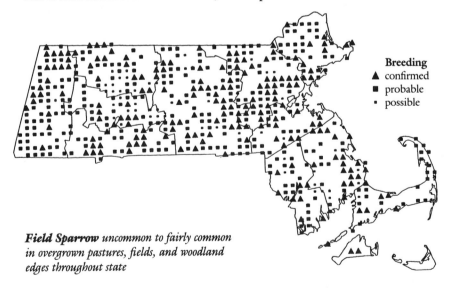

Breeding
▲ confirmed
■ probable
. possible

*Field Sparrow uncommon to fairly common in overgrown pastures, fields, and woodland edges throughout state*

in the state than Chipping Sparrows. Fortunately, however, they have quickly adapted to clearings beneath power lines and other disturbed areas that are regenerating to shrub growth. They typically avoid suburban habitats, as well as the higher hill country of western Massachusetts. Nonetheless, they are relatively widespread on the mainland but are less common on Cape Cod and Martha's Vineyard and absent from Nantucket. Sample densities: 65, South Groveland, 8 June 1991 (Stymeist, VO); 48, South Groveland, 10 June 1990 (Stymeist, VO); 21 pairs, Wellesley, June 1954, but only 8 pairs there in 1955 (Freeland); 25 +, East Longmeadow, 31 July 1966 (Weigand); 22 residents, South Peabody, 16 May 1983 (Heil). *Egg dates:* 8 May–12 June.

**Nonbreeding:** In spring, most migrant Field Sparrows occur in April, although it is often difficult to distinguish arriving migrants from residents. *Spring maximum:* 16, South Peabody, 2 April 1976 (Heil). During the fall, Field Sparrows typically associate with other sparrows in weedy fields, and most migrants have departed by late October. *Fall maxima:* 60, Truro, 29 September 1974 (Petersen); 60, Framingham, 16 October 1976 (Hamilton). *Winter maxima:* 103, Buzzards Bay CBC, 14 December 1974; 95, Taunton-Middleboro CBC, 26 December 1987; 91, Uxbridge CBC, 31 December 1988.

# Vesper Sparrow   *Pooecetes gramineus*

**Range:** Nearctic; breeds from central British Columbia, northern Manitoba, southern Quebec, and Nova Scotia south to central eastern California, central Arizona, Missouri, and North Carolina. In the eastern United States, winters from southern Illinois, Pennsylvania, and Connecticut south to central Florida and Mexico.

**Status:** Uncommon and local breeder; uncommon to fairly common migrant. Rare and erratic in winter.

**Breeding:** Vesper Sparrows have very specialized habitat preferences for breeding and have consequently declined considerably in Massachusetts since the late 1800s, due primarily to the disappearance of these habitats. They seem to require barren or rocky fields, particularly those with open, sandy patches and very short grass. Occasionally they will nest around the borders of agricultural areas, and they still breed in small numbers on extensive moors on outer Cape Cod. During July 1978, 28 singing Vesper Sparrows, as well as a nest with 4 young, were discovered in a short grassy area being managed for Mourning Doves and Northern Bobwhites in the pine barrens of the Myles Standish State Forest in Plymouth (MBO staff). Nesting has been more or less continuous in that area since that time; however, the numbers have declined. Vesper Sparrows apparently breed in similar habitat on Long Island (P.A. & F.G. Buckley, pers. comm.) so it is possible that they could be overlooked as breeders elsewhere in the pine barrens of southeastern Massachusetts. In addition to these known breeding areas in southeastern Massachusetts, Vesper Sparrows continue to nest in small numbers and in widely scattered localities in western Massachusetts. Sample densities include: 4, Plainfield, 2 June 1990 (Rancatti); 4, Worthington, 3 June 1990 (Rancatti); 3, Agawam, 5 June 1991 (Allen). *Egg dates:* 15 April–11 August.

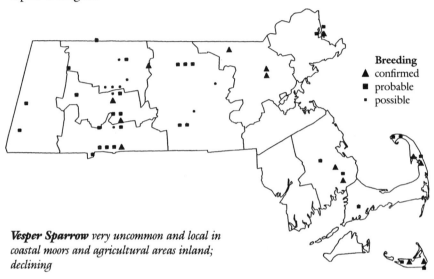

**Breeding**
▲ confirmed
■ probable
• possible

*Vesper Sparrow very uncommon and local in coastal moors and agricultural areas inland; declining*

**Nonbreeding:** Vesper Sparrows are generally uncommon as migrants in both spring and fall, and the decline in the breeding population seems to be commensurate with a pronounced decrease in migratory totals since 1955. *Spring maxima:* 50, Granby, 19 April 1965 (Logan); no count since 1970 has exceeded ten away from known breeding areas. *Fall maxima:* 50, Plum Island, 16 September 1956 (Gardler); 35, Marconi Station, South Wellfleet, 6 October 1974 (Cornwell); 22 +, Marconi Station, South Wellfleet, 13 September 1980 (Heil). Vesper Sparrows are of irregular occurrence in Massachusetts during winter. Because they feed mainly on weed seeds, their survival in Massachusetts depends, in part, on the amount of snow cover. In snowless winters, a few probably overwinter regularly. *Winter maxima:* 7, Nantucket CBC, 3 January 1981 (Nikula); 6, Halifax, 27 February 1989 (Anderson); 2, Halifax, 15 January 1984 (Petersen, Anderson).

# Lark Sparrow   *Chondestes grammacus*

**Range:** Nearctic; breeds from western Oregon east to southern Manitoba, central Minnesota, and southern Ontario south to northern Mexico, central

Alabama, and western North Carolina. Winters from California, southern Arizona, central Texas, and southwestern Louisiana to El Salvador, and occasionally along the Atlantic Coast north to southern New England.

**Status:** Rare but regular fall migrant; occasional in winter and very rare in spring.

**Occurrence:** Of the western passerine species that occur primarily as fall migrants in Massachusetts, the Lark Sparrow is one of the most frequent. Always preferring open, barren habitats, including weedy and plowed fields and sandy areas near coastal thickets, the majority of Lark Sparrows in Massachusetts are found close to the immediate coast. For example, of nearly 200 reported between 1954 and 1968, only 8 were from localities more than ten miles inland. After a peak reached during the late 1950s and 1960s, the number of Lark Sparrow reports in Massachusetts has declined considerably. There are approximately ten spring records of Lark Sparrows in Massachusetts, which span the dates 28 April–21 May, three of which are from inland locations—i.e., 1, Princeton, 30 April 1954 (Smith); 1, Pittsfield, 6 May 1956 (Schumacher); 1, Littleton, 17 May 1964 (Bradley).

During fall, Lark Sparrows are rare before mid-August and after early October, with most reports occurring between late August and late October. *Fall maxima:* 5, Plum Island, 18 September 1965 (VO, RNEB); 14, coastal Massachusetts, September 1955 and 1965 (RNEB). Since 1954, there have been approximately twenty-five records of Lark Sparrows during January and February, six of these from inland locations.

# Black-throated Sparrow  *Amphispiza bilineata*

**Range:** Southwestern Nearctic; breeds from southern Oregon, southwestern Wyoming, and northwestern Oklahoma south to southern Baja California and central Mexico. Winters from southern California, southern Nevada, and central Texas south through the remainder of the breeding range.

**Status:** Vagrant: two sight records.

**Occurrence:** During the period 1959 to 1963, Black-throated Sparrows, which previously had not been known to stray significantly east of their breeding range, were found in Wisconsin, Illinois, Ohio, Massachusetts, and New Jersey (Bull 1963). The Massachusetts records are as follows: 1, North Amherst, 12 April 1963 (Snow, fide Carleton, AFN 17: 394); 1, Amherst, 14 April 1963 (Ward, fide Carleton, AFN 17: 394). Though neither of these reports was ever confirmed by an experienced ornithologist, the details of the observations and the coincidence in time and space provide compelling evidence of their authenticity. Black-throated Sparrows have subsequently been reported in Louisiana, New Jersey, Virginia, and Florida (AOU 1983).

# Lark Bunting   *Calamospiza melanocorys*

**Range:** Western Nearctic; breeds from southern Alberta and southwestern Minnesota south to southeastern New Mexico, northern Texas, and western Oklahoma. Winters from southern California, central Arizona, and north-central Texas south to central Mexico. Rare fall visitor to the Atlantic Coast.

**Status:** Rare fall visitor; very rare in spring.

**Occurrence:** Lark Buntings have been most frequent in Massachusetts since 1955, prior to which time there were only five records for the state. Since then, they have occurred nearly annually, primarily in September and October, with a maximum count of four during September 1970 (Heil 1977). Lark Buntings prefer open and barren habitats, and in Massachusetts they are most often found at the immediate coast, frequently within sight of the ocean.

There are very few inland Massachusetts records to date—e.g., 1 "abnormal, diseased, sick, and tame to the point of stupidity," Wayland, 11 November 1947 (Griscom 1949); 1, Millis, 16 October 1979 (Cassie). Spring records are very rare—e.g., 1, Marshfield, 9 June 1907 (May); 1, Plymouth, 5 May 1969 (fide Petersen); 1, Marshfield, 18–21 May 1969 (Harrington, Petersen, VO); 1, Newbury, 2 June 1971 (Kenneally); 1, Nantucket, 22–25 May 1982 (Gardner). The fall records span the dates: 1, Plum Island, 23–25 July 1988 (P. and F. Vale); to 1, Lynn, 5 December 1977 (Vickery, BMS #x03–169). The only winter record is of a bird that survived in Newburyport, 22 December 1950–14 April 1951 (Arakelian et al).

# Savannah Sparrow   *Passerculus sandwichensis*

**Range:** Primarily Nearctic; breeds from northern Alaska, northern Mackenzie, northern Quebec, and northern Labrador south in the West to Mexico and Guatemala and in the East to Missouri, central Ohio, western Maryland, and northern New Jersey. Winters from southern British Columbia, Oklahoma, southern Illinois, and southern New England south to El Salvador, Cuba, and the Cayman Islands.

**Status:** Locally common breeder; very common to abundant migrant. Uncommon but regular in winter.

**Breeding:** The preferred breeding habitat of the Savannah Sparrow includes the open moorlands of Cape Cod and the Islands, sand dunes along the coast, agricultural fields in the Connecticut River valley and Berkshires, and grassy fields adjacent to airports. Sample densities: 25 breeding pairs, Muskeget Island, May 1981 (Heil); 40 (including young), Plum Island, 16 July 1979 (BOEM). *Egg dates:* 21 May–29 June.

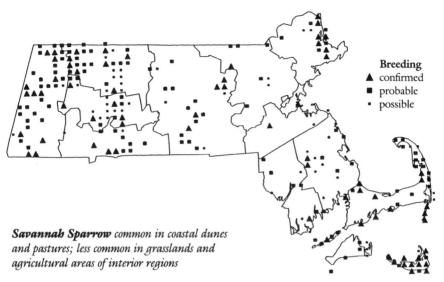

*Savannah Sparrow common in coastal dunes and pastures; less common in grasslands and agricultural areas of interior regions*

**Breeding**
▲ confirmed
■ probable
• possible

**Nonbreeding:** Savannah Sparrows are among the most numerous migrant sparrows in Massachusetts during April and from late September to October. They are especially common along the coast and in the Connecticut River valley. *Spring maxima:* 150 +, Truro, 13 April 1974 (Veit, Perkins, Hamlen); 150, Dover, 24 April 1976 (Hamlen). *Fall maxima:* 250 +, Middleboro, 15 October 1989 (Lynch et al); 230, Squantum, 13 October 1989 (Brown); 200 +, Salisbury, 22 October 1978 (Veit); 200, Salisbury, 28 September 1979 (Kasprzyk); 150, Framingham, 21 September 1977 (Forster); 150 +, Concord, 26 September 1981 (Walton). *Winter maxima:* 205, Buzzards Bay CBC, 14 December 1991; 64, Martha's Vineyard CBC, 22 December 1989; 62, Nantucket CBC, 2 January 1977; 50, Martha's Vineyard, 16–19 February 1979 (Lincoln et al); 47, Cape Cod CBC, 29 December 1974; 40, Bridgewater-Halifax, 15 January 1984 (Petersen, Anderson).

**Subspecies:** The "Ipswich" Savannah Sparrow, *P. s. princeps*, breeds on Sable Island, Nova Scotia, and winters along the Atlantic Coast from Massachusetts to Georgia. It is a locally common winter resident in Massachusetts, where it is restricted to sand dunes, beaches, and salt marshes at the immediate coast. There is at least one documented inland record: 1 photographed, GMNWR, Concord, 10 October 1966 (Garrey, photos at MAS). *Winter maxima:* 21, Plum Island, 3 December 1983 (Heil); 16, Tuckernuck Island CBC, 31 December 1981 (Veit, Ebersole); 15, Plymouth Beach, 21 December 1974 (Petersen).

# Grasshopper Sparrow  *Ammodramus savannarum*

**Range:** Nearctic; breeds locally from eastern Washington, southern British Columbia and Manitoba, southern Quebec, and central New England south to southern California, Texas, and Florida; also to the Greater Antilles and northern South America. Northern populations are migratory; on the East Coast, winters north to North Carolina, rarely to Massachusetts.

**Status:** Rare to uncommon local breeder; rare or rarely detected spring migrant and uncommon fall migrant. Very rare in early winter but occasionally surviving the entire season.

**Breeding:** Grasshopper Sparrows nest almost exclusively in fields and moorlands with very short grass and a scattering of small bushes. Because such habitats tend to be transitory, loose colonies of Grasshopper Sparrows often appear and disappear rather abruptly. A general decline in Massachusetts occurred between 1900 and 1955 due to the drastic reduction in farmland. They are still fairly common in open moorland on the Elizabeth Islands, where sheep are regularly grazed, and also in the short grass surrounding airports, including Westover Air Force Base in Chicopee, Barnes Airport in Westfield, Hanscom Field in Bedford, and Otis Air Force Base on Cape Cod. A few isolated pairs also breed around agricultural fields and pastures in Pepperell, Worcester, South Dartmouth, and at a few sites in the Connecticut River valley and eastern Berkshire County. Sample counts: 40+, Naushon Island, 23–25 June 1980 (Sorrie); 25 pairs, Pasque Island, June 1978 (fide Veit); 8 pairs, Tuckernuck, June 1976 (Veit). Recent counts from mainland sites include: 16 singing males, Westover Air Force Base, July 1984 (Merrill); 12, Westover Air Force Base, 6 July 1990 (Allen); 9 pairs, Crane Wildlife Management Area, Falmouth, July 1984 (Heil); 4 pairs, Hanscom Field, Bedford, July 1984 (Heil).

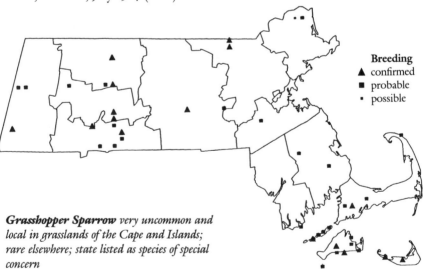

**Breeding**
▲ confirmed
■ probable
• possible

*Grasshopper Sparrow very uncommon and local in grasslands of the Cape and Islands; rare elsewhere; state listed as species of special concern*

**Nonbreeding:** As spring migrants, Grasshopper Sparrows are rarely detected away from known breeding localities so the following records are noteworthy: 1, Plum Island, 19 May 1953 (Hill, Petty); 1, Concord, 20 May 1972 (Bemis); 1, Plum Island, 24 May 1975 (Johnson); 1, MNWS, 29 April 1983 (Heil). The earliest arrival dates for breeding birds are: 1, South Hadley, 5 April 1943 (Saunders); 1, Williamsburg, 5 April 1943 (Graves). Resident birds normally depart by mid-September, and the first migrants are seldom reported until mid-October, when they are seen both on the coast and at inland localities. *Fall maxima:* 5 or 6, Nantucket, 14 October 1979 (Veit); 3, Truro, 24 October 1976 (Petersen); 12, Nantucket, throughout October 1980 (Veit). Grasshopper Sparrows are rare but regular into late December—e.g., 1, Winthrop, 15 December 1974 (Abbott); 1, Rockport, 24 December 1976 (Heil). There are enough midwinter and early spring records to suggest that the species must occasionally overwinter successfully—e.g., 1, Peabody, 31 January 1966 (Palmer); 1, Halifax, 5 February 1989 (Petersen); 1 collected, Wayland, 21–22 March 1953 (Morgan, Wiggin, MCZ #279410); 1, Springfield, 22 March 1953 (Guyett); 1, Middleboro, 24 March 1991 (Ludlow et al).

# Henslow's Sparrow  *Ammodramus henslowii*

**Range:** Eastern Nearctic; breeds from eastern South Dakota, central Minnesota, southern Ontario, and Massachusetts (rarely) south to eastern Kansas, northern Kentucky, and northern North Carolina. Winters mainly along the coast from southeastern Texas and central Florida to South Carolina.

**Status:** Rare to very rare, erratic, and local breeder; very rare migrant.

**Breeding:** Henslow's Sparrows breed in damp fields heavily overgrown with tall grasses, sedges, and low shrubs. Optimum habitats are increasingly rare in Massachusetts, either because these fields are being destroyed for development or because they are gradually becoming too heavily overgrown for Henslow's Sparrows. In 1954 and 1955, Henslow's Sparrows bred at South Egremont (5 pairs), West Newbury (3 pairs), East Hadley (1 pair), Mt. Greylock (1 pair), and Amherst (1 pair) (all fide RNEB). Most of those localities were deserted by about 1965, and none of them are currently suitable for nesting. Pairs were suspected to be breeding at the Leicester Airport in 1965 (fide Emery) and at Chilmark, Martha's Vineyard, in 1957 (Keith) and 1960 (Keith). More recently, 2 pairs definitely bred at the Leicester Airport, 1973 and 1974 (Blodget, Petersen, et al), and at least four singing males were present in West Newbury, 18 May–10 August 1974 (Stymeist, Leverich, Robinson, Johnson). From then until 1983, there were no summer records of Henslow's Sparrows in Massachusetts. The most recent suggestion of local nesting occurred when 4 singing males were present at Fobes Hill, Windsor, August and early September 1983 (Stemple,

Blodget, Kellogg, et al). There have been no known breeding attempts since that time. *Egg dates:* 25 May–6 August.

**Nonbreeding:** The Henslow's Sparrow is among the most rare and inconspicuous migrants that occur in Massachusetts. Until the early 1960s, they were regularly reported during late September and October at the outer coast, but their recent scarcity now makes all reports of significant interest. Spring records (since 1965): 1 banded, MBO, 16 May 1976 (MBO staff); 1, Plum Island, 30 April 1983 (Schlinger). A sample of fall records (since 1965) includes: 1, Chatham, 28 October 1965 (Clem); 1 banded, MBO, 22 October 1968 (Anderson et al); 1, Nantucket, 11 October 1979 (Veit, Litchfield); 1, Truro, 15–17 October 1980 (Nikula, Goodrich); 1, Squantum, 18–19 October 1981 (Brown); 1, Wayland, 27 September 1983 (Hines, Walton); 1, Lancaster, 10 October 1986 (Lynch et al); 1, Concord, 15 September 1991 (Paine). Despite the scarcity of the Henslow's Sparrow as a migrant, there are at least three winter records: 1 banded, Sandwich, 23 January 1954 (Burbank); 1, Brookline, 19 December 1982–15 January 1983 (Wilson, Mueller, Komar, et al [see Komar 1983]); 1, Wayland, 1 January 1983 (Hines).

**Subspecies:** A single Massachusetts specimen exists for the western race of the Henslow's Sparrow, *A. h. henslowii*—i.e., 1 collected, Osterville, 6 November 1874 (Brewster, BMS #13935).

# Le Conte's Sparrow  *Ammodramus leconteii*

**Range:** Nearctic; breeds from southern Mackenzie, central Manitoba, northern Ontario, and southern Quebec south to central Montana, northern North Dakota, eastern Minnesota, and northern Michigan. Winters from western Kansas, southern Illinois, and South Carolina to southern Texas, southern Mississippi, and northern Florida.

**Status:** Vagrant: at least fourteen records.

**Occurrence:** Beginning in the 1980s, there has been an apparent increase in the number of occurrences of fall migrant Le Conte's Sparrows on the Atlantic Coast. In Massachusetts, these migrants often appear in habitats similar to those in which they breed—dense, grassy meadows, either at the uppermost reaches of salt marshes or around the borders of freshwater ponds. The records are as follows: 1, Truro, 19–25 October 1969 (Clem, Bailey, et al); 1, Eastham, 18 November 1970 (Kenneally); 1 collected, MBO, 4 September 1971 (Anderson 1975, MCZ #330035); 1, Eastham, 25 March–14 April 1972 (Pease, Nikula, et al); 1, Nantucket, 7 October 1980 (Veit); 1, Monomoy, 10 October 1980 (Goodrich, Nikula); 1, Newburyport, 31 October 1982 (Heil, Smith); 1, Plum Island, 21 October 1983 (Ferren et al); 1, Orleans, 16 December 1984 (Heil, Cape Cod CBC); 1, Newburyport, 27 September 1986 (Heil); 1, Newburyport, 4–20 February 1989 (Petersen et al); 1, South Peabody, 13–14 October 1990 (Fitzgerald, Rines); 2, Northampton, 28 September 1991 (Gagnon, VO). There is a single published, but largely ignored, record for spring: 1 "seen on a lawn with White-throated Sparrows," Marblehead Neck, 5 May 1953 (Snyder, Searle).

## Sharp-tailed Sparrow  *Ammodramus caudacutus*

**Range:** Nearctic; breeds (*A. c. nelsoni*) in freshwater marshes of the interior from eastern British Columbia and southern Mackenzie southeast to southeastern South Dakota and northwestern Minnesota; (*A. c. altera*) around the shores of James Bay; (*A. c. subvirgata*) in salt marshes along the south shore of the St. Lawrence River and along the coasts of New Brunswick, Nova Scotia, Prince Edward Island, and south to southern Maine; (*A. c. caudacutus*) along the Atlantic Coast from southern Maine south to southern New Jersey; and (*A. c. diversa*) in North Carolina. The species as a whole winters on salt marshes along the Gulf and Atlantic coasts north to New York and, more rarely, to Massachusetts.

**Status:** Locally common to very common breeder; common migrant in coastal salt marshes and rare, but regular, migrant inland in freshwater marshes. Rare in winter.

**Breeding:** Sharp-tailed Sparrows are widespread breeders in the salt marshes along the Massachusetts coast, where they normally build their nests under tufts of *Spartina patens*. The largest numbers occur in the Parker River marshes of Essex County, the Sandy Neck Marsh, Barnstable, and the Nauset Marsh, Eastham. Scattered pairs also breed in smaller salt marshes, such as those on Muskeget and Tuckernuck islands, in Belle Isle Marsh, East

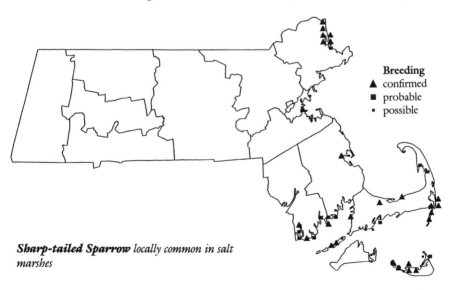

**Breeding**
▲ confirmed
■ probable
· possible

*Sharp-tailed Sparrow locally common in salt marshes*

Boston, and in marshes along the North River in Marshfield. Brewster (1906) described their historic breeding in the Charles River marshes, Cambridge, in 1869. Sample densities: 125, "in a small section of the Plum Island marshes," 1 June 1945 (Karplus); 31, in a quarter-mile section in the Barnstable marshes, 17 June 1944 (Snyder). Hill (1965) extrapolated a staggering total of 1,000 pairs in the Sandy Neck marshes, Barnstable. *Egg dates:* 24 May–14 June.

**Nonbreeding:** Resident Sharp-tailed Sparrows arrive in Massachusetts during the second week of May, and most have departed by early September. More northerly breeders occur as coastal migrants in late May to early June and again in September and October. Spring peak counts are usually difficult to define due to confusion with resident birds. A few migrants are occasionally seen at inland freshwater marshes during these same time periods. *Fall maxima:* 80, Plum Island, 6 October 1957 (Nash); 75+, Scituate, 20 October 1968 (Litchfield). During mild winters, a few Sharp-tailed Sparrows survive the entire season in Massachusetts, especially on Cape Cod and the Islands and near the mouth of the North River in Scituate. *Winter maxima:* 12, Cape Cod CBC, 18 December 1989; 7, Scituate, 28 March 1959 (Fox, Howland); 4, Plum Island, 18 February 1980 (Martin).

**Subspecies:** It is apparent from specimen evidence that at least four distinct races of the Sharp-tailed Sparrow occur in Massachusetts. However, because of the similarity between these races, it is often impossible to distinguish them with certainty in the field. The MCZ possesses only five unambiguous Massachusetts specimens of *A. c. nelsoni*—i.e., 1, Revere, 23 October 1883 (MCZ #192923); 1, Wareham, 28 September 1884 (MCZ #1599); 1, West Barnstable, 9 February 1901 (MCZ #15390); 1, Barnstable, 8 February 1901 (MCZ #15588); 1, West Barnstable, 6 February 1901 (MCZ #55307). These records suggest that *A. c. nelsoni* is a rare but regular fall migrant and that it is rare and irregular in winter in Massachusetts.

The MCZ also houses seven Massachusetts specimens of *A. c. altera*, which span the dates 8 October to 2 November, plus a single specimen taken at Scituate, 27 February 1955 (MCZ #291109). None of these specimens appear to be positively distinguishable from *A. c. subvirgata*, and the February specimen looks most like a worn specimen of *A. c. nelsoni*. It seems likely, therefore, that *A. c. altera* is rare but regular in fall in the state but that distinguishing *A. c. altera* from *A. c. subvirgata* may often not be possible with certainty. It further appears that the bulk of the migrant Sharp-tailed Sparrows in Massachusetts are of the race *A. c. subvirgata*. Fifteen existing spring specimens of *A. c. subvirgata* at the MCZ span the dates 15 May to 13 June, while forty fall specimens exist for the period from 3 September to 5 November. Inland specimen records of the race are: 3, Wayland, 20 May 1952 (MCZ #279413, 279084, and 279085); 1, Springfield, 15 May 1863 (MCZ #6206); 1, Wayland, 18 October 1952 (MCZ #279414).

There is a single winter specimen: 1, Scituate, 27 February 1955 (MCZ #293223).

In summary, specimen evidence suggests that inland Sharp-tailed Sparrow migrants in spring are mostly *A. c. subvirgata*, and in fall they may be *A. c. subvirgata*, *A. c. altera*, or *A. c. nelsoni*. Most winter records, all from the coast, seem to be *A. c. nelsoni*, but undoubtedly also include *A. c. subvirgata* or *A. c. altera*. *A. c. caudacutus* is found chiefly in salt marshes on the coast from mid-May to early September, and *A. c. subvirgata* is the common form between mid-September and November. During late May and early June, Massachusetts coastal marshes probably contain a mixture of breeding *A. c. caudacutus* and migrant *A. c. subvirgata*.

# Seaside Sparrow  *Ammodramus maritimus*

**Range:** Eastern Nearctic; breeds along the Atlantic and Gulf coasts from southern New Hampshire south to northern Florida and west along the coast to southern Texas. Winters primarily within breeding range.

**Status:** Uncommon and very local breeder; uncommon migrant. Very uncommon and erratic in winter.

**Breeding:** Seaside Sparrows are near the northern limit of their breeding range in Massachusetts. Nonetheless, regular breeding has been confirmed in South Dartmouth (intermittent since at least 1945); in the Barnstable marshes (25 pairs estimated in 1976 [Pease]), where they have been more or less continually present since 1940; on Monomoy (at least 2 pairs nesting in 1976, 1977, and 1980 [Petersen, Forster, et al]); and on Plum Island (up to 10 pairs intermittently breeding since 1952). Seaside Sparrows seem to prefer the wettest portions of salt marshes for nesting, usually occurring in stands of *Spartina alterniflora* at the upper edges of a marsh. *Egg dates:* 8 June–17 July.

**Nonbreeding:** Seaside Sparrows are rarely detected during migration away from their known breeding areas in Massachusetts. The following spring records are notable exceptions: 1 banded, Manomet, 29 April 1977 (MBO staff); 1, Plymouth Beach, 21 May 1977 (Petersen); 1, Nahant Thicket, 17 May 1982 (Heil). The highest counts for the year occur in late fall and early winter. *Fall maxima:* 22, Nauset, Eastham, 28 November 1958 (Fox, Smart, et al); 12, Provincetown, 4 October 1977 (Veit, Litchfield, Heil); 11, Scituate, 17 November 1957 (Fox). There is only a single inland record: 1, GMNWR, Concord, 5–7 September 1981 (Walton 1981). Despite being at the northern limit of their range in southern New England, a few Seaside Sparrows regularly attempt to winter in the state. *Winter maxima:* 20, Cape Cod CBC, 3 January 1960; 20, Fort Hill, Eastham, 12 January 1972 (Nikula); 20, Scituate, 30 December 1967 (Higginbotham, Marshfield CBC); 4, Newburyport CBC, 29 December 1991.

## Fox Sparrow  *Passerella iliaca*

**Range:** Nearctic; breeds from Alaska, northern Manitoba, and northern Labrador south, in eastern North America, to north-central Quebec and Newfoundland. Winters from coastal Maine south to central Florida on the East Coast.

**Status:** Uncommon to occasionally abundant migrant; exceedingly variable in abundance from year to year. Uncommon in winter.

**Occurrence:** Fox Sparrows are rather shy, and they seem to prefer dense thickets and heavy shrubbery more than weedy fields and open areas. They migrate through Massachusetts during late March and early April and again in late October and early November. In a typical season, they have one of the most precise migration windows of any Massachusetts passerine, and significant flights invariably seem to be associated with weather conditions that ground large numbers of migrants. In some seasons, even the most active observer will scarcely record a single migrant Fox Sparrow. During the late 1950s, several enormous spring flights occurred in Massachusetts, the likes of which have not been duplicated since. Fox Sparrows are invariably more numerous on the mainland than they are on Cape Cod and the Islands. *Spring maxima:* 900, Cape Ann, 7 April 1956 (Jodrey); 700, Sudbury River valley, 22 March 1959 (Morgan); 117, Granby, 19 March 1966 (Yenlin); 40, Mt. Auburn Cemetery, Cambridge, 13 April 1978 (Taylor); 20, Amherst, 16–18 March 1989 (Ortiz); 17, Holden, 27 March 1989 (Lynch). *Fall maxima:* 50, Hancock, 24 October 1954 (Hendricks); 28, Lexington, 12 November 1983 (Stymeist); 26, Lynn Woods, 19 November 1977 (Heil). Fox Sparrows are usually uncommon after early winter, a notable exception being: 49, throughout Massachusetts, February 1966 (RNEB). *Extreme date:* 1 collected, Topsfield, 20 May 1954 (Griscom, PMS #7441).

## Song Sparrow  *Melospiza melodia*

**Range:** Nearctic; widespread throughout most of North America. Breeds, in eastern North America, from northern Manitoba and southwestern Newfoundland south to South Carolina and northern Georgia. Winters south to southern Florida and southern Texas.

**Status:** Very common breeder and migrant; common winter resident.

**Breeding:** Song Sparrows are among the state's most widespread and numerous birds. They nest in a remarkable variety of habitats but are most abundant in disturbed, secondary-growth areas, at forest edges, and in the scrub forests of the southeastern coastal plain. Sample densities: 384, GBBBC, 13 June 1981; 64, Longmeadow, July 1968 (Yenlin); 57, Bolton Flats, 10 June 1990 (SSBC); 51, Truro-Wellfleet, 10 June 1960 (Tudor); 47, Plum Island, 24 June 1987 (Oliver). *Egg dates:* 30 April–29 July.

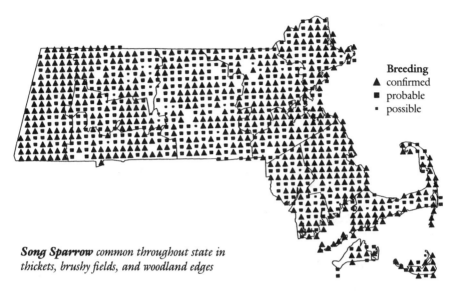

**Breeding**
▲ confirmed
■ probable
· possible

***Song Sparrow*** *common throughout state in thickets, brushy fields, and woodland edges*

**Nonbreeding:** Although some Song Sparrows are resident in Massachusetts, there is a definite passage of migrants through the state from late March to early April and again in September and October. ***Spring maxima:*** 220, Westport-Acoaxet, 31 March 1979 (Heil); 150, Plum Island, 13 April 1974 (Cornwell); 125, Salisbury, 29 March 1991 (Leahy); 74, Mt. Auburn Cemetery, Cambridge, 31 March 1974 (Stymeist). ***Fall maxima:*** 400, Plum Island, 17 October 1965 (Forster); 300, Plum Island–Salisbury, 18 October 1964 (Petersen); 150 +, Middleboro, 15 October 1989 (Lynch et al). ***Winter maxima:*** 449, Greater Boston CBC, 16 December 1990; 365, Buzzards Bay CBC, 14 December 1991; 336, Nantucket CBC, 30 December 1990; 331, Martha's Vineyard CBC, 3 January 1989; 100, Chilmark, 12 February 1965 (Willmann); 50, Nantucket, 4 January 1964 (Heywood).

## Lincoln's Sparrow  *Melospiza lincolnii*

**Range:** Nearctic; breeds from southern Mackenzie, northeastern Manitoba, northern Labrador, and Newfoundland south, in eastern North America, to northern Michigan, central New England, and Nova Scotia. Winters in the south-central United States north to central Missouri and northern Georgia; also south to El Salvador and Honduras.

**Status:** At least one breeding record. Uncommon migrant; very rare in winter.

**Breeding:** A nesting Lincoln's Sparrow was discovered, and the young were banded and photographed in Florida, Berkshire County, during June and July 1981 (Stemple, see BNWM 20:41–42). This is the only confirmed breeding record for Massachusetts.

**Nonbreeding:** During migration, Lincoln's Sparrows are most often found in dense, wet thickets in spring and in weedy fields in fall. Perhaps because Lincoln's Sparrows migrate southwest from New England to their wintering grounds, they often tend to be more common inland than on the coast and Islands. Spring migrants pass through in May—latest, 1, Dana, 2 June 1991 (FBC)—and fall migrants are most common during September and October. *Spring maxima:* 15 dead, Prudential Tower, Boston, 4 May 1968 (Howard); 9, Plum Island, 19 May 1967 (Forster). *Fall maxima:* 31, New Braintree, 2 October 1983 (Jenkins); 28, Barre-Hardwick, 14 October 1979 (Jenkins); 18, North Adams, 29 September 1975 (McNair); 17, South Peabody, 17 September 1981 (Heil); 16, Sudbury River valley, 8 October 1989 (Forster); 15, Wellfleet, 24 October 1976 (Nikula); 10, Truro, 22–31 September 1974 (Nikula).

Since 1980, there have been an increasing number of reliable late fall and early winter records of the Lincoln's Sparrow in Massachusetts, including several on CBCs—e.g., 1, Gloucester, 1 January 1980 (Heil); 1, Buzzards Bay CBC, 17 December 1983; 1, Wellesley, 9 December 1983–5 January 1984 (Ewer et al); 1, Marshfield CBC, 27 December 1987; 1, Greater Boston CBC, 18 December 1988; 1, Newburyport CBC, 29 December 1991.

# Swamp Sparrow   *Melospiza georgiana*

**Range:** Nearctic; breeds from southern Mackenzie and northern Saskatchewan east to southern Labrador and Newfoundland south to eastern South

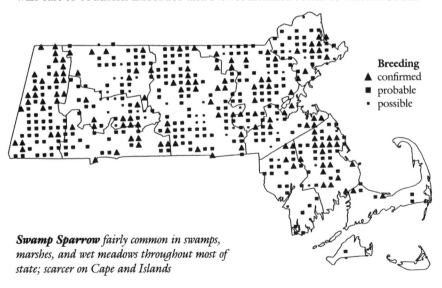

Breeding
▲ confirmed
■ probable
· possible

*Swamp Sparrow fairly common in swamps, marshes, and wet meadows throughout most of state; scarcer on Cape and Islands*

Dakota and southeastern West Virginia. Winters in the southeastern United States north, on the East Coast, to eastern Massachusetts.

**Status:** Common breeder and occasionally very common migrant; uncommon in winter.

**Breeding:** Swamp Sparrows breed in cattail marshes, brushy wet meadows, and emergent shrubbery adjacent to ponds throughout the state, although they are uncommon on Cape Cod and are absent from the Islands. Sample densities: 50 males, Baldwinville, July 1966 (O'Regan); 31, Bolton Flats, 8 July 1990 (Lynch et al); 29, West Bridgewater–Raynham, 8 June 1986 (SSBC); 27, Brookfield, 23 July 1967 (Yenlin). *Egg dates:* 13 May–14 July.

**Nonbreeding:** During migration, Swamp Sparrows are numerous in the same types of habitats in which they breed, as well as in weedy fields and waste areas with other migrant sparrows, especially in fall. In spring, both residents and migrants begin arriving in early April, and, by late May, migration is usually over. *Spring maxima:* 300, Nahant, 10 May 1948 (Griscom); 50, Boston Public Garden, 19 May 1967 (Emery); 45, Lynnfield, 19 April 1954 (Freeland); 40, Sudbury River valley, 24 April 1949 (Morgan); 30, Nahant, 12 May 1959 (Argue). The highest counts of the year are normally obtained during the peak of fall migration in October. *Fall maxima:* 200, East Boston, 7 October 1977 (Zendeh); 120 +, Framingham, 8 November 1976 (Hamilton); 120 +, GMNWR, 15 October 1988 (Lynch et al); 80 +, Fowl Meadow, Milton, 3 October 1973 (Veit); 75, South Peabody, 11 October 1979 (Heil). *Winter maxima:* 63, Mid-Cape Cod CBC, 28 December 1989; 58, Concord CBC, 1 January 1969; 52, Uxbridge CBC, 30 December 1989; 47, Concord, 10 January 1960 (Alden, Dana); 42, Plymouth CBC, 27 December 1990; 3, Pittsfield Sewer Beds, 25 February 1956 (Schumacher).

# White-throated Sparrow   *Zonotrichia albicollis*

**Range:** Nearctic; breeds from southeastern Yukon, northern Manitoba, central Quebec, and southern Labrador south to central British Columbia, central Minnesota, northeastern Pennsylvania, and northern New Jersey. Winters from southern New Mexico, eastern Kansas, southern Ohio, and Massachusetts south to southern Texas, the Gulf Coast, and northern Florida.

**Status:** Common breeder from Worcester County west; rare and local in eastern Massachusetts. Very common to abundant migrant; uncommon winter resident, especially numerous near the coast.

**Breeding:** White-throated Sparrows are primarily birds of northern coniferous forests and forest openings. In Massachusetts, they also maintain low breeding densities in stands of Red and White pine, as well as in slash areas created by logging activities. They are common breeders in Berkshire County, east to the higher elevations in Worcester County, and occasionally in Red Maple and White Cedar swamps in eastern Massachusetts. In western Massachusetts, it is not uncommon to record between 5 and 15 birds per locality in summer. *Egg dates:* 20 May–14 July.

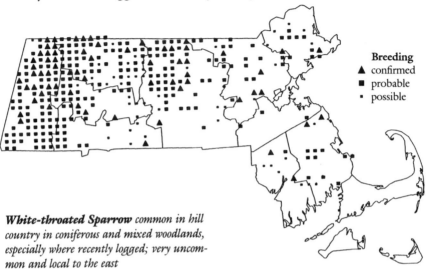

**Breeding**
▲ confirmed
■ probable
▪ possible

*White-throated Sparrow common in hill country in coniferous and mixed woodlands, especially where recently logged; very uncommon and local to the east*

**Nonbreeding:** White-throated Sparrows migrate through Massachusetts in enormous numbers from late April to early May and again in October. The numbers recorded, however, fluctuate considerably from year to year. *Spring maxima:* 2,000, Boston Public Garden, 5 May 1953 (Argue); 1,500, Nahant, 22 April 1948 (Kelly); 500+, Newburyport, 4 May 1968 (BBC); 500, Provincetown, 23 April 1977 (Nikula); 424 dead, Prudential Tower, 7 May 1968 (Howard). *Fall maxima:* 1,000+, Provincetown, 27 October 1976 (Nikula); 850, Mt. Auburn Cemetery, Cambridge, 12 October 1966 (Stymeist); 300, Boston Public Garden, 30 October 1976 (Greenman).

White-throated Sparrows often survive the winter in Massachusetts, especially in the temperate areas surrounding Buzzards Bay, although their overall numbers are highly variable from year to year. *Winter maxima:* 831, Concord CBC, 2 January 1976; 485, Cape Cod CBC, 19 December 1975; 390, Concord CBC, 31 December 1989; 341, Buzzards Bay CBC, 17 December 1988; 305, New Bedford CBC, 30 December 1989; 286, Buzzards Bay CBC, 16 December 1989.

# Golden-crowned Sparrow  *Zonotrichia atricapilla*

**Range:** Western Nearctic; breeds from western coastal Alaska and south-central Yukon south to northern Washington and southern Alberta. Winters mainly along the Pacific Coast from southern British Columbia to southern California.

**Status:** Vagrant: nine records.

**Occurrence:** Unlike other western vagrant species whose occurrence is primarily in fall, Golden-crowned Sparrows have been detected surprisingly often in spring. These spring records most likely represent birds that wintered in eastern North America and went undetected until the spring migration. The records for Massachusetts are: 1 immature male collected, Bedford, 23–26 January 1928 (May, Riese, May [AK 1928: 222–223]); 1 adult, Edgartown, Martha's Vineyard, 21–30 April 1955 (Thomas, Hough, Worden, et al); 1 immature, Weymouth, 1 November 1959–15 April 1960 (Sylvester, Harrington, et al); 1, Mattapoisett, 14 April 1965 (Stowell); 1 adult, Mt. Auburn Cemetery, Cambridge, 27 April–10 May 1966 (Eusden, Troy, Stymeist, et al—Fray & Eusden 1966); 1 immature, Duxbury Beach, 9–10 October 1979 (Jackson, fide Petersen); 1, Orleans, 18–24 April 1980 (Brown, Bailey, photo at MAS); 1, Holyoke, 27 January–9 April 1982 (Stone et al); 1 immature, South Dartmouth, 14–26 January 1990 (Gove et al).

# White-crowned Sparrow   *Zonotrichia leucophrys*

**Range:** Nearctic; breeds from northern Alaska, northern Manitoba, northern Quebec, and Labrador south in the western United States to southern California and northern New Mexico, and in eastern North America (*Z. l. leucophrys*) to central Manitoba, southeastern Quebec, and northern Newfoundland. Winters from southern British Columbia, Kansas, and Massachusetts (rarely) to Florida, the Bahamas, Cuba, Jamaica, and northern Mexico.

**Status:** Uncommon to very common migrant with numbers fluctuating considerably from year to year; most common in fall. Rare but regular in winter.

**Occurrence:** Although spring migrants may appear in almost any open habitat during the peak of migration in mid-May, in some years, fewer than five individuals are reported during the entire month. *Spring maxima:* 35, Plum Island, 14 May 1956 (Kleber); 27, Nantucket, 13 May 1956 (Dennis); 26, Plum Island, 18 May 1967 (Forster). The peak of the fall migration is reached in the middle of October, when migrants are most common in weedy fields and waste areas. *Fall maxima:* 350 +, Nantucket, 3–23 October 1980 (Veit); 250, outer Cape, 13 October 1958 (Gardler); 200, Plum Island, 17 October 1965 (Emery et al); 150, Monomoy, 8 October 1973 (Goodrich).

Although White-crowned Sparrows are rather rare in winter, they do occasionally survive the entire season in Massachusetts. *Winter maxima:* 17, eastern Massachusetts, January 1976 (BOEM); 12, Nantucket CBC, 18 December 1977; 5, Danvers, throughout January 1979 (Pyburn et al).

**Subspecies:** *Z. l. gambelii*, which breeds from Alaska and central Keewatin south to British Columbia and northern Manitoba, is a vagrant to Massachusetts, with at least twelve records since 1955. Most have been found among flocks of other White-crowned Sparrows. Recent reports include: 1 banded and photographed, South Natick, 6 April 1977 (Landre, Taylor, photos at MAS); 1 adult collected, Tuckernuck Island, 2 November 1980 (Veit); 1, Ipswich, 7 December 1980 (Heil).

## Harris' Sparrow *Zonotrichia querula*

**Range:** Nearctic; breeds from northwestern Mackenzie and southern Keewatin south to northeastern Saskatchewan and northern Manitoba. Winters in the central United States from southern Minnesota and eastern South Dakota south to southern Texas. Of rare but regular occurrence on migration on both coasts of North America.

**Status:** Very rare migrant; occasionally winters at feeders.

**Occurrence:** Harris' Sparrows are most frequently found in Massachusetts at feeding stations in late fall and winter. Midfall occurrences suggest that individuals wander about until settling in at feeding stations—e.g., 1, Northampton, 8–12 October 1950 (E. and C. R. Mason); 1, Lincoln, 4–5 December 1950 (Wellman, Elkins, Griscom); 1, Chatham, 20–28 October 1959 (Copeland, Earle); 1, Nantucket, 25–31 October 1968 (Andrews et al); 1, Edgartown, Martha's Vineyard, 12 October 1974 (Wynn); 1, Framingham, 11–12 October 1975 (Hamilton); 1, Truro, 28–29 September 1983 (Comeau, Nikula). Some individuals that appear in fall remain throughout the entire winter—e.g., 1, late December 1979–1 May 1980 (Sorrie, VO). There are at least two records of spring migrants, or birds that went undetected in winter—i.e., 1 collected, Hingham, 21 April 1929 (May, AK 1929: 392); 1, West Tisbury, Martha's Vineyard, 11–15 May 1965 (Hancock).

## Dark-eyed Junco *Junco hyemalis*

**Range:** Primarily Nearctic; the race *J. h. hyemalis* breeds from western Alaska, southern Keewatin, northern Ontario, and Labrador south to central British Columbia, Wisconsin, southern Ontario, Connecticut, and, in the Appalachian Mountains, to northern Georgia. The western race, *J. h. oreganus*, breeds in coniferous forests from southeastern Alaska south to western Nevada and northwestern Wyoming. Winters from southern Canada south to northern Mexico, the Gulf Coast, and northern Florida.

**Status:** Fairly common breeder east to Worcester County; rare and local breeder in eastern Massachusetts. Very common to occasionally abundant migrant; common winter resident.

**Breeding:** Dark-eyed Juncos typically breed in coniferous and mixed forests. As a result, they are widespread in Berkshire County eastward to the higher elevations in Worcester County. Anywhere from 5 to 20 juncos per locality may be found in a day during the breeding season in western Massachusetts. They have also been recorded as casual nesters as far east as Weston (Smith 1964), Dover, Milton, and Annisquam. *Egg dates:* late May–mid-June.

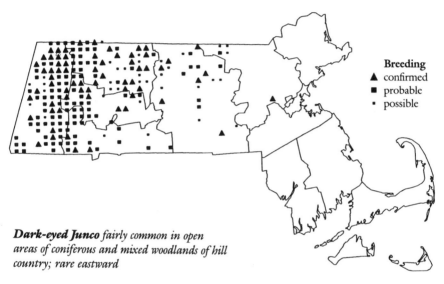

**Breeding**
▲ confirmed
■ probable
· possible

*Dark-eyed Junco fairly common in open areas of coniferous and mixed woodlands of hill country; rare eastward*

**Nonbreeding:** Although their numbers fluctuate from year to year, juncos are always common to abundant in both spring and fall throughout Massachusetts during migration. *Spring maxima:* 300, Mt. Auburn Cemetery, Cambridge, 6 April 1975 (Stymeist, Emery); 250, Mt. Auburn Cemetery, Cambridge, 31 March 1973 (Robinson); 250, Mt. Auburn Cemetery, Cambridge, 18 April 1974 (Stymeist). *Fall maxima:* 1,500+, Truro, 4 October 1975 (Martin, Veit); 1,000+, Truro, 29 October 1976 (Moore, Veit, Martin). During the winter, juncos are often concentrated near suburban bird feeding stations. *Winter maxima:* 2,295, Millis CBC, 22 December 1985; 2,237, Springfield CBC, January 1965; 2,118, Concord CBC, 26 December 1970; 1,893, Northampton CBC, January 1965.

**Subspecies:** The "Oregon Junco," *J. h. oreganus*, is a rare but regular migrant and winter visitor in Massachusetts. Reports in the 1950s and 1960s averaged five to ten per year, whereas more recently only 1 to 2 per year are reported. They are almost invariably found among flocks of *J. h. hyemalis*.

Most reports are probably referable to *J. h. cismontanus*, of the central Rocky Mountains; however, both *J. h. cismontanus* and *J. h. oreganus* are represented in the Museum of Comparative Zoology collection.

## McCown's Longspur   *Calcarius mccownii*

**Range:** Nearctic; breeds from southeastern Alberta, southern Saskatchewan, and North Dakota south to southeastern Wyoming and northwestern Nebraska. Winters from central Arizona and central Oklahoma south to northern Mexico.

**Status:** Vagrant: one record.

**Occurrence:** The state's only record of a McCown's Longspur is: 1, discovered in a Bridgewater cornfield, 9 January 1977 (Petersen 1976). During its stay until 26 January, the bird was seen by hundreds of observers and was eventually trapped, banded, and photographed (AB 31: 309). Copies of the photographs are on file at Massachusetts Audubon. Unfortunately, the photograph published in *American Birds* (31: 294) is of a Lapland Longspur that was erroneously identified as the McCown's Longspur.

   An old record of a specimen bought at the Boston Market, 7 January 1877 (E.A. and O. Bangs), and said to have been taken in Ipswich (Townsend 1905), was rejected by Griscom and Snyder (1955) on the grounds that there was no proof that it had in fact been collected in Massachusetts.

## Lapland Longspur   *Calcarius lapponicus*

**Range:** Holarctic; breeds, in North America, from northern Alaska and Ellesmere Island south to southern Alaska, northeastern Manitoba, northern Ontario, and northern Quebec. Winters from southern Canada south to southern California, Oklahoma, and Maryland.

**Status:** Locally common migrant and winter resident.

**Occurrence:** Lapland Longspurs frequent expansive open habitats such as beaches, agricultural fields, and salt marshes, where they are often found in association with Snow Buntings and Horned Larks, most notably at the immediate coast and in the Connecticut River valley. In spring, there is occasionally a pronounced movement of northward-bound migrants during March and early April. *Spring maxima:* 50, Middleboro, 27 March 1988 (Petersen); 30, Northampton, 19 March 1955 (Johnston). Longspurs usually arrive during the last few days of September and build up to peak numbers during November and December. *Fall maxima:* 80, Newbury, 5 December 1990 (Perkins); 60, outer Cape Cod, 25–28 November 1960 (Fox, Smart); 10,

Bolton, 23 October 1977 (Merriman). Numbers stabilize at favored localities in midwinter; however, the counts vary considerably from year to year. *Winter maxima:* 300, Salisbury, 9 January 1959 (Kieran). *Extreme dates:* 1, Plum Island, 18 September 1977 (Denison); to 1, Scituate, 22 June 1986 (Petersen); 1, Monomoy, 17 May 1984 (Nikula); 1, Plum Island, 11 May 1974 (Petersen, Forster).

## Smith's Longspur   *Calcarius pictus*

**Range:** Nearctic; breeds from eastern central Alaska southeastward across arctic Canada to northern Ontario. Winters in the southern Great Plains from southern Iowa south to eastern Texas.

**Status:** Vagrant: one sight record.

**Occurrence:** A Smith's Longspur in winter plumage was found at Salisbury Beach, 12 October 1968 (Leahy), and was convincingly described in writing (details on file at MAS). On the East Coast, Smith's Longspurs have also been recorded in New York, Connecticut (Bulmer 1969), Maryland, South Carolina, and New Jersey.

## Chestnut-collared Longspur   *Calcarius ornatus*

**Range:** Nearctic; breeds from southern Alberta and southwestern Manitoba south to western Kansas and western Minnesota. Winters from northern Arizona and northern Louisiana south to northern Mexico.

**Status:** Vagrant: four records.

**Occurrence:** The first Massachusetts record of the Chestnut-collared Longspur was a single individual that was collected at Magnolia, 28 July 1876 (Townsend 1905). Additional records are: 1, North Beach, Chatham, 3–6 January 1975 (Goodrich, Nikula, Clem, Bailey, Petersen, Sorrie, Harrington); 1 immature female banded and photographed, Nantucket, 12–16 October 1979 (Veit, Perkins, Litchfield, Andrews, photo in AB 34: 141); 1 photographed, Duxbury Beach, 23–25 October 1991 (Abrams, VO, photo in AB 46: 167). Of the prairie longspurs, this species has occurred on the Atlantic Coast the most frequently.

## Snow Bunting   *Plectrophenax nivalis*

**Range:** Holarctic; breeds, in North America, from northern Alaska and Ellesmere Island south to northern Labrador and northern Quebec. Winters south to northeastern Utah and North Carolina.

**Status:** Common to locally abundant migrant and winter resident.

**Occurrence:** Snow Buntings are characteristic birds of beaches and barren fields during late fall and winter. They appear in peak numbers in early November and gradually diminish during the course of the winter. Spring migrants are usually difficult to distinguish from wintering birds. They are most numerous at the coast and in the Connecticut River valley. *Maxima:* 1,000, Salisbury Beach, several years in early November (RNEB, BOEM); 1,000, East Hadley, 19–22 February 1956 (Eliot); 1,000, Monomoy, 13 November 1981 (Goodrich); 700, Barnstable, 11 November 1973 (Pease); 450, Bolton, 27 February 1982 (Merriman). *Extreme dates:* 3, Brewster, 3 September 1956 (Isleib); to 1, Katama, Martha's Vineyard, 21 July 1988 (Whiting); 3, Chatham, 21 May 1966 (fide Bailey); 1, Chatham, 15–21 May 1960 (Copeland, Bailey).

# Bobolink   *Dolichonyx oryzivorus*

**Range:** Nearctic; breeds from central British Columbia, central Ontario, and western Newfoundland (recently) south to northeastern California, central Nebraska, central Illinois, northern West Virginia, and New Jersey. Winters in central and southern South America.

**Status:** Locally common breeder but decreasing. Common spring and occasionally abundant fall migrant.

**Breeding:** Bobolinks breed in open grassy pastures but have declined considerably since the mid-1900s, when agricultural land was much more widespread in Massachusetts. Today they are still common where there is suitable breeding habitat in Berkshire County, in the Connecticut River valley, in the northeastern parts of both Worcester and Essex counties, and at scattered localities in Plymouth County. They are generally scarce on the coastal plain, except for a few pairs that regularly attempt to nest at Chilmark, Martha's Vineyard, and 5 pairs that attempted to nest at Nantucket from 1980 to 1982 (BOEM). Early mowing of hayfields is a threat constantly facing the breeding attempts of Bobolinks in many Massachusetts locations. *Summer maxima* (recent): 175 +, Ipswich, 28 July 1974 (Berry); 114, NBBC, 15 June 1980; 75 +, Princeton, 22 July 1976 (Taylor); 60 +, Bolton Flats, 10 June 1990 (Anderson, SSBC). *Egg dates:* 1–8 June.

**Nonbreeding:** In spring, Bobolinks begin arriving in Massachusetts during the first week of May, and peak numbers of migrants and residents are recorded during the second and third weeks. *Spring maxima:* 400, Plum

*A bird of farm fields and grasslands in summer, the **Bobolink**, with its rollicking song, is slowly fading from many areas as local agriculture declines. Nonetheless, during fall migration, hundreds are occasionally heard passing overhead at night.*

▷

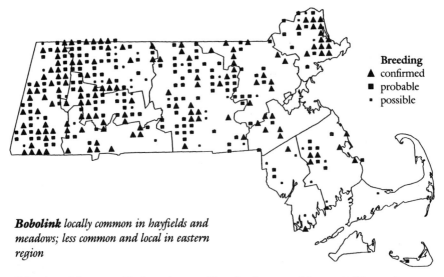

**Bobolink** *locally common in hayfields and meadows; less common and local in eastern region*

Breeding
▲ confirmed
■ probable
▪ possible

Island, 13 May 1978 (Roberts); 280, Framingham, 19 May 1978 (Forster); 200+, West Newbury, 18 May 1974 (Stymeist et al); 50, GMNWR, 1 May 1982 (Porter).

Prior to fall migration, Bobolinks begin gathering in large flocks by late July, reaching peak numbers in late August before departing for the south during September. Most are gone by late September. During autumn migration, they congregate in cornfields and weed fields, both at the outer coast and inland near their breeding areas. *Fall maxima:* 1,500, Halifax, 4 September 1984 (Petersen); 1,134, Newton, 5 September 1981 (N. and O. Komar); 500+, Southwick, 2 September 1972 (Bartlett); 475, Framingham, 6 September 1979 (Forster); 366, Hadley, 7 September 1972 (Gagnon); 250, Nantucket, 29 August 1980 (Veit). *Extreme dates:* 1, Marshfield, 28 April 1991 (Ludlow); to 1, Concord Sewer Beds, 11–17 December 1983 (Hines, Walton); 1, Truro, 11 November 1973 (Veit, D'Entremont).

# Red-winged Blackbird *Agelaius phoeniceus*

**Range:** Primarily Nearctic; breeds from south-central Alaska, northern Saskatchewan, central Manitoba, southern Quebec, and southwestern Newfoundland south throughout the United States to Costa Rica. Winters in much of the southern portion of the breeding range north to Washington, Nebraska, and Massachusetts.

**Status:** Locally abundant breeder and abundant migrant. Uncommon and irregular in winter, with frequent survival in mild seasons.

**Breeding:** Red-winged Blackbirds are primarily marsh blackbirds, but pairs also nest in the upper portions of salt marshes and in dense thickets and shrubbery in wooded swamps. The largest nesting colonies are in extensive cattail marshes, such as those at the Great Meadows National Wildlife Refuge, Concord. Sample densities: 305 males, Littleton, June 1960 (Bolton); 300, Bolton Flats, 10 June 1990 (Anderson, SSBC); 90 males, Great Barrington, June 1964 (Simmons). After they have finished nesting in late July, they become somewhat inconspicuous until late September, when massive flocks congregate prior to southward migration. *Egg dates:* 10 May–18 June.

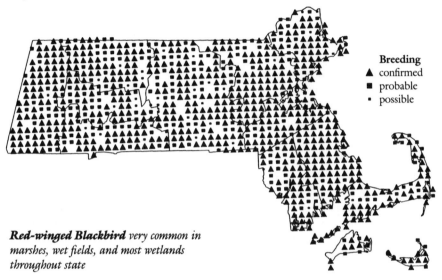

**Breeding**
▲ confirmed
■ probable
· possible

*Red-winged Blackbird very common in marshes, wet fields, and most wetlands throughout state*

**Nonbreeding:** During mild winters, flocks of male Red-winged Blackbirds are occasionally seen in late February—e.g., 1,000, Middleboro, 27 February 1975 (Wilson); 1,000, Lanesboro, 26 February, no year given (McNair 1978); 125 +, Middleboro, 20 February 1984 (Petersen). However, during a typical season, the majority of spring migrants are not ordinarily recorded until the second or third week of March. *Spring maxima:* 18,000 +, West Newbury, 12 March 1977 (Veit); 5,000, Concord, 22 March 1971 (Swift et al); 3,000 +, Hatfield, 3 April 1970 (Yenlin).

In the fall, Red-winged Blackbirds congregate into large flocks during September and October, with the largest counts usually occurring in late October. *Fall maxima:* 200,000 blackbirds (two-thirds of which were Redwings), Dartmouth, 23 October 1972 (Willoughby); 20,000, Wayland, 24 October 1967 (Mazzarese); 7,000 +, Ipswich, 21 October 1984 (Berry); 6,000 +, Framingham, 23 October 1977 (Forster); 5,000, Concord, 10 November 1985 (Forster); 4,200 flying south in 20 minutes, Wayland, 23 October 1965 (Forster).

The number of Red-winged Blackbirds surviving the entire season in Massachusetts varies considerably from year to year, depending upon the relative severity of the season. They are commonest on the southeastern coastal plain in this season. *Winter maxima:* 300, Littleton, 8 January 1980 (Baird); 200, Abington, throughout January 1974 (Pearson); 50 wintering, West Roxbury, 1972–1973 (Stymeist, Martin). In Berkshire County, where Red-winged Blackbirds often frequent feeders in the winter, no more than three have survived the season at a single locality (McNair 1978); survival has also occurred in wetlands.

## Eastern Meadowlark   *Sturnella magna*

**Range:** Nearctic and Neotropical; breeds from southwestern South Dakota, northern Michigan, south central Quebec, and central Nova Scotia south to central Arizona and the southeastern United States into Central and South America. Winters from central Wisconsin, southeastern Ontario, and central Nova Scotia south to the southern United States.

**Status:** Locally uncommon to fairly common breeder and migrant, but decreasing. Erratic in winter; most frequent and numerous on the southeastern coastal plain.

**Breeding:** The habitat preferences and history of the Eastern Meadowlark in Massachusetts parallel those of the Bobolink. Following a period of maximum abundance in the 19th century, during which time agriculture and dairy farming were at their peak in Massachusetts, Eastern Meadowlarks gradually declined as breeders in the state. The highest remaining densities are in the rural farming districts of eastern Berkshire County, the Connecticut River valley, the Sudbury River valley, and the Middleboro-Bridgewater area of Plymouth County. Scattered pairs also regularly breed at a number of airports throughout the state. *Egg dates:* 21 April–28 June.

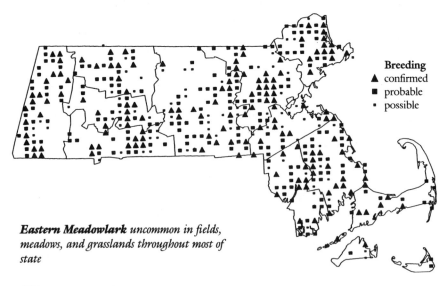

Breeding
▲ confirmed
■ probable
• possible

*Eastern Meadowlark uncommon in fields, meadows, and grasslands throughout most of state*

**Nonbreeding:** In spring, Eastern Meadowlarks arrive in Massachusetts during March and April; however, distinguishing migrants from residents is often difficult. *Spring maxima:* 100, Granby, 26 March 1955 (Ballman); 29, Halifax, 26 March 1989 (Forster); 19, Bridgewater, 10 March 1991 (d'Entremont); 16, Ipswich, 18 April 1987 (Berry, BBC); 16, West Newbury, 18 May 1985 (BBC); 9, Hardwick, 25 March 1989 (Lynch). In fall, migrants regularly congregate in salt marshes and open moorlands along the coast, where some often remain for winter. *Fall maxima:* 111, Nauset, Eastham, 23 October 1968 (Bailey); 34, DWWS, Marshfield, 27 November 1991 (Aversa); 21, Eastham, 23 November 1991 (Nikula); 14, Framingham, 28 September 1990 (Forster); 12 +, Truro, 15 October 1989 (Nikula). Winter survival inland has only been recorded for particularly mild and snowless winters. *Winter maxima:* a total of 388 was reported in Massachusetts during February 1960, including: 130, South Dartmouth, 21 February (fide Emery); 208, Cape Cod CBC, 19 December 1976; 74, Northampton CBC, 2 January 1967; 72, Marshfield CBC, 29 December 1991.

# Western Meadowlark   *Sturnella neglecta*

**Range:** Primarily western Nearctic; breeds from central British Columbia east to northwestern Ohio and western New York south to Texas and Arizona. Winters in the southern portion of the breeding range south to Mexico.

**Status:** Rare and erratic visitor: 25 records between 1957 and 1974; scarce or absent before and since.

**Occurrence:** Although Griscom & Snyder (1955) refer to an 1898 record from Taunton, the first recorded Western Meadowlark in Massachusetts this century was a bird seen and heard singing in Pittsfield, 8–19 July 1944 (Eliot et al). The species then went unrecorded until one appeared in Burlington, 2 June 1957 (Argue, Beattie). Between then and 1974, twenty-three Western Meadowlarks have occurred in Massachusetts, mostly from the Connecticut River valley and Essex County (e.g., Boxford, Rowley), but also including four records from the southeastern coastal plain—i.e., 1, Wellfleet, 8 June 1964 (Bailey); 1, Katama, Martha's Vineyard, 17 July 1967 (Forster); 1, Truro, 7 June 1970 (Jenkins); 1, South Wellfleet, 10 May 1971 (Cunningham). These records all pertain to males identified on the basis of their distinctive song and occurring between the dates 21 April and 17 July, with one exception: 1, Salisbury Beach, 11 October 1971 (Forster). Since 1974, Western Meadowlark occurrences in Massachusetts seem to have stopped rather abruptly. The most recent record is: 1 singing male, Squantum, 25–27 April 1981 (Brown et al).

## Yellow-headed Blackbird   *Xanthocephalus xanthocephalus*

**Range:** Western Nearctic; breeds from western Oregon, north-central Saskatchewan, central Manitoba, and southern Ontario south to southern California, southern New Mexico, northwestern Arkansas, and central Illinois. Winters from central California, central Arizona, and central Texas south to Mexico. Rare, but regular, fall migrant on the Atlantic Coast between Nova Scotia and Florida.

**Status:** Rare to very uncommon, but regular, fall migrant; very rare in spring and winter.

**Occurrence:** In Massachusetts, Yellow-headed Blackbirds are most often encountered during late August and early September on Cape Cod and the Islands. Although historically they were rarer in spring than in fall, recently, they are being reported with increasing frequency in spring. Griscom and Snyder (1955) knew of no spring records, but since 1955 there have been over thirty-five reports, the majority of which fall in March, April, and May. Spring occurrences are not as restricted to the southeastern coastal plain as the fall reports, and over ten records of single birds exist from inland localities, frequently at feeders, west to New Salem, 3 April 1964 (Lawrence), and Williamstown, 19–20 March 1960 (Raymond, Treadway, Hendricks).

   Between the years 1951 and 1981, one-hundred-seven Yellow-headed Blackbirds were seen in Massachusetts in the period 2 August to 12 December, with sixty-three of these reports falling between 15 August and 15 September. Of these records, there are approximately ten from inland localities, which clearly reflects the species' coastal affinity in autumn. The westernmost records are: 1, Cheshire, 12 October 1954 (Brierley); 1, Williamstown, 23 October 1975 (McNair). All records are of either one or two individuals, the majority of which are immature birds. Since 1959, there have been at least eleven Massachusetts winter records, most of them at feeders during the period between 29 December and 21 February.

## Rusty Blackbird   *Euphagus carolinus*

**Range:** Nearctic; breeds from northern Alaska, central Mackenzie, northern Quebec, central Labrador, and Newfoundland south to central Alaska, central Manitoba, southern Ontario, and central New England. Winters from southern North Dakota, southern Michigan, and southeastern New York south to eastern and northern Florida.

**Status:** Rare and local breeder in Berkshire and Franklin counties. Common to abundant migrant inland; much less numerous at the outer coast. Rare but regular in winter.

**Breeding:** During the late 1970s, McNair and others first found small numbers of Rusty Blackbirds nesting in the northeastern part of Berkshire County, and the first nest was collected there at Tyler Swamp, Savoy State Forest, 19 May 1977. A second nest with four eggs was found in Florida, 19–29 May 1977. In 1978, a pair was found feeding young at Borden Mountain, Savoy (Quinlan). From investigations conducted during the period 1980 to 1982, it would seem that Rusty Blackbirds probably breed regularly in small numbers at higher elevations in Berkshire County. *Egg dates:* 19–29 May.

**Nonbreeding:** Migrating Rusty Blackbirds are most numerous in wooded swamps, with the largest counts in Massachusetts in both spring and fall often coming from the Sudbury River valley. Griscom and Snyder (1955) refer to a "split migration" in spring, "with flocks appearing in early March, and again from late April to early May"; however, recent records fail to adhere closely to this pattern. In recent years, Rusty Blackbirds seem to be reported rather evenly during the period mid-March to early May, the majority of migrants usually passing through in April. *Spring maxima:* 2,000, Princeton, 5 April 1960 (Hunt); 1,000, Westford, 1 April 1940 (Abbott); 500, Ipswich, 1 April 1940 (Hill); 175, Sudbury River valley, 12 April 1975 (Forster); 115 in one-half hour, Middleboro, 27 March 1968 (Anderson); 30, Provincetown, 23 April 1977 (Nikula).

In the fall, the peak period of Rusty Blackbird migration usually occurs during the first two weeks of October. *Fall maxima:* 2,000, Newton, 26 October 1946 (Karplus); 1,500, Concord, 12 October 1940 (Griscom). Recent totals have been much lower—e.g., 500, Littleton, 6 October 1970 (Baird); 450, "Brookfields," 8 October 1977 (Blodget, Meservey); 300, Concord, 11 October 1981 (Petersen). Counts of 25 to 50 represent typical daily maxima for Cape Cod and the Islands during October.

Rusty Blackbirds are generally uncommon to rare in winter in Massachusetts, and those that do survive often go undetected because they retire to dense wooded swamps and spring-fed brooks, where birders rarely venture in that season. For example, during the blizzard of early February 1978, Heil counted 45 Rusty Blackbirds at Tapley Brook, South Peabody, suggesting that they had been driven out of other more heavily snow-covered swamps. *Winter maxima:* 80+, Whitman, 10 February 1985 (Petersen); 75, Martha's Vineyard, 26 February 1978 (Alden et al); 27, South Peabody, 16 February 1980 (Heil); 24, Wayland, 16 January 1964 (Morgan); 24, Orleans, 20–21 January 1968 (Lund); 20, Marshfield, 29 January 1984 (Petersen); 16, Nantucket, 2 January 1977 (Veit).

# Brewer's Blackbird *Euphagus cyanocephalus*

**Range:** Primarily western Nearctic; breeds from central British Columbia, southern Manitoba, and western Ontario south to southern California, central New Mexico, northern Iowa, and northwestern Indiana. Winters from southwestern British Columbia, eastern Montana, Kansas, northeastern Mississippi, and western North Carolina south to central Mexico.

**Status:** Rare fall migrant or winter visitor.

**Occurrence:** The first occurrence of a Brewer's Blackbird in Massachusetts was: 1 male, Easthampton, 30 October 1958 (Stone, Eliot). The following year, a second bird was reported in Hadley, 23–24 March 1959 (Keith). These were apparently isolated occurrences because the next Brewer's Blackbird did not appear in Massachusetts until 1973, when two immatures appeared in East Orleans, 27–28 October (Petersen, Goodrich, Bailey, Petersen 1974). A second immature bird occurred that fall in Truro, 7 November 1973 (Forster et al).

Since 1973, there have been more or less annual reports of Brewer's Blackbirds in Massachusetts. The majority of these have occurred in October and November, although a scattering of winter records exist from the period December to April. Most birds are found in farmyards near the coast, similar to habitats frequented by Brewer's Blackbirds in the West. An immature at Bridgewater, 4 October 1977 (Petersen), was the first record for Plymouth County, and one at South Peabody, 27 September 1980 (Heil), was the first record for Essex County. *Fall maxima:* 4 (2 males, 2 females), Truro, 24–31 October 1976 (Veit, Litchfield, et al); 3–5, Truro, 21 October 1977 (Nikula, Goodrich, Bailey); 3, Marshfield, 24–25 October 1981 (Altman et al). Recent records for winter and spring include: 2 males, Katama, Martha's Vineyard, 14 February–6 March 1976 (Daniels, Stymeist, Veit, et al); 1 male, Katama, Martha's Vineyard, 17–26 February 1978 (Sargent, Stymeist, et al); 1, Nantucket, 3 April 1978 (Andrews). In addition, one or two birds successfully spent the entire winter of 1978–1979 and 1979–1980 at Katama, Martha's Vineyard (Laux et al).

# Boat-tailed Grackle *Quiscalus major*

**Range:** Nearctic; resident along the Atlantic Coast from New York southward, throughout peninsular Florida, and west along the Gulf Coast to southeastern Texas; casual north to Nova Scotia.

**Status:** Vagrant: one sight record.

**Occurrence:** The appearance of two female Boat-tailed Grackles at Newbury, 24 April 1986 (Forster [see Forster 1986], Seeckts) represents the only acceptable record of this salt-marsh blackbird in Massachusetts. The season, habitat, and precedent of the species' presence in Connecticut and Rhode Island in 1985 suggested that these birds were this species rather than the Great-tailed Grackle (*Q. mexicanus*).

# Common Grackle   *Quiscalus quiscula*

**Range:** Nearctic; breeds from northeastern British Columbia, southern Mackenzie, central Saskatchewan, northeastern Ontario, and southwestern Newfoundland south, east of the Rocky Mountains to central Texas and southern Florida. Winters in the southern portion of its range north to southern Minnesota, southern Michigan, and southern New England.

**Status:** Common to very abundant breeder and migrant. Local and very uncommon in winter.

**Breeding:** The Common Grackle is one of the most widespread and numerous nesting birds in the state. Family groups are familiar sights on practically any suburban lawn in Massachusetts during July and August, before the birds collect into flocks prior to fall migration. These postbreeding flocks typically gather in nocturnal roosts, which gradually increase in size as the season progresses—e.g., 1,360 in one hour, West Acton, 31 July 1960 (Bolton); 1,400, Lynnfield, 27 August 1960 (Dillaway). *Egg dates:* 2 May–1 June.

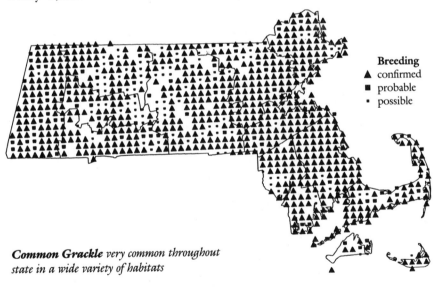

Breeding
▲ confirmed
■ probable
• possible

***Common Grackle*** *very common throughout state in a wide variety of habitats*

**Nonbreeding:** Because a substantial number of grackles regularly winter north to central Connecticut, the first spring migrants in Massachusetts often arrive as early as late February. A brief spell of unseasonably warm weather at that time almost invariably results in the arrival of migrant grackles, particularly in the Connecticut River valley and in southeastern Massachusetts. In spring, peak migration occurs in late March and early April. *Spring maxima:* 13,000, Sudbury River valley, 1 April 1950 (Parker); 7,000+, Concord, 2 April 1974 (Forster); 5,000+, Hadley, 18 March 1966

(Yenlin); 4,000+, Waltham, 19 March 1977 (Stymeist); 3,500+, Natick, 18 March 1989 (Taylor). In fall, grackles habitually gather in enormous roosts that reach maximum size during late October and early November. These great roosts often diminish dramatically during mid-November, and by December grackles are generally scarce in Massachusetts. The number of grackles entering these gigantic roosts is very difficult to estimate, but the following counts provide an order of magnitude. **Fall maxima:** "one million," Oxford, 23 November 1962 (Gibson); "one million," Oxford, 2 November 1968 (FBC); "maybe one million," headed for a roost along the North River, Pembroke, 26 October 1979 (Petersen); 200,000, Methuen, 1 November 1989 (Hogan, VO); 100,000, Lynnfield, 28 October 1973 (Keenan). Establishing accurate counts of blackbirds en route to communal evening roosts is difficult because the birds may alter their flight lines from one day to the next; however, the following counts from Middleboro probably reflect the dramatic departure of migrants bound for a Pembroke roost: 113,000, 27 October; 10,000–25,000, 29 October; 0, 31 October (Lloyd-Evans). Common Grackles probably winter regularly in small numbers in the milder sections of Massachusetts, but they often go undetected unless they are discovered at a roost. **Winter maxima:** 1,002, Martha's Vineyard CBC, 3 January 1989; 800, Wellesley, 19 January 1966 (Leverett et al); 500, Orleans, throughout January 1977 (Nikula).

## Brown-headed Cowbird   *Molothrus ater*

**Range:** Primarily Nearctic; breeds from southeastern Alaska, northern British Columbia, northern Alberta, southern Manitoba, central Quebec,

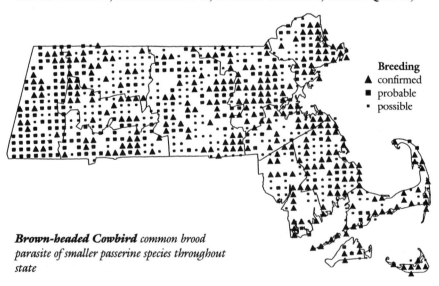

Breeding
▲ confirmed
■ probable
• possible

*Brown-headed Cowbird common brood parasite of smaller passerine species throughout state*

and southern Nova Scotia south to southern California, central Mexico, Louisiana, and central Florida. Winters from northern California, Kansas, the southern Great Lakes, and southern New England south to Florida and southern Mexico.

**Status:** Common and widespread breeder and abundant migrant. Locally fairly common during winter.

**Breeding:** During summer, Brown-headed Cowbirds are most numerous around farmlands, but they are increasingly widespread in a variety of other habitats, where they have been documented to parasitize the nests of a remarkable assortment of songbird species. Increasing evidence suggests that this species may be playing an important role in the decline of certain interior forest-nesting species (Terborgh 1989). *Egg dates:* 15 May–1 July.

**Nonbreeding:** In spring, migrating cowbirds appear in Massachusetts during March and April, with peak counts usually occurring in late March. *Spring maxima:* 800, Weymouth, 8 March 1977 (Hatch, Veit, et al); 600, Spencer, 4 April 1960 (Crompton); 600, Granby, 22 March 1969 (Yenlin); 600, Bridgewater, 16 March 1980 (BBC, Davis). After breeding, flocks of cowbirds gradually build up during early fall, and peak counts are normally made in October. *Fall maxima:* 30,000, Wayland, 24 October 1967 (Mazzarese); 5,000, Sudbury River valley, 25 September 1955 (Morgan, Stackpole); 5,000, Springfield, 3 November 1965 (Cavanaugh); 2,000 +, Eastham, 22 August 1968 (Harris).

In winter, cowbirds are most abundant in the lowlands of the Connecticut River valley, but they regularly winter in scattered localities throughout the state. *Winter maxima:* 3,020, Springfield CBC, 30 December 1967; 3,000 +, Springfield, 22 January 1968 (Bates); 1,329, New Bedford CBC, 30 December 1973; 500, Pittsfield CBC, 2 January 1967.

# Orchard Oriole  *Icterus spurius*

**Range:** Primarily eastern Nearctic; breeds from southeastern Saskatchewan, southern Manitoba, central Wisconsin, southern Ontario, and Massachusetts south to northeastern Colorado, western Texas, northeastern Mexico, the Gulf Coast states, and northern Florida. Winters from southern Mexico south to northern South America.

**Status:** Local and uncommon breeder but apparently increasing since 1975. Uncommon spring and very rare fall migrant.

**Breeding:** Forster (1975) has described the breeding status of the Orchard Oriole in Massachusetts, emphasizing the erratic fluctuations of the Massachusetts population during the historical period and concluding, "The [Orchard] oriole has apparently extended its breeding range northward because of population pressures in the more southerly portion of its range."

Since 1975, Orchard Orioles have increased in Massachusetts. For example, the first Worcester County breeding record was established at Hardwick, 23 June 1977 (Forster), when an adult was seen with two fledged young. Then, two pairs nested on Nantucket in 1980 (Perkins), and as many as ten pairs were found on the GBBBC, 14 June 1980. At least four pairs bred in South Peabody in 1982 (Heil), and additional pairs were found breeding in Framingham and Wellesley during 1981 and 1982 (Forster). By 1990, Orchard Orioles were found breeding at widely scattered localities throughout much of Massachusetts. *Egg dates:* 28 May–25 June.

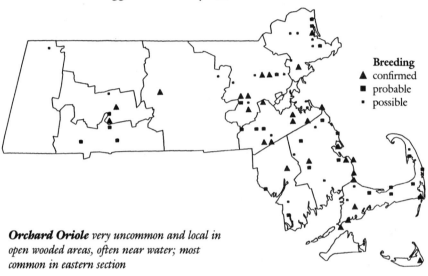

Breeding
▲ confirmed
■ probable
• possible

*Orchard Oriole very uncommon and local in open wooded areas, often near water; most common in eastern section*

**Nonbreeding:** Most resident Orchard Orioles arrive in Massachusetts in mid-May. Migrants are routinely seen at Mt. Auburn Cemetery, Cambridge, during May, and single birds are occasionally reported in April following coastal storms—e.g., 1, Newton Highlands, 17 April 1952 (Rost). *Spring maxima:* 41 reported, throughout Massachusetts (including 6 in the Connecticut River valley, 2 in Pittsfield, 3 in Vineyard Haven, 1 on Cape Cod), May 1967 (RNEB); 37 reported, eastern Massachusetts (including 7 at MBO), 6–31 May 1980 (BOEM). The highest count for a single locality on one day is: 7, Mt. Auburn Cemetery, Cambridge, 23 May 1976 (Leverich et al).

In the fall, the Orchard Oriole is one of the earliest Massachusetts nesting birds to depart, most having disappeared from the state by the end of July. As a result, they are particularly rare as migrants during fall. *Fall maxima:* 10 banded, Manomet, 10–22 July 1980 (MBO staff); 3, Tuckernuck Island, 13 August 1977 (Veit, Litchfield). *Extreme dates:* 1, Lambert's Cove, Martha's Vineyard, 16 April 1969 (Kelley, Rogers); to 1, Chatham, 26 September 1967 (Copeland). Anomalous summer reports, probably of nonbreeding wanderers, include: 1 male, Plum Island, 17 June 1972 (Petersen); 2 (1 adult male and 1 immature male), Provincetown, 4 July 1964 (Gammel).

# Northern Oriole  *Icterus galbula*

**Range:** Primarily Nearctic; breeds from southern British Columbia, central Alberta, southern Ontario, and central Nova Scotia south to west-central Oklahoma, central Louisiana, northern Georgia, and western South Carolina. Winters mainly from southern Mexico to northern South America, with a few individuals in the United States north, in the East, to southern New England.

**Status:** Fairly common breeder throughout the state. Common to very common spring and early fall migrant; very uncommon to rare in winter.

**Breeding:** Northern Orioles are conspicuous and widespread in suburban and rural habitats throughout much of the state. For nesting, they prefer elms and other shade trees adjacent to fields, forest clearings, and other open areas, but they are generally absent from densely forested areas. They are scarce on Nantucket. *Summer maxima:* 29 pairs, Wellesley, throughout June 1955 (Freeland, VO); 55, South Groveland, 8 June 1991 (Stymeist, VO); 50, West Newbury, throughout June 1955 (deWindt); 23, South Groveland, 10 June 1990 (Stymeist, VO); 18 males, Watertown, 13 June 1985 (Hall). *Egg dates:* 24 May–4 July.

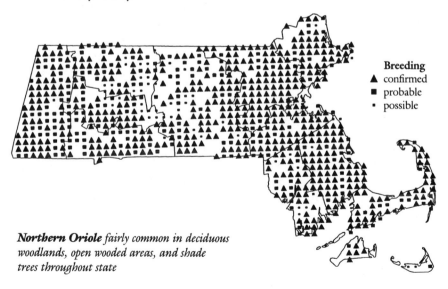

Breeding
▲ confirmed
■ probable
• possible

*Northern Oriole fairly common in deciduous woodlands, open wooded areas, and shade trees throughout state*

**Nonbreeding:** After a punctual arrival in early May, peak counts of spring migrant orioles occur by midmonth. Occasionally, individuals appear much earlier, usually following coastal storms in April—e.g., over thirty records, 3–24 April, with the majority occurring on the southeastern coastal plain. *Spring maxima:* 200, Essex County, 12 May 1979 (Stymeist); 137, Wellesley, 16 May 1964 (Leverett et al); 100 +, Essex County, 14 May 1955 (Griscom et al); 60, Wellesley, 19 May 1968 (Petersen). In the fall, adult Northern Orioles have largely departed from Massachusetts by early August; however, large numbers of immatures are occasionally found at land-bird traps along the outer coast during the last two weeks of August. *Fall maxima:* 200 +, Monomoy, 9 September 1968 (Harris et al); 75, Chatham, 3 September 1962 (Gardler); 65, Monomoy, 30 August 1965 (Forster). Adult males are rarely reported after August (Baird 1966), so that, 1, East Orleans, 1 January 1972 (Petersen) is most unusual.

Northern Orioles are frequently recorded at feeding stations and in fruit-laden thickets into late December—e.g., 21, eastern Massachusetts, December 1979 (BOEM)—and they occasionally survive the entire winter on the southeastern coastal plain and in the Connecticut River valley—e.g., West Springfield (1966); Springfield (1969); Middleboro (1969); East Orleans (1974); Rowley (1977); and Wayland (1989) (all fide RNEB or BOEM). *Winter maxima:* 7, Westfield, throughout January 1958 (Smith et al); 5, Framingham, 3–12 January 1976 (Hamilton).

**Subspecies:** The western subspecies, *I. g. bullockii*, breeds east to the western edge of the Great Plains and winters from western Mexico to Costa Rica. There are a number of well-substantiated records of "Bullock's" Northern Orioles for Massachusetts, including: 1 immature male, Falmouth, 2 December 1952–24 April 1953 (Collins et al); 1 adult male, Marblehead, 1 January–15 April 1954 (Snyder et al); 1 adult male, Osterville, 24 April 1954 (Johnson, Bagg, Collins); 1 dead, MNWS, 14 April 1957 (Dee, Griscom); 2 immature males, Monomoy, 6 September 1957 (Buckley, Isleib, Smith, Harte); 1 adult male photographed, Wellesley, 28 February–3 March 1959 (Chandler et al); 1 adult male, Vineyard Haven, 27 December 1961 (Smart, Keith, Sargent, et al); 1 immature male dead, South Salem, 19 November 1966 (Snyder); 1 immature male photographed, Abington, November 1975–22 February 1976 (Lynde, Petersen, Sorrie, et al, photos at MAS). Five separate individuals were reported in Massachusetts during December 1966 and January 1967, and the specimen obtained in November 1966 suggests that a bona fide incursion to Massachusetts occurred that winter. Reports of this race in Massachusetts seem to have diminished since about 1970.

# Common Chaffinch  *Fringilla coelebs*

**Range:** Palearctic; breeds throughout north temperate Eurasia south to the Mediterranean region, Iran, southern Russia, and western Siberia. Winters south to northern Africa and southwestern Asia.

**Status:** Vagrant: two records.

**Occurrence:** The first record involved a bird that was present in Chatham from 1–3 April 1961 (Reynolds, Copeland, Bailey), where it was identifiably filmed in color. The second individual was seen and photographed in Windsor, 26–27 March 1988 (Rockoch, photo in BOEM 16: 215). The highly migratory behavior of this abundant and wide-ranging Palearctic species makes it an excellent candidate for vagrancy. Chaffinches have also been recorded in spring in Maine (1980) and New Hampshire (1989).

## Brambling  *Fringilla montifringilla*

**Range:** Palearctic; breeds from northern Scandinavia, northern Russia, and northern Siberia south to southern Scandinavia, central Russia, and the Kamchatka Peninsula. Winters from the British Isles and the southern edge of the breeding range south to northern Africa, the Middle East, Iran, India, China, and Japan. Vagrant to North America (Banks 1970) but of regular occurrence in the Aleutian Islands and western Alaska.

**Status:** Vagrant: three records.

**Occurrence:** The first two Bramblings to occur in Massachusetts were found in the Connecticut River valley during the winter of 1961–1962. A male initially appeared at a farm in South Hadley, where it fed with House Sparrows, 29 November–7 December 1961 (Sessions, Eliot), then later moved to a feeder in Florence, where it remained until 18 March 1962 (Budgiare). Meanwhile, a second bird appeared at a feeder in Richmond, 18 February 1962, where it remained until 6 April (Annin). The Richmond bird was banded and color photographed in the hand. The third record involved an immature male that visited a feeder and was photographed in Mansfield during February 1979 (Everett, photos at MAS). As with the Common Chaffinch, the Brambling is highly migratory in the Old World, so its appearance as a vagrant in North America should not be viewed as totally unlikely.

## Pine Grosbeak  *Pinicola enucleator*

**Range:** Holarctic; breeds, in North America, from western Alaska and central Mackenzie, northern Manitoba, northern Quebec, and northern Labrador south to central California, central Manitoba, southern Ontario, and sporadically in northern New England. Wanders south during irruptions, in the East, to Virginia and the Carolinas.

**Status:** Erratic winter visitor; at times very common but usually rare to uncommon.

**Occurrence:** Pine Grosbeaks are among the least common of the northern finches to occur in Massachusetts. Major flight years have been widely separated—e.g., 1892–1893, 1930–1931, and 1950–1951 (Griscom & Snyder 1955). The only major flights since then were in 1961–1962, when 401 were recorded on eleven Massachusetts CBCs (fide AFN), and 1977–1978, when at least 1,000 appeared in eastern Massachusetts during December-January (BOEM). During flight years, even when the flights are light, Pine Grosbeaks often seem to first occur in late October and November, only to apparently disappear until midwinter, when they may reappear at widely scattered localities throughout the state. In Massachusetts, Pine Grosbeaks feed largely upon the seeds and buds of ash, elm, and maple, as well as upon crab apples, viburnum berries, and the fruits of a variety of other ornamental plantings. During the great flight of 1892–1893, Brewster (1906) noted over 500 Pine Grosbeaks in Cambridge and estimated that the city "must have harbored several thousands." The flocks that he observed fed almost exclusively upon ash seeds, a preference that was also noted during the 1977–1978 flight. *Winter maxima* (recent): 390, Framingham to Concord, 15 January 1978 (Forster, Hamilton); 200 +, Boxford, 21 January 1978 (Palmer); 177, Concord-Sudbury, 15 January 1978 (Walton). *Extreme dates:* 4, Savoy State Reservation, 19 July 1980 (Carroll, Lynch); 2, Windsor, 21 July 1980 (Carroll & Lynch 1980).

# Purple Finch   *Carpodacus purpureus*

**Range:** Nearctic; breeds from northern British Columbia, central Manitoba, central Quebec, and Newfoundland south to southern California in the mountains, southern Saskatchewan, central Minnesota, northeastern Ohio and Pennsylvania, and southeastern New York. Winters in the southern portion of its range south to southern Arizona, southeastern Texas, and central Florida.

**Status:** Common to uncommon nesting resident; most numerous west of Worcester County. Uncommon to fairly common migrant; irruptive, occasionally very common in winter.

**Breeding:** Purple Finches breed throughout the state, although they tend to be local in eastern Massachusetts, where they prefer to build their nests in ornamental conifers, especially spruces. In the western part of the state, where they are more widespread, breeding commonly takes place in mature mixed forests as well as in suburban habitats. In suitable habitat, from 5 to 10 Purple Finches can frequently be encountered in a day during early summer. Sample densities: 31 pairs, Wellesley, throughout June and July 1955 (Freeland et al); 14, Granville, 12 June–9 July 1987 (Kellogg). *Egg dates:* 10 May–19 June.

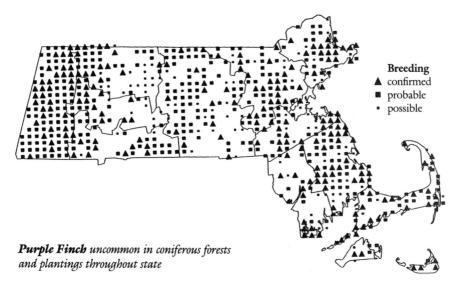

**Purple Finch** *uncommon in coniferous forests and plantings throughout state*

Breeding
▲ confirmed
■ probable
· possible

**Nonbreeding:** Migrant Purple Finches typically pass through Massachusetts in late April and May and from late September to early November. Their numbers are highly variable from year to year, with large numbers periodically remaining throughout the winter—e.g., 2,000 banded in Massachusetts, winters of 1939–1940 and 1941–1942 (Griscom & Snyder 1955); 1,500 banded statewide, winter of 1950–1951 (op cit). In years of great irruptions (e.g., 1883–1884, 1950–1951), up to 50 birds may be seen passing overhead each day; however, in most seasons, daily migration totals are considerably lower. For a complete discussion of the 1939–1940 winter invasion (see Weaver 1940). *Winter maxima* (additional): 612, Concord CBC, 2 January 1983; 457 banded, Adams, 1958–1959 (Brierley); 125, Wayland, 5 March 1983 (Robinson); 90, Framingham, 9 January 1983 (Forster).

# House Finch  *Carpodacus mexicanus*

**Range:** Primarily Nearctic; breeds from central British Columbia, north-central Wyoming, and western Nebraska south to central Mexico. Introduced to New York in 1940. Now breeds from Illinois, southern Ontario, southern Quebec, Vermont, and southern Maine south to Missouri, Georgia, and South Carolina. Winters within the breeding range and south to Mississippi and Alabama.

**Status:** Locally common to very common resident; some migration or dispersal, especially in fall.

**Breeding:** House Finches were introduced to Long Island, New York, during the early 1940s (Bull 1964). The first birds to be recorded in Massachusetts were in Berkshire County, when 2 were seen at Bartholomew's Cobble, Ashley Falls, 15 June 1955 (Bailey), where breeding was first confirmed in 1958 (Bailey). The next records were: 1 male, Cotuit, 10–30 January 1963 (Higgins, Donald); 1 female, Easthampton, 5 May 1964 (Riedel); 1, South Chelmsford, 1–15 December 1964 (Cail); 1, Needham, 1 December 1964 (Sargent); 20, Orleans, 3 January 1965 (Baird). Since then, House Finches have continued to expand their range in Massachusetts, and they are now widespread throughout suburban and semiurban habitats, where they frequently nest in dense conifers, as well as in gutters, under eaves, and in hanging flower pots (Burt 1968). They are most numerous on the southeastern coastal plain, in the western suburbs of Boston, and in the southern Connecticut River valley. *Egg dates:* late March–July.

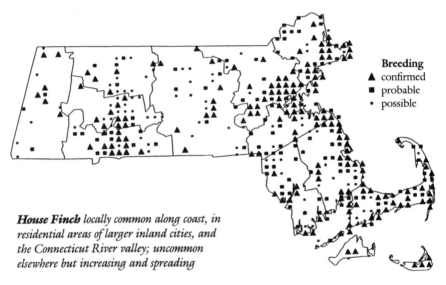

Breeding
▲ confirmed
■ probable
· possible

*House Finch locally common along coast, in residential areas of larger inland cities, and the Connecticut River valley; uncommon elsewhere but increasing and spreading*

**Nonbreeding:** House Finches are at least partially migratory, as has been demonstrated through extensive banding programs, particularly those done in Lexington 1970–1974 (Smyth) and Rockport 1977–1983 (Norris). Smyth (Sorrie 1975c) banded a total of 2,218 birds between 1970 and 1974, most of these in Lexington. The majority of the banded individuals were hatching year birds that were trapped between July and October. Some of these birds were recovered as far away as Virginia and Maryland, but "a substantial majority" were recaptured within 10 to 15 miles of the banding site. Norris (unpublished data) similarly banded 5,404 House Finches in his Rockport backyard between 1977 and 1983. The majority (2,838, or 53 percent) of these birds were caught during July and August. Of those recaptured in fall, almost 100 percent were hatching-year birds, which suggests that most movements involve the dispersal of young. Norris (pers. comm.) reported recoveries from as far away as Maryland, New Jersey, and Virginia.

Because most of these birds were banded as immatures, these records may primarily involve one-way dispersal of young; however, the following returns suggest that at least some House Finches are regularly migratory—i.e., 1 banded, Poquoson, Virginia, 2 March 1981, and retrapped at Rockport, 21 May 1981; 1 banded, Spotswood, New Jersey, 19 December 1982, and retrapped at Rockport, 13 April 1983 (fide Norris). The largest counts of House Finches are generally obtained in winter, when they congregate at feeders and other suburban food sources. ***Winter maxima:*** 1,372, Northampton CBC, 16 December 1990; 1,350, Concord CBC, 27 December 1991; 1,166, Cape Cod CBC, 18 December 1988; 995, Greater Boston CBC, 15 December 1991; 974, Concord CBC, 30 December 1990; 754, Uxbridge CBC, 29 December 1991.

# Red Crossbill   *Loxia curvirostra*

**Range:** Holarctic; breeds, in North America, from southern Alaska, central Ontario, and northern Minnesota east to the Gaspé Peninsula, Newfoundland, and Nova Scotia and irregularly south, in the East, to southeastern New York on the Atlantic Coast. Wanders erratically south to the southeastern United States, mainly during winter.

**Status:** Rare breeder following major winter flights. Erratic winter visitor; occasionally common.

**Breeding:** Griscom and Snyder (1955) documented the confirmed instances of breeding of the Red Crossbill in Massachusetts through 1955. All such breeding has followed major winter irruptions—e.g., Tyngsboro, 1875; North Truro, 1889 (female collected with well-developed eggs); Marblehead, 22 April 1917 (Brewster); nest and eggs blown down, Rockport, 3 March–6 April 1949 (Snyder); one fledgling obtained as specimen from nest, East Gloucester, March–April 1952 (Snyder). More recent breeding evidence includes: 15 adults and juveniles at feeder, Chatham, 3 June 1973 (Forster, Saunders); 2 pairs feeding young, Abington, May 1976 (Pierson); adults suspected of breeding, Framingham, May 1978 (Forster). ***Egg dates:*** late March–6 April.

**Nonbreeding:** During irruptive winter flights to Massachusetts, Red Crossbills are found most often in Pitch and Japanese Black pine groves on Cape Cod and the Islands. They are comparatively scarce inland west to Berkshire County, where McNair (1978) reported 115, 3 November 1969, as the largest flock ever found there. Recent winter flights have occurred in 1963–1964, 1969–1970, 1972–1973, 1973–1974, 1975–1976, and 1977–1978. The magnitude of these irruptions seems comparable to those reported by Griscom and Snyder (1955) for the years 1890 to 1955. ***Maxima:*** 479, Cape Cod CBC, 29 December 1963; 350, Nantucket CBC, 30 December 1973; 52, Nantucket, 29 May 1974 (Veit, Andrews).

**Subspecies:** The subspecific identification of Red Crossbills in Massachusetts suggests the origins of birds involved in southward irruptions. *L. c. sitkensis* breeds along the Pacific Coast from central and southeastern Alaska south to northwestern California. Specimens of this form were taken in Massachusetts during the major Red Crossbill incursion of 1887–1888 (Griscom 1937b), 1900, 1919–1920 (8 specimens from Chatham, Godfrey 1945), and 1940–1941. Between 9 March and 9 April 1941, Griscom and others identified 69 *L. c. sitkensis* out of 89 Red Crossbills in the greater Boston area and took 4 specimens (Griscom 1941b). In addition, 15 "probable" *L. c. sitkensis* were seen in Northampton, 31 March 1941 (Eliot, Griscom, VO). *L. c. pusilla*, a less clearly marked subspecies, is the breeding form of Newfoundland. One of this subspecies was collected in Springfield, January 1860, and flights occurred in the winters of 1919–1920 (Bent 1920) and 1932 (Griscom & Snyder 1955). The most recent specimen of this race was taken at Amherst, 25 March 1950 (Baird).

# White-winged Crossbill   *Loxia leucoptera*

**Range:** Holarctic; breeds, in North America, from central Alaska, northern Mackenzie, northern Quebec, and northern Labrador south in eastern North America to northern New Hampshire, Maine, and Nova Scotia. In winter, wanders south to North Carolina on the East Coast.

**Status:** Erratic winter visitor; occasionally fairly common. Rarely recorded during summer.

**Occurrence:** As is the case with certain other winter finches, White-winged Crossbills seemed to occur in much larger numbers prior to 1955 than they have since that time. Griscom and Snyder (1955) reported enormous flights in 1933–1934 (300 per day in Essex County) and February 1953 (reported from 100 localities in the state in flocks of up to 50). Winter reports in BOEM indicate that the largest recent flights include: approximately 150, eastern Massachusetts, 1973–1974; approximately 150 (with 14 in Wellesley as late as 18 May [Ewer]), eastern Massachusetts, 1975–1976; 199, Worcester, 1977–1978; 191, Boston, late December and approximately 140, eastern Massachusetts, 1981–1982.

An especially early flight occurred in August 1969—i.e., 1, Monomoy, 25 August (Petersen); 225, seen feeding in spruces, Brewster, 28 August (Petersen); 8 seen flying west, Tuckernuck Island, late August (Veit). Unlike the Red Crossbill, this species is generally more frequent inland than on the coast, perhaps due to its preference for Eastern Hemlock cones. Although nesting of White-winged Crossbills has not been reported in Massachusetts, there are summer occurrences—e.g., 1 fledgling, Annisquam, late May 1974

(Wiggin); 3 adults seen in a White Cedar swamp, West Bridgewater, 8 June 1986 (Petersen); 1 juvenile on the roadside, Adams, 8 July 1991 (Petersen).

# Common Redpoll   *Carduelis flammea*

**Range:** Holarctic; breeds, in North America, breeds from northern Alaska, northern Mackenzie, eastern Baffin Island, and southern Greenland south to James Bay and Newfoundland. In winter, occurs south to Virginia and Arkansas, occasionally farther.

**Status:** Erratic winter visitor and resident; occasionally abundant.

**Occurrence:** In Massachusetts, Common Redpolls are most numerous in open weed fields, weedy hollows among coastal dunes, and alder thickets near streams and at bird feeders. A few appear in Massachusetts nearly every winter, usually in small flocks. Periodically, however, great winter incursions occur. Recent major winter flights to Massachusetts took place in 1937–1938, 1946–1947, early winter 1949, 1952–1953, 1973–1974, 1975–1976, 1977–1978, and 1981–1982. Griscom and Snyder (1955) reported flocks of 2,000 to 2,500 birds from both eastern Massachusetts and the Connecticut River valley during the flights prior to 1955. No flocks of that magnitude have been encountered since the 1940s. The largest recent irruption was in 1973–1974, when more than 1,000 redpolls were reported in eastern Massachusetts during February (BOEM). During the flights of 1975–1976, 1977–1978, and 1981–1982, no more than 500 to 1,000 were found each year, and most flocks numbered fewer than 100 birds (BOEM). Very often, large numbers of redpolls do not appear until late January or February, suggesting that they may attempt to winter elsewhere, only moving into Massachusetts when they encounter food shortages in midwinter.

# Hoary Redpoll   *Carduelis hornemanni*

**Range:** Holarctic; breeds, in North America, in northern Alaska, northern Mackenzie, northeastern Manitoba, Southampton Island, and northern Quebec. Winters mainly in the breeding range, occasionally south, in the East, to southern Michigan and New Jersey.

**Status:** Rare and erratic winter visitor.

**Occurrence:** Hoary Redpolls have occurred in Massachusetts exclusively during major flights of Common Redpolls, and Griscom and Snyder (1955) listed nineteen specimens taken in the state prior to 1947. Although as many as nineteen have been reported during the course of a single winter, relatively few have been clearly photographed or remained in one place long enough to permit study by a number of observers. Nonetheless, it seems safe to conclude that Hoary Redpolls probably occur more or less regularly in Massachusetts during major flights of Common Redpolls. Recent records of unambiguous Hoary Redpolls include: 3, Lincoln, 16 February 1969 (Baird); 1 banded, Littleton, 6 April 1970 (Baird); 1 banded, Littleton, 12 March 1972 (Baird); 1, Eastham, 16–20 February 1974 (Petersen et al); 1, Duxbury Beach, 6 February 1982 (Petersen, Anderson); 1, Lancaster, 13 February 1982 (Merriman); 1, Framingham, 22 February 1982 (Hamilton et al); 1, Plum Island, 6 February–31 March 1982 (Roberts, Petersen, Veit, Heil); 2, Concord, 1–12 March 1982 (Walton); 1, Littleton, 3–24 March 1982 (Baird); 1, IRWS, 13 March 1982 (Heil); 1, Watertown, 4 February–31 March, 1987 (Stymeist). Note that none of these individuals were recorded earlier than February.

**Subspecies:** The AOU (1983) currently recognizes two subspecies of the Hoary Redpoll, *C. h. exilipes* of North America and *C. h. hornemanni* of Ellesmere, Bylot, and Baffin islands, as well as Greenland. Troy (1985) has shown that there is continuous morphological variation between *C. h. exilipes* and *C. flammea flammea*, the North American race of the Common Redpoll. Thus, it would appear that *C. f. flammea* and *C. h. exilipes* may represent a single variable species. If so, then *C. h. hornemanni* might represent either a distinctive form or a completely separate species. In either case, *C. h. hornemanni* was reported from Massachusetts during the major redpoll flight of 1968–1969 (Finch, AB 23: 456).

# Eurasian Siskin   *Carduelis spinus*

**Range:** Palearctic; breeds in Europe from northern Scandinavia and western Russia south to the British Isles, southern France, and Turkey and in eastern Asia from Manchuria and Sakhalin south to northern Japan. Wanders irregularly in winter south to northern Africa, Iran, Egypt, and southern China. Vagrant to North America (Borror 1963).

**Status:** Vagrant: three records.

**Occurrence:** The first Eurasian Siskin to appear in Massachusetts was closely studied in Cambridge, 11–17 August 1904 (Brewster 1906). It was identified as "a male, apparently adult, with the characteristic black areas of the throat and forehead well developed, if somewhat less extensive than in spring birds." A second bird was photographed at a New Bedford feeder, March 1969 (Johnson), and the slides are on file at the Massachusetts Audubon Society. A third individual, a male, was banded at Rockport, 5 May 1983 (Norris). Other records of Eurasian Siskins in eastern North America in 1983—e.g., 1, St. Pierre Island, 23 June; 1, Bloomfield, New Jersey, February–March (fide AB)—suggest that an irruption of this species within its European range may have occurred during the winter of 1982–1983 (McLaren et al 1989).

# Pine Siskin  *Carduelis pinus*

**Range:** Nearctic; breeds from southern Alaska east to Labrador and New-foundland south, in eastern North America, to central Illinois, northern Ohio, Pennsylvania, and southern New Jersey; nesting sporadic in southern areas of the range east of the Rockies. Winters, in the East, south to Florida and Texas.

**Status:** Occasional breeder. Erratic migrant and winter resident; occasion-ally common to very common.

**Breeding:** Following pronounced southward winter incursions, Pine Siskins are regularly found nesting in Massachusetts—e.g., from March to May 1976, nesting pairs were found in Abington, Wellesley, and Framing-ham (fide BOEM); in April 1978, 4 nests were found in Waltham and 3 in Cambridge (Stymeist); and, on 14 May 1978, 1 pair with 3 young was seen in Middleboro (Anderson). Information gathered by the Breeding Bird Atlas Project shows that from 1974 to 1979, nesting Pine Siskins were concentrated in the Sudbury River valley, the Connecticut River valley, and Berkshire County. Nests have most often been located in tall ornamental conifers, especially Norway and Blue spruces. It is likely that Pine Siskins also nest fairly commonly in coniferous woodlands, where they are un-doubtedly often overlooked. *Egg dates:* uncertain; probably in late March and April.

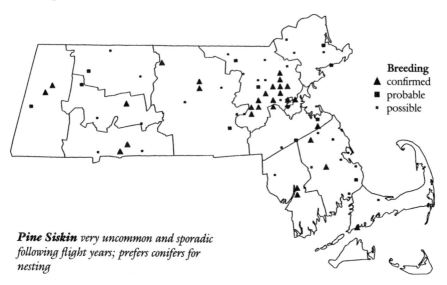

**Breeding**
▲ confirmed
■ probable
· possible

*Pine Siskin very uncommon and sporadic following flight years; prefers conifers for nesting*

**Nonbreeding:** Although siskins are very erratic in their annual abundance in Massachusetts, the seasonal timing of their flights is usually fairly predict-able. Southbound migrants normally appear during late September and

October and reach peak numbers during late October and November. In most flight years, the bulk of these birds winter south of Massachusetts, as reflected by a diminished local abundance by December. Returning migrants occur during March and April, but never in the numbers noted in fall. *Maxima:* 1,258, Concord CBC, 2 January 1977; 1,000, Provincetown, 23 October 1977 (Veit et al); 900, Nantucket, 10–20 October 1980 (Veit, Andrews); 600, Athol, 2–3 February 1990 (Frageau et al).

## American Goldfinch  *Carduelis tristis*

**Range:** Nearctic; breeds from southern British Columbia, southern Manitoba, southern Quebec, and southern Newfoundland south to the southern Great Plains, central Georgia, and South Carolina. Winters from southern Canada south to northern Mexico and Florida.

**Status:** Common breeder, migrant, and winter resident.

**Breeding:** American Goldfinches are among the latest bird species to breed in Massachusetts, with most individuals nesting between mid-July and September. Because of the conspicuous courtship antics of the males, they are also among the most conspicuous summer residents in the state. They are often most numerous in open, disturbed habitats, especially near overgrown weedy fields. Sample density: 117, MCCBBC, 20 June 1982. *Egg dates:* 10 July–early September.

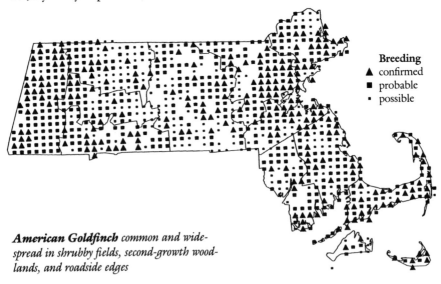

Breeding
▲ confirmed
■ probable
• possible

*American Goldfinch common and widespread in shrubby fields, second-growth woodlands, and roadside edges*

**Nonbreeding:** Because American Goldfinches are present in Massachusetts year-round, defining periods of migration and migratory peaks is difficult.

Nonetheless, there usually are indications of migration activity during early spring and midfall. Unlike Pine Siskins and Purple Finches, goldfinches do not move southward in cohesive irruptions during winter. Very large flocks are occasionally encountered in midwinter, but these seem to be the result of their attraction to abundant localized food sources rather than a response to massive seed failures to the north of Massachusetts. For example, during winters when unusually large flocks occurred in Massachusetts—e.g., 1948–1949, 1949–1950, and 1953–1954—goldfinches were not generally recorded abundantly elsewhere in the Northeast. Conversely, large numbers reported on Long Island, New York, in February 1964 (Bull 1974) were not reflected by big flocks in Massachusetts during the same period. In winter, goldfinches frequent weedy fields and are regularly attracted to feeders where thistle seed is provided. *Winter maxima:* 1,425, Concord CBC, 30 December 1972; 1,000, Beverly, 19 February 1950 (F. and K. Elkins); 918, Cape Cod CBC, 1 January 1950; 899, Concord CBC, 2 January 1983; 300, Wayland, 10 February 1950 (Elkins); 300, Middleboro, throughout March 1950 (Romaine); 250, Sunderland, 2 February 1949 (Baird).

# European Goldfinch   *Carduelis carduelis*

**Range:** Palearctic; resident throughout much of temperate Eurasia. Introduced on Long Island, New York, and elsewhere in the Northeast in the late 1800s and early 1900s. More recent records throughout the Northeast probably represent escaped cage birds (AOU 1983).

**Status:** Very rare visitor; most presumed to be escapes. Apparently introduced near Boston during the mid- or late 1800s, but extirpated by about 1900 (fide Griscom & Snyder 1955).

**Occurrence:** The first Massachusetts record of the European Goldfinch was a male seen in Cambridge, 28 February 1865 (Allen). Brewster later collected a pair with "reproductive organs well developed," also in Cambridge, 21 April 1875. There were then several other records from towns in the greater Boston area between 1875 and 1898, and a nest with five eggs was collected in Worcester, July 1890 (Brewster 1906). Griscom and Snyder (1955) imply that European Goldfinches were recorded more or less continuously in eastern Massachusetts until 1938, and Eliot (1933) reported four or five individuals from the Connecticut River valley between 1930 and 1932. The latter included an individual banded at a Westfield feeder, 29 January 1930, which remained until 11 March, and then presumably returned the following winter, 6 January 1931 (fide Bagg & Eliot 1937). Since then, a scattering of Massachusetts European Goldfinch records has been omitted from the literature on the grounds that they most likely involved escaped cage birds.

## Evening Grosbeak   *Coccothraustes vespertinus*

**Range:** Primarily Nearctic; breeds in a narrow belt from British Columbia across Canada to southern Quebec and south in the mountains of western North America to central California and southern Mexico. In eastern North America, breeds south to northern Minnesota, northern Wisconsin, northern New York, and northern New England. Winters in much of the breeding range south to the central United States and irregularly farther south.

**Status:** Two definite breeding records. Uncommon to very common, but irregular, migrant and winter resident.

**Breeding:** Although Evening Grosbeaks bred in Connecticut and New Jersey as early as 1962 (Bull 1974), the first breeding record in Massachusetts was not positively confirmed until 1980. In that year, a pair of adults was seen feeding young in Pittsfield, 16 July (Shampang). They have been more or less continuously present in the Pittsfield area during the summer since then, with two pairs seen all summer in 1983, although breeding has not subsequently been proven in that area. The most recent breeding record involved a pair that brought 2 juveniles to a feeder at Princeton, 4–5 July 1991 (Poor).

**Nonbreeding:** Evening Grosbeaks were unrecorded in Massachusetts prior to a major irruption that occurred in the winter of 1889–1890 (Forbush 1929). Historically, they were restricted as breeders to the northwestern portion of North America, but their population gradually advanced southeastward during the period from 1854 (when first collected in Toronto) to 1887 (when first taken in upstate New York). Beginning in early January 1890, the winter irruption of 1889–1890 brought numerous small flocks of 5 to 12 birds to Massachusetts, as far east as Revere Beach, as well as to several other towns in the greater Boston area. They appeared in small numbers each winter after that, until a second major irruption occurred in 1910–1911 (op cit). Griscom and Snyder (1955) indicate that they were first recorded in numbers on Cape Cod in 1950 and that by 1953 they had reached Nantucket. The largest incursions to reach Massachusetts since 1955 were in the winters of 1969–1970 and 1971–1972, when more than 14,000 were found on Massachusetts Christmas Bird Counts. Migrating Evening Grosbeaks are seen in greatest numbers during late October and November and from mid-April to early May. Because they migrate diurnally in compact, noisy flocks, they are particularly conspicuous. In winter, flocks feed on buds, ash seeds, and various fruits of ornamental plantings but readily switch to a diet of sunflower seeds when they are offered at backyard bird feeders.

*The flamboyant **Evening Grosbeak** is an irregular winter visitor that was first recorded in Massachusetts in 1889 as a wanderer from the Northwest. In winters when the species is abundant, it regularly consumes quantities of sunflower seeds at backyard bird feeders.*  ▷

## House Sparrow   *Passer domesticus*

**Range:** Nearly cosmopolitan due to introduction; breeds over much of inhabited North America. For the most part, resident within its range.

**Status:** Very common to abundant resident around cities and farmlands.

**Breeding:** House Sparrows were first accidentally introduced to Boston in 1858 and then intentionally in 1868 and 1869, supposedly to help reduce the population of Gypsy Moths and other insect pests (Griscom & Snyder 1955). Brewster (1906) graphically described the initial effects of the rapidly expanding House Sparrow population upon several native bird species, especially Tree Swallows, House Wrens, and Eastern Bluebirds. The adverse effects of competition created by House Sparrows upon these native cavity-nesting species are still evident today. House Sparrows reached their peak abundance in Massachusetts during the period 1890 to 1915, after which they gradually declined. Due to the replacement of horse-drawn carriages by the automobile and the gradual decline of farming, a widespread abundance of oats and other seeds no longer existed as a ready food source for the sparrows. *Egg dates:* February to September; two to three broods yearly.

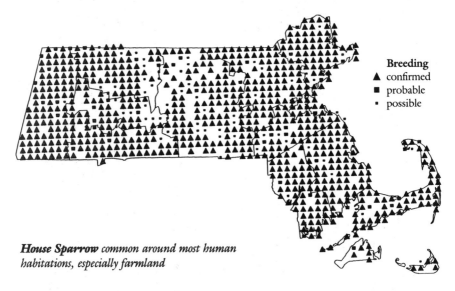

Breeding
▲ confirmed
■ probable
▪ possible

*House Sparrow common around most human habitations, especially farmland*

**Nonbreeding:** Despite any decline in House Sparrow numbers since 1915, they are still widespread and locally abundant, with most birds concentrating around feeding stations in urban areas and also around the few dairy farms that remain in Massachusetts. The largest totals are recorded by Christmas Bird Counts, particularly those in Concord, Northampton, and greater Boston—e.g., 1,564, Concord CBC, 27 December 1991; 1,365, Northampton CBC, 17 December 1978; 1,352, Greater Boston CBC, 15 December

1991. House Sparrows are partially migratory, as evidenced by several observations of them during the fall at coastal localities, where they do not breed—e.g., "4 flying to a vanishing bearing of approximately 300 degrees True on morning of 18 October 1979, Eel Point, Nantucket" (Veit).

# Bibliography

Abbot, J. M. 1946. The White-faced Storm Petrel off Cape Cod. *Auk* 63: 251.

Able, K. P. 1973. The changing season. *American Birds* 27: 19–23.

Alexander, W. B. 1963. *Birds of the Ocean*. New York: G. P. Putnam's Sons. 306 pp.

Allen, F. H. 1937. Western Grebe in Massachusetts. *Auk* 54: 376–379.

Allen, F. H. 1941. Louisiana Heron in Massachusetts. *Auk* 58: 91–92.

Allen, J. A. 1869. *Notes on Some of the Rarer Birds of Massachusetts*. Salem, MA: Essex Institute Press. 49 pp.

Allen, J. A. 1878. A list of the birds of Massachusetts, with annotations. *Bulletin of the Essex Institute* 10: 3–37.

Alsop, F. J., III, and E. T. Jones. 1973. The Lesser Black-backed Gull in the Canadian Arctic. *The Canadian Field-Naturalist* 87: 61–62.

American Ornithologists' Union. 1957. *The A.O.U. Check-list of North American Birds*, Fifth Edition. American Ornithologists' Union. 691 pp.

American Ornithologists' Union. 1983. *The A.O.U. Check-list of North American Birds*, Sixth Edition. American Ornithologists' Union. 877 pp.

Ames, P. L., and G. S. Mersereau. 1964. Some factors in the decline of the Osprey in Connecticut. *Auk* 81: 173–184.

# Bibliography

Anderson, H. C. 1968. A Forster's Tern in New Hampshire. *Records of New England Birds* 24(7): i-ii.

Anderson, K. S. 1975. First Massachusetts specimen of Le Conte's Sparrow. *Auk* 92: 145.

Anderson K. S. 1982. Marbled Murrelet: a first Massachusetts record. *Bird Observer of Eastern Massachusetts* 10: 349–352.

Anderson, K. S., and H. K. Maxfield. 1967. Warbler returns from southeastern Massachusetts. *Bird-Banding* 38: 218–233.

Andrews, J., and L. Taylor. 1983. Results of the 1982 spring migration watch. *Bird Observer of Eastern Massachusetts* 11: 75–81.

Andrews, J. W. 1978. Relative abundance analysis: a technique for assessing bird count data. *Bird Observer of Eastern Massachusetts* 6: 112–117.

Andrews, J. W. 1981. A post-breeding roost of American Robins. *Bird Observer of Eastern Massachusetts* 9: 319–321.

Andrews, J. W. 1982. A Winter roost of Long-eared Owls. *Bird Observer of Eastern Massachusetts* 10: 13–22.

Andrews, J. W. and L. E. Taylor. 1982. Warbler migration study: May 1981. *Bird Observer of Eastern Massachusetts* 10: 79–83.

Andrews, R. (compiler). 1990. *Coastal waterbird colonies: Maine to Virginia 1984–85— An update of an atlas based on 1977 data showing colony locations, species, and nesting pairs at both time periods. Part 1. Maine to Connecticut.* U.S. Fish and Wildlife Service, Newton Corner, Massachusetts.

Arvidson, D. R. 1986. What is so rare? *Bird Observer of Eastern Massachusetts* 14: 79–80.

Arvidson, D. R. 1986. Another Massachusetts first: Red-billed Tropicbird. *Bird Observer of Eastern Massachusetts* 14: 241–243.

Arvidson, D. R. 1991a. Wild barnacles in quiet Osterville. *Bird Observer of Eastern Massachusetts* 19: 25–26.

Arvidson, D. R. 1991b. Another wild goose chase: addendum to the Osterville barnacles. *Bird Observer of Eastern Massachusetts* 19: 147.

Atwood, F. 1975. Fish Crows in Massachusetts. *Bird Observer of Eastern Massachusetts* 3: 95–96.

Audubon, J. J. 1870. *The Birds of America, From Drawings Made in the United States and their Territories.* Vol. V. New York: G. R. Lockwood and Son.

Austin, O. L. 1940. Some aspects of individual distribution in the Cape Cod tern colonies. *Bird-Banding* 11: 155–169.

Bagg, A. C. 1932. Ruby-crowned Kinglet feeding young in Massachusetts. *Auk* 49: 486.

Bagg, A. M. 1955. Airborne from gulf to gulf. *The Bulletin of the Massachusetts Audubon Society* 39: 106–110, 159–168.

Bagg, A. M. 1969. A summary of the fall migration season, 1968, with special attention to the movements of Black-capped Chickadees. *Audubon Field Notes* 23: 4–12.

Bagg, A. C., and S. A. Eliot, Jr. 1937. *Birds of the Connecticut Valley in Massachusetts.* Northampton: The Hampshire Bookshop. 813 pp.

Bailey, W. 1955. *Birds in Massachusetts. When and Where to Find Them.* South Lancaster: The College Press. 234 pp.

Bailey, W. 1968. *Birds of the Cape Cod National Seashore and Adjacent Areas.* South Wellfleet: Eastern National Park and Monument Association. 120 pp.

Bailey, W. 1968. Migrating Red-shouldered Hawks over Cape Cod. *Records of New England Birds* 23(12): i.

Baird, J. 1958. Yellow-throated Warblers collected in sycamores along the Delaware River in New Jersey. *Urner Field Observer*, January.

Baird, J. 1963. The Changing Seasons: A Summary of the Fall Migration (1962). *Audubon Field Notes* 17: 4–8.

Baird, J. 1966. A late adult male Baltimore Oriole. *Records of New England Birds* 22(12): i.

Baird, J. 1968. A United States record of the Black-tailed Godwit. *Auk* 85: 500–501.

Baird, J. 1968. A partially albino Song Sparrow. *Records of New England Birds* 24(9): ii.

Baird, J., A. M. Bagg, I. C. T. Nisbet, and C. S. Robbins. 1959. Operation recovery— report on mist-netting along the Atlantic coast in 1958. *Bird-Banding* 30: 143– 171.

Baird, J., and I. C. T. Nisbet. 1960. Northward fall migration on the Atlantic Coast and its relation to offshore drift. *Auk* 77: 119–149.

Baird, S. F. 1887. Occurrence of Cory's Shearwater *(Puffinus borealis)* and several species of jaegers in large numbers in the vicinity of Gay Head, Massachusetts, during the Autumn of 1886. *Auk* 4: 71–72.

Balch, L. G., H. D. Bohlen, and G. B. Rosenband. 1979. The Illinois Ross' Gull, *American Birds* 33: 140–142.

Banks, R. C. 1970. Records of the Brambling in North America. *Auk* 87: 165–167.

Beardslee, C. S., and H. D. Mitchell. 1965. Birds of the Niagara Frontier Region. *Bulletin of the Buffalo Society of Natural Sciences*. Volume 22. 478 pp.

Benkman, C. W. 1987. Food profitability and foraging ecology of Crossbills. *Ecological Monographs* 57: 251–267.

Bennett, A. 1989. A Massachusetts first: Allen's Hummingbird on Nantucket. *Bird Observer of Eastern Massachusetts* 17: 21–24.

Bent, A. C. 1920. Flight of Newfoundland Crossbills. *Auk* 37: 298.

Bent, A. C. 1932. *Life Histories of North American Gallinaceous Birds*. Orders Galliformes and Columbiformes. Smithsonian Institution United States National Museum Bulletin 162. Washington, D.C. 490 pp.

Bent, A. C. 1937. *Life Histories of North American Birds of Prey*. Order Falconiformes (Part 1). Smithsonian Institution United States National Museum Bulletin 167. Washington, D.C. 409 pp.

Bent, A. C. 1938. *Life Histories of North American Birds of Prey*. (Part 2). Orders Falconiformes and Strigiformes. Smithsonian Institution United States National Museum Bulletin 170. Washington, D.C. 482 pp.

Bent, A. C. 1950. *Life Histories of North American Wagtails, Shrikes, Vireos, and Their Allies*. Order Passeriformes. Smithsonian Institution United States National Museum Bulletin 197. Washington, D.C. 411 pp.

Bierregaard, R. O., Jr., A. Ben David II, T. D. Baird, and R. E. Woodruff. 1975. First northwestern Atlantic breeding record of the Manx Shearwater. *Auk* 92: 145– 147.

Binford, L. C. 1978. Lesser Black-backed Gull in California, with notes on field identification. *Western Birds* 9: 141–150.

Bird, J., and M. Payne. 1981. A Chuck-will's-widow on Stellwagen Bank. *Bird Observer of Eastern Massachusetts* 9: 194.

Blodget, B. G. 1976. A decade of gull control at Wachusett Reservoir. *Chickadee* 46: 27–28.

Blokpoll, H., R. D. Morris, and P. Trull. 1982. Winter observations of Common Terns in Trinidad, Guyana, and Suriname. *Colonial Waterbirds* 5: 144–147.

Bock, C. E., and L. W. Lepthien. 1972. Winter eruptions of Red-breasted Nuthatches in North America, 1950–1970. *American Birds* 26: 558–561.

Bohlen, H. D. 1975. Ash-throated Flycatcher in Illinois: summary of records east of the Mississippi River. *Auk* 92: 165–166.

Bond, J. 1980. *Birds of the West Indies*. Boston: Houghton Mifflin Company. 256 pp.

Borden, R., and H. A. Hochbaum. 1966. The establishment of a breeding population of Gadwall in Massachusetts. *Records of New England Birds* 22(3): ii.

Borror, A. C. 1963. European Siskin (*Carduelis spinus*) in Maine. *Auk* 80: 201.

Bourne, W. R. P. 1953. On the races of the Frigate Petrel (*Pelagodroma marina* [Latham]) with a new race from the Cape Verde Islands. *Bulletin British Ornithology Club* 73: 79–82.

Bourne, W. R. P. 1955. On the status and appearance of the races of Cory's Shearwater *Procellaria diomedea. Ibis* 97: 145–149.

Bourne, W. R. P. 1955. The Birds of the Cape Verde Islands. *Ibis* 97: 508–556.

Brewster, W. 1879. The terns of the New England coast. *Bulletin of Nuttall Ornithological Club*: IV: 13–22.

Brewster, W. 1906. *The Birds of the Cambridge Region of Massachusetts*. Memoirs of the Nuttall Ornithological Club. No. IV. Cambridge, Nuttall Ornithological Club. 426 pp.

Brooks, W. D. 1934. Brown Pelican in Massachusetts. *Auk* 51: 77.

Brooks, W. S. 1917. A new record for New England. *Auk* 34: 86.

Brown, R. G. B., D. N. Nettleship, P. Germain, C. E. Tull, and T. Davis. 1975. *Atlas of Eastern Canadian Seabirds*. Ottawa: Canadian Wildlife Service. 220 pp.

Bryant, W. L. 1929. Lewis' Woodpecker in Rhode Island. *Auk* 46: 113–114.

Buckley, P. A., and C. F. Wurster. 1970. White-faced Storm Petrels (*Pelagodroma marina*) in the North Atlantic. *Bulletin British Ornithological Club.* 90: 35–38.

Buckley, P. A., and F. G. Buckley. 1981. The endangered status of North American Roseate Terns. *Colonial Waterbirds* 4: 166–173.

Buckley, P. A., F. G. Buckley, and M. Gochfeld. 1975. Gull-billed Tern: New York State's newest breeding species. *Kingbird* 25: 178–183.

Bull, J. 1963. Black-throated Sparrows in the eastern United States. *Auk* 80: 379–380.

Bull, J. 1964. *Birds of the New York Area*. New York: Harper & Row, Publishers. 540 pp.

Bull, J. 1974. *Birds of New York State*. Garden City: Natural History Press. 655 pp.

Bulmer, W. 1969. First record of Smith's Longspur in Connecticut. *Auk* 86: 345.

Burnett, F. L., and D. E. Snyder. 1954. Blue crab as starvation food of oiled American Eiders. *Auk* 71: 315–316.

Burt, Mrs. H. E. 1968. House Finch nests in Massachusetts. *Records of New England Birds* 24(10): ii.

Carroll, S., and M. Lynch. 1980. A summer sighting of Pine Grosbeak (*Pinicola enucleator*) in Massachusetts. *Bird Observer of Eastern Massachusetts* 8: 199.

Chadbourne, A. P. 1889. An unusual flight of Killdeer Plover (*Aegialitis vocifera*) along the New England Coast. *Auk* 6: 255–263.

Chalif, E. L. 1947. Northern Eider on Martha's Vineyard. *Auk* 64: 633.

Chandler, E. H. 1953. A breeding record for the Ring-necked Duck in Massachusetts. *Auk* 70: 86.

Chartier, B., and F. Cooke. 1980. Ross' Gull (*Rhodostethia rosea*) nesting at Churchill, Manitoba, Canada. *American Birds* 34: 839–841.

# Bibliography

Clark, W. S. 1974. Second record of the Kestrel (*Falco tinnunculus*) for North America. *Auk* 91: 172.

Collins, J. W. 1884a. Notes on certain Laridae and Procellariidae of the New England Coast. *Auk* 1: 236–238.

Collins, J. W. 1884b. *Notes on the habits and methods of capture of various species of seabirds that occur on the fishing banks off the eastern coast of North America, and which are used as bait for catching codfish by New England fishermen.* Rep. U.S. Fish Commission for 1882: pp. 311–335.

Confer, J. L., and K. Knapp. 1981. Golden-winged Warblers and Blue-winged Warblers: the relative success of a habitat specialist and generalist. *Auk* 98: 108–114.

Conover, B. 1944. The races of the Solitary Sandpiper. *Auk* 61: 537–544.

Cory, C. B. 1888. The European Kestrel in Massachusetts. *Auk* 5: 110.

Cottam, C. E. 1939. Food habits of North American diving ducks. Washington D.C.: U.S. Dept. of Agriculture Technical Report #643.

Cottrell, G. W., Jr. 1949. The southern heron flight of 1948. *The Bulletin of the Massachusetts Audubon Society* 33: 101–104 and 155–160.

Cramp, S., (Ed.) 1977. *Handbook of the Birds of Europe, the Middle East and North Africa.* The Birds of the Western Palearctic Vol. 1. Ostrich to ducks. Oxford: Oxford University Press. 722 pp.

Cramp, S., W. R. P. Bourne, and D. Saunders. 1974. *The Seabirds of Britain and Ireland.* New York: Taplinger Publishing Co., Inc. 287 pp.

Crandall, L. S. 1915. Gray Sea Eagle off Nantucket. *Auk* 32: 368.

Davis, D. E. 1960. The spread of the Cattle Egret in the United States. *Auk* 77: 421–424.

Davis, W. E., Jr., and K. C. Parsons. 1982. The Clark's Island heronry. *Bird Observer of Eastern Massachusetts* 10: 125–131.

DeSante, D. F. 1973. An analysis of the fall occurrences and nocturnal orientations of vagrant wood warblers (*Parulidae*) in California. Unpublished PhD dissertation. Stanford, California, Stanford University.

DeSante, D. F. 1983. Vagrants: When orientation or navigation goes wrong. *Point Reyes Bird Observatory Newsletter* 61: 12–16.

Devillers, P. 1977. The skuas of the North American Pacific Coast. *Auk* 94: 417–429.

Donahue, P. K. 1976. Field identification of Western Sandpipers in Massachusetts. *Bird Observer of Eastern Massachusetts* 4: 104–107.

Drury, W. H. 1973a. Population changes in New England seabirds. *Bird-Banding* 44: 267–313.

Drury, W. H. 1973b. *The importance of movements in the biology of Herring Gulls in New England in population ecology of migratory birds.* A symposium. Wildlife Research Report 2, U.S. Department of Interior, pp. 173–212.

Drury, W. H. 1974. Population changes in New England seabirds. *Bird-Banding* 45: 1–15.

DuMont, P. G. 1973. Black-browed Albatross sightings off the United States east coast. *American Birds* 27: 739–740.

Duncan, C. D., and R. W. Havard. 1980. Pelagic birds of the northern Gulf of Mexico. *American Birds* 34: 122–132.

Dunn, E. K. 1981. Roseates on a lifeline. *Birds* 8: 42–45.

Eliot, S. A., Jr. 1933. European Goldfinch in western Massachusetts. *Auk* 50: 366.

Eliot, S. A., Jr. 1941. Mourning Warbler breeding in central Massachusetts. *Auk* 58: 410–411.

Emery, R. P. 1966. A late record of the Louisiana Heron in Massachusetts. *Records of New England Birds* 22(12): i-ii.

Emilio, S. G., and L. Griscom. 1930. The European Black-headed Gull (*Larus ridibundus*) in America. *Auk* 47: 243.

Ernst, R. 1948. Gnatcatchers present problems. *The Bulletin of the Massachusetts Audubon Society* 32: 305–308.

Erwin, R. M., and C. E. Korschgen. 1979. *Coastal waterbird colonies: Maine to Virginia, 1977—An atlas showing colony locations and species composition*. U.S. Fish and Wildlife Service, Biological Services Program. FWS/085–79/08. 647 pp.

Evered, D. S. 1985. Pacific (and Arctic) Loon identification. Difficulty, unfamiliarity, and a little bit of confusion. *Bird Observer of Eastern Massachusetts* 13: 10–14.

Faxon, W. 1889. On the summer birds of Berkshire County, Massachusetts. *Auk* 6: 39–46, 99–107.

Faxon, W., and R. Hoffman. 1900. *The Birds of Berkshire County, Massachusetts*. Privately printed. 60 pp.

Fay, S. P. 1910. Canvas-back in Massachusetts. *Auk* 27: 369–381.

Finch, D. W. 1969. Northeastern maritime region. *Audubon Field Notes* 23: 447–457.

Finch, D. W. 1978. Black-headed Gull (*Larus ridibundus*) breeding in Newfoundland. *American Birds* 32: 312.

Finch, D. W., W. C. Russell, and E. V. Thompson. 1978. Pelagic birds in the Gulf of Maine. *American Birds* 32: 140–155.

Foley, J. 1967. A wintering Clay-colored Sparrow in Massachusetts. *Records of New England Birds* 23(5): ii.

Forbes, H. S., and J. D. O'Regan. 1960. Nesting of Louisiana Waterthrush and White-throated Sparrows in eastern coastal Massachusetts. *Auk* 77: 92.

Forbush, E. H. 1916. *A History of the Game Birds, Wild-fowl and Shore Birds of Massachusetts and Adjacent States*. Boston: Wright and Potter Printing Company, State Printers. 636 pp.

Forbush, E. H. 1925. *Birds of Massachusetts and other New England States*. Massachusetts Department of Agriculture. 481 pp.

Forbush, E. H. 1927. Ibid. Vol 2. 461 pp.

Forbush, E. H. 1929. Ibid. Vol 3. 366 pp.

Forster, R. 1975. Orchard Orioles in Massachusetts. *Bird Observer of Eastern Massachusetts* 3: 92–94.

Forster, R. 1980. The identification and occurrence of "Portlandica" type Arctic Terns in Massachusetts. *Bird Observer of Eastern Massachusetts* 8: 91–93.

Forster, R. 1982. Status of the Red-necked Grebe in Massachusetts. *Bird Observer of Eastern Massachusetts* 10: 325–327.

Forster, R. 1986. Sighting of Boat-tailed Grackle (*Quiscalus major*) in Massachusetts. *Bird Observer of Eastern Massachusetts* 14: 206–207.

Forster, R. 1987a. Sighting of an Anhinga (*Anhinga anhinga*) in Massachusetts. *Bird Observer of Eastern Massachusetts* 15: 263–264.

Forster, R. 1987b. Why was it a Cox's Sandpiper? *Bird Observer of Eastern Massachusetts* 15: 282–284.

Forster, R. 1989. First United States sight record of Little Egret (*Egretta garzetta*). *Bird Observer of Eastern Massachusetts* 17: 239–244.

Foster, F. A. 1917. *Muscivora tyrannus* (Linn.) in Massachusetts. *Auk* 34: 337.

Fray, H. R., Jr., and D. B. Eusden. 1966. Golden-crowned Sparrow in Massachusetts. *Records of New England Birds* 22(4): ii.

Garrison, D. L. 1940. Northern Skua in Massachusetts. *Auk* 57: 567–568.

Gill, F. B. 1980. Historical aspects of hybridization between Blue-winged and Golden-winged Warblers. *Auk* 97: 1–18.

Gill, F. B., and W. E. Lanyon. 1964. Experiments on species discrimination in Blue-winged Warblers. *Auk* 81: 53–64.

Godfrey, W. E. 1945. Sitka Crossbills in Massachusetts. *Auk* 62: 151.

Godfrey, W. E. 1966. *The Birds of Canada*. Ottawa: National Museums of Canada. 428 pp.

Godfrey, W. E. 1973. A possible shortcut spring migration route of the Arctic Tern to James Bay, Canada. *The Canadian Field-Naturalist* 87: 51–52.

Gordon, M. S. 1955a. A western North Atlantic record for the Frigate Petrel (*Pelagodroma marina hypoleuca*). *Auk* 72: 81–82.

Gordon, M. S. 1955b. Summer ecology of oceanic birds off southern New England. *Auk* 72: 138–147.

Grice, D., and J. P. Rogers. 1965. *The Wood Duck in Massachusetts*. Massachusetts Division of Fisheries and Game.

Griscom, L. 1923. *Birds of the New York City Region*. New York: The American Museum of Natural History, Handbook Series No. 9. 400 pp.

Griscom, L. 1937a. European Dunlins in North America. *Auk* 54: 70–72.

Griscom, L. 1937b. A monographic study of the Red Crossbill. *Proceedings of the Boston Society of Natural History*. Vol. 41, No. 5: 77–210.

Griscom, L. 1941a. Two Yellow Warblers new to Massachusetts. *Auk* 58: 100–101.

Griscom, L. 1941b. Second flight of the Sitka Crossbill to Massachusetts. *Auk* 58: 411–413.

Griscom, L. 1949. *The Birds of Concord*. Cambridge: Harvard University Press. 340 pp.

Griscom, L. 1955. The Yellow-billed Cuckoo flight of 1954. *The Bulletin of the Massachusetts Audubon Society* 39: 151–156.

Griscom, L., and D. E. Snyder. 1955. *The Birds of Massachusetts. An Annotated and Revised Check List*. Salem: Peabody Museum. 295 pp.

Griscom, L., and G. Emerson. 1959. *The Birds of Martha's Vineyard*. Sponsored by the Massachusetts Audubon Society, Portland, Maine: The Anthoenson Press. 164 pp.

Griscom, L., and E. V. Folger. 1948. *Birds of Nantucket*. Cambridge: Harvard University Press. 156 pp.

Gross, A. O. 1923. The Black-crowned Night Heron (*Nycticorax nycticorax naevius*) of Sandy Neck. *Auk* 40: 1–30 and 191–214.

Gross, A. O. 1927. The Snowy Owl migration of 1926–27. *Auk* 44: 479–493.

Gross, A. O. 1940. The migration of Kent Island Herring Gulls. *Bird-Banding* 11: 129–155.

Gross, A. O. 1944. The present status of the Double-crested Cormorant on the coast of Maine. *Auk* 61: 513–537.

Gross, A. O. 1956. The recent reappearance of the Dickcissel (*Spiza americana*) in eastern North America. *Auk* 73: 66–70.

Hagan, J. M., III, and D. W. Johnston. 1992. *Ecology and Conservation of Neotropical Migrant Landbirds*. Washington, D.C.: Smithsonian Institution Press. 609 pp.

Hagar, J. A. 1936. Rare shorebirds on the Massachusetts coast. *Auk* 53: 330–331.

Hagar, J. A. 1941a. Double-crested Cormorant breeding in Massachusetts. *Auk* 58: 567–568.

Hagar, J. A. 1941b. Little Blue Heron nesting in Massachusetts. *Auk* 58: 568–569.

Hagar, J. A. 1946. Black Skimmer breeding in Massachusetts. *Auk* 63: 594–595.

Hagar, J. A. 1969. History of the Massachusetts peregrine falcon population, 1935–57. In J. J. Hickey, ed., *Peregrine Falcon Populations, Their Biology and Decline.* Madison: University of Wisconsin Press. pp. 123–131.

Harrington, B. A., and R. I. G. Morrison. 1979. Semipalmated Sandpiper migration in North America. *Studies in Avian Biology* 2: 83–100.

Hatch, J. 1982. The cormorants of Boston Harbor and Massachusetts Bay. *Bird Observer of Eastern Massachusetts* 10: 65–73.

Hatch, J. J. 1982. The heronries of Boston Harbor. *Bird Observer of Eastern Massachusetts* 10: 133–135

Hatch, J. J. 1984. Rapid increase of Double-crested Cormorants nesting in southern New England. *American Birds* 38: 984–988.

Hayman, P., J. Marchant, and T. Prater. 1986. *Shorebirds: An Identification Guide to the Waders of the World.* Boston: Houghton Mifflin. 412 pp.

Heil, R. S. 1977. A sight record of the Lark Bunting and its historical occurrence in Massachusetts. *Bird Observer of Eastern Massachusetts* 5: 192–194.

Heil, R. S. 1980. An avian fallout and the first state records for Black-chinned Hummingbird and Lucy's Warbler. *Bird Observer of Eastern Massachusetts* 8: 61–64.

Heil, R. S. 1981. An avian fallout and the first Massachusetts records for Black-chinned Hummingbird and Lucy's Warbler. *American Birds* 35: 139–141.

Heil, R. S. 1983a. The eighty-third Audubon Christmas Bird Count (New England). *American Birds* 37: 380–382.

Heil, R. S. 1983b. Observations of two apparent hybrid gulls in Massachusetts. *Bird Observer of Eastern Massachusetts* 11: 137–141.

Hendricks, B. 1970. Puffin in Berkshire County. *Bird News of Western Massachusetts* 10: 90.

Henny, C. J., and H. M. Wight. 1969. An endangered Osprey population: estimates of mortality and production. *Auk* 86: 188–198.

Hersey, F. S. 1913. Sabine's Gull in Massachusetts. *Auk* 30: 105.

Hiam, A., and M. Sutherland. 1979. Ground-nesting and related behavior of Nighthawks (*Chordeiles minor*) in Massachusetts. *Bird Observer of Eastern Massachusetts* 7: 98–105.

Hill, N. P. 1965. *The Birds of Cape Cod, Massachusetts.* New York: William Morrow and Company. 364 pp.

Hill, N. P. 1976. Sharp-tailed Sparrows in Massachusetts. *Bird Observer of Eastern Massachusetts* 4: 42–43.

Holmes, R. T., T. W. Sherry, and F. W. Sturges. 1986. Bird community dynamics in a temperate deciduous forest: long-term trends at Hubbard Brook. *Ecological Monographs* 56: 201–220.

Holt, D. 1986. A summary of Short-eared Owl breeding status in Massachusetts. *Bird Observer of Eastern Massachusetts* 14: 234–237.

Holt, D. W., J. P. Lortie, B. J. Nikula, and R. C. Humphrey. 1986. First record of Common Black-headed Gulls breeding in the United States. *American Birds* 40: 204–206.

Houston, C. S. 1981. *Owl Banding.* Seminar presented at the Nuttall Ornithological Club.

Howard, D. V. 1966. Robin Nest Survey. *Records of New England Birds* 22(10): ii–iv.

Howard, D. V. 1967. Five years of mist netting (1962–1966) at Round Hill, Sudbury, Massachusetts. *Records of New England Birds* 23(2): iii–vi.

Howard, D. V. 1967. The 1967 Robin nesting season. *Records of New England Birds* 23(9): ii-iii.

Howard, D. V. 1968. Robin nest survey 1963–1968. *Records of New England Birds* 24(6): i-iv.

Howe, R. H., Jr., and G. M. Allen. 1901. *The Birds of Massachusetts*. Cambridge: Nuttall Ornithological Club. 154 pp.

Humphrey, P. S., and K. C. Parkes. 1959. An approach to the study of molts and plumages. *Auk* 76: 1–31

Jehl, J. R., Jr. 1963. An investigation of fall-migrating dowitchers in New Jersey. *The Wilson Bulletin* 75: 250–261.

Johnsgard, P. A. 1981. *The Plovers, Sandpipers and Snipes of the World*. Lincoln: University of Nebraska Press. 493 pp.

Johnsgard, P. A., and D. Hagemeyer. 1969. The Masked Duck in the United States. *Auk* 86: 691–695.

Kadlec, J. A., and W. H. Drury. 1968. Structure of the New England Herring Gull population. *Ecology* 49: 644–676.

Karplus, M. 1947. Massachusetts alcids. *The Bulletin of the Massachusetts Audubon Society* 31: 21–32, 119–126, and 151–159.

Kasprzyk, M. J., R. A. Forster, and B. A. Harrington. 1987. First Northern Hemisphere record and first juvenile plumage description of the Cox's Sandpiper (*Calidris paramelanotos*). *American Birds* 41: 1359–1365.

Keith, A. R. 1964. A thirty-year summary of the nesting of the Barn Owl on Martha's Vineyard, Massachusetts. *Bird-Banding* 35: 22–31.

Keith, A. R. 1968. A summary of the extralimital records of the Varied Thrush. *Bird-Banding* 39: 245–276.

Kellogg, P. P. 1962. Vocalizations of the Black Rail (*Laterallus jamaicensis*) and the Yellow Rail (*Coturnicops noveboracensis*). *Auk* 79: 698–701.

Kerlinger, P., M. R. Lein, and B. J. Sevick. 1985. Distribution and population fluctuations of wintering Snowy Owls (*Nyctea scandiaca*) in North America. *Canadian Journal of Zoology* 63: 1829–1834.

Komar, N. 1983. A winter record of Henslow's Sparrow in Massachusetts. *Bird Observer of Eastern Massachusetts* 11: 111–114.

Kress, S. W., E. H. Weinstein, and I. C. T. Nisbet. 1983. The status of tern populations in northeastern United States and adjacent Canada. *Colonial Waterbirds* 6: 84–106.

Lambert, K. 1977. Black-capped Petrel in the George's Bank area. *American Birds* 31: 1056.

Lanyon, W. E., and J. Bull. 1967. Identification of Connecticut, Mourning, and MacGillivray's Warblers. *Bird-Banding* 38: 187–194.

Lauro, A. J., and B. J. Spencer. 1980. A method for separating juvenal and first-winter Ring-billed Gulls (*Larus delawarensis*) and Common Gulls (*Larus canus*). *American Birds* 34: 111–117.

Leahy, C. 1982. *The Birdwatcher's Companion: An Encyclopedic Handbook of North American Birdlife*. New York: Hill and Wang. 917 pp.

Lee, D. S., and J. Booth, Jr. 1979. Seasonal distribution of offshore and pelagic birds in North Carolina waters. *American Birds* 33: 715–721.

Lee, D. S., D. B. Wingate, and H. W. Kale II. 1981. Records of tropicbirds in the North Atlantic and upper Gulf of Mexico, with comments on field identification. *American Birds* 35: 887–890.

Lee, D. S. 1984. Petrels and storm-petrels in North Carolina's offshore waters:

*Bibliography*

including species previously unrecorded for North America. *American Birds* 38: 151–163.

Lincoln, F. C. 1925. Some results of bird banding in Europe. *Auk* 42: 358–398.

Lloyd-Evans, T. 1981. Chickadee invasion. *Bird Observer of Eastern Massachusetts* 9: 289–291.

Lowery, G. H., Jr. 1974. *Louisiana Birds*. Third edition. Baton Rouge: Louisiana State University Press. 651 pp.

Mackay, G. H. 1891. The habits of the Golden Plover (*Charadrius dominicus*) in Massachusetts. *Auk* 8: 17–24.

Mackay, G. H. 1893. Observations on the knot (*Tringa canutus*). *Auk* 10: 25–35.

Mackay, G. H. 1895. The terns of Muskeget Island, Massachusetts. *Auk* 12: 32–48.

McLaren, I. A. 1981. The incidence of vagrant landbirds on Nova Scotian Islands. *Auk* 98: 243–257.

McLaren, I. A., J. Morlan, P. W. Smith, M. Gosselin, and S. F. Bailey. 1989. Eurasian Siskins in North America—distinguishing females from green-morph Pine Siskins. *American Birds* 43: 1268–1274.

Maher, W. J. 1974. Ecology of Pomarine, Parasitic and Longtailed jaegers in Northern Alaska. *Pacific Coast Avifauna* no. 37. Los Angeles, Cooper Ornithological Society. 148 pp.

Mason, C. R., and W. B. Robertson, Jr. 1965. Noddy Tern in Massachusetts. *Auk* 82: 109.

Mayr, E., and L. L. Short. 1970. Species taxa of North American birds. Cambridge, Massachusetts, *Publication of the Nuttall Ornithological Club* 9: 1–127.

McDaniel, J. W. 1973. Vagrant albatrosses in the western North Atlantic and Gulf of Mexico. *American Birds* 27: 563–565.

McNair, D. 1978. *The Birds of Berkshire County*. Unpublished manuscript. 168 pp.

Miliotis, P., and P. A. Buckley. 1975. The Massachusetts Ross' Gull. *American Birds* 29: 643–646.

Monroe, B. L., Jr., and A. Barron. 1980. The Fork-tailed Flycatcher in North America. *American Birds* 34: 842–845.

Montevecchi, W. A., E. Blundon, G. Coombes, J. Porter, and P. Rice. 1978. Northern Fulmar breeding range extended to Baccalieu Island, Newfoundland. *The Canadian Field-Naturalist* 92: 80–82.

Moore, M. C., and S. B. Light. 1976. A record count of Blackbellied Plovers at Newburyport. *Bird Observer of Eastern Massachusetts* 4: 125.

Morgan, R. S. 1966. Notes on nesting bluebirds in Lincoln, Massachusetts. *Records of New England Birds* 22(9): ii-iv.

Morimoto, D. C. 1987. *Calidris paramelanotos*: A perplexing story. *Bird Observer of Eastern Massachusetts* 15: 286–288.

Morris, R. O. 1906. The Rough-winged Swallow (*Stelgidopteryx serripennis*) breeding near Springfield, Massachusetts. *Auk* 23: 463.

Morrison, A. W. 1967. Sandhill Crane in Acton, Massachusetts. *Records of New England Birds* 23(10): ii.

Morrison, R. I. G., T. H. Manning, and J. A. Hagar. 1976. Breeding of the Marbled Godwit, *Limosa fedoa*, in James Bay. *The Canadian Field-Naturalist* 90: 487–490.

Morrison, R. I. G., and B. A. Harrington. 1979. Critical shorebird resources in James Bay and Eastern North America. *Transactions of the 44th North American Wildlife and Natural Resources Conference* pp. 498–507. Wildlife Management Institute, Washington, D.C.

Morse, D. H. 1978. Populations of Bay-breasted and Cape May Warblers during an outbreak of the Spruce Budworm. *The Wilson Bulletin* 90: 404–413.

Murphy, R. C., and W. Vogt. 1933. The Dovekie influx of 1932. *Auk* 50: 325–349.

Nero, R. W. 1980. *The Great Gray Owl, Phantom of the Northern Forest*. Washington, D.C.: Smithsonian Institution Press.

Nettleship, D. N. 1976. Gannets in North America: present numbers and recent population changes. *The Wilson Bulletin* 88: 300–313.

Nettleship, D. N., and R. D. Montgomerie. 1974. The Northern Fulmar, *Fulmarus glacialis*, breeding in Newfoundland. *American Birds* 28: 16.

Nichols, C. K. 1955. Hudson-St. Lawrence Region. *Audubon Field Notes* 9: 10–14.

Nickerson, A. W. 1978. Sighting of a Franklin's Gull in Vineyard Sound, Massachusetts. *Bird Observer of Eastern Massachusetts* 6: 222–223.

Nikula, B. 1980a. Massachusetts non-resident terns. *Bird Observer of Eastern Massachusetts* 8: 95–101.

Nikula, B. 1980b. Observation of a Little Stint (*Calidris minuta*) in Massachusetts. *Bird Observer of Eastern Massachusetts* 8: 187–188.

Nikula, B. 1982. First record of Swainson's Warbler (*Limnothlypis swainsonii*) in Massachusetts. *Bird Observer of Eastern Massachusetts* 10: 219–220.

Nikula, B. 1988. Birding Chatham, Cape Cod. *Bird Observer of Eastern Massachusetts* 16: 124–132.

Nikula, B. 1992. The great gannet wreck of '91. *Bird Observer of Eastern Massachusetts* 20: 84–90.

Nisbet, I. C. T. 1970a. Autumn migration of the Blackpoll Warbler: evidence for long flight provided by regional survey. *Bird-Banding* 41: 207–240.

Nisbet, I. C. T. 1970b. Band recoveries of the Blackpoll Warbler. *Bird-Banding* 41: 279–281.

Nisbet, I. C. T. 1971. The Laughing Gull in the northeast. *American Birds* 25: 677–683.

Nisbet, I. C. T. 1973. Terns in Massachusetts: present numbers and historical changes. *Bird-Banding* 44: 27–55.

Nisbet, I. C. T. 1976a. The colonization of Monomoy by Laughing Gulls. *Cape Naturalist* 5: 4–8.

Nisbet, I. C. T. 1976b. Early stages in postfledging dispersal of Common Terns. *Bird-Banding* 47: 163–164.

Nisbet, I. C. T. 1978. Population models for Common Terns in Massachusetts. *Bird-Banding* 49: 50–58.

Nisbet, I. C. T., and J. Baird. 1959. The autumn migration of the Double-crested Cormorant through eastern New England. *Massachusetts Audubon* 43: 224–227.

Nisbet, I. C. T., and W. H. Drury, Jr. 1967. Orientation of spring migrants studied by radar. *Bird Banding* 38: 173–186.

Nisbet, I. C. T., and W. H. Drury, Jr. 1967. Weather and migration. *Massachusetts Audubon* 52: 12–19.

Nisbet, I. C. T., W. H. Drury, Jr., and J. Baird. 1963. Weight-loss during migration. Part I: deposition and consumption of fat by the Blackpoll Warbler (*Dendroica striata*). *Bird-Banding* 34: 107–159.

Nisbet, I. C. T. 1980. Status and trends of the Roseate Tern *Sterna dougallii* in North America and the Caribbean. Unpub. report to USFWS, Newton Corner, MA, Massachusetts Audubon Society, Lincoln, MA

O'Sullivan, J. 1977. Report on rare birds in Great Britain in 1976. *British Birds* 70: 405–453.

# Bibliography

Palmer, R. S. 1949. Maine birds. *Bulletin of the Museum of Comparative Zoology.* Vol. 102. Cambridge: Harvard College. 656 pp.

Palmer, R. S., (Ed.). 1962. *Handbook of North American Birds.* Vol. 1. New Haven: Yale University Press. 567 pp.

Palmer, R. S., (Ed.). 1976. Ibid. Vols. 2, 3. 521, 560 pp.

Parker, H. C. 1939. Atlantic Fulmar in Worcester, Massachusetts. *Auk* 56: 326.

Parker, J. W., and J. C. Ogden. 1979. The recent history and status of the Mississippi Kite. *American Birds* 33: 119–129.

Parker, S. A. 1982. A New Sandpiper in the Genus Calidris. *South Australian Naturalist* 56: 32.

Parkes, K. C. 1953. The Yellow-throated Warbler in New York. *Kingbird* 3: 4–6.

Petersen, W. R. 1971. *A preliminary study of scoter migration in southeastern Massachusetts.* Research Report No. 1. Manomet Bird Observatory, Manomet, Massachusetts.

Petersen, W. R. 1974. A note on Brewer's Blackbird in New England. *Bird Observer of Eastern Massachusetts* 2: 55–56.

Petersen, W. R. 1976. A sight record of McCown's Longspur in Massachusetts. *Bird Observer of Eastern Massachusetts* 4: 163.

Petersen, W. R. 1977. A breeding record for the Acadian Flycatcher in Massachusetts. *Bird Observer of Eastern Massachusetts* 5: 162–164.

Petersen, W. R. 1981. Massachusetts Rallidae: A summary. *Bird Observer of Eastern Massachusetts* 9: 159–173.

Petersen, W. R. 1982. Massachusetts waders: past and present. *Bird Observer of Eastern Massachusetts* 10: 113–120.

Petersen, W. R. 1985. A second record of Little Stint (*Calidris minuta*) in Massachusetts. *Bird Observer of Eastern Massachusetts* 13: 278–280.

Petersen, W. R. 1988. New England Region. *American Birds* 42: 1267–1270.

Peterson, R. T. 1954. A new bird immigrant arrives. *National Geographic* 56: 281–292.

Peterson, R. T. 1980. *A Field Guide to the Birds.* Boston: Houghton Mifflin Company. 384 pp. Fourth Edition.

Phillips, A. R. 1975. Semipalmated Sandpiper: identification, migrations, summer and winter ranges. *American Birds* 29: 799–806.

Pitelka, F. A. 1950. Geographic variation and the species problems in the shorebird genus *Limnodromus. University of California Publications in Zoology* 50: 1–108.

Potter, E. F., J. F. Parnell, and R. F. Teulings. 1980. *Birds of the Carolinas.* Chapel Hill: The University of North Carolina Press. 408 pp.

Powers, K. D. 1979. Lesser Black-backed Gull *Larus fuscus* in Labrador waters. *The Canadian Field-Naturalist* 93: 445–446.

Powers, K. D. 1983. *Pelagic Distributions of Marine Birds Off the Northeastern United States.* NOAA Technical Memorandum NMFS-F/NEC-27, U.S. Dept. Commerce; NOAA, Woods Hole, Massachusetts. 201 pp.

Powers, K. D., and J. Cherry. 1983. Loon migrations off the coast of the northeastern United States. *The Wilson Bulletin* 95: 125–132.

Powers, K. D., and J. A. Van Os. 1979. A concentration of Greater Shearwaters in the western North Atlantic. *American Birds* 33: 253.

Prater, A. J., J. H. Marchant, and J. Vuorinen. 1977. *Guide to the identification and ageing of Holarctic Waders.* British Trust for Ornithology Field Guide 17. Beech Grove, Tring, Herts, British Trust for Ornithology. 168 pp.

Purdie, H. A. 1882. *Rhynchops nigra*—an early record for the New England coast. *Bulletin of Nuttall Ornithological Club* 13: 125.

Richards, R. J. 1986. Bird Sighting. *Bird Observer of Eastern Massachusetts* 14: 78.

Richardson, W. J. 1972. Autumn migration and weather in eastern Canada: A radar study. *American Birds* 26: 10–17.

Richardson, W. J. 1978. Reorientation of nocturnal landbird migrants over the Atlantic Ocean near Nova Scotia in autumn. *Auk* 95: 717–732.

Ridgway, R. 1885. A new petrel to North America. *Auk* 2: 386–387.

Riedel, D. A. 1966. A flock of cardinals. *Records of New England Birds* 22(11): i-ii.

Rimmer, D. and R. Hopping. 1991. Forster's Tern nesting in Plum Island marshes. *Bird Observer of Eastern Massachusetts* 19: 308–309.

Robbins, C. S., B. Bruun, and H. S. Zim. 1966. *Birds of North America*. New York: Golden Press. 340 pp.

Robbins, C. S., D. Bystrak, and P. H. Geissler, 1986. *The Breeding Bird Survey: Its First Fifteen Years, 1965–1979*. U.S. Dept. of the Interior, Fish and Wildlife Service, Resource Publication 157. Washington, D.C. 196 pp.

Roberson, D. 1980. *Rare Birds of the West Coast of North America*. Pacific Grove, CA: Woodcock Publications. 496 pp.

Roberts, P. M. 1979. The Broad-winged Hawk flight of September 13, 1978. *Bird Observer of Eastern Massachusetts* 7: 137–144.

Roberts, P. M. 1990. Spring hawk migration in Massachusetts. *Bird Observer of Eastern Massachusetts* 18: 12–22.

Roberts, T. S. 1955. *Manual for the Identification of the Birds of Minnesota and Neighboring States*. Minneapolis: The University of Minnesota Press. 738 pp.

Robertson, W. B. 1969. Transatlantic migration of juvenile Sooty Terns. *Nature* 225: 632–634.

Robinson, L. J. 1977. The Red-bellied Woodpecker in Massachusetts—a case history of range expansion. *Bird Observer of Eastern Massachusetts* 5: 195–199.

Rosenwald, J., II. 1986. How about that tail? *Bird Observer of Eastern Massachusetts* 14: 238–240.

Rowan, M. K. 1952. The Greater Shearwater *Puffinus gravis* at its breeding grounds. *Ibis* 94: 97–121.

Rowlett, R. A. 1980. Observations of marine birds and mammals in the northern Chesapeake Bight. U.S. Fish and Wildlife Service, National Coastal Ecosystems Team, Slidell, Louisiana. FWS/OBS-80–04. 87 pp.

Salomonsen, F. 1965. The geographical variation of the Fulmar *Fulmarus glacialis* and the zones of marine environment in the North Atlantic. *Auk* 82: 327–355.

Salomonsen, F. 1976. The South Polar Skua (*Stercorarius maccormicki*) saunders in Greenland. *Dansk. Ornith. Forening Tidsskrift* 70: 81–89.

Samuels, E. A. 1864. *Descriptive Catalogue of the Birds of Massachusetts*. Boston: Wright and Potter, Printers. 15 pp.

Sharrock, J. T. R., comp. 1976. *The Atlas of Breeding Birds in Britain and Ireland*. Berkhamsted, England: T. and A. D. Poyser. 479 pp.

Sherman, K. 1981. *Zooplankton of Georges Bank and adjacent waters in relation to fisheries ecosystem studies*. Third informal workshop on the oceanography of the Gulf of Maine and adjacent seas. University of New Hampshite, pp. 40–43.

Short, L. L., Jr. 1963. Hybridization in the wood warblers (*Vermivora pinus* and *V. chrysoptera*). *Proceedings of the 13th International Ornithological Congress*: 147–160.

Short, L. L. 1965. Hybridization in the flickers (*Colaptes*) of North America. *Bulletin of the American Museum of Natural History* 129: 307–428.

Smith, C. E. 1964. Nesting of Worm-eating Warbler and Slate-colored Junco in eastern Massachusetts. *Auk* 81: 96–97.

Smith, C. E. 1966. Red-headed Woodpeckers nesting in Massachusetts. *Records of New England Birds* 22(5): ii-iii.

Smith, C. E. 1968. Status and movements of Tufted Titmice in Weston, Massachusetts. *Records of New England Birds* 24(3): ii-iii.

Smith, N. G. 1966. Evolution of some arctic gulls (*Larus*): an experimental study of isolating mechanisms. *The American Ornithologists' Union-Ornithological Monographs* 4: 1–99.

Smith, N. G. 1982. Lesser Black-backed Gull in Panama. *American Birds* 36: 336–337.

Snyder, D. E. 1953. A great flight of Dovekies (*Plautus alle*). *Auk* 70: 87–88.

Snyder, D. E. 1958. Recent occurrences of the Manx Shearwater in Massachusetts. *Auk* 75: 213–214

Snyder, D. E. 1960. Great Black-backed Gulls killing Dovekies. *Auk* 77: 476–477.

Snyder, D. E. 1961. First record of the Least Frigate-bird (*Fregata ariel*) in North America. *Auk* 78: 265.

Snyder, D. E. 1964. *Icterus bullockii* in Massachusetts. *Auk* 81: 92–94.

Sorrie, B. 1975c. The House Finch in Massachusetts. *Bird Observer of Eastern Massachusetts* 3: 192–193.

Sorrie, B. A. 1974. Probable nesting of Yellow-breasted Chats in Sandwich. *Bird Observer of Eastern Massachusetts* 2: 74.

Sorrie, B. A. 1975a. Alder and Willow Flycatchers in Massachusetts. *Bird Observer of Eastern Massachusetts*. 3: 48–50.

Sorrie, B. A. 1975b. Boreal Chickadee invasions. *Bird Observer of Eastern Massachusets* 3: 165–166.

Spear, L. B., M. J. Lewis, M. T. Myres, and R. L. Pyle. The recent occurrence of Garganey in North America and the Hawaiian Islands. *American Birds* 42: 385–392.

Spencer, P. M. 1967. A partial albino male Parula Warbler. *Records of New England Birds* 23(4): iv.

Spitzer, P., and A. Poole. 1980. Coastal Ospreys between New York City and Boston: a decade of reproductive recovery 1969–1979. *American Birds* 34: 234–241.

Spitzer, P. R., R. W. Risebrough, W. Walker II, R. Herandez, A. Poole, D. Puleston, and I. C. T. Nisbet. 1978. Productivity of Ospreys in Connecticut—Long Island increases as DDT residues decline. *Science* 202: 333–335.

Stanton, P. B. 1977. Eider Duck transplant experiments on Penikese Island. *Transactions of Northeast Fish and Wildlife Conference* [No. 34] pp. 65–70.

Stein, R. C. 1963. Isolating mechanisms between populations of Traill's Flycatchers. *Proceedings of the American Philosophical Society* 107: 21–50.

Stemple, D. 1990. Terek Sandpiper at Plum Island. *Bird Observer of Eastern Massachusetts* 18: 286–290.

Stemple, D., J. Moore, I. Giriunas, and M. Paine. 1991. Terek Sandpiper in Massachusetts: First Record for Eastern North America. *American Birds* 45: 397–398.

Stone, W. 1937. *Bird Studies at Old Cape May: An Ornithology of Coastal New Jersey.* Vols. I, II. New York, Philadelphia: Delaware Valley Ornithological Club. 941 pp.

Strahler, A. N. 1966. *A Geologist's View of Cape Cod.* Garden City: The Natural History Press. 115 pp.

Stymeist, R. H. 1979. A MacGillivray's Warbler in Lexington, Massachusetts. *Bird Observer of Eastern Massachusetts* 7: 18–20.

Sykes, P. A., Jr. 1974. Florida Burrowing Owl collected in North Carolina. *Auk* 91: 636–637.

Taylor, E. 1975. September swifts. *Bird Observer of Eastern Massachusetts* 3: 161–163.

Thayer, J. E. 1905. Water-Thrush (*Seiurus noveboracensis*) nesting in Lancaster, Massachusetts. *Auk* 22: 418–419.

Terborgh, J. 1989. *Where Have All the Birds Gone?* Princeton: Princeton University Press. 207 pp.

Townsend, C. W. 1905. *The Birds of Essex County, Massachusetts*. Memoirs of the Nuttall Ornithological Club No. III. Cambridge: Nuttall Ornithological Club. 352 pp.

Townsend, C. W. 1929. Breeding of the Yellow-crowned Night Heron (*Nyctanassa violacea*) at Ipswich. *Bulletin of the Essex County Ornithological Club* 11: 27–30.

Townsend, C. W., and F. H. Allen. 1933. Breeding of Leach's Petrel on Penikese Island. *Auk* 50: 426–427.

Trimble, B. 1968. Aberrant Wilson's Petrel on the Newfoundland Grand Banks. *Auk* 85: 130.

Troy, D. M. 1985. A phenetic analysis of the red polls *Carduelis flammea flammea* and *C. hornemanni exilipes*. *Auk* 102: 82–96.

Trull, P. 1983. Shorebirds and noodles. *American Birds* 37: 268–269.

Tuck, L. M. 1961. The Murres: their distribution, populations and biology. Ottawa, *Canadian Wildlife Service Report Series* No 1.

Tuck, L. M. 1968. Recent Newfoundland bird records. *Auk* 85: 304–311.

Tyler, W. M., M.D. 1915. The Cape May Warbler in eastern Massachusetts. *Auk* 32: 104.

U.S. Fish and Wildlife Service. 1987. Endangered and threatened wildlife and plants: determination of endangered and threatened status for two populations of the Roseate Tern. *Federal Register* 52: 42064–42071.

U.S. Fish and Wildlife Service. 1989. Recovery plan for Roseate Tern, *Sterna dougallii:* northeastern population. Newton Corner, Massachusetts. 86 pp.

Van Tyne, J. 1926. An unusual flight of Arctic Three-toed Woodpeckers. *Auk* 43: 469–474.

Veit, R. R. 1973. Sighting of a Black-browed Albatross. *Bird Observer of Eastern Massachusetts* 1: 137–138.

Veit, R. R. 1976. Recent changes in the range and distribution of Cory's Shearwaters in North American waters. *Bird Observer of Eastern Massachusetts* 4: 72–73.

Veit, R. R. 1976. Sighting of a Eurasian Curlew (*Numenius arquata*) in Massachusetts. *Bird Observer of Eastern Massachusetts* 4: 138.

Veit, R. R. 1978. Some observations of South Polar Skuas (*Catharacta maccormicki*) on Georges Bank. *American Birds* 32: 300–302.

Veit, R. R., and W. R. Petersen. 1982. First and second records of Rufous-necked Sandpiper (*Calidris ruficollis*) for Massachusetts. *Bird Observer of Eastern Massachusetts* 10: 75–77.

Veit, R. R., and L. Jonsson. 1984. Field identification of smaller sandpipers within the genus *Calidris*. *American Birds* 38: 853–876.

Veit, R. R. 1988. Why don't Red-billed Tropicbirds nest on Martha's Vineyard? *Bird Observer of Eastern Massachusetts* 16: 11–15.

Veit, R. R. 1989. Vagrant birds: passive or active dispersal? *Bird Observer of Eastern Massachusetts* 17: 25–30.

Viator, H. A. 1958. My game of solitaire. *The Bulletin of the Massachusetts Audubon Society*. Vol. 42: 3–4.

Vickery, P. D. 1977. The spring migration, April 1-May 31, 1977. *American Birds* 31: 972–977.

Vickery, P. D. 1978. *Annotated Checklist of Maine Birds*. Falmouth: Maine Audubon Society. 20 pp.

Vickery, P. D., D. W. Finch, and P. K. Donahue. 1987. Juvenile Cox's Sandpiper (*Calidris paramelanotos*) in Massachusetts, a first New World occurrence and a hitherto undescribed plumage. *American Birds* 41: 1366–1369.

Vickery, P. D., and R. P. Yunick. 1979. The 1978–1979 Great Gray Owl incursion across northeastern North America. *American Birds* 33: 242–244.

Walton, R. 1981. Inland record of Seaside Sparrow. *Bird Observer of Eastern Massachusetts* 9: 317–318.

Walton, R. K. 1984. *Birds of the Sudbury River Valley—An Historical Perspective*. Lincoln: Massachusetts Audubon Society. 220 pp.

Watson, J. B. 1910. Further data on the homing sense of Noddy and Sooty Terns. *Science* 32: 470–473.

Weaver, R. L. 1940. The Purple Finch invasion of northeastern United States and the Maritime Provinces in 1939. *Bird-Banding* 11: 79–104.

Wilson, W. H. 1988. Weather and long-distance vagrancy in Red-billed Tropicbirds. *Bird Observer of Eastern Massachusetts* 16: 139–142.

Wingate, D. B. 1973. *A Checklist and Guide to the Birds of Bermuda*. Bermuda: Island Press, Ltd. 36 pp.

Winkler, K. 1988. Notes on a Hammond's Flycatcher. *Bird Observer of Eastern Massachusetts* 16: 133–138.

Woods, R. W. 1970. Great Shearwater *Puffinus gravis* breeding in the Falkland Islands. *Ibis* 112: 259–260.

Wright, H. W. 1909. *Birds of the Boston Public Garden*. Boston: Houghton Mifflin Co. 238 pp.

Wright, H. W. 1921. Bohemian Waxwing (*Bombycilla garrula*) in New England. *Auk* 38: 59–78.

Wynne-Edwards, V. C. 1935. On the habits and distribution of birds on the North Atlantic. *Proceedings of the Boston Society of Natural History* 40: 233–346.

Yank, R., and Y. Aubry. 1985. The winter season: Quebec region. *American Birds* 39: 148–150.

# Index

Pages listed in the index refer only to the locations of individual species accounts. The names of birds and the systematic order used throughout the text follow *The A.O.U. Checklist of North American Birds,* Sixth Edition (1983), and all subsequent supplements published in *The Auk* through 1992.

# Index

# Index

# Index

# Index

# Index

Waterthrush
  Louisiana, 412
  Northern, 411
Waxwing
  Bohemian, 365
  Cedar, 366
Wheatear, Northern, 347
Whimbrel, 175
Whip-poor-will, 275
Whistling-Duck, Fulvous, 90
Wigeon
  American, 106
  Eurasian, 106
Willet, 170
*Wilsonia*
  *canadensis,* 419
  *citrina,* 418
  *pusilla,* 419
Woodcock, American, 201
Woodpecker
  Black-backed, 288
  Downy, 285
  Hairy, 286
  Lewis', 281
  Pileated, 291
  Red-bellied, 283
  Red-headed, 282
  Three-toed, 287

Wood-Pewee
  Eastern, 293
  Western, 293
Wren
  Bewick's, 337
  Carolina, 335
  House, 337
  Marsh, 341
  Rock, 335
  Sedge, 340
  Winter, 339

*Xanthocephalus xanthocephalus,* 464
*Xema sabini,* 228
*Xenus cinerus,* 173

Yellowlegs
  Greater, 167
  Lesser, 168
Yellowthroat, Common, 417

*Zenaida*
  *asiatica,* 253
  *macroura,* 254
*Zonotrichia*
  *albicollis,* 451
  *atricapilla,* 452
  *leucophrys,* 453
  *querula,* 454

*Birds of Massachusetts* was composed in 10 point Galliard, a contemporary typeface based on traditional designs. Galliard was created by Matthew Carter in 1980 and is licensed by the International Typeface Corporation.

The illustrations for *Birds of Massachusetts* were produced using a combination of techniques. Initially, an ink line drawing was produced on coquille board. Solid black areas were added with a watercolor brush and the midtones laid in with a black "china-marker" crayon, which, when drawn across the textured surface of the coquille board, creates a unique halftone texture. Finally, by means of an overlay on the original art, a 30 percent gray tone was added to portions of the design.

*Birds of Massachusetts* is printed on 60 pound Canadian Pacific Offset, Smooth, manufactured by the Canadian Pacific Paper Company. Printing and binding was done by BookCrafters USA, Inc.